Consumer market research handbook

CONSUMER MARKET RESEARCH HANDBOOK

2nd edition

Editors: **ROBERT M. WORCESTER**
JOHN DOWNHAM

VAN NOSTRAND REINHOLD COMPANY
New York - Cincinnati - Toronto - London - Melbourne

**Published by Van Nostrand Reinhold Company Ltd.,
Molly Millars Lane, Wokingham, Berkshire, England**

*Published in 1978 by Van Nostrand Reinhold Company
A Division of Litton Educational Publishing, Inc.,
450 West 33rd Street, New York, N.Y. 10001, U.S.A.*

*Van Nostrand Reinhold Limited
1410 Birchmount Road, Scarborough, Ontario, M1P 2E7,
Canada*

*Van Nostrand Reinhold Australia Pty. Limited
17 Queen Street, Mitcham, Victoria 3132, Australia*

Library of Congress Cataloging in Publication Data
Main entry under title:

Consumer market research handbook.

Includes bibliographical references and index.
1. Marketing research—Addresses, essays, lectures.
I. Worcester, Robert M.
HF5415.2.C62 1978   658.8'34   78–6925
ISBN 0–442–30237–1

Printed and bound in Great Britain
by W & J Mackay Limited, Chatham

7100930375

Contents

Preface to the Second Edition

In the preface to the original edition, I noted that for some years practitioners and users of market research in Great Britain had deplored the lack of a comprehensive summary of consumer research techniques and applications. At the time of writing (1971) there were many books available which treated this or that aspect of the subject, but evidently none that were widely considered to be comprehensive.

Thus, when approached in 1969 by the original publishers to take on the task of such a work, I found widespread appreciation of the need for the book among potential contributors, and an almost universal willingness on the part of the acknowledged experts in the fields who were asked to contribute their experience and thought to set aside time and commercial pressures in order to share their expertise with others. We saw the potential audience for the book in three distinct groups: the general marketing student, as a reference, and as a text for advanced course; practitioners, including those working in research and advertising agencies and on the staffs of manufacturing and service companies; and finally, those executives in agencies and companies who are charged with responsibility for the use and application of research findings.

At the outset, it was clear that the book would necessarily be a large one indeed if it was to have any claim whatsoever to being reasonably comprehensive. For this reason, I first turned to the task of gathering a team of advisory editors together whose functions included both the assumption of responsibility for an individual section of the book and also service as a board of editors. The section editors for the first edition included Liz Nelson, Paul Harris, John Downham and Bert de Vos.

While the focus of the book is British, an effort has been made to include references to work being done in America, Europe and elsewhere. Another decision made early on was that the contributors were to be drawn entirely from the ranks of practising market researchers rather than from academics. It was felt that the annealing process of commercial experience would lend strength to the fundamental purpose, which is to provide guidance to the efforts of those studying, doing and using commercial market research. In a way, our theme became one of, 'But will it help him to understand the problem tomorrow morning at 9.30?' Obviously, even a work of this size cannot be comprehensive. It is intended to be reasonably instructive in each of the subjects covered, and also to give guidance as to where to extend the search if more information is needed.

The organization of the volume became almost chronological in the process of conducting a study. We felt the overall content could be broken into what has, by sheer magnitude of the contributions, become two parts; the first devoted to the techniques of consumer market research and the second to the use of research. Further, each part, we originally felt, lent itself to further subdivision, the 'techniques' half being split into two sections: 'Collecting the Data' and 'Analysing the Data'. The second half was divided into 'Consumer Research Applications' and 'Media Research'. This, then, was the concept behind the original organization of the book.

In the Second Edition we took into account several suggestions from contributors and many from readers. We dropped the sections as such, as it was felt that the two parts provided enough division. Chapters on desk research and models were added; all chapters were revised, some more than others; several were combined with others, thus enabling them to be somewhat shortened. We corrected some 27 typographical errors, most caught by K. Kitahara, who translated the first edition into Japanese.

Sadly, since the first edition two of our colleagues have died, Gerry Arnott and Mike Burrows. We miss them as contributors and as friends. We have asked Brian Hughes to revise Gerry's chapter on Trade Research, and my colleague Roger Stubbs has updated Mike Burrows' chapter on Financial Relations Research.

Thanks are due to each contributor and especially to John Downham who willingly took up co-editing responsibility for the Second Edition, to McGraw-Hill for the idea in the first place and to Van Nostrand Reinhold Company for carrying the book to the second edition, and I am indebted to the Literary Executor of the late Sir Ronald A. Fisher, FRS, to Dr. Frank Yates, FRS, and to Oliver and Boyd, Edinburgh, for permission to reprint tables from their book, *Statistical Tables for biological, agricultural and medical research*. Finally, thanks to my wife, Joann Worcester, who did the prodigious job of reading the proofs and compiling the index to the Second Edition.

Robert M. Worcester
London, 1978

Part I. Techniques of market research

Introduction

This section, as in the First Edition, concentrates on marketing research techniques. While the section is aimed principally at practitioners and students of market research, it may also prove useful to the market research user as a guide to the methods by which the answers he seeks are obtained.

The section is written around the time sequence involved in carrying out a market research project. Thus, it starts with defining the problem and gaining the necessary background information before going on to techniques employed to solve marketing problems.

An attempt has been made to cover all of the major research techniques now employed perhaps at the sacrifice of depth in the analysis of the use and limitations of each technique examined. Each contributor has attempted to show the purpose of the technique covered in the chapter, its advantages and disadvantages, how it actually operates and, in each case, where to look for further information.

Definition of Problems and Client Involvement

Marketing research is characterized by its use of orderly scientific procedure. A discussion of techniques, therefore, must begin with the first step of that procedure, i.e. define the problem. There is a saying that, 'when your marketing problems are known, they are half solved'. The role of the researcher in helping to define problems is crucial. When the researcher is properly involved, he will be able to suggest not only which technique is most applicable but what data need to be gathered. He can separate out the essential data from 'interesting information'. He can also say when market research cannot assist in the solution of the problem. Proper involvement by the researcher can overcome the common pitfall of expecting too much from research.

Marketing research data can be helpful in predicting the future, but as yet not with any degree of accuracy. Marketing research cannot yet make decisions. The marketing man must still operate in the area of uncertainty.

3

Thus, looking ahead, market researchers will become more involved in making decisions; they will become more involved in clients' problems both before research is carried out and afterwards. There will be more of a continuous relationship between researchers and marketing men. The more that the continuous relationship concept develops, the more researchers will be asked to solve problems which are not of the bushfire type. Much problem solving will then be not of the 'outright difficulty' type. Research should be involved in the recognition of hitherto unnoticed opportunities and, often, research can provide the most profitable type of problem solving.

A chapter new to the Handbook, on desk research, begins to define the problem. Chapter 2 is concerned with qualitative and psychological techniques. Having defined the parameters of the problem from the research point of view, chapter 3 goes on to experimental design and models. Models are included in this section, but only briefly discussed, since this subject is more thoroughly treated in Part II of this book. Chapter 4 provides a 'short course' on sampling, chapter 5 covers survey questionnaire design using personal interviews. It seemed necessary to cover interviewing and field control in chapter 6 before discussing other widely-used techniques, audits (chapter 7), consumer panels (chapter 8) and omnibus surveys (chapter 9). The point of view that retailer research is closer in its techniques to consumer rather than industrial research has been taken. Thus, trade research as well as retail audits is covered in chapter 7.

The previous near total dependence on the personal interview is already becoming less marked and is likely to diminish further in the future. There are already signs of a greater inclination to postal, telephone, or self-completion techniques. Thus, chapter 10 deals with mail surveys and other techniques such as telephone surveys and observation.

Certainly, large users of research do not rely upon one technique alone. They use a combination of panels and audits, panels and surveys, audits and surveys. If any general point can be made out about choice of techniques, it is that if the client does not know much about his market or indeed much about a particular problem, he is best advised to use desk research and qualitative research and to proceed from that stage learning more and more about his market as he proceeds.

The stage has now been reached when the data have been collected by using the techniques described. What the user requires now is that the data are analysed quickly and efficiently so that the maximum amount of usable information is obtained. He also wishes to know how accurate the results are and whether the results are 'real' or can just be explained as random fluctuations. In addition, the user needs to be told of the complex inter-relationships of various parts of the data. Only when he has been given all these things is he able to use the research results with confidence, and be sure that they can profitably assist in the marketing decisions. Of course, any analysis of the data is only as good as the data that have been collected. No amount of 'playing with numbers' can get over such problems as questions asked in a biased way, questions missing from the questionnaire and incorrect measuring techniques.

In the last two decades tremendous advances have been seen in the analysis of market research surveys. Most of this has been due to the advent of the computer, which has brought speed and flexibility to the handling of data. This advance, though bringing obvious advantages, is not without its drawbacks. Previously, the researcher had, because of time and cost considerations, to limit the number of tables produced from any survey, and thus it forced him to think objectively about the analysis. It was necessary to consider only the most important hypotheses about the data, and this had the effect of disciplining the researcher in his approach to survey analysis.

Now, as the on-cost of producing a large amount of survey tabulations or extra analyses is small, there is a tendency to analyse 'everything by everything' and just 'see what comes up'. In some cases, where a new topic is being investigated, for example, this may pay dividends; but as has been pointed out[1] this testing of a large number of hypotheses simultaneously has to be handled carefully to avoid incorrect conclusions being drawn from the data. With this reservation, however, it must be stated that the increasing technological nature of survey analysis methods has mainly had a good influence on the analysis and interpretation of market surveys. Nowhere is this more true than in the use of advanced statistical techniques to discover important and complicated relationships in the data that have been collected (see chapter 14).

Chapter 12 describes what happens to a batch of questionnaires that have been completed. It tells how the questionnaires are checked, and how the data are transferred to a medium, such as punched cards or paper tape, which is used as input to an electronic computer. The methods of analysis given are mainly in terms of a general 'one off' quantitative survey. The temptation was resisted to include the special problems and methods of specific types of surveys such as qualitative surveys or panels and audits. Details of the analysis of data from such sources are given in the chapters devoted to them or in the references given in those chapters.

The next chapter (13) is concerned with elementary statistics obtained from survey tabulations and the testing of statistical hypotheses using a group of testing procedures which comes under the general heading of significance tests. These are used to explain whether observed differences in the data are due to the errors of sampling. It is well known, however, that the total error in any survey result comes from non-sampling errors, e.g. non-response and measurement errors, as well as sampling errors. Market researchers have paid too little attention in the past to estimating these non-sampling errors. Attempts have been made to quantify such errors[2] and to build them into a framework for estimating total survey error[3], but not much of this work has passed into current practice. The results of surveys are sometimes used as input to market forecasting exercises, especially when a survey has been repeated over a number of years. There is a body of statistical techniques subsumed under the heading of time series analysis, which can assist the researcher whose statistical analyses of surveys include future projections of market size, etc. Details are not included in this section's chapters as this would have taken too much space, and it was thought that such techniques were more often used by the statistical specialists in marketing departments than by the average market researcher. For those who wish to read about such techniques three references[4,5,6] are given at the end of the book.

Chapter 14 deals with the more advanced statistical techniques used to analyse market research data. The techniques go under the general heading of multivariate analysis. In most cases no single thing determines what makes consumers buy the products they buy or makes them behave in a certain way. The influences on consumers are many and varied, including such things as past behaviour and attitudes to the product. It is not surprising, therefore, that multivariate statistical methods, i.e. those which examine a large number of survey characteristics simultaneously, are widely used by survey analysts. The methods used are mathematically complicated but the description of them in this chapter involves only simple algebra.

Finally, I would like to again draw the reader's attention to the contribution of Liz Nelson and Paul Harris, section editors in Part One of the First Edition, whose original thoughts and contribution were so substantial and who did the substantial and significant job of collating the chapters which for the most part comprise the chapters that follow.

Robert M. Worcester

1. Desk research

Nigel Newson-Smith

Desk research is not the exclusive activity of market researchers. In a monograph on desk research written for the Incorporated Society of British Advertisers, Peter Anderson remarked that 'all business executives tend to be desk researchers'. More and more, business management is concerned with sifting, absorbing, and interpreting information to aid business decisions. However, while market researchers do not have proprietorial rights over desk research, they do reckon to have special talents in undertaking it; their skills are in collecting data, organizing it, and interpreting it against a brief; these are the primary skills required in desk research.

Desk research usually yields different data from those generated by field research, but on those occasions when it covers the same ground, desk research is very significantly cheaper. It avoids the main cost element in field-work, relying heavily on data other people have already collated.

Normally grouped with desk research are sales statistics, sales forecasting, and some forms of telephone surveys. For the purpose of this chapter, the first two are omitted as specialist techniques which often find their way into the market researcher's province, simply because they may suit the researcher's numerical and analytical skills. Analysis of one's own sales data, and forecasting, are, of course, relevant elements in many desk research projects. Telephone *survey* methods (as opposed to using the telephone to obtain expert assistance or factual data) are discussed in chapter 10.

Desk research is that which can be conducted from behind one's desk or by interviewing experts to obtain data; to this extent it is the antithesis of field research. The raw material for desk research is other people's data, not original data generated by a first-time survey or other original research techniques. Because of this, desk research is often referred to as the use of 'secondary data'. This is rejected here because the raw material for much desk research is *primary* in the sense that an original survey generates primary data and also because, within desk work, there are primary and secondary sources: sources which produce their own data (a survey organization, trade association, etc.) and those which quote information generated by others (typically the national and trade press).

One of the essential differences between desk research and most field research is in the prior assumptions made. Implicit at the start of a field survey is the assumption that the answer does not already exist in an available form. There is no point in indulging in relatively expensive sample survey interviewing to discover the level of tape-recorder ownership if the answer already exists somewhere other than in the secure hands of one's competitor. In contrast, a desk research project assumes at the outset that such information is available somewhere. The field researcher's skill is in knowing how to ask which sample of people the right questions. The desk researcher's skill is in knowing which information sources are likely to be the best starting points for the search. The common skills follow: that of organizing the resultant data and of interpreting them in such a way that they becomes useful, not just interesting, to the client.

A later section entitled 'Integration of Results with Field Studies' raises the issue of the relative status of desk and field research in consumer—and industrial—marketing contexts. The points to be made here are:

(a) While many (rightly or wrongly) feel that industrial market research has much to learn from consumer research in the conduct of sample surveys, it is probably true that those concerned with consumer research matters have more to learn from their industrial colleagues about the use and practices of desk research.
(b) If this is so, the common practice of relying on junior researchers to 'do a quick desk study' whilst their seniors get on with the (frequently) more interesting tasks of conducting a field survey needs to be severely questioned.

Following this introduction the chapter is split into two sections: the first dealing with the uses and practices of desk research—what is desk research, what it can do, who undertakes it and in what circumstances; the second covering the all-important question of sources of information—with no sources there can be no desk research. The chapter deals with the British scene, with a small sub-section devoted to considering overseas data sources. This is because, while the practice is broadly similar the world over, the sources used vary not only in title, but in origin, from country to country.

Uses and Methods of Desk Research

The process of desk research involves the receipt and (sometimes) translation of a question, the reference to internal or published source material and/or contact with a human source, the organization and evaluation of the resultant information, and its synthesis and interpretation. In everyday terms, you look up the answer or ask someone; the principle is simple. The practice, however, can be involved and time-consuming.

The uses of desk research

If we accept that desk research is an all-embracing information gathering and using process, then the uses are almost endless. It can be applied to any aspect of a commercial problem from the seeking of planning permissions to the examining of wage differentials.

Most lecturers and writers on the subject will point to three clear applications within the narrower aspect of consumer market research:

(a) to provide a background for a field study or other marketing activity;
(b) as a substitute for a field study;
(c) as a technique in its own right;

A fourth application is important, namely:

(d) acquisition studies.

To Provide a Background

Many consumer research proposals open with a statement suggesting that, prior to a field study, a search of the existing literature on the subject will be undertaken. The rationale will either be to orientate and educate the research executive or to avoid unnecessary repetition where research might have already been done. The learning application is of self-evident value: an informed executive is more likely to achieve a relevant field study than an un-informed one. In this context, desk research would take the form of checking out news reports, statistics, published surveys, etc., which together would provide a reasonably balanced picture of the market under study. This would be an informal process which would not necessarily have to be structured.

Probably the most frequent background usage of desk research is in its sampling application; the most obvious example would be the case of a field study of owners of a particular consumer durable item owned by a minority of the population. Data showing the level of ownership would be an essential prerequisite of efficient sampling which would be further helped if these data also described the type and location of such owners.

The scene-setting, or background sketching, facility of the desk research function is also frequently used by New Product Development management. A manager can resort to desk research for comparative descriptions of potential markets, or for a detailed analysis of a particular market as a first step to judge whether investment in prototype production, concept creation, field research, brainstorming, etc. (whichever is considered the right starting point) is likely to be worthwhile. Such questions as:

how big is the market?
is it expanding?
is it a concentrated or fragmented market?
is advertising heavy?

are nearly always capable of speedy answer (see also 'Acquisition Studies' below).

Similarly, many an annual marketing plan is preceded by a desk research review of a market, a reappraisal of all that is known about the market situation, to judge whether assumptions and conventional wisdom still have a factual basis.

As a Substitute for a Field Study

Desk research cannot, of course, fulfil the field research role of putting supplier in direct touch with consumer. Indeed it would be as wrong to infer knowledge of consumer behaviour from a study of production statistics as it would from a single group discussion. Direct contact with the consumer, however, is not always necessary: *vide* the retail audit technique.

Where desk research can be a useful substitute is on the occasion when a serious study, or perhaps re-analysis of existing research data, can lead to perfectly valid conclusions about the market. Many a New Product Development executive has discovered that a bank of product test results will reveal fundamental truths about how the consuming public looks at a product, and their attitudes to it. The interpretation of a campaign evaluation survey can be helped by a fresh look at the results of the copy test, avoiding a further survey designed to discover why the campaign appeared to have a specific effect. Here, then, is the role of desk research as a re-user of field research data, trying to ensure that new research is not undertaken if the answer can be shown to exist already.

As a Technique in its Own Right

As distinct from occasions where desk research can adequately substitute for a field research project, there are cases where desk research is, in fact, an improvement on the field alternative. To many in the business consumer market research can be weak when it comes to an accurate description of market parameters. The first two questions potential new entrants to a market will ask are: how big is the market? and at what rate it is growing? Sampling and question technique difficulties with consumer panels and other consumer surveys can, on occasion, render them inefficient when it comes to estimating the total size of a market. Practical difficulties in the coverage of retail audits can similarly render them inefficient devices for measuring a total market. Where the market is diffused between different types of retail outlet or different types of consumer, the measurement problem intensifies. The best example of these difficulties is seen in the food market, where significant consumption occurs in the catering sector, which is notoriously difficult to measure.

In difficulties such as these, desk research frequently produces not just better data, but probably 'correct data', lacking the disadvantage of inbuilt sampling error. Published statistics are generally freely available to describe the size of most of the markets with which industry is concerned. Data can be retrieved from the publication of statistics by a relevant government department or trade association, from trade periodicals, published market research results (these do suffer from the potential problems of sample surveys described above) and so on. From these sources it is usually possible to provide good 'hard' data about market dimensions. Market trend data can only be established from historical evidence of the kind which field research cannot gather retrospectively.

Acquisition Studies

A common method of expansion is by acquisition or merger and in this area desk research is of great importance. First, most of the data required to aid a buy/no-buy decision are available from a number of printed sources. Second, the security requirements of an acquisition appraisal are extreme, and field research is incipiently less secure than desk research because more people have to be involved. In the case of an acquisition appraisal, the sort of data required are:

(a) *Company Description* company history
financial structure
financial performance
ownership and directorate
plant location
production techniques
number of employees, etc.,

and thereafter match many of the data requirements for a new product study:

(b) *Products and Markets* competitive activity
advertising and marketing, etc.

Most of the data required under (a) will be contained in:

company reports
share registers
financial analysis surveys
brokers' reports
commercial directories
technical press.

In category (b) the trade press
official statistics
published survey data

are all additional sources. In all cases, however, a personal contact will help add meaningful flesh to the bones; but remember, even a carefully worded question can risk security.

The scope of desk research — what sort of information?

The main-stream desk research project may well involve the description of a new consumer goods market which a manufacturer is considering entering. The sort of brief to which the researcher could be working might be as follows (FR indicates a probable requirement for field research results):

Objective What and who is the study for? What are the constraints? In conjunction with what should this be read?

Definition What is included in and excluded from the product field? (This might include a technical product specification.)

Market Size Volume and value estimates; the importance of exports and imports.

Rate of Development The same data over time (perhaps the last 5 to 10 years).

Competition A list of present producers and their brands and pack sizes. A price list. Estimates of brand share, preferably showing movement over time (FR). Launch activity.

Distribution Types of retail outlets involved (FR); Participation by wholesalers (FR); Retail and wholesale margins.

Advertising Levels Volume of advertising by brand, by media.

Consumers Purchasing, usage, or attitude data; product test results (FR).

Apart from relatively large-scale formal projects preceded by a written brief, much desk research activity is centred around specific questions such as:

What is the average confectionery retail margin?
How many toy shops are there in Lancashire?
Who manufactures plastic bottle closures?
What were last year's profits of my main competitors?
What is the volume of TV advertising on cosmetics?
Who are the major shareholders in XYZ Ltd?

Most frequently, however, researchers are faced with the question 'Will you tell me all you know about . . .?' A nonsense question. A frustrating question. A question which is not meant. What *is* meant is 'Tell me all *I* want to know about . . .' This requires in response a set of questions, the answers to which form the brief; and for any multi-question brief a written one is essential. The briefing process is therefore the same as for a field research project.

A note on sources

What are all these information sources, and where are they found? This chapter concludes with an abbreviated list, but in fact the sources are so many and various that an exhaustive list is just about impossible to produce. One of the best was compiled by Elizabeth Tupper and Gordon Wills under the title 'Sources of UK Marketing Information' (Ernest Benn, 1975). The book runs to 166 pages, most of which are devoted to listing and describing actual data sources. This book is regarded as an essential component of any marketing information department.

Briefer lists are contained in 'Principal Sources of Marketing Information' (Times Newspapers) by Christine Hull, 'A Monograph on Desk Research' (ISBA) by Peter Anderson, in various government pamphlets, and in textbooks on market research.

The desk researcher

In the case of field research, the careful user will consider the limitations of the technique before acting upon the results, or even commissioning a study. With desk research, however, one is much more in the hands of the researcher himself. The proposal is likely to include the statement: 'we will scan all relevant published materials and contact appropriate trade associations, etc.' which is vague. Unfortunately, there is little more that can be said at that stage, short of listing publications and individuals to be used as initial contacts. Desk research is rather like a treasure hunt; there might be a sense of achievement at each point on the trail, but the winner is the one who stays the course, using each clue to find the ultimate reward: it is not possible to map the entire course in advance. To this extent, the researcher is a detective; he needs qualities of nosiness, persistence, a fair degree of scepticism, even a streak of ruthlessness. Above all, he (or she, because experience suggests that women make better desk researchers than men; perhaps their patience helps) needs to keep an eye on the ball and not be diverted by tidbits of information which appear on the way—collecting fascinating but irrelevant information.

First, scepticism. Early in any project, the researcher will find conflicting pieces of evidence, or at least data which are difficult to reconcile. A government might publish reports of an annual production of 400 000 tons, but the latest article by an expert in the trade magazine might suggest only 300 000 tons. A trade federation might record sales of £6 million, implying a price of £15 to £20 a ton, which the researcher recognizes as either side of the truth. These apparently conflicting pieces of evidence must be faced and subjected to several questions:

(a) Are any of the figures misprints?
(b) Have I/they got the definitions right? Are we talking of domestic consumption or is institutional usage included? Are the product definitions the same? Is the retailer's profit margin included or not?
(c) Which figure seems more *reasonable*? It is far safer to accept a sensible answer than a surprising one.
(d) Which source is, in principle, more likely to be right? Which has an axe to grind? Which could have the wool pulled over its eyes?

13

(e) Where did the data come from in the first place? Have I got a primary or secondary source of information here?

(f) (In the context of a telephone or face-to-face contact) was I speaking to the expert/author or was it just the boss/assistant?

Faced with conflicting evidence, these questions spring easily to mind, but if there is only one source, or, more particularly, if all the sources agree, it requires an effort to don the mantle of scepticism. Nevertheless, an essential, if not endearing, quality required of the desk researcher is a healthy dose of scepticism (an attitude requiring proof before acceptance) if not cynicism (a predilection for fault-finding); this is where persistence comes in. Just because a fact is headlined in the press or published by the government does not *per se* make it true. The art is to discover where the press obtained the information or how the government calculated these statistics in the first place. In the latter case, the Central Statistical Office's quarterly 'Statistical News' provides a useful guide to developments in government (and some other) statistics.

Next, ruthlessness. It was Bacon who said 'knowledge itself is power'. (In fact what he really said was 'nam et ipsa scientia potestas est'.) If this is true, then there are two implications to the desk research situation. Much of the process, as we shall see, involves the use of people as sources, and to obtain information from individuals is at once difficult and easy, and for the same reason. On the one hand, people are generally much more willing to give information than one might suppose (most experienced fieldworkers confirm this), largely because communicating knowledge is an effective means of demonstrating power. On the other hand, to part with information is to an extent to part with power and it is for this second reason that the desk researcher needs to add ruthlessness to his persistence, to make sure that he is getting not only the truth but the whole truth. Part information can some-times be as dangerous as wrong information. Because many of the data used for marketing decision-making are confidential, important sources are closed to the would-be competitor, customer, or supplier researching in the same area. Commercial espionage is clearly out. The solution to the problem is in the building of a personal network of trustworthy contacts who agree to share information which, while not available to the general public but probably accessible to the professional researcher at a cost in time and/or money, can safely be shared on a reciprocal basis. It is possible to assume this information-sharing role without giving away secrets or behaving in any way improperly, and many businessmen operate on this basis much of the time. An important caveat is that the desk researcher, like any other market researcher, must be relied upon to behave with propriety and rise above any suspicion of either gaining or using the information improperly; to do this and remain a good researcher, he will have to have considerable freedom to make contacts without necessarily revealing who they are. One finds that librarians and information officers frequently subscribe to a network of their opposite numbers in the government, agencies, editorial offices, manufacturing companies and so on. This is one reason why they are so frequently able to answer a variety of questions at what appears to be uncannily short notice. (Who is X Ltd's sales manager; who is the major importer of jute; what is the average summer temperature in Scotland; what directorships does Lord T . . . p have?)

Evaluating the results

The problems attached to the evaluation, establishing the cost effectiveness, of desk research study match those of evaluating any study. An earlier section has briefly suggested the considerations involved in trying to evaluate an individual piece of information. When looking at the results as a whole, the normal process of looking at a report from the viewpoints of understandability, believability, usability, etc. apply.

Integration of results with field studies

Desk research plays a more important part in the industrial market research scene than in consumer research. There are probably two reasons for this. Industrial market research budgets are smaller, and the comparative cheapness of desk research makes it a particularly attractive proposition; and, more importantly, desk research is frequently a more apposite technique for the solution of industrial marketing problems. Industrial marketing problems are generally less separable from technical problems, and the more esoteric aspects of consumer marketing (consumer attitudes, etc.) are absent. It is for these reasons that a typical industrial market research report will contain the results of both desk research and field research, neither taking precedence over the other. On the other hand, the typical consumer research project which sets out to describe a market scene will very rarely contain the results of a desk project. In those cases where it does, the desk results will frequently be relegated to a separate appendix volume. There are several reasons for this; primarily that desk research and field research are frequently the responsibilities of different executives and the nature of the estimates resulting from the two techniques is different. The reliability of field research results is often expressed in terms of sampling error, whereas the reliability of desk research results cannot be quantitatively expressed. In spite of this common practice of separation, most researchers would agree that a complete marketing appreciation would be more valuable if the two sets of results were combined. That is to say, a description of consumer attitudes and consumer behaviour could be seen in its proper perspective if accompanied by an estimate of market size and rate of growth, together with a description of the distribution situation and marketing activity. Such an approach would imply the raising of a research report to the level of a marketing appreciation. Whilst this is not always desirable, it is a healthy discipline for a field research report to be introduced by an outline of what is known of the market so that the results could be viewed in perspective.

Organizing an information unit

Any sensible executive will ensure that the information which flows across his desk is categorized in such a way as to aid its future use. He will make sure that he has to hand relevant books, journals and references which will help him do his job. This library of information forms the basis of an information section, and a market research manager will add to it a number of statistical references, for example The Annual Abstract of Statistics (HMSO).

Of a different order is setting up a professional function to be the information base for a commercial or other operation. Time and money are required to achieve this: time, because each information section needs to be organized according to the requirements of its clients and only experience will show what the information demands are likely to be; money, because the purchase of printed data sources can be a costly business. An information function, while selective in its purchases and subscriptions, has to anticipate queries and briefs if it is to answer them quickly, and in order to do this must speculate—some of the speculative expenditure will inevitably prove wasted. A fully-fledged system will also need full-time staff to scan, retrieve, index, and file. Finally, and perhaps surprisingly, the capital involved in cabinets, cupboards, shelving, etc. can amount to a considerable sum.

One further point is on the need for flexibility. A company's information needs change over time according to whether it is acting aggressively or defensively, diversifying or rationalizing, concentrating on marketing or production. Such operational or philosophical changes need to be accompanied by a change in the information base. The contrast is therefore between the cheap and relatively easy task of maintaining an informal library of limited scope and that of building and running a professional information system.

Developments

Because the desk research process is basically a straightforward and simple one, the opportunities for *technical* development are limited. The obvious area for improvement has, disappointingly, received little attention: the opportunity for more automatic data handling. Storage and retrieval systems have changed relatively little over the last ten years or so. The use of microfilms, and of mechanical indexing, has been slow to develop.

The real area of change, however, is that of data availability. Government departments, particularly since the creation of the Business Statistics Office and Central Statistical Office, are increasingly making data available outside their own departments. Further, more and more companies are prepared to exchange information and even publish it. The most noticeable change is seen overseas. About 10 years ago, commercial information in Britain was better in quality and quantity than in most other countries of the world, with the exception of the USA, but now, although Britain is still amongst the leaders in the practice of field research, generally available commercial information is of a higher standard and more generally available in many European countries.

Sources

The printed word

Printed data sources are legion and most of this section is limited to a description of the type of data available from broad categories of publications. It is in no way exhaustive; it sets out to exemplify and to set the reader on the course of chasing valuable data by giving a sketch-map and some starting points. The building-up of a list of sources for just one market area is a long and painstaking business, involving, as it does, careful comparison and evaluation as well as organizing and cataloguing. While there is no real alternative to building up the list on the basis of experience there are one or two short-cuts already in existence which will help; such lists as:

  Daily List of Government Publications (HMSO)
  Sources of Economic and Business Statistics (Heinemann)
  Sources of UK Marketing Information (Ernest Benn)
  Principal Sources of Marketing Information (Times Newspaper)
  Willing's Press Guide (Thomas Skinner Directories)
  Current British Directories (CBD Research Limited)

Additionally, most trade organizations and Economic Development Committees have a fund of data which they publish, for example:

  Marketing Abstracts (Paper Industries Research Association)
  Trends in Catering (National Economic Development Office)

A walk around an HMSO shop will give a good idea of the availability of official publications.

The major sources are listed below under 10 headings*. Further discussion of some of these sources is to be found in T. P. Prout's 'Industrial Market Research Yearbook' (Gower).

(i) *General Government Publications* (all available from HMSO)

  Annual Abstract of Statistics
  Abstract of Regional Statistics
  Monthly Digest of Statistics

---

* In many cases the main source of real information will be the issuing offices or actual author rather than the printed data—a later section comments on the value of personal contact.

Social Trends
Economic Trends
Statistical News
Overseas Trade Statistics
National Income and Expenditure ('Blue Book')

In varying degrees of detail, these sources give statistical data on the key demographic, social, economic, industrial, etc., areas. Perhaps more importantly, they attribute sources and point the reader to the relevant government department for further data or expansion. For anyone likely to have a continuing interest in the business operating environment, the Annual Abstract of Statistics is essential for both its data and its list of sources; it is also a fascinating volume in its own right, covering amongst other subjects the climate, illegitimacy rates, the extent of infectious disease, air travel data, import-export statistics, educational data and so on.

(ii) *More Specialized Government Publications* (all available from HMSO)

Census of Population (and annual estimates)
Census of Distribution
Business Monitor series
Family Expenditure Survey
National Food Survey
Department of Employment Gazette

Census data, even if they are sometimes out of date, are essential to sampling procedures. The expenditure surveys similarly provide valuable background data for those marketing consumer goods and asking the question 'what sort of people are spending how much on what goods?' One of the key sources is the Business Monitor, which describes British industry sector by sector to give, in most cases, apparent consumption (i.e. production + imports — exports) data in considerable product detail covering, for example, toys (cardboard or paper toys, table games, modelling kits, mechanical toys, etc.), leather goods (luggage and travel goods, handbags, saddlery, harness, etc.), and sports goods (gymnasium equipment, golf balls, sports gloves, fishing tackle, etc.).

(iii) *Other Official Publications*

Trade and Industry (from HMSO)
Inland Revenue Annual Report and Statistics (from HMSO)
Monopolies Commission Reports (from HMSO)
Economic Development Committee Reports (NEDO)

To this list one can add many other HMSO publications such as Government White Papers, old Prices and Income Board reports (a fund of quite accurate information) and many reports by the Departments of Trade, Industry,

Environment, Health, Agriculture, etc., all of which impinge on many industries and marketing operations. 'Trade and Industry' is a weekly publication which reports on, amongst other matters, recently published official statistics and is probably the best source of keeping up to date with recently published official data.

(iv) *Quasi-Official Publications*

Trade Association Year Books
Current British Directories (CBD Research)
Directory of British Associations (CBD Research)
Councils, Committees and Boards (CBD Research)
Other Directories
Jane's Major Companies of Europe (Macdonald and Jane's)
Who Owns Whom (O. W. Roskill)
Kompass Register of British Industry & Commerce (Kompass Publishers)

This category contains many source lists and moves from government information nearer to the commercial field. Most commercial concerns belong to the relevant trade association (Food Manufacturers' Federation, etc.) and receive their publications. There are also other trade associations and groups including

The Advertising Association
Incorporated Society of British Advertisers
Institute of Practitioners in Advertising
Confederation of British Industry

not forgetting, of course,

Market Research Society
Industrial Marketing Research Association

Current British Directories and Directory of British Associations are self-evidently valuable elements in the library of anyone with a continuing interest in the flow of data.

(v) *Some Trade Research Associations*, such as

Paper Industries Research Association
Fruit and Vegetable Canning Association

supplement their basic technical research function with the provision of industry statistics and the operation of information services, news bulletins, etc.

(vi) *Trade Press*

The Grocer
Morning Advertiser

Caterer and Hotel Keeper
Confectionery Trade News
Beauty Counter
Chemist and Druggist
Cabinet Maker and Retail Furnisher
Packaging News
Toy Trades

as well as those in industrial fields, such as,

Plastics and Rubber Weekly
Paper Trade Journal
The Engineer

The list is almost endless (numbering over 2000) and is to be found in several directories, including Willing's Press Guide (Thomas Skinner Directories).

Again, most companies are aware of the various trade periodicals covering their industries; in fact, many industries are covered by more than one periodical and the art is to sort out the key publications to reduce reading time. Certainly the average trade periodical is a valuable source of data, particularly of competitors' activities.

(vii) *The Press*

National Newspapers (probably not local newspapers)
The Economist
Investors Chronicle

The national press is an excellent medium for getting early news of, for example, market developments, and the more serious papers contain business sections, special articles and supplements and run information services which can be of particular interest. A word of caution: the press is produced at high speed and relies on people as prime information sources and, because of these two factors, can make large factual errors. It is recommended to check the data before acting upon them. The author would isolate the Financial Times as by far the best source of complete continuing and reliable information for the businessman, but have a care, even these pink pages are sometimes subject to error! Press cutting services will read and abstract from the press according to a predetermined brief for a fee. Also worth examining is the Research Index (Business Surveys Ltd.) which indexes both newspaper and periodical items by industry and by company.

(viii) *Subscription Sources*

Retail Business (Economist Intelligence Unit)
Marketing in Europe (Economist Intelligence Unit)
Long Range Planning Service (Stanford Research Institute)
Mintel (Maclaren)
IPC Marketing Manual (International Publishing Corporation)

20

These are all additional sources of industrial or commercial information which are sold on a syndicated basis at prices ranging from less than £100 to over £2000 annually.

They are probably of most use to those companies with a very wide range of commercial interests, and while the subjects covered do reflect to a degree the commercial interests of their clients, the publishers reserve the right to produce articles on any subject which seems to them to be appropriate. One big advantage of these services is that they construct the reports. Such reports are extremely valuable start-points for examining a new industry or market, but of comparatively little value when describing a market with which the reader is already familiar.

(ix) *Published Surveys*

These range from the free to the commercially priced, from those published in the daily press to those available on request, and from the general to the particular. The British Travel Association publishes annually the findings of its travel survey which is in the form of statistics on holiday-making by British citizens. Two examples of published data which are abstracted from a syndicated research project are the JICTAR television viewing data and the results of the AGB Home Audit of consumer durable ownership. Many market research agencies have a bank of back-data or syndicated research results which are available on subscription, the size of which is related to the contemporaneity of the data.

(x) *Financial and Allied Services*

Extel Services
British Middle Market Directory (Dun and Bradstreet)
Guide to Key British Enterprises (Dun and Bradstreet)
Companies House
Stockbrokers' Reports
Bank Reviews

The first three are specialized financial services which provide, according to different contractual arrangements, analyses of company performances, credit rating services, etc. These services would form part of any examination of acquisition candidates, of customers, or of competitors. One notable feature of the last few years is of the up-grading of quality and quantity of stockbrokers' reports on industrial sectors and on companies within them. Many brokers' research departments are now quite sophisticated units, providing a wealth of detailed data describing market situations of use to many marketing managers, not just financial analysis. It is surprising how much businessmen still regard as confidential information about their subsidiary companies which is filed at Companies House and which is therefore available to the general public.

21

Internal sources

Insofar as two characteristics of desk research are its relative cheapness and the relative speed with which results can be obtained, the most effective sources of information can exist within the researcher's own office or that of his client. Internal data sources can be split into a number of categories which can be briefly described as:

Sales statistics
Field sales reports
Past market research data
The company library

The problem with these sources is that they are usually organized for specific purposes not necessarily connected with desk market research. Sales statistics are produced largely for sales and distribution control purposes; field sales reports (a valuable contribution to measuring, for example, competitors' activity) are again produced for sales management tactical purposes; market research reports are commissioned to solve either *ad hoc* problems or to undertake continuous monitoring measurement; and the information library is usually a source of scattered book shelves containing government reports, trade periodicals, etc. for general reference. As a result, although there is a wealth of information in most commercial offices, it is frequently easier to obtain the same information from outside sources, wasting both time and money. The desk researcher could profitably invest some time in trying to organize these many internal data sources in such a way that they can become a proper data base for very cheap and very quick desk research. (See also 'The Spoken Word' below.)

Overseas sources

Countries overseas have the same sort of information coverage as Britain, the coverage, completeness and contemporaneity varying proportionately with the degree of industrialization. Most industrialized countries are served by government and other official statistics, by data from trade associations and periodicals as well as from financial institutions, and by the media. The one area of difficulty is of company financial data where different local accounting obligations and procedures apply—in these cases the international banks are helpful.

Transnational or multi-national research is aided by those organizations specializing in international desk research; organizations such as:

The Economist Intelligence Unit (London and Brussels)
Gordon International Research Associates (Geneva)
Stanford Research Institute (Menlo Park (California), London and Zurich)
Battelle Institute (Columbus (USA), Geneva and Frankfurt)
Business International (New York and Geneva)

It is difficult even to begin the task of listing overseas information sources. Instead it is best to suggest a few opening courses of action for those undertaking this sort of desk research for the first time.

Apart from the use of international directories and research specialists, the first step which many have found useful is contact either with their own embassy in the country of concern, or with that country's embassy in their own capital. The status and competence of commercial members of the embassy staff have risen very significantly in the last few years. Frequently, contact with our embassies is best managed by talking to the Export Services Division of the Department of Trade, which exists specifically to help British business with their export-geared information requirements. Local Chambers of Commerce operate throughout the world with varying degrees of effectiveness and helpfulness. Most sizable companies have a continuing contact with their merchant bank which is likely to have overseas offices or associates which again can provide useful first-base information or initial contacts. On the statistical front, there are several international agencies such as:

The United Nations (and its satellites, FAO, ILO, etc.)
Organisation for Economic Co-operation and Development (OECD)
European Economic Community
European Free Trade Area

which regularly produce a mass of statistics of a commercial nature. The big problem in this area is that of time-lags, many of the data being as much as several years out of date.

The European Society for Market Research (ESOMAR) can, through its membership in many countries, provide help by pointing the researcher in a useful direction. There is naturally a number of generally available data sources with international or multi-national coverage.

Reference works would include:

Hints to Businessmen series (B.O.T.B.—Department of Trade)—
covering most countries
Bibliographies of Market Surveys (UNCTAD/GATT)
World Directory of Industry & Trade Associations (UNCTAD/GATT)
Yearbook of International Associations (U.I.A. Brussels)
International Directory of Market Research Organisations (Market
Research Society)
International Directory of Published Market Research
(B.O.T.B./Research and Finance Management (International) Ltd.)
Business Information Sources (University of California Press/Centre for
Business Information, Paris)

Europe in particular is covered by:

Directory of European Associations (CBD Research)
Europa Yearbook (Europa Publications)

European Directory of Market Research Surveys (Gower Press)

Eurofood (Agra-Canadean Publications) and AGRA Europe (Agra Europe London) covering agriculture and food.

Sources of Statistics for EEC and EFTA (Dept. of Trade)

Sources of Statistics for Market Research (OECD)

Statistics Europe (CBD Research)

European Directory of Business Information Sources and Services (Centre for Business Information, Paris).

Many of the company analysis services cover several countries, for example:

Moodies Services—covering many countries throughout the world

Dun & Bradstreet—several services in USA and Europe

Kompass Registers—cover virtually all European countries

Who Owns Whom (O. W. Roskill)—volumes covering European companies and overseas subsidiaries of N. American companies.

Beyond these initial contacts and international references, the process of searching for data sources and undertaking desk research is the same worldwide.

The spoken word

Most experts lay emphasis on the use of personal contact as a data source and they are right to do so. Individual people are the primary source of all information—however, people are fallible, and can be inefficient and lazy. It is wise to double check every piece of spoken evidence. Where individual personal contact is invaluable is in the ability to point to data sources. Within an information department, each member leans on the experience of each other member. Probably the most overlooked source is that of personnel in one's own organization—not only do they have skills and experience, but also many have prior experience in other fields. This is where the ferreting, dogged nature of the desk researcher is so important . . . and so is an element of cheek—the Chairman may be the only source of information, in which case he must be asked.

This last point brings the discussion round to complete the circle. The chapter opened with the comment that businessmen are desk researchers; we close with the thought that they are data sources as well.

The involvement of specialist market researchers reflects a need for useful information, whether desk or field techniques are used. The basic skills of organizing and integrating data are common to desk and field researchers, differing only as to the data collection technique, and many commercial questions are best answered by a blend of the two techniques in the hands of one research team.

2. Qualitative research and motivation research

Peter Sampson

Qualitative research is usually exploratory or diagnostic. It involves small numbers of people who are not sampled on a probabilistic basis. They may, however, be selected to represent different categories of people from a given target market or section of the community. In qualitative research no attempt is made to draw hard and fast conclusions. It is impressionistic rather than definitive. Quantitative research, on the other hand, is concerned with large numbers of people, usually members of some carefully drawn sample that is representative of a larger population. The data obtained are quantified on some basis to indicate the numbers and proportions of sample members who fall into different response categories. A degree of statistical significance is usually attributed to quantitative data and within the confines of a known margin of error, its conclusions are generalized to the population universe represented by that sample.

Motivational Research

Motivation or motivational research is not synonymous with qualitative research. Very often, motives are sought and explored by qualitative techniques, but these techniques are used for a wide range of purposes other than being concerned with motives. Equally, motivations can be quantified.

The concept 'motive' is a complex one in the field of psychology. Motivation explains *why* specific behaviour takes place. Gellerman[1] has commented that 'The first and most important thing to be said about motives is that everybody has a lot of them, and that nobody has quite the same mixture as anybody else'. This observation merely points to the fact that every individual is unique, which is of little consolation to the market researcher who is concerned with identifying groups, segments, target audiences, etc., on the basis of some common characteristics. Notwithstanding, sufficient people seem to have enough in common for us to recognize fairly homogeneous groups on the basis of certain parameters that include motives, thus making the identification of these valuable.

Early psychological theories of motivation took an 'animalistic' viewpoint, with the emphasis upon biological or physiological needs such as hunger, thirst and sex. Motivation towards the satisfaction of these needs or drive states may be regarded as being universal, automatic and self-regulatory. However, they provide little explanation of social or consumer behaviour. Social or 'secondary' drives may be regarded as explaining a good deal of the variation in human behaviour. They are enduring characteristics of the individual, but vary in strength from time to time, depending upon the extent of arousal or satiation. There is general agreement among social psychologists that there are six major social drives or motives. These are the:

(a) affiliation motive (the desire to be associated with or to be in the presence of other people);
(b) acquisition motive (the desire to possess or hoard material things);
(c) prestige motive (the desire to be highly regarded by other people);
(d) power motive (the desire to control or influence other persons);
(e) altruism motive (the desire to help others);
(f) curiosity motive (the desire to explore and investigate one's surroundings).

It has been said that motives tell us why people behave as they do, but there is rarely a simple, single explanation for human behaviour. This is especially the case with the type of consumer behaviour studied by market researchers. Here, we are more likely to be concerned with discovering the reasons why people behave as they do in terms of a number of variables, some of which go to make up this complex psychological construct, 'motive'. For example, we can employ characteristics such as demographic variables (sex, age, socio-economic class, etc.) behavioural variables (e.g. heavy, medium, light consumption) and, in addition, those closer to motivation like attitudinal, personality and life-style variables. In consumer behaviour terms, there are also situational or 'market place' variables like advertising, word-of-mouth influences, in-store activity and so on. Consumer behaviour may be thought of as a function of both the person and the environment, that is personal factors like attitudes, motives and personality traits and these external situational factors.

In the market research context, motivations are important, but only in conjunction with other information. Lunn[2] distinguishes two categories of person variables:

(a) relatively specific requirements that reflect the importance given by the consumer to product attributes;
(b) more general *motives* and attitudes that are, nevertheless, close to product context, e.g. traditionalism, economy-mindedness, experimentalism, and health-consciousness. They may be regarded as 'broad consumer values' that influence and *motivate* consumers.

The Uses and Limitations of Qualitative Research

Some research problems require a more flexible approach than can be provided by the standardized interviewing techniques offered by a structured questionnnaire. Under these circumstances, qualitative research may be employed. The writer[3] has listed ten common examples of the use made of qualitative research techniques:

(a) to obtain some background information where absolutely nothing is known about the problem area or product field in question;
(b) in concept identification and exploration;
(c) to identify relevant or 'salient' behaviour patterns, beliefs, opinions, attitudes, motivations, etc.;
(d) to establish priorities amongst categories of behaviour and psychological variables like beliefs, opinions, and attitudes;
(e) generally defining problem areas more fully and formulating hypotheses for further investigation and/or quantification;
(f) during a preliminary screening process in order to reduce a large number of possible contenders to a smaller number of probable ones;
(g) to obtain a large amount of data about beliefs, attitudes, etc., as data input for multivariate analysis studies;
(h) conducting post-research investigations or 'post mortems' to amplify or explain certain points emerging from some major study, without having to repeat on a large scale;
(i) in piloting questionnaires to test comprehension, word forms, the 'memory factor', etc.;
(j) where we cannot discover in a simple, straightforward way like direct questioning, why people behave as they do because the field of enquiry is personal or embarrassing in some way. In these circumstances some 'oblique' approach is called for, where projective questioning techniques may be used in a qualitative research setting.

Often qualitative research is required to stand by itself as the basis for decision making. That is, either cost or timing constraints prevent quantification or, indeed, quantification is felt unnecessary. Here, the researcher must exercise more caution and interpretative skill than is the case where more limited demands are placed upon qualitative research because of subsequent quantification taking place.

One of the major drawbacks of qualitative research is its intrinsic subjectivity. After a qualitative study has been conducted and presented, often, especially if the issues are subtle rather than black and white, there may exist the feeling that another researcher may have obtained a different answer. Some guard against this is to design the study to incorporate a means of cross-validation, albeit a fairly unsophisticated one. That is, to use some form of semi-quantitative method (easily done with four–six groups upwards, where the researcher is dealing with 30+ respondents) as a check on the subjective content analysis[4].

The Techniques of Qualitative Research

In qualitative research, respondents are either interviewed individually or in small groups. The main interview types are the:

(a) individual 'depth', or intensive interview, lasting upwards of one hour;
(b) group interview or group discussion, lasting between one and two hours, usually, except for longer interview formats like brainstorming and synectics;
(c) the semi-structured interview and shorter interviews (20–30 minutes) of the elicitation type;
(d) decision protocol interview[5,6]
(e) repertory grid interview.

In addition, there is a range of techniques that extend beyond interviewing, overlapping into areas of quantitative research. Techniques like perceptual mapping and item-by-use are borderline qualitative-quantitative approaches, but of sufficient relevance to justify brief mention at the end of this chapter.

The individual 'depth' or intensive interview

Many practitioners argue that the term 'depth' interview is a misnomer in that it is too often used generically to describe a wide range of different types of interviews. A suggested classification of interview types that covers a range of possibilities is put forward, covering such diverse descriptions as clinical, free, focused, non-directive, extended, unstructured, semi-structured, intensive[7].

Collectively, these interviews represent an interview type that may be described as *less-structured-more-intensive* than a standardized question-naire-administered interview. The classification delineates three broad types:

(a) true depth or clinical interview that corresponds to the psycho-therapeutic interview and requires far longer than a single session, and is, strictly speaking, outside the scope of conventional market research (Sheth[8] argues that 'the intense loyalty to Freudian psychology' which has characterized much motivation research has been largely responsible for the failure of it to contribute to consumer psychology generally);
(b) non-directive interview where, although the interviewer retains the initiative regarding the course of the interview, the respondent is given maximum freedom to respond in the manner he wishes, within reasonable bounds of relevancy;
(c) semi-structured, or focused interview, where the interviewer is required

to cover a specific list of points and, although the respondent is allowed to respond freely, a much tighter control is exercised by the interviewer in order to maximize the collection of relevant data. Specific areas may be focused upon. The interviewer (or researcher) has determined *a priori* the sort of questions to which he requires answers and is merely seeking the appropriate responses from the respondent.

The group interview or group discussion

In the case of the group discussion we are concerned with a number of respondents or group 'participants' brought together under the direction of a 'group leader' or 'moderator'. There is no correct size for any group. The number of participants may vary according to the type of participant, the subject matter for discussion and the group leader's preference. For example, with highly articulate and fluent professional people, the ideal size is perhaps five or six participants. With members of the public, seven or eight would be preferred. Under certain circumstances, like conducting a group discussion among elderly people or groups of inarticulate people, and dealing with a subject not likely to be of great interest to them, the number may be increased from nine to twelve. It is important to remember, though, that the value of any particular group discussion is quite independent of its size. Another question often asked is whether participants should be seated around a table with the leader at the head, or on chairs in a circle. In the author's experience it makes no difference at all. Given the accommodation available, people should be seated as comfortably as possible in full view of each other and the leader. If they are required to write anything down or fill in questionnaires, a table is necessary.

Whereas, in the case of the individual intensive interview, the flow of response is from the respondent to the interviewer, with the group interview the leader should play a relatively more passive role since the prime concern is group *interaction*. Each participant is encouraged to express their views, and is likewise exposed to the views of fellow group members. The leader says as little as possible and merely guides the course of discussion by, first, ensuring that participants are in fact discussing issues relevant to the problem or subject matter in question, or at least do not stray too far from this. (Often a move off at a tangent can be profitable but if in the judgement of the moderator this is not proving so, the group is refocused towards the issue under investigation.) Second, ensuring that each person participates fairly equally, which means encouraging less forthcoming members of the group, suppressing the loquacious, and seeing that no leadership force emerges from the group and takes over effective control. Goldman[9] has described five characteristics of the group discussion:

(a) the interaction among group members stimulates new ideas regarding the topic under discussion that may never be mentioned in individual interviewing;

29

(b) group reactions provide the opportunity to observe directly, the group process;

(c) the group provides some idea of the dynamics of attitudes and opinions;

(d) discussion often provokes considerably greater spontaneity and candour than can be expected in an individual interview;

(e) the group setting is emotionally provocative in a way that an individual interview cannot be.

Brainstorming and synectics represent special examples of group interviews. In attempting to increase the involvement of individuals in the group situation, increase the amount of group interaction, reduce the inhibition of group members and encourage creative thinking, brainstorming and synectics techniques may be employed.

In the brainstorming group a heterogeneous collection of participants is selected (compared to the usually fairly homogeneous group of participants in the conventional group discussion). Typically, if the problem was one concerned with an infant food product, instead of merely talking to mothers of infants, the brainstorming group would encompass men, women, young, old, married and unmarried and those with and without children. Rather than just sit down at a table or in a circle around the moderator, they may get up and walk about, break up into smaller groups, enact various role situations, etc. Whereas the average length of group discussion is $1\frac{1}{2}$–$1\frac{3}{4}$ hours, the brainstorming group would be likely to continue for much longer, perhaps three or four hours. The conventional group discussion would normally be a one-off affair but the brainstorming group may meet on several occasions or regularly over a period.

Synectics is a more recent method of directing creative potential towards the solution of problems (Gordon[10]). Synectics means, literally, the joining together of different and apparently irrelevant elements. In the group interview sense this means participants. These must be drawn from a wide spectrum of educational, academic, social, and work backgrounds. They must, however, have one thing in common, the ability to think creatively. The synectics process harnesses this diverse source of creativity, directing it towards the group goal which may be the solution of a problem or generation of ideas.

Participants may be screened for high 'creativity' or 'divergent thinking' (Getzels and Jackson[11], Hudson[12]) or 'lateral thinking' (de Bono[13]) in a number of ways. The synectics process involves a number of mechanisms, including the requirement that participants employ four different types of analogy thought processes. For a detailed discussion of what is involved in synectics the reader is referred to Gordon[10].

The synectics groups that the writer[14] describes are a very considerable modification of the Gordon approach. They involved five participants, carefully screened, and two moderators. The groups were undertaken on an *ad hoc* basis whereas the approach really required a continuous and regular operating group run over a lengthy period of time. The author concluded that in the context of generating new product ideas the synectics approach might be of value.

The elicitation interview

For most people, many of the attitude dimensions listed in lengthy scale batteries are irrelevant or 'unimportant' because they do not enter into the purchase and brand choice decision situations. Those that really matter will be few in number. The important attributes are those that contribute to the overall determination of buying behaviour— *these are the ones that matter.*

By asking respondents open-ended questions, like 'When you actually go out to buy _____ (product category) and you are in the shop, what things about _____ help you to decide what type of brand to buy? (Keep on probing) — I mean, what do you take into account when buying _____?'

and

'If you had to describe _____ to a friend who did not know what sort of product it was, how would you describe it? (Probe) What else would you say about it?'

'Top of the mind' or salient attributes are elicited[15] for *both products and brands*, that appear to relate to reasons for purchase and purchasing behaviour. These are examined and the key ones incorporated in an attitude battery for subsequent quantitative research.

Each respondent is able to rate about six items. On the basis of 12 items covered, with each respondent rating a selection of six; 50 observations per item will be obtained from 100 elicitation interviews.

The decision protocol interview

In the last couple of years, increasing attention has been directed towards the consumer decision process. That is, the series of steps leading up to the act of purchasing a particular product or brand. Traditionally, researchers have questioned consumers sometimes long after the event in an attempt to re-construct, by inferences, these decision processes. More realistic, however, is the Decision Protocol interview[5,6] conducted at the time of decision-making and/or actual purchase with the view to identifying the factors that led to a particular decision being taken and the linkages between those factors.

A weakness of present methods of motivational research is that they tend to be based exclusively on 'Why?' questions asked long after the event. Often, this type of data is generally inadequate. Decision Protocol Interviews are the means used in a point of purchase situation to elicit the pattern of decision making.

They involve a combination of observation and in-store interviews. That is, after gaining the co-operation of store owners, interviewers are sited strategically near the display of products in question. They observe (or cameras record) purchasing behaviour. Respondents are then interviewed, the reasons for their behaviour determined and the pattern of their decision process constructed[5,6].

About 30 decision protocol interviews using a combination of observation and questioning are usually sufficient.

The repertory or 'Kelly' grid technique

Criticism of traditional exploratory research techniques from the standpoint of their subjectivity and the occasional failure to obtain responses in the 'true language of the consumer' led to the development of the repertory grid interview in the context of market research. The repertory grid technique was felt to be a much better way of locating attitude scale items or 'constructs', from which semantic differential scales for multivariate analysis procedures could be devised. The methodology involves ranking stimuli.

A detailed discussion of personal construct theory is outside the scope of this chapter. The interested reader is referred to Kelly[16], Bannister[17,18], Frost and Braine[19], Bannister and Mair[20], and Riley and Palmer[21].

In market research practice, for most exercises, the repertory grid interview varies little from the original Kelly approach in its basic form. The respondent is presented with a list of stimuli numbering from a half dozen or so to a maximum of around 30. Somewhere in the region of 16 to 20 is about optimum. A wide variety of different types of stimuli may be used. For example:

(a) products, e.g. tea, coffee, milk, drinking chocolate, etc.;
(b) brands, e.g. Lyons, Typhoo, Brooke-Bond, Tetley, etc.;
(c) concept statements, e.g. 'slow-roasted coffee granules', etc.

Stimuli may be presented in the form of word labels, written statements, drawings, photographs, actual packs or products, advertisements, etc.

After removing any stimuli from the list the respondent has not heard of, or on some other grounds that require exclusion, three stimuli are presented to the respondent, who is asked to state one way in which two of them are alike and yet different from the third. The basis for similarity (the emergent pole) and the difference (the implicit pole) are recorded. The remaining stimuli are then sorted, equally between the two poles. Then another three stimuli are presented and the respondent asked to state *another* way in which two of them are alike and different from the third. The interviewer continues to present the respondent with different triads until the respondent can no longer think of any reason why two items are different from the third. When this occurs, the respondent's repertoire of constructs is said to be exhausted and the interview completed. The triads are selected according to some random procedure that ensures identical triads are never repeated.

With the repertory grid the interview situation resembles more a test than an interview. Considerable skill is required to administer such a test. A good interviewer or 'tester' is not necessarily a good 'depth interviewer' or vice-versa. The information sought and collected is extremely specific. Although repertory grids may be administered in conjunction with an individual intensive interview, if the grid is executed properly, it should be exhaustive and, at the end of it, both the respondent and the interviewer will have had enough. The case for combining repertory grid interviews and individual intensive interviews is a weak one, if either is to be done properly, but there may be special circumstances where this is justified. For example, we may have a problem that can be explored initially, albeit in a somewhat speculative way, by conducting a short (perhaps highly focused) intensive interview followed by a repertory grid test using no more than half a dozen stimulus items.

A major drawback of the repertory grid interview is the tendency for some responses to be utterly valueless in terms of the type of information being sought. Two types of such responses are found. First, there are those which are too descriptive or irrelevant, and secondly, those which are too evaluative. Examples of the first type are:

(a) 'Those two come in bottles; that one comes in a cardboard packet';
(b) 'Those two are made by ABC; that one is made by XYZ'.

Typical of the second type are:

(a) 'I like those two; I don't like that one'.

Given a response like, 'My children like those two; they don't like that one' the researcher is able to transpose this into something that could form a scale, such as, 'Is liked by children'—'is not liked by children'.

This particular example shows up another problem that is faced in utilizing grid responses. According to Kelly, 'Is liked by children—is not liked by children' is not a proper construct, whereas 'Is liked by children—is liked by adults' is a construct.

Similarly, responses like 'Fizzy—not fizzy' and 'Fizzy—still' may often be obtained. A good deal of editing, rephrasing, etc., is usually required. This is bound to reduce the overall objectivity of the exercise in that an element of subjective interpretation is called for. (A categorization for the different types of responses provided by repertory grids is described by the writer elsewhere[22].)

Figure 2.1 shows a typical completed grid sheet.

A single repertory grid sheet such as this will, on its own, tell the researcher very little. A series of these (any number from say, 12–40 or 50 is usual, depending on time/cost factors and the problem in hand) is content analysed by sorting, classifying, and listing the items. The collection of items obtained from the set of repertory grids would be used to form scales for subsequent attitude research. They may also be computer analysed[21].

Repertory Grid Sheet / EMERGENT POLE (√)	TEA	OVALTINE	COCA-COLA	COFFEE	LUCOZADE	WATER	DRINKING CHOCOLATE	MILK	RIBENA/BLACKCURRANT	SOUP	ORANGE SQUASH	MILK SHAKE	IMPLICIT POLE (×)
Harmful to teeth	(×)	√	(√)	×	(√)	×	√	×	√	×	√	×	Not harmful to teeth
Add sugar	√	(√)	×	(√)	×	(×)	√	×	×	×	(√)	√	Do not add sugar
Comes in bottles	×	×	(√)	√	(√)	×	(×)	√	√	×	√	×	Comes in other containers
Not stimulant	×	√	×	(×)	√	(√)	√	√	√	√	√	√	Stimulant
Opaque	√	√	×	×	×	(×)	√	(√)	×	(√)	×	√	Clear
Nutritive value	×	√	×	×	√	√	×	(√)	√	(√)	(×)	×	No nutritive value
Can drink through straw	×	×	√	√	√	×	×	(√)	×	(×)	√	(√)	Cannot drink through a straw
Not addictive	×	√	(×)	×	√	(√)	√	(√)	√	√	√	√	Addictive
High calorie content	(×)	(√)	×	×	√	×	(√)	√	√	×	×	√	Low calorie content
Derived from plants	(√)	×	×	(√)	×	×	√	×	√	√	√	(×)	From other source
Dairy product	×	(√)	×	√	×	×	(√)	√	√	(×)	×	√	Not dairy product
Fizzy	×	×	√	×	(√)	√	×	√	(×)	×	(√)	√	Still
Cannot buy frozen	Could not divide equally					×	(√)				(√)	(×)	Can buy frozen
Thirst quenching	√	(×)	√	×	×	(√)	×	×	√	×	√	(√)	Not thirst quenching

Fig. 2.1

Descriptions of the use of the repertory grid in market research exist. Frost[23] has described an interesting use of the repertory grid technique in respect of television programs. Clemens and Thorton[24] describe the role of the repertory grid as the first stage of a 'gap analysis' approach to locate new product ideas. Sampson[3] describes how repertory grids were used to obtain pack image dimensions for male toiletries.

These examples of the use of repertory grids and, indeed, their commonest use, employ the rotated triads approach. This need not be so. A simple variation is to have one fixed element in a succession of different triads, e.g. abc, abd, abe, acd, ace, ade. Equally, although Kelly suggested that the minimum context within which a construct can be formulated comprised three elements, the grid approach can be used with just two stimuli being presented. Yet a further variation is to 'fix' one pole, and ask the respondent to supply the other, rather than supply both poles.

Completed grids may be regarded as data sheets that provide lists of actual or potential semantic differential scale items. It has been suggested that immediately after obtaining constructs, the interviewer may transform these into five, six, or seven-point scales and undertake a further scaling exercise with the same respondent. The writer[3] has argued that considerable editing and tidying up of verbalized constructs is necessary in order to produce meaningful scale items.

As far as scale item construction is concerned, the repertory grid has been criticized[25] for 'dredging up' irrelevant and non-salient dimensionality, making further refining essential. For this reason, its use has largely been superceded by the Elicitation Interview when the requirement is to find quickly and inexpensively the most salient product attributes and features.

Problems Encountered During the Interview Situation and How They May Be Overcome

The writer[3] has described the various problems that may be encountered during the interview situation which serve to distort the accuracy of responses. These barriers to communication are:

(a) psychological barriers, i.e. the memory factor, emotional factors, and unconscious or repressed material;
(b) language barriers;
(c) social barriers.

Different Types of Interview Situations

The use of projective techniques

Within the context of the individual intensive interview or conventional group discussion, use is very often made of a wide range of projective techniques.

Oppenheim[26] suggests that suitably designed projective techniques can penetrate some of the following barriers:

(a) barrier of awareness—when people are unaware of their own attitudes and motives;
(b) barrier of irrationality—to overcome the rationalizations that people make when they talk about themselves;
(c) barriers of inadmissibility and self-incrimination—when people are disinclined to admit things in a conventional interview situation;
(d) barrier of politeness—when respondents are disinclined to be critical because they are, by nature, polite and tend to behave so towards the interviewer.

By projective technique is meant the utilization of vague, ambiguous, un-structured stimulus objects or situations in order to elicit the individual's characteristic modes of perceiving his world or of behaving in it (Chaplin[27]). The underlying theory of projective questioning is that in certain circumstances it is impossible to obtain accurate information about what a person thinks and feels by asking him to explain *his* thoughts and feelings, but this information can be obtained by allowing a respondent to project these on to some other person or object. Some examples are given below.

(a) *Sentence Completion Tests.* The respondents are asked to complete statements like 'Women who give their families tinned vegetables are . . .', 'People who don't have bank accounts are . . .', 'Women who use Lux Toilet Soap . . .';

(b) *Word Association Tests.* The respondent may be presented with a list of stimulus words and, for each one, asked to say what he thinks about when he sees the word;

(c) *Fantasy Situations.* The respondents may be asked to imagine that they are motor cars, lawn mowers, or boxes of chocolates and describe their feelings;

(d) *Cartoon Completion.* The respondent is shown a cartoon similar to a comic strip with 'balloons' indicating speech. Usually, two people are shown in conversation but only one balloon contains speech. The respondent's job is to fill the other balloon with his idea of what the other person is saying.

(e) *Draw a Picture.* A respondent may be asked to draw or sketch a picture. Often reported studies describe how people with bank accounts, when asked to draw the interior of a bank, draw what appears to be a friendly place, whilst people without bank accounts tend to draw rather awesome and grim interiors.

(f) *Picture Interpretation* This technique is based upon the Thematic Apperception Test (TAT) which, along with the Rorschach Ink Blot Test, must rank as the most widely known and used projective test in clinical work. Here the respondent is shown a picture—either a line drawing, illustration, or photograph—that is rather ambiguous and asked to say what is going on or tell a story about what is illustrated.

(g) *The Friendly Martian.* Many research situations are concerned with low interest and low ego-involving products and subject matter. People may not perceive differences to exist, or genuinely opt for 'the most convenient' or even behave randomly. Alternatively, these inferences may be expressed rationalizations rather than true reasons for underlying behaviour. Here, the Friendly Martian can be useful.

Questioning forms like:

'Well suppose a Martian had landed in the middle of the High Street and wanted to open a bank account. All four major banks are there, what do you think he'd do?'
(Why? and so on) or

'Now if a Martian landed, went into a tobacconist and found he couldn't get King Size cigarettes (his regular brand) what would he do?' (Smoke a smaller size of that brand, another King Size brand (What?) etc.)

The depersonalization of the participant into some neutral embodiment offers considerable scope for oblique questioning of this nature.

In projective questioning, the individual's responses are not taken at face value, i.e. with the meaning that the respondent would expect them to have, but are interpreted in terms of some pre-established psychological framework. It is here that projective tests have come in for major criticism. A considerable degree of subjectivity is exercised in the interpretation of responses to projective tests, and very often 'experts' may be in disagreement amongst themselves. For an extremly detailed review of projective techniques, the reader is referred to Murstein[28].

Abelson's 'role rehearsal' technique

An interesting exploratory research technique is that described by Abelson[29]. In practice, role rehearsal consists of asking respondents, in a group discussion situation, to alter their behaviour pattern in some extreme way by offering an incentive for them to do so. Abelson describes a study where he asked housewives to serve chicken three times a week for a year to their family in return for $15.00 a week, and an agreement not to tell them that this arrangement had been made. According to Abelson, the approach yielded useful information on the reactions of the individuals to this offer, in terms of perceived obstacles and problems they would face, which gave some insight into their attitudes. Studies undertaken using this approach to see just how loyal consumers were to their regular brands, have brought to light some interesting information. The offer can be progressively increased in the attempt to break down strong brand loyalty. Failure to achieve this transfer at a given size of offer, and the reasons why a person will not switch brands, illustrated why brand loyalty was so strong. Furthermore, the group situation provided some interesting interaction between the 'disloyals' who caved in at the offer of a small incentive and the 'loyals' who either held out for a larger incentive or remained loyal at 'any price'.

Immediately after this section of the interview has taken place (and it is recommended that it is towards the end of a group session) respondents are told that the offer was really fictional. Participants appear to enter into the spirit of the exercise and do not mind being misled.

The Selection and Training of Interviewers

Many of the basic requirements for individual intensive interviewing are the same as for interviewing with a standardized, structured questionnaire (see chapter 6). However, over and above these basic skills, additional skills are required because non-standardized interviewing is a more complex task and the quality of information is to a much greater extent dependent upon the skill of the interviewer. Precisely what these are is difficult to determine and there is a distinct lack of any detailed research on this question.

There is a general agreement that 'depth' interviewers must be very carefully selected and thoroughly trained (Berent[30]). However, on the question of on what basis selection should be made and the type of person that makes a good interviewer, there is less agreement. Berent argues for selecting qualitative interviewers from amongst the 'normal quantitative field force'. He lists the necessary qualities as:

(a) the ability to relax in the interviewing situation;
(b) a friendly manner;
(c) the ability to instil confidence;
(d) to like people and be interested in them;
(e) to be broadminded.

He considers that people with strong ideas about politics, religion, or morals and people with a conventional and narrow outlook are likely to be unsuitable. Whereas the first set of qualities are obviously desirable, and narrowness and rigidity a likely disadvantage, it is difficult to imagine why the possession of strong views should be a drawback, providing the interviewer has sense enough to keep his or her views from entering into the exchange.

From the standpoint of selecting 'depth' interviewers, Berent argues in favour of having intelligent people without academic qualifications rather than psychologists. Many practitioners have expressed a preference for graduates, especially in one of the social sciences and, particularly, psychologists. This preference one way or the other must be regarded as very much a personal one. There is no conclusive evidence to suggest that graduates are better than non-graduates and graduates in one discipline better than any other.

As far as training is concerned, some basic instructions in interviewing methods like achieving rapport, questioning approaches, prompting and probing, is absolutely vital. The trainee interviewer should be made to listen to tape recordings of an experienced interviewer's work and to undertake a number of trial interviews on different subjects, with different respondents. These should be tape-recorded and subject to criticism by the training officer in the presence of the trainee. Even among interviewers who exhibit a flair for this sort of work, the commonest mistakes are invariably to ask leading questions and the failure to probe. This can be corrected if they are pointed out. Trainee interviewers should be allowed to listen to the recordings of other trainees and, through constructive criticism, improve their own performance and that of their fellow trainees. Even with experienced interviewers it is a good idea to comment constantly on their work and run refresher courses in order to develop their skills and improve their performance still further.

With group discussions, many of these considerations in respect of selection and training apply. Certainly, there is far more to conducting a group interview than merely sitting round a table with a group of people and getting them to talk. Failure to achieve interaction will result in a series of dialogues between participants and the group leader. With inexperienced group leaders this often tends to happen.

Individual group interviewing styles, even among experts, can vary. Moderating a group discussion is rather like driving a car. One can accelerate, slow down, steer the group in a different direction, change gear and arrive in the right place, go around in circles or get hopelessly lost. Just as some moderators are skilled enough to take part in a Monte Carlo Rally, others manage to reverse into their own garage doors.

Assessing Performance

Apart from fairly obvious errors, like asking leading or loaded questions and the failure to probe when this was clearly called for, a skilled qualitative researcher can, by listening to the tape recording of an interview, usually make a fair assessment of the interviewer's performance from the general run of the interview and the nature of the data (notes and/or edited transcripts perhaps) provided by the interviewer. Obviously, not all interviews will be good ones. Even the most skilled interviewer can have an 'off-day' or, more commonly, a poor respondent or a poor group. Experience will help overcome these. If a respondent is very poor at communicating and verbalizing, there is a strong case for terminating the interview and finding another respondent.

The Use of Tape Recorders

At one time there was disagreement about the advisability of using tape recorders for individual depth interviews; there is no disagreement about using tape recorders for groups, where they are considered essential. Berent[30] felt that the advantages (a complete record of the interview obtained without effort by the interviewer who is thus able to concentrate on the actual interview without worrying about recording information) are outweighed by the disadvantages. He described these as:

(a) the likelihood of the respondent becoming inhibited and selfconscious;
(b) tape recorders attract the interest of other members of the family;
(c) the likelihood of interruptions through tape recorder failure or having to change a tape;
(d) transcription is arduous and costly.

Wilson[31] stated that a tape recorder at an interview creates anxiety and inhibits the discussion.

The writer[32] has opposed these viewpoints and argued that the advantages of using a tape recorder outweigh the disadvantages. A friendly relaxed approach and manner and the clear guarantee of anonymity by the interviewer can very quickly allay any suspicion and anxiety about the tape recorder on the part of the respondent. True, there are some individuals who flatly refuse to have an interview recorded but, in the author's experience, they represent less than one per cent of people approached. Moreover, it is likely that some of these people would refuse to be interviewed without a tape recorder. That tape recorders attract other members of the family does not appear to be a major disadvantage. Interviewers should be instructed always to conduct the interview with the chosen respondent *alone* and preferably in a quiet part of the house. Unfortunately, the home environment of some people does not always allow this. In some circumstances there is only one available room in the house which may have to be shared with children and other adults. The interviewer is instructed to be as polite as possible in restraining other members of the family from joining in. Another problem in crowded homes is the television set, which the interviewer would politely ask to be turned off. If the circumstances under which the interview has to be conducted are too unfavourable, an appointment to carry this out at another time may be made or another respondent found. However, if the respondent happens to be one of an extremely small minority located only after a long and intensive search and the only time and place the interview can be obtained is a room full of children, adults, dogs, cats, and a television set, there may still be a strong case for going ahead.

In the case of individual intensive interviews, making the interviewers produce a 2000–3000 word edited transcript, including the most interesting verbatim comments, rather than produce a complete verbatim transcript, is often a satisfactory compromise.

In a study to determine the effect of accuracy of response in survey interviews by using tape recorders, Belson[33] concluded that

. . . the use of the machine was rarely a source of overt objection. Despite possible expectations to the contrary, this is the common experience of others reporting on the use of tape recorders in interviews.

. . . for the sample as a whole, the tape recording of the interview did not appear to reduce the accuracy of respondent estimates.

Video-Tape Recording

For group discussions and individual interviews in the past few years, increasing use has been made of video-tape recorders to provide a visual as well as sound recording. A special filming studio is required as are skilled technicians to film, record, and set lighting. Participants must be told that they are being filmed and, providing that the camera is sited in some unobtrusive place (like a hole in a wall, and operated from the adjoining room) they do not manifestly appear to be adversely affected. The precise effect that filming has could, however, be the subject for some empirical research.

Video-taped groups have been found to be especially useful with children (playing with toys, eating sweets, etc.) and adults who are required to use their hands or undertake some other activity like eating, drinking, smoking, opening packs, etc. Filming merely to record facial expressions to supplement voice intonation and verbal responses is, in itself, likely to be of little value in cost-benefit terms.

Analysis and Interpretation

The results of an interview or group discussion may be regarded as the results of communication between the interviewer and the respondent and, in the case of the group discussion, between respondents themselves. Communication may be analysed by a technique known as 'content analysis'. Berelson[34] defines content analysis as 'a research technique for the objective, systematic and quantitative description of the manifest content of communication'. Berelson describes 17 types of use of content analysis that in some way or another call for the quantification of content elements like words, themes, characters, items, and space-and-time measures. (It is outside the scope of this chapter to discuss approaches to content analysis in detail. The interested reader is referred to Berelson[34], and Holsti, Loomba and North[35].)

The content analysis forms of Berelson and others have been primarily concerned with the analysis of written documents and items of communication, like newspapers. Some attempt at quantification lies behind the analysis. With the analysis of qualitative research interviews, the objective of content analysis is to abstract the relevant and important data without quantifying. Precisely how this should be done and the criteria that should be used is an area that has been neglected by market researchers until recently. Papers have appeared discussing sophisticated methods of linguistic content coding[36,37], and the problem of interpretation generally[38]. The analysis and interpretation of qualitative data is very much an individual skill possessed more by some researchers than others.

The Psychological Interpretation of Qualitative Data

At the simplest level, analysis of overt content, 'content analysis', represents the most objective treatment. If one is looking for clues as to what behaviour is relevant to a particular problem or product field purely in a descriptive sense or what 'attitude dimensions' appear salient, this will suffice. It is when the researcher is asked to explain *why?*, why people behave as they do, why people hold the attitude they do and so on, that the question of interpretation becomes a contentious one. The non-psychologist has his own private viewpoint, experience, perception, insight, call it what you will. The psychologist has all these things, and, in addition, a familiarity with a body of theory derived from many and conflicting schools of thought. Rarely do we have, amongst contemporary market research psychologists, an exclusive commitment to a school of thought like Freud, Adler, Jung, Rank, etc. There may, however, be a tendency to incline slightly towards a particular viewpoint. Very often a 'psychologists's interpretation' may be full of conclusions like '*a hoarding or collecting instinct* is, therefore, necessary in order to save the coupons from the cigarettes smoked'. Or, 'they were also more *guilt-ridden*, than smokers of X'. The reader or user must be very careful to look for, discuss and be satisfied by, sufficient evidence to support conclusions like these which, on the face of it, always appear speculative.

It has been argued that the psychologist or more appropriately, perhaps, the social scientist, can find good utilization of his skills in data collection. His discipline can also be of value in data interpretation. What is of greater value than these learned skills is a sense of pragmatism when it comes to interpreting data, in terms of appreciating what it is going to be used for, either to provide hypotheses for future testing, data for some subsequent research input (i.e. scale items) or the basis upon which some decision will be made. Here an appreciation of marketing implications is invaluable.

The Choice Conflict — Which Technique?

There may often be a choice conflict, over which to use for a given problem, between the two major techniques, individual intensive interviews and group discussions and the repertory grid approach, and elicitation interviews as alternatives. While certain points may be made that can guide technique selection, the deciding factor is sometimes a personal preference, but most often a question of logistics.

As a general rule, individual intensive interviews provide more 'depth', i.e. compared to a group discussion where 'breadth' is provided. This is not implying 'depth' from the standpoint of probing the unconscious mind. It is obvious that a one-to-one interview lasting between one and two hours will generate more information appertaining to the individual than in the case where seven or eight people are interviewed collectively for the same time. If it is necessary to obtain information *in considerable detail* about people's past and current behaviour, their beliefs, opinions, and attitudes, then an individual intensive interview may be preferred. If certain broad indications are sought, a group discussion may be more appropriate. In some instances, this could mean undertaking some group discussions initially to obtain a broad understanding of the problem area and *then* undertaking individual intensive interviews either to obtain more detail, information in greater depth, or to focus on specific issues.

Historically, it has often been argued that in specific instances, where the nature of the subject matter precludes the likelihood of a group of people discussing it, individual interviews would be called for. In practice, we find that there are very few subject areas where group discussion participation is found embarrassing and it is possible to conduct groups on such hitherto taboo subjects as contraception, sanitary protection and so on. The problem here is not that people refuse to discuss personal matters in the presence of others but that the amount of inhibition which does exist tends to produce a rather superficial discussion. Thus, although we are able to talk to groups of people about sanitary protection, it is likely that we could obtain much more information from an individual interview situation. The whole area of financial research presents a similar problem. Whereas people are prepared to discuss their finances in the presence of others, they are much more forthcoming when interviewed alone. The rule must be, therefore, that if detailed information on personal matters is required, individual depth interviews are to be preferred to group discussions.

The repertory grid technique has been claimed to be the most appropriate one [24,23,19] where the problem is merely to obtain image and attitude dimensions for subsequent scaling exercises. The writer[3] has shown how, for a given problem, group discussions and repertory grids proved equally satisfactory, with neither being exhaustive in generating pack image dimensions. Current thinking suggests that, where possible, both groups and/or individual interviews should be used in conjunction with repertory grids to ensure that the total dimensionality of the product or problem field is located[22]. For locating salient attributes and product features, the elicitation interview is unquestionably the most cost-effective.

In deciding how many of what type of interview to be carried out, time and cost considerations are likely to be the determining factors. For example, in the case of group discussions there are sometimes good reasons for not mixing social classes, particularly DE and ABC_1, in which case class composition of groups may be on some basis like:

$$AB$$
$$C_1$$
$$C_2$$
$$DE$$

or

$$ABC_1$$
$$C_2DE$$

or

$$AB$$
$$C_1C_2$$
$$DE$$

However, there is little evidence to support the viewpoint that men and women should not be mixed for most general discussions or that a spread of ages (excepting extremes) is disadvantageous.

If some regional split is sought (although it is unreasonable to expect the group discussion technique to do more than provide the hypothesis that 'there may be regional differences') it is unlikely that the number of groups to be carried out will allow for all possibilities. For example, a two-class, two-age split in two areas would require *eight* groups. In many instances this would be undertaken but, in others, some compromise would be effected like:

south ABC_1	. . .	under 35 years
south C_2DE	. . .	over 35 years
north ABC_1	. . .	over 35 years
north C_2DE	. . .	under 35 years

A group discussion can cost anything between £250 to £350 in the United Kingdom depending upon:

(a) who is being recruited, i.e. housewives are easy to find and recruit but women over 65 years with a full set of teeth are not;
(b) whether verbatim transcripts are required and whether a detailed report is to be provided;
(c) the amount of travelling time, expenses, and overnight accommodation involved;
(d) who actually conducts the group session. There are many psychologists acting as consultants scattered throughout Britain, acting as 'sub-contractors' who can conduct groups for a relatively low cost. In the author's experience some of these people are very competent but others are not;
(e) whether participants are to be paid. It now appears fairly standard to pay respondents, even for nothing else than to provide them with an incentive

for turning up, although if they use their own cars, respondents can be put to some personal cost. Payment varies from £2 for housewives coming to a morning or afternoon session, to £3 for, say, an evening session and as much as £5 for some considerable inconvenience.

Drakeford[39] has questioned whether payment or, indeed, the whole manner of recruiting, tends to attract certain types of respondent. This may be so but in the context of a qualitative research exercise where no generalization should be made for the total population, it is unlikely to be a major drawback to this sort of research. What is undesirable, though, is the 'professional' group discussion participant whose regular attendance can lead to her providing what information she thinks the moderator wants to hear.

Similarly, with individual intensive interviews costing between £40–£75 and repertory grid interviews costing between £20–£30, time and cost considerations will be important in determining numbers.

The writer has never found a case for conducting dozens of individual depth interviews since, after a certain point, they become extremely repetitive. Depending upon how categories are broken down, 5–6, 10–12, 20–24 seem adequate for most purposes. For example, if the subject was credit cards, something like

men card owners	=	10
women card owners	=	10
men non-owners	=	10
women non-owners	=	10

would probably be adequate. If time and money were vital considerations, a total of 24 (six in each group) may suffice. Certainly, one should not need 20–25 in each category.

With repertory grids, it has been shown by the writer[22] that high divergers produce, on average, twice as many constructs as low divergers, which could suggest that it is more worthwhile to undertake fewer repertory grid interviews than one would normally expect exclusively among respondents who are high divergers.

For deriving product attributes, the elicitation interview is extremely efficient.

Some Quasi-qualitative Techniques

Perceptual mapping

People cannot ordinarily provide accurate and reliable data about relationships among objects such as competing products and brands. The evidence of this is considerable[40].

Additionally, data may be spurious. For example, metric data (such as that derived from scaling approaches) make a number of assumptions about the properties of means, the differences between ratings, etc. Non-metric procedures (or 'lower order' data) make fewer assumptions about the nature of the data; these are techniques in which the only operations used are comparisons such as 'greater than', 'less than', 'similar to', etc. Non-metric procedures operate on a more meaningful conceptual level—that of paired comparisons and rank orders.

The approach is to present stimuli to respondents, pairwise, and for each pair, a similarity/dissimilarity measure is obtained. (The total number of pairwise comparisons usually made is $n(n-1)/2$, and where n is large, an incomplete block is presented.) The criteria used for determining similarity is irrelevant. This represents the underlying perceptual structure and is to be inferred from the perceptual organization features.

For each respondent, a rank order of descending dissimilarity is obtained, and for N respondents, these rank orders are subject to one of several computer algorithms, e.g. M–D Scal, Guttman and Lingoes SSA, SSAR and SSAP, Torgerson and Young's TORSCA or Carroll and Chang's INDSCAL. Each of these is a differently conceived piece of software that will result in the same effect, namely and literally a 'map' that positions the stimuli. These are positioned in relation to X and Y axes according to statistical goodness of fit measures[41].

Since any product can be visualized as composed of attributes or properties, they may be projected into 'perceptual' or 'attribute' space, being a configuration of how the objects are perceived in relation to each other. The 'nearness' of any two brands in attribute space may be regarded as an opera-

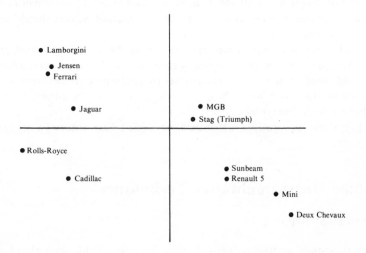

Fig. 2.2

tional measure of their competitiveness. The axes are interpreted as the dimensions or attributes.

The example in Fig. 2.2 (a constructed one) represents a two dimensional space scenario: n-dimensional space can be determined. The above example, based on motor cars, shows four 'clusters' of stimuli. The obvious interpretation would be that the vertical axis represented 'power', running High–low, North–south, and the horizontal axis represented 'price', running High–low, West–east. Thus we have a cluster of High Power/Low Cost cars (MGB, Stag) and so on.

Clearly such a research approach is far removed from individual intensive interviews and group discussions and some researchers would argue that in no way is perceptual mapping a qualitative technique. However, despite these objections and the fact that perceptual mapping can be extended into more complex analyses, the simple production of maps to show relationships is often a valuable exploratory device and with their interpretation open to subjective judgement the data may be regarded as 'more soft than hard'.

Item-by-use

In a complex market it is often necessary to obtain a structure of what products are used for what use occasion, in particular, in the context of understanding 'what really competes with what?'

Historically, the researchers' usual approach has been to undertake several group discussions to provide some background. More recently, a technique called item-by-use[40] has been used to provide a picture of the competitive structure of a market. Essentially it provides information about:

(i) what products compete with what, i.e. it breaks a product field into inter-competitive and intra-competitive brands/types, etc.;
(ii) which uses or consumer needs are similar;
(iii) which groups of products or brands are satisfying or seeking to satisfy which consumer needs.

There are normally three stages to an item-by-use study.

Stage 1 Preliminary interviews (10–20 say) to develop questionnaire structure;
Stage 2 Main fieldwork consisting of about 40 interviews;
Stage 3 Computer analysis.

The purpose of Stage 1 is to develop comprehensive lists of items (products) and uses. The end result is to develop a structure of the form of Fig. 2.3. The first column lists the stimulus items, the second, the uses for which that item is put by each respondent and column three indicates alternative/substitute items for that use.

ITEM	USE	ITEM
Potato chips	'Elevenses'	Biscuits Piece of cake Bar of chocolate Toast & Jam/Marmalade
	When friends drop round	'Twiglets' Peanuts Olives Cocktail biscuits
	In a pub	Sandwich Sausage on stick Peanuts
Nuts and raisins	At the cinema	Popcorn Cashew nuts Chocolates
	When watching TV	Sweets/chocolate Beans on toast Bowl of soup

Fig. 2.3

A Final Note*

The whole area of qualitative research is one which has received an increasing emphasis in recent years. But until very recently little attention was devoted to methodology. It is an area which appears to be familiar to almost everybody but really known and understood by a much smaller number of market researchers. To the many, it is a field of market research which lacks subtlety and requires little skill. To the expert it is the complete reverse.

* For an interesting review of the history of motivation research, see Collins and Montgomery[43].

3. Experimental designs and models

James Rothman

This chapter is divided into two distinct parts: experimental design and models. The researcher must consider the question of experimental design and models before proceeding to the choice of sampling techniques, sample size or questionnaire design, hence the placing of these two subjects early on in this section.

Experimental Designs

The role of experiments in marketing

According to Enis and Cox[14] the future will see experiments being used more frequently as an aid to reaching marketing decisions. An experiment can be defined as an attempt to measure the effect of a given stimulus or to compare the effects of different stimuli. There is a sense in which, on this definition, all market research can be considered to be an experiment; since any question is a stimulus. If we believed that the questions we ask are completely understood and answered absolutely correctly by every respondent, then the sense in which market research was an experiment would be trivial. However, we know from the research carried out by Belson[1] and others that, in many cases, respondents do not understand questions or do not answer them correctly. In other words, we should try to make as few assumptions about our questions, and the answers we are likely to get from them, as possible. This means that even when preparing basic questionnaires we should bear in mind the principles of experimental design.

To take an obvious example, if we wanted to test two advertisements to find out which of them was the more persuasive, we could, if we believed that respondents always answered questions correctly, just show the two advertisements to each respondent and ask them which of the two they thought would be more likely to make them buy the product. However, life is not as easy as that and we have to find a suitable experimental procedure for testing the two advertisements, such as splitting our sample in two, exposing one advertisement to each half of the sample and then, possibly, measuring their buying behaviour after the exposure.

One point which it is convenient to make here is that in most market research we are more concerned with comparing the effects of different stimuli, rather than with making an absolute measurement of the effect of a single stimulus, and this is probably particularly true of those areas where experimental design can be used. Thus, for example, we are more likely to be asked to say which premium offer would have the better effect on sales rather than to attempt to estimate the absolute sales increase that will be achieved by a given premium offer. Consequently, much of this chapter will be concerned with experimental designs for the purposes of making comparisons.

Definition of experimental design

If a given stimulus were always followed to exactly the same extent by exactly the same effect, and the effect of the stimulus could be measured with perfect accuracy, then experimental designs would probably not be needed. However, in most of our work, the measurements we make of the effects of stimuli are affected by many other factors. In a product test, for example, we will not find that everybody prefers one product by exactly the same amount to the other product; instead, we will find that some people like one product and some like the other and, moreover, that other factors such as the order in which the products are tried will affect our results. An experimental design, then, is a method of planning experiments in such a way that the sampling error can be measured and the results are affected as little as possible by random errors and are not confused by other factors.

Techniques for achieving good experimental designs

There are four basic ways of achieving the objectives of a good experimental design. First, we can remove or minimize these sources of error, e.g. we can reduce the effect of between-interviewer variation by ensuring that all our interviewers have been carefully trained. Again, if we are doing some type of split-sample operation we can remove the effects of between-polling district variation by ensuring that the sample is split exactly in half in each polling district. Second, if we cannot remove these random fluctuations, then we can attempt to control them, in other words, attempt to allocate them equally between the samples receiving the different stimuli. This is not always as easy as it sounds, particularly when there are many different sources of fluctuations and the number of experimental units we have is limited. One of the things which we will be talking about are the types of experimental design which are useful in these circumstances. Third, besides controlling the effects of some types of fluctuation we can measure their effect and make due allowance for them, e.g. if we want to compare the effectiveness of two different forms of packaging for a product by using two samples of stores and putting the product on sale in each of the stores in one of the forms of packaging, then we have two alternative possibilities for splitting the sample and analysing the result. Firstly, we can try to match the stores by ensuring that for every store in one sample there is a store in the other sample which is identical to it in terms of turnover, type location, etc. However, although we might be able to match our stores in terms of type of location, it is very probable that we could not match them exactly in terms of their turnover. In these circumstances, it may well be a better procedure to measure the effect of turnover on sales of the product before comparing the effects of the two different packages. Finally, if all else fails, the least we can do is to ensure the effects of these fluctuations are randomized. In other words, even if in our store test the store managers all refused to declare their turnovers, we can still assign the stores to the samples in a random fashion rather than, for example, allowing each store manager to put on sale the package he likes best. These, then, are the four procedures which we have at our command for reducing the effect of fluctuations on our measurements: we can attempt to remove or reduce these effects; attempt to control them; attempt to measure their effect separately and make allowance for them or, at the very least, ensure that there are no systematic errors and that the effects are randomized.

Conditions for good experimental designs

However, besides this there are four other requirements which we must bear in mind when we design our experiment. First, we should design our experiment in such a way that it will have adequate precision, i.e. we must employ enough experimental units on each treatment. This is the familiar problem of ensuring that our sample size is adequate so that we do not conclude that there is no significant difference between the effects of the stimuli when, in fact, the difference between them is sufficiently large to be of commercial importance. Second, the results should be applicable over a wide range, e.g. if we are comparing the effectiveness of two advertising campaigns, each of which contains a number of advertisements, then it is obviously not adequate merely to compare one advertisement from one campaign with a single advertisement from the other campaign. These two advertisements might be freaks and, whereas campaign A might in general be better than campaign B, one advertisement from campaign B might still be better than another given advertisement from campaign A. Third, as stated earlier, we must in any experiment be able at the end of all this to calculate the error in our measurements and to assess the significance of the comparisons which we make. Finally, the conditions in which the experiment is conducted must be such that the results are capable of real life application. All experiments are artificial to some extent so whether or not a particular experiment is too artificial needs to be either a matter of judgement or the subject of an empirical comparison with another experiment which, although more realistic, would be too costly for regular use.

Types of experimental design

Split Runs. The simplest form of experimental design is the split run. This is the arrangement in which, say, half the sample is administered one stimulus and half the other.

In market research, split runs, in spite of their simplicity, can be extremely useful, e.g. one form of assessing the likely demand for products at different prices is to ask respondents to indicate their likelihood of buying the product if it were on sale at a given price. The price quoted can be varied between respondents and the information derived used to plot a demand curve. Again, split sample techniques can be used to test the effects of alternative question wordings and, hence, to set upper and lower bounds for the prevalence of a given opinion or attitude.

Split runs should only be used in cases such as the above where, for one reason or another, it is not advisable to administer both stimuli to the same respondent since otherwise this would be the more sensitive design.

In designing split runs, two alternatives are possible, either each interviewer can be instructed to administer all the stimuli rotating them across respondents with different starting points for different interviewers, or the different stimuli can be issued to the different interviewers for administration.

From a theoretical standpoint the former method is always preferable since it eliminates between-interviewer variance; and also if, as is usual, different interviewers operate in different sampling areas, it eliminates between-area variance. From a practical point of view, on the other hand, the former method puts a heavier strain on the interviewer and, if the sample is to be split into more than three segments, it may be necessary to adopt the second approach.

'Before and After' Test. The second elementary experimental design frequently used in market research is the 'before and after' test in which a measurement is made and a stimulus is administered, either by artificial means, such as posting an advertisement to respondents, or by real life means, such as a test advertising campaign after which a measurement survey is conducted.

Two forms of 'before and after' survey are possible: that in which the second measurement survey is conducted on the same respondent as the first, and that in which it is conducted on a different sample of respondents.

Here again, the first method is theoretically preferable. However, unless the interval between the two surveys is long, there is the danger that the initial survey may itself act as a stimulus, e.g. respondents asked a brand awareness question may become conditioned and take a greater interest in brand advertising for that product group after the interview than they did before.

52

For these reasons most 'before and after' surveys are conducted on different samples of respondents.

In this instance, as for split sample tests, there are two alternatives, the second survey can be conducted in the same sample points as the first or a fresh sample of points can be drawn. From a sampling point of view the first method is preferable. However, if the initial survey is itself likely to create so much interest that the respondents talk to their neighbours about it and so condition them it may be necessary to use the second one. A further refinement of the 'before and after' survey is to carry out an additional control survey, that is a before and after survey taking place at the same time as the test survey but in which the respondents have not received the stimulus material during the interim period. The advantage of doing this is that a correction can be made for other changes that may have been taking place during the intervening period apart from the administration of the test stimulus, e.g. there may have been competitive advertising during the interim period or, in some circumstances, changes in the weather may have affected the results of the survey. Here again, the question arises as to whether the control survey should be carried out in the same area as the test survey.

The answer this time normally depends on the way in which the stimulus has been administered. In general, the principle is to have the control sample as close to the test sample as can be achieved whilst avoiding the danger of 'carry over' effects. However, if the stimulus has been administered in a real-life situation, the control area will have to be different, say a different television area or a different newspaper circulation area to that used for the test survey.

If the control area is widely separated from the test area, the researcher must then consider carefully if it may not indeed be so widely separated that it will be unlikely to have received the same external stimuli as the test area. If this is the case, then the use of the control area will only confuse rather than assist the interpretation of the results of the experiment. Ideally, this type of problem can be overcome by the use of several test and control areas. In the UK this is possible, but expensive, for local press advertising but virtually impossible for national press or television.

At this point we need to think carefully about the role of the 'before' surveys in the test and control areas. If a number of areas are used, can we not say that if they have been properly selected the 'before' surveys are redundant since we know that the results ought to be the same for both the test and the control areas? Why not use a special case of the split runs described above — an 'after only' design?

In certain circumstances the 'after only' design will indeed be better. The use of 'before and after' designs stems from the fact that the 'before' units can often be matched more closely with the 'after' ones than the test units can be matched with the controls. Thus, if we think conditioning effects will balance out, we might even be able to use the same units for both stages of the research. The following approximate rules can be used to reach a decision on the best design:

1. Is the correlation between the before and after stages expected to be greater than 0.5?
   If 'no', use an 'after only' design.
   If 'yes',
2. Will the amount by which this correlation exceeds 0.5 be greater than half the correlation expected between the test and control units?
   If 'no', use an 'after only' design.
   If 'yes', use a 'before and after' design.

Split runs and 'before and after' studies are relatively simple experimental designs. We now proceed to the more complex designs which are occasionally used in market research.

Latin Square Designs. This design normally arises when the effects of a number of alternative stimuli need to be compared, and the units over which they are to be administered are known to differ along two different dimensions. One may wish, for example, to carry out a store test on an item with a very high rate of sale, in four stores for one week only. The sampling unit in this case is a week in a store. If we label the four different test stimuli A, B, C, and D, it will be seen that if an arrangement as shown in Fig. 3.1 is employed, each test stimulus has been employed once in each week, and once in each store. Arrangements such as this, where the design can be represented by a square with the same letter appearing just once in each row and each column of the square, are known as 'Latin squares'.

More advanced versions of the same type of design known as 'Graeco Latin squares' can be used to control the sample across three or more dimensions.

The arrangement shown in Fig. 3.2, which might be used to test a product sold at four different prices W, X, Y, Z, in four different stores, in four different weeks from four different types of display stands A, B, C, D, is an example of the 'Graeco-Latin square'.

Store

		1	2	3	4
	1	A	B	C	D
	2	B	D	A	C
Week	3	D	C	B	A
	4	C	A	D	B

Fig. 3.1

Fig. 3.2

As will be noted, designs of this type can be used either to control the tests across a number of different dimensions or to enable the researcher to test two or more variables such as prices, display stands or pack designs at the same time. At first glance, it may seem that testing two different variables in the same test should halve the effectiveness of the sample and consequently no advantage would be gained. In fact, whilst the accuracy of a test of several variables using the same experimental units is slightly less effective than a test across just one variable, the loss of efficiency is relatively small and more information is gained.

Factorial designs

A related type of situation which is also found in market research is that in which a product or an advertisement can be considered as being made up of a number of different factors; e.g. a food product may be considered as containing two or more flavouring ingredients in differing proportions, together with different levels of a texturizing process. Again, in an advertisement, alternative visuals may be under test together, with the inclusion or absence of some specific product claim or free offer and the use or non-use of the company logotype as well as the brand name. In these circumstances, we may wish to measure the influence of each of these factors separately — in technical language, their main effects. In addition, we may also wish to see if the presence or absence of one variable influences the effect of another, known in technical language as an 'interaction' affect.

Interaction effects can, of course, arise at several levels; e.g. in the food product sample quoted above, if both flavouring ingredients were present together, the product might receive a high appreciation score, but if either were present separately, the product might receive a lower than expected appreciation score and could even do worse than if neither were present at all. Effects of this nature are known as 'first order interactions', a 'second order interaction' being the differential effects produced by combinations of three variables taken together, and so on.

55

If every combination of factors is tested, we have a so-called 'complete' factorial design which enables us to measure all main effects and all interactions. If we have a large number of different factors to test, the number of combinations required can become large, especially if we need to test these at more than two basic levels, such as present and absent or high concentration and low concentration; e.g. a test of the effects of three different flavouring ingredients at three different concentration levels would require the preparation of 27 different test products.

Whilst sample sizes used in most market research studies are sufficiently large to accommodate this sort of number of test items, the cost of their production can be high. In these circumstances, an incomplete experimental design can be employed. For example, with a design such as that shown in Fig. 3.3 it will be seen that using only nine different test products we have enough information to enable us to measure main effects and first order interactions for three different ingredients A, B and C each used at three concentration levels 1, 2 and 3.

$$
\begin{array}{lll}
A_1B_1C_1 & A_2B_1C_2 & A_3B_1C_3 \\
A_1B_2C_2 & A_2B_2C_3 & A_3B_2C_1 \\
A_1B_3C_3 & A_2B_3C_1 & A_3B_3C_2
\end{array}
$$

Fig. 3.3

In many tests it is reasonable to assume that higher order interactions will be small compared with the main effects and the first order interactions, and the cost savings achievable by the use of incomplete factorial designs more than offset the slight risk of making this assumption. Several works in this area such as Cox[2] contain examples of such incomplete experimental designs for various combinations of factors and levels.

Paired comparisons

An experimental design frequently found in market research is the paired comparison design in which respondents compare two different products or other stimuli. Use of these designs will also be discussed in chapter 15. A point which is worth making here, however, is that in a situation in which three or more products are to be assessed by means of a test of this nature, two alternatives are available:

(a) one product can be selected as a standard and each of the others can be tested against this;
(b) each product can be tested against every other one.

It will be seen that, in general, the second method known as the 'round robin' method involves a larger number of tests than the first. For this reason, some researchers have been tempted to use the first method. Nonetheless, it can be shown that the 'round robin' method is more efficient and can, in some circumstances, even yield information which is lost completely when the first method is used. Say, for example, we have the three products to be tested, A, B and C and the research budget permits the use of a total sample of 300 respondents. The first approach then would be to test A against C and B against C using a sample of 150 respondents for each test. On this basis, our information about the performance of A and B would be derived from 150 respondents. On the other hand, we could use the 'round robin' technique of testing A against B, B against C, and A against C, using three samples each consisting of 100 respondents. In this case, information on the performance of each of the three test samples is based on 200 respondents so that the variance is reduced by a quarter. In addition, when this is done, it may be found that product A performs better than one would expect when tested against B, but worse than one would expect when tested against C. This might arise if the different pairings encourage respondents to make comparisons along different dimensions; e.g. if A and B are similar in colour but different in flavour then when B is tested against A, respondents tend to express their flavour preference, rather than their colour preference and vice versa when B is tested against C. In these circumstances, the so-called effect of non-additivity described above can be observed. Whilst the interpretation of these non-additivity effects is often difficult, the presence of this type of effect may not be noticed and valuable information lost if the system of testing against a standard is employed.

The method for analysing 'round robin' tests is summarized in chapter 12 in this handbook.

Carry-over effects

These occur when the use of one stimulus affects the results obtained with another; e.g. if, in a store test, one particular stimulus administered in one week gives a high rate of sale, then this may pre-empt potential purchases that might have been made in a later week so that the effect observed for the stimulus administered in the store in the following week will be artificially depressed.

If a Latin square design is used the size of these carry-over effects can be measured if the test is continued for an additional week, without changing the stimuli between the stores. If there were no carry-over effects the sales observed in the last week should be the same as those observed in the previous week. The difference between the sales in the two periods shown represents a measure of the carry-over effects delivered by each stimulus which can be then used to correct observations made in the previous weeks[3].

Difference tests

In product tests especially, the researcher may find himself attempting to test for preference between products before it has been established whether or not the ordinary user is capable of detecting any difference between the test products. In some cases we may even be more concerned to know whether people notice a difference between the products than to know which they prefer; e.g. in existing products, the possibility of substituting a cheaper ingredient for a more expensive one can arise. However, if buyers notice the difference, the product may lose some of its franchise even if the majority of users preferred the product with the cheaper ingredient. Designs to test whether people are capable of noticing the difference between test products are known as 'difference tests'. The most common form of these is the so called 'triadic difference test' in which respondents are given three samples to try and informed that two of these are the same and one is different, and then asked to guess or state which one is the odd one out. If each of the three test products is selected by a third of the sample, the conclusion can be reached that there is no real difference between the two versions of the product. If, on the other hand, the odd one out is selected by significantly more than a third of the respondents, the opposite conclusion can be drawn. It should be noted that this type of test, since it is based on a variance of one third times two thirds, i.e. two ninths, is slightly more sensitive than a conventional product test where, if there is no preference between the two products, the variance would be one quarter.

One point to be noted in the use of this type of test is that it is important that respondents are informed that one of the three products in the triad is different from the other two. A frequent temptation is merely to ask respondents if they can notice any difference between the three and to say which one is the odd one out. This, however, means that respondents who notice a slight difference but are reluctant to commit themselves, and therefore claim that they can detect no difference, are eliminated so that the test results are distorted.

The sensitivity of difference tests can be increased by giving respondents more samples to assess; e.g. respondents may be given five samples to try and asked to sort the products into one group of three and another group of two. Analysis methods for this type of test which gives credit to respondents not only for getting a completely correct result but also a partial result such as A, B in one group and A, B, B in the other are given by Greenhalgh[4]. Another type of difference test is to ask respondents to test a number of test samples and say for each one whether or not it is the same as a standard which they are given to try.

The advantage of these more elaborate techniques is that not only do they enable a greater test precision to be obtained from a given sample size but they also enable respondents to be identified as good or poor discriminators. On the other hand, in the conventional triadic difference test, since even a non-discriminator stands a one in three chance of getting the right answer it is normally not possible to identify discriminators in a situation in which, say, 30 per cent of the population can discriminate and the remainder not.

Analysis of experiments and choice of sample size

Apart from the case of the simple split run with a two-way split where a conventional student 't' test can be employed, the standard method of analysing the results of experiments in which experimental designs have been employed is the analysis of variance or, where the test result is known to be correlated with some characteristic of the sample unit which it is not possible to stratify out completely in the experimental design, the analysis of covariance. This last method can be reduced to an analysis of variance of deviations about a regression line.

Details of these analysis techniques are given in chapter 12. One point, however, that should be made here is that it is often mistakenly believed that the size of samples to be used in an experiment is the minimum size of sample that can be accommodated within the experimental design. Thus, if the experimental design indicated is a four-by-four Latin square, then the experiment could be conducted on a basis of sixteen sample units. This, however, is merely the minimum size of sample that can be used. The size of the sample that is necessary must still be calculated on the same basis as for any other survey (see chapter 4). Whilst experimental designs can be more efficient than conventional sampling procedures because of the way in which they stratify out the between and within unit variance, the improvement in efficiency is usually not large and it is still necessary to estimate the within unit sampling variance and, hence, derive the size of sample that is required for any given degree of accuracy. This size of sample is then achieved by means of duplicating the experimental design, i.e. by repeating the experimental design for the required number of times.

Generally speaking, it is more efficient if the replications differ from each other, e.g. if it is calculated that 32 sample units are required and the sample design is to be two four-by-four Latin squares then the Latin squares employed should be different from each other.

Examples of the use of experimental designs

Voting Experiment

In August 1964, when the two main political polls showed different parties in the lead, Sales Research Services Ltd. carried out an experiment to test the hypothesis that political polls had a band-wagon effect encouraging voters to vote for the party which they believed stood the greatest chance of winning. A continuous survey sample was split into three equal sub-samples and each of these sub-samples was asked a standard voting intention question together with another question designed to estimate turnout. The introduction to the questions, however, differed between the sub-samples, one being told that the latest survey showed that the Conservative party was most likely to win, the second that the Labour party was most likely to win and the third being given no information on recent survey results.

The results of the experiment showed no significant difference between the sub-samples on voting intention. On turn-out, however, the experiment showed that supporters of a particular political party showed greatest determination to vote when told that the opposing party was in the lead and least determination to vote when told that their own party was in the lead. The differences were very small; nonetheless, this example is of interest since it illustrates how a simple experiment can often throw more light on a controversy than can the most powerful argument.

More recently N.O.P. used a similar experiment to show the way in which the results of the referendum on Britain joining the EEC might be affected by the wording used on the ballot paper[15].

Store Front Tests

The next experiment illustrates the way in which a suitable experimental design for the stimulus material under study can be used to test a general concept, i.e. to ensure that the results of the experiment are applicable over a wide range. The purpose was to determine whether the style and quality of shop-front design influenced attitudes towards stores such as grocers and drapers. Each member of a panel of designers was asked independently to assign pictures of shop-fronts to one of three categories, good modern, bad modern and old-fashioned design. A check was made to ensure that designers agreed on their assignment of photographs and a few pictures where there was substantial disagreement on their category were rejected. From the remaining pictures, three examples of each design style were selected. A Latin square design was then used to assign the pictures into groups of three in such a way that each group contained one example of each design style and that each picture appeared once with each of the pictures in either of the other two categories.

An omnibus survey sample was then split into nine equivalent sub-samples, each sub-sample being shown one of the groups of three pictures and asked to select the shop-front they thought best on a number of different aspects. Scores for the different shop fronts were then summed over the categories in which they appeared to yield ratings for each of the nine pictures and these ratings, in turn, were summed to yield average ratings for the design styles.

The results showed that, whilst clear differences emerged for the different design styles, it was possible for particular examples of a design style to yield inaccurate results; e.g. on drapery stores the overall preference scores were as follows:

good modern	48%;
bad modern	23%;
old-fashioned	29%

The average scores for three individual photographs, however, were:

good modern (photograph A)	38%
bad modern (photograph C)	27%
old-fashioned (photograph B)	43%

If these three shops only had been tested, because the good modern design was a relatively inferior member of the good modern design category whilst the old-fashioned shop was a superior member of its category, we would have reached the wrong conclusion.

An Exhibition Test. It was required to obtain data at low cost on the effects of different types of stimulus which can, for the purposes of this example, be considered as different prices, on the rate of sale of a product. Advantage was taken of an exhibition at which the product was placed on sale. The exhibition lasted for four weeks and the Mondays, Tuesdays, Wednesdays and Thursdays of each week were selected as test days on which sales of the product were measured. A Latin square design was used to allocate the prices to days of the week in such a way that each price was administered once on each day of the week and once in each of the four weeks that the exhibition lasted. A count was also maintained of the number of people visiting the stand on each day of the week.

From analyses of the results it was possible to produce what amounted to a demand curve for the product and also, as a by-product, to investigate the effect of day of week and week of exhibition on the sale of the product.

Store Tests. Similar techniques to the above are used to assess the effects of varying stimuli on the rate of sale of the product. The use of stores rather than an exhibition enables greater flexibility and more realism to be achieved albeit at a higher research cost. Normally speaking, a period of a week or a month rather than a day is used as the test period so as to accumulate an adequate number of sales under each stimulus without the necessity of introducing too many changes into the stores. A good account of such a test is given by Woodside and Waddle[16].

Dummy Stores and Laboratory Experiments. Another area in which test designs are frequently used is in test centre experiments in which respondents are asked to visit a centre for the purposes of research; e.g. in these centres 'find time' tests can be administered to compare the time it takes to find a brand in alternative pack designs on self-service style shelving. In these experiments the position of the test product on the shelves can be varied in accordance with the experimental design to ensure that the results are not biased by this factor.

Factorially Designed Product Tests. An important area for the use of experimental design is in the field of product tests. Products can be made up on the basis of a factorial design, whether complete or incomplete, with the proportions of key ingredients being varied or alternative processing systems being altered. These products can then be tested against each other using a 'round robin' design and from the results a score for each product calculated. These scores are then subjected to an analysis of variance so that the effect of each factor is tested to see whether it has a significant influence on product preference and the presence or absence of interactions are also explored. Tests of this nature are valuable not only in that they enable an optimum formulation of a product to be reached but because they can throw light on respondents verbal statements as to their reasons for preference in a product test.

Postal Surveys and Mail Order Advertising. Here, too, experimental designs are valuable. A factorial design can be used in the pilot of a postal survey to test the effect on response rates of such factors as the wording of a covering letter, questionnaire layout, inclusion or absence of a question on a sensitive subject, etc. Many studies of this nature have been reported, e.g. Sheth and Roscoe[17]. Further details on mail surveys are given in chapter 10. A similar approach can be used in testing advertising designed to achieve a direct mail type of response.

Models in Marketing Research

Definition of the term model

A model is a set of assumptions about the factors which are relevant to a given situation and the relationships which exist between them. The term model is normally taken to mean one in which the assumptions are stated explicitly and relevant conclusions can be drawn by deductive (usually mathematical) methods. Hopefully, the model has also been tested in various ways by adducing evidence in favour of the initial assumptions or by testing conclusions drawn from the model. (By assumptions here we include both those in which one can be reasonably confident because they are based on repeated observation and those for which the only evidence is 'common sense' or introspection.)

The role of models in research and marketing

The first way in which models are used in market research is that virtually every method of analysing research results involves a set of assumptions about the data which is equivalent to the use of, at the least, an implicit model. Usually, for example, when a scale question is employed an average score implies the assumption that the scale is of equal interval, i.e. the difference between the fourth and fifth position on the scale is assumed to be equivalent to the difference between, say, the first and second position. Methods are, of course, available for checking the equal interval assumption and experience has shown that even if a scale is not exactly of equal interval, the departures from this property are not normally sufficient to affect the conclusions one draws from the results. Nevertheless, it is important to realize that this assumption is being made.

Another example of the way in which we assume a model when analysing research results (including, of course, those from experimental designs) is the assumption of the order of interaction present in the data. As we have seen, incomplete factorial designs are frequently employed on the assumption that interactions above a certain order are unlikely to be important. Again, we normally assume that the data inter-relate in a certain way, e.g. we might assume that, within a certain range, liking of a soft drink can be calculated by some equation of the type: 'appreciation score equals constant times quantity of flavour component one plus constant times quantity of flavour component two plus a small interaction effect'. We do not countenance the concept that the appreciation score might be a function of these quantities multiplied together rather than added together, i.e. we assume an additive rather than a multiplicative model. By and large, most of these assumptions are justified by the fact that, within the sort of range of variables normally found in the market research situation, it can be shown that models are reasonably robust to departures from these assumptions. Models can be used to help describe the current state of a market, to aid understanding of the reasons for the way in which it develops or as a means of predicting what will happen in the future under alternative assumptions.

Principles of behavioural models used in market research

Behavioural models in market research perform three main functions:

(a) the construction of such a model prior to the carrying out of a survey can assist in ensuring that all the relevant data are collected and, in addition, can prevent the construction of over-long questionnaires asking 'interesting' but irrelevant questions;
(b) they can simplify the analysis of the survey results by enabling the answers to several questions to be combined in a meaningful fashion and ensuring that only relevant analyses are conducted on them;
(c) they reduce the gap between the market research report and the marketing decision it is intended to assist.

One point which should be noted about models in market research is that, whereas the conventional operational research model normally has to use data which are already available and consequently restricted by the form in which the data are produced, the market researcher building his own model can choose the method for collecting and analyzing the data to suit the requirements of the model exactly and, consequently, is not restricted in this fashion. Normally, for example, an operational researcher using data on the prevalence of a certain characteristic analysed by age and class would not be able to incorporate in his model the possibility that there is an interaction effect between age and class so that the characteristic is prevalent amongst say, young working class individuals and older middle class individuals. The researcher, on the other hand, is free to decide whether he wishes to have his analyses conducted in terms of class within age or on these characteristics taken separately. This leads to the first of our distinctions between different types of models used in market research, i.e. the distinction between global and individual models.

Global or individual models

A macro or global model is one which takes data in their conventional form for a population or a sample and attempts to relate it to other characteristics under study. An individual or micro model, on the other hand, takes each individual or unit in a sample in turn and relates the characteristics of that individual to the factor under study; it then combines the results for the individuals in the sample to produce a final result; e.g. in assessing a media schedule, a global model might simply work with conventional readership and duplication data, whereas an individual or simulation model would take each individual in the sample, calculate his expected number of exposures from the campaign, relate this to a response function and thus calculate the average response for the total sample.

The individual simulation technique has the advantage of allowing all the complexities in the data to be taken into account. On the other hand, the global model is simpler to operate; it can be more readily understood and, providing it is a correct representation of the situation, is likely to yield more accurate results than would a simulation technique. The best method is probably to work from an individual model and to attempt to build up from this an appropriate global model; e.g. the original inspiration for Ehrenberg's[5] NBD theory of consumer purchasing behaviour was that a negative binomial distribution of consumer purchases within a period would result if the assumption was made that each individual's purchases within a finite period would follow a Poisson distribution, whilst the long term frequency of individuals' purchasing behaviour followed a gamma distribution.

Formal and informal models

It should be noted that not all behavioural models used in market research follow or are expressed in exact mathematical terms; e.g. various models of the advertising process such as the DAGMAR model[6] have been hypothesized. Whilst purists may wish to argue whether models of this type are, in fact, worthy of the name, such a discussion is outside the scope of this

64

chapter. It should, however, be noted that a model is only useful in so far as it is expressed sufficiently precisely either for the model itself to be validated or for one or more of the conclusions that can be drawn from it to be verified.

Occasions or people

Many behavioural models used in market research work on the principle that people can be divided into types, e.g. buyers or non-buyers of brand A. An examination of the buying behaviour for most products, however, would indicate that truly brand loyal buying behaviour is relatively uncommon; consequently, models which assign probabilities of buying brand A on a given occasion to individuals and, hence, work in terms of expected numbers of buying occasions rather than in terms of people, must be considered to be more realistic. Again, in interpreting test results, the conventional model is that they indicate, say, that 60% prefer brand A to brand B; unless further evidence is available a more precise model could well be that brand A is preferred to brand B on 60% of the occasions on which it is tested. This is related to the next distinction between models traits and types.

Traits or types

It is often convenient to divide people up into different type groups, e.g. housewives who enjoy cooking and housewives who cook as a duty, people willing to try new things, people not willing to try new things, and so on. However, if these characteristics are studied in detail, it is often more likely that they will be found to be traits which people may have to a greater or lesser extent rather than type groups into which people may or may or not fall. The difference is shown in Fig. 3.4.

Frequency distribution of a trait   Fig. 3.4   Frequency distribution of a type

Segmentation and taxonomic models normally work on the type rather than the trait principle. In many instances, the type assumption is a convenient approximation and may well not distort the research results. However, if the type assumption is being made, it is important to verify either that it is valid or that the interpretation of the results is unlikely to be affected greatly if the trait principle is, in fact, more appropriate.

State or dynamic models

Most models used in market research work on the principle of finding an explanation for behaviour in terms of attitudes or other characteristics and then assume that if an individual's characteristics or attitudes can be changed, his behaviour will alter in the direction predicted by the model. Models of this nature can be described as static since they assume that the system is not altered by its dynamic characteristics. There is, in fact, very little evidence in favour of this assumption and, indeed, the work of, for example, Hovland[7] tends to support the view that attitudes may continue to change long after the stimulus causing that change has been removed. It would seem reasonable, then, to suppose that the same process of change might apply to behaviour.

The discussion now current as to whether or not changes in attitudes precede or follow changes in behaviour is, of course, related to the same question. Whilst researchers may be forced to continue to use static models and to make the static assumption until workable procedures for developing and operating a dynamic model have been discovered, it is still necessary that the nature of the static assumption should be clearly recognized.

Points in space

Congruity or Dominance

Coombs[8] has pointed out that data used in the social sciences can be considered as being represented by a series of points in space. It is convenient to consider models used in market research in these terms. Thus, for example, many models work on the congruity principle, i.e. that individuals will tend to purchase products which come close to their requirements. Other models, however, work on the dominance principle, i.e. that individuals will tend to purchase the product which in their space can be represented by a point farthest along one or more evaluative axes. A congruity model can be used as an approximation to an evaluative one by placing the requirement points at the extremes of the dimensions but normally an evaluative model cannot be used to approximate a congruity one.

Measures of Distance

Once the space with which we are concerned occupies more than one dimension, we have to consider the method by which distance will be measured, either for the purpose of determining relative congruity or dominance. The obvious form of measure to employ is the so-called Euclidean measure, that is to say the distance as the 'crow flies' between the two points. Those who recall Pythagoras' theorem will appreciate that this measure of distance, depending as it does on the sum of the squares of distances along each dimension, is essentially a quadratic function. Many marketing models, however, employ linear functions. The effect of using a linear instead of a quadratic function is equivalent to the use of what is called a 'city block' measure of distance, i.e. the distance between two points where one has to travel between them along a grid of roads running at right-angles to each other. There is no evidence to suggest whether subjective distances are

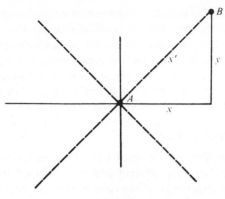

Fig. 3.5

most appropriately measure by 'city block' or Euclidean measures. It should, however, be noted that, whereas the Euclidean measure of distance is robust to rotations of the dimensions which constitute the space, the 'city block' measure is not. This will be seen more clearly if we consider Fig. 3.5. In this diagram, it will be seen that the Euclidean distance between the two points A and B will be the same regardless of whether the orientation of the axis is chosen to be the solid lines or the dotted lines. If a 'city block' measure of distance is employed, however, the distance between the two points in the one case will be $x + y$, whereas in the other case, it will be $\sqrt{x^2 + y^2}$ which will be seen to be smaller. Further transformations of the distance measure may be required to account for the relationship between behaviour or attitudes and the distance measure. A special case of such transformations are threshold models under which changes in distance below a certain level produce no effect.

Orthogonal or Oblique Axes

If data are to be represented by a system of points in space, it is necessary to consider whether the axes used to represent these points should be orthogonal or oblique. Using a static model it is possible to determine whether two measures are orthogonal or oblique to each other by considering whether or not they are correlated across respondents. However, the fact that two dimensions are correlated in the static case does not necessarily mean that they would also be correlated in the context of a dynamic model; again they might be orthogonal for one population and oblique for another. There is, therefore, some justification for systems of market segmentation or other types of models which use correlated measures, such as scores on different scales, as if they were, in fact, orthogonal to each other. Moreover, if a 'city block' system of measurement is employed, there is no reason for supposing that the 'streets of the city' must run at right angles to each other. So long as they run parallel to the axes of the system, whether or not the axes were

67

orthogonal in this model would be irrelevant. For small correlations between measures in the static case, the question of whether the distance measure employed should or should not correct for the obliqueness of the axes, is relatively unimportant. If, however, the measures do show correlations with each other which are greater than, say, 0.3 it is important either to consider carefully whether or not a correction should be applied or to verify that the model is, in fact, robust to the alternative assumption.

The Dimensional System Itself

Most behavioural models used in research tend to assume that all individuals employ the same dimensional system and, frequently, it will be found that they further assume either that all individuals agree on their perception of the world but their requirements differ; or that individuals have the same requirements but differ in their perception of the world, i.e.

(a) all individuals would agree on the way in which different products rate on a particular factor, but whilst some would want a product with a high score on that factor, others would want a product with a moderate or even a low score; or

(b) all individuals are agreed that a certain factor has an evaluative content so that a high score on it is always considered to be a good thing, but that individuals differ as to which products possess this quality to the greatest extent and, thus, differ in the items they purchase.

In most instances, however, the true situation is probably that individuals differ both in their requirements and in their perceptions and models which allow both these assumptions are preferable to the more restricted type which enables only one or the other assumption to be made. Again, it is normally recognized that the weights applied to different dimensions can vary; thus, in calculating a distance measure, dimension A might be given twice the weight to that applied to dimension B. In some models the assumption is made that these weights are the same for all individuals whilst other models enable the weights to be varied between individuals so that for some, dimension A might be more important than dimension B, whereas for others the opposite would be true.

Further to these complications, however, there is also the possibility that the dimensionality of the space itself may differ between individuals. This may simply be a matter of the rotation of the dimensions differing between them. If so, correct results can still be achieved if a Euclidean space is assumed. On the other hand, it is also possible that, whereas factors A, B, and C are salient for one individual, for another three totally different factors, say D, E, and F might be salient. In theory, the question of saliency can be overcome if the importance weights can be varied between individuals. This may, however, mean that the number of dimensions that may need to be studied can become unduly large either for the analysis itself or for measurement purposes.

Interactive or non-interactive models

In addition to the above, a further complication is that most behavioural models will assume that there is not interaction between the scores on different dimensions. Some models of individual behaviour, however, work on a hierarchical basis such as that shown in Fig. 3.6. It will be seen that this type of model is equivalent to assuming a high degree of interaction between the dimensions.

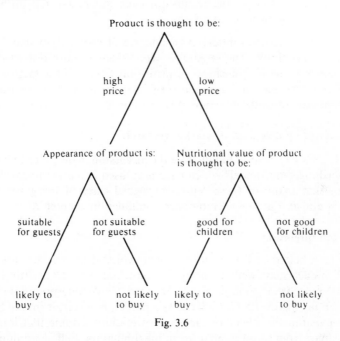

Fig. 3.6

In theory, this can be overcome by treating the interaction components as additional dimensions. In practice, however, the number of dimensions that are created becomes too great for the model to be usefully manipulated. At this point, then, it may be convenient to depart from considering data as a representation of points in space and employ other approaches. In this case, though, we need to consider whether or not the system of hierarchical needs has the same arrangement for different individuals.

General model

To sum up, the most general behavioural model would need to incorporate the following:

(a) a congruity principle instead of or as well as an evaluative one;
(b) the possibility for individuals to differ both in their perceptions and requirements;

(c) the incorporation of a dynamic element for the time that has elapsed since the change of attitude took place;

(d) the possibility for individuals to differ in the importance weight which they assign to different dimensions and even to differ in the dimensions which they select as salient;

(e) the incorporation of interaction terms whose weights differ between individuals;

(f) the interpretation of the results for each individual in a probabilistic rather than a deterministic fashion.

It is doubtful whether a model of this degree of generality would ever be a practical proposition. The researcher who selects a more restricted model must, however, be in a position to justify his choice of the factors that he considers to be relevant. It would seem that the availability of the model determines too often the selection of relevant factors rather than the reverse.

Examples of models used in market research

Finally, it may be helpful to illustrate the discussion in the preceding sections by describing some models which have been used in market research. It will be seen that many of these represent special cases of the general model outlined above. Further examples are contained in chapter 20.

Table interpretation

As we have stated earlier, even those who would deny that they are using a formal model may well be using an informal one. Conventional table interpretation is a good example of this. Table interpretation itself is discussed in chapter 12. Considered as a model, however, it should be noted that conventional systems of table interpretations assume that interaction effects apart from those catered for in the tabulation itself, are unimportant. Furthermore, if the same variable is tabulated on a number of different factors, straightforward table interpretation tends to ignore the effects produced by correlations between these factors. Thus, a report may state that young housewives tend to buy brand A more than older ones and those with young children tend to buy brand A more than women with older children or adult families. The analysis, however, does not consider whether both of these factors influence separately the purchase of brand A or whether housewives with young children tend to have the characteristic merely because they are also younger.

Models of attitude change

Models of attitude change clearly have considerable relevance to advertisement planning and testing and they are frequently referred to when interpreting research results both in test situations and before and after surveys. They have, however, tended not to be used directly in market

70

research. The reason for the lack of direct use of models of attitude change is probably twofold:

(a) the client, quite correctly, is interested in influencing behaviour and not attitudes and, consequently, models which relate attitudes or attitude change to behaviour are likely to be considered more useful;

(b) most models of attitude change normally have a qualitative rather than a quantitative format and, consequently, are not suitable for direct use.

A typical example of a model of attitude change is the Rosenberg and Abelson[9] balance model. This assumes that, if an object is associated in a positive fashion with a second object towards which the respondent already has an attitude, the attitude he will adopt towards the first object will be similar to that which the individual holds towards the second one. Conversely, if the two objects are negatively associated then the attitudes between the two objects will diverge.

The St James' model[10]

This is a model which was widely adopted in UK market research. The model can be categorized as a 'city block' distance type of model since it states, in effect, that individuals will buy the brand of a product which comes closest to their requirements using a 'city block' distance measure. The procedure for employing the model is as follows. Respondents rate brands using say, a battery of semantic differential scales, they also rate on the same battery of scales the characteristics they would wish an ideal brand to possess. The scale scores then are factor-analysed to yield a smaller set of orthogonal or, more usually, oblique factors. For each respondent the absolute distance between his rating of each brand and of his ideal is calculated and a regression is then conducted using these distances as independent variables and the likelihood of buying the brands as the dependent ones. This likelihood is estimated either from claimed purchase data or from respondent's preference ratings. This regression is then used to derive the importance weights to be associated with the different dimensions for all respondents. Whilst the obvious measure of these importance weights might seem to be the regression coefficients themselves, the classical version of the model employs, in their place, the squared correlation coefficients between the dependent and independent variables. The results from the model are normally expressed in terms of the average distance scores for each brand from the ideal along each dimension together with the derived importance weight for that dimension and these two measures can be summarized by multiplying them together.

The Fishbein model[11]

This differs from most research models in that it concentrates on the act of purchasing the brand rather than on the brand itself and allows for the incorporation not only of beliefs about the brand but also of normative beliefs, i.e. beliefs about how the respondent himself feels he ought to behave or about how he feels others, whose opinions he considers important, would expect him to behave. Each respondent scores first his opinion of the importance of different belief statements to the decision under consideration and then of the extent to which he believes the brand under study possesses them. These two scores are multiplied together for each respondent and then summed, again for each respondent, across belief statements. A check is then made to verify that the sum of these products is correlated with the respondent's overall attitude towards the act of purchasing the product measured on a separate set of scales. A similar procedure is adopted with respect to the normative beliefs.

Finally, the relative weight to be assigned to attitudes to the purchasing act and to the normative beliefs is obtained by means of a regression between these two functions with behavioural intention as a dependent variable. It should be noted that this is the first occasion on which a regression is used in the model. The correlations between the attitudes towards the act and the beliefs/importance products is a direct and not a multiple correlation derived from a regression equation.

The model, then, does incorporate an internal check on its own validity which avoids the danger that, with a large number of variables, high multiple correlations can be produced merely by capitalizing on random effects.

The NBD/LSD model of consumer purchasing behaviour

This model, which was originally developed by Ehrenberg[12], states that the number of purchasing occasions for an individual within a certain period follows a particular statistical distribution known as the negative binomial distribution. Moreover, where the penetration of the product or brand is relatively low, the distribution of purchasing occasions for buyers of the product follows an even simpler distribution known as the 'logarithmic series distribution'.

From these laws it is possible to derive a number of interesting conclusions about, for example, the number of individuals who, having purchased in one period, will cease to purchase in a following one, or the relative number of buyers to be expected in two periods of differing lengths. The occurrence of these distributions has been observed in a wide range of product fields and in overseas countries as well as in the UK and consequently it can, perhaps, claim to be the best founded of all market research models.

Television viewership

Another model derived by Ehrenberg and Goodhardt[13] is that for the duplication encountered between viewers of two television programs. This states that the number of individuals seeing both programs is (subject to small discrepancies, and with the exception of programs closely following each other or occurring at the same time on the same day of the week) pro-

72

portional to the product of their ratings. Moreover, the constant of proportionality is dependent only upon the days of week and the channels over which the programs are broadcast. This model is a valuable aid to television media scheduling since it enables duplication factors to be calculated readily.

4. Sampling

Martin Collins

The Theory of Sampling

Sampling is an essential ingredient of market research and can be justified on a number of grounds. In terms of practicality, it would simply not be feasible to establish the habits, views or requirements of every member of the population each time market research was called upon. Again, quite clearly, the cost of such a mammoth exercise would be prohibitive. Less obviously, sampling allows us to concentrate our attention upon a relatively small number of people and, hence, to devote more energy to ensuring that the information collected from them is accurate.

We do not even need to excuse sampling in these terms; it should not be regarded simply as a more or less unsatisfactory substitute for total coverage. Over the years, both the theory and the practice of sampling have developed to the extent that we are in possession of a reliable means of learning about the whole from a study of only a part. Properly conducted, sampling will produce results which are, for all practical purposes, as good as those which would emerge from a fully exhaustive study.

The use of sampling processes does, nevertheless, bring problems with it. Most of these lie in details of a particular use; they are not inherent in the overall process. This is an area where quantity can certainly not replace quality; the biggest is not necessarily the best. Before looking at some aspects of sample design, however, we must consider the pattern of theory underlying our use of sampling. This theory is basically concerned with chance and its inevitable effects upon data drawn from a sample. Without some appreciation of these effects, sample results become dangerously prone to misinterpretation.

Sampling error

If we measure some property, say height, for every member of a population, we produce answers which are indisputable facts (given, of course, that our measuring instrument is accurate). A measurement based upon a sample, in contrast, can provide only an *estimate;* an estimate which may be more or less close to the true population value being studied. It is an unfortunate fact that the estimate is unlikely to be exactly correct.

Suppose we have a 'population' of nine men:

Alf, aged 26; Dave, 29; George, 25;
Bert, 21; Ernie, 22; Harry, 20;
Charlie, 21; Fred, 24; Ian, 28.

By studying the whole of this population we can state the fact that their average age is 24. We might, however, wish to estimate this average using a sample of only three of the nine men. Putting all the names in a hat and withdrawing three of them, we produce, perhaps, a sample consisting of Alf, Fred and Harry. This sample will give us an estimate of the average age of our population of just over 23 — not far from the truth. This is, however, only one of the samples which we might have drawn from the hat. We might have chosen Alf, Dave and George to arrive at an estimate of rather under 27, or Ernie, George and Harry with an estimate of just over 22 and so on. In all, there are 84 different samples of three men which we could happen to draw; samples which would yield us estimates of the average age of our population ranging from under 21 to almost 28. Of all these possible samples, only six would actually yield a correct answer.

Clearly, then, sampling involves a risk; we stand a 6-in-84 (or 1-in-14) chance of getting the answer exactly right whilst, at the other extreme, the possibility exists that we might be almost four years astray. When we produce some measurement on the basis of a sample, therefore, we must qualify it; how accurate is it likely to be; what is the risk of its being wrong by more than some stated amount?

The science of sampling theory is concerned with this problem, the element of chance and probability, and is based upon two main properties. First, if we

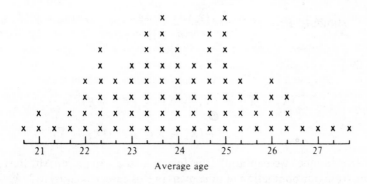

Average age

Fig. 4.1

took all the possible samples of three men from our population of nine and averaged out the 84 different estimates of age, this average would be exactly equal to the correct population value (a fact which can be verified by the more disbelieving reader). Second, the scatter of the various samples estimates about this overall average (and, hence, about the correct answer) will tend to follow a known pattern, called the *normal distribution*. This pattern can be seen in Fig. 4.1, where the 84 different sample estimates from our example are plotted, each X representing one sample estimate. Thus, one sample yields an answer of $20\frac{2}{3}$, two yield estimates of 21 and so on. We are dealing here with very small numbers. Even so, we see the clustering of the estimates around the true value and the emergence of something like the bell-shape of the normal distribution.

The standard error

With reasonably-sized samples, then, we know how the various possible answers will be scattered, in terms of their mid-point and the shape of their distribution about this mid-point. We must now investigate the likely extent of this scatter; when we select just one of the many possible samples, how wrong might we be?

The precise extent of the scatter of the different sample estimates could only be measured by actually drawing all the possible samples and studying the answers they yield, hardly a practical or worthwhile proposition! We can, however, obtain a good estimate from the results of a single sample, an estimate which we call the *standard error*.

The standard error of a sample estimate is a measure of the extent to which chance may influence its accuracy. It is calculated as follows:

where X_1 is our measurement for the first person in the sample, X_2 the measurement for the second person and so on, X_i being the measurement for the ith person; where $\bar{X}$(x-bar) is the average of these measurements (i.e., our sample estimate) and where n is the sample size:

$$\text{standard error of } \bar{X} = \sqrt{\frac{\sum (X_i - \bar{X})^2}{n(n-1)}}$$

Note that

$$\sum (X_i - \bar{X})^2 = (X_1 - \bar{X})^2 + (X_2 - \bar{X})^2 + \cdots$$

$$+ (X_i - \bar{X})^2 + \cdots (X_n - \bar{X})^2$$

As an example, we can apply the formula to a sample of Alf, Bert and Charlie from our population of nine men. In this case, n is equal to 3, X_1 is 26, X_2 is 21 and X_3 is 21.

$$\bar{X} = \frac{\sum X_i}{n} = \frac{26 + 21 + 21}{3} = 22\frac{2}{3}$$

$$\text{standard error } (\bar{X}) = \sqrt{\frac{\sum (X_i - \bar{X})^2}{n(n-1)}}$$

$$= \sqrt{\frac{(26 - 22\frac{2}{3})^2 + (21 - 22\frac{2}{3})^2 + (21 - 22\frac{2}{3})^2}{3 \times 2}}$$

$$= \text{approximately 1.7 years}$$

If our sample estimate takes the form of a percentage, say p, the formula is much simpler:

$$\text{standard error } (p) = \sqrt{\frac{p(100 - p)}{n}} \quad \text{or} \quad \sqrt{\frac{p \cdot q}{n}} \quad \text{where} \quad q = 100 - p$$

We might estimate, for example, from a sample of 100 adults that 50 per cent of all adults are men. The standard error of this estimate is:

$$\text{standard error } (p) = \sqrt{\frac{p \cdot q}{n}} = \sqrt{\frac{50 \cdot 50}{100}} = \sqrt{25} = 5 \text{ percentage points}$$

Confidence limits

We use our calculation of the standard error to construct statements which must qualify our sample estimate in terms of its probable accuracy. Such statements are couched in terms of *confidence limits* and take the general form:

Our sample estimate is p. We are C per cent confident that the true population value lies between $p - a$ and $p + a$.

Various levels of confidence (i.e., C), may be adopted. We might talk about the 90 per cent confidence limits, a range of values within which we are 90 per cent confident the true population value lies (i.e., there is only a 10 per cent risk that it lies outside these limits). Alternatively, we might refer to the 95 per cent confidence limits, the range of values within which we are 95 per cent confident the true population value lies. The more confident we wish to be, however, the wider the range of values we quote must be.

Confidence limits are calculated by multiplying the standard error by some value and adding the result to the sample estimate to obtain the upper limit, subtracting the result from the sample estimate to obtain the lower limit. The multiplier to be used depends upon the level of confidence required:

Level of confidence required	Multiplier of standard error
50%	$\frac{2}{3}$
68%	1
87%	$1\frac{1}{2}$
90%	$1\frac{2}{3}$
95%	2
99%	$2\frac{1}{2}$
99.7%	3

If we require the 95 per cent confidence limits of an estimate, therefore, we define these as being our sample estimate plus or minus *twice* its standard error.

Influences on the size of the standard error

There are two main factors which influence the size of the standard error of a sample estimate. The first is the amount of variation, or scatter, exhibited by the population being measured. The more variation there is the greater the standard error of a sample estimate will be. The second is the size of the sample. A larger sample will produce a more precise estimate, i.e., an estimate with a smaller standard error. The two are not in direct proportion, however; to halve the standard error we must *quadruple* the sample size, since the error varies inversely with the square root of the sample size.

It is important to note that, for most practical purposes, the size of the population being studied can be ignored. Only when the sample represents 10 per cent or more of the total population need we apply a correction factor. This factor, the *finite population correction*, has the effect of reducing the standard error:

where n is the sample size and N is the population size,

$$\text{true standard error} = \sqrt{1 - \frac{n}{N}} \text{ times the basic standard error.}$$

Bias

It was stated earlier that the average of all the possible sample estimates will be exactly equal to the true population value. In fact, this will only be true provided the sampling method used does not involve *bias*.

The standard error measures only random discrepancies, the inaccuracies which might arise purely from the element of chance involved in any sampling operation. Bias is a second type of error, one which cannot be measured by the standard error. Its existence implies that, if we were to measure every possible sample selected by our biased method, the average of their estimates would *not* be equal to the true population value. As a result, the existence of a bias in a sampling procedure will invalidate the exercise.

Bias arises, basically, from the use of a sampling method which does not allow every member of a population an equal chance of contributing to the sample estimate. To avoid bias, every individual must have a known chance of being selected. If, for some practical reason, this chance is not equal for every member of the population, the final sample estimate must be adjusted by applying differential weights to each informant's response, such that:

Where P_i is the ith person's probability of being chosen, n is the sample size and N the population size, the weight to be applied to the ith person,

$$W_i = \frac{n}{NP_i}$$

Sampling in Practice

The theory of sampling discussed above underlies the practical processes of sampling in market research. It is, however, tempered by considerations of cost and practicability. Thus, the design of a sampling method cannot be concerned only with maximizing accuracy in the simple statistical terms we have discussed. The problem can be expressed as a need to maximize statistical accuracy for a given expenditure, within certain constraints of practicability and data quality. This requirement leads to modifications of the simplest form of random sampling (e.g., a lottery) and, even in some instances, a complete departure from the principles of random sampling. These modifications and departures demand adjustments to the calculations set out above.

Clustering

Clustering is one of the major modifications normally made to the simple random process. It is the process whereby interviews are not spread throughout the population but are concentrated into groups, e.g., into a restricted number of constituences or in certain administrative districts. This procedure is, of course, absolutely essential to the practicability of survey conduct. It is an example of the consideration of cost-effectiveness: the additional expense which would be involved in conducting a survey without clustering would be so great as to outweigh the advantages which would be gained in terms of precision.

Clustering will certainly reduce the precision of sample estimates. The extent of this reduction will depend upon the number and size of the clusters used and the homogeneity of members of each cluster (generally related to the area covered by a cluster). It would be foolish to attempt to formulate hard and fast rules since these could not give adequate consideration to such practical considerations as the desirable interviewer workload. Certainly, however, it is generally inadvisable to cluster interviews into areas smaller than polling districts. If areas as small as this are used, the number of interviews in each cluster should probably not exceed 15 to 20. If larger areas are used, the number of interviews might be increased to say, 25 or 30. Beyond this point clustering ceases to be cost-effective. Additional interviews within a relatively homogeneous area will add little new information.

Weighting

Samples are sometimes drawn in such a way that differential weights need to be applied in order to yield unbiased estimates, e.g., in order to increase the number of interviews in some specialist group without, at the same time, increasing the number of interviews with other groups of the population which are already adequately represented.

Except in special cases, too complex to be dealt with in this chapter, the effect of any such weighting will be to reduce the accuracy of the resultant estimates. Certainly, there should be good reasons before weighting is adopted for any sample design and excessively large weighting factors should be avoided. (Opinions differ as to a proper definition of excessively large in this context but a weighting factor of five or six would probably be regarded as a desirable limit.)

Stratification

One complexity normally found in survey design, stratification, is not a harmful one. This is a process used to ensure that different strata of the population (e.g., regions, age groups) are represented in a sample in the correct proportions. This is achieved either at the selection stage, by selecting a separate sample in each stratum or, less satisfactorily, at the analysis stage, by a process known as post-survey stratification, where differential weighting is used to ensure appropriate representation in the sample.

Stratification will normally have the effect of reducing the standard error of a sample estimate. The extent of this contribution will depend upon the relevance of the stratification factor or factors involved. Thus, a stratification by region will only help when the property or characteristic being measured varies much more between the different regions than it does within any given region.

The design factor

The overall effects of any complexities in a sampling design are summarized by the *design factor*, which is used to multiply the simple standard error calculation. Thus, if our basic calculation yields a standard error of four per cent and our sampling method has a design factor of two, the true standard error is $(4 \times 2 =)$ 8 per cent.

The design factor, despite its potential significance, tends to be ignored, largely because its calculation is complex and because the design factor can be different for each variable measured. Even the National Readership Survey, however, has been estimated as having an average design factor in the order of 1.4, and this is recognized as being a particularly good sample design. Many random samples have design factors of two or even more. The calculation of the design factor for every survey can certainly not be recommended as a practical proposition. Safer than totally discounting it, however, is making some arbitrary allowance by always multiplying the basic standard error calculation by a factor of, say, 1.5.

The precise sampling method used will certainly have a profound effect upon the accuracy of our sample estimates and, hence, upon the conclusions we can draw from them, e.g., a sample of 1000, yielding an estimate of 5 per cent for some proportion, has a simple standard error of about 1.6 per cent. In a well-designed sample, with a design factor of about 1.5, the real standard error would actually be about 2½ per cent, whilst, with a less efficient sampling method with a design factor of about 2, the real error would be over 3 per cent.

The importance of the design factor can, perhaps, best be appreciated in financial terms. Suppose we ask two research agencies to quote for conducting a survey amongst a random sample of 2000 informants. One agency might quote us £20 000, the other £15 000; costs per interview of £10 and £2.50. The more expensive quotation might, however, include provision for a technically better sampling method. Supposing the two have design factors of 1.4 and 1.8 respectively, we might go through the following calculations to show that the more expensive quotation in fact provides better value:

	Agency A	Agency B
(a) quote	£20 000	£15 000
(b) sample size	2000	2000
(c) design factor	1.4	1.8
(d) effective sample size $= b \div c^2$	1020	617
(e) cost per effective interview $= a \div d$	£19.61	£24.31

In practice this calculation will only rarely be possible. But one must be aware that the cheapest does not necessarily represent the best value.

Bias in sampling

The design factor provides a useful summary of the effects of details of sample design. Like the standard error itself, however, it relates only to random or chance fluctuations and errors and we must still consider elements of practical sampling which might produce errors of another type, namely, biases.

One important potential source of bias in a sample is the *sampling frame*, the list from which the sample is selected. This list may be incomplete or inaccurate, with the result that some members of the population do not have their due chance of being selected for the sample.

To avoid bias from this source, one must clearly take all possible steps to ensure that the sampling frame is completely accurate. More important, it must be recognized that such complete accuracy is unlikely and a sampling method must take account of any residual errors in the frame used. This is a point which will be discussed further when we turn to the use of the electoral registers in sampling, certainly the most widely used sampling frame in UK survey research.

A second major source of bias is *non-response*. In no survey is an interview successfully achieved with every person selected for the sample. Indeed, we count ourselves as having been successful if we manage to interview 80 per cent of the selected individuals, even after making allowances for 'deadwood' — selections no longer available for inclusion for one reason or another. In the remaining 20 per cent or more of selections we will meet with refusal to co-operate or simply failure to contact the person involved.

Clearly, non-response must be kept to a minimum, involving us in the use of well-trained interviewers and of methods which maximize the likelihood of contact being made with selected informants. Whatever our efforts, however, some non-response will remain. Bias will then be introduced if those people who do not respond differ from the respondents in respect of the characteristics being measured.

By definition, bias is not measurable, although various methods are used to assess the probability of its existence. None of these can lead to anything more than a fairly subjective assessment, however, and it is such a subjective opinion which must always temper the scientifically drawn conclusions of a sample survey.

Quota sampling

Thus far we have discussed only various forms of random (or 'probability' or 'pre-selected') sampling. One can probably say, however, that the majority of commercial survey research in the UK is not done through such methods. A random sampling procedure will result in an interviewer being issued with a list of names and addresses of pre-selected informants. Contacting and interviewing these people is never easy and is an expensive process. In many market research projects this expense is felt to be simply not justified.

The most common form of non-random sampling is the *quota sample*. In this form of sampling, the interviewer receives, instead of a list of names and addresses, a quota to fill. This will instruct her to conduct a set number of interviews with people in various categories, e.g. six interviews with women, aged under 35, in the AB social grades. Generally, it is much easier for the interviewer to achieve this target than to interview an equivalent number of pre-selected informants. The main advantage of quota sampling lies, then, in cost-saving. Not only will the interviewer's work rate be much higher (perhaps even doubling that achieved with random sampling) but also one is saved the not inconsiderable expense of actually drawing a sample, e.g., from the electoral registers.

A concomitant advantage lies in the speed which is possible with the use of quota sampling. First, time can be saved at the stage of setting-up a survey because no names and addresses have to be selected. Second, time can be saved in the field; an average assignment for an interviewer working to a quota is probably three days, whilst effective random sampling usually demands a minimum assignment of five days.

These advantages must be weighed against the undeniable disadvantages. In theory, the main disadvantage is that the idea of sampling errors cannot be applied to this type of sample because it does not satisfy the conditions which define an unbiased random sample. In practice, however, sample estimates are useless without some statement of their accuracy and we tend to apply the same theory. Various attempts to qualify this approach by the application of arbitrary design factors have been suggested, although there is no conclusive evidence to show that quota sampling necessarily produces estimates which are less precise than those produced by random sampling.

A far greater danger is that bias may be introduced. Within the framework laid down by the survey designer in terms of quota controls, the interviewer has a good deal of freedom in choosing her informants. As a result, certain sections of the populations are likely to be over-represented in the sample: those who are easy to contact and interview, people who are at home a lot, who are readily accessible at work and, especially, those whose jobs demand an accessible presence with a good deal of waiting time (firemen, inspectors at bus garages, police station sergeants, etc.) and those who most obviously fit the required quota — the stereotype AB; those aged from 20 to 25 to fit a quota cell of 16 to 34; and those whose appearance is more acceptable to the interviewer.

This danger cannot be removed, although it can be minimized by the thorough indoctrination of interviewers as to the requirements of survey research and by the application of controls. Such controls might include restrictions on clustering of informants, quota limitations on non-working women, on people working in non-manufacturing industries, etc.

In judging quota sampling, it must be remembered that the criticisms levelled at the approach are, in practice, also true of most random samples. With an achievement or response rate of only 75–80 per cent or less, the average random sample is certainly exposed to many of the biases attached to the quota sample. Again, the people successfully interviewed are likely to be those who are most accessible. This factor is of importance when the survey subject is related to accessibility, e.g. leisure pursuits, drinking, etc. In such instances, it may well be that the biases incorporated in a well-designed quota sample which allows interviewing at work will be less severe than those arising in a random sample which depends upon availability at home.

There are other forms of non-random sampling, which generally share the advantages and disadvantages of quota sampling, e.g. random-route sampling is frequently used. In this approach, an interviewer is instructed to follow a predetermined route, calling on households at a set interval. At its worst, this method is open to even greater errors than a quota sample; at its best it becomes virtually as expensive as a random sample. Alternatively, streets or blocks are selected at random and the interviewer is then instructed to fill a quota, usually defined in terms of sex and age, within the selected area. One should not be led by the rather confusing name given to this form of sampling, *quasi-random sampling* into thinking of it as a randomized method. It is open to all the biases arising from inaccessibility and may well be less satisfactory than the *at work-interview* quota sample.

Sample Size

Just as the statistical theory underlying sampling allows us to compute the accuracy of an estimate made on the basis of a sample of a given size, so the operation can be reversed in order to calculate the sample size which would be required in order to yield a set level of accuracy. The formula to be used in this case is:

$$\text{sample size } (n) = \frac{k^2 DF^2 p(100 - p)}{L^2}$$

So, in order to calculate our required sample size, we must pre-set the following four terms:

k: k is used here to denote the multiple associated with the standard error in defining confidence limits. Its value will depend upon the level of confidence (or, conversely, the level of risk) acceptable in the qualifying statement. Thus, if the user of the research demands 95 per cent confidence in its results within certain limits, the value of k to be used is 2.

L: L represents the other term in the qualifying statement, the limit (above or below the estimate) within which the required level of confidence holds. Taking k and L together, if we demand a result the accuracy of which we are 95 per cent confident to within plus or minus 4 per cent, we insert values of 2 for k and 4 for L.

DF: DF is the design factor of our sample design. If this is not known, we take an arbitrary value of about 1.4 (such that $DF^2 = 2$).

p: *p* is the answer we expect to obtain. Clearly, we are unlikely to be able to state this precisely but a reasonable estimate may be possible on the basis of earlier research or knowledge of correlated measures. If no estimate of *p* can be made, it should be set at the level at which it will have the maximum effect on sample size: 50 per cent.

As an example, we might be asked to provide an estimate of the proportion of the population who wear spectacles. We are asked to provide an estimate which is accurate to within two per cent with only a five per cent risk of greater inaccuracy. Our calculation is then:

$$n = \frac{2^2 \times 1.4^2 \times 50(50)}{2^2}$$

$$= \frac{4 \times 2 \times 2500}{4}$$

$$= 5000$$

All too often, the result of such a calculation is a sample size which would go beyond the budget for the research. At this point, it is up to the research user to amend his demands either by accepting a greater risk of error outside the given limits (e.g., by taking the 90 per cent confidence limits) or by widening the actual limits.

The effect of such revision will be quite marked. If the demands in the foregoing example were revised so that a range of accuracy of plus or minus five per cent and a risk of greater error of ten per cent were acceptable, the sample size required would be reduced from 5000 to rather over 500:

$$n = \frac{1.64^2 \times 1.4^2 \times 50(50)}{5^2}$$

$$= \frac{2.7 \times 2 \times 2500}{25}$$

$$= 540$$

There are, however, other ways of reducing the total sample size required and, hence, cutting the cost of the research. Three approaches are outlined below.

Sequential sampling

The basis of this method is the gradual building up of a sample by a series or sequence of subsidiary sampling operations until the point is reached where a sufficiently conclusive answer can be drawn from the research. The approach is most often used where the result needed from research is an answer to the question of whether a characteristic is held in a population at a level above or below some threshold or critical level. We might, for example, be conducting research to define the circulation area of a regional newspaper. Our approach is to divide up the likely area into zones and to include a zone in the defined area if household coverage by our paper is at least 10 per cent. As a first step, we might conduct, say, 400 interviews in each zone. In one zone this might yield an estimate of 20 per cent coverage. With our sample size, this estimate has a standard error of 3 per cent (assuming a design factor of 1.5) and we can be very confident that the true coverage in this zone is above the threshold level. In another, more marginal, zone we might obtain an estimate of 14 per cent coverage. This estimate would have a standard error of around 2½ per cent and, hence, 95 per cent confidence limits of about 9 to 19 per cent. On this basis, we could not reach a firm decision as to whether the zone should or should not be included in our definition of the circulation area.

Applying our formula for the calculation of required sample sizes would show us that we would require a sample of about 700 households to give us enough precision to make a firm decision about the meaning of an estimate of 14 per cent. On this basis, we conduct a second phase of interviewing in this zone in order to increase our sample base. For safety, we might add a further 400 interviews, bringing our combined sample for the zone up to 800. If our estimate is still 14 per cent, the larger sample will now permit us to say with more than 95 per cent confidence that coverage in this zone is, in fact, above the threshold limit. Clearly, the advantage of this approach lies in the economy which is possible when a relatively small sample yields a sufficiently accurate result. Larger samples are only used when they are found to be essential.

Disproportionate sampling

In most surveys our interest is not restricted to opinions or behaviour reported by the total sample. We also need to know about certain subsections of the population, e.g. in assessing reaction to a new version of a product, the manufacturer will wish to know how users of the brand, as a special category, react. If these users make up only a relatively small proportion of the total population, we will need a large total sample in order to obtain sufficient accuracy within the group of users of the brand.

Economies can be achieved in such a situation by the use of disproportionate sampling. Very simply, we would interview more users in our sample than would be warranted if we followed the population proportions. Thus, if a brand was bought by about 25 per cent of the population, we might interview all the users we came across but only one in three of the non-users (apart, of course, from asking the questions needed to establish non-use). In this way, our total sample would be equally divided between users and non-users. If this approach is adopted, it is important to remember that the results for the total sample will be meaningless until the correct proportions are restored to the sample by differential weighting of the groups affected.

Multi-phase sampling

Few surveys set out to measure only one characteristic. When a number of different properties are to be estimated, it may well be that we can attach varying demands of accuracy to them. Thus, we might conduct a study to measure both purchasing behaviour and attitudes in a product field. The accuracy demanded of the purchasing data might be such that 1000 interviews would be required, whilst 500 would suffice for some rather less stringent demands placed upon the attitudinal data. In order to economize both in the field and in data processing, we can apply the purchasing questions to a sample of 1000 informants but only apply the longer questionnaire including attitudinal measures to alternate informants.

Some Mechanics of Sampling

This chapter has so far only outlined some of the many ways in which sample designs may vary. Because of the number of options available (many of which are a matter of personal preference rather than scientific judgement) it is not possible to give an authoritative 'blow-by-blow' description of exactly how a sample should be drawn. The methods which follow are selected only as examples of the mechanics of drawing samples in order to illustrate some of the basic principles.

A sample of adults (aged 15 and over)

Let us suppose that our brief is to select a sample of 1000 adults aged 15 and over, clustered into 50 wards. Our method is as follows:

Step 1. A sampling frame of administrative districts is drawn up. This is a full listing of the districts, grouped (or stratified) under headings and subheadings (e.g. area type within region). Against each district we give its population and then, through the list, we add a cumulative population figure:

Conurbation	POPULATION	CUMULATIVE
District I	56 345	56 345
District II	32 070	88 415
District III	64 813	153 228
District IV	57 962	211 190
District V	48 054	259 244
Other urban		
etc.,		
etc.		

Step 2. We can now move on to the selection of our 50 interviewing areas by a process known as sampling with *probability proportional to size*. This process can best be explained by reference to a simpler example.

Suppose we have four towns, A, B, C, and D, from which we wish to select two as interviewing areas. Our sampling frame is:

	POPULATION	CUMULATIVE
Town A	4500	4 500
Town B	7000	11 500
Town C	6000	17 500
Town D	2500	20 000

First, we divide the total population of the four towns by the number of interviewing areas required: $20\,000/2 = 10\,000$. The result is known as our *sampling interval*. Using a table of random numbers we select a random number between 1 and our interval, i.e., between 1 and 10 000 — let us say 7325. This number determines our first interviewing area, in which the 7325th person in our list lives — town B. (Town A houses the 1st to the 4500th persons, town B the 4501st to 11 500th, and so on.) Next, we add our sampling interval to the random number. The result, 17 325, then determines our second area, town C, which houses the 17 325th person in the list.

In our main example, then, we would divide the total population of our universe by 50, the number of areas required, in order to obtain a sampling interval. We would select a random number between 1 and this interval to define the first area to be used. We would then add the interval to determine our second area, add it again to determine the third and so on, until we have our fifty areas.

Step 3. At this point, we have selected 50, administrative districts and must now move on to the selection of wards, again with probability proportional to size. Within each selected administrative area, we list out the wards, in descending order of size:

	POPULATION	CUMULATIVE
Town B, ward I	2500	2500
II	2000	4500
III	1500	6000
IV	1000	7000

We now refer back to the number which led us to select the area for the sample. In our simple example, this was 7325 in the case of town B. This we described as a pointer to the 7325th person in our full list. This person is the $7325 - 4500 = 2825$th person in town B. In the same sense as before, this person is housed in the second ward of town B.

The effect of sampling with probability proportional to size is to give a large area a greater chance of selection than a small one. As a result, we can interview an equal number of informants in each of our selected areas, regardless of the relatives sizes of the areas, and still meet the need to give an equal chance of selection to every member of the population.

Step 4. We now turn to the selection of individual informants for our sample, using the electoral register. We do this by a process known as *serial sampling.* We divide the total number of electors registered in our selected ward by the number of interviews required in that area (plus some allowance for non-response). In our example, we require 20 interviews in each ward. Making an allowance for non-response, we will give the interviewer 25 names within her area, so we divide the population of the district by 25 to yield a sampling interval. As before, we turn to a table of random numbers for a number between 1 and this interval. This number selects our first informant; if the random number is N, we take the Nth person listed in the register for the district. Adding our interval, say, K gives our second selection — the $N + K$th person in the list. We continue in this way, adding our interval repeatedly until we have our full list of 25 names and addresses. (The process is rendered fairly easy by the fact that every person in the electoral register bears a serial number.)

Step 5. We are now left with only one problem, i.e. that the electoral register is not a full or completely accurate sampling frame. It will not list the youngest adults, those too young to vote, nor will it list some other special categories of residents not qualified to vote. The register is six months out of date by the time it is published and is 18 months out of date before it is replaced. During this interval, some of those listed in it will have died or left the country; far more will simply have moved their residence since it was compiled.

If our final sample is to provide unbiased estimates we must take account of non-electors amongst our defined universe of people aged 15 and over and of the mobile members of the population. This is done as follows. The interviewer is given the list of selected names and addresses. She calls at an address and interviews the named person if he is still resident there. If he is not, even if he has only moved to the next street, she does not attempt to contact him. Whether the named person still lives at the address or not, the interviewer prepares a list of all the adults who are resident in his household (or in the space formerly occupied by his household). She compares this list with the list given in the electoral register for the address. If she finds a resident adult who is not entered in the register, she seeks an interview with him (even if she has already taken one interview at the address with the originally selected person). If she finds more than one such non-registered person, she selects one of them at random for interview. This can be done either by the use of a selection chart or by the use of the 'birthday rule', selecting for interview the person whose birthday is the next to come round.

Step 6. This process of covering non-electors disrupts the equal probabilities in our sample. In order to restore these, we must apply differential weighting at the analysis stage, multiplying the responses of each non-elector interviewed by the fraction:

$$\frac{\text{number of non-electors found in household}}{\text{number of electors registered for household}}$$

This is just one way in which a sample of individuals can be selected and it is by no means universally adopted. Details of a somewhat different approach can be found in the Technical Appendix of the National Readership Survey. Of course, not all surveys use samples of individuals; many are concerned with households. These surveys involve us in an extra problem in the selection of names and addresses from the electoral register.

We proceed as above for steps 1, 2, and 3, resulting in our selection of interviewing areas. Step 4 is, however, quite different. We obtain an interval by dividing the total electorate of the area by a number three times the number of households to be interviewed, so, if we require interviews with 15 households in the area, we divide by $3 \times 15 = 45$. Then, as before, we take a random number and proceed to select our list of 45 individuals from the electoral register. We then check each person on our list and, if they are the first person listed at their address, we take that address for our sample; if not, we reject it. In this way, we ensure that each address in the electoral register has only one chance of being selected for our sample. In this instance, we ignore the problem of non-electors since it will be far less serious. (There are few households made up entirely of people not eligible to vote.) The problem of mobility does not arise because we are selecting addresses and we interview whoever lives there.

A new problem does, however, arise in that some addresses will be shared by more than one household. The normal procedure in such a case is to list all the households found at the address. If only one is found, that household is interviewed. If two are found, both are interviewed and the next address on the list is deleted in compensation. If three households are in residence, all three are interviewed and two addresses are delected in compensation. If there are more than three households at the address, three of them are randomly selected for interview and two addresses are deleted from the list.

5. Questionnaire design

Jean Morton-Williams

Every stage of a market research survey is of vital importance if valid conclusions are to be drawn from it. But the design of the questionnaire is certainly one of the most critical phases. If the required information is not covered or if the questions are posed in such a way that they make nonsense to the respondent, no amount of clever interviewing or ingenious analysis can produce useful results.

This chapter is mainly concerned with the design of structured questionnaires for use in face-to-face interviews. It does not deal with the development of guides for depth interviewing nor with the problems of questionnaires for special populations, such as retailers or professional investors, since these are covered in other chapters.

The aims of this chapter are modest; it attempts to lay down a few tentative general principles, to indicate some of the hazards met in collecting information of various kinds and to describe some of the main techniques used at present, especially in the area of attitude measurement. But in the last analysis questionnaire design cannot be learnt from books; it is a skill that has to be acquired through experience. The best method of learning the skill is to write a questionnaire, to go out and interview people with it and then to analyse it oneself.

Unfortunately, it is usually only at the trainee stage of a researcher's career that there is the opportunity to do this. Researchers are usually too busy and under too much pressure to delegate to be able to find the time to go out into the field; the result is that they tend to become remote from the realities of the interviewing situation. A considerable amount of useful 'feedback' from the field can be obtained, however, if full use is made of that invaluable ambassador between researcher and respondent, the experienced interviewer. 'Debriefing' conferences after pilot studies can provide the opportunity for the researcher to learn how respondents reacted to the questionnaire, which questions caused difficulties and whether all sectors of the population to be covered by the survey could understand and answer validly. It is unfortunately true that a questionnaire must be designed to be comprehensible to the least able respondents.

Planning the Questionnaire

The precise ground to be covered by a questionnaire arises from the brief. The first step is to decide what *specific* information is required in order to solve the marketing problems and to answer the questions raised in the brief.

There are often limitations of money and time which dictate the length of the questionnaire, quite apart from considerations of the amount of time that members of the public might be prepared to spend in being interviewed! Of all the information that *could* be useful, it is necessary to have some means of assessing what should be given priority. The brief obviously provides the main criteria for assessing what is most important, but exploratory research can also contribute; the insight it provides into the market leads to the development of hypotheses about motivation which the survey may be required to validate. Information to test the hypotheses must be gathered in the questionnaire; e.g. depth research suggested that women who used a lot of a certain brand of disinfectant were particularly conscientious housewives who had babies or very young children. To test this hypothesis it was necessary to include a measure of the extent to which they were conscientious housewives and also to make sure that full details of household composition were collected.

Before starting to formulate actual questions, it is advisable to list in detail *all* the information that the questionnaire will be designed to obtain; this gives a broad indication of its length and enables a review to be made at an early stage of the degree of detail that can be covered. It is also a valuable aid to organization of the various sections and of the order in which questions will be asked. If the subject is complex and different groups within the sample need to be asked different questions, it is helpful to use a flow chart as set out in Fig. 5.1 to plan the questionnaire and to ensure that all the ground is covered with the optimum efficiency.

In planning the content, the requirement of the analysis stage must be borne in mind. If the views of the brand-loyal are to be compared with the views of those who constantly change brands, questions must be included to identify the brand-loyal and the changeable. If hypotheses are to be tested about the motivations that lead housewives to be heavy users of disinfectant, then some measure of amounts of disinfectant used must be included.

Some General Principles

A questionnaire is a tool for the collection of data from respondents. If it is to be an efficient tool it must fulfil six functions; these are:

92

(a) maintaining the respondent's co-operation and involvement;
(b) communicating with the respondent;
(c) helping the respondent to work out his answers;
(d) avoiding bias;
(e) making the interviewer's task easy;
(f) providing a basis for data processing.

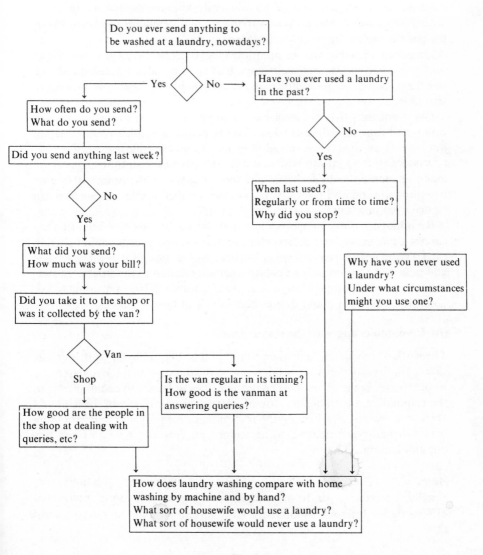

Fig. 5.1

(a) Maintaining the respondent's co-operation

Maintaining *rapport* during the interview is obviously an important part of interviewing skill but the questionnaire can help or hinder the interviewer's task. The longer it is the more is demanded of the respondent in terms of time and attention. No absolute rules can be laid down about length; a housewife might be prepared to spend an hour and a half talking about her children and what she feeds them on but be bored and exhausted after half an hour's questioning on an uninteresting topic involving unfamiliar and difficult concepts; the average working class housewife will soon become antagonistic if questioned closely about the relative merits of different forms of investment for people paying different levels of income tax.

Questionnaires that are boring or that try to get people to give their views on topics that are beyond their scope lead to respondents breaking off the interview before it is completed. An uncompleted interview is usually unusable.

Questionnaires that are long but on topics of interest to the respondent cause problems of a different kind. Many people are able to spare half an hour when an interviewer knocks on the door, even during the day; but relatively few can spare an hour and it is often necessary for the interviewer to make an appointment to carry out the interview. This necessitates more travelling around and radically reduces the number of interviews which can be achieved in a day.

Respondents sometimes become bored during an interview because they cannot perceive any overall structure or sense to the questionnaire. Having each section introduced to them gives them the feeling that they know what is going on and also usefully orientates them in relation to the subject matter; e.g. (after a series of questions about using a laundry) 'Now I'm going to ask you a few questions about doing the washing at home . . .'

(b) Communicating with the respondent

The work of Payne[1] in the United States and of Belson[2] in Great Britain has shown that respondents often fail to grasp the question that the researcher is trying to ask. Some of the most common causes of failure to communicate to the respondent are ambiguity, use of unfamiliar words, use of difficult and abstract concepts, overloading the respondent's memory and understanding with too many instructions, using vague concepts and trying to ask two questions in one.

Ambiguity. Everyone tries to avoid using ambiguous questions but, equally, everyone finds from time to time that a question is interpreted differently by different respondents. Only careful piloting can guard against this.

Use of Unfamiliar Words. A study by Belson and the author when in the

BBC's Audience Research Department[3] indicated that many words which appear to be in quite common use are in fact not properly understood, e.g. words such as 'incentive', 'proximity' and 'discrepancy' are known by only about half the population whereas words such as 'paradox' and 'chronological' are known by only about a fifth. Although the context in which a word is used can sometimes help people to understand the word, often the effect is reversed and the unfamiliar word prevents comprehension of the whole sentence.

Use of Difficult and Abstract Concepts. Research in the field of education has shown that both intelligence and educational level are related to the degree to which people are able to think in terms of abstract concepts. Most researchers and their clients are intelligent and highly educated and the use of abstract concepts is second nature to them. They often find it difficult to grasp that the mode of thinking of a large proportion of the population differs quite markedly from theirs.

In a pilot survey, respondents were asked to say what region of the country they felt they belonged to; they were then shown a map with a region marked on it and asked whether they agreed with this definition of their region. It was apparent that those who had not travelled about the country much, whose friends and relatives came from a small nearby area and who had not had an extensive education in geography and the reading of maps had no concept of a region as such; they were able to think only in terms of their neighbourhood or town. Their answers to the series of opinion questions which followed on how things were run in their region could have referred only to the more limited area where they lived. For the main survey it was essential to identify those who could not grasp the key concept of region or quite invalid conclusions might have been drawn.

Those not used to abstract concepts tend to turn them into concrete concepts. An interviewer asked, 'How would you feel if your neighbour didn't use disinfectant?' 'Oh, I'm sure she does,' replied the respondent, 'she's ever such a clean woman!'

Overloading the Respondent's Memory with Too Many Instructions. When an interviewer reads out a question, the respondent has to remember what has been said long enough to work out the answer. People's short-term memory varies considerably and some people find it quite difficult to hold even two ideas in their head at the same time.

Every time a respondent is asked to rate a brand on an attribute he has to hold two ideas in his head, the name of the brand and the scale dimension that he is to apply to it; it is common practice to help him by presenting one or other on a card. But many questions are loaded down with explanatory and conditional phrases that confuse rather than clarify; e.g. 'Do you read regularly any daily newspapers; that is, at least three out of every four issues? By 'read' I mean read or look at?'

Using Vague Concepts. Vague questions tend to produce confusion in the respondent or else equally vague answers. The question 'Do you think your house is the right sort of house for your family?' was interpreted by some as meaning 'Do you like your house?' whereas others counter-questioned 'What do you mean? "Right" in what sense?'

Trying to Ask Two Questions in One. It is often tempting to try to save time in an interview by letting one question be submitted under another and hoping that the respondent will say if the question is inapplicable to him; e.g. 'How many hours did you spend at work last week?' instead of; 'Did you do any paid work at all last week?' 'How many hours did you work?' which makes quite clear that we are asking about any form of paid employment and not simply about the regular job or about unpaid work.

(c) Helping the respondent to work out his answers

Sometimes the mental tasks which the respondent has to perform in answering the questions put to him are quite arduous. Some of the difficulties that respondents experience are related to the problem of communicating that have already been discussed, e.g. if he is asked to hold a number of defining concepts in his head while trying to work out his answer, not only does he find it difficult to grasp the question but he may forget some of the concepts and make a mistake, a mistake which may not be apparent from his answer.

Generalizing. Survey research aims to draw a fairly broad picture of people's behaviour and attitudes; to do this, a certain amount of detail has to be ignored or glossed over. Question design often reflects this need; instead of being asked to give full and precise information about his behaviour or attitudes, the respondent is asked to generalize: 'How would you rate the performance of your car overall?' asks the interviewer. 'Well, the acceleration is very good but it doesn't pull well on the hills' replied the respondent. 'How would you rate the performance *overall*?' prompts the conscientious interviewer. But the respondent may not know how to add together 'very good' for acceleration and 'rather poor' on hills to form an overall rating.

Questions about the respondent's 'usual' behaviour also ask him to make a generalization. If his behaviour is very variable, it may not make sense to him to do so.

Mathematical Concepts. Asking the respondent to say 'on average' how many times he buys sweets in a week demands that he has a clear idea of the variability of his behaviour from week to week and then applies an arithmetical concept to the data. Most respondents would fail on both counts. In order not to reveal their ignorance and because they want to oblige the interviewer, many would say what they 'usually' do or what they did last week, which might or might not approximate to the concept the researcher had in mind in asking the question. Requesting people to work out proportions is likely to cause similar difficulties unless kept very simple, e.g. 'Less than half, about half, more than half'.

Memory.   Respondents are sometimes asked to perform prodigious feats of memory. They are asked to remember where, when and how they purchased something, how much they paid for it and where they saw it advertised. They are asked to remember what magazines they have read during the past month, when, exactly, they last decorated a room of their house, what brand of paint they used, and so on.

Trying to remember something that has been more or less forgotten or has merged into a number of other similar acts, demands considerable mental effort and concentration. Respondents are not always willing or able to make this effort.

What little research has been done on this subject (Belson[4]) suggests that memory is fairly accurate where behaviour is regular, e.g. where magazines are bought on subscription, but much less accurate for the occasional departure from regularity, or for the person whose behaviour follows no regular pattern.

Pilot questioning as to how certain the respondent feels that he has remembered accurately is no proof that he has in fact done so but suggests that the relatively rare and important event is more precisely remembered than the trivial, often repeated event. The purchase of a car may be remembered in some detail for years whereas the purchase of a packet of cigarettes may be forgotten 24 hours later.

Steps can be taken to optimize memory accuracy by getting the respondent to recreate in his mind the total context in which the event occurred and by asking only those for whom the event occurred very recently to try to remember the details of it. But, however skilful the questioning, it will still remain likely that many respondents will not give accurate information. Pilot checks can at least establish whether the respondent thinks he remembers what he actually did. Beyond this, retrospective question and answer techniques cannot go; diaries, home audits or observation techniques have to be used instead.

Indicating the Answers Required.   An important part of helping the respondent both to understand the question and to arrive at his answer is to make sure that he knows what type of answer is required. There are basically two types of questions, 'open-ended', to which the respondent replies in his own words, and 'pre-coded' where he chooses his answers from those provided. It should be clear to him which type of answer he is meant to be giving. If the question is 'pre-coded', all the alternatives should be presented to him either verbally by the interviewer or on a card. Bias can result if only the positive or only the negative answers are presented.

A practice that should be avoided in most circumstances is that of asking a question in 'open-ended' form and then requiring the interviewer to code the answers into a set of pre-codes given in the questionnaire. This procedure works very well for simple factual data, e.g. 'How long have you lived in this house?'; but for more complex questions, and in particular for attitude questions, it should be the respondent's task to decide which one of a set of pre-codes best represents his views. The interviewer is unlikely to be able to assess the respondent's reply fully or to code it accurately while in the midst of coping with the interview.

The Use of Cards.   Cards can be a valuable aid to the respondent in helping him to work out his answer. They can be used to help him grasp and remember the concepts in the question and can indicate to him the response categories from which he is to choose his answer. Sometimes, the card bears a list of items, such as brand names, and the respondent is asked to pick items from the list in answer to the question put by the interviewer; e.g. 'Which of these brands have you ever used?' or 'Which of these brands are particularly good for colds?'.

Alternatively, the card presents a series of response categories and the respondent picks the one which expresses his opinion of a proposition put to him by the interviewer; e.g. 'I am going to read out some statements that people have made about doing the washing. Please tell me how much you agree or disagree with each one; pick your answer from this card'.

If items are to be put in order of preference, each item should be put on a separate card, otherwise it is difficult for the respondent to remember which items he has already selected. Separate cards are also useful if a second question is to be asked about some items; e.g. 'Please sort these cards into two piles, those brands you think you might use and those you would avoid' and 'Now from those you might use, select the three you would be most likely to use'.

'Open Ended' Questions tax the skill of the interviewer even more than other types. She has to record the respondent's answer verbatim and simultaneously consider whether the answer makes sense in terms of the question that has been asked and whether it is likely to be fully intelligible to someone in the office who was not present at the interview. She also has to ensure that the respondent has said all he has to say on the subject.

The answer to open questions must be recorded verbatim, otherwise 'interpretation' on the part of the interviewer is likely to distort the respondent's views.

If the respondent gives an answer which does not make sense in terms of the question that was asked, the interviewer should *repeat the question as it is written on the questionnaire*; she should not re-word or explain it since this would mean that each respondent was not being asked the same question. At most, she should change the emphasis in order to stress that part of the question which the respondent seemed to misunderstand.

If an answer is vague or lacking in specific detail, the interviewer should 'probe', i.e. ask questions to obtain further information. It is in this area of interviewing skill that thorough training is most necessary since it is essential that probes should be of a very general kind; e.g. 'In what way . . . ?' 'Can you explain about the . . . a little more fully?'. Even if the respondent has already talked in the course of the interview about the subject of the question, the interviewer should not assume she knows the answer and that it is safe to ask a leading question; e.g. if the respondent says 'I wasn't satisfied with the way the machine washed my husband's shirts', the probe should be, 'Can you explain that a little more?' or 'In what way were you not satisfied?' not 'Is that because it didn't get the collars and cuffs clean as you mentioned earlier?'.

When the respondent has fully elucidated the first answer given, the interviewer should not assume that that is all he has to say on the subject but ask 'Anything else?' or 'Any other reasons?' before moving on to the next question.

If the researcher wishes to obtain reasonably full answers to open-ended questions, plenty of space must be left on the questionnaire. The interviewer will not believe that verbatim answers with careful probing are really required if there is room on the questionnaire for only about ten words.

The importance of the interviewer's role in putting over open-ended questions and probing to elucidate the answers means that the usefulness of open-ended questions in self-completion questionnaires, e.g. in postal surveys, is very limited. They can be used in telephone interviews but there are difficulties in hearing accurately and in maintaining *rapport* with the respondent while probing and writing down the answer. It would, therefore, be unwise to use a questionnaire that consisted almost entirely of open-ended questions for a telephone survey.

(d) Avoiding bias

The way in which a question is written can bias the answers obtained if it presents only one side of an issue to respondents. In a public opinion poll on the Common Market a question took the following form:

> 'Before taking their final decision about joining the Common Market, Norway, Denmark and Ireland will each have a referendum in which all the people will be able to say whether they want to join or not. Do you think that Britain should do the same?'

Not surprisingly, a large majority said 'Yes'. It is pretty certain that very different results would have been obtained if the opposite position had been incorporated into the question: 'When France, Germany, Italy, Belgium, Luxembourg and Holland decided to form the Common Market, they each left the decision entirely to their Parliaments. Do you think Britain should do the same?'

In this particular case, it would have been fairly easy to construct a question that presented both sides of the issue, though it might have been necessary to have used a visual aid to put it over in full.

Bias can also occur when examples are used to indicate to the respondent what sort of information is required. The examples are nearly always mentioned more frequently than other points in the answers.

Both of these types of biased question usually arise because the researcher has difficulty in framing a brief and comprehensible question on a rather difficult issue. The answer may be to break the question down into a number of subsidiary parts that lead up to the main point and to make full use of visual aids.

(e) Making the interviewer's task easy

The task that the interviewer has to perform can be made easy or difficult by the way the questionnaire is laid out. A badly laid out questionnaire leads to mistakes on the part of the interviewer: for example, it may lead her to ask wrong questions, put questions incorrectly or record the answers incorrectly.

There is a fairly widespread belief that respondents are put off by the sight of a questionnaire several pages long; efforts are made to make the questionnaire look as short as possible by using small print and cramping the questions together. But it is doubtful whether a five-page questionnaire looks less intimidating to the respondent than one of ten pages and the interviewer's task is made much more difficult for no good reason. Many interviewers are in their forties and fifties and find it difficult to read very small print; lack of space between pre-coded answers (especially vertically) leads to errors in recording answers, and lack of space in which to write down the answers to open-ended questions means that the interviewer is forced to paraphrase instead of recording verbatim.

How the question is to be asked should be indicated in the way it is laid out, including the point at which cards should be introduced. The questions should be in lower case and the instructions to the interviewer in capital letters, e.g.

> SHOW CARD   On this card are the names of some brands of
> toothpaste. Which ones would you say are particularly
> good at making your teeth white?
> PROBE: Any others?
> REPEAT FOR EACH ITEM IN TURN

The instructions to the interviewer to omit certain questions on the basis of the respondent's responses to other questions are usually called 'skip instructions'. A good method, and one that minimizes error, is to indicate which question should be asked next against each set of response categories. It is then a simple matter to indicate that different response categories lead on to different questions (see questionnaire example at end of chapter). This method obviates the necessity for lengthy verbal instructions ('IF YES ASK Q.2,

IF NO GO TO Q.30'), or arrows, which tend to be confusing and difficult for the typist to draw accurately.

(f) Providing a basis for data processing

A great deal of time and money can be saved if the questionnaire is laid out in such a way that the data can be punched on to cards straight from the questionnaire without being transferred to another sheet. Open-ended questions obviously have to be coded at a later stage but for all those questions to which answer categories are given, code numbers can be provided and the interviewers asked to ring the relevant number to indicate the respondent's answer during the course of the interview. The questionnaire example at the end of this chapter indicates how this can be done so that it is easy for the interviewer to see which code she should ring and also easy for the card puncher to read. (In this example, the numbers in brackets indicate on to which punch-card column the answers to each question are punched.)

The Use of Piloting

There are two main types of piloting, methodological pilots which are specifically designed to provide data for the development of measuring tools such as attitude scales, and questionnaire pilots designed to ensure the efficiency of the questions. Methodological piloting is discussed in the section on measuring attitude and beliefs. This section deals only with questionnaire piloting.

Piloting plays a vital part in questionnaire development but it too often consists only of getting some interviewers to conduct a few interviews 'to see if the questionnaire works'. Simply using a questionnaire will reveal the most obvious ambiguities and incomprehensions because the respondent will ask questions or give answers which clearly indicate incomprehension; but questionnaires can apparently work quite well in that respondents give what appear to be reasonable answers while, in fact, there are wide variations in interpretation or even complete misunderstandings hidden below the surface.

Interviewers should be specially trained in the requirements of piloting. It is useful, however, to use some relatively inexperienced interviewers on pilots, as well as highly skilled and experienced ones, because they throw more light on the sorts of problems which the less experienced interviewer is likely to come across in the field.

Pilot questionnaires should be laid out with plenty of space so that interviewers have room to record any spontaneous comments or explanations that respondents give while working out their answers. Interviewers should be instructed to write in all comments made by the respondent and any alterations made to the wording of the question or additional explanations that they gave in order to help the respondent understand. (This often reveals that the purpose and meaning of the question was not clear to the interviewer.) The interviewer should also follow up some of the questions by asking 'Can you tell me what you understand by this question (or statement)?' and 'Can you tell me what you had in mind when you answered . . .?'. This probing reveals the hidden ambiguities and misunderstandings. Questions involving memory can be followed up by 'How clearly can you remember this particular purchase? What fixed it in your mind?'.

To go back over the whole questionnaire in this manner can be very time-consuming; it is sometimes carried out at a separate operation, a different interviewer calling back on the respondent later on in the day. Often, however, just key questions are picked out for this treatment and they are followed up during the course of the interview or, if this disrupts the flow too much, at the end. The interviewer might say 'We are trying out this questionnaire and want to make sure that the questions make sense, so can I go back quickly over some of the answers you gave?'. This positions the process as a trial of the questionnaire and not an examination of the respondent's ability to understand. The amount of time taken can be reduced by dividing the questions to be examined in detail among the interviewers so that each deals with only three or four.

It can also be useful to ask interviewers to tape record some of their pilot interviews so that the researcher can listen to the interview and hear for himself what difficulties came up.

Apart from studying the pilot questionnaires and listening to tape recorded interviews, it is useful to have reports from the interviewers working on the pilot in which they summarize their findings under a number of headings provided by the researcher. These might be:

'selling' the survey and persuading the respondent to take part;
the opening questions;
the length of the interview;
the flow of the interview;
any particularly difficult questions;
any problems of interviewers' instructions;
any layout problems.

Questions for Behavioural Information

Information on consumer behaviour is usually required in order to give a picture of where and when the product is being bought, how it is used and into what context of more general behaviour its usage fits. It is also needed in order to provide a basis for discovering what sorts of people use the product in terms of characteristics and attitudes. For this latter purpose, it is usually necessary to identify particular 'behaviour groups' for use in tabulation, such as present and past users, heavy and light users, and so on. These groups must be precisely defined and questions asked to identify them.

The main difficulties in designing questions to collect behavioural information concern the problem of getting respondents to remember accurately and trying to get them to distinguish between what they 'usually' do and what, precisely, they did last time. There can also sometimes be difficulties in getting respondents to generalize about their behaviour. Techniques other than question-and-answer surveys have to be used when accuracy is essential. The information collected from surveys can be only an approximation. The researcher's job is not only to make the approximation as close as possible but also to have some idea from piloting as to what kind of errors are likely to occur.

Some of the most common types of behavioural questions and their problems can be discussed separately.

Product Group Definition. Before asking people whether they have ever used a product, make sure they know what is included, e.g. in asking housewives whether they have ever used a laundry, it may be necessary to ensure that they understand that this does not include launderettes or dry cleaning. In asking people whether they have ever taken a tonic, indicate whether tonic wines, doctors' prescribed tonics or vitamin pills, etc., are included or not. Make sure that they understand that by 'ever used' you means tried once and gave up as well as used regularly.

Frequency Questions. When a respondent is asked to say 'how often' he does something or 'how many times' he does it within a particular time period, he is usually being asked to generalize about his behaviour since there is almost certain to be some irregularity. The tendency is for him to give his *ideal* behaviour, from which he may frequently deviate; e.g. a person may think that the proper number of baths he ought to take in a week is four, though more often than not he may only get around to taking two, but may quite honestly believe that he usually takes four baths a week. Furthermore, he may be reluctant to admit that he only took two last week. To obtain accurate information it may be necessary to ask a series of questions, e.g. 'Quite a lot of people find it difficult to take as many baths as they wish because of shortage of time or because they're tired, or for other reasons; do you ever find you miss baths for this sort of reason?'. This can then be followed up with questions about the number of baths taken last week, preferably by getting him to recreate the week in his mind rather than by just asking him to give the number of baths taken; e.g. 'Now would you think back over last week, and tell me on which days you happened to take a bath?'.

Questions which proceed from what the respondent 'usually' does to what he 'happened to do last week' assist accuracy because he is less tempted to falsify his account of what he did last week on the grounds that it is atypical. It must be remembered, however, that what the respondent claims he 'usually' does is likely to represent his ideal rather than his average behaviour.

'Where?' and 'When?' Questions. Questions which ask where a product was purchased or where advertising for the product was seen are particularly subject to memory failure unless the event was a particularly important one for the respondent or clearly linked to a date. Because it is difficult to remember precisely, the respondent tends to say what he thinks was most likely to be the case.

Time tends to contract in memory with the result that people tend to remember events as having happened more recently than they really did. Difficulties of remembering lead respondents to substitute what they think they *usually* do for what they actually did. In answer to questions such as 'When did you last buy a bottle of disinfectant?' respondents are likely to claim that they bought one within the last seven days because they feel that it ought to be part of their once a week grocery purchasing and they know that they bought some not very long ago. Yet estimates of the total disinfectant market based on those claiming to buy within the past seven days are usually of the order of four times the most optimistic estimate of the market based on sales information.

'How Much?' Questions. Respondents can sometimes remember how much of a product they bought or used on a recent occasion as long as the units are clear cut, but they frequently cannot remember how much they paid for it (especially if the item was part of a larger bill) and are usually unaware of bottle or can sizes, especially when a number of size variations are available. Metrication has further confused this issue.

Brand Names. In some product fields where brand attachment is not strong, respondents sometimes cannot remember accurately which brand they last purchased or have in the house at present. Brands of stockings or tights are rapidly forgotten and a kitchen check might reveal confusion between 'Sunfresh' and 'Suncrush' and between 'Daz' and 'Surf'.

Measuring Attitudes and Beliefs

The measurement of attitudes is a vast subject that can only be touched on in this chapter. For a more comprehensive review of measuring techniques and also for papers on the main theories of attitude, the reader is referred to Fishbein[5].

It is useful to distinguish between the more general 'life-style' attitudes, such as attitudes towards the job of being a housewife or towards saving, and the more specific attitudes to brands or products. The term 'image' is reserved for these more specific brand evaluations.

The relationship between attitudes and beliefs

Attitudes can be defined as emotionally toned evaluations about events, objects or activities. They are *evaluations* because they assess things as good or bad, desirable or undesirable. They are *emotionally toned* in that the events, objects or activities with which the attitudes are connected arouse pleasure, joy, pain, anger, fear, anxiety, etc.; e.g. people who hold the attitude that saving money is a very good thing are likely to feel happy when they have a lot of money deposited in a Building Society and very anxious when they have no money saved.

The direction that the evaluation of the object or event takes, however, and the type of emotion felt is likely to be affected by a person's *beliefs* about the object, event or activity. If he believes that having money saved gives security, he is likely to feel anxious if he has no savings. If, on the other hand, he believes that one can only save by stinting one's family, he may feel guilty of meanness if any money accumulates in the bank. This last example demonstrates that beliefs can also carry evaluations.

Fishbein[6] has pointed out that it is important in attitude research to distinguish between evaluations of the subject that is being investigated, beliefs about it and evaluations of these beliefs. All three may be included implicitly within one measuring technique. Sometimes, this results in a valid measure of attitude because everyone agrees with the evaluation placed on the belief. The statement 'Coloured people are less intelligent than white people', for example, is a statement of belief. Everyone may agree, however, that intelligence is a desirable and admirable attribute; therefore anyone who agrees with the statement is giving a low evaluation to being coloured. The belief statement 'Coloured people are more athletic than white people' may not carry the same evaluation for everyone and those who agree with it are not necessarily giving a high evaluation to coloured people. The evaluation attached to the belief would, in this case, have to be measured separately in order to know whether it was contributing positively, negatively or neutrally to the overall evaluation of the subject being studied.

Saliency of attitude

One of the problems of investigating attitudes with structured questionnaires is that it is difficult to avoid putting words into people's mouths. It is impossible to ask someone whether he agrees or disagrees with a proposition without putting the subject of the proposition into his mind. He may agree strongly with the proposition, yet he may never have given the matter any thought before. The term 'saliency' is used to describe the extent to which a particular attitude is actively in people's minds before the interviewer asks specific questions about it.

The saliency of an attitude is usually measured by a series of open-ended questions which progressively 'home in' on the target attitude. In a study of attitudes to the noise of aircraft around Heathrow[7], for instance, respondents were asked a series of questions designed to discover whether aircraft noise was sufficiently annoying for it consciously to affect their pleasure in living in their home; e.g. 'What do you dislike about living around here?'; 'If you could change just one thing about living round here, what would it be?'; 'Have you ever thought of moving away from here? Why?' and 'What are main kinds of noise you hear round here?'. No mention of aircraft or aircraft noise was made in the interview until all these questions had been asked. The answers to these questions indicated the extent to which people were consciously aware of aircraft noise as a source of disturbance.

Dimensionality of attitudes

Open-ended questions can indicate whether a particular subject is uppermost in people's minds and what the main opinions are that people hold about the subject; but they can at best be only crude indications of how people feel. In particular, open questions cannot assess how *strongly* people feel about a subject.

The main purpose of measuring attitudes in market research is usually to be able to make *comparisons* between the attitudes of different groups of consumers, e.g. users and non-users of the product or brand. To make valid comparisons between groups, it is essential to be able to measure the position of *all* the people in the groups on the attitude, to measure whether they are favourable or unfavourable in their attitudes and how strongly they feel about it. This implies that attitudes are *dimensions* along which people can be positioned. This concept of the dimensionality of attitudes underlies all the main techniques of attitude measurement.

Attitudes and opinions that are simple, clear-cut and readily accessible to conscious introspection can be measured by single questions, e.g. people's optimism about their future financial prospects was measured by a simple self-rating scale, 'Over the next five years or so, do you expect your financial situation to:

improve a lot;
improve a little;
stay about the same;
get a bit worse;
get a lot worse?'

The more complex and fundamental attitudes which underlie specific opinions cannot be so easily measured, however. It is unlikely, for instance, that people would give a valid answer if asked to rate themselves on the extent to which they were conscientious housewives or concerned with maintaining their financial independence. This is partly because people are not usually aware of these broader attitudes and therefore cannot introspect accurately about them, and partly because these broad attitudes are *generalizations* about the people and, as already discussed, people find it very difficult to generalize.

The broad underlying dimensions of attitude are usually measured by batteries of questions which measure different aspects of the attitude and are then combined in some way to give an overall measure of the underlying attitude. The main methods of forming attitude batteries are discussed later in this chapter, but first it is necessary to consider the basic ingredients of attitude measurement, the questioning methods used in the interview situation.

Questioning techniques

The most common basic tool of attitude measurement is the *rating scale*, by which the respondent is asked to indicate his position on a dimension of opinion. Other techniques involve the ascription of adjectives to concepts, or vice versa, or a choice between alternative attitudinal positions. Rating scales can be verbal, numerical or diagrammatic. Verbal rating scales may take the form of the 'financial optimism' scale given above in which a single clear-cut concept is rated on a specific scale which embodies an attitude to the concept or a belief about it. Alternatively, a more complex concept may be presented which embodies the attitude or belief. The respondent is then asked to say whether he agrees or disagrees and how strongly (or whether he believes it to be true or untrue). Several concepts may be presented one after the other and the respondent may be asked to use the same response framework for replying to each; e.g. 'Tell me how much you agree or disagree with each of these statements:

(a) everyone should disinfect their drains every day;
(b) only those in old houses need use disinfectant;
(c) those who use a lot of disinfectant must be dirty people'.

A 'no opinion' or 'don't know' category should be provided for the interviewer to use if the respondent is unable to give an answer, though it need not necessarily be offered to the respondent.

Belson[8] has investigated the effects of the order in which categories are presented in verbal rating scales on the distribution of answers along the scale. He found that the positive answers were more frequently endorsed when they were presented at the top of the scale than when the scale was reversed and the positive answer appeared at the bottom. Putting the negative response categories at the top of the scale tended to give a better distribution of answers across the categories. There are, therefore, advantages in presenting the negative categories first, provided that it does not lead to confusion for the respondent.

There is no case for varying the order of presentation of rating scales from one interview to another, since this could lead to a situation where apparent differences in attitude between sub-groups of the sample were due to there being more people in one group than in the other having the scales presented in a particular way.

Numerical Rating Scales take several forms. Respondents may be asked to give scores out of ten or out of five. They might be asked, for instance, to score a cake mix that they have just tested on a number of attributes such as ease of making, lightness, tastiness and so on. Alternatively, they might be asked to score different brands according to their suitability for some purpose.

In using scoring systems the evaluation to be placed on the top score must be indisputable. (A product could not be scored for 'sweetness' for instance, because respondents cannot be certain whether the top point of the scale meant 'too sweet' or 'just right'.) Shorter scales are usually preferable to longer scales since it has been found that people tend to use only part of longer scales. Scores out of ten tend to carry particular connotations from school marks in that a score of five is often regarded as a low score rather than as the mid-point; the respondent may in effect use only the top half of the scale. The top and bottom point of a numerical scale should be defined verbally in order to avoid variability of interpretation between respondents.

Diagrammatic Rating Scales are as varied as the imaginations of the research people who invent them. They may be representational or abstract. The example in Fig. 5.2 below is a simple way of measuring pure evaluation independently of descriptive content by a representational scale; 'Which of these faces best expresses how you felt about the sweetness of the product?' In this example, the most favourable response means 'just right' while the least favourable response might mean 'too sweet' or 'not sweet enough'. It would clearly be necessary to ask those who gave a poor rating what was wrong with the sweetness of the product.

Fig. 5.2

Diagrammatic scales can present the dimension as a set of categories:

or as a continuum:

The respondent is simply asked to indicate his position on the scale. Numerical values can easily be assigned to respondents' positions on the scales that are presented with categories, but continuous scales present more of a problem. It is usually necessary to impose categories on the continuum for scoring purposes. The argument in favour of continuous diagrammatic scales is that they do not impose a set of categories of a pre-defined size and number. On the other hand, in common with all diagrammatic scales, they tend to involve the respondent in abstract thinking and to present ideas in a way that is unfamiliar.

Semantic Differential Scales are very popular in measuring brand, product or company images. These combine elements of both verbal and diagrammatic scales.

The technique was developed by Osgood[9] to investigate the meaning which concepts had for people. He presented concepts, e.g. 'the American nation' or 'coloured people', and asked respondents to rate them on seven-point scales, the end points of which were defined by pairs of adjectives:

good | | | | | | | | bad

strong | | | | | | | | weak

Market researchers have adapted the technique by using a brand, product or company name as the concept and often using quite complex descriptive and evaluative phrases to define the ends of the scale. The advantage of the technique is that several brands can be quite rapidly rated on several different scales (say four brands on 15 scales or six brands on ten scales) and comparisons made between them. Often, the respondent is shown how the scales are to be used and is then asked to fill them in himself. Numerical values can be assigned to the scale positions and comparisons made between the various brands (or between users and non-users of a brand) in terms of mean scores.

The pairs of adjectives or phrases used to define the ends of the scale should, of course, be very carefully selected to be relevant to the market being investigated. The Kelly Repertory Grid technique, described by Sampson in chapter 2 on Qualitative and Motivational Research, is often used to throw up attributes and to define the scale ends.

Some people prefer to use only 'monopolar' scales, such as 'sweet—not sweet' while others may use 'bipolar' scales, such as 'sweet—sour' where appropriate. The mid-point of the scale has different meanings for these two types of scale. On monopolar scales, the mid-point is simply a step on the scale from 'not sweet' to 'sweet', whereas on a bipolar scale the mid-point is a neutral point meaning 'neither sweet nor sour'. It can also be used to represent a 'no opinion' point on bipolar scales while a separate 'no opinion' category is necessary for monopolar scales.

Five-point rather than seven-point semantic scales are usually used in market research on the grounds that five points are easier for the interviewer to explain and for the respondent to grasp. Inspection of respondents' answer patterns on seven-point scales certainly seems to suggest that many fail to use all the positions but confine their answers to the extreme position and one other on each side of the mid-point. The meaning of the scale positions on five-point scales can easily be described by turning it into a verbal rating scale.

Interviewers need to be carefully instructed on how to explain semantic differential scales to respondents. A few trial examples should always be provided to make sure that the respondent has understood.

Ascription of Adjectives to brands is another questioning technique for measuring brand images. The respondent is handed a list of brands and asked to say which of them fit a particular adjective well; e.g. 'Which of the brands on this list are particularly sweet?' or 'And which are not at all sweet?'.

By presenting both ends of an attribute, as in the above example, a simplified brand rating can be achieved; i.e., a brand is rated either as 'particularly sweet' or 'not at all sweet' or, by implication, as neither one nor the other.

Two measures for each brand on each attribute can be derived from this: 'image strength', which is the proportion of the sample mentioning the brand as being either sweet or not sweet and 'image direction', which is the proportion of those mentioning it as sweet or not sweet who assign it to each side of the dichotomy.

Joyce[10] has indicated that this simple technique is quicker and easier to administer in the field than semantic scales, that it provides sharper discrimination between brands and that it is more sensitive in pinpointing changes in brand images over time. It is not suitable, however, for making comparisons between brands which differ markedly in share of the market and familiarity, since the unfamiliar brands tend to be swamped by the familiar brands and thus are not mentioned.

Presenting Alternative Attitude Positions is a useful technique for explaining the relative importance of conflicting values. Most people would agree, for instance, with the proposition that they ought to save when the country is in financial difficulties, yet many people do not do so because they feel that inflation makes saving pointless. If two propositions are presented as equally sensible alternatives, the tendency to agree glibly is reduced and the respondent is forced to think out his position, e.g.;

'Which of these two statements do you agree with most?' (SHOW CARD AND READ):

'People should save money when the country is in financial difficulties', or 'It's better to spend your money when the country is in financial difficulties because prices keep going up.'

Similarly, most people would like to consider themselves to be safe and careful drivers and also to be skilful and confident drivers, but the relative degree of importance which an individual motorist attaches to these descriptions could indicate differences in driving attitudes and values. Motorists were, therefore, asked to choose between a number of opposing adjectives, as follows.

As a motorist, would you rather be described as:

considerate or quick-witted;
confident or safe;
careful or skilful?

Which of these descriptions would you object to more:

timid or foolhardy;
aggressive or hesitant;
impatient or slow?

One of each pair of words described a more introverted type of motorist while the other described a more extrovert type. Each word was paired with another which, in the opinion of a panel of judges, was equally favourable or unfavourable.

The use of projective techniques in attitude measurement

Most projective techniques are not suitable for use in attitude measurement in structured questionnaires. The majority require open-ended answers, which cannot be used as efficient means of measurement, and often require a high degree of subjective interpretation. (See chapter 2 for a description of the use of projective techniques in qualitative research.)

Indirect questioning techniques can, of course, be used in structured questionnaires, such as asking the respondent to say what sort of person would or would not use a particular product or brand. Most of the different measurement techniques described above could be applied within this framework; semantic differential scales, for instance:

used by hard-working   used by lazy
housewives   housewives

Such questions as: 'If your car were to become a person, what sort of person would it be?' can also be structured in the same way.

Sentence completion can be used in a structured form in which the respondent is asked to select one of several alternative ways of finishing a sentence, but this moves away from the truly projective nature of the technique and it becomes simply another method of presenting a scale or a series of propositions.

Attitude batteries

The development of attitude batteries that combine the answers to several questions so as to measure a general underlying attitude usually requires special preparatory work. To ensure that the items that go into the battery all contribute efficiently to the measurement of the attitude it is usually necessary to try out a large number of items in a methodological pilot study of 100 to 200 respondents and then to apply various criteria for selecting those items which are the most appropriate. This procedure is commonly called 'attitude scaling'.

There are four main types of attitude scaling techniques:

(a) the Thurstone method of 'equal-appearing intervals';
(b) the Likert method of summated ratings;
(c) Guttman cumulative scales;
(d) scales based on factor analysis.

The last is the most commonly used in market research nowadays.

Each will be described briefly in turn but the reader is referred to the relevant literature for a fuller exposition.

Thurstone Scaling[11] involves devising (or collecting from free interviewing) a large number of opinion statements on the attitude subject. Preferably about 100 statements are collected. The attitude dimension to be measured is broadly, but clearly, defined. A panel of at least 100 people is then asked to rate the opinion statements on an 11-point scale according to how favourable or unfavourable each one is in terms of the attitude to be measured.

Those items are selected from each of the 11 scale positions about which there is most agreement from the judges. Each item is given a weight according to its median scale position. It is called the method of 'equal appearing intervals' because the 11 groups into which the judges divide the statements are meant to be equally spaced along the favourable/unfavourable continuum. The scale, now reduced to about 20 items, is then ready for use. Respondents are asked simply to endorse all the statements with which they agree. They are given a score on the attitude dimension by averaging the scale weights of all the items they have endorsed. This method of scaling is very laborious and its validity depends on the judges being drawn from the same population as that on which it is intended to use the scale. The average member of the public is likely to have some difficulty in acting as a judge without his agreement or disagreement with the statement influencing or confusing his judgement.

Likert Scaling[12] also starts with a large number of opinion statements but, instead of a panel of judges, a sample of respondents is asked to rate each statement on a verbal scale from 'agree strongly' through a 'no opinion' mid-

112

point to 'disagree strongly'. The answer categories are given weights from one to five or five to one depending on whether the statement is positive or negative in relation to the underlying attitude. Each respondent is then given a score by summing the weights attached to each of his answers. Items are then selected for inclusion in the final scale by applying a criterion of internal consistency; a group of respondents with high scores and a group with low scores (say the top and bottom 10%) are selected and their answers to each item are compared. The means for each item for each of the two groups are computed and the items which show the biggest difference between the means are retained.

Guttman Cumulative Scales[13] utilize the hierarchical property of questions that lie at different points along the same attitude dimension. A simple example illustrates the principle: if we ask people to say whether they are (a) over 20 years of age, (b) over 40 years of age, or (c) over 60 years of age, their answers will form a 'scalogram' pattern in that all those over 40 would also endorse that they are over 20, and those who are over 60 would endorse that they are over both the lesser ages. If the answers are hierarchic, a person's answer pattern can be deduced from his overall score.

To discover whether the scalogram pattern exists, the items are placed in order of the number of people endorsing each along one dimension of a sheet of paper and the individuals are placed in order of number of items endorsed along the other dimension and their answer patterns entered in the matrix.

The 'scalogram analysis' is usually performed using a special scalogram board which allows individual items or people to be shifted about slightly in order to optimize the scalogram pattern. The closeness with which a series of questions approaches perfect scalability is measured by the coefficient of reproducibility which is assessed by the following formula:

$$\frac{\text{number of errors}}{\text{number of questions} \times \text{number of respondents}}$$

A value of about 0.90 for the coefficient of reproducibility is usually taken as the lower acceptable limit for inferring scalability.

Guttman scales have the property of being strictly 'unidimensional', i.e. of measuring one, and only one, underlying dimension of attitude. In practice, it is extremely difficult to develop a satisfactory Guttman scale to measure attitudes unless the attitudes to be measured have a logical hierarchical foundation, as attitudes to aircraft noise do. In the study of the effects of aircraft noise round Heathrow already quoted[7], a Guttman scale of annoyance was used. This took the form of a series of questions about the effects of aircraft noise, e.g. 'Does the noise of aircraft ever wake you up? Interfere with conversation? Make your television flicker?' etc., followed by, 'When this happens, how annoyed does it make you feel?'. It can be argued that the louder the aircraft passing overhead, the wider the range of disturbances caused and the more annoyed people are likely to be; the scale is thus in a sense based on the hierarchic nature of noise measurements.

The 'unidimensionality' of Guttman scaling is an attractive concept to many people but, except in rare cases, it is extremely difficult if not impossible to develop a Guttman scale that both scales well according to his criterion and ends up containing items that have a high degree of face validity.

Scales Based on Item Intercorrelations are more generally used nowadays in survey research. The Thurstone, Likert and Guttman scaling techniques all depend on the subjective definition by the researcher of an attitude dimension and then set out to develop a scale for measuring it. But, however thorough the initial exploratory research, it is not easy for a researcher to obtain a completely clear understanding of the structure of attitudes; what he identifies as a single broad attitude dimension may in fact consist of two separate dimensions which have little relationship to each other. Conversely, what he thought to be two distinct dimensions may turn out to be so closely related that they can be combined for all practical purposes.

Scaling techniques based on the intercorrelations between attitude items enable the researcher to test out and refine his hypotheses about the structure of attitudes in the particular field being investigated; they also give him the opportunity of identifying attitudes at different levels ranging from very specific opinions to very broad general 'life style' attitudes.

Factor analysis is the statistical method most widely used in the development of attitude scales; its application in the field of market research has grown rapidly with the availability of well-tried programs for the technique for large computers which has brought the cost down within the reach of most attitude survey budgets.

There are different types of factor analysis of which the one most appropriate to attitude scaling problems is that known as 'principal component analysis'. (Experts might argue that this is not really a form of factor analysis at all but a separate technique. Colloquial usage has led, however, to principal component analysis being called 'factor analysis'.) The basic function of principal component analysis is quite easy to grasp without there being any necessity to understand the mathematics underlying it. Its use, therefore, need not be confined to statisticians. It can be applied when there are a lot of different measurements for the same sample of people. In attitude research it can, for instance, be applied to semantic differential scales, to ratings applied to opinion statements or any other measurements provided the total sample is rated on each item.

The first step is to calculate the correlation between each and every other item. The matrix of correlations provides the input for the principal component analysis. (A program for calculating the intercorrelations is usually an integral part of any factor analysis program.)

Principal component analysis sorts all the measurements into a number of

114

groups or 'factors' on the basis of the extent to which they are measuring common ground. This is assessed by examining within the computer each person's pattern of answers for all the items and identifying the items which tend to have common patterns. The assumption is made that items which are shown to belong to the same factor are measuring something in common, e.g. an underlying attitude dimension. Examination of the content of the items usually indicates fairly clearly what the underlying dimension is.

In addition to grouping attitude items into factors and indicating any which do not fit the factors, a 'factor loading' is given to each item. This is a figure from -1.0 to $+1.0$ which indicates the extent to which each item is associated with the dimension underlying the factor. The factor loading is therefore an indication of the efficiency with which each item measures the underlying factor. Another measure given by most programs of factor analysis indicates how much of the total variance of all the items is accounted for by each of the factors.

Principal component analysis can be used to help identify the relevant attitude dimensions and to examine the efficiency of specific items in measuring the attitude dimensions.

In a study of attitudes to savings[14], a number of hypotheses about the attitudes that led people to save were developed on the basis of a qualitative study. A list of about 25 statements of opinion were derived from the depth interviews and administered to a sample of 130 members of the public in a methodological pilot. The results were subjected to principal component analysis. A 'four-factor' solution grouped the statements broadly as had been expected from the qualitative study but indicated which statements were the most efficient at measuring each factor. The four factors are listed below together with names which were given them after the content of the main items had been examined to identify the common element underlying them.

FACTOR I   Temperamental difficulty in saving

Loading

—0.75   I have never been able to save.

—0.74   Unless you have some specific reason to save, it's better to spend and enjoy it.

—0.69   I believe in enjoying my money now and letting the future take care of itself.

—0.63   I don't feel it's necessary to save just now.

—0.55   I can't help spending all I earn.

FACTOR II   Sense of solidity

Loading

—0.81   If you've got a bit of money saved you are not so likely to be pushed around.

—0.72   Your opinions carry more weight if you've got money saved.

—0.68   You don't feel successful until you've got money saved.

—0.54   I'd like to feel I was worth something.

FACTOR III Concern with independence

Loading

—0.85   I hate to feel I might have to ask someone for financial help.
—0.80   I hate to feel that a minor emergency could cause me financial embarrassment.
—0.54   Money not needed should be saved rather than spent on luxuries.
—0.43   It would worry me if I had no savings at all.

FACTOR IV Feeling of financial security

Loading

—0.65   I feel it's unlikely I shall have any financial emergencies in the near future.
0.54   I always feel there might be a financial emergency at any time.
—0.45   I can't help spending all I earn.

Items can be selected from each factor to use in the main survey to measure the attitudes which have been identified. The number of items selected depends on the degree of reliability desired (the more items, the more reliable the measure) and the amount of space available in the questionnaire. Each respondent can be given a score for each attitude by using the Likert method of weighting each response category and summing the weights. A further refinement is to weight each item by its factor loading so that the more important items in measuring the attitude play a bigger part in the overall score.

Principal component analysis is often applied to measures of brand image using semantic differential scales. It is usually used in a methodological pilot to identify the main image dimensions and to provide a basis for reducing the number of scales to be included in the main survey.

Although factor analysis methods add a number of refinements to attitude scaling, some would argue that some of these (e.g. using factor loadings to weight the items) are unnecessary. McKennell[15], for instance, points out that, except where the structure of attitudes is particularly complex, a study of a correlation matrix of all the attitude items, perhaps aided by relatively simple techniques such as McQuitty's Hierarchical Linkage or Coefficient Alpha, can identify the main dimensions of attitude measured by the items as effectively as factor analysis without imposing a particular mathematical model on the data (as is implicit in the choice of a method of factor analysis). Both McQuitty and Coefficient Alpha work with average correlations; the reader is referred to the literature for details[17,16].

The 'priority evaluator' approach

A study of attitudes, especially if related to other information about people and to their behaviour, can provide a considerable degree of understanding as to why people behave as they do and buy the products they buy. But some purchasing decisions are very complex because the object being purchased has several aspects which are important to the purchaser. A holiday, a car or a new house must meet the purchaser's requirements in several respects. Often, however, the purchaser's choice is limited by what is available and by considerations of price. A broad understanding of his attitudes and motivations may therefore not give a very good indication of what his purchasing behaviour is likely to be. In addition we need to know to which attributes he gives priority and how he trades off one against the other to arrive at his choice. The Priority Evaluator approach has been developed to cope with this complex kind of decision[18].

The first step is to identify the four to six main features that people take into account in making their choice; in choosing a package holiday, the main aspects to be considered might be the crowdedness of the resort, type of hotel, nearness to the sea and the sort of food served. For each of these aspects, a scale could be devised to indicate the various possibilities available to purchasers. For example, the following types of hotel might be listed:

round-the-clock room service, several bars and lounges, swimming pool, variable meal times;
day time room service, one bar and lounge, small swimming pool, fixed meal times;
breakfast time room service, bar-lounge, no pool, fixed meal times;
pension-type hotel, fixed meal times.

It is apparent that each of these categories will have different implications for the price of the holiday: the next step is therefore to attach a value to each category in each scale which represents the contribution that choosing that category would make to the total cost of the holiday. When this procedure has been followed for each set of categories, it can readily be seen that selecting one category from each set will indicate a particular type of holiday against which a price can be set. The values allocated can vary from scale to scale; for instance, type of hotel might be more important than the other three scales in determining price of holiday, and this would be reflected in higher values being attached to it.

This set of four scales could then be used in a number of ways: first, respondents might be asked to rate their last holiday on each scale. By adding the numerical values assigned to each category indicated, the number of 'points' that that holiday was worth can be arrived at. Respondents might then be asked to indicate what changes, if any, they would have liked to have made to their holiday without altering its overall price; in other words, they are given the chance to alter the categories chosen by 'trading-off' one against the other; e.g. someone might decide that he would prefer a less crowded resort and that to obtain it he was prepared to accept a lower standard of amenity in the hotel.

Respondents might then be asked how much they were prepared to spend on their next holiday and be given a number of points to represent this; they would then be asked to allocate the points across the four scales to indicate again what mix of categories they would like to buy.

To help respondents in the task they are asked to do, the different scale categories are often illustrated with line drawings to put them over realistically. In addition, the respondent is given a set of counters which represent the points he has to allocate.

Careful preliminary work has to go into devising and testing out the scales and their categories; interviewers need full briefing and training in how to administer the scales; respondents need to be allowed time to learn what they have to do and to consider their choices carefully; it is therefore apparent that this technique cannot simply be grafted on to an attitude survey. But it does provide a useful method for more focused studies of the ways in which consumers make complex choices.

Classification of Respondents

It is usual practice to collect personal details about the respondent and his household at the end of the interview, such as age, occupation, socio-economic class, household composition, etc. The purpose of this information is to provide:

(a) control over the sample;
(b) a check on the sample;
(c) profile descriptions of sub-groups of the sample;
(d) breakdown groups for analysis.

(a) Control over the sample

Many market research surveys are based on quota sampling in which the interviewer is asked to find so many men and so many women, so many in each age group, so many in each socio-economic group, and so on. To check that the sample has been correctly constituted, it is necessary to record on the questionnaire the details of the variables used in controlling the selection of respondents. Region, town size and urban/rural classification is usually controlled by the allocation of interviewing areas and is not left to the discretion of the interviewer; these data are often identified on the questionnaire by a quota number. The interviewer, however, has to select respondents from within her area to fit the quota she has been given using, perhaps, three or four variables, some of which may be 'interlocking', e.g. her age and social class quota may be specified separately for men and women, thus making them interlock with sex.

(b) A check on the sample

It is practical to use only a small number of variables in selecting a quota sample. The variables chosen are obviously those which are considered to be

118

most relevant to the particular survey; there may, however, be others which have some relevance but which could not be used as controls without making sample selection extremely difficult and expensive; for example, housewives might be selected using age, socio-economic class and working status as controls; in such a case, it would be likely that a cross-section of mothers with children in different age groups would also be obtained because this is related to age and working status. The socio-economic class control should also ensure a correct proportion with the use of a car, but both these variables could usefully be checked against published statistics based on large random samples to ensure that no bias has crept in.

When random sampling methods are used, it is also useful to check the distributions of the classification variables against those collected from other large-scale random-sample surveys or against census data in order to ensure that sampling error, refusals, or problems in contacting people have not resulted in bias.

(c) Profile description of sub-groups of the sample

Much of the value of survey research comes from making comparisons between sub-groups of the sample that show different purchasing, usage or attitude patterns. An important use of classification data is to provide profile descriptions of these different sub-groups in the market.

(d) Breakdown groups for use in analysis

In examining survey results, it is also often relevant to compare the purchasing, usage, and attitude patterns of different segments of the population; analysis may therefore be carried out using classification variables to define breakdown groups. This underlines again the point made earlier that it is essential to consider the requirements of analysis in some detail when the questionnaire is being designed.

Classification variables for inclusion

The classification variables that should be included in the questionnaire will depend on the particular requirements of the survey for controlling and checking the sample and for providing profile descriptions and breakdown groups. A classification manual produced by Social and Community Planning Research[19] lists the following variables for each of which there is an established system of classification and published population statistics.

Area variables:

geographical region;
type of area;
density of population;
socio-economic index;
person per room index.

Accommodation variables:

type of accommodation;
type of tenure;
length of residence;
age of building;
number of rooms;
accommodation amenities;
garage facilities.

Household variables:

household size;
household structure (alternatives A and B);
gross household income;
socio-economic group of head of household (as shown in The Classi-
    fication of Occupation)[20];
socio-economic grade of household (used in National Readership
    Surveys);
types of vehicle owned;
household vehicle ownership;
household possessions.

Individual variables:

age of individual;
sex of individual;
status in the household;
relationship to head of household;
marital status;
activity status, e.g. working full/part-time, retired, studying, etc.;
socio-economic group;
personal income (gross or net);
terminal education age;
education qualifications;
type of school attended;
driving characteristics.

There may be others, not included in this list, which are important in a
particular case. The National Readership Survey[21] provides information on a
number of variables of interest to specific markets, e.g. pet ownership,
possession of gardens.

There are several arguments in favour of using standard methods of classification wherever possible[22]; apart from enabling proper sample control and
checking to be maintained, it ensures at least some comparability between
surveys taken at different times and on different subjects. The National
Readership Survey[21] is the most widely-used source of information for
setting quota controls in the market research field and, because it is the main

Name		(10)–(12)
Address	Quota District Number	
	Quota District Name	

	Age:	(13)
	16–24	1
	25–34	2
Position in family: (19)	35–44	3
head of household 1	45–64	4
housewife 2	65+	5
other adult 3		
Occupation of head of household	Class: A	6
	B	7
	C1	8
	C2	9
(20)	D	0
Informant: not working 1	E	X
┌──── working 2		
↓	Sex:	(14)
Is there a pension scheme with Yes 3	male	1
your job? No 4	female	2
IF YES: are deductions made Yes 5	Status: married	3
from your pay for it or not? No 6	┌── single/widowed/divorced	4
	↓	
	Are you engaged or planning Yes	5
Do you have an income of your Yes 7	to get married? No	6
own? ┌─No 8		(15)
	IF MARRIED 0–2 years	1
(Skip to age)	How long have you 3–5 years	2
	been married? 6–10 years	3
IF YES: Which of these income	Longer	4
groups do you come in?		

			Total	Earns
(CARD 9) (Gross income)				
Yearly (*Weekly*) (21)			(16)	(17)
–£1500 (under £30) 1	(a) *Total in household:* One		1	1
£1500–£1749 (£30–£34.95) 2	Two		2	2
£1750–£1999 (£35–£39.95) 3	(b) *How many of them* Three		3	3
£2000–£2249 (£40–£44.95) 4	*are wage earners?* Four		4	4
£2250–£2749 (£45–£49.95) 5	Five		5	5
£2750–£3249 (£50–£62.95) 6	Six+		6	6
£3250–£3750 (£63–£71.95) 7				
£3750+ (£72+) 8	Is your home: (READ OUT)			(18)
	rented furnished			1
	rented unfurnished			2
Do you pay tax at the standard (22)	being bought on mortgage			3
rate of 0.41p on any of your Yes 1	fully paid for and owned			4
income? No 2	or rent free with the job?			5
Don't know 3				
	Interviewers name:			
(23)	Date of interview: / /			
Do you pay surtax? Yes 1				
No 2	Length of interview: mins.			
Don't know 3				

source of media information, is also a standard to which other survey data are often compared; for this reason the conventions set up by it for defining classification variables are generally established in market research.

As the typical 'classification page' of a questionnaire (p. 121) indicates, the questions which the interviewer should ask in order to collect the classification information are not always specified. This is a practice which can be carried too far since it relies overmuch on the assumption that all interviewers have received the same type and amount of training. It also depends heavily on interviewers remembering definitions accurately while trying to conduct the interview. Collection of enough detail on occupation of the head of the household to classify his socio-economic group accurately is probably the item that suffers most from this practice.

Appendix: Excerpt from National Savings Survey Questionnaire

No.	Question	Answer	Code	Skip to
36.	SHOW CARD 5 Can you tell me, very roughly, how much money you have saved or invested altogether in these forms of saving?	£50 or less £51–£200 £201–£500 £501–£1000 £1001–£3000 More Don't know	(69) 1 2 3 4 5 6 7	37
37.	In which form of saving do you have *most* money?	Only one form held Premium Bonds National Savings Certificates Building Society P.O.S.B. Ordinary Account P.O.S.B. Investment Account Bank Deposit Account National Development Bonds Defence Bonds Unit Trusts Stocks and Shares Trustee S.B. Ordinary Account Trustee S.B. Special Investment A/c Local Authorities Other	(70) 1 2 3 4 5 6 7 8 9 0 X V (71) 1 2 3	38
38.	SHOW CARD 6 What is this saving for? For any of these purposes (CARD) or for other purposes?	For emergencies For meeting large household bills For holidays, Christmas, etc. For security in later life To provide an income Other	(72) 1 2 3 4 5 6	39

No.	Question	Answer	Code	Skip to
39.	Why did you choose that particular form of saving? PROBE		(73)	
				40
			(74)	
	IF ONLY ONE FORM OF SAVING, GO TO Q. 41. IF MORE THAN ONE, ASK FOR EACH REMAINING IN ORDER OF SIZE: ASK SEPARATELY FOR ALL OTHER TYPES OF SAVING HELD	(WRITE IN TYPE) Type of saving.................................	(10)	
40. a	SHOW CARD 6 What are the savings in ....for?	For emergencies For meeting large household bills For holidays, Christmas, etc. For security in later life To provide an income Others	(11) 1 2 3 4 5 6	
b	SHOW CARD 5 What are the savings ....for?	(WRITE IN TYPE) Type of saving.....................................	(12)	
		For emergencies For meeting large household bills For holidays, Christmas, etc. For security in later life To provide an income Others	(13) 1 2 3 4 5 6	
c	SHOW CARD 6 What are the savings in ....for?	(WRITE IN TYPE) Type of saving.....................................	(14)	
		For emergencies For meeting large household bills For holidays, Christmas, etc. For security in later life To provide an income Others	(15) 1 2 3 4 5 6	

		Held (16)	0–2 (17)	3–5 (18)	6–10 (19)	11+ (20)	CR (21)	
41. a	SHOW CARD 7 Are there any types of saving on this list which you held in the past but no longer hold?	None	1	1	1	1	1	1	
		Premium Bonds	2	2	2	2	2	2	
		Nat. Sav. Certs.	3	3	3	3	3	3	
b	IF YES: ASK FOR EACH HELD How long ago did you cash the last of them:	Building Society	4	4	4	4	4	4	
		P.O.S.B. (O)	5	5	5	5	5	5	
		P.O.S.B. (I)	6	6	6	6	6	6	
	Within the last 2 years	Bank Deposit A/c	7	7	7	7	7	7	42
	3–5 years ago	Nat. Devel. Bonds	8	8	8	8	8	8	
	6–10 years ago	Defence Bonds	9	9	9	9	9	9	
	or longer	Unit Trusts	0	0	0	0	0	0	
		Stocks and Shares	X	X	X	X	X	X	
		Trustee (O)	V	V	V	V	V	V	
			(22)	(23)	(24)	(25)	(26)	(27)	
	(CR = Can't remember)	Trustee (I)	1	1	1	1	1	1	
		Local Authority	2	2	2	2	2	2	
		Other	3	3	3	3	3	3	

No.	Question	Answer		Code	Skip to
				(28)	
42.	Do you yourself pay any life insurance premiums?		Yes	1	43
			No	2	45
43.	Can you tell me about how much you pay per month in premiums?		£1 or less	3	
			£2 to £5	4	
			£6 to £10	5	44
			£11 to £20	6	
			More	7	
			Don't know	8	
44.	In general, do you think of your life insurance as a method of saving or just as insurance?		A method of saving	9	
			Just insurance	0	45
			Don't know	X	
				(29)	
45.	Do you have a current bank account at present?		Yes	1	46
			No	2	

SHOW CARD 8

No.	Question	Answer	(a) Most	(b) Very	Skip to
46. a	Which of these is *most* important to you in choosing a form of saving or investment?				
			(30)		
b	Which others would you also consider to be *very* important?	A chance for the capital to grow	1	7	
		Complete security of the capital	2	8	
		A high interest rate	3	9	
		Tax concessions on the interest	4	0	47
		Quick and easy to get your money out	5	X	
		(Don't know)	6	V	

No.	Question	Answer		Code	Skip to
				(31)	
47.	Do you think of yourself as being	READ:	Well off	1	
			Fairly well off	2	
			Neither well off nor hard up	3	48
			A little bit hard up	4	
			Very hard up	5	
			(Don't know)	6	
48.	Over the next couple of years, do you think your income/your family income will:	READ:	Increase a lot	7	
			Increase a little	8	
			Decrease	9	49
		or	Stay about the same	0	
			(Don't know)	X	
				(32)	
49.	Do you feel that your future financially is:	READ:	Completely secure	1	
			Very secure	2	
			Fairly secure	3	50
			Rather insecure	4	
			(Don't know)	5	

124

No.	Question	Answer	Code	Skip to
50.	I am going to read a pair of statements. Will you tell me which you feel is closest to your opinion:		(33)	
a	When the country is in difficulties:			
		People should save all they can	1	
	OR	People would be wiser to spend before inflation makes prices rise	2	
		(Don't know)	3	
	CONTINUE WITH REMAINING PAIRS			
b	When the country is in difficulties:			
		People should buy government sponsored savings	4	
	OR	You should still buy the type of saving which suits you best	5	
		(Don't know)	6	
c		I prefer not to buy Government savings when the wrong Party is in power	7	
	OR	The Party in power does not affect my choice of savings at all	8	51
		(Don't know)	9	
d		I never consider how the money I save is being used	0	
	OR	I would only choose savings methods which I felt would make good use of my money	X	
		(Don't know)	V	
e			(34)	
		Your savings are put to best use by the Government	1	
	OR	Your savings are put to best use by private enterprise	2	
		(Don't know)	3	
51. a		It is best to spread your savings	4	
	OR	It's best to put all your savings in one good form	5	(b)
		(Don't know)	6	52
b	Can you tell me why you think that it's best to ....?		(35)	
				52
			(36)	

6. Interviewing and field control

John F. Drakeford

The Role of the Interview in Survey Research

Most survey research requires the collection of information or observations from representative samples of particular populations. These samples can comprise individual members of the public where information, when aggregated, aims to reflect the behaviour or opinions of the *total* population or *sub-samples* of it (e.g. housewives, AB class male householders, single working women). Alternatively, these samples can comprise individuals within specialist groups, such as manufacturers, retailers, businessmen, where information may be needed either about the behaviour and opinions of these respondents as individuals, or about the establishments (e.g. companies, shops, etc.) that they represent.

Irrespective of the *type* of information to be collected, virtually all of this work, if postal surveys are excluded, demands *personal* contact of some kind between an interviewer and a respondent. The fundamental importance of this requirement can not be overstated; as far as the sponsor of a particular survey is concerned, this *personal* contact between an interviewer and a respondent is nearly always the *only* direct link he has with the user or potential user of his products or services. In certain circumstances, particularly in small (usually industrial) markets or where the identity of customers or potential customers is already known, it may be possible for a manufacturer to establish this direct personal contact himself or through his representatives; indeed in some specialist fields a complete *census* of customers or potential customers may be possible, and there is no need to use sample survey methods. In situations like these, it is not uncommon for salesmen to be used to report back to management with information collected by them from customers or potential customers. There are a number of serious dangers in this approach, principally that representatives or salesmen are almost certainly not able to collect relevant information, nor trained to collect it in a systematic and controlled way. They may often have a particular axe to grind; the special relationship between salesmen and customers or potential customers is almost certain to introduce bias in the way questions are asked, the way they are answered, and the way the aggregated results are interpreted. Where a research sponsor seeks information from a 'mass market', it is, of course, impossible for him to have direct contact in this way. Nevertheless, the dangers of ever using 'committed' or involved people as interviewers, without adequate training and control in the special kind of personal content required in survey research, cannot be overemphasised.

It must be stressed that, in this chapter, we are concerned with the role of *professionally trained research interviewers* who alone should be responsible for this vital phase in any project.

Putting the Interview in Context

The need for information in survey research to be collected most often by *personal* contact of this kind must be seen against the background of how particular surveys are structured and planned. The complex nature of survey research nowadays, and the need to employ specialists at various phases in a project, means that the questionnaire, recording form, diary, or inventory designed for use by the interviewer cannot be planned solely with him or her, or indeed the respondent, in mind. Of particular importance here is the need to appreciate that:

(a) the survey sponsor will have his own special requirements in terms of the information or observations he needs to collect;
(b) the researcher in control of the project who is translating these requirements into practical survey methodology will have open to him a wide range of techniques and procedures;
(c) the questionnaire, recording form, diary or inventory incorporating these must be usable by the interviewer in a face-to-face situation, and comprehensible to the respondent;
(d) completed documents must be capable of processing through a number of different routines — *manual* checking and editing, listing open-ended responses, preparing a code frame, coding itself, and *mechanical* transfer to punched cards, computer tapes;
(e) the resultant findings must be capable of interpretation in depth, and of *real use* to the survey sponsor.

Any project, therefore, will pass through a number of phases, and no one phase can be allowed to dominate; even the *best* questionnaire must be something of a compromise, in needing to take account of these various requirements.

In the recent past, a great deal of attention has been paid to new techniques and procedures in questionnaire design, and to ways of assembling and analysing the data collected in the most meaningful (albeit often highly complex) way, with all the refinements in, for instance, multivariate analysis that the widespread and still growing use of computers can bring. Less attention than it deserves has perhaps been paid to the vital *interviewing* phase in survey research, and the clear need to impose on this standards of the highest quality.

Field Organizations

The most important types of field organization in countries with well developed research facilities are as follows:

(a) Those integrated totally into large independent research practitioner companies. There is a central Field Management Organization (usually at head office), and a structure of field supervisors and interviewers on a national basis.

(b) Similar field 'structures' belonging to large research companies but where these are 'hived' off as separate independent companies. Such field organizations are of course used on a day-to-day basis by the 'parent' research company, but this structure provides the opportunity to present 'fieldwork only' as a speciality to those buyers wishing only to make use of the fieldwork element outside their own company, or to subcontract fieldwork to one specialist, data processing to another, and so on.

(c) 'Specialist' field forces of a totally independent kind, not linked to any research company offering a full range of services, and not usually offering anything other than fieldwork, with the appropriate administrative back up.

(d) The field forces built up and employed privately and regularly by manufacturing companies or advertising agencies.

(e) Finally, there are the 'private lists' of supervisors and interviewers held by many research buyers *and* practitioners. These lists have been built up over time, and constructed to fit a user's particular needs (e.g. a team of properly trained group discussion recruiters; teams of interviewers in selected towns capable of administering hall tests; interviewers specializing in unstructured interviewing work with businessmen, doctors, etc.).

In buying fieldwork as part of a complete project 'package' or if buying fieldwork only, a researcher will have to satisfy himself as to the standards of that organization or individual interviewer (see later check list for buyers). Many interviewers (who are, after all, very often freelance) work for several field forces and are therefore exposed to and controlled by different field organizations with different standards, different procedures. Sometimes this can cause problems, especially if an interviewer is on the books of several field forces and works fairly regularly for them. As an insurance policy, therefore, the research buyer needs to know how many interviewers are in *regular* work for a particular field force (as opposed to just names on a list), and ideally how many different organizations each interviewer works for regularly. Essentially, a compromise will need to be reached since, for economic reasons, very few research organizations of any kind can these days afford an 'exclusive' field force, or one where interviewers are on a permanent salaried basis.

The need for training and control

If the need for professionally trained interviewers in survey research is accepted, it follows that detailed attention has to be paid to the ways in which these interviewers are selected, trained and subsequently controlled in their day-to-day work. This is necessary especially because:

(a) the range of problems that survey research is called upon to solve is extensive and varied;

(b) to the researcher planning a project, an ever growing corpus of survey techniques, interviewing methods, and analysis procedures is available. These can be used in various combinations with equal effectiveness to solve a particular problem; in other words, the ways in which different research organizations will use the techniques available in attempting to solve similar or even identical problems will vary; indeed it is unreasonable to suggest that there should always be a single, standard method of approach;

(c) the characteristics of respondents from whom information is to be collected, or about whom observations are to be made, will vary widely within a particular survey, and even more *between* surveys;

(d) whatever standards are imposed on the interviewers by adequate selection, training and quality-control, interviewers will themselves vary in being members of field forces with different structures, in their own personal characteristics and backgrounds, in the depth and variation of initial training and subsequent retraining, in the types of survey in which they may specialize, and in the frequency with which they are engaged.

These variations in types of research, characteristics of respondents, and structure and methods of field forces, can only emphasise further need for a high degree of overall efficiency in day-to-day fieldwork and, wherever possible, the aim of standardizing and further improving basic procedures.

For the interested student, there is available a range of data on the importance of maintaining very rigorous basic procedures, particularly the valuable experimental work conducted and reported on by W. A. Belsen (see suggested reading list).

Types of Interviewer and Interviewing

The wide-ranging nature of survey research includes many projects where it may be inappropriate to use part time interviewers in a field force, however well trained and controlled they may be, for 'conventional' face-to-face interviewing.

Such projects will need information collected by:

(a) Structured or unstructured interviews, especially in *industrial and commercial companies*, with top level management or employees who need to be approached because of the specialist (often highly technical) nature of the information they can provide. In industrial research surveys, for instance, it is often desirable to employ specially selected and trained interviewers of a rather higher calibre than those used on research surveys of a fairly standardized and conventional kind. These interviewers may also need to have some technical knowledge of the particular survey topics being investigated.

(b) Group interviewing, or single interviews of an extended and unstructured kind, most often described as 'group discussions' or 'depth interviews'. Work of this type is usually of an exploratory nature where attitudes and beliefs are examined and collated, but in an unquantified way, in order to elicit hypotheses for further study, or to ensure that the full range of attitudes and beliefs are extracted early enough to ensure inclusion in a subsequent quantified stage of research. Here, ideally, psychologists or sociologists specially trained in this type of work should be used, particularly where the topics to be explored are of a particularly personal, delicate or intimate nature. It is, of course, not uncommon for researchers without special psychological or sociological training to be used for work of this kind and, indeed, this has some value if the main purpose is to inform the researcher planning and controlling a survey about the way in which people behave and think about the particular topic. There are, however, great dangers in relegating this type of interviewing to inexperienced researchers, who will fail to appreciate often enough the subtleties of approach required and the all important and difficult task of extracting the appropriate data, and putting the right emphasis on it in subsequent stages of research.

(c) Telephone interviewing, a fast growing method of data collection. In surveying the general public the (relatively) low level of telephone ownership has tended to inhibit researchers in Britain, but recent experiments suggest that many of the obstacles can be overcome. In any event, in certain subsections of the total population telephone ownership is very high and in business of any kind it is virtually total. The objections to using part-time interviewers for telephone work can be overcome *provided that* careful training is given. In terms of supervision, of course, a very high degree of control can be achieved in interviewers' work at a central point equipped with a number of telephones.

The task of a conventional field force

Having said this, it is nevertheless true that the great majority of survey research projects are likely to use interviewers who belong to field forces of the kinds described earlier. Before dealing with how these field forces operate, it is worthwhile reviewing the range of tasks which such interviewers can be called upon to carry out. Major areas of activity include:

(a) the selection and recruitment of individual members of the public to attend research sessions, e.g. group discussions, hall tests, advertising testing, etc.;

(b) the selection and recruitment of individuals to be members of a panel required to report, over a lengthy period, on purchasing behaviour, etc.;

(c) shop audits and domestic pantry checks, where interviewers are required to inspect and check ranges of products held and to calculate from invoices, or other records, sales volume, purchasing rates, etc.;

(d) courtesy calls, made from time to time on individuals reporting as panel members, to check on performance, answer queries, and possibly to reactivate disinterested panel members;

(e) exploratory interviewing, often of a fairly unstructured nature, sometimes at the pilot stage of a project, where experiments are being conducted on the design and content of a questionnaire or recording form, whose final version will subsequently be used in a major survey;

(f) conventional face-to-face interviews where behavioural or attitude and opinion information is being collected;

(g) invitations to members of the public to participate in product testing, where existing or new products are to be placed in homes for subsequent use over a controlled period;

(h) telephone interviewing, either to collect information on the spot using a structured or unstructured questionnaire, or to arrange an appointment for a subsequent face-to-face interview;

(i) industrial or commercial interviewing;

(j) observing, counting and classifying individuals, and/or vehicles, in traffic studies, parking studies, shop research, etc.

The varying nature of the types of task interviewers are called upon to perform further emphasises the need to maximize efficiency of field force operations and to impose stringent interviewer control.

Field Management Organization

Head office organization

The administration of a field force engaged on this varied work requires a carefully structured central organization from which field work can be planned, and to which individual interviewers and supervisors must report.

The complexity of this central organization will, of course, vary with the size of the field force and the nature of its work.

In a small field force, perhaps operated by a manufacturer solely for his own research puposes, full-time salaried or part-time interviewers may work only in a particular town or region of the country. Such a force will require only a small head office team to control adequately the comparatively few interviewers involved; indeed, these interviewers will be seen personally by head office staff fairly frequently. It is worth noting here that there are in fact very few exclusive field forces operated by manufacturers or advertising agencies. In larger, mostly nationally spread, field forces of the type operated by many independent research organisations, teams of several hundred interviewers will be employed, often regularly for several days of the week, on repeat surveys, panels, omnibus surveys and so on, but nevertheless usually on a part-time rather than a full-time basis. Field organization here must be on a much larger scale, and there will often be separate field managers at head office looking after separate teams of interviewers, some of whom will operate 'across the board' on a wide variety of projects, and some of whom will be confined to continuous audit and panel work for which they will be specially trained.

The work of head office field staff in larger organizations is likely to be sectionalized, different staff members having different responsibilities. These separate sections of responsibility will include:

(a) the selection, training and retraining of interviewers;
(b) costing surveys, negotiating rates of pay with interviewers, and ensuring prompt payment on delivery of completed work of an acceptable standard;
(c) booking interviewers for survey work or arranging for them to be booked through supervisors;
(d) despatching work material;
(e) day-to-day supervision and control of interviewers in the field;
(f) the receipt and checking of completed work;
(g) following up substandard work, arranging for reinterviewing or substitute interviewing, checking on suspect interviewers, etc;
(h) administrative matters concerned with quality control, training sessions, briefing conferences, etc;
(i) the continual updating of the *interviewer manual* on basic procedures.

Supervisors

The volume and complexity of this work in large field forces will also almost certainly necessitate a supervisory level, interposed *between* head office staff and individual interviewers. Supervisors of this type will usually have had considerable depth of interviewing experience previously, and will often be employed in their supervisory role on a full-time salaried basis. They will be in frequent contact with head office staff and responsible, usually on a regional basis, for controlling a team of interviewers in their areas on the basis of 10–25 interviewers per supervisor. The interviewer to supervisor ratio is crucial. This control will include the allocation of work to individuals in an area, attending briefing conferences, dealing with queries arising from interviewers about research projects or from head office about interviewers, maintaining supervision in the field and assisting in interviewer training. In a large field force, a supervisor has a very real part to play in maintaining interviewer efficiency and morale, and it should be emphasised that supervisors' allegiance *must* be firmly to the head office and not to individual interviewers for whom they are responsible.

Maintaining sufficiently frequent personal contact with interviewers working relatively infrequently, or with those in remote areas, can be a real problem. Maintaining interviewer efficiency and morale is considerably helped by the existence of a supervisory force, and by the attendance of interviewers at briefing conferences and training sessions. Nevertheless there is *no substitute* for head office contact with individual interviewers as often as is practicable. Personal briefings held at head office or regionally on major *ad hoc* surveys or at suitable intervals on audit and panel work, with attendance by head office field force and research executives handling projects, have a most important role to play here.

The Selection and Training of Interviewers

Selection

National and local press advertising, spontaneous application and 'word of mouth' recommendation are the main ways in which prospective interviewers can be contacted initially. If selection is to be effective, at least one personal interview with each candidate, certainly at the supervisory level, will be required. The qualities and basis characteristics that go to make up a successful interviewer, notwithstanding the necessary training to follow initial selection, are such that it is extremely dangerous to engage new interviewers (even if they claim extensive past experience) by correspondence, without this important face-to-face contact.

At this exploratory stage it is important to compile key information about a prospective candidate. If the candidate is later selected, trained and used as a member of the field force, this information should be stored in an interviewer 'data bank' or 'card index' system, and these aggregated records *must* be updated from time to time.

The key information to be sought from a prospect should include at least the following:

a photograph;
full name and address;
sex and age;

social grade;
marital status;
family composition;
car ownership/usage;
telephone details;
educational attainments;
previous business experience, if any;
previous (general) research experience;
previous interviewing experience;
number of field forces worked for (past and current);
types of survey experience;
suitability if appropriate for specialist work (e.g. shop audits, telephone
    interviewing, group discussion, recruitment and hostessing);
voice (type, accent, etc.);
dress and manner.

In compiling this information—obviously only at a personal interview—the candidate's general attitude to market research and interviewing can be explored. The first interview will lead to a decision on whether or not the candidate is suitable for training, and remember here that irrespective of past experience some retraining is probably desirable.

Formal training

Formal 'in office' training is advisable as a first stage. Whether this is undertaken at supervisory level in the regions or at head office will depend on the size and structure of the field force, and the number of candidates coming forward at a particular time. The duration of such a formal training session will vary from one field force to another, but there will be general agreement that such training shall occupy not less than two, preferably up to five, days.

The formal training course, after a suitable introduction to the nature and purpose of survey research and the way in which interviewing is integrated with the other phases of the project, will include:

(a) instruction on basic *sampling procedures* to be followed, use of maps to determine boundaries and grid references, sampling at preselected addresses, the concept and implementation of random walk sampling and quota sampling methods;
(b) *questionnaire design* with particular emphasis on how to ask questions, strict adherence to the written content, prompting and probing, questionnaire routing, skips and recording demographic and other classification data;
(c) *methods of introduction* to a potential respondent, how to deal with queries about survey sponsorship, keeping respondents to the point, clarifying vague replies, dealing with unsuitable respondents, possible refusals, and with queries as to why respondent was chosen for interview;

(d) *methods of quality control* used by the field force (supervisor checks, postal checks, office check, editing, etc.), and steps that are taken on queries or suspect work;

(e) *administrative details about procedures* for interviewer booking; briefing methods, allocation of work, receiving return of completed work, methods of payment and the relationships and method of contact between the interviewer, supervisor, and head office staff.

As part of this formal training, interviewers should be encouraged to conduct 'in office' interviews with dummy questionnaires; demonstration interviews will be given by head office staff and supervisors and, ideally, some system of rating interviewer performance even at this early stage should be devised. It is helpful to tape record demonstration and test interviews and to play these back during the training sessions. If training is on a large enough scale, initial criticism of performance here should be actively encouraged. It is well worth while at the close of such formal training sessions also to administer short written tests to interviewers, which will further assist in decisions about potential for further training.

Training in the field

Formal first-stage training of the kind described above will eliminate applicants who for one reason or another are below standard or, less dramatically, felt to be suitable only for certain types of survey work.

There is, however, no substitute for training in the field and prospective interviewers passing successfully through formal training need to move on rapidly to this phase before final decisions are taken about their acceptability for future work.

Most often, training in the field will be conducted by a supervisor (who will of course have been similarly trained in the past) in which she herself will demonstrate various interviewing techniques in the field with the trainee observing; this will be followed by test interviews by the trainee in the presence of the supervisor and, finally, if at all possible, the assessment by the supervisor of a batch of interviews completed by the trainee on her own. This assessment can be achieved by a detailed examination of completed questionnaires, a full discussion with the applicant of any problems encountered, or by supervisor call-backs on the respondent interviewed during this test phase. The stark reality of this training in the field will almost certainly show which trainees may have mastered the theory adequately enough but are unlikely in practice to be of a sufficiently high standard.

Formal and field training of the kind described above should be regarded as *the least* that should be done to ensure competent performance, once successful candidates have been enlisted for future work. Obviously, during the first few weeks in the field, a new interviewer will have to be supervised and controlled very closely, to ensure that standards are being maintained.

Both the formal and field training described are essential for new interviewers; they are also advisable as a method of retraining and bringing up to date older established members of a field force.

All supervisors and interviewers working in the field must be supplied with identity cards indicating details about themselves and the organization for whom they are working. Apart from a need from time to time to convince doubtful respondents about the authenticity of a particular study, the use of such cards is invaluable in demonstrating that interviewers are *not* 'saleswomen in disguise'. Examples of (non-research) organizations masquerading as interviewers conducting a survey, where the real purpose (either immediate or in a later follow up) is selling, are unfortunately not infrequent. Any way therefore which helps to make this important distinction between survey research and selling must be encouraged, since our industry depends very heavily on the voluntary (and usually free) co-operation of members of the public, and we all have responsibilities to them. In Britain the MRS Code of Conduct sets out these in detail and all supervisors and interviewers need to be made aware of what they are.

The interviewing manual

To complement training, all interviewers need to be supplied with a manual which sets out in detail general procedural rules and methods to be followed on the various types of project that the interviewer is likely to encounter. Basically, these rules will comprise those dealt with fully at the initial training session, but, of course, they will need to be amended frequently and brought up to date by head office staff as new procedures and new techniques are developed.

Any interviewers engaged on repeat surveys or on audit and panel work will need to be supplied with detailed instructions about checking methods to be used, products, prices and pack sizes to be checked, and so on. Every interviewer must be encouraged to master the contents of the manual and to use it for day-to-day reference in the field, prior to attempting to contact their supervisor or head office to resolve queries. In addition to the manual carried, an interviewer is, of course, likely to be supplied with further instructions in writing specific to each project, even with an additional personal briefing.

Briefing Interviewers

As we have said, contact between interviewers and head office staff or supervisors needs to be maintained as frequently as possible. Formal training or retraining sessions held periodically, however, will tend to deal mostly with basic issues of a general nature. On each specific survey special briefing procedures need to be adopted to deal with problems and procedures peculiar to that survey. This briefing can take one of a number of forms depending on the complexity of the project, the extent to which it introduces new requirements, the number of interviewers required to work on the project, and the time available for pre-field work instruction.

Briefings on panel and audits work

Where interviewers are in contact regularly with panel members, reporting weekly, monthly or quarterly on individual shops or homes, basic interviewing and checking procedures are unlikely to vary substantially from period to period. Keeping the instruction manual on a project of this kind up to date should allow these procedures to be followed satisfactorily each time a contact is made. This does not mean, of course, that an interviewer may not receive additional instructions for each new visit or that the normal quality control checks in the field will not be imposed.

There will be a need to call interviewers working on such projects for refresher briefings together from time to time, in order to discuss problems which arise, the implementation of new checking techniques, and so on. In continuous audit or panel work it is essential for slackness and boredom to be avoided. Here, either random or specially timed supervisor checks on interviewers will prove invaluable in ensuring the maintenance of accuracy.

Survey briefings

Where special *ad hoc* surveys are concerned, briefing practices will vary more widely. On major surveys, particularly those involving fresh interviewers or new survey techniques, it is certainly of considerable value to brief all interviewers personally, either at head office or regionally, with research staff and head office field staff and area supervisors in attendance. Such briefings, however, are costly and the time required for them prior to commencement of field work may not be available.

Personal briefings

Where they take place, these personal briefings will comprise:

(a) a detailed description by the appropriate member of head office staff of the background to, and the nature and purpose of, the survey. If the content of the survey is of a technical nature it is sometimes useful to have the client himself present to answer questions;
(b) instructions about how respondents are to be selected for interview with particular emphasis on any changes in standard procedures for pre-selected address sampling, random routes, or quota controls;
(c) an exposition of the questionnaire to be used, to ensure that interviewers fully understand the nature of the questions, how they are to be asked, question routing, skips, etc.;

(d) general discussion with interviewers of any problem arising;
(e) test interviews, either between pairs of interviewers chosen at random on the spot or by interviewers with a member of head office staff;
(f) further discussion of any additional problems arising;
(g) the allocation of work material and discussion of any administrative problems relating to field work dates and deadlines, methods of payment, and so on.

Ideally, personal briefing of this kind should be attended by head office representatives; where this is impracticable, similar personal briefings can be run at supervisor level on a regional basis. Ideally, personal briefings can only really be considered unnecessary where *all* interviewers concerned have worked fairly recently on an identical or very similar project.

Postal and telephone briefings

These are necessary substitutes for personal briefings in many cases, and in certain circumstances can be regarded as adequate, provided interviewers so briefed are encouraged to raise any queries immediately with their supervisors or with head office, so that these can be dealt with before field work commences. In all cases like this it is essential that the interviewer *thoroughly reads and completely understands* the written instructions that will have been supplied with the work material. It is worthwhile also building in the additional safeguard of inspecting the first batch of each interviewers work to decide whether any interviewers should be debarred from continuing.

Pilot briefing

A special comment about briefings on pilot research is worthwhile, because here both the requirements and the procedures tend to be different. At the planning stage on major projects, it is a widespread practice for a research organization to test and develop a number of versions of a questionnaire in draft, prior to agreeing the version to be used in the main survey.

Pilot interviewing may be needed at various stages, with a highly structured and almost final draft which has been worked on for some time by head office staff who may also have, themselves, tested earlier versions by pilot interviews in the field or with a much more flexible document which now needs further refinement with the guidance of interviewers who have used it in the field. On normal survey work, the very fact that interviewers are required to adopt a consistent approach, and not to deviate from written instructions and the printed questionnaire, makes some interviewers unsuitable for use in exploratory pilot work. What is required here is a much more flexible approach, where interviewers are actively encouraged to use their initiative, and to report back to head office staff about the best way in which questions can be phrased or ordered in a questionnaire and whether there are any significant errors or omissions. It follows that supervisors themselves or interviewers of the highest calibre are likely to be best suited for this pilot work. After pilot briefing and pilot field work, debriefing sessions, where each interviewer is invited to contribute to further improvements in questionnaire design prior to the main survey, can be invaluable.

Quality Control

A rigorous and planned approach to selecting and training interviewers, and the implementation wherever possible of briefing sessions prior to field work, will do much to ensure that high standards in the field are maintained. However, there are great differences between theory and practice in interviewing, not least because of the very real stresses that are imposed on interviewers in the course of their work. Interviewing with the very best type of questionnaire is not easy, and having also to combat such factors as bad weather, complex instructions, difficult quotas, difficult respondents, tiredness, etc., adds to the stress in the field—something which it is all too easy to forget as an office-based researcher. Indeed, in setting up quality control systems, there is no substitute for field experience, and all those concerned with research planning or head office field organization need to spend occasional days in the field; this is always valuable, even if not always enjoyable!

No matter how carefully a project is planned, the nature of the project itself, the characteristics of the respondents and differences between interviewers or, indeed, variation in performance of a single interviewer from day to day can and often do give rise to problems in interviewing that could not have been foreseen. It is necessary, therefore, to impose additional checks against these eventualities, with the aim of maintaining overall performance in the field at the highest possible level.

Control by supervisors

The ratio of supervisors to interviewers will, of course, vary from one field force to another, and, indeed, with variations in project nature and interviewers there can be no correct level of supervision. The ratio must be such that no single interviewer goes too long without contact with and checks by, the supervisor on projects, quite apart from additional contact through briefings and training sessions. A considerable amount of time here will be devoted by supervisors to the control of new interviewers or interviewers whose performance for some reason is suspect.

Control imposed by supervisors will usually take the form either of accompanying interviewers on an assignment, or of conducting spot checks on respondents and re-interviewing them as soon as possible after their first interview, or else of scrutiny of completed work before it is passed back to head office for subsequent processing. Accompanying interviewers in their work has some advantages, particularly in terms of ensuring that no deviations are occurring in the basic methods laid down, and is useful on the one hand for keeping interviewer morale high, and on the other for making it clear that field force management are concerned on a continuing basis with maintaining the standards of performance of individual interviewers. However, the advantages of this type of control are limited; any interviewer can have an 'off day', or be at a stage in a project where unusual difficulties appear to be arising, atypical of a more normal situation. A more useful form of control is spot checks at random on interviewers' 're-calls' on respondents, to establish first whether the interview took place, and second how it was conducted in broad terms, how long it took, and so on. Such spot checks will need to be conducted rapidly after the first interview, otherwise a respondent may reflect changes in behaviour or opinion of a real nature which give the false impression that a first interview was inaccurate in some way. There is some merit in having completed work routed through supervisors before transmission to head office. This will ensure that genuine problems can be dealt with quickly and suitable corrective action taken. Checking of this kind may not be practicable for all interviewers all the time, but is useful even if based on some system of rotation. In practical terms, how much of this scrutiny can be achieved at the regional level will depend on how many interviewers supervisors have under their control and variations, over time, in workload.

Postal checks

It is a widespread practice to send prepaid postcards or letters to respondents to enquire whether an interview was carried out and the opportunity is often taken to ask additional questions. Such a postal check, however, can only be a partial check, and extreme care has to be taken in the selection of any check questions to be asked, otherwise differences in response will be apparent which are quite unrelated to interviewer performance. In theory, it is possible to conduct 100% postal checks on all work of all interviewers all the time, but this is extremely costly, cumbersome and probably unnecessary, because the very nature of postal checks means that replies from respondents themselves will never be at the 100% level. A more common approach is to:

(a) select batches of interviewers in rotation over time, and submit all their work on one survey to postal checks at the 100% level; or
(b) check a randomly selected proportion of all interviewers' work on all surveys, but at a much lower level, say 10–20%.

Both of these approaches have advantages and disadvantages; actual practice will depend on the nature of the surveys being conducted by a particular field force, the number of interviewers involved, and background knowledge at head office of individual interviewer performance over time.

Check editing

Even if some scrutiny of completed work is undertaken at the supervisor level, it will be essential to impose further check editing procedures on work that has reached head office for subsequent processing. This check editing can again be operated in various ways, by sampling either proportions of interviewers or of their work; it will concern itself principally with sources of error such as:

(a) failure to adhere to sampling instructions — the failure to select appropriate individuals at preselected addresses or failure to complete set quotas of work;
(b) the omission of vital demographic data such as age, occupation, income level, socio-economic class, family size, etc.;
(c) the omission of specific questions, or failure to follow correctly routing instructions through a questionnaire;
(d) a tendency, most often apparent on open-ended responses, to generate inadequate or vague replies.

Apart from the additional measure of control this check editing imposes on a day to day basis, it is of considerable importance as a basis for head office to build up a backlog of performance data about each interviewer. These data will come from a number of sources, and need to be compiled into readily available records which show, for each interviewer, such aspects of performance as:

(a) levels of response rate by respondents to postal checks carried out;
(b) any evidence from these of possible falsification of interviews (e.g. interviewing someone other than the alleged respondent recorded) or of 'making-up' replies for interviews which never took place;
(c) the number of errors found in recording classification data;
(d) the levels at which omission or misrouting occur;
(e) rates per day achieved in initial contacts and in successfully completed interviews.

Ideally a data bank of information of this kind should be compiled to enable performance of individual interviewers to be compared with average performance. The aspects of performance listed above can be built into this system, as also can analyses on particular projects of the kinds of responses different interviewers are obtaining to questions. Obviously if suspicion is aroused at any stage about an interviewer's performance, through supervisor checks, postal checks, check editing, or cumulative evidence from the data bank, immediate follow-up action will need to be taken.

The aim of quality control of this kind must be to minimize errors and maintain individual interviewer standards at the highest possible level. Deliberate cheating, despite all the precautions taken, is extremely difficult to detect. In general, the evidence is that such cheating is at a low level, not least because this very rigorous approach to quality control that most research organizations adopt.

In order to be effective, of course, it is absolutely *vital* that *all* interviewers are fully aware that these various checks are made and they should be equally aware of the penalties which can follow from substandard performance; in particular, knowledge that blacklists of interviewers exist and then confidential information about individual performance is exchanged among research organizations.

A Check List For Buyers

Some readers, as members of independent research organizations or specialist field companies, will be actively engaged with the problems of interviewing and field control on a day-to-day basis, especially if their responsibilities include operating and controlling a field force. Most of these will already be well aware of the problems in interviewing that can arise, and will be implementing the quality control procedures described here. Other readers, however, as sponsors of survey research, will be buying expertise from independent research organizations or specialist field forces. They will, no doubt, be equally concerned about the problem in research of maintaining high interviewing standards, and will wish to satisfy themselves that the organizations from whom they buy research are, in fact, adopting acceptable control procedures where appropriate. Perhaps a useful way to summarize what has been said is to present, particularly for the benefit of these readers, a check list of points which need to be borne in mind when checking upon the credentials of a particular research organization. Such a check list would certainly include the following:

Research Planning and Design:

(a) Is the right degree of emphasis placed upon the interviewing phase of a project, compared with the other phases through which the project has to go?
(b) How are questionnaires, recording forms, diaries or inventories laid out, and by whom are they designed?
(c) Has the designer any interviewing experience, and has he or she at any stage piloted the questionnaire?
(d) Are instructions to interviewers comprehensive; and who drafted them?
(e) Are the sampling procedures to be used in the project feasible in the field?
(f) How are interviewers instructed on these sampling procedures and under what circumstances, if any, are they allowed to deviate from instructions?
(g) What checks are imposed to ensure that a sampling plan is followed?

Field Control

(a) How is field management at head office organized in general and in relation to the implementation of a particular project?
(b) How much contact is there between head office staff and the supervisors and interviewers?
(c) What documentation exists as a control on contact rates, interviewing rates, etc.?
(d) How is supervision in the field organized and how are queries that arise in the field dealt with?
(e) What is the ratio between supervisors and interviewers and what responsibilities have the supervisors for maintaining adequate interviewer standards?
(f) What procedures are followed in briefing interviewers, either personally, by post or telephone?
(g) How well are these procedures supported by written material of a general kind (e.g. interviewer manual) or of a kind specific to the survey (e.g. instructions, call-sheets, etc.)?

The Interviewers:

(a) What is the composition of the field force and how has it been built up?
(b) How are the interviewers initially selected?
(c) How are they trained, either at formal training sessions or in the field?
(d) How frequently are the interviewers seen by head office staff and supervisors?
(e) Are they aware of the nature and depth of the quality control procedures conducted?
(f) What are their terms of employment and how are they paid?
(g) How regularly do the interviewers work for the organization?
(h) To what extent do they work also for other field forces?
(i) What methods of identification are carried?

Quality Control:

(a) What checks are imposed on interviewers while work is in the field and how are the problems and queries resolved?
(b) How often and at what level are supervisor spot checks, postal checks, revisits to respondents conducted as further control measures?
(c) What are the check-editing procedures once work has been returned to head office and how are queries and suspect interviewing dealt with?
(d) Has the organization been able to build up a data bank on individual interviewer performance; if so, what does this data bank comprise?

While the vital importance of controls on interviewing will be recognized, the way these are imposed will vary from one organization to another. Clearly, no perfect system of control can exist, in a situation where survey research deals with such a wide variety of projects and where the composition and structure of field forces necessarily differs. The aim, however, must be to achieve the best possible combination of controls, consistent with the nature of the field force, the money available, and the time span (often relatively short) over which particular projects are conducted.

7. Trade research

Brian Hughes

Trade research is a collective term for a series of specially developed techniques serving the needs and objectives of marketing management at the various stages of the distribution network. Just as the elementary methods of consumer research have been adapted and improved to gear them more specifically to particular problems, so the basic techniques of research among the distributive trades have been refined from the original to meet current demands. This chapter deals with the basic techniques and illustrates a few of the applications and developments that have occurred. It makes no attempt to be comprehensive.

Of all the expenditure on trade research, by far the most is spent on retail and wholesale audits; the remainder is probably divided evenly between distribution checks and *ad hoc* research at the point of sale, in particular surveys among the retail trade. Almost inevitably, therefore, the emphasis in this chapter will be upon trade audits. For those who are particularly interested in the latter, the reader is referred to Melhuish, Nowik and Yates[1-3].

Trade audits

With few notable exceptions, most manufacturers requiring national retail audit data subscribe to the services offered by those research agencies that specialize in these studies. A few manufacturers, however, continue to conduct their own, largely for reasons of frequency of reporting, speed of preparation, the need for product panels rather than shop indices and the volume of information required. In test markets, i.e. audits in test towns or TV regions, perhaps a few more manufacturers venture to carry out the audit measurements independently, even though there are adequate facilities available from the specialist agencies who almost invariably have active (sometimes dormant) panels of shops in their territories. It is with this concentration of syndicated audit facilities among a few specialist research agencies in mind, and the continuing existence of some manufacturers

145

independently conducting their own, that the following pages attempt to serve the interest and needs of readers.

The use of retail audits to management

Information from retail audits is vital to marketing management in the areas of both strategic and tactical decision making.

Information leading to strategic decision making can frequently be obtained by simple observation of long-term trends indicated by this source. These trends enable management to predict with some accuracy the size of the market in which the company is operating currently and in the future. It can tell management how the company is performing relative to its competitors in terms of market share and, within the overall picture of market share, it can pick out dramatic movements by individual brands, brands of a certain type, formulation, or price range, perhaps indicate a need for the company to review its product mix, its pricing policy, where it should concentrate its promotional expenditure, etc.

Provided the company possesses the other information necessary to assess which brands are likely to be profitable and which relatively unprofitable in the long term, retail audit can contribute to a large extent in successful long-term profit planning. To put it another way, retail audit data can provide a framework of basic knowledge of market movements to which may be linked a myriad of other marketing factors—such as raw material prices and availability, machinery and labour requirements, competitive strengths and weaknesses—and, equally important, movements in consumer behaviour and retail attitudes to equip a company with signposts to find the direction in which profitability is most likely to lie in the long term.

The use of audit data in a tactical role is also essential, although this use tends to be evaluative of what has happened in the past as much as predictive as to what is to happen in the future, e.g. management will look back on recent promotional campaigns to assess their effectiveness and, by building up a picture composed of evaluations of several such recent performances, be better able to select those courses of short term activity which are effective. Likewise, this study of past action can help management avoid the more obvious pitfalls, e.g. the repetition of clearly disastrous sales promotions. Perhaps the major short term value is the ability to read quickly and to act upon competitive successes and failures.

In summary, audit data, imperfect though it may be in part, is one of the best aids at the disposal of marketing management for keeping informed about the market place in a quantitative, relatively unbiased way, month by month and year by year.

Collecting the information

The technique of auditing is simple and straightforward. The auditors visit the sample shops at predetermined intervals and at each visit they count the

146

Shop name
address

1. BRAND: NAME SIZE VARIATION		A Lge	A Hdv	B Lge	B Lge 2p off
2. Sales last audit		224	82	43	12
3. Brand code	6·11	010.121	010.141	010.221	010.324
4. Price information	12·14	7p	4p	10½p	10½p
5. Delivery details since last audit — Whole-sale	15·19				
Cash and carry	20·24				
Direct and head office	25·29	96 / 96 / +8 / +8 — 288	36 — 36		+8 / +8 / +8 — 144
6. Opening stock	30·34	71	73	89	132
7. Opening stock plus deliveries	(5+6)	359	109	89	276

8. Stock this audit and use of display material		Forward	Reserve	D	Forward	Reserve	D	Forward	Reserve	D	Forward	Reserve	D
	a. Counter												
	b. Shelf	9			7			12			27		
	c. Window												
	d. Floor												
	e. S/S Stand												
	f. Dumper												
	g. Storeroom		144						40			30	
9. Total stock a.-g. incl. 35·45		9	144		7			12	40		27	30	
10. Closing stock 46·50		153			7			52			57		
11. Sales this audit (7 minus 10) 51·55		206			102			37			219		
12. Special information													
13. Comments													

Fig. 7.1 An example of an audit form.

stock and record deliveries to the shop since their last visit. Sales during the interval between visits is simply calculated thus:

PAST STOCKS + DELIVERIES − PRESENT STOCKS = SALES

It should not be inferred from this bald statement that auditing is easy; considerable discipline and an organized approach are essential to obtain accurate estimates. Auditors must be trained to examine each stock location searching for the brands that make up the product class. As these are observed and counted they must be recorded separately against the location in which they are found so that stock in dump bins, shelves, or self service stands, i.e. in the selling area, can be distinguished from that held in the stockroom, the yard, or elsewhere, i.e. out of the selling area. The same care and attention is necessary in annotating delivery information. Each invoice, delivery note, or daybook entry must be scrutinized to be certain that all relevant delivery information is collected. Each delivery must be recorded against the source of purchase to distinguish between the conventional wholesaler, cash and carry, head office, or direct from the manufacturer. The whole operation must be systematic, deliberate, and rigorous for errors in stock counts, or missed invoices will give false sales readings, possibly leading to a misinterpretation of the expanded results. Additional data are also collected by the auditors, selling price, promotional packs, special offers and any other information that could be of value. Thus, for each sample shop, a pattern of trading in the period is prepared; when added to the data collected from other sample shops a comprehensive picture of the market as a whole is constructed.

An example of an audit form is given in Fig. 7.1.

Preparing the data

Each entry and calculation made by the auditors in the shops must be subject to rigorous examination at the processing centre, each notation of stocks and deliveries, addition and calculation of sales for each brand size and type, must be physically checked. The most recent sales must be compared with the previous sales history of that brand and size in that shop and only if it is 'reasonable' or anomalies explained by known activity such as promotions or price changes should it be used in the preparation of the report. The auditor's notes are of great importance here to help account for changes or unusual levels of sales, deliveries or stocks following marketing activity. The emphasis at the processing centre, as in the field work, must be upon accuracy and thorough checking.

Once this scrutiny is completed, totals are made up of the stocks, the deliveries, and the sales for all the shops for each of the 'itemized' brands and sizes separately (collectively for that group of less important brands that are to be shown in the report as 'all others'). For small audits, such as those in test towns, the bulk of the processing is then complete except for the totalling of the shops found to be either in stock or to have made sales during the period of the various brands. These small audits are the exception, however. Most audit data need to be grossed or expanded to universe levels. The process of totalling is common to both small and large 'national' audits, except that in the latter case the shops are first sorted into cells (shop type within area) and then totalled. For each cell the value of the universe is known and the expansion is simply:

$$\frac{\text{UNIVERSE}}{\text{SAMPLE}} \times \text{SALES (OR STOCK OR DELIVERIES)}$$

By adding the expanded cell data, area totals and shop type totals are obtained and, thus, a representation of the national market is constructed.

The bulk of national audits today, of course, are processed by computer and the methods vary in detail from the one described. But whatever facility is used it is essential that the most stringent checks are applied at every stage.

The data provided

Though each of the service companies, and those manufacturers who conduct their own audits, have developed their own distinctive style of table

148

presentation, the same basic data are common to them all. A description of these essential tables is followed by a brief outline of some of the additional analyses that are possible.

Consumer sales are sales made over the counter to customers during the audit period and shown both on a sterling or cash paid basis and as volume when the expression is package or weight. These tables normally also feature the share of the market accounted for by each itemized brand.

Retailer deliveries or purchases from wholesalers and manufacturers made by the shop during the audit period and normally expressed as volume on a package or weight basis.

Retail stock, the stock of the product encountered at the last shop check, expressed in packages or weight.

Stock cover, a tabulation of the length of time stocks will last, based upon current rates of sale. With seasonal products, this table is more meaningfully presented in terms of anticipated future sales which is not difficult to calculate once sufficient back data are available.

Average stocks and average sales per shop handling, literally averaging the total stock and sale by the number of shops in current distribution in order to present the true-life situation of the stockist.

Average prices paid by consumers, as the heading implies, a simple average of all the items and brands based upon prices encountered at closing stock.

Distribution, which takes two forms, the first, 'numerical', is based upon the proportion of shops handling the product at some time during the audit period (maximum), and subsequently the proportion actually in stock (effective) at the end of the period, the difference between the two figures being the shops 'out of stock'. The same basic information, but calculated upon the proportions of total annual grocery turnover represented by the shops handling it and 'in stock' at the end of the period, is termed 'sterling distribution'.

Showings, or information about the display material encountered in the shops at the last check. This is usually divided into groups, e.g. advertising material, which would include showcards or mobiles, self-selection, incorporating dispensers, outers from which customers make their own selection and dump bins and, lastly, stock presentations, pyramids, or features.

These basic tables represent the bulk of the tables provided as standard in most audit reports both from research agencies and by those manufacturers conducting their own audit. Each of these is analysed or broken down by region, either television area, the Registrar General's standard regions, or into individual or combinations of the manufacturer's sales divisions. Further analysis by shop type or form of organization, multiple, co-operative and independent, the latter divided by size, or membership of voluntary group, is also normal. By this means, a total and composite picture of the retail trade is obtained.

There are several other useful tabulations which can be prepared from the basic data, some examples of these follow.

Forward and reserve stocks, which is a simple division of the stock levels already annotated but divided between that which is in the forward selling area, the shop itself and, thus, available to the consumer, and that which is in the stock or storeroom.

Source of delivery, a broad division of the volume of retail deliveries from the three main sources, wholesaler, manufacturers, and the multiple head office.

Frequency distribution of shops selling at individual prices, literally an annotation of the proportions of stockists selling each brand size at given prices and most useful when contrasted with frequency distribution of prices paid.

Frequency distribution of prices paid, when the volume sold at each price can be compared with the proportion of stockists selling at these prices so that the extent and impact of price cuts, promotions, and dealing can be better assessed.

Frequency distribution of stock, which either shows the proportion of stockists holding given levels of stock, or is expressed as stockists holding levels equal to given weeks' sales (stock cover). From this, an analysis can be made of marginal stockists.

Marginal stockists, which identifies the areas and shop types holding minimal stock levels, either in absolute or relative stock cover terms.

Marginal purchases analysis, another frequency distribution analysis of the amounts delivered to retailers during the audit period.

Analyses of combination of brands stocked puts into real terms the extent to which individual brands are competing together in stores.

Cumulative distribution, a useful measure to check on the developments in distribution of new brands and the extent to which new stockists are being attracted and old stockists failing to re-order. It is particularly appropriate in test market evaluations.

There are many other forms of special analyses, each designed to answer a specific problem. No useful purpose will be served in making an exhaustive list in this chapter; a little thought and some ingenuity is all that is required to conceive yet another presentation, more meaningful or pertinent to the matter in hand. For those who buy a syndicated service, the client executive allocated to the account is the most useful source for discussion, consultation, and general advice in the matter of special analyses. He can warn of the problems and difficulties and he understands the extent to which the audit information can be reliably adapted.

Omitted from the list of basic and supplementary tables is 'back data'. For manufacturers entering a new product field much useful background can be obtained from past history; all retail audit companies will sell back data at a discount, obviously at a greater discount if a forward contract is entered into.

Special analyses of back data, however, are not generally available and the cost of re-analyses is normally prohibitive.

The sample

The types of sample used in retail audits fall into two distinct types, those that mirror a particular trade or type of shop, e.g. grocers, chemists, or hardware, and the, at present, relatively specialized which attempt to reflect the characteristic distribution of a product class, e.g. confectionery, or tobacco. In the latter, a combination of store types is used in the panel of shops, grocers, confectionery/tobacco/newsagents, cinemas, public houses, canteens in factories and offices, restaurants, garages, etc., all linked in such proportions that the data represent the totality of outlets selling the product.

When investigating the sample of outlets covered by A. C. Nielson, Retail Audits, Stats MR, and any other audit firm, it is advisable to check the representativeness of the sample. It has been impossible for audit firms to gain the co-operation of *all* large multiple grocery groups, large chemists such as Boots and important food outlets such as Marks & Spencer. Obviously, the lack of representativeness can affect estimates of turnover by units and volume. Therefore, when assessing the validity of the estimates, the user is well advised to look for minimum/maximum estimates with some indication of 'best guess'.

More and more interest is being shown by manufacturers in a 'product class' index. A manufacturer of aerosol air fresheners, for example, can buy an audit sample which reflects the distribution of the product, adequate numbers of grocers, chemists, and hardware stores all linked by the research agency, audited at the same time and processed and presented to the client as fully representative of the product class distribution and, thus, a market totality.

While this development of product sample as opposed to shop type sample continues, there are several basic rules followed by all the agencies and those few manufacturers who conduct their own audits, in constructing their samples. Figure 7.2 describes more than adequately the problem that faces the sample designer. From it can be seen the problem posed by attempting to reflect just one type of shop. Later, the application of this same principle is used with modifications when a product class sample is drawn but the same basic principles must be enforced.

The fundamental rule is to sample the volume of sales, rather than the number of stores. The principle used is simple and effective and the method titled 'disproportionate' sampling. While Fig. 7.2 simplifies the problem and ignores the modification normally made to account for variations in size and organization within the type of shop, it describes adequately the basic rules followed by most designers of audit samples. This is to audit most where most of the sales lie.

Taking the concept a stage further, where the sample attempts to reflect the

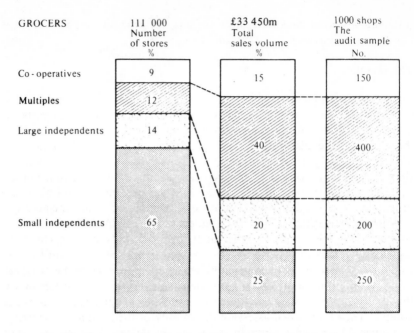

Fig. 7.2   The relationship of sales volume, number of stores and audit sample.

whole spectrum of sales of the product class, a sample could be constructed in the following manner (see Fig. 7.3). Here, the considerations of adequate sample cell size and the need to expand the data to national estimates force the designer to reflect the total sales volume of the product only in each shop type, and within each to contain sufficient of the various organizations to give approximately equal cell bases in order to provide the most reliable estimates consistent with the economies of a modest sample.

Whatever type of sample is favoured (product class or shop type index) it is clearly important that the sample itself should be, as far as possible, stable; inevitably with rebuilding, reorganization, sickness, and expiry of leases, there will be sample losses from time to time and these are unavoidable, but positive steps must be taken to keep refusals to co-operate further to a minimum. Some companies operating audits make a point of providing panel retailers with information, all make payments for the facility, make appointments for the following visit, are courteous and take care to trouble the retailer as little as possible consistent, that is, with collecting the correct information. Recruitment of replacement shops must be carefully policed to ensure that the refusal rate is not so large as to warp the results. Regular sample censuses or large distribution checks are essential periodically to check that the sample shops continue to reflect the universe.

All companies who operate audits guarantee that the identity of organizations and the individual shops who co-operate with them will be preserved

152

| OUTLETS | | 143 000
Number of
stores selling
the product class
% | £90m
Total
sales volume
of product class
% | 1000 shops
The audit
sample to measure
product class |

Grocers — Co-operatives: 6, Multiples: 17, Independents: 32 (55); Chemists — Co-operatives: 3, Multiples: 15, Independents: 12 (30); Hardware: 15 (15). Total sales volume: 48, 31, 21. Audit sample: 150, 150, 180, 160, 150, 210.

Fig. 7.3 An example where the audit sample attempts to reflect the product class sales.

and under no circumstances revealed to anyone. This is an assurance which all research agencies involved in this type of work respect most thoroughly.

Frequency of reporting

Most of the national syndicated audit services are geared to preparing reports every two months; for nearly all the major manufacturers this frequency is adequate since the basic object is to study trend data. There are, however, several product classes for which more frequent reports are desirable, particularly seasonal ones where a 'burst' pattern of reports is more appropriate. Examples of these would include soups in winter, salad cream and mayonnaise in summer, paints and decorating materials in spring and autumn, and so on. Of course, the level of stock held in the retail trade at the end of the season is the most important item of data to manufacturers. Increased frequency of reporting is more expensive, however, and unless the time required by the agency to prepare the reports is considerably shortened, a more frequent service is difficult to use fully and properly.

In test market audits where the sample of shops is comparatively small and the processing simple, audits are generally available at four-weekly intervals. Indeed, this is usually demanded since the object of test audits is often to measure short term activity or to obtain quick assessments of competitive tactics. An audit can be prepared to report even more frequently, but this is

153

inevitably by special arrangement, and one example occurred some years ago when a national audit of approximately two hundred grocers was set up to audit daily, though reports were prepared only each week. The project ran successfully but once the pattern of sales by day of week was established and the seasonal differences observed, the auditing frequency dropped to weekly for reasons of cost. In national audits a bimonthly report is normal; more frequent reports can be arranged, at a price.

Client service

One of the attractions of buying from a syndicated service is that most companies that provide audits to manufacturers and distributors feature, as part of their service, the availability of a client service executive. It is his duty to maintain regular and frequent contact with clients in order to ensure that the data obtained from the audit are related to current problems and presented in the most easily understood way.

In contrast, the client service executive can never know more about the client's business than the client himself. Although he can only advise the client he can compare current market situations with what has occurred in others, since one of the duties of a client service executive is that he serves a number of non-competitive accounts and that he has a wide experience of the problems that face manufacturers, gained from practical experience. The experienced client service executive is not concerned with theories but with the practical, profitable, successful selling of his client's product. His purpose in life can be summarized as the responsibility to provide his client with the precise marketing intelligence necessary to aid the taking of sound marketing decisions. The value of his service, however, is directly correlated to the degree to which he enjoys his client's confidence and all who consider subscribing to a retail audit service need to be satisfied that the client service executive allocated to their account is a man with whom they feel they can discuss fully the problems of the company, in order to profit from that man's experience.

Validation

This is a necessary exercise to gauge the extent to which ex-factory shipment is being recorded by the audit. It forms the basis of the level of confidence that can be put upon the results, it indicates the adjustment necessary to account for differences and, of prime importance, the interpretation and use that can be made of the information about the market as a whole and competition, both strategically and tactically.

The calculation should be made at least half-yearly, more frequently for seasonal products, but always using moving annual totals of consumer sales and factory shipments in order to smooth the figures and avoid freak results caused by the inevitable varying time lapse between shipment and delivery to

154

Table 7.1

| PRODUCT | CHANGE IN STOCKS | | | | Over-counter sales (5) | Total (4) + (5) (6) | Factory despatches (7) | per cent (6) to (7) (8) | 1967/68 per cent | 1966/67 per cent | 1965/66 per cent | 1964/65 per cent |
	Retail (1)	W/S (2)	H.O. (3)	Total (4)								
Brand A	+28.4	+21.4	+0.3	+50.1	1693.4	1743.5	1752.0	100	100	98	96	101
Brand B	+1.6	−6.2	−2.2	−6.8	891.7	884.9	998.6	89	89	88	91	77
Brand C	−0.1	−7.6	+4.7	−3.0	1398.9	1395.9	1341.5	104	100	97	98	100
Brand D	−10.8	−10.2	−4.5	−25.5	354.0	328.5	333.7	98	99	129	—	—
TOTAL ALL BRANDS	+19.1	−2.6	−1.7	+14.8	4338.0	4352.8	4425.8	98	98	96	96	99

the store. Basically the formula is:

$$\frac{\text{CHANGES IN STOCKS} + \text{CONSUMER SALES}}{\text{FACTORY SHIPMENT}}$$

In Table 7.1 it can be seen that in the ideal situation, using audit information from a sample designed to reflect the full spectrum of outlets (a product class audit rather than a type of shop index, e.g. grocers), the changes in stock retail, wholesale, and multiple head office levels are all taken into account. Individual companies will need to make other adjustments. If the audit information available relates to only one type of shop, say grocers, and significant company sales are made through other outlet types, some allowance for the unaudited sales volume must be made. Other adjustments, not featured in Table 7.1 should be made for sales through particular important retailers known not to co-operate with the audit.

As a general rule the higher the distribution and the greater the sales volume, the better the validation is likely to be.

Costs

It is most important to realize that the nature of an audit is its measurement of changes in the market over time, and that its value, therefore, is long term. Though it can, no doubt, help to resolve immediate problems, its real worth is the facility it gives management to observe, understand, and profit from changes both in the market as a whole and the individual parts of the market, pointing out areas of opportunity and weakness. It is essentially a continuous research vehicle and becomes integrated in company marketing thought. Once available as an aid to planning and market assessment, it is insidious in that it becomes difficult to conceive of ever having been without it.

The cost of an audit, whether as part of a syndicated service, a specially set up 'exclusive' panel or a test market, naturally reflects the complexity and amount of work involved. The number of shops, the frequency of visits, literally the volume of individual brands to be itemized and their incidence or distribution, the size of the market under study, the degree of breakdown required, the extra analyses, the interpretative function provided as part of the service and the length of contract, are all components of the cost. Some economies can be made by asking competing agencies for quotations and making use of the slightly different specifications, the different sample sizes providing the greatest opportunity for economy.

Case histories

Such is the confidential nature of the relationship between the research agency providing retail audit facilities and their clients (and the jealously guarded examples held by the manufacturers who conduct their own audits) that the illustrations of the practical use of audit information is limited to the

156

few that follow. Nonetheless, they serve adequately to show the practical use
of the data.

Case History 1

Quite apart from the special analyses of audit information carried out by the
service company for a particular manufacturer, there are obvious gains in
information and a fresh understanding of changing market characteristics to
be made by reassembly of the standard data. In the following example the
grouping of individual brands with an empirical but meaningful (to the
manufacturer) reassembly of the data revealed to him the growth in a
particular sector of the trade. A number of individual minor brands had been
seen to be enlarging but the full significance of this growth was only demonstrated when the data were re-presented (see Fig. 7.4). Re-analysis of audit
information by pack size, price, product type, company, or other meaningful
grouping should be carried out as a matter of course, in order to get the most
from the data and to determine the early indications of change.

Fig. 7.4   Case History 1.

Case History 2

Confident of success following pre-tests of his commercial, the manufacturer
required reassurance so tested the sales effectiveness of the advertising for his
new product by buying time in all television areas except the Midlands.
Linked with the television campaign was a heavy sales drive to obtain

Table 7.2 Case history 2

	London	South	West	Lancs	Yorks	Tyne	Scotland	Midlands
Brand A								
Sales share								
Pd 1	23	25	10	8	16	23	27	25
Pd 2	27	23	20	14	24	14	23	14
Pd 3	54	53	62	69	48	44	42	23
Sterling distribution								
Pd 1	81	82	60	79	61	53	55	56
Pd 2	85	86	61	80	69	58	70	53
Pd 3	92	94	84	90	75	79	82	69

(Courtesy A. C. Nielsen)

distribution. The data in Table 7.2 show that, although there was apparent increase in distribution for the brand in the Midlands, the consumer reaction was much less marked than in the areas where television had been used.

Case History 3

This example features the use of audit data to assist management in forward planning. The figures shown in Table 7.3 are indices on a bimonthly moving annual total basis, in sterling turnover, for the total market.

In making the first forward projection, management took simply the average of the growth for the first seven periods, 10.6%. At that time, distribution was already high at 85% numerical, 94% by value and it was assumed that advertising expenditure, as a percentage of sales, would remain constant at 22% as it had been in the two earlier years. With the benefit of hindsight, the final projected figure of 447 was remarkably close to the actual market size reached of 451, although there were signs in the periods immediately following the projection that the market had begun to slow down indicating that the projection would overstate. Management thus elected to make a second projection once again based on the average growth, this time for the preceding twelve months, which was 9.6%. There had been a marked increase in advertising expenditure, however, which, as a proportion of sales, now stood at 33%. Further, distribution had improved and for the last four periods of the projection stood at 88% numerical and 97% sterling

Table 7.3 Case history 3

Moving Annual Totals

Actual	100	110	123	134	147	163	182	198	212	230	255	284	319	361	411	451
First projection								201	222	245	261	300	332	367	405	447
difference								+3	+10	+15	+6	+16	+13	+6	−6	−4
Second projection											279	306	336	368	405
difference										−5	−13	−25	−43	−46

(Courtesy A. C. Nielsen)

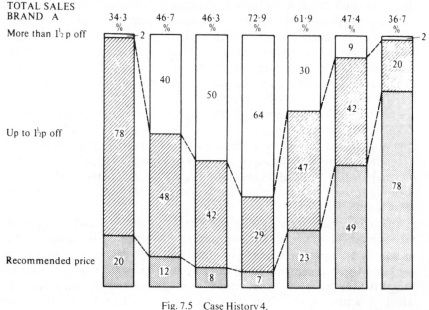

TOTAL SALES
BRAND A

| More than 1½ p off | 34·3 % | 46·7 % | 46·3 % | 72·9 % | 61·9 % | 47·4 % | 36·7 % |

Fig. 7.5   Case History 4.

(by value). Both these factors contributed towards the substantial difference between the two estimates and also from the actual market levels achieved.

Case History 4

Sales of a recent nationally launched brand were seen to develop at a very fast rate (see Fig. 7.5). It was known from salesmen's reports that the brand was being dealt in heavily with selected retailers and was also being supported by a national 'money-off' offer. The intention was clearly to encourage trial. Analysis by price noted by the auditor at closing stock enabled sales to be analysed in detail, which revealed the very extensive below-the-line activity and entirely explained the rise in sales. Though backing at these levels could clearly not be maintained, the brand leader countered by more modest retail dealing and consumer offers, reducing the impact of the new brand and, as support was withdrawn, the brand reverted to its pre-promoted level.

Invoice Analyses

As the name suggests, these are analyses of the delivery notes and invoices of goods bought by the retailers or wholesalers. No attempt is made to count stock, unlike the full retail audit and, consequently, tabulations are limited. This is adequate, however, for some product classes, the notable example being the full range of ethical pharmaceuticals. To all intents and purposes the retail stock level of the bulk of ethicals is constant, the retailer either ordering specifically for each prescription or replenishing his limited stock promptly. Obviously, the vast range of items prohibits any but the largest chemists carrying adequate stocks and one consequence of this is the remarkable wholesale service provided to chemists, twice daily. In this trade, then, stocks are constant and thus deliveries to the retailer are equivalent to over-the-counter sales to the customer.

The technique offers several advantages in that retailer co-operation is not strained, it is cheaper since the auditor does not need to spend time stock counting, and it should be faster since fewer analyses or tabulations are necessary. Where it is reasonable to assume that stocks are either constant or immaterial since their sale is imminent because of their nature, such as when shelf life is short, an invoice analysis is a useful and cheap alternative to the retail audit.

The next logical stage in the development of invoice analysis is already taking place in America. The research agency involved in pioneering the method is taking advantage of the (relatively) high degree of stock control exercised by distributors, to sell the concept of invoice analysis to manufacturers. The service is not confined to samples of retailers but reflects the whole structure of the distributive chain—wholesalers, head offices, and individual shops. It is fast, less expensive, and highly successful.

This application in the UK is likely to be slower, the less 'organized' end of the trade is larger and could be some time before the process of rationalization makes this technique more obvious. However, there are products that could already be adequately measured by invoice analysis such as cigarettes, perishables such as sausages, whole cheeses, fresh and chilled meat, bacon, fish, fresh fruit, and vegetables, and other merchandise which should only be handled by shop staff. Currently the sales or deliveries of most of these products are not recorded or available to management even though organizations for their promotion and marketing exist. It can only be a matter of time before this development is generally available here.

Distribution Checks

The battle for distribution and shelf space is continuous. While manufacturers seek to maintain or increase availability to retain a competitive edge and to obtain representative facings, the retailer strives to rationalize the range of brands held and to reduce stock levels to a minimum.

Accurate information about distribution is therefore vital, particularly during times of competitive activity. As already stated, information about distribution is available from retail audit but not every manufacturer buys audit information for all his products and even those who subscribe to a retail audit sometimes do so on a limited scale, such that many products (principally minor competitors) are shown grouped. There is also a clear limit to the breakdowns possible because of the relatively small samples used; audit data on distribution are simply not sufficiently detailed for the diagnostic information required by manufacturers with distribution problems. To remedy deficiencies or assess competitive pressure it is necessary to examine shops of a particular type in a particular area, e.g. multiple grocers in the Midlands, co-operatives in Scotland. Only with this information can manufacturers pinpoint weaknesses and strengths and direct the sales force or distributor to specific defined targets.

Clearly, then, large numbers of outlets must be sampled, the number dependent on the breakdowns required, around 3000, for example, to measure distribution among four types of grocer in the eight major television regions and the remainder of the country. Using such a sample size to its maximum efficiency by 'equal cell sampling' would yield for each area sample a total of 336 shops each containing 84 shops of each of the four types—co-operatives, multiples, symbol independents, and other independents—the imbalance of the sample being restored at the expansion stage to provide correctly weighted national and area totals and within these, the shop-type totals.

The basic data obtained from a distribution check show simply the proportion of shops of a particular type in a particular area found to be in stock at the time of the fieldwork. This is the equivalent of numerical distribution obtained from a retail audit. Putting a value to the distribution, in other words to attempt to show the volume of sales represented by the shops stocking, is more difficult since retailers are most unlikely to give reliable information about their turnover. Some approximation can be made, however, by basing the calculation upon the numbers of staff employed. Thus, distribution achieved in a shop staffed by ten persons is worth ten times the distribution value of a shop staffed by one person. Other devices include square footage of the shop, rateable value, number of check-outs or cash registers, all reflecting, to a greater or lesser extent, the volume of business carried out. In addition to these two basic tabulations a number of additional analyses are also possible. If, in addition to the simple annotation of shops stocking, a listing is made of the prices at which the various brands are being sold, three useful further tables can be constructed, i.e. the:

(a) range of prices at which individual brands are being sold;
(b) proportion of stockists selling at each point in the range;
(c) 'average' price and the degree of dispersion about the mean (the standard deviation).

By some further work by the interviewer in the store, other helpful analyses can be prepared:

(d) counts of 'facings' on shelf-service shelves to obtain the share held by each brand stocked;
(e) the incidence of displays, special features, dump bins;

(f) special packs, 'flash' packs, old and new labels;

(g) by questioning, to establish the source of supply, i.e. the use of cash and carry wholesalers by symbols and other independents.

Most distribution checks can be carried out by observation, certainly in the case of self-service and supermarket grocers and the products are on the shelves, if in stock. This was confirmed by a recent survey designed to measure the incidence of stock in the reserve area (storerooms, stockrooms, and yards) not being on sale in the forward selling area. Checks were carried out at two-hourly intervals over five days among a sample of 300 stores on a high volume range of products. Only late on Saturday afternoons and the early opening hours on Monday mornings was it found that any significant proportions (between four and ten per cent) of brand stockists were out of stock in the forward selling area. By midday on Monday, only two per cent of the stores had failed to relocate the brands. The advantage of observation rather than questioning is the facility to carry out checks among particular multiple groups whose managers would perhaps refuse information were they to be questioned.

Several research agencies offer syndicated distribution checks. These are carried out periodically three or four times a year; most feature calls on a continuous sample, a form of panel operation. Syndication enables the cost to an individual client to be kept to the minimum but requires complying with predetermined field dates and sample demographics. Information is processed relatively quickly, the full report is normally despatched within three weeks, preceded by advance information on key items available a few days earlier by telephone.

A summary of several circumstances that have precipitated a number of recent distribution checks follows, rather than illustrations or case histories. Basically the efficiency of distribution policies, strategies, and tactics need to be reliably measured by distribution checks. Many manufacturers experiment with varying cover and call rates, merchants are concentrated in some areas and thinned out in others, free mail-outs for immediate initial distribution are increasingly used as are commando sales forces. The effect on distribution of bonusing and dealings needs to be offset against the cost and the sales achieved. Reciprocal trading agreements are developing in outlets controlled by competing manufacturers, each naturally anxious to establish independently the levels achieved. The development of line extensions and varieties (the umbrella brands) is another frequent reason for distribution checks. Salesmen's reports of competitive price activity need to be assessed for extent and depth. Reported growths in distribution from retail audit reports are sometimes checked out by larger sample distribution surveys. One syndicated service carries out a number of these studies in named outlets to verify developments and to obtain measures of facings.

162

Trade Surveys

An increasing amount of research is being carried out in the retail trade as competition between manufacturers intensifies and as the structure of the trade changes (with greater concentration of buying power among voluntary groups, combines and larger individual retail organizations). Notwithstanding these changes, manufacturers have become increasingly aware of the need for more information about the needs and attitudes of the retail trade than can be provided by feedback from the sales force.

The selection of trade channels and the motivations and performance of retailers have an important influence on the effectiveness of every other marketing decision of the manufacturer. The co-operation and support of the retailer is obviously crucial for such activities as special point of sale displays and certain types of consumer promotion. Trade surveys are therefore carried out to examine attitudes in connection with the image of the company and its competitors, its products, pricing policies, selling methods, distribution policies, advertising and promotional policies, trade incentives, etc. In other words the range of topics covered in trade surveys can be as broad as that covered in consumer research. Similarly, the techniques of trade surveys differ little in principle from those of consumer research. It is important, however, to draw out the distinction between trade and consumer research arising out of the different characteristics of the two universes. A fundamental distinction lies in sampling procedures.

Sampling in trade surveys

Samples of retailers have to be taken from a heterogeneous universe with a high degree of concentration in size, type and geographic location. Figure 7.2 illustrated the skewed distribution of turnover by shop type. In terms of geographic location it is found, for example, that about a half of all small grocers are located in the Midlands, Lancashire and Yorkshire television regions. These characteristics suggest the use of non-probability or quota sampling methods in trade research in order to achieve adequate representation of all types. This involves dividing or stratifying the universe into more homogeneous groups and then selecting a random sample from within each. An example of such a sampling frame would be type of trade × form of organization × turnover over size within region.

Two main problems arise in this type of sampling exercise. First, precise definition of the characteristics or types can be difficult. Errors can easily occur; for example, the distinction between a department store and a furniture store, wholesalers that are both cash-and-carry and conventional. Second, it is necessary to have information on the sampling frames, ideally a complete list with details of all significant characteristics. Only in this way can the results be aggregated to give estimates of the whole population. Unfortunately, this is difficult with the current paucity of relevant census data, particularly with the constantly changing characteristics of the retail and wholesale trade. Steps have been taken by the Department of Trade, largely at the instigation of the Market Research Society, to meet the need for information in these areas. In addition, the television contractors conduct their own censuses and re-analyse and update Department of Trade estimates.

Often the most useful source for filling sample frames are directories and trade registers such as Benn's Hardware Directory, the Chemists Register, the Self-Service and Supermarket Directory, Classified Telephone Directories and curiously, but not ominously, fairly exhaustive listings can be obtained through the Inland Revenue and local authority rating lists. Directory lists can be easily obtained from many sources (e.g. Current British Directories: C.B.D. Research), but care must be exercised in using directories as most are bound to be out of date before they are in print and some, particularly trade association membership lists, contain many serious omissions.

It is difficult to generalize about the appropriate sizes of samples in trade surveys. Smaller samples of perhaps only 200 respondents often suffice compared with the usual sample size of 1000 in consumer surveys. However, the important determinants of sample size are obviously the objectives of the study and accuracy required, the nature of the universe and the number of categories or sub-samples to be analysed.

Interviewing in trade surveys

Apart from the difficulties of sampling set out above, another major problem in conducting trade surveys is the correct identification of a respondent, particularly in studies of buying procedures. In multiple or co-operative retail outlets buying decisions are rarely taken at the retail manager level. Moreover, buying decisions taken at the head offices of multiples or co-operatives may not be the responsibility of a single individual. In these situations, several interviews may be undertaken within a single organization. More generally, the scope of trade research can be usefully extended by questioning not only the retailer, but also his staff and his customers as they make their purchases, go through check-outs or emerge from the store. A recent study of trade incentives by an oil company included interviews with forecourt attendants and workshop staff as well as garage proprietors. It is obviously vital in such studies that the permission and co-operation of the manager is obtained.

Contacting the appropriate respondents and arranging appointments for interviews is obviously crucial to secure a high rate of successful interviews. Generally speaking, a higher interview success rate is achieved when interviews are pre-arranged as opposed to 'cold calls'. The quickest and most efficient way of arranging interviews is by telephone and especially for identifying the correct respondent. The retailer is a busy man and his time is limited. While it follows that a short interview will have a lower rate of failure to complete, successful interviews extending well over an hour are frequently achieved. Obviously peripheral questions should be edited from the questionnaire and as much information as possible obtained by observation rather than questioning. The brands stocked, the number of fixtures, floor displays, product locations, and space, the use of particular forms of promotion material can all be observed or noted and need not require questions to be put to the retailer. Where possible, however, observations should be correlated by the retailer and vice versa.

Interviewing in trade surveys is often structured but semi-structured or non-directive interviewing can be more productive. While the latter is not structured in the sense that precise questions are formulated in advance and asked in given sequence, non-directive interviews are not casual discussions; there is usually a high degree of precision in both the questioning and classification of results. There can be problems of communication in trade survey interviewing. It is obviously important to use the language and idiom of the section of the retail trade under study. Expressions which are familiar to managers of multiples are not necessarily as well known to the independent. Grocery terms are not those in common use among the hardware trade. Restricted to the grocery trade only, the following examples have been found to be confusing even within that trade and serve to illustrate the very real need for preparation and care in this area:

allocation	in-store promotion	return
backing card	lines	run
broken bulk	long runs	shelf talker
bonus	marketed	shrink wrap
cover	merchandise	spectacular
direct	movement	splits
expanded	offer	stack
fixture	operator	stand
flash pack	pack	stand strips
floor display	period	stock loading
group	promotion	units
indirect	quote	volume

The above has implicitly been concerned with face-to-face interviewing. The techniques of postal questionnaires and telephone interviewing can be used to advantage in trade surveys, perhaps to a greater extent than in consumer research. The use of postal questionnaires is covered in chapter 10, and it is sufficient to say that the same rules and pitfalls of using postal questionnaires in consumer research apply in trade surveys.

On the other hand, use of the telephone in trade surveys does not suffer many of the problems apparent in consumer research. Telephone ownership is not a source of sampling bias since every retailer, virtually without exception, is on the telephone. Telephone interviewing enjoys the obvious benefits of time and cost savings and because the telephone is so much a part of business life, interviews are conducted under familiar and almost normal circumstances. There are two main disadvantages of using the telephone in trade surveys. Firstly, there are the obvious limitations on certain types of questioning, especially those where visual aids are usually necessary, e.g. image rating scales. Secondly, it is not possible to assess the physical environment of the respondent that in personal interviewing provides valuable classification data and illuminates the answers of respondents.

To summarize, trade suveys confront the researcher with a number of additional problems not generally encountered in consumer research. Some of these problems require imagination and creativity while others can only be resolved in a pragmatic way. Above all, however, the advice and recommendations applying to research given elsewhere in this volume should be employed with utmost rigour in trade surveys. A clear understanding of the problem, care in constructing the questionnaire, pilot interviews to check interpretation and flow, relevance of questions, the ability of the respondent to answer the questions and the adequacy of the sample must all be thoroughly checked out before the main fieldwork starts

8. Panel research

John Parfitt

This chapter is concerned with panels. Like so many common English words placed in a market research context, its special research meaning is entirely familiar to the practitioners and confusing to the layman. Its nearest common meaning is a list of names (doctors, jurors, etc.), but in its research meaning this list of names has to be performing certain functions for certain desired objectives before it takes the form of a panel.

There are a wide variety of panel techniques available in Great Britain and some are permanent and some short term. Their functions and characteristics are described later in this chapter. All these panels have two common distinguishing characteristics with regard to the type of data they are designed to obtain and the method of obtaining it:

(a) Panels are based on a representative sample of individuals or households from the universe being studied (e.g. all private households, all households with TV sets, all cigarette smokers, etc.). Each individual or household panel member records (or permits the recording of) their complete activity in some factual aspect of consumer behaviour, such as their purchases in a defined range of consumer products or their television viewing.

(b) This measurement is ideally a continuous process over time, by virtue of retaining the same sample of respondents over the full period of measurement and obtaining from them a continuous and complete record of the required data. The collection of these data has, therefore, to be at regular and frequent intervals.

There are two basic objectives of panels, whatever specific data they are designed to collect. These are to:

(a) collect detailed and accurate information of the anatomy of consumer

167

behaviour and the characteristics of the consumers; in other words, to obtain such precise information about the behaviour of each consumer or group of consumers that the differences in behaviour can be clearly recognized and the relevant characteristics recorded. This refers, of course, to basically factual data about behaviour and not attitudinal data and in this respect panels offer the possibility of much greater accuracy and detail than is normally possible from single-call-interviewing techniques.

(b) obtain information on the dynamics of consumer behaviour over time. The continuous study of the behaviour of individual consumers over time, made possible by the panel techniques, enables measurements to be made of the consistencies and inconsistencies of consumer behaviour, exact measurements of the frequency and volume of purchases/ viewing/reading (whatever is being measured) and the response to given stimuli—advertising, brand launches, program changes, or whatever.

Why Use Panels?

It requires little knowledge of research to see that these can be difficult objectives to obtain in full. The problem of respondent co-operation alone is a formidable one. Panels require a lot of 'know-how' to be run efficiently and, above all, they are expensive to operate. It is relevant to ask, therefore, why bother to set up panels anyway, what use do they have and in what sense do they have advantages over research techniques that may be cheaper and easier to operate? After all, sample size for sample size it will be far cheaper to call on a sample of respondents only once and interview them on, say, their purchasing behaviour for the last three months than to set up a panel that records these data for three months, so what advantages do panels offer for the extra money and time?

The answer to this question is in two parts:

(a) Panels have marked advantages in the amount and accuracy of the data that can be obtained from one source, compared with the normal alternative of single call interview techniques (see 'Technical considerations in panels').

(b) The depth of analysis of the dynamics of consumer behaviour possible from the continuous nature of panel measurements offers unique opportunities to understand the ways in which the consumer behaves under given stimuli (see 'Analysis of panel data').

The Marketing Need For Panel Data

The wide range of panel and repetitive survey services currently available in Great Britain has grown not out of the steady widening of technical research knowledge as to how to operate them, since this was known substantially long before the majority of the services began (even if it has been polished en route), but out of the marketing need and, therefore, demand for the data they provide. The first of these services to be launched in Great Britain was the household consumer panel technique (the Attwood panel started in 1948). In fifteen years from 1955 and, particularly, in the six years from 1964 to 1970, many other panel services have been set up to meet specific marketing requirements for data. What were the marketing requirements which caused the development of the consumer panels?

A recent leaflet published by Arthur D. Little Inc. makes the challenging statement: 'Marketing managers are being inundated with data but starved of information'. The distinction drawn by the writer is between data (facts about the world) and information (answers to specific questions). In measuring consumer purchasing and attitudes, one is gathering 'data' (as defined) but one is also gathering them selectively with a view to transmuting them into 'information' (as defined). There are certain recurrent questions in marketing which the manufacturer's research department knows to be of perennial interest and, therefore, facilities have been created to provide the 'data' which will yield the necessary 'information'. The questions are of the type:

> How many people buy my product?
> How much do they buy?
> Who are my competitors?
> How strong are they?
> Are we/they gaining or losing?
> What sort of people buy our/their products?
> Is any brand responsive to promotion?
> Has it regional/shop-type strengths and weaknesses? etc.

Marketing people are very interested in the detailed anatomy of the market and also in its dynamic characteristics. Monitoring services of various sorts have grown up to satisfy this need and among these the consumer panel technique.

The type of service which has evolved reflects the nature of the need. A mail order house, for instance, obtains a great deal of information from its own internally collected statistics. The exact response to any advertisement may be determined right down to the last unit sold and the name and address of each customer. A seller of expensive consumer durables such as Rolls-Royce may go even further and seek to maintain a 'cradle to grave' record of each vehicle that leaves the factory. A soap powder manufacturer, on the other hand, may sell 5 million units per week of a big brand and, without some fairly elaborate system of data collection, he will have little idea of the final destination of these packets after his own transport and distribution organization has offloaded them at the delivery point. Similarly, apart from a few rather barren industry statistics, supplied by his trade association, he will have little knowledge of what his competitors are doing. It is with the information needs of manufacturers at this 'low cost/repeat purchase' end of the spectrum rather than at the 'high cost/consumer durable' end that consumer panels are mainly concerned.

The manufacturer who is interested in the market standing of low-cost repeat purchase items is faced with two main choices of data source. He may choose a method which takes a measurement at some point in the chain of wholesale and retail distribution. Commercial services are available which measure such things as warehouse withdrawal (mainly in the US), retail sales, retail distribution (retail audits and distribution checks). Such techniques are described elsewhere in this volume. His alternative is to pick a method which goes directly to the final link in the chain, the consumer, and again there are many commercial services which take measurements at this point. They fall into two broad categories—interview survey techniques, and continuous consumer panels. Some of the relative merits of interview surveys and panels with regard to the accuracy and detail of the data that can be obtained from respondents are discussed in a later section. For the time being it is sufficient to mention that it is the continuity of the data supplied by consumer panels that gives them particular value in providing marketing information.

People's actions are often a better guide to their character than their expressed opinions. Consumer panels are concerned mainly with consumer *behaviour*, i.e. actions not opinions. Again, a motion picture conveys more information than a snapshot. A snapshot of a hundred housewives might reveal that thirty of them were wearing hats. A second picture of another hundred might turn up the same proportion of hat-wearers. What does one conclude?, that 30% of housewives wear hats? A continuous film record of the behaviour of one of these groups might show that all its members wear hats, but that they do so only 30% of the time. Such a finding would be entirely consistent with the snapshot evidence, but might well lead to different conclusions, particularly if one happened to be a hatter. Consumer panels are *continuous:* they aim to cover *all* the purchases of each panel member over time in the field under study.

Thus, the consumer panel technique operates by confining itself to the collection of basically factual data about consumer purchasing behaviour, containing the minimum of respondent bias or conditioning resulting from seeking opinions or searching the respondents' memories about purchasing behaviour, and transmuting it by analysis into marketing 'information' for the study, not only of the detailed anatomy of the market but also of the dynamics of consumer behaviour over time.

The Types of Panel Services Available

Continuous consumer purchasing panels

The majority of permanent panel services are purchasing panels, based either on samples of households or individuals. The principals of these

170

operating in Great Britain in 1978 were:

Panel service	Date of formation	Reporting sample size	Data collection method	Type of data collected	Standard reporting periods
Attwood Consumer Panel	1948	4800 households	Postal diary	Purchases of household consumer goods	4-weekly and/or quarterly
AGB Television Consumer Audit	1964	5800 households	Home audit	Purchases of household consumer goods	4-weekly
TCPI (Individuals Panel)	1973	8000 adults 1500 children	Postal diary	Purchases of personal consumer goods	One or two monthly
Attwood AMSAC Personal Panel	1970	12 000 individuals	Postal diary	Purchases of personal consumer goods	
RSGB Baby Panel	1967	1150 mothers with babies	Diary and interviewers	Purchases of of consumer goods for use by babies	4-weekly and/or quarterly
RBL Motorists Panel	1964	4000 individual motorists	Postal diary	Purchases of petrol, oil and car accessories	4-weekly
Agridata Farming Panels	1971	Two Panels of 1500 and 2500 farmers respectively	Personal Interview	Purchases of sprays, fertilizers, feeds etc.	Quarterly
AGB Index	1978	11 500	Personal	Spending habits, savings, insurance	Monthly

There are two basic alternatives for collecting data in consumer purchasing panels. These are the home audit and the diary method.

The Home Audit.   A panel is recruited and agrees to one main condition, i.e. that once a week (or at some other agreed interval) the panel member will admit an auditor into her home and will permit her to check household stocks of any product field in which she may be interested. Secondary conditions are that the panel member will save up used cartons, wrappers, etc., in a special receptacle provided by the auditor and that she will also answer a short questionnaire when the auditor calls (since some required information about the purchase will not be obtainable from the package alone). The auditor then checks all household stocks and *marks* the packets that have not been marked in previous weeks. She then checks the receptable for used packs, ignores anything that has been marked at a previous call, and adds to the total any used pack which has not been marked. Thus, the purchases for the week are counted as all packets found in stock, in use or in the empty packet receptacle, that had not been marked at previous calls.

The Diary Method.   A panel member is recruited and undertakes to record in a preprinted diary all purchases, made either by herself or by other

171

members of the family, in certain nominated product fields. Every week (or at some agreed interval) she returns the diary to the research company. She may or may not be provided with a receptacle for used packets (as an aid to memory). If she normally receives and returns diaries by post, she will be visited periodically by a representative of the research company so that the contact is kept 'alive' and is not allowed to grow stale, and to provide an 'educational' function where necessary. Some diary panels rely on interviewer collection of the diaries anyway—this is more expensive but it does combine some advantages of both systems.

All operators of consumer purchasing panels use one or other of these methods of data collection but predominantly it is the diary method that is used. A great deal has been said about the advantages of the one method or the other in the collection of panel data and remarkably little has been written for publication. The home audit method appeals to the imagination more as an objective method putting less burden on the panel members than the diary method, which may be subject to problems of understanding, memory, and fatigue. In practice, the differences between the two methods appear to be much less marked than they appear to be in theory, i.e. judging from parallel data from the Attwood panel (postal diary) and the TCA panel (home audit). Nevertheless, there are differences and the principal advantages and disadvantages of the two data collection methods appear to be as follows:

(a) Postal diary collection methods are cheaper to operate than home audits and, as the method is not dependent on regular personal calls, the sample does not need to be so closely clustered as for home audits. A part of these two advantages disappears when interviewers are used for diary collection.

(b) The initial panel recruitment rate is probably higher for the home audit method than for the diary method. In both cases recruitment is by personal interview. How important this factor is is a moot point bearing in mind that in the USA national diary panels are usually recruited by mail and produce a 10–15% recruitment rate, compared with, say, 50% for diary panels in Great Britain and higher for home audit panels; and yet the American panels are reported to produce very reliable purchasing data.

(c) The continuity of panel membership is probably higher for the home audit method than for the postal diary method. A 'drop out' rate of 25–30% per annum can be expected from a postal diary panel and 10% has been quoted for home audit panels, although this latter figure sounds low allowing for the normal rates of death and home-removal in this country. The use of interviewers to collect diaries almost certainly reduces the 'drop out' rate below the level quoted above for diary panels, since it is known that regular calling has a beneficial effect on continuity of panel membership.

(d) Home audits are entirely dependent on getting regular access to the home

172

for the collection of data, which postal diary panels are not. On the other hand the non-receipt of a diary for a particular week calls for very quick action from the research company to collect the diary if the record is not to be lost.

(e) The two methods have different advantages and disadvantages in the collection of certain types of data. Thus, home audits record very accurately any promotions, special offers, etc., marked on the pack. Pickup of other promotions is adequate but probably no better than diary records. Foodstuffs which are bought loose and consumed quickly are hard to check in home audits, and wrappers which may start to smell after a brief storage may be missing from the audit bin and missed from the audit. These present no particular problem in a diary record. Diaries are probably better than audits at picking up the purchases of 'other family members', e.g. the teenage daughter's personal bottle of shampoo or father's extra tube of toothpaste packed in the overnight bag may well be missed even in a conscientious audit.

(f) The diary method can cover a wider range of goods and services than the home audit method as such, since it is not dependent on physical evidence of purchases for its data collection. Thus, it can collect data on products with important unbranded sectors, like eggs, sausages and cheese, or products difficult to audit in the home, like paint or garden products, or services like hairdressing, cinema visits, or dry cleaning. Naturally, these data can be collected on home audits also but only by the introduction of diaries or by interviewer-administered questionnaires.

Although both audit and diary panels have their imperfections, both methods have over long periods been shown in Great Britain to provide accurate market share and trend data over a wide range of product fields. The technical weaknesses do not manifest themselves to any very great extent if the aim is simply to produce aggregate market share data by weekly or quarterly periods; and this was the type of service which the panel companies were originally set up to supply. Indeed, the bulk of their income is still derived from the sale of such standard reports.

Of the continuous consumer purchasing panels operating in Great Britain in 1975 one, the TCA panel, relies on the home audit method and the remainder on the diary method, with or without interviewer collection of diaries. Two are household panels (the Attwood Consumer Panel and the AGB home audit panel) set up for the collection of purchasing data on products which are basically for household use. In these panels it is the housewife who is recruited for co-operation in the collection of the data, both because she is usually the most readily available of the household members and also because she will normally be the main agent of purchase for products of this kind. The Attwood consumer panel did for some years rely on supplementary data from diaries issued to other household members for recording purchases of a more personal kind, e.g. shampoos, toilet soaps, records, etc. This was done on the grounds that these are purchases which the housewife might not otherwise be aware of and therefore would not record in her household diary. The logical development of this technique is the most recent development in continuous panel services—personal panels.

Two personal panels have been set up on a national basis—the AGB TCPI and the Attwood AMSAC panel. The method of operation of these is basically similar to that of household diary panels except that the data are collected from individuals rather than households and the range of products on which data can be collected goes far beyond what is considered to be feasible from a household panel, e.g. it includes cigarettes, confectionery, etc., which are essentially personal purchases for personal consumption often beyond the home. The principal problem in collection of these types of data is to ensure that the panel members record their purchases as soon after making them as possible, since the frequency of purchase is often far higher than for products normally recorded in household panels; and the evidence of purchase, i.e. packaging, often disappears quickly after purchase as does the memory of the purchase. Experimental work has suggested that a more portable form of diary than is necessary for a household panel is a valuable aid to complete and accurate recording of personal purchases of this kind.

Two other continuous consumer purchasing panels mentioned in the summary—the RSGB Baby Panel and RBL Motorist Panel—are essentially aimed at special interest groups (mothers with babies, and motorists) but otherwise work on normal diary panel lines. The motorist panel comes closer to a personal panel than the others and relies on a small-size diary which can be kept in the car to ensure that petrol and oil purchases are recorded as soon after they are made as possible. The baby panel has particularly acute recruitment problems, compared with the normal run of panels, since only mothers with young babies are of interest and they need to be recruited as soon after the birth of the child as possible. And once the baby is over two years of age panel membership is no longer required.

The Agridata Farming Panels are a very special form of panel and come into the boundaries of the techniques covered in this chapter. Quarterly personal interviews with the farmers establish purchases of products necessary for farming—chemicals, sprays, animal health products, feedstuffs, etc. Both diaries and invoice auditing had been used to collect the data before the personal interview was adopted.

Short-term consumer purchasing panels[1]

Unlike the continuous panels, the short-term consumer purchasing panels do not usually operate on a syndicated service basis. They are designed for a specific purpose, usually only for one client, and their duration is determined by the measurements necessary to answer the marketing problems for which they were set up. A minimum of twelve weeks and a maximum of a year are the usual limits of these short-term panels. The objectives of these are numerous but the most important of them are:

(a) To measure test marketing activity, particularly in terms of product penetration and repeat purchasing, in test towns or in small areas where the continuous panel services do not yield samples of a sufficient size.

(b) To test out alternative marketing choices, e.g. alternative promotional activities, in controlled conditions in order to determine which is likely to be the most efficient in general use, or to discover whether existing policies could be modified without detriment to the product's sales. To do this, different matched panels are subjected to the different marketing pressures under observation and the purchasing behaviour of the samples are compared, usually in penetration and repeat purchasing terms. There are sometimes as many as half a dozen matched panels under observation at the same time, although the number is usually only two or three. They may all be located in the same district or town, or sometimes they are located in different areas depending on how closely the stimuli being applied can be confined to the households under observation. Thus, a test of different advertising campaigns usually has to take place in several areas, as the advertising cannot be confined to small districts; whereas a comparison of different promotional activities can often be carried out within the same district or town.

(c) A third use of short-term consumer panels is where information is required from the panel households or where they are subjected to special marketing pressures which would be considered conditioning and detrimental to the future buying behaviour of permanent panel members. Thus, purchasing behaviour collected from the panel may need to be related to information on their attitudes to the product or awareness of its advertising, etc. This is perfectly feasible with a short-term panel. Indeed the application of awareness and attitude questions at the end of the panel's life is a standard feature of the technique, whereas such information obtained from a permanent panel might be considered harmful to the representativeness of the panel's future buying behaviour.

The data collection methods employed in short-term panels are much the same as those described earlier for the continuous panel services. The principal difference is that the recruitment rate for short-term panels is usually higher than for permanent panels since more respondents are prepared to participate in panels when they know exactly how long it is for, and when the burden of data required from them is relatively small.

Television-viewing panels

The television-viewing panel technique was developed by Nielsen in the USA and, at the time of the start of commercial television in Great Britain, by TAM. This service is now operated by AGB on behalf of JICTAR.

The panel is recruited from households with television sets and the primary

175

measurement is achieved by means of a meter attached to the set which records on a tape the time when the set is turned on or off and the station it is tuned to. This information alone gives no indication of the actual audience and this is usually obtained by means of a viewing diary in which the viewing times of the individual household members (and guests) are recorded. From these data are estimated the total household viewing audiences to each channel in each ITV area and also the household composition of these audiences. The methods have remained virtually unaltered in the over 20 years since commercial television began in Great Britain. One important exception in data collection is that meter tapes are now returned by post, instead of being collected every Monday by an employee of the research company.

By consumer purchasing panel standards panel sizes in each area are comparatively small, as is shown below, and this can be attributed to the comparative simplicity and stability of television viewing behaviour compared with the complexities of consumer purchasing behaviour.

JICTAR panel sample sizes in each ITV area:
Television meter households in each area

London	350	Central Scotland	200	Ulster	100
Midlands	300	North East England	200	Border	100
Lancashire	300	Wales and the West	200	South West England	100
Yorkshire	300	East of England	200	North East Scotland	100
		Southern	200		

Total in Great Britain 2650 households

The recruitment rate for television viewing panels and the continuity of panel membership is traditionally higher than for consumer purchasing panels (particularly of the diary panels). This can be attributed to the smaller burden on the respondents, the relatively greater attractiveness of television panel membership and to the higher rewards offered. This subject of television viewing panels is covered in greater depth in chapter 25.

Consumer product consumption panels

In the same way that consumer purchasing behaviour is complex and liable to exaggeration and over-simplification in single-call interview situations so, too, is consumer consumption behaviour of the products they buy or make. The pattern of product consumption, the uses to which products are put, the occasions of consumption, who consumes them, in what quantities and with what other products, etc., can be measured most accurately over time by means of a panel. These are normally very short-term panels set up long enough to allow for running-in and the normal cycle of consumption behaviour, for which an average period may be eight weeks duration, dependent on the average frequency of consumption and purchase of the product under observation.

176

Like short-term purchasing panels, the panels to measure product consumption are usually set up for one specific purpose and for one client. The purpose normally requires some disguise as far as the respondent is concerned to avoid over-reporting of consumption behaviour, and this is usually achieved by measuring a wider range of product consumption than is required for the study. The scope of product consumption panels is wide. In the experience of the author examples of them give some illustrations of the size, subject, and duration of panels of this kind. Panels set up to measure the preparation and consumption in the home of soups and canned puddings had a sample of 1000 housewives and lasted for eight weeks. During this time, housewives recorded the occasions of serving the products, details of other foods eaten with them, who ate them, full details of the product served, etc. An edible fats consumption panel consisted of 1000 housewives and lasted for three weeks (some in winter, spring, and summer) and obtained full details and the quantities of the purpose for which butter, margarine, etc., was used. A clothes washing habits panel of 300 housewives ran for six weeks and obtained full details of the washes carried out, the main clothes categories washed and of the washing products used.

It is normal at the finish of the panel operation to interview the respondent in order to obtain attitude and awareness data and to relate these to consumption habits.

Shopping panels

This research technique is really a variant of the consumer purchasing panel. It has been developed in the USA and is relatively widely used there. The example currently available in Great Britain is the Forecast Mini-Test-Market Service. The panel consists of a demographically controlled example of housewives in a town (Forecast have a 500-housewife panel in both Southampton and Manchester, for instance) who have expressed their willingness to purchase products from a travelling shop. The travelling shop is, in fact, run by the research company and calls on each housewife once a week. Each housewife is regularly supplied with a brochure containing illustrations of all the products and brands she can purchase and an order form (which, in effect, is the equivalent of a panel diary). The operation carries the usual range of brands in each product field it covers, and these are at carefully controlled but competitive prices. In addition, however, it introduces new brands or varieties which are not available on the general market and using the brochure as an advertising medium and applying normal promotion schemes where necessary it promotes these products to the panel. The result is that it usually achieves an abnormally high penetration for the new brand, compared with what would probably happen in a real test market situation. It provides, however, a realistic impression of the likely repeat purchasing rate the brand would achieve in the market. It is on this latter measurement that the panel largely depends for its assessment of whether the brand would be successful or not if it were launched. It is, therefore, not a substitute for a consumer purchasing panel in a test marketing situation, but rather it permits an earlier measurement to be made of a brand's likelihood of success prior to test marketing.

Product testing panels

Product testing panels are more in use in the USA than in this country. Their title is slightly inaccurate since they are usually used for collecting data quite as much as for testing products. They lack many of the common characteristics of the panels so far described since there is seldom any continuity in the data collection or product testing functions; their continuity is solely in the fact that a particular sample of respondents of known characteristics is retained for a semi-continuous miscellany of research enquiries. They are at their optimum use when the cost of interviewer field work for national enquiries is at its maximum in relation to postal costs (as in the USA or France) and for this reason have made rather less headway in Great Britain where travelling distances and field work costs are comparatively low. Their principal use in Britain has been by manufacturers running their own panels, and this has been primarily to retain the maximum control and secrecy in their product development.

Technical Considerations in Panels

Sample selection

As panels are intended to operate for a considerable length of time, if not indefinitely, considerable care is applied in sample selection at recruitment. The Attwood consumer panel, for example, was based on 250 local government sample district clusters of 16 households in each. These were selected in a four-stage stratified random sample, the last stage of which was the selection of addresses at a fixed interval from the electoral registers of wards selected at the third stage. The resulting sample was proportionately correct by four town size groups within 15 control areas in the country and demographically balanced within each of the 15 areas.

It is not sufficient, however, just to exercise this care at the initial recruitment stage. Similar controls have to be applied in two other panel-sampling procedures. The first of these relates to panel maintenance, i.e. the replacement of households which are removed or remove themselves from the panel. This is a continuous process and each removed household has to be replaced by another with similar demographic and area characteristics. To provide these 'quotas' a large number of households selected by the methods described above have to be surveyed and held in readiness for the occasion when they need to be used as panel replacements.

The second sampling procedure relates to actual reporting periods. Any

178

panel has a reserve over and above its basic reporting number to allow for slow or non-return of purchasing records in any one period. This reserve (usually about 10%) has to be large enough so that in any period a fully balanced area and demographic sample of reporting households can be drawn within a minimum waiting period, otherwise panel reporting would be delayed whilst the returns from demographically deficient groups were awaited.

The validity of panel data

The fact that panel recruitment rates may vary from as little as 10 to 15% of initial contacts in postal recruitment in the USA to around 50% for diary panels in Great Britain and higher for home audit panels has already been discussed. Thus, there are a lot of people who refuse to join panels, and this sometimes raises doubts about the representativeness of those who do. A source of evidence which suggests that panels are representative comes from some experimental work to create psychological or attitude grouping scales with which to classify panel housewives. An initial set of attitude scales designed ultimately to be related to consumer purchasing behaviour on the panel were applied initially to a random sample of 3600 non-panel housewives. The results obtained from the random sample and later from the panel housewives show a close similarity in attitude groupings, as may be seen in Table 8.1.

The extremes of each scale are composed largely of different housewives. It is not unreasonable to assume that if the consumer panel sample was fundamentally unrepresentative of the domestic household population then significant differences would appear in these attitude scales and, in its turn, in purchasing behaviour.

In theory, the simplest way to test the validity of purchasing data obtained from panels is to compare them with data obtained from other sources. In practice this is difficult, partly because very little other reliable information is available and, where it is available, it is often hard to make direct comparisons with panel results. This is because household consumer panels measure only purchases taken into the home and, in some fields, this excludes important areas of consumption beyond the home. Where such information does exist, and it is usually in the form of total production figures for the retail market, then the panel results (grossed-up) normally range from about two-thirds to 100% of these tonnages, depending on how much purchasing occurs beyond the home. In the case of flour, for instance, where there is little non-domestic consumption of retail packs the panel pick-up is virtually 100%. In the case of toilet soaps, where there is much more consumption of the retail pack beyond home, then the panel pick-up is about 90%, and so on. In general, with one or two notable exceptions, consumer panels reflect total domestic purchasing of products with accuracy, where valid comparisons can be made.

Table 8.1   *A comparison of attitude groupings in a random sample of the total housewife population and among Attwood Consumer Panel members*

Attitude scale:	Rigidity in housework		Traditionalism in housework		Economy consciousness		Conservatism in shopping	
	Random sample 100%	Consumer panel 100%	Random sample 100%	Consumer panel 100%	Random sample 100%	Consumer panel 100%	Random sample 100%	Consumer panel 100%
Total housewives								
No. of housewives falling into each group on the scale								
1. Very rigid/ traditional/ economy conscious/ conservative	9%	7%	13%	12%	10%	10%	10%	10%
2.	13%	12%	21%	24%	38%	35%	13%	13%
3.	22%	24%	29%	29%	24%	31%	44%	48%
4.	35%	35%	25%	24%	16%	16%		
5. Flexible/modern minded/not economy conscious/not conservative	21%	22%	11%	11%	11%	8%	33%	29%

Source: Attwood Consumer Panel, Great Britain.

180

The question of whether panel housewives get conditioned in their purchasing behaviour by long membership of the panel is one on which some direct evidence can be produced. Two separate studies are shown which, while not being fully conclusive, do at least provide no evidence of this type of conditioning. The first example is taken from the STAFCO consumer panel in France and it compares two demographically matched samples of panel households; the first long-serving panel members (five years or more) and the second more recently recruited members. Two potential types of conditioning are studied; the first that panel membership tends to induce greater brand loyalty, and the second that it tends to produce greater price consciousness and, therefore, more attention is paid to obtaining price advantages (see Tables 8.2 and 8.3).

Table 8.2 *Average number of brands purchased—by length of panel membership*

	(Brands purchased in a 12 week period)			
	Dentifrice	Margarine	Toilet Soap	Washing Powder
Long service panel members (recruited 1955–1960)	1.23	1.29	1.45	1.98
Shorter service members (recruited 1961–1964)	1.22	1.31	1.42	1.98

Table 8.3 *Average price paid per 100 grms—by length of panel membership*

	Average price paid in a 12 week period (francs per 100 grms)			
	Dentifrice	Margarine	Toilet Soap	Washing Powder
Long service panel members (recruited 1955–1960)	2.05	N.A.	0.77	N.A.
Shorter service members (recruited 1961–1964)	2.09	N.A.	0.77	N.A.

Source: STAFCO Consumer Panel 12 weeks ending
27 December, 1964.

This study at least shows that there is no progressive conditioning of panel housewives. The behaviour of the longer serving panel members is virtually identical with that of shorter service members. A similar study carried out in the Attwood panel in Germany showed similar results. It does not, however, preclude the possibility that all the conditioning occurs in the first few months of panel membership and thereafter ceases. The second analysis is taken from the Attwood Consumer Panel in Great Britain at the time when the basic sample size was increased from 2000 households to 4000. The purchasing levels in 25 product fields were compared between the old 2000 panel (containing a high proportion of long service members) and the newly recruited 2000 panel (who by definition were all short-service members) to see whether any variations which occurred were beyond those which would be attributed to chance after allowing for the variations in the range of chance differences which would occur for fields of different size and frequency of purchase. In fact, 13 of the fields showed some upward movement in total purchases and 12 showed some downward movement, but in only two cases were these movements statistically significant. These results suggest that even during the first year of panel membership there are no basic differences in product purchasing levels from those obtaining after longer service.

Table 8.4   Normalized deviates of percentage differences between purchasing levels of old and new panels

Normalized deviate	over −2	−2 to −1	−1 to 0	0 to 1	1 to 2	over 2	Total fields
Actual	0	3	9	7	4	2	25
expected	0.6	3.4	8.5	8.5	3.4	0.6	25

If conditioning does not seem to occur to any great extent in practice—and in general terms the evidence suggests that a continuous consumer panel is a representative measuring instrument—there still remains the fact that consumer panels do tend to have minority areas of unrepresentativeness. There are at least three known minorities of the domestic population that consumer panels tend to under-represent. These are the two extremes of the population, the very prosperous and the very poor (particularly the very poor and old). The third group are the fluctuating and transitory households composed mainly of young single men (or women) living particularly in the centres of the larger cities. It is likely that these groups tend to be under-represented to some extent in most market research samples.

Continuity of reporting

As one of the principal advantages of panels is the continuity of the data, clearly continuity of reporting by panel members is of paramount importance. This is particularly true of the more sophisticated analyses of panel data, which rely heavily on complete continuity of reporting by the panel members included.

Continuity is directly influenced by three factors: the rewards offered for panel membership, the degree of interest the panel members have in participation, and the ease with which they can supply the data required. Probably all panel operations offer some reward for the services of the members; these range from direct money payments, through stamp schemes in exchange for gifts, to free television set maintenance in the case of

182

television-viewing panel members who own their own sets. Clearly, there are limits set by the commercial viability of the panel operation itself to the size of the payments to its members. Suffice it to say that the payments themselves can hardly be regarded as the 'rate for the job' and therefore continuity is very much dependent on the interest of the panel member.

The degree of interest the panel members have is a very important factor. There is little doubt that frequent visits by friendly auditors/interviewers has an important effect, as does the exchange of chatty notes between a *nom de plume* at head office and the panel members (the Americans are so much better at this than researchers in Great Britain). A cordial relationship between the panel member and the panel company is at least as important as the payments.

The interest of the panel members is very much influenced by the ease with which they can supply the data required of them. Confusion about what they are supposed to do, even on small points, is a great destroyer of interest. People essentially like to co-operate and do not like to be made to feel inadequate to what has been set them, by a failure to understand what they are supposed to do. Clarity, particularly in diary layout, is vital. One special feature of this factor is the problem that respondents usually do not understand that to report a non-purchase is as important as reporting a purchase, i.e. a genuinely empty audit bin is as important as a full one. There is a danger, particularly in the early stages of panel membership, that respondents will create purchases or find packages rather than report nothing. Thus, in short-term panels in particular it is necessary to cover a wide enough range of products for most of the sample to have purchased at least one item per diary-reporting period (usually weekly); for the rest it is a matter of respondent education that a non-purchase is as interesting as a purchase.

The Volume and Accuracy of Panel Data, Compared with Interview Surveys

Panels are used to measure aspects of consumer behaviour which are complex and variable, e.g. purchasing or viewing behaviour over time and where a relatively high degree of accuracy in the measurement is required. This second point is important because, for instance in the measurement of purchasing behaviour, for many purposes the high degree of accuracy and detail offered by a panel may not be necessary to obtain the information required for a particular marketing decision. In such cases, and there are many, using a panel might prove to be an expensive luxury and a cheaper simple interview survey would suffice adequately.

How complex and subtle purchasing behaviour can be is often not fully appreciated. This is illustrated in Figs. 8.1 and 8.2. In Fig. 8.1 the purchases of 350 households in seven product fields (of high purchase frequency) over two consecutive eight-week periods is studied by individual households,

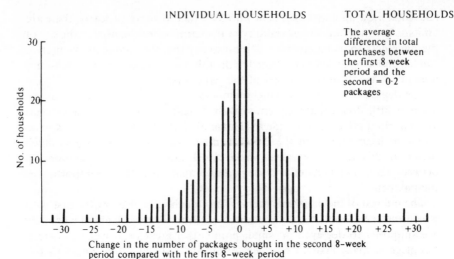

INDIVIDUAL HOUSEHOLDS TOTAL HOUSEHOLDS

The average
difference in total
purchases between
the first 8 week
period and the
second = 0·2
packages

No. of households

Change in the number of packages bought in the second 8-week
period compared with the first 8-week period

Fig.8.1 Individual household variations in purchasing levels in the total of seven product fields
between one 8-week period and the next. Source: Attwood Consumer Panel.

showing the amount of variation in total purchases between the first and
second periods. The average change for the total sample over these two
periods was negligible—from 21.3 to 21.5 packages per household, or an
increase of less than 1%. However, in 49% of the households studied
purchases changed by more than 20%, thus illustrating that even in the most
apparently stable market situations there is considerable and diverse movement below the surface.

Fig. 8.2 Proportion of purchases of a washing powder brand
made on promotions. Source: Attwood Consumer Panel.

Figure 8.2 illustrates the purchases of a brand of washing powder over the period of a year and the proportion of these purchases that were made with promotions. The complexity of this situation speaks for itself, and it is only part of the picture since the problem of purchases of competitive brands is ignored in this illustration.

It is generally accepted among researchers that if you interview a respondent asking him (or, more likely, her) to recall purchasing behaviour in a consumer product field, there is a strong likelihood that the frequency and quantity of purchases will tend to be exaggerated and the complexity of purchasing behaviour over-simplified. This hypothesis was tested in an experimental research study[2] in which 1000 consumer panel housewives were interviewed about their purchasing behaviour in 12 product fields and the data obtained were compared with the data recorded by the same housewives in the panel to which they belonged. The results obtained from this study suggested the following conclusions:

(a) that respondents when interviewed are prone to exaggerate their purchasing behaviour;
(b) this exaggeration is very closely related to the respondent's average frequency of purchase of the product. Thus, the more frequently a respondent actually purchases a product the more accurate he/she is likely to be in recalling that frequency and, conversely, the less frequently a product is purchased the more likely that the purchasing behaviour will be exaggerated;
(c) in its turn this conclusion has two effects. The first is that products with a high average frequency of purchase tend to be exaggerated least in interview surveys. Table 8.5 summarizes these findings from the experimental study. The second effect is that within any product field the gap between the volume of purchases of high- and low-frequency buyers is artificially narrowed in an interview situation because the latter tend to exaggerate their purchases more than the former;
(d) there is dramatic over-simplification of brand switching behaviour over time in an interview situation. Broadly, respondents tend to equate their most recent brand buying behaviour to their 'normal' behaviour over time, whether this is accurate or not.

Broadbent and Mooney in their follow-on to this study[3] point out that for certain purposes (in this case selection of print media against light, medium, and heavy buyers of products) the exaggeration obtained at single-call interviews does not distort the rank order of purchase volume too seriously and does not, therefore, invalidate the results obtained. This may be so, but as this is a relatively insensitive use of purchasing data it does not alter the fact that a high degree of exaggeration and distortion of purchasing behaviour is present in purchasing data obtained from single-call interviews; and for many of the studies of purchasing behaviour required from panel data such distortion would seriously affect the accuracy of the results obtained.

Table 8.5   The relationship between average frequency of purchase and interview exaggeration of total purchase volume

Product field	Average frequency of purchase		Interview exaggeration factor—volume of purchases (panel diary returns = 100)			
	Average interval between purchases— weeks	Rank order	Panel housewives when interviewed		Matched non-panel housewives*	
			Exaggeration factor	Rank order	Exaggeration factor	Rank order
Tea	1 week or less	(1)	116	(1)	136	(2)
Margarine	1.1	(2)	128	(3)	123	(1)
Washing powders	3.0	(3)	124	(2)	143	(4)
Washing-up liquids	3.5	(4)	178	(5)	210	(5)
Baked beans	4.5	(5)	152	(4)	140	(3)
Toilet soap	4.9	(6)	208	(9)	261	(8)
Canned soups (summer)	5.3	(7)	200	(8)	298	(10)
Instant coffee	6.2	(8)	179	(6)	245	(7)
Jam	9.4	(9)	194	(7)	235	(6)
Dentifrice	9.7	(10)	217	(10)	282	(9)
Floor and furniture polish	15.9	(11)	292	(11)	396	(11)

* A Matched Sample of 1000 housewives who were not members of the Attwood panel were also interviewed, using the same questionnaire as for the panel housewives. In general they exaggerated their purchasing behaviour more than panel housewives and this is attributed to the fact that the latter had a better idea of their purchasing behaviour from their habit of recording it in the panel diaries. The rank order of exaggeration is, however, similar.

As well as the accuracy possible in panel techniques in obtaining the sheer volume of purchasing, or consumption habits, or television viewing data or whatever over time, there is also an advantage in comparison with interview surveys in the volume of ancillary data that can be obtained. This advantage is, as yet, relatively unexploited. Because a panel sample is by definition available over a long period these ancillary data can be collected, and perfected, at intervals and not cause respondent fatigue which might result from their collection at one-point in time as would be necessary in single-call interview surveys. These ancillary data fall into two distinct categories:

(a) consumer classification data for the better identification of types of consumer behaviour. Into this category fall all the normal demographic characteristics of the consumer which would be collected as a matter of course in the recruitment of a panel. In addition there is a vast range of classification characteristics which might prove relevant to the purposes of the panel, the ownership of goods and services, leisure time activities, shopping habits, consumption habits, income and occupational categories, etc. It has also proved possible to obtain psychological or attitude classifications of panel members. The advantage of the panel technique is that classification data can be collected and tried by analysis for its relevance and usefulness in isolating consumer behaviour characteristics and, if found wanting, can be rejected or modified. It is a continuous process;

(b) ancillary data which are known, or suspected, to have an influence on consumer behaviour and therefore can be collected alongside the main data of the panel and applied to get a better understanding of processes of consumer activity. Into this category comes the collection of readership and television-viewing data for application to consumer purchase panels, and holiday and other travel activities in relation to motorist panels.

As far as the collection of ancillary data from the single source of the panel is concerned, there is still a considerable potential to be tapped. This should be one of the major areas of development of panel techniques.

The Analysis of Panel Data

Panels, whether they are short-term or continuous, provide an almost indigestible mass of data which have to be translated into a limited amount of information which can be absorbed and acted upon. This is, of course, true of almost all research work but it is a particularly acute problem for panels simply because of the sheer volume of data flowing in as a continuous process. The efficient use of panels, therefore, lies in the standard and relevance of the analyses obtained from the data.

The analyses derived from the data of consumer purchasing panels can be conveniently divided into three groups:

(a) standard trend analyses produced at regular intervals, usually four weekly, which show the progress of the market and of its principal brands;

(b) 'simple' special analyses designed to show the anatomy of the character- istics of purchasing behaviour and of the consumers. These are not usually produced on a continuous basis but rather as and when required, usually when some significant change is thought to have occurred in the market which requires further study:

(c) 'complex' special analyses designed to examine the fundamental patterns of consumer behaviour, particularly in relation to specific bursts of major marketing activity.

The remainder of this section illustrates examples of analyses in the three groups.

Standard trend analyses

These differ in detail from one purchasing panel operation to another but are similar in purpose and provide the content of the basic reports. The normal reporting period is four weeks, long enough to provide enough data of significance to analyse and short enough to show trends while there is still time to take action. In special and urgent cases data may be produced on a weekly basis, but this is rare.

The analysis tables in the four weekly report shows the number of buyers in the total product field in the period and the buyers of each of the brands and subsections (if any) of the field. A similar table shows the total quantities purchased (again by brands) expressed in whatever quantity measure is most appropriate to the field—expenditure, weight, packets, standard units, etc. The current four-weekly period is usually shown alongside similar data from previous periods, going back for perhaps as long as a year, and this provides a ready reading of trends. Other data may also be shown in the report where this is relevant to the interpretation of the trends, such as the proportion of purchases made in different types of consumer promotions, etc.

The trend analyses of purchasing panel data are the essential preliminaries to all other panel analysis work. They provide the broad picture of the market but they are not the *raison d'être* of panels since similar information could be obtained from other research techniques, e.g. shop audits, regular *ad hoc* surveys, and they make no use of the real advantage of panels, their continuity of reporting.

'Simple' special analyses

The term 'simple' is derived not from the ease with which the analysis is provided (it may in fact be relatively difficult to provide) but from the nature

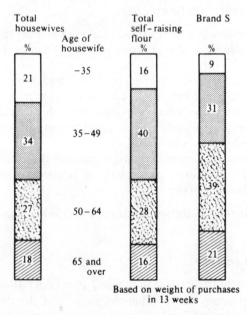

Fig. 8.3   Self-raising flour purchases, by age of housewife.

of the information it supplies. The examples given here are not meant to provide a comprehensive list of the analyses that are possible but are meant to be illustrative of the range of analyses.

The first example, in Fig. 8.3, relates consumer demographic characteristics to purchasing behaviour. In this particular example it relates the weight of total self-raising flour purchases in 13 weeks to the age of house-wife purchasers for the total market and one particular brand. The brand in question shows a higher average age of purchaser than the total market. This is a particularly simple example of the great range of consumer classification analyses possible from panel data. A second example is shown in Fig. 8.4, which relates the quantity of purchases of baby products in a 12-week period to whether the baby is the first, second, third, etc., in that family. Clearly, experience in bringing up babies influences purchasing behaviour.

Panels habitually collect a lot of associated data about the item purchased—for example, the price paid, the day of the purchase, and the type of shop from which it was made and whether any promotions were involved. These data provide useful information.

In Fig. 8.5 a series of analyses have been summarized to show the trend in importance of the different types of outlets in the growth of a fast-moving food product. It shows clearly that the rate of growth of purchases of the product differs markedly from one type of outlet to another and gives a clear warning light to any brand which is not keeping pace in the outlets expanding at the fastest rate. It does, incidentally, give strength to the point made in the

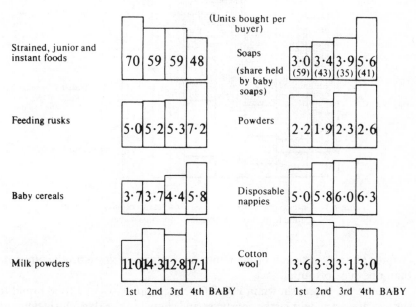

Fig. 8.4   The volume of purchases of a range of baby products related to whether the baby is the first child or not. Source: RSGB Baby Panel.

189

Percentage of total
Household purchases,
by volume, from
each source of purchase.

Large multiple grocers

Other grocers

Co-operatives

Woolworths

Other outlets

Year 1 2 3 4 5 6 7

Fig. 8.5   Consumer purchases by type of outlet in a rapidly expanding
food field. Source: Attwood Consumer Panel.

chapter on trade research of the importance of measuring a product in more
than one type of outlet.

Another example, shown in Fig. 8.6, relates purchases of a food brand to
the average price paid by the consumer and shows a clear elasticity of demand
related to price. The brand was a premium priced product and it should be

Fig.8.6 The relationship of the volume of purchases of food Brand C to the average price paid by the consumer. Source: Attwood Consumer Panel.

emphasized that the same degree of price elasticity might not be present for a lower priced brand in the same market or for any brands at all in some other product field.

'Simple' analyses begin to lose some of their simplicity once they get into the realm of defining 'users' and 'non-users' of a product. There was a time when many marketing men would divide their world quite simply into these two categories. The brand had a franchise, which could be termed 'users' and beyond them were a lot of people who could be termed 'non-users'. Marketing skill consisted of persuading the 'non-users' that your brand was really very good, then inducing them to sample it, after which experience of the sterling qualities of the brand they would be convinced of the error of their ways and would be converted into 'users'.

Analysis of panel data showed that this was a grossly oversimplified view of a fast-moving consumer goods market. Firstly, what is a user? Does she have to buy once only to qualify or does she have to buy twenty times? Does she have to take all her purchases in the product field in your brand or only part of them—if part, then what proportion would you settle for? Secondly, how much substance is there in the belief that persuasion will induce trial, which will in turn induce loyalty to the brand? Experience shows that the trial/conversion process can happen when a significant innovation hits the market place, but that more often than not there is a constant battle for position going on between closely matched brands, with smallish strongholds being held on a long-term basis and much of the territory in a more or less fluid state, being held sometimes by one brand and at other times by another, and with no brand making permanent gain.

Fig. 8.7   Analyses of frequency of purchase—examples from instant coffee and self-raising flour. Brand S. Source: Attwood Consumer Panel.

Fig. 8.8   Continuity of purchasing over a 6-month period—example of a brand leader in the toothpaste market. Source: Attwood Consumer Panel.

The following analysis examples illustrate some of the purchasing behaviour characteristics described above.

Figure 8.7 shows the frequency of purchase of buyers of instant coffee and the buyers of a brand of self-raising flour. In both cases it is a relatively small minority of buyers who account for a majority of total purchases of the product.

Figure 8.8 shows a measure of continuity of purchasing, i.e. a form of loyalty measurement, for a leading brand of toothpaste in which it will be seen that nearly half the quantity of the brand purchased in a six month period was accounted for by less than 20% of the buyers who were 'loyal' to the brand, and that 46% of the buyers were moving in or out of the market for the brand and accounted for only a small proportion of the total purchases.

The user/non-user concept of a market is replaced, therefore, in analysis terms by the two concepts of 'market penetration', i.e. those who buy the brand at least once in a given time period, and 'brand loyalty'. Brand loyalty is subject to a number of interpretations depending upon the analyses used. The analysis of continuity of purchasing in Fig. 8.8 is a relatively crude

Fig. 8.9   The extent to which buyers of toilet soap are completely loyal to one brand in a 13-week period.
Source: Attwood Consumer Panel.

definition, and the type of analysis which examines total purchases in a product field for each individual panel member in a given period of time and then expresses purchases of a given brand as a proportion of the total comes closer to an exact definition. This has its problems, however, since very light buyers tend to show brand loyalty merely because they have less opportunity to switch brands, and in this type of analysis need to be isolated from the heavier buyers.

Figure 8.9, which shows the extent to which buyers of toilet soap are loyal to one brand, illustrates both the relatively limited extent of 100% loyalty to a brand in a highly competitive market and, what we have already seen, that a high proportion of the buyers in any field accounts for only a small part of total purchases.

There are many other forms of special analyses, each designed to answer specific problems and the illustrations here are meant only to indicate a little of the possibilities of 'simple' analyses from panel data. Nothing has been said at all of many of the analysis types regularly produced from panel data of which the following is a list of examples:

(a) purchases by size of pack;
(b) quantity of the product bought on each purchase occasion;
(c) day of the week on which purchases are made;
(d) extent to which different individual consumers purchase products with the same 'family' brand name, e.g. Lux, Ajax, Heinz, etc.;
(e) the limits of duplication between brands by which consumers confine their purchases to a limited group of the total brands available;
(f) the extent of purchasing 'own label' brands compared with nationally advertised brands, among consumers who shop at supermarkets;
(g) loyalty to flavours rather than brands in certain food fields;
(h) price consciousness by demographic groups;
(i) the relationship of quantity of purchases to size of household.

'Complex' special analyses

The dividing line between 'simple' and 'complex' analyses of panel data is not an easy one to define and there is probably little to be gained from pursuing the definition to the bitter end anyway. Included in the latter category are the analyses which call for the collection of special ancillary data from panels, e.g. media exposure data, attitude grouping data, etc., or which examine the fundamental characteristics of consumer behaviour for the purpose of a more complete understanding of the complex processes by which marketing stimuli influence purchases.

The first example of this type of analysis is of the use of readership and television viewing data collected from panel housewives to measure the influence of advertising on purchasing behaviour. The principle employed in this analysis is to isolate the purchasing behaviour of housewives exposed to a particular advertising campaign from those who were not.

Table 8.6   The sales effect of a press campaign for brand X, by readership categories

	Total housewives		Heavy readers		Medium readers		Light readers		Non-readers	
	Volume of purchases	Brand share index	Volume	Brand share	Volume	Brand share	Volume	Brand share	Volume	Brand share
Q4 1964*	100	100	100	100	100	100	100	100	100	100
Q4 1965	106	105	115	116	112	109	104	106	96	95
Q4 1966	91	97	107	112	102	111	75	84	90	91

* Before press campaign began.

Source: *Attwood Consumer Panel, Great Britain.*

In this particular example, involving a food product brand, a press advertising campaign spread over a two-year period has been superimposed on the normal television advertising support for the brand. A common sample of panel housewives who were reporting their purchases over the full two years has been selected and these have been classified according to their likely exposure to the advertising (based on their readership of the publications used in the campaign) into heavy, medium, light, and non-reader categories.

The purchases of the brand (in volume and market share) were measured in the quarter year prior to the start of the press campaign and in the same period in the two succeeding years, as shown in Table 8.6.

After the first year of the advertising campaign the volume of purchases and share indices have a consistent relationship with the amount of exposure to the press advertising—those not exposed showing a decline in purchases, those most exposed showing the greatest increase in purchases. By the end of the second year there had been an absolute decline in purchases of the brand for reasons beyond the control of this particular press campaign. The only groups whose purchases have not fallen below the 1964 level are the heavy and medium reader groups. It would seem that in the second year light readership was not sufficient to counteract the tendency for purchases of the brand to decline.

There is a further analysis which has been extracted for this study and this relates to the relative effectiveness of the press advertising on housewives who have (or have not) been exposed heavily to the television advertising for the same brand. The television advertising is a relatively common element running through the whole period of the study, including the period before the press campaign began (Q.4, 1964). Table 8.7 illustrates this analysis. The readership groups have been split into two (rather than four) in the interests of sample size.

Almost all the increase in purchases among the heavy and medium reading groups is confined to those who had *not* already been exposed heavily to the television advertising. The implication of this is that the television advertising had already raised the level of purchasing of its heavy viewers as far as it was

Table 8.7   The trend of purchases of brand X by the volume of exposure to the TV and press advertising

Readership:	Heavy and medium readers				Light and non-readers			
Television:	Heavy and medium viewers		Light and non-viewers		Heavy and medium viewers		Light and non-viewers	
	Volume	Share	Volume	Share	Volume	Share	Volume	Share
Q4 1964*	100	100	100	100	100	100	100	100
Q4 1965	105	105	123	119	97	99	105	103
Q4 1966	96	104	113	119	83	91	80	83

* Before the press campaign began.

Source: *Attwood Consumer Panel, Great Britain.*

likely to go before the press campaign began. Certainly, the general level of purchases of the heavy and medium ITV viewers was some 10% higher than that for the light and non-ITV viewers before the press campaign began.

The second analysis example is drawn from relating an attitudinal classification of panel housewives to their purchasing behaviour. The principle adopted in this approach is that housewives with identical demographic characteristics show considerable differences in purchasing behaviour and it is possible and, indeed, likely that these relate to differences in fundamental attitudes to activities like shopping, housework, cooking, trying new products, etc., which in their turn reflect in their purchasing behaviour. If this hypothesis is correct, and the attitudes which relate to the differences in the purchasing behaviour can be measured, this will have an important bearing not only in understanding the marketing approach to be made to purchasers of a particular product but also in identifying where potential purchasers are most likely to be found. Table 8.8 shows an analysis based on experimental work on the Attwood Consumer Panel where two types of floor and furniture polish (wax and aerosol) show similar demographic profiles among purchasers but strongly contrasting attitude profiles. This type of analysis is represented in the continuous consumer panel services at the present time only by experimental work; it is not offered as a regular service but it is an important indicator of the direction in which these services can develop in the

Table 8.8   Social class and attitude to housework profiles of purchasers of two types of polish

	Social class				Attitude to housework scale				
	AB	C	D1	D2E	1 Very traditional	2	3	4	5 Modern- minded
Proportion of housewives buying:				100 = Average level of buying of the polish types					
Wax polish	134	111	94	93	110	110	105	84	68
Aerosol polish	170	110	98	85	45	91	100	109	146

Source: *Attwood Consumer Panel, Great Britain.*

future. There are, of course, limits to the extent to which attitude data can be collected in the permanent panels without conditioning future purchasing behaviour; but general attitude data not related directly to questions on brand or product purchasing are certainly well within these limits. Such limitations do not apply to short-term panels, where the attitude questioning is confined to interviewing immediately after the end of the panel operation, and this service is regularly applied in short-term panels to provide an additional dimension in the interpretation of the purchasing data[1].

The remaining examples of 'complex' analysis of panel data are derived from the study of the underlying patterns of consumer purchasing behaviour using a model which predicts future market share by measuring the likely penetration and the likely repeat purchasing rate for the brand under study. The analysis was originally devised to predict the share of newly launched brands but has since been developed to study the longer term effects of promotions, or advertising campaigns, or other marketing activity for established brands.

The launch of 'Signal' toothpaste is shown in the next example. Figure 8.10 shows the penetration and repeat purchasing rate achieved by the brand in the weeks following the launch of the brand. They show two characteristics which are common to virtually all analyses of this kind:

(a) After a time the cumulative penetration of the brand, i.e. the number of people buying the brand for the first time, shows a declining rate of increase. Once the shape of the curve is determined and a declining rate of increase is observed, it is possible to make a reasonable estimate of the ultimate likely penetration.

(b) The repeat purchasing rate is calculated by taking the total volume of purchases in the product field made by people who have tried the brand under study and expressing the repeat purchases of that brand as a proportion of these total purchases. This repeat purchasing rate usually declines in the early weeks after a first purchase and eventually begins to level off. When this levelling-off occurs it is possible to calculate what the equilibrium market share of the brand will be.

In the Signal example the estimated ultimate penetration was 37%, i.e. 37% of all dentifrice buyers would try it at least once in the reasonable future, and the repeat purchasing rate settled down at around 40%, i.e. after curiosity had been satisfied those who had tried Signal would, on average, repeat purchase the brand four times out of 10. Forty per cent of 37% would yield a market share of 14.8%. Figure 8.11 shows that this share was reached some three or four months after the prediction was made and remained a valid share prediction for over two years.

There are a number of refinements and qualifications to this analysis which were not included in this early example and there is not space in this chapter to deal with them. Readers who wish to pursue them should read the published work on this subject[4].

197

CUMULATIVE PENETRATION OF SIGNAL

100% = Total dentifrice buyers in 26 weeks

Estimated ultimate penetration — 37%

First estimate made here

Final estimate made here

Cumulative percentage of households trying Signal at least once

Number of weeks after launch of Signal

REPEAT PURCHASES OF SIGNAL

100% = Total field purchases by buyers of Signal

Estimated ultimate level — 40%

Repeat purchases of Signal as a percentage of total field purchases

Number of weeks after the first purchase of Signal

Fig. 8.10   The cumulative penetration and repeat-purchasing rate for Signal in the period immediately after its launch.

The product of the penetration × repeat purchase analysis has proved to give a forward estimate of market share which has been found to be very reliable in frequently purchased product categories. The accumulation of many examples of the analysis has also contributed to a greater understanding of the way consumer purchasing responds to marketing stimuli. In particular, one 'rule' that has emerged has important implications. This 'rule'

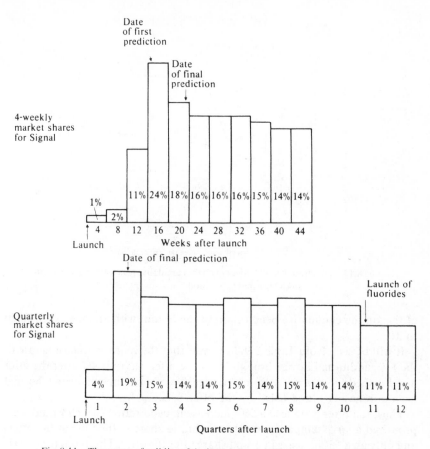

Fig. 8.11   The extent of validity of the brand share prediction made for Signal.
Source: Attwood Consumer Panel.

is that on average the later a buyer enters the market for a brand for the first time the lower her repeat purchasing rate will be and the smaller the contribution to the future brand share. Thus, it can be concluded that any attempt to improve the penetration of a brand, e.g. with a particularly attractive promotion, will not yield a repeat purchasing rate for buyers brought in by the promotion higher than the rate of the marginal buyers existing before the promotion began; and in all probability it will be lower.

An example to illustrate this concept is taken from an established detergent brand, brand L. In the normal way the brand would penetrate about 20% of the buyers in the market in, say, a six-month period and achieve an average repeat purchasing rate of 25% (which would be normal in a highly competitive relatively disloyal market with five or six major brands to choose from), thus indicating that its market share is around 5%. In this example a 50% price-cut promotion was introduced and Fig. 8.12 illustrates the effect

Fig. 8.12 The effect of a 50% price cut on the cumulative penetration of detergent Brand L. Source: Attwood Consumer panel.

of this on the cumulative penetration of the brand, with an increase from 20 to 31%.

It will be seen from Table 8.9, however, that the repeat purchasing rate of the 11% additional buyers brought in by the offer was only 4% after the offer had finished, compared with an average of 25% for those buyers who had been purchasing brand L before the offer began.

Thus, the offer produced a 55% increase in penetration (which would have produced a large temporary increase in brand share at the time of the offer) and only an 8.5% increase in brand share after the offer. This is not to say that that was an unsatisfactory result for the offer but purely that the long-term effects, measured in terms of repeat purchasing, are very much more subdued than the immediate increase in penetration would suggest. There is also reason to believe that the immediate penetration effects of marketing activity

Table 8.9   *The contribution made to the ultimate share of brand L by buyers introduced by the offer*

BRAND L (50% price cut offer)	Ultimate penetration	×	Repeat purchasing rate	×	Buying rate index	=	Ultimate brand share
Before introduction of the offer	20%	×	25%	×	1.03	=	5.15%
After introduction of the offer							
buyers before offer	20%	×	25%	×	1.03	=	5.15%
buyers after offer	11%	×	4%	×	1.01	=	0.45%
							5.60%

200

are not necessarily a very good guide to the strength of the longer-term effects; a promotion, for instance, that yields a relatively high immediate increase in penetration does not necessarily make the biggest contribution to the longer term strengthening of that brand's market share.

The Continuous Study of the Underlying Patterns of Consumer Purchasing Behaviour

Somewhere locked in the panel data accumulated over the years lie the answers to a range of marketing questions. Some important work has been carried out to extract the essence of these data and find marketing 'laws', e.g. Ehrenberg[5], but for the most part the more sophisticated analysis of panel data has been carried out primarily to pursue specific and 'limited' objectives, such as to predict the future share of a new brand or to measure the sales effect of a particular advertising campaign. The analyses have been relatively expensive to carry out and, therefore, no attempt has been made to introduce them as a matter of course at each point of major change in advertising, promotion, etc. A data bank of case histories in a particular market would reveal far more of the fundamental factors influencing purchasing behaviour in that market than the occasional isolated analysis, however sophisticated. The increasing use of panel raw data for computer analysis by client companies must eventually lead to this situation and, assuming that the appropriate ancillary data mentioned in this chapter are also by then regularly available, panels will at long last be used to their full advantage. Panel analysis will then fully serve its dual purpose, to provide:

(a) immediate data on the development of trends and consumer characteristics in the market—the traditional rôle of panels;
(b) the more fundamental data on how consumers react to given marketing activity to determine how they are likely to react to future marketing activity.

9. Omnibus surveys

J. P. H. Kendall

The fieldwork costs for most market research surveys are very high. In some surveys, they can reach 80% of the total expenditure. A more detailed examination will reveal that these costs are incurred almost entirely in making contact with the respondent, whereas the length of the eventual interview will only marginally influence expenditure. In other words, a survey amongst 2000 women, asking one question only, will cost almost as much as a survey of similar design and sample size asking 30 questions. This situation arises because the majority of interviewer time is taken up in travelling to the place of interview and attempting to make contact with the respondent, and only a relatively small percentage with the actual questioning. It is primarily the relatively high costs of making contact and the insensitivity of costs to the length of the questionnaire that have given rise to what are called omnibus or syndicated surveys.

An omnibus survey is similar to an *ad hoc* survey with the exception that the questionnaire, instead of being devoted entirely to one research project, is made up of a number of sub-questionnaires, each one being a survey in its own right. These sub-questionnaires, with a few reservations indicated below, can be on entirely different subjects and deal with different aspects of those subjects. By this device it is possible to share the costs of interviewer time between several different surveys and thereby very substantially reduce the expenditure on each project. Although cost is the main reason for the development and use of this kind of survey, there are other reasons for using them which are indicated later in this chapter. Furthermore, omnibus surveys are defined here in a fairly narrow sense and there are associated areas which are considered briefly in the section below called 'Other Forms of Syndicated Research'.

As is frequently the case with cost saving ideas, particular care must be taken to ensure that these are genuine savings and that in the end an even greater expenditure has not been involved. Whilst there are many market research problems which can be solved using these approaches, there are also problems where the omnibus survey would not be appropriate, even though at first sight it may appear to offer a cheaper alternative. The major part of this chapter is concerned with indicating the advantages and disadvantages of this type of survey, and to assist the reader in deciding whether the omnibus survey is appropriate for his particular problem.

Basic Methods of Operation

In theory it would be possible for any researcher to set up an omnibus survey. All that is required would be to find a number of other researchers concurrently planning a survey with similar sample designs and to create one master questionnaire from the individual questionnaires. In practice, the problems of obtaining agreement on all aspects of the survey design and the financial commitment involved are such that few individual researchers would attempt this. The field is left to market research companies who, by weighing up the likely demands and offering space on a master questionnaire, carry out the planning, fieldwork and analysis of these omnibus surveys themselves. These research companies usually undertake their omnibus surveys at frequent intervals on a standard sample size and design. The researcher can, therefore, select from a range of such services the sample design and timing that he believes to be most appropriate. The services offered by research companies vary widely, in terms of the frequency with which they carry out these surveys, the sample size, the type of sample interviewed and the methods of working. (A list of actual examples can be found at the end of this chapter.)

Most research companies place certain restrictions, particularly on the type and number of questions which can be asked on their omnibus surveys. The restrictions vary from company to company and it would be necessary in practice to check with each research company. Such areas which should be considered are:

(a) the number of questions permitted;
(b) use of prompt cards and other additional materials;
(c) number of code positions permitted;
(d) confidentiality of results;
(e) position in the master questionnaire;
(f) classification details that can be collected;
(g) range of cross analysis available.

The above method of operation, whereby a research company offers service to the clients and takes the risk of not filling the questionnaire, is by far the most common method of operating omnibus surveys. One other approach is the research company undertaking a survey on a particular project but willing to allow one or two additional clients to add questions to the end of their questionnaire. This is most common where the major research project is a continuous one and, therefore, the company is able to offer the service at regular intervals. This can be considered similar to the normal omnibus surveys with one of the clients having a substantial part of the questionnaire.

Aspects of Design

Questionnaire

Questionnaire design has been fully examined in chapter 5 and it is assumed that the reader is aware of the major problems. There are some aspects peculiar to omnibus surveys which are considered here in more detail.

The first point to remember when designing questions for an omnibus survey is that the questions will be appearing with many others, often in completely different fields. Unless the questions happen to be first in the master questionnaire, for example, the final question from the previous research will occur immediately before the researcher's questions. It is, therefore, advisable to begin the questions for any particular subject with an opening indicating to the respondent that the following questions will be in a new field. The following sequence of questions could occur if attention is not paid to this particular point.

Q Which of the following brands of toothpaste have you heard of? (Show list.)

Q And which brand of toothpaste did you last purchase?

Q And could you tell me the names of all the brands of toothpaste that you have in the house at present?

Q Have you flown in an aircraft in the last twelve months? If 'No', go to Question 12. If 'Yes' ask:

Q On the last occasion that you flew in an aircraft, from where and to where did you fly?

The above questions may have appeared perfectly reasonable to the client interested in toothpaste usage and the client interested in obtaining travel information, but to the respondent, the switch without warning from one subject to another, is liable to create considerable confusion, and will undoubtedly effect the accuracy of his response. The use of an opening paragraph, 'I would now like to change the subject and talk about something completely different . . .' can help this difficulty, but the reader should always remain aware of this problem.

Even where there is an adequate introduction to any changes of subject in the questionnaire, it is clearly desirable to keep these changes to a minimum. This is largely the task of the research company offering the syndicated service to arrange this, so that clients may find their questions refused for a particular period or placed in such a position in the questionnaire so as to avoid clashing with another client. Although this is usually carried out responsibly by the research company, it is advisable for the client to try to check which product field is being used immediately before and immediately after their particular questions. This is sometimes difficult as, for reasons of confidentiality, the research company may not be willing to disclose details of other clients.

Invariably, the more complicated the question technique, the less likely it is that an omnibus survey will be adequate. It is difficult to be exact as the complexity of other questions in the questionnaire is relevant. An interviewer should be able to handle one or two difficult questions but there is clearly a limit, particularly if each client uses different types of questions. There is also a limit to the amount of additional material an interviewer can carry around with her in the form of prompt cards, samples and so on. It is, therefore, particularly desirable to use the simplest possible questions when using omnibus surveys, even if this involves increasing the total number of questions.

Coding

Coding problems are similar to those used for ordinary *ad hoc* surveys. It should be remembered that most research companies will charge for the number of positions used on the coding of their questionnaires. The costs involved are usually relatively small and it would be an unwise researcher who limited the amount of coding he required merely on the grounds of cost. Unlike an *ad hoc* survey where the client can leave the coding entirely to the research company, in an omnibus survey the client should be prepared to define the exact coding positions he requires at the same time as indicating the questionnaire requirements. He should also make his requirements on whether, for open-ended questions, the questionnaire should be pre-coded or whether coding should be carried out after the interview.

Analysis

In theory, it is possible to undertake any form of analysis on an omnibus survey which would be feasible on an ordinary *ad hoc* survey. In practice, the researcher is advised to use the standard analysis package offered by the company if he is to keep within reasonable costs. Most research companies operating omnibus surveys will offer, at very low cost, an analysis giving most standard breakdowns; most will charge a substantial additional fee for any analysis required which is not of a standard pattern. Furthermore, the requirements for additional analysis tend to affect the timing of results as well as the overall costs. If additional analysis is required, it is recommended that this be kept separate from the main body of the report and issued at a separate time, otherwise the client will find that his major results are delayed awaiting more detailed analysis.

Sampling

The primary problem facing the user of omnibus surveys in the area of sampling is that to all intents and purposes the sample is decided and fixed by the research company offering the service and the client cannot make modifications. This raises problems both in the areas of the design of the sample and in the selection of respondents. As far as the design is concerned, in the author's experience, the sampling design of omnibus surveys tends to be less rigorous than some used in *ad hoc* surveys. This does not imply inaccuracies as there are many different approaches possible in sampling presenting equally satisfactory alternatives. However, any particular problem may demand certain requirements from the sample or, at least, indicate a priority in forming the sample frame. The number of call-backs made on a random sample, for example, can vary from none to as many as five, depending on the requirements of the sampling design. Clearly, a survey which is concerned with a problem relating to the absence from the home of the individual to be interviewed (such as a survey into the habits of the working woman) will have a high priority for as many call-backs as possible. However, a survey into the brand image of different dog foods might not place multiple recalls with as high a priority.

It is always possible for the researcher to look at the various alternative omnibus surveys and select one that comes nearest to his requirements, and in most countries there are a range of surveys offered. Unfortunately by their very nature these surveys tend to be designed on the basis of the average requirement. There is a tendency not to satisfy any individual requirements particularly if they are slightly out of the ordinary. It cannot be too strongly emphasized that the researcher should be prepared to investigate fully the exact sample specifications of the various omnibus surveys and not assume that, since there are many other reputable companies using the survey, it necessarily fills his own particular requirements.

As an omnibus survey is likely to be repeated at frequent intervals with the same sample design, it is possible for a research company to examine the design and to rectify inaccuracies or, at least, give an indication of the errors involved. This is usually not possible on an *ad hoc* survey, partly by virtue of the fact that only one survey will take place, also because the total costs of any particular additional analysis must be borne on that one survey, whereas for an omnibus survey the costs can be spread over several surveys.

Interviewers

Since the research company is operating the omnibus survey on a continuous basis, it should be particularly easy for the company to recruit and train competent interviewers. Yet probably because one of the prime reasons for using omnibus surveys is the cost element, interviewers used for them do not always measure up to those used in *ad hoc* surveys. The researcher should question the research company in depth on the interviewers they use and their method of operating. There is an undesirable tendency for interviewers, for example, not to receive a personal briefing on the omnibus survey. To some extent this can be justified as the interviewers will have become fully acquainted with the omnibus survey problems and therefore a personal briefing is not so essential. In the author's opinion, there will still be problems on most questionnaires which warrant a briefing directly between the executive organizing the survey and the interviewers.

Costs

It will have been apparent from the beginning of this chapter that the primary reason for using an omnibus survey is to save money. Figure 9.1 below indicates for a typical survey of varying questionnaire length the appropriate expenditure for that survey if it was carried out on an *ad hoc* basis or on an omnibus survey basis. It will be noticed that there will be a point when the questionnaire becomes so long that, even from a cost point of view, it is cheaper to do the survey on an *ad hoc* basis.

Although costing systems vary from company to company, most

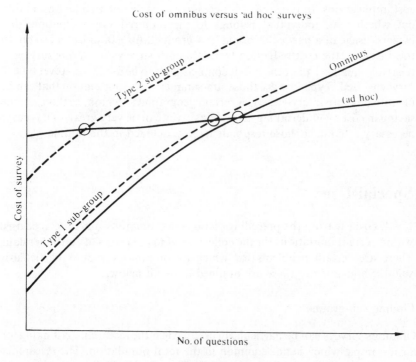

Fig. 9.1   Cost of omnibus versus *ad hoc* surveys.

companies operate on the following principles:

(a) a basic joining charge, usually about £50 to £100;
(b) a cost per question, sometimes with a discount for a number of questions;
(c) a cost for each position of coding—usually not very large in relation to (a) and (b);
(d) additional costs for extra analysis, extra reports, open-ended questions, and so on.

Care should be taken by the researchers to ensure they have included costs which may not at first appear relevant. It is essential, for example, to define the universe to be sampled before approaching the various companies. In an *ad hoc* survey it is often possible to restrict the survey entirely to the required population, at least after the initial contact. In an omnibus survey, it is usually necessary to pay for the total sample covered and, if the required sample is a small percentage of the total, then the costs will rise proportionally for the omnibus survey as is indicated by the dotted lines on the graph above. It will be noted that the researcher should not reject omnibus surveys purely on the grounds that the interviewing will take place on a wider sample than is required for his particular research. It may still be cheaper to use the omnibus survey rather than the *ad hoc* approach.

One can distinguish between two types of sub-sample with very different cost implications. In type one it is necessary to carry out an interview to find out whether an individual belongs to the required sub-population: dog owners' usage of a particular brand of a product, for example, and so on. In this instance, the cost reduction from omnibus surveys to *ad hoc* surveys is relatively small, as all of the initial contacts need to be made, whatever type of survey is used. Type two are those sub-samples of the population that can be identified before interview, e.g. a certain geographical region. In this case, the saving in cost by undertaking an *ad hoc* survey can be very great, as it is never necessary to contact those respondents not included in the sample.

Special Uses

It will be clear from the preceding sections that omnibus surveys can be used within certain limitations for the collection of many forms of consumer data. There are certain problems for which an omnibus survey is particularly suitable and some of these are outlined in detail below.

Finding sub-groups

Omnibus surveys can be particularly useful when the researcher is looking for a sub-sample which is not common in the total population. The researcher may wish to carry out an interview only, for example, with housewives who own a particular type of washing machine. Clearly, in these instances it is extremely expensive to find the sub-groups by means of an *ad hoc* survey as the total number of contacts will have to be very large indeed. It is possible to ask questions concerning the attributes (which in the above sample would be the type of washing machine owned) on an omnibus survey where the sample is large. In this way, the costs of finding a sub-group may be very significantly reduced. Having obtained a subsample of the required type, it is possible to carry out the interview with this sample on the omnibus survey itself or, because of the restrictions already outlined in relation to omnibus surveys, it may be necessary to carry out a second interview. The costs of the second interview will be substantially reduced in that the interviewer will have a list of respondents known to belong to that particular sub-group. The cost savings of this mode of operation are not always as large as might at first sight appear, for two reasons; first, the members of the sub-group will be geographically widespread in accordance with the original omnibus survey sample and so a considerable amount of travel will be necessary at the second interview; second, not every member interviewed on the first occasion will be available because of absence or refusal at the second interview. If the respondent can be given a questionnaire to return by post at the first interview, so that no second interview is needed, these reservations do not apply and a substantial cost saving may be made.

Sequential or cumulative sampling

Since most omnibus surveys are carried out on a continuous basis, it is possible to build up a very large sample by adding the same questions to a series of consecutive omnibus surveys. This is of value when building up a sub-group of the population (as above) in order to obtain a sufficiently large sample for accurate measurement.

A second use of omnibus surveys in this area is one which, at least in theory, could save substantial expenditure. Most surveys are carried out to estimate the proportion of the population or a sub-group of the population which has a particular attribute or make a particular comment. This estimate is subject to sampling error which depends on the sample size and the actual population proportion being estimated. This latter statistic is usually unknown. By using an omnibus survey series it is possible to cumulate samples until a sufficiently large sample is obtained to give the required degree of accuracy. As soon as this degree of accuracy has been achieved no further purchases of omnibus survey space are made. The risk of having a sample that is too small and with an insufficient degree of accuracy, or a sample which is unnecessarily large incurring a considerable excess cost, is avoided. This approach appears to be rarely used in practice. Probably this is partly because most surveys include a range of estimates each requiring different sample sizes and partly because the time of the survey would be seriously delayed by waiting for repeat results in order to make the accumulation. Finally, another reason may be the unfortunate, but general, lack of interest in the degree of accuracy of the results obtained.

Experimental designs

In chapter 3 the many aspects of experimental design are outlined in detail. It is worth noting that a number of these designs are easily incorporated into the omnibus survey and some market research companies offer such designs as part of their standard omnibus survey. The simple experiment, for example, of a split-run between two samples to test, say, an alternative form of question can be easily incorporated into an omnibus survey. The advantage in using omnibus surveys for this type of experiment lies primarily in the availability of the design. Again, many researchers use them as a form of pilot survey for their main research project.

Unfortunately, the facilities for such experiments are limited by the omnibus operators themselves and the researcher will find considerable degrees of difference between the various omnibus research companies in the extent to which they can carry out the more complicated forms of experimental design. Where an omnibus survey does include these facilities, the actual design should be checked to ensure that it is adequate, for example, when a research company offers a split-run facility, the researcher should examine carefully the method used by the research company for obtaining the two matched samples as it may be found that their method does not adequately match the sample in terms of the variable to be measured. An example of this occurs when the sample is split by sampling points so that there is a tendency for different interviewers to be involved in the two matched samples, as opposed to the alternative method where each interviewer alternates between the two variations. Clearly, any problem concerned with measuring the effect of interviewer bias between two questions will not be so adequately measured by the former of these two approaches.

Time series

Many problems require a variable to be measured over a period of time; for example, a researcher may be interested in the purchasing trend for a particular product; or he may wish to measure average purchases over a period of time where he suspects the purchase rate varies from one time period to another. In both examples, it is then necessary to undertake a continuous series of surveys. The omnibus survey may well be the cheapest and easiest form of research for both. The advantages of cost and organization are more in favour of the omnibus survey although there are the same restrictions as usual on the number and type of questions.

It is important to distinguish two types of fieldwork timing offered by market research companies. Some companies carry out literally continuous interviewing every day, every week, and every month. Other surveys are repeated at given intervals but the interviewing is not evenly spread out over that interval; for example, the interviewing for a monthly omnibus survey may be carried out in the first week of each month. When using omnibus surveys to obtain time series, it is clearly necessary to obtain these details on the timing of fieldwork.

Advantages and Disadvantages

Already a number of advantages and disadvantages have been indicated to the reader. In this section there is a summary of the major advantages and disadvantages of omnibus surveys.

Summary of advantages

The primary advantage to the researcher in the use of an omnibus survey is that within the limitations of the number and complexity of questions, there will be a substantial saving in cost compared with carrying out the survey on an *ad hoc* basis. Another important advantage is that the use of omnibus surveys can often be carried out more quickly. First of all, the work of preparation before undertaking the fieldwork can be considerably reduced since the sampling and fieldwork will have already been organized, unlike an *ad hoc* survey where it is often necessary to begin with a newly designed sample and to make special arrangements for fieldwork. Second, because the survey is usually spread over a number of clients, it is possible to use more interviewers, so reducing the fieldwork time. This is particularly true when a very large sample is required as, in *ad hoc* surveys, interviewing may have to be spread over a long period of time in order to avoid overloading the field-work staff. Third, analysis of results is usually quicker after the survey has finished because a greater degree of automation in the production of results is possible. The saving in time here is probably not very substantial, particularly if the alternative *ad hoc* research company is selected for their ability to produce fast results. Finally, a certain degree of 'bottle-necking' occurs in availability of interviewers for *ad hoc* projects with the result that a researcher may have to wait until there is vacant fieldwork time. With omnibus surveys it is usually possible to commission an immediate survey.

The design of an omnibus survey should be reliable as it will have been used by a substantial number of different companies. Thus, the various aspects of design of the surveys will have been examined critically by a wide number of people. This is particularly useful for the researcher who does not have time to go into the facilities and reliability of a particular research company in detail. This may occur in international research where research is conducted at some distance from the country concerned. In theory, this should be a substantial advantage for the researcher as it is rarely possible for him to examine in great detail the sample design of a particular research company for an *ad hoc* project. However, the author should add in caution that, in his experience, whereas the variation in quality between different omnibus surveys is less than the variation obtained in undertaking an *ad hoc* project, it is not true to say that the omnibus research designs are in general any better. Indeed, there is some evidence that the design of these surveys is less efficient than for some *ad hoc* projects. Omnibus surveys do, to some extent, serve to ensure that the researcher does not undertake a survey using a particularly inferior design although it does not act, as might be hoped, as a guarantee that the research design is more than adequate.

Because the research company is carrying out a continuous series of these omnibus surveys, it is possible for the company to invest a substantial amount in their design, particularly in the areas of sample design. Furthermore, it is possible for the research company to indicate the effect of errors contained within their particular sample design because they will have already carried out a series of tests. Thus, for example, it will probably be possible for an omnibus research company to indicate the clustering of the sample design. This advantage of carrrying out the research on a continuous basis should enable them to improve not only aspects of sampling but also such problems as the production of reports, analysis of results, training of interviewers and so on.

Another advantage of omnibus surveys occurs when a researcher is interested in carrying out multi-national research. Partly because the survey operator is able to invest in the design of his surveys it is simpler to operate a similar service in a number of different countries. It is, therefore, possible to use the omnibus survey approach in different countries, virtually simultaneously, and to obtain results which would be more nearly comparable than if an *ad hoc* survey was undertaken in each individual country.

Summary of disadvantages

The most obvious limitation of the omnibus survey is the number of questions which can be asked on it. First, in order to achieve a cost saving, the number of questions must be restricted or it will be as cheap to undertake a full scale *ad hoc* survey. Second, because the omnibus survey operator is unlikely to allow any one client to dominate a particular questionnaire, there may well be a limitation on the number of questions permitted to one client. Finally, of course, there is a limit to the total length of a questionnaire used by an omnibus operator and this in itself may limit the individual users. A second disadvantage closely associated with this is the inability of the omnibus survey to handle complex questions. Some researchers claim that any question can be asked in a simple form. However, most would agree that there are a number of problems that are best solved with a more complex type of question. In addition, the more complex questions may entail supplementary equipment such as prompt cards and this in itself is usually restricted on an omnibus survey.

Any survey that involves carrying around any substantial quantity of material, such as products for placement or advertisements for testing, may well put a burden on the interviewers which they would be unable to handle. This bars a number of types of research project from using the omnibus survey approach.

Any survey requiring an unusual or specific sample design is not suitable for an omnibus survey as no operator can adapt the sample design for any individual user. Similarly, if a particular target is required the omnibus survey may not be the best way of achieving it. However, in both these cases it is possible that a sub-group of the total omnibus survey will give the required results and it may be cheaper to use an omnibus survey and to discard unnecessary information.

Any other peculiarity in the total survey design that is essential to a particular project may, of course, prohibit its use on an omnibus survey; for example, a survey requiring a series of interviews with the same respondent will be unlikely to be suitable. Requirements for specific fieldwork dates are another example, although some companies will permit questions for part of the fieldwork period.

Although in theory it should be possible to receive as detailed a report and as comprehensive an analysis from an omnibus as from an individual *ad hoc* survey, in general, if such a facility is required, it is probably more advisable to use an *ad hoc* survey. The operators of an omnibus survey do not usually wish to give an extensive analysis service other than the normal forms of analysis which are required for most surveys and they do not usually wish to give a detailed marketing report. Furthermore, the types of executive who operate such surveys are not necessarily the researchers who would be required for a more detailed and extensive analysis of the problem.

Problems to watch

In addition to the disadvantages outlined above, there are a few other problems in the use of omnibus surveys of which the user of this type of research should be aware. One of these is the omnibus survey operator who is offering a service which is not fully operational. Some research companies, in order to set up an omnibus survey on a working basis without initially investing funds in that service, form their first few omnibus surveys by attempting to persuade clients to join before they have finally made it a viable proposition. In some instances this may be the only practical way of getting a survey operational, e.g. an unusual minority group survey. Unfortunately, some research companies do not make it clear whether the omnibus surveys offered are going concerns or of the nature mentioned above. It is, therefore, possible for a researcher to place questions on an omnibus survey which, for various different reasons, never actually takes place. Although the researcher

213

is unlikely to involve himself in any expenditure, it is more than probable that he will have difficulty in maintaining his timetable. The researcher should always enquire from the research company the status of the omnibus survey and, if possible, obtain some guarantee that the survey will take place even if sufficient clients are not forthcoming.

The next problem concerns the sampling frame used by the research company. Particular care should be taken by the researcher to ensure that the sample is as required and no researcher should ever assume that any particular omnibus survey will match his own particular requirements. For some reason, researchers appear to accept research company statements about the design of omnibus surveys far more readily than if they were carrying out an *ad hoc* survey themselves. This may be because they would be unable to change the system even if they found it was unsatisfactory; although, of course, they are always at liberty to move to another omnibus operating company. However, even if the researcher continues to use that omnibus survey it may be possible to make an allowance for differences between what is required and what is actually happening. The researcher, for example, might require adults over the age of 21 whereas the omnibus survey might contain all adults over the age of 15. In this instance, it would be extremely simple for the researcher to deal with the difference but only if he realized that such a difference existed.

Another problem requiring care has already been outlined in some detail previously, i.e. the positioning of the questions within the omnibus question-naire. The researcher should always discuss with the omnibus company ways of overcoming the difficulties of positioning effects of these questions and should ensure that his questions do not suffer from the fact that they are on an omnibus survey. Far too often the research company is left to choose the layout of the questionnaire itself and the result is that in many instances questions are placed in inappropriate places.

One final problem worth mentioning is that, in the experience of the author, a number of omnibus surveys are operated on a less efficient basis than the average *ad hoc* survey, although this is difficult to establish in practice. Exactly why this should be so is difficult to determine, as one would expect that the investment possible on an omnibus survey would enable the many aspects of design, such as sampling, to be more critically examined than in most *ad hoc* surveys. The probable reason for this is that omnibus surveys are still regarded by a number of researchers as a form of cheap research. For some reason they are willing to accept a lower standard of results from such research than from an *ad hoc* survey which would involve a greater expenditure. The majority of research companies operating omnibus surveys will tend to disagree for obvious reasons, although they would probably agree that in *ad hoc* research there is a far greater breadth in the quality of the surveys between the best and the worst than on omnibus research surveys. The research company will correctly point out that it can only operate an omnibus survey on the basis of obtaining a wide range of clients and, therefore, the quality of these

214

surveys is a reflection of the average quality of the requests from their various clients. So long as the researcher recognizes the situation he will have little difficulty in carrying out these surveys. If he is not wary he may well be disappointed in the results.

Other Forms of Syndicated Research

It has been the main purpose of this chapter to consider the omnibus survey where the questionnaire is a combination of smaller questionnaires designed by a variety of different clients and with the total research project being administered and controlled by a research company which sells space on this master questionnaire to the different clients. Two variations should be mentioned. First of all, there are a number of research companies that operate omnibus surveys strictly limited to one particular type of research but still allowing for a variety of clients and a variety of different questionnaires on the same master questionnaire. An example of this is the Advertising Planning Index (API) operated by the British Market Research Bureau. On this survey it is possible for clients to obtain information on brand awareness, attitudes and so on. Each client has questions on the master questionnaire but the questions are of a standard form and designed by the research company so that the whole questionnaire follows a consistent pattern. In some instances it is possible to add a few additional questions on these question- naires in exactly the same way as for an ordinary omnibus survey. Since this is designed for a specific purpose the number of additional questions is limited. The second type of syndicated research occurs when a research company carries out a survey and sells the results, either in part or in its entirety, to a number of different clients. An example of this is the consumer panel. This type of syndicated research is covered elsewhere in this book and except in certain specialized areas it is not common practice for a research company to carry out its own research project and then sell the results to a number of different clients.

Examples of Existing Services

It is difficult to present a practical list of omnibus surveys currently in existence. Companies operating such services are continually changing and as many as four or five companies come into existence each year and an equal number drop out. Furthermore, companies change, from time to time, aspects of the design of these surveys such as the sample design or the coverage. Despite these difficulties, it is felt useful to give some indication of the companies operating this type of service.

Table 9.1 below indicates the current situation with regard to service being offered by companies in Britain. This has been made as comprehensive a list

Table 9.1 *Examples of UK omnibus surveys*

Name of company	Sample size	Coverage	Type of sample	Cost standard unit	Frequency
British Market Research Bureau	1000	Adults, 15+, national	Random walk	£385	Weekly
Gallup Poll	1000	Adults, 16+, national	Quota	£530	Weekly
MAS Survey Research Ltd.	2400	Adults, 16+, national	Random	£1200	Weekly
NOP Market Research	2000	Adults, 15+, national	Random	£1100	Weekly
Research Surveys of GB	2000	Adults, 16+, national	Random location	£890	Weekly

as possible of surveys based on samples of the total adult population. It is strongly recommended that the reader checks the individual facts with the research companies for himself. With regard to costs, the expenditure clearly depends on the type of questions demanded by the researcher. In order to get some meaningful comparison on costs, a standard questionnaire was designed which involves the following (based on total adult population as far as the survey would permit):

(a) three pre-coded questions using one column of punch card;
(b) two open-ended questions using two columns of punch card;
(c) standard analysis and report.

It has already been mentioned earlier in this chapter that a valuable use of an omnibus survey is in the commissioning of international market research.

Table 9.2 *Examples of omnibus surveys in different countries*

Country	Research company	Sample size	Type of sample	Total £
Australia	Roy Morgan Research Centre	1100	Random	870
Austria	GFK + Fessel	2000	Random	2356
Canada	CanadianFacts Co Ltd	3150	Random	5000
Denmark	AIM Markedsanalyse	2400	Random	808
Finland	Suemen Gallup	2000	Random	1159
France	Sofres	2000	Random	2351
Germany	GFK	2000	Quota	1839
Greece	Institute for Research & Communication	2400	Quota	537
Holland	Nederlandse Stichting Voor Statistiek	2400	Random	2291
Italy	Demoskopea	2000	Quota	1106
New Zealand	Research Marketing Services Ltd	2000	Quota	1429
Norway	Norsk Gallup	1600	Random	1021
Spain	Instituto ECO	3000	Random	1185
Sweden	IMU	2000	Random	1747
Switzerland	AES	2000	Quota	2584
USA	Gallup	3000	Random	2248

It would clearly be impossible to give as comprehensive a list for the whole world as had been attempted for the UK above; but in order to give an indication of the scope and possibilities of such surveys, an example is given in Table 9.2 of one omnibus survey operator, in several countries, with a similar cost estimate to that given for the UK companies above. It should be emphasized that this does not in any way indicate approval for these particular research companies, nor does it imply that there are not other equally, if not more, appropriate omnibus research companies in each country.

10. Telephone, mail and other techniques

Leonard England

Of the chapters in this section of the book, the majority are basically concerned with forms of market research which imply personal confrontation of interviewer and respondent. It is probably impossible ever to estimate the proportion of all consumer market research carried out in this way, either by volume or by number of contacts, but an estimate of 75–85% (cost or volume) seems reasonable enough. What is more, changing and developing techniques are unlikely to alter this proportion to any dramatic extent in the years to come in Great Britain, although in the USA, Canada, Australia and New Zealand a trend towards telephone interviewing (especially by WATS line) has developed over the last few years.

Most of the research which does not involve the direct interview is, in fact, related to measurement of television viewing by means of meters (chapter 25) or the auditing of shops by various forms of counts (chapter 8). Over a very wide range of problems, however, there are occasions when standard forms of interviewing become inappropriate. This chapter is concerned with such occasions.

In general terms three such situations call for the use of techniques other than standard interviews. The *first* of these operates when those to be interviewed are likely to be acutely difficult to contact, probably because each person of relevance to the survey is a long way away from all the others, possibly because a large number of interviews are required almost simultaneously. In these instances use is likely to be made of:

(a) telephone surveys;
(b) mail surveys.

These approaches also come into their own when the universes concerned are ideally suited to this form of approach, e.g. surveys on current subscribers for telephone companies or surveys on known users of direct mail.

218

The *second* situation occurs when surveys involve the co-operation of respondents over a long period of time or when the interviewer is unable to be present for the whole of the interview time. The need here is for:

(c) self-completion questionnaires.

The *third* area operates when it is thought likely that standard techniques will fail to uncover the basic reasons involved in decision making. In many cases (see chapter 2) qualitative work will mean that any questionnaire developed will allow useful and relevant answers to emerge rather than those

Table 10.1.

Method	Some Uses	Some Advantages	Some Disadvantages
(a) Telephone	(i) When simultaneous interviews needed (ii) When individual calls are very far apart	Cost Speed	Lack of rapport Interviews must be fairly short Cannot use show cards, pictures Low incidence of telephone ownership
(b) Mail	When respondents are difficult to contact	Cost No interviewer "interference"	Unrepresentative sample Lack of control of questionnaire completion
(c) Self-completion	When interview should be completed but interviewer cannot be present	Cost Accuracy of reporting close to action reported	As with mail surveys (e.g. misunderstanding bias; only short questionnaire possible)
(d)(i) Psycho galvanometer	When respondent unlikely to be aware of own responses	Prestige and similar answers need not be considered	Unreal surroundings Little data about why Cost of large samples
(ii) Tachistoscope etc.	To test detailed physical behaviour, particularly of eye reaction	Ability to measure action in a detail not available by other methods	Unreal surroundings Little data about why Cost of large samples
(e) Count	When requirement implies total numbers of people involved in certain actions	Cost Speed Large samples	Little data about 'why' No analysis possible by profile of individual
(f) Observation	When the concern is more with *how* people act than *why*	Direct observation of what people do rather than what they *say* they do	Cost Sample structure
(g) Participant observation	When only information at a very detailed level is of value	Depth of response	Very high cost and very long time taken Problems of representative sample

which are superficial and 'unexpected'. There are, however, occasions when respondents themselves have, perhaps, no idea of what they do let alone why they do it: or where they are unable to report accurately how they order a pint of beer, how long it takes them to cross a road or why they buy brand X rather than brand Y and so on. For these occasions the following techniques might need to be considered:

(d) the use of ironmongery;
(e) counts;
(f) observation;
(g) anthropological participation.

These seven techniques each have a section to themselves, but the sections differ considerably in length, with by far the greatest attention being paid to mail surveys. These are far more widely used than any of the other approaches and are probably growing in popularity (as are telephone surveys) although they are of far *less* importance than a study of technical literature would imply. Experimental work of any kind involving face-to-face interviews is very expensive, even when respondents are 'captive' such as other students of the same universities. But mail surveys involving change of questionnaire length, change of words, change of incentives and so on are ideal for simple (and often extremely valuable) theses or papers. Because so many of these exist, there is a real danger of ignoring the fundamental weaknesses in the technique which can very rarely be overcome.

Table 10.1 summarizes very briefly disadvantages not merely for postal surveys but also for all other techniques considered in this chapter: but it shows too the main uses to which each technique can be put and the main advantages which they are generally assumed to have. In a final section some general comments are made on the value of, and the problems involved in, techniques other than direct interviewer–respondent confrontation.

(a) Telephone Surveys

No researcher training can be complete without the classic story of one of the earliest of all surveys, carried out to predict the results of the American presidential elections. The survey was conducted by telephone only, the sponsors being unaware that those with telephones were richer and more likely to vote Republican. The result was wildly wrong; yet personal interviews carried out at the same time by another organization showed how clearly opinion polls could predict voting patterns.

By now, nearly everyone in the USA has a telephone, but the proportion in Great Britain is still no higher than 40%, thus clearly precluding their use for any form of survey involving a cross-section of the whole population or for groups other than those for which there is reason to suppose that telephone ownership is almost universal. If this were the only problem, it is true that almost all interviews with executives or professional people *could* be carried out by telephone; it could also be used with groups for whom a telephone is essential, e.g. builders, individual car hire operators and so on.

There are, however, further problems with telephone interviews. Whether or not more useful results are produced, it is a fact of modern research that there is an increasing use of aids—pictures of mastheads of papers, illustrations of advertisements, lists of scales or words to choose from and so on. No technique involving aids can be used on the telephone, and to send the aids through the post in advance, as is sometimes suggested, inevitably raises an unknown degree of bias because of the advance knowledge provided in the respondent.

More important than either of these limitations is the difficulty of establishing rapport through a telephone. Those likely to be available for telephone interviews are also those most likely to need to be reassured as to the credentials of the interviewer, the purpose of the survey and so on; the interviews which finally emerge may be of the highest quality but only if the respondents are first satisfied on points such as these. It is true here that a letter can provide advance warning and explanation and a pre-arranged time for the call can be made, but even this provides far less rapport than that of a responsible interviewer fully briefed to explain the purpose of the survey and the importance of the respondent's personal contribution.

When all this is said, it remains true that the telephone interview plays a major part—and probably one of increasing importance—in the researcher's armoury. We are not concerned in this book with industrial research, but in the consumer field there are many surveys which involve interviews with those almost certain to be on the telephone but equally likely to be hard to contact personally—owners of expensive cars, of deep freezers, readers of business papers, users of credit cards and so on. Lists selected from clients' records would probably provide the framework of the survey, but even with a car and by making prior appointments an interviewer would usually be hard put to it to do more than two such interviews an evening. If a great deal of data is required, then the costs involved in personal contact are worthwhile. What happens, however, if one's only concern is a comparatively simple piece of information? Do they belong to one particular professional group? Can they remember the context of a commercial recently shown on television? Have they had particular forms of trouble with their car? And indeed the cost differential becomes even more dramatic when a before-and-after interview may be involved in order to assess changing views as a result of an advertisement and two such calls are necessary.

There are refinements and rather more special uses of this approach. While in general simultaneous recall techniques never seem to have found much favour, the telephone is ideally suited (again, if the nature of the sample to be interviewed justifies it) for calls immediately after a television program or related to an evening newspaper advertisement where it is essential to check recall within a given period after exposure, and where a large number of calls must be done in a short time. Probably even more important, as with many other techniques discussed in this chapter, is the use of the telephone interview *in conjunction with* the personal interview. It might, for example, be sensible to ask a few extra questions *after* a launch to those selected from a pre-launch survey as the most likely users. These additional questions can be asked by telephone to all recorded originally as having the use of a telephone; other interviews would have to be carried out personally.

It is the writer's contention that telephone surveys by their nature can never be as efficient as the personal interview; even with coincidental recall the theoretically correct solution must be to use a very large number of interviewers for a very short time. But two points must be set against this.

The first is that very many steps have recently been taken to improve the quality of telephone interviewing, efforts which have been assisted partly by the involvement of able researchers[1] and partly by the steady increase in the proportion of the population able to be reached by telephone. The second is that, in practical terms, the cost differential is sometimes so great and the efficiency loss so small that telephone interviewing may well become a perfectly reasonable solution. On certain types of interviewing with small minority sample, for example, personal interviews might well cost £20.00 to £30.00 each, while telephone calls could cost only £4.00 to £5.00. If 200 or 300 such interviews are required, then the use of the telephone becomes almost inevitable.

(b) Mail Surveys

It has already been noted that mail surveys generate a disproportionate amount of technical comment, at least in part, because they are easy and cheap to use as the basis of experiment. For the same reason they seem always to be the amateur's first do-it-yourself approach to market research. 'Let's do our own survey' almost always develops into home-made questions circulated for postal reply. Inevitably such an approach usually produces results that are not merely irrelevant but also dangerous; for postal surveys very easily provide misleading results if the questions are ambiguous or if those who reply are not a true cross-section of the target market.

There remain, of course, many right reasons for carrying out mail surveys. The *first* of these is the simple one that there may be no other method of carrying out a survey economically. To contact all those who have bought waste-disposal units or invalid chairs in the last month would imply a survey of a cost which no manufacturer is likely to be able to contemplate. But a properly organized, professionally controlled survey can provide a good deal of relevant data at a reasonable price. To take a quite different example, to interview people leaving a theatre is a very complex problem, for all interviewing has to be jammed into ten or 15 minutes: to leave questionnaires in programs ensures a larger, if not disinterested, sample.

An outstanding example of the success of a survey carried out by post which would be too expensive by other means is the regular 'Target Group Index' run by the British Market Research Bureau[2]. Technically, perhaps, this can be counted as a self-completion questionnaire (considered in the next sub-section) since the postal questionnaire is prefaced by a personal visit from an interviewer. But when the 'briefing' is completed, respondents are asked to provide broad details of their buying habits about some 350 different products. And they do. Personal interviewing time is, in consequence, cut to a fraction.

The second instance when it is right to use mail occurs when the sample is, by its nature, involved in using mail; in consequence, a postal questionnaire is the natural means to carry out a survey. A study, for example, amongst members of a book club, used to filling in a monthly questionnaire to state which books they required, or among those who have recently completed a quiz-type competition, would best be done by post, for people would answer in their own time and in their own way. Were interviewers to call, their sample might not even be as good because these people could well contain a disproportionate number of those acutely difficult to contact by normal means, living either in inaccessible points or in communities.

The third reason for using mail is related to the questionnaire itself. Most questions asked in interviews expect an off-the-cuff reply: detail is usually obtained by means of a whole series of subsidiary questions rather than by obtaining a more lengthy considered reply. But there are studies better done if the respondent has plenty of time either to think out the answers he intends to give (If you had £100 to spend on your garden, how would you spend it?) or to work out detailed answers (Where did you go on holiday in each of the last ten years; or buying habits in the TGI detail referred to above).

General approach

The whole approach to mail surveys must, of course, be as closely geared to the potential respondent as is the case with any other type of survey: at its crudest, either with post or personal interviews, the busy housewife must somehow be pushed to answer even a small number of questions, although the enthusiast talking about his hobby may, with great pleasure, answer a 20-page questionnaire. But just as the financial advantage of a postal survey is the absence of the face-to-face interview, so its technical disadvantage is that the respondent is faced not with somebody helping, cajoling, co-operating in interview completion but with a questionnaire which can be filled in tomorrow just as well as today. The art of a good postal survey is to humanize it as much as possible to show that even if real people are not delivering it they have at least written and are concerned whether you reply or not.

Wherever possible, therefore, postal questionnaires should be accompanied by a personal indication of concern—ideally personally addressed to an individual, certainly signed by an individual from the company concerned. Follow-up reminder letters, probably becoming more and more personal and friendly, also serve this purpose.

So, of course, do incentives, the area covered by so much experimentation. What happens if one sends personally stamped envelopes instead of reply paid? if one adds a ballpoint or a postal order? if one offers a small lottery prize? or a large one? All extras are effective, providing higher response rates, though final effectiveness is likely to be governed more by other factors such as general interest in the subject of the study or length and comprehensibility of the questionnaire. But all incentives are, in any case, a reflection of care and concern: anything which shows that the agency sending the questionnaire realizes that it is going to a human being is likely to increase the likelihood of reply.

It is clearly impossible in a few pages to describe the techniques involved in coping with mail surveys—indeed, one of the standard books on mail surveys is almost as long as the present volume[3]. What is vital, at all stages of administration, is to keep a tight control on speed and nature of return, methods of sending reminder letters while continuing to show concern for the confidentiality of reply (if this is necessary), checking whether the 'right' person is replying—often within the household an unexpected or irrelevant member may reply.

The sample

The greater the care the greater the likely response rate. Clearly this is vital for reasons already mentioned, the permanent worry that those who do not answer are different in kind from those who do. And while a *prima facie* case may be made out for assuming a representative sample has been obtained when those returned reflect those despatched on known data (e.g. ratio of men to women) this does not alter the basic worry that they may not do so on the essentials of the survey—usually that of interest in the subject covered.

Very high success rates can be obtained either when one is dealing with enthusiasts (such as owners of new cars) or when all the processes concerning control of the survey are applied very rigorously—the Government Social Survey have many examples of such successes[4]. Given that these *are* achieved, then a major advantage of postal interviewing—selective sampling—can be fully utilized. In most personal interviews a *representative* sample of the population is selected either because the geographical scatter of specialist groups makes interviewing only such people prohibitively expensive, or because at the beginning of the survey there is no means of defining use or interest. Postal surveys are more likely to begin with lists, the very existence of which define respondents. And it is, of course, just as cheap to send out 1000 questionnaires to 1000 towns as it is to send them out all to one square mile.

It is possible, in consequence, to concentrate on sections of the potential which would repay special study. A survey on mail order buying, for example, might involve 500 customers: a random selection would, perhaps, provide 300 buying once every year, 150 buying once every three months and 50 buying every month—in other words, most replies would be from irregular buyers, whereas clearly the views of the heavy spenders are of greatest interest. A postal survey can 'over-weight' the heavy spender by making sure that half the interviews are sent out to monthly spenders, a quarter each to less relevant, less frequent groups. Computer weighting can bring figures back to a representative sample but the most vital group is no longer based on very small numbers.

This is a technique which is of particular relevance in follow-up surveys where postal questionnaires are used either in series on the same people or to gain further data from those already personally interviewed once. Here a very full office study can be made to decide on those people of particular inter-est—and the right people can be selected rather than those financially most convenient.

The questionnaire

But with postal surveys—indeed, as with any survey—value ultimately depends on the extent to which questions asked can provide the data required. And there are in postal surveys a whole series of problems not shared by personal interviewing. In particular, these are:

length
intelligibility
bias

It is probably true that most personal interviews are longer than they should be, but whether or not this is the case there is little difficulty, with a well laid out questionnaire and a well trained interviewer, of going through 15-20 pages of questions. It *is* possible too with postal surveys, especially with specialized interested groups (such as readers of 'Which?' or people discussing their main hobby). But the problem becomes a far more complex one to persuade the respondent to go on and on.

Much can be done to this end by making the pages interesting and the com-pletion of questions more of a game. Cartoons and drawings can help, as can changes of typeface. But probably more important than any of this is the need for an *obvious* sense of purpose. Why am I being asked this question? What is the point of all these stupid additions?

One aspect of 'intelligibility'—the second important consideration in a postal questionnaire—is precisely to explain why questions are being asked and why answers are important. But it is much more than this. The routing of any questionnaire is complex (see chapter 6), increasingly so when the person who answers has none of the experience of such problems gained by the trained interviewer, and cannot be assumed to understand instructions of the kind 'Answer Q.5(b) unless you have said "No" to Q.3(b)'. Lay-out again can help greatly but cannot get rid of the problem.

Perhaps even more important within the framework of intelligibility is the question of semantics. A good interviewer will automatically probe to discover how the respondent is interpreting such words as 'room' or 'week' (indeed, such words should probably not occur in a good questionnaire anyway) or what is meant by 'company director' or 'frequently'. But this form of probing cannot be done in a postal questionnaire. Piloting becomes increasingly important—and yet, because the questionnaire must *look* simple, many, both clients and practitioners, assume that it *is* simple and do not bother.

A covering letter explaining the reasons and purposes of the questionnaire is usually a very great help, and can indeed explain certain inherent problems within the main document. But this too, of course, must not merely be human (never 'Dear Sir or Madam') but must also be intelligible.

To explain is in itself sometimes to create bias—the third, and perhaps the most intractable of the problems of postal questionnaires. The essential difficulty here is caused by the fact that with a postal questionnaire the respondent may answer questions in any order he cares to, and certainly is likely to have read the whole of the questionnaire before he begins to answer it at all. Now it is often vital in a personal questionnaire that the respondent begins by answering in general terms—which is your favourite washing powder?—before the main concern of the survey becomes obvious—what do you think of Persil? Once she knows of the interest in Persil, the housewife's objections and biasses could well overload all parts of the survey. In personal interviews this can be avoided: in postal surveys it cannot. Nor without very acute difficulty can any form of rotation be applied to lists of attributes, brands, etc., to prevent top names being more frequently chosen.

For precisely the same reason it is impossible to ask—at least in this simple form—any questions such as 'What brands of paint have you ever heard of?' Between reading the questionnaire and answering it, a period of anything from a few hours to a few weeks, the respondent will be conscious of brands of paint, will be more aware (but to an unknown degree) of commercials, press advertisements, posters, even shop displays: even brands *used* are likely to be increased as memory is jarred—or simply as other members of the family are asked to add their memories to make the questionnaire a joint effort.

The essentials in mail surveys

Maximum involvement and maximum value from a postal questionnaire can probably be gained by use of these principles[5]:

> rouse curiosity;
> make importance clear;
> make relevance *to the respondent* clear;
> be easy to understand;
> be interesting;
> be easy to complete;
> be easy to return.

But with all this it must be clearly understood that answers from a postal questionnaire are different in kind from those of a personal interview—less

226

spontaneous, more considered, less affected by the involvement of a third person, more likely (however high the response rate) to over-emphasize the interested. None of these points necessarily vitiates or even devalues answers given—indeed, it has been shown above that while, for example, time taken to think can vitiate replies to some types of questions (Name as many brands as you can think of) it adds value to others (How would you spend £100 on . . .?). But they do make it important to realize that the variations which do exist imply that the answers given are not always measuring the same thing in postal surveys as in personal ones.

(c) Self-Completion Questionnaires

All mail surveys are, of course, self-completion questionnaires. Reference should also be made, however, to other forms, particularly to the fact that self-completion questionnaires can be of considerable value *in conjunction with* standard interviewer studies as part of what is, in effect, one questionnaire. In these circumstances they are not usually sent by post but left by the interviewer.

This is particularly the case in product tests. In some cases, the test can be made on the spot; in others it does not matter a great deal if comments are not collected until the interviewer returns to obtain views on the product. There is an intermediate group of cases, however, when the *immediate* reaction of the housewife, and perhaps also of her family, is of considerable importance. As examples of this we may cite:

(a) a cough mixture left with people to take when they got a cough. Although those taking part were asked to contact the market research company as soon as the cough developed to arrange a personal interview, some report on the immediate interchange of cough and remedy seemed essential and this was done by means of a form left with the respondent.

(b) a new product which involved unfamiliar cooking patterns. When the housewife was in the process of making it, it was essential that she should also make a note of snags which she encountered, the immediate results and the immediate comments of the family.

(c) a paired comparison test of two cigarettes. To do the test while the interviewer waited would make it most unreal. To leave it to the respondent in his own time was far more realistic provided that he was sure to record what his feelings were at the time rather than recalling them at a later stage.

An alternative approach involves the self-completion questionnaire as a form of *aide-memoire*. Development of new products may be assisted by knowledge of how current products are used in a detail for which memory may be dangerous except over very short periods. A new form of instant coffee, for example, may depend for its success on how many cups are made at any one time, or a new baby food on whether the mother usually prepares food for the baby at the same time as food for adult members of the household. Recording of this kind is, of course, close to the diary panels considered in chapter 8, but there is no need for a panel to be involved, the respondent being asked to co-operate only in a single study.

This approach is also of value on occasions where respondents would be *able* to tell the interviewer their answers but might be somewhat embarrassed to do so. Probably this is less important today than it was even ten years ago, e.g. on a recent survey a few sudden questions on brands of contraceptives used appeared to cause very little problem even though both interviewers and respondents were specifically told to omit these if they wished. On the other hand, answers thought to be *socially unacceptable*, e.g. strong approval of South African apartheid policies, could well be expressed by some people more forcibly on a piece of paper than to a total stranger.

Self-completion interviews of the kinds so far considered assume completion in the home. A separate use of the same technique is involved when self-completion means mass-completion. The most obvious instance of this is that of theatre tests when a representative sample is invited to see a series of films interspersed by commercials. At various stages in the performance the audience is invited to answer questions usually about the products concerned in the advertisements. Which would they buy? What do they see as particular advantages and disadvantages of each?

Questionnaires are distributed for self-completion primarily because of the expense and time involved in the simultaneous personal interviewing of all people in a theatre, but in consequence the approach suffers from most of the same limitations as any other form of self-completion and mail question-naire. It does, however, have one major advantage over other forms. In the course of an evening, respondents may well fill in half a dozen *separate* simple questionnaires. However, they have filled in the first ones unaware of what is to follow. This removes the bias which sometimes can exist in any form of self-completion survey caused by respondents knowing in advance what further questions he is likely to be asked.

(d) Ironmongery

In the techniques so far considered, the main variations from the standard interview approach are in the *method* of data collection rather than in what is collected. Whether the interview is asked personally, or left for the respondent to fill in, or posted, or asked over the telephone, the question-and-answer approach applies, and the information collected is recorded and coded in a standard form. For the techniques now to be discussed in this chapter, this no longer applies; the interviewer is no longer a recorder of what is said, the respondent is no longer necessarily expected to provide in words or writing what she is doing and saying and thinking. Actions are now speaking rather than words. Hardware and counts and observation imply the use of an interviewer to report what is happening; they watch, they do not ask.

In operations of this kind, much help can be given by the use of mechanical equipment; indeed, in some instances such equipment can, in fact, provide data which could not be obtained in any other way. Almost without exception, however, apart from the use of television meters*, such 'hardware' has been found to have only limited uses in market research and the last five years have probably witnessed no new gadgetry of even passing importance. A description of how some current machinery works may in itself indicate the reason for the limitations.

We must include in this category the *camera*. On occasions this may be used only to provide still photographs, e.g. for use in a survey covering a representative sample of kitchens to discover the extent to which there was room in them (if necessary after rearrangement) to add extra durable goods. It is more likely, however, to be a moving record. One case using this technique was carried out by the London Transport Executive[6]. The object of the study was to assess the proportion of the population given the opportunity to view posters on bus sides. On special buses following randomly selected standard routes, cameras were placed above the advertisement used as a test. By replaying the film thus made available it was possible to analyse in part the nature of the potential audience (defined as those passing the bus and at least part facing it) and from this to make deductions as to the total audience.

Such a survey naturally cannot be concerned in any way with whether respondents did see the advertisement concerned, only with whether they had the *opportunity*. Much of the equipment devised is more specifically concerned with what the eye does, in fact, see and what it passes to the brain. For a year or so in the early 1960's work with special equipment was carried out on subliminal advertising and the effect of messages displayed too fast for the eye apparently to see but yet probably absorbed; and at a later stage there was a belief that data as to the state of mind of a purchaser in a supermarket could be disclosed by recording the 'blink rate'. A concealed special camera recorded the speed at which the shopper blinked; the slower the blink rate the more 'hypnotized' by choice she was said to be, the more open to suggestion. A separate technique widely discussed a few years ago involved pupil dilation, the average percentage change in this being assumed to measure the degree of interest in the advertisement or display being studied[7]. On another study—this time not involving a camera—fingerprints were recorded to test

---

* Although audience measurement devices are of the same kind as those considered in this section, they are the subject of separate discussion in chapter 25. It is perhaps relevant to point out, however, one basic argument against such machines is very similar to that considered here; the fact that the television is on is recorded by the meter, but this on its own tells us nothing about who is in the room and whether, in fact, they are watching.

page traffic on a magazine. All these 'machines' are now generally discredited.

The *psychogalvanometer* remains with us and has been used far more[8]. The respondent watches television or reads copy, 'wired' by means of small suction cap electrodes fitted to the back of his hand. These are connected to a machine recording sweat variations. Precise nervous reactions are thus recorded to what he is seeing. As with many other techniques considered in this chapter, the main objection is the question of what any reaction means. In certain cases, it must be admitted, tape recording provides *in parallel* what the respondent is saying as his reactions are being recorded on the psychogalvanometer, but this again does not necessarily mean that the respondent will behave in a predictable way in a subsequent behavioural situation.

The *tachistoscope*[8] is far more widely accepted although it is probably far less used than five or ten years ago. This machine tests to calibrations of one hundreth of a second the reaction of a respondent to what he sees though a shutter; it may be a test of the comparative legibility of pack or label design or the extent to which one pack stands out against all its competitors, or the *part* of the advertisement which is most likely to be seen first. A simple tachistoscope measures a single stimulus at a time, but further developments with stereoscope or binocular models allow the exposure of two stimuli simultaneously with independent and variable light densities and, at the same time, allow tests to be made on eye dominance. Other things being equal, it is assumed that the name or the display which is recognized in the fastest time is the most likely to be successful. However, other things rarely are equal, of course, and there is a good deal of evidence that the most effective advertisement is the one which is less likely to be seen immediately but is studied in detail when it is. Used side by side with other techniques, however, the tachistoscope can be of considerable importance.

All these techniques are, in fact, best used in conjunction with direct interviewing. A rather newer form of eye camera can *only* be used in such conjunction by a procedure known as DEMOS[9]. This springs from the need to be able to relate what is remembered in advertisements to what has definitely been seen. Is complete lack of recall of an advertisement due to the fact that the respondent has not, in fact, seen it all, her eye having completely overlooked the page; or has she seen it and found it so totally uninteresting that she has no recollection of having seen it? By means of an ingenious lay-out of mirrors and camera the respondent is watched unobserved as she turns the pages of a magazine, and a record is made of the time she has taken page by page, and area by area. A later questionnaire considers her recall of advertisements and relates this to what she has seen and how long she has spent reading it. This is a case where mechanical aids are used to assist the interviewing technique rather than to replace it. There are other forms of hardware with much the same purpose, and in the foreseeable future portable video machines or cassettes may be attached to television sets to allow this kind of advertising testing to be carried out in the more realistic surroundings of the respondent's own home. There are already, however, other useful aids of this kind; to take one example, the purchase of any major item—a car, a house—involves the consideration of a number of factors on which the buyer must place varying stress to keep within his budget. He is unlikely, for example, to be able to afford a house which meets all his requirements, or even most of them. What 'premium' does he place on the number of rooms, or nearness to the shops, or proximity of other houses? In market research terms it is usual that one ranks such attributes in order of importance but can rarely force the respondent into a position where he can put a cash value on what he has chosen.

Gerald Hoinville[10] has developed an appliance which in some ways resembles the children's general knowledge game where plugs connected to the right answer to a question bring on a light. In the market research context, within a box are illustrated a series of different attributes which people might bear in mind when buying, say, a house. Against each there is a price. The respondent is given pegs to represent money which he can use, as he likes, to 'buy' advantages. What he has bought lights up, the other attributes remain dark. What is important about this technique is that it reveals to the respondent that his willingness to 'buy', for example, garage space and a corner site may mean that he has no money left to ensure nearness to a bus route or that he is not overlooked. The technique at the moment is a crude one, but is useful as an illustration of a way in which, in the future, hardware may develop as an aid to interviewing rather than as a replacement.

(e) Counts

Between the use of mechanical equipment and of observation lies the simple count. 'Simple' is, perhaps, a misnomer if the count technique is assumed (as is technically possible) to embrace almost all forms of audience meter recording and retail audits. Occasions exist, however, when a count carried out by interviewers can provide more useful data than an actual interview.

At the beginning of the Second World War civilians were supposed to carry their gas-masks wherever they went[11]. These were, however, cumbersome and most people chose to forget them. On certain occasions it was noticed that the proportions carrying them seemed to rise sharply, and a study of the news on the progress of the war revealed what appeared to be a consistent relationship between the proportions carrying gas-masks and the state of general morale. Counts were consistently carried out to assess morale until such time as the fear of gas attack so abated that few people carried masks on any occasions at all. This technique could not be validated since direct questioning (at a time when it might have been thought unpatriotic to be depressed) revealed that the stated comments of the general public showed a far closer relationship to the official attitude of 'do or die'. In more recent applications, however, the same technique has been used in a number of projects to provide data difficult to collect in other ways; to take one example, operational research has apparently established that pedestrian subways will not generally be used when the time taken to travel through the subway is markedly longer than that taken above ground. It is highly doubtful, however, if people consciously realize this fact, and certainly they would not have been able to answer with any precision before a particular subway was built. Simple timing of road-crossing under laboratory conditions were meaningless when little was known about traffic flows or the difference in speed of crossing at different times of day.

An unpublished survey of this kind was conducted with the traffic entering and leaving one of London's main railway stations. Brief interviews first established the proportions likely to be crossing given roads where subways were planned, and preliminary counts checked the numbers crossing such roads at various times of the day. Then, using a random selection technique and stopwatch, interviewers timed pedestrians from the moment they *reached* the curb they planned to step off to the moment they were able to *step on to* the opposite one. Average times were calculated and it became apparent that subways costing many thousands of pounds would be unlikely to be used at least for some years to come; for the most part people did not have to wait long enough to make them likely to go down one flight of steps and up the other.

Counts can also establish data which would, again, not be forthcoming from direct questioning because of difficulties of obtaining either correct samples or answers unaffected by memory or fear of consequences of reply. The 'dustbin audit' of AGB described in chapter 8 is one such example. In similar vein, however, it is possible to estimate the extent of all-day parking in meter areas by checking registration numbers of cars either remaining on one meter (with the meter being fed) or moving very short distances. It is a simple matter on the computer if regular counts are held through the day to record the time at which a car enters the area and the time at which it leaves it, and by so doing to calculate the extent to which meters are used by all-day parkers. Direct questioning presents alternative problems.

Counts suffer from the same problems as many other techniques described in this chapter: they record but they do not explain. There are many cases, however, where accurate reporting is all that is, in fact, required and where direct interviewing will not provide such clear data.

(f) Observation

The research use of investigator observation was made widely known in this country as a result of work before the war by Mass-Observation: basically its founders, Tom Harrison and Charles Madge[11] argued that there were very many areas of knowledge in which people would not answer correctly, either because they did not know the correct reply or because they would be unwilling to tell from embarrassment or from various reasons of prestige.

In the 30 or so years since the founding of Mass-Observation many arguments have weakened the original thesis. Their early work was epitomized by vivid descriptions of public events such as wrestling matches and election meetings or of private and family matters, but these are now covered more simply, if not more efficiently, by the use of documentary film, particularly in television. Techniques of asking questions have improved and extended, and in parallel with this the principle of the question-and-answer survey has become more widely accepted; respondents are thus less reticent in revealing intimate information or that which is difficult to collect, and motivation research has helped to define in what areas questions are appropriate. A recent study by an anthropologist, for example, provided vivid and important data on class variations in food habits, including the significance of liquid content and of the shape of the foods most often served. The technique used to obtain this material involved observation over a period of months at all meals within individual families. Before the last 20 years or so such an elaborate research procedure would almost certainly have been necessary: but it is very difficult to believe that in the 1970's a carefully constructed questionnaire would not have provided the same data at one tenth of the cost. Nevertheless, the need for observation remains. Observation has been described[12] as a primary tool of social enquiry which becomes a scientific technique when it:

(a) serves a formulated research purpose;
(b) is planned systematically;
(c) is recorded systematically and related to general propositions;
(d) is subject to checks and controls on validity and reliability.

In the intense forms of the technique, which are mainly anthropologically inspired, there are a separate set of problems discussed later. Simpler techniques, however, are now gaining wide favour again. Many recent developments, for example, involve a skilled investigator watching some simple household process to find areas for new product development. At what stage, for example, in her cleaning routine does the housewife find something difficult to clean with which a new gadget might help[13]? Are there new products which the housewife could use as instant or convenience foods which would help her with her regular meals? This can be expanded widely in many areas. No housewife could probably tell exactly how much salt or cornflour she uses in simple recipes and she would be unlikely even to admit that she often guessed; certainly, for whatever reasons, estimates from direct questionnaires are almost always very inflated. Observation, however, particularly when its main purpose is masked, can provide better data on how the housewife acts.

Few beer drinkers would know in exactly what terms they asked for their beer—they would *think* or *report* that they said 'Half a light ale, please', when what they probably said was 'The same again, Fred'. Nor would they always know the extent to which what they had ordered was, in fact, supplied. Do they get the same in all pubs, for example, when they ask for a 'pint of the best' or 'half of keg'? To brewers this is vital in terms of advertising copy and in the extent to which criticism of their product perhaps springs from the wrong product being provided by the barman.

Observation techniques are also of use in studying more detailed behaviourist patterns. A recent study[14], for example, related the actual driving of motorists to their driving personalities assessed by a series of psychological questions. The driving assessment involved three observers taking drivers on a standard test route, one in the front giving instructions as to where the driver was to go, two in the back recording handling of gears and clutch, use of side mirrors, number of times the car concerned overtook or was overtaken and so on. The driver knew that he was being studied but the system was so simple and the observers so well concealed that it seemed almost certain that after the first few minutes driving behaviour became normal.

There remain two basic problems about all observation work. The first is that the cost involved, not only in observation but in writing up and training, usually implies limited regional areas or small sample bases, and the critics can, in consequence, always fault it on the grounds that what has been found out would not apply elsewhere. Most of the early work done by Mass-Observation, for example, concentrated on studying one Lancashire town in great detail, and even though a few further towns were studied with less concentration there is little evidence available to indicate that what emerged from one town was true even for another ten miles away, let alone for another part of the country.

It is also true (although not for participant observation) that studies can only report on what happens and draw conclusions from this, excluding the 'why's' of what is done. Sometimes these speak for themselves, like the elaborate treating rituals found in many pubs whereby all those involved in groups find themselves, at the end of the evening, having paid out the same sums; but others are open to a series of different interpretations. Work was carried out, for example, on the selection of books from public libraries. People were observed at a distance; details including the extent to which they read titles, looked at books, the parts of the book which they looked at and so on were noted. What did it mean if a person picked up a book, looked at the cover, read the last page and put it down again? That he had read it already? That it had an unhappy ending? That there were too many long words or too many pages? All these interpretations were possible, none could be accepted as definitive; and probably the reader, even if he had been asked, would not have been able to unscramble his motives.

One must also stress that these forms of observation require training and that few interviewers, however skilled at questionnaire techniques, are able to carry out this sort of work. It is necessary to spot and record the relevant detail and to report it in quite objective terms. An interviewer may well be used to writing down precisely what has been said; it is quite a different thing to decide herself what should be recorded about actions rather than words.

(g) Participation

In the observation techniques so far described the interviewer has served in the function of an impartial observer—almost an automaton—and an essential of the observer's function has sometimes been that those observed do not know that they are being observed. We have seen that one of the serious limitations of such techniques lies in the fact that little or no information is obtained for the *reasons* behind the actions observed.

It does not follow, however, that the observer *has* to be anonymous. There is a sense in which any group discussion involves an observer playing a role in the exploration of the subject of the study and certainly in synectic groups this aspect becomes increasingly important (see chapter 2). Even if we exclude this field, however, this section must include reference to what may be called participant observation. This technique owes much to the early work of the anthropologists and ethnologists and, again, was introduced into the market research field by Tom Harrison (who would probably not have drawn the division made here between participant and non-participant observation[15]). It is now widely accepted by journalists and users of the documentary (witness the television film on the Royal Family where journalists and cameramen accompanied the Queen through private and public engagements over a long period) but its research uses are even more strictly limited than those of simpler forms of observation, almost entirely because of the length of time involved in laying the groundwork.

Many sociological studies make great use of the continuous observation of a single family to reveal, for example, kinship patterns or socialization of children, but it is not often that market research needs to explore issues at such depth. An observer using this approach must first find a family he thinks will be likely to illustrate the problems with which he is concerned: he has then to persuade them to accept him into the family circle for all events, weddings, funerals, quarrels and so on, and he must then continuously ask his questions slowly and carefully so as not to destroy any mutual trust or create suspicion. And when results are written up he is open to constant criticism, which is extremely difficult to answer, that had he taken a family in a different road, let alone a different town, the conclusion which he had drawn would not have been the same. He must prove too that his presence has not affected the situation.

There is little doubt of the value of these techniques at the academic level and it is probable that the method has considerable uses in market research not so far really exploited; for example, for studies of shops and their customers or reactions to given events taking place over a short period. It seems unlikely, however, that it will ever be of very general importance in the market research armoury.

The above, of course, assumes that the researcher must be 'injected' into a group and must make himself accepted by it; but what if a series of observers all report on their own family circle in which they are already accepted? This again was a technique developed by Mass-Observation in the years before the Second World War and used fairly widely until the end of that war. Some hundreds of people reported monthly on what they themselves were doing, and how those with whom they were directly concerned were reacting to events.

Changes in social climate and in sociology itself tended to make this work increasingly less useful and it is doubtful if there could be a revival in this approach except in specialized areas such as the recording of dreams or fears. Reports were inevitably subjective, to a degree which made it difficult to know what weight to put on individual comments, however graphically expressed; but perhaps more important was the fact that in the mid-thirties there were many working class people anxious to express themselves in this way but unable to get a job which allowed them to do so; today the increasing influence of higher education has meant that panels of observers of the kind considered here become more and more composed of teachers and civil servants, precisely those groups most likely to be willing to answer mail and other forms of questionnaire when the need arises.

Some General Comments

Much of this chapter has been devoted to stressing the drawbacks of techniques described, most of which are, in fact, attempts to cope with some of the more complex problems facing the researcher: sometimes, how can I get the answer at a cost which is reasonable—sometimes, how can I get the answer when the respondent himself does not know it?

Telephone and mail surveys are 'cheap' in that they make feasible surveys which could not be considered by personal contact: but this does not alter the fact that almost always they retain the snags—of being unrepresentative, of presenting problems of answer interpretation—which make many hesitate to use them. And at the other end of the scale, use of hardware or participant observation produces costs per 'interview' which are so high as to preclude uses of samples of more than 50 or 60, too small to satisfy any statistician.

It is probable that the researcher will always have to live with these problems, and the only practical solution is the compromise of the largest and 'best' sample which is feasible within the prescribed budget. Certainly, if the techniques employed seem to be producing results not obtainable by other methods but appearing to be of real use, the argument for using them in whatever detail possible seems a strong one.

A second point is, perhaps, more fundamental although not often discussed. A convention of market research (although it is obviously open to much argument, especially from the psychologists) is that the nature of the direct interview is such that it provides information only at *one* level of consciousness or communication and that this is a useful level. There are many others which could be used from the subconscious world of dreams to the

236

purely formal one of polite and meaningless conversation. In another dimension, the interview usually (though by no means always) involves an immediate answer to an immediate question while, to take an extreme, the anthropological approach to a subject may be discussed intensively over weeks. A 'deeper' answer is not necessarily a 'better' one or, in more practical terms, one of which greater use can be made, but it is not measuring the same thing.

Similarly, while a good deal of evidence is to hand that interviewer personality makes less difference to the nature of answers provided than was at one time assumed, the degree and nature of the rapport must in some way show through the answers to any study. This rapport must be different if, on the one hand, the 'interviewer' is a person who lives as part of the family circle for months, if on the other he is seen as the hand on the switch of the psychogalvanometer. Again, the 'best' approach must, to some extent, be recommended on pragmatic grounds.

For all their weaknesses and unsolved difficulties of comparison, do the special techniques considered here offer something not otherwise able to be provided? If they do, then there is a reason for using them. If they do not, there is none.

11. Coding, editing, and processing of market research data

G. W. Roughton

In earlier chapters techniques have been described for obtaining market research data. These techniques mostly provide raw data. Before the data can be used in most types of surveys they must be converted from their raw state into finished tabulations. These show the practitioner what the findings of the survey are, and will allow statistical and other appropriate tests to be applied. This usually involves coding, editing and processing. Editing is carried out to correct or remove obvious logical or factual errors in the raw data; coding, to classify informant responses in terms of a predetermined coding frame, and processing, to produce summaries of the results as well as cross tabulations to show the presence or absence of relevant relationships in the data. It may be useful to begin by considering the more common forms of data.

Forms of Data

By far the most common document in market research is the interviewer-administered questionnaire. These consist of lists of pre-coded and open-ended questions. In pre-coded questions, interviewers mark or 'code' the appropriate pre-printed answer to show into which of the categories (pre-codes) printed on the questionnaire the informant's reply falls. To a question such as 'Have you purchased a washing-machine in the past twelve months?', an obvious set of pre-coded answers would be 'Yes', 'No' and, for the sake of completeness, 'Don't know'. It is important to include categories such as 'don't know' so as to leave as little doubt as possible in the interviewer's mind as to the category into which the particular answer should be placed. Badly designed pre-codes will mean that the interviewer has some difficulty in fitting answers into the pre-coded list. As a result, errors may be introduced by inadvertently forcing answers into pre-codes to which they do not belong.

In open-ended questions, informants' replies are written out by the interviewer. There may be some probing with answers of several sentences. In other cases, where a question is purely a factual one, an open-ended answer may consist of only one or two words; for example, a question about consumption could elicit a number as an answer.

Generally, it is unwise to use pre-codes where the interviewer, unless specially trained, is required to exercise any degree of judgement in determining into which category the answers should fall. On the other hand, pre-coding greatly reduces processing time and the cost of coding. It also tells the interviewer the kind and detail of answers you are expecting. Questionnaires involving a mixture of open-ended and pre-coded questions with space for the answers to be either coded or written in by the interviewers, are by far the most common form of questionnaire administered in market research. Some brief notes are given below on other types of document. In certain kinds of study, e.g. postal surveys, a self-completion questionnaire is used. They are largely pre-coded and extremely simple. Although they are different in certain respects from interviewer questionnaires, the steps through which they subsequently pass are exactly the same.

Instead of, or in conjunction with, carrying out interviews using a questionnaire, interviewers may record the activities or behaviour of informants on specially designed transfer or other forms of document involving such things as mark sense cards and optical reading. Mark sense cards are a special form of punch card (punch cards are fully described later in this chapter) measuring about $3\frac{1}{4}$in.$\times 7\frac{3}{8}$in. on which a number of small rectangular boxes are printed. Each box may be marked with a line using a special graphite pencil. These marks can then be interpreted by appropriate card reading devices. Optical reading enables marks placed in special boxes on ordinary paper to be similarly interpreted. The speed, reliability and flexibility of optical reading is, however, very much more highly developed than mark sensing.

There are other more advanced methods of data recording which are appropriate for large scale or repetitive types of project where there is ample time available to design the entire data recording procedure. One of the better known examples is the use of special meters to record household television viewing.

Editing

The first stage through which the data must pass is editing. It is a truism to say that not every interviewer will ask and correctly record answers to every question that should have been asked of every informant. Nor, indeed, will every informant necessarily be so obliging as to answer every appropriate question. The result is that survey data are normally less than perfect. Although one could reject data which contained any errors at all, this would mean that a considerable amount of useful information was being thrown away simply because of possibly one or two trivial errors at some stage in its collection. The purpose of editing is to reduce or remove the effect of these minor errors. Some common causes of errors are as follows.

Poorly Designed Questionnaires and/or Instructions. These invoke the GIGO principle familiar to all in the computer world (Garbage in = Garbage out). There is usually little, if anything, that can be done at the editing or coding stage to retrieve fundamental survey design errors. There is little remedy for missing questions, or incorrect instructions. The best thing to do is to try to make as much use as possible of the data which have been correctly obtained (see chapter 5).

Poor Quality Interviewing. Poor quality interviewing, and the consequent poor quality answering are probably the principal causes of errors that can be corrected at the editing stage. It is often possible for an experienced editor to patch up the questionnaire which has been badly completed by an interviewer who may have been working on a doorstep in bad weather. Despite this, the GIGO principle applies to poor quality interviewing. Although editing can ameliorate the effect, it cannot remove it. The justification for editing in these circumstances is that it is wasteful to reject a questionnaire which has been reasonably well administered, but on which one particular question may not have been correctly asked. The more common types of data error arising from poor quality interviewing are discussed below. Procedures for dealing with these are, to some extent, a matter of judgement. Policies vary from one organization to another. Some of the more common practices now in existence are noted.

Types of error

Missing Data

For a variety of reasons, it frequently occurs that an interviewer omits to ask a question which she should have asked. In these circumstances, one might begin by attempting to infer the answer from other data on the questionnaire. There are certain circumstances in which this is possible, but there are, of course, dangers if this is taken too far. Alternatively, one may raise a specific 'not answered' category or perhaps base answers to the question at the tabulation stage only on those informants who actually answered the question rather than on those who should have answered it. In either of these cases the questionnaire is accepted in its present form, and passes through the editing stage. However, it may be of vital importance that an answer to the question concerned is obtained. In these circumstances the questionnaire has to be returned to the interviewer with a request for them to obtain the missing information from the informant. Timing and other administrative considerations may cause difficulties in this latter approach. Interviewers are not particularly co-operative in returning to ask informants one of two additional questions, particularly if the interview was a long one. Often, it is not possible to obtain the information in any case.

Incorrect Logic

This occurs when a question or group of questions are answered which should not have been answered or are not answered when they should have been. This latter case obviously comes under the heading of missing data. In the former case, a decision has to be made whether to use the information which should have been collected; in other words, should the logic of the questionnaire be amended to fit the response pattern which appears to exist on the questionnaire? This enables one to accept the redundant data as a sort of bonus. The alternative is to delete the redundant answers, maintaining the original logic of the questionnaire. It is difficult to give a general ruling on which procedure to adopt as it would depend upon the objects of the survey, the size of the sub-bases required for meaningful analyses, and what sort of logical errors are occurring. Generally, however, greater homogeneity in the data will result if the original logic in the questionnaire is adhered to, and the 'bonus' data are rejected.

Informant Misunderstanding

It is sometimes clear to an experienced editor that an informant has misunderstood the question. This will usually result from bad questionnaire design. Sometimes it is possible for the editor to infer the answer from the data given but, if not, it may be possible to distinguish between those informants who have understood the question correctly and those who have not. If an appropriate code or codes are raised to indicate this, then answers to the partially misunderstood question can be based only upon those informants who have understood it correctly. The resultant data are generally more useful than combining answers of those who have understood with answers of those who have misunderstood.

Inconsistent or Erroneous Answers

It frequently occurs that informants will change their mind during the progress of an interview. As a result, it becomes clear that answers given towards the end of the interview are inconsistent with those given at the beginning. It is a matter of judgement as to what should be done in these circumstances. Informants do change their minds, particularly as a result of intensive questionning, which can condition them on a subject, if not actually educate them. One opinion is that to edit out these sort of inconsistencies is to force an unreal pattern of consistency upon the answers. In other cases obviously erroneous factual answers may arise. The editor must determine

241

whether these are due to incorrect recording by the interviewer or arise from the answers to the questions themselves. In the latter case, the fact that the informant has given an erroneous answer may itself be an important item of data. In certain other cases, however, the recording of obviously erroneous data does cause trouble; e.g., in computations of consumption it is important that pack sizes, prices, etc., are correctly recorded. Not to do so would mean that market size estimates, the calculation of which are fraught with difficulties even with proper data, are likely to be badly effected.

Frivolous Data

Occasionally it is obvious to an editor that an informant has been insincere in the conduct of the interview. Questionnaires of this kind really should not be submitted by interviewers. These questionnaires should be withdrawn. Questionnaires in which the informant has obviously lost interest and has given up half-way should similarly be withdrawn.

Editing may be carried out as a separate operation or in conjunction with coding. It may be carried out manually, mechanically or electronically. It is extremely rare for data to be useable without some form of editing. The aim of editing is to do whatever is legitimately possible in dealing with errors of the type listed above. In dealing with these errors, most of them can be dealt with by modifying the input, i.e. the raw data. In certain cases, however, when basing tabulations on those who have answered rather than those who should have answered a question, for example, it is possible for the editing to be carried out, in effect, at the output or table stage. Editing the input data is obviously more thorough, and will ensure that the results of the survey are more consistent. However, editing of the output data is very much quicker and less costly. It is normal, therefore, to make decisions early on in the editing process as to what type of errors are to be dealt with by modifying the input and what kind are to be dealt with at the output stage. At the moment, we are concerned only with editing the raw data at the input stage. The principle reasons for editing should now be clear but it may be useful to review them briefly.

Editing can in many circumstances improve the data themselves. Second, the effect of unedited data upon the inexperienced can be disturbing. Many laymen studying survey data have doubts about the legitimacy of taking samples of a population rather than carrying out a census. They are not aware of the various stages through which the data have gone and they may, indeed, find the results highly distasteful. It is not uncommon, therefore, for considerable importance to be attached in these circumstances to minor obvious faults in the data. It is important, in order to establish the proper level of confidence in the data themselves, that they should appear to be accurate.

Trivial errors, e.g. resulting in percentages adding to less than 100, e.g. 96, 97, etc. will rarely effect any conclusion likely to be drawn from the data. However, if trivial errors are obvious in the final tabulations which, in the view of the reader could be put right with only five minutes effort, then it obviously conveys a slipshod and unsatisfactory impression.

On the other hand, 100% consistency gives a delusion of accuracy that is not real and is fairly time consuming to achieve. It is important that users of data should be aware that they have limitations, but at the same time have complete confidence in what they see before them. Editing has to draw a happy medium between pressing a completely unreal rigidity upon data and at the same time preventing the more obvious idiocies appearing in the final output.

Editing can be carried out manually, in which case an 'editor' goes through each data document amending it in accordance with the set of editing instructions. It can be carried out mechanically on a machine such as a counter sorter or electronically using an appropriate computer program.

Methods of editing

Manual Editing

In manual editing each survey document is thoroughly examined by an editor who is fully conversant with the conditions the document should meet. The editor must have a complete written set of instructions, setting out each condition the document is to satisfy, and what they are to do in the event of the condition not being satisfied. As little as possible must be left to the judgement of the individual editor. Different individuals will edit differently, and this will introduce differences into the data which arise from differences between editors rather than in the data themselves. Comprehensive written instructions will avoid this. Editing will involve raising or deleting codes on the original survey document. It is essential that this should be carried out in a distinctive colour, e.g. green, which the interviewers had been specifically told not to use. It is then clear afterwards, on any particular document, exactly what editing has been done. In this way it is also possible for a supervisor to examine the work done by any particular editor.

Editing instructions should take the editor systematically through the questionnaire or other document showing for each question in the order on the questionnaire what should have happened. The editing instructions will, therefore, follow the logic of the questionnaire. It is customary to lay them out in a stylized format and for these to include coding instructions for the open-ended question as and when they come up. (Coding is discussed separately later on in this chapter but is, in fact, almost invariably carried out simultaneously with editing.) Written instructions are also important to users of the data, so they know what editing has been done. The precise form in which editing instructions are written vary from one organization to the other. However, an example of some typical editing instructions are given below in Table 11.1.

Manually editing, say, 1000 questionnaires, each one of which comprised a

Table 11.1 *Some typical editing instructions*

Question	Editing/coding instructions	Code category	Code	Col
	Classification. Occupational grouping. Check group ringed against Occupation of Head of Household Age. One pre-code to be ringed between V–2 in C.10 Children. Code V or X to be ringed in C.11 Product tried first. Code V or X to be ringed in C.12 Area. One pre-code to be ringed in C.13			
1	At least one pre-code to be ringed in C.14.			
2 (a)	Code V or X to be ringed in C.18 All coded X in C.18. Code V or X to be ringed in C.19			
3	Check that following sections are asked of correct members of the household by checking with Q.1 as to the composition of the household. At least one pre-code to be ringed in relevant columns. If N/A leave blank Columns 21, 23, 25, and 27 will not be used.	Milk .... 8 All other foods 9		20 and 22 and 24 and 26

20-minute interview might typically require 80–100 manhours to complete by an *experienced* editor. It is perhaps important to say that editing is something that requires experience to be done effectively and accurately. Although it is simple in concept, it can prove tedious and demanding to inexperienced people. The use of unskilled students or other office staff for this function can sometimes result in a greater number of errors being introduced into the data than had been removed.

Manual editing must be used where any element of judgement has to be exercised by the editor; in other words, where it is not possible by means of a simple set of logical rules to say what should happen in a given set of circumstances. This will occur whenever an editing instruction lays down that the editor should try to infer the answer to the question from elsewhere in the questionnaire without specifying where. Manual editing has the advantage that it can be started during the course of the fieldwork, often in sufficient time for interviewers to be informed of the more obvious errors which are occurring. The editor can exercise judgement as to whether or not to accept a questionnaire in total, and is in a better position than any mechanical or electronic method to assess the overall plausibility of a survey document. It is easier for them to write appropriate reports to interviewers on the quality of the work that has been done.

The principal drawbacks with manual editing are that it is usually more costly than other methods and, though it is rarely critical in the timing of a survey, it requires more manhours. Editors, being human, also make errors and it sometimes happens that errors are still found in data which have been 100% manually edited.

Mechanical Editing

Mechanical editing is possible where data have been transferred to punched cards. It is carried out on the cards rather than on the original document, using punch card unit record equipment, principally the counter sorter. This is a device which enables one to sort cards into groups, dependent upon whether or not holes appear on particular parts of the card. (A fuller explanation of punch cards is given later in this chapter.) It is therefore possible to check whether informants with a hole on one part of the card also have a hole, or holes, on some other parts of the card. This enables thorough and exhaustive logical checks to be carried out. Clearly, little judgement can be exercised in respect of individual informants. What the procedure does is to isolate those informants, i.e. cards, which contain a particular error and additional codes may then be raised on the cards concerned. This type of editing is extremely quick and effective for logic checking. It is therefore inexpensive and there is little or no room for error (assuming the machine is working correctly, which is not always the case). Instructions are necessary only in the form of punch card logic.

Computer Editing

Computer editing is similar to mechanical editing. The principal difference, however, is that whereas only one editing instruction can be executed at one time on the counter/sorter, several hundred can be executed at one time on the computer. Computer editing is very much faster, more accurate, and far more complex logical instructions can be specified. A certain amount of skill is normally required in setting up jobs running on the computer, and this is best handled by an appropriate bureau. A number of the computer programs for cross-tabulation have a certain number of built-in editing features. Nowadays, this is the principal form of editing carried out.

In an editing operation, a rigorous attitude must be taken to the question of replacing missing data. Legitimate inference is generally acceptable but, at a certain point, inspired guesswork can begin to add information to the data not inherent in its original collection. At a certain point, this would clearly become unethical.

The effect of guessing answers, and thereby inserting missing data, is to introduce a random element into the results. It is as though there had been a reduction in the effective sample size on which the survey was based. Clearly to amend two or three questionnaires out of 1000 on each question is not likely to cause any differences to the results of the survey, but may tidy up one or two irritating inconsistencies. However, since tabulations are often based upon sub-samples, a correction rate of 1% in a total sample can easily transfer itself into a correction rate of 20% on a sub-base, and clearly a figure of the latter magnitude would be totally unacceptable.

An important element of editing is to provide a method of checking on the quality of the interviewing. In many organizations, editors will compile reports on interviewers' work which can be forwarded to fieldstaff who can take appropriate remedial action. Computerized methods enable analyses by interviewer to be carried out automatically. The advantages of this latter form of quality control are obvious but are beyond the scope of organizations without the appropriate data processing facilities. Editors can often provide useful information on the quality of questionnaire design and layout and if their advice, though from a lowly source, is heeded some useful minor improvements to questionnaires may result.

Coding

In open-ended questions, it is common to obtain a wide variety of answers. It is usually necessary to group these answers together in some way. This is the first function of coding. The second function is to assign numeric or other codes to each category of answers so as to allow subsequent mechanical or electronic processing of the results. Grouping of answers is required because few practitioners can cope with responses to a question where there are dozens of different answers. The proportion of informants giving each answer is often extremely small and many of the answers are either very similar or convey exactly the same sense. Grouping enables the practitioner to see the wood for the trees.

In order to carry out coding, it is necessary to prepare clear printed instructions on both the groupings of answered and on the codes which are to be subsequently assigned to each group. A coder (who may also be the editor) then compares the actual answers on each questionnaire with the various categories given on the coding frame. The coder then decides into which category or categories the informant's answer falls and then assigns the appropriate code or codes. The codes assigned are usually written on the questionnaire and, as with editing, a distinctive colour should be used for this purpose. Part of a typical coding frame might look as shown in Table 11.2.

Before coding can begin it is necessary to prepare a coding frame. This involves taking a sub-sample of the data and producing an exhaustive listing of all the answers obtained from each question which requires coding. At this stage no attempt is made to group the answers although it will rapidly become clear that there is a considerable overlap both in words and sense between some of the separate answers which are listed. Each time an answer is found on a questionnaire the entry on the listing sheet is marked. This will give a very rough count of the number of times each particular answer has occurred.

The disparate answers are then inspected and appropriately grouped

4(b) and 5(b)	Code for R.42 in Cols. 21 and 22 Code for M.51 in Cols. 25 and 26	Not enough taste/flavour..........	V	
		Powdery taste/uncooked taste....	X	
		Disliked oatmeal taste/like porridge...............................	0	
		Too dry.....................................	1	21
		Too mushy/soggy......................	2	
		Dislike appearance/looked horrible...............................	3	and
		Disliked fruit/raisins hard..........	4	25
		Too bitty/lumpy.........................	5	
		Too much fruit/raisins...............	6	
		Not enough fruit/raisins.............	7	
		Not a good texture/coarse/ not smooth............................	8	
		Takes too long to eat.................	9	
		Disliked the nuts.......................	V	
		Disliked flakes of oatmeal..........	X	
		Stuck in teeth............................	0	22
		Too heavy/stodgy......................	1	
		Too sweet.................................	2	and
			3	
			4	26
			5	
			6	
		Just disliked it (unspec.).............	7	
		Other dislikes............................	8	
		DK/NA/nothing disliked..........	9	

together. There are certain problems in preparing coding frames which are discussed below.

In producing the preliminary exhaustive listing referred to above, a proper sample of the data should be taken. This should consist of at least 100 questionnaires. If the first 100 questionnaires that are received are taken, it will quite often happen that this is in no way representative of the total number. It may over-represent the work of certain interviewers, certain areas or certain time periods. Although timing considerations often press for coding to be carried out simultaneously with the latter stages of fieldwork, a poorly-designed coding frame would frequently result. What then happens is that answers are found in subsequent questionnaires for which no code has been generated at the time that the coding frame was devised. Although coding frames should always provide for the addition of codes when necessary, it will quite frequently happen that coders will put answers for which there is no code into an 'others' category. It will usually be found, therefore, that coding frames based upon a poor sample of total data will have a higher proportion of answers coded as 'others'.

The actual formation of codes can derive from the data themselves and are therefore oriented round the replies which informants give; alternatively they may be oriented round the objectives of the survey. A question on informants' comprehension of an advertisement, for example, can be coded on the replies they gave or in terms of whether, from their reply, they appeared to understand a specified message in the advertisement.

In certain cases, a combination of the two is required. In these circumstances two separate sets of codes may be used for the question(s) concerned with double coding in each case. Whatever form of coding is adopted, however, it is important that the coding frame should be considered in the light of survey objectives, and in the light of whether or not an analysis of the answers to the question in terms of the codes proposed will provide useful and actionable data. Failure to do this will often result in a feeling of 'so what' when the results are examined.

The designer of a coding frame must find a compromise between having a sufficiently large number of codes to provide sensitive discrimination between different answers, and too few codes, which result in coders tending to lump answers together in the same categories, even though there may be important, though subtle, differences between them. The best way to avoid this is for the practitioner to examine the preliminary listing in terms of survey objectives, and the proposed coding frame. At the same time the proposed codes should be examined to ensure that they are not ambiguous as this also reduces the efficiency of the coding.

Like editing, coding may in concept seem a comparatively simple operation. However, unless it is carefully organized and appropriately skilled staff used, the quality of the results can be extremely poor. It is not particularly easy to find staff with the intellectual ability to carry out interpretive work of this kind who are also willing to accept its tedious nature. In actually organizing coding, it is important that careful control is kept of the code sheets, so that in the event of additional codes being added after coding has started, this is transcribed on to all the coding sheets in use. It is not an uncommon practice for the supervisor responsible to keep all coding sheets and to hand these out on a daily basis to the coders concerned. In addition, the supervisor must ensure that coding is carried out consistently; that each coder will code a particular response in the same way(s). This requires thorough checking of each coder's work at the beginning of the coding operation. Consistency grows over time within a particular team of coders.

Another method of ensuring consistency is for a particular question or set of questions to be entirely coded by one coder, another question or set of questions by a different coder and so on. Though greater consistency is achieved, more time is involved in the total coding operation. In some cases, a mixture of both methods is used. This is applicable where the majority of questions are straightforward but where there are perhaps one or two questions requiring a very high degree of consistency or special technical knowledge. In these cases, the latter questions may be reserved for one specially appointed coder.

Analysis

Once data have been edited and coded they are ready for analysis. The object of analysis is to summarize individual items of data, questionnaires or whatever, so that the practitioner can readily know how many informants in the sample gave each of the possible replies to each question. These summary data are usually presented in the form of tables which may show the results not only for the sample as a whole, but also for sub-groups of it, e.g. for males and females separately, young people/old people, etc. This kind of cross-tabulation is extremely important in discovering relevant relationships within the data, and is nowadays carried out more and more extensively. An example of a typical table is given in Fig. 11.1.

Analysis may be carried out by hand, by mechanical methods, or by computer. Although, nowadays, computers are the principal method of analysis, the three methods are described in some detail below. Hand and mechanical methods do have applications, particularly for the smaller, more simple surveys, though for certain kinds of operations, and especially where multivariate methods (see chapter 13) are being used, computers are the only method of analysis.

Hand analysis

Hand analysis involves the preparation of outline tables or hand summary sheets. One or more of these sheets is prepared for each question. The replies to questions are written down the left-hand side of the sheet with appropriate columns, across the sheet for any cross-tabulation that may be required. This latter point is explained more fully later on.

Analysis is carried out one question at a time. Using the appropriate hand summary sheet, every questionnaire is examined and an entry made on the appropriate line of the hand summary sheet corresponding to the answer(s) given to that question. It is customary in many organizations for the marking of the summary sheet to take the form of five bar gate scores—four upright marks, with the fifth marked across, e.g. ||||| |||||, ||, etc. Each complete 'gate' represents five responses. This simplifies subsequent counting-up. Where more than one answer is possible to a question the sum of scores against each response will add to more than the total number of questionnaires involved. In order to ensure that this is not due to errors in summarizing, it is normal to provide at the bottom of the sheet concerned appropriate 'overlap' categories. Thus, when the two entries to the sheet are made for one question, an additional entry is also made to a category called 'Overlap 1'. Where three entries are made, the additional category would be made to a category called 'Overlap 2', etc. In this way, a record is kept of the extent of multi-coding of replies. On completion of the summarizing the replies and overlap scores are added up. The overlap scores are further weighted by 1, 2, 3, etc., according

TABLE DISTRIBUTION OF PRODUCT X AND PRODUCT Y
ANALYSED BY FORM OF ORGANISATION · SELF SERVICE · ESTIMATED SALES PER WEEK
BASE ALL GROCERS INTERVIEWED IN GREAT BRITAIN

TABLE NO 2
QUESTION

COLUMN PERCENTAGES

RESPONSES		Total	FORM OF ORGANISATION				SELF SERVICE			-£100	ESTIMATED SALES PER WEEK			Not Given
			Co-operative	Multiple	Volunt Chain	Independent	+2000 Sq. ft.	-2000 Sq. ft.	Count. Serve		-£200	-£500	+£500	
		2724 ·	409 ·	611 ·	632 ·	1072 ·	436 ·	700 ·	1588 ·	223 ·	531 ·	811 ·	1068 ·	91 ·
PRODUCT X	IS	14 ·	9	23	18	12	24	16	12	4	7	16	24	14
	TOS	3 ·	3	3	3	2	3	5	2	1	2	4	3	4
PRODUCT Y	IS	29 ·	38	33	34	24	43	35	25	15	23	30	40	20
	TOS	5 ·	5	4	5	6	5	4	5	5	6	6	4	1

PROJECT NO 2839   REF 1/61/70 1485

Fig. 11.1   Example of a table showing distribution of products X and Y in grocers.

to the number of overlaps they represent to give the number of replies which were second (or more) replies. This figure is subtracted from the total replies. The result should be equal to the number of questionnaires which have been summarized. This kind of checking is essential in hand analysis. It is extremely easy for errors to creep in, particularly when this kind of work is done quickly or by inexperienced staff.

In hand summarizing, questionnaires are first bundled into groups or batches. Each bundle is counted and the total number of questionnaires written on each bundle. Each person summarizing then deals with one particular question, i.e. summary sheet, going through one bundle at a time. On completion of each bundle the cumulative scores including overlaps can be counted and checked. Not only does this emphasize the need for accuracy all the time, but if the recording of replies for each bundle is kept separate on the summary sheet then it is an extremely easy matter to put any errors right by only going through the bundle in error. Not to follow this kind of procedure means that if checking is left to the end, and errors are found, it is necessary to resummarize every bundle for the question(s) in error.

When it is desired to carry out cross-tabulations in which replies to one question are analysed either by classification information or replies to other questions, it is essential to sort the questionnaires into bundles corresponding to the breakdowns involved. This must be done one break within the other. This ensures that the figures within each breakdown add back to the same total figure as well as keeping the actual summarizing to a minimum. As an example, let us suppose it was desired to analyse some data by two area codes, three age groups and two social classes, the questionnaires would be sorted into twelve bundles of the following composition:

Bundle	Area code	Age group	Social class
1	1	16 to 34	ABC1
2	1		C2DE
3	1	35 to 54	ABC1
4	1		C2DE
5	1	55+	ABC1
6	1		C2DE
7	2	16 to 34	ABC1

etc.

Results for each bundle would be summarized within separate columns on the summary sheets. The replies would then be added up within each column. From these subtotals the breakdown total is obtained. Thus results for areas 1 and 2 are obtained by adding the subtotals for columns 1 to 6, and 7 to 12 respectively on the summary sheets for the 16–34 age groups by adding columns 1, 2, 7 and 8, etc. This method obviously ensures that inconsistencies across breakdowns are removed. Where this method cannot be followed, hand analysis should be used for surveys with comparatively small samples (under 200).

It is clear from the foregoing that hand analysis has certain limitations; for example, it frequently happens that on examining data, the practitioner requires different or additional tabulations. In hand analysis this involves repeating the above operations, perhaps with the questionnaires bundled in a different way or ways. Rigorous control is essential if errors are to be avoided. The process lacks flexibility and requires tight quality controls. However, it does have some advantages. It can be extremely quick in producing rough results to, say, a few key questions, e.g. which product was preferred in a product test. Summarizing may be carried out simultaneously with booking-in of questionnaires from the field. Because of higher fixed costs associated with other forms of analysis, including the possible need for special equipment, or the need to deal with outside suppliers, hand analysis can be extremely economic to practitioners carrying out only occasional surveys on limited samples.

Most survey organizations, however, use hand analysis mainly for advance results, analysing pilot surveys and handling certain kinds of complex data, e.g. depth interviews, calling for special interpretative techniques. It is not recommended procedure for the ordinary type of survey.

Card punching, tape, document reading

Both mechanical and electronic methods of analysis involve converting the original data into some other medium. This conversion itself is usually carried out by machines, which may be manually operated. Whatever the medium into which the data are transferred, its resultant format is entirely rigid. This must be taken into account in the design of the original questionnaire or other survey document. Failing this, it may be necessary for the data to be manually transferred to a special transfer sheet from which the subsequent transformation takes place.

The principal medium at present is punch cards. The most commonly used card measures approximately $7\frac{3}{8}$in. $\times$ $3\frac{1}{4}$in. and is notionally divided into 80 columns. On each column a rectangular hole or set of holes may be punched in any of 12 positions. Cards may be singly punched, in which case there will be a maximum of one hole per column, or multi-punched where there may be any number of holes punched in up to all 12 positions. The latter case is rare, and should be avoided as some card reading devices (principally the mechanical ones) cannot read columns with more than a specified number of positions punched. The bottom ten positions on any column are referred to by the numbers 0 to 9 respectively. The top two positions are referred to variously as V and X, A and B, Y and X and 12 and 11, etc. Nomenclature varies from one organization to another. Columns are referred to by the numbers 1 to 80. An example of a punch card is given below in Fig. 11.2. Any position on a card can, therefore, be defined by its column number and hole code, e.g. column 13, code 1, or 13/(1), column 61, code 2 or 61/(2) etc. Thus, analysis can be specified in a form such as: give a count of the number of times each code position on, say, column 48, contains a hole (a hole corresponds to a particular answer either already printed on the questionnaire, or subsequently assigned when the coding frame is prepared). Such counts may be based on all the cards for the survey or only on a sub-group, e.g. those with, say, 2 punched on column 14. This enables extremely complex logical filtering to be carried out. The assignment of columns and codes on a questionnaire is an integral part of its design. Figure 11.2 shows how this was done for a code sheet. When codes are printed directly on the questionnaire, the punch operators punch the cards from the questionnaire itself.

Instead of card, paper tape is occasionally used. Paper tape is normally about $3/4$ in. in width, and punching devices allow for a varying number of holes (eight is common) to be punched across the width of the tape. Whereas a punched card contains a fixed number (80) of columns regardless of the number of columns required per questionnaire (many questionnaires require more than one card to accommodate all the data obtained), paper tape can provide as many 'columns' as are required per item. One record is punched consecutively after another on the same tape, one reel of tape being capable of accommodating a large number of records. Although tape can show cost savings and avoidance of the matching problems sometimes associated with multi-card data, it can only be processed by computer. Preliminary processing by mechanical methods is not possible. It is also relatively less common than card; in consequence, skills in structuring questionnaires for tape may be less common, and equipment suitable for processing tape less universally available. Furthermore, the fact that one card column can accommodate 12 codes means that the answers to many questions can be very conveniently punched on one column. A reduction to eight codes reduces the number of questions which can be so accommodated. The use of one column for a complete set of answers to a question greatly simplifies checking and analysis specifications.

An alternative method is to punch directly onto magnetic tape. This method of data preparation is increasing in other fields. It does, however, further restrict both the organizations which can punch the data in the first place and those who can subsequently process it. Because of the density with which the data are packed on the tape, one reel of tape (usually 2400 feet) can accommodate a very large amount of data. The precise amount depends upon the format of the data and certain technical considerations but could be the equivalent of 60 to 70 000 eighty-column punch cards. Generally, however, the same points apply as to paper tape.

All of the above methods involve the data being read by an operator who then punches keys on special machines which make the appropriate holes or entries on whatever medium is being used. Experienced operators can expect to achieve punching speeds of 6 to 7000 key depressions per hour on market research questionnaires, although for short periods or on simple work, e.g.

Fig. 11.2   An 80 column punch card.

transfer sheets, speeds may be very much higher. Alternatively, for badly structured questionnaires or where the punch operator is asked to check the data as they are punched, the rate may fall, sometimes considerably. After data are punched, it is customary as a quality-control measure for all or part of it to be repunched on verifying machines. In the case of cards the original cards are fed into the machine and the punching operation repeated. However, instead of actually punching the card, the image of the column punched on the verifying machine is compared with what is already on that card 'column'. If the two are the same, the card moves to the next 'column'. If they are different, a red light (the method varies from machine to machine) appears and the operator can then check that column to identify the error. The principles are the same for paper and magnetic tape, although the actual procedures are slightly different. A typical survey involving, say, 1000 punch cards may involve some 100 000 key depressions requiring perhaps 20 to 30 hours for punching and verification.

Document reading devices are beginning to provide an alternative method of translation for certain kinds of questionnaire. Instead of the document being read by human operators they are read by a machine which generates, usually, a magnetic tape of the data read. These may be used directly as input to a computer or converted back mechanically into punch cards or paper tape. Document reading cuts out the need for verification, and enables data to be transcribed very much more quickly. However, considerable care must be taken in the design and printing of the document to be read. Interviewers must take greater care in marking questionnaires. In certain, but not all, cases an error in marking means filling in a fresh questionnaire. The quality of printing required, particularly in the registration of the answer spaces with respect to the top and side of the paper, is beyond the scope of most organizations with only the normal stencil or small offset printing facilities. This method will provide a substantial increase in speed at the processing stage but takes slightly longer to set up at the design stage. Recent technical development in readers is rapidly making them suitable for a wide variety of *ad hoc* surveys. It is probable that this form of transfer will become much more important in the future.

Given, then, that the data have been transferred to a suitable medium, analysis may now be carried out mechanically or by computer. Mechanical methods replaced hand summarizing in the early 'fifties' and were the predominant analysis method for well over ten years. Mechanical methods are still used for many kinds of smaller surveys.

Mechanical analysis

The principal machines used in mechanical analysis are counter/sorters, tabulators and statistical analysis machines. These machines are (or were) made by IBM, ICL, and other suppliers of punched card equipment.

The best known mechanical device is the counter/sorter. This is a machine which consists of a hopper into which punched cards can be placed, and thirteen output pockets into which the cards fall after passing through the machine. As the cards go through the machine they pass under a bar with 80 serations on it on which a small brush is mounted. The mounting of the brush is usually spring-loaded. The brush may be moved along the bar by the operator and placed on any one of the 80 positions on the bar which correspond to the 80 column position on the card. As the cards pass under the brush they pass over a metal roller with the brush exerting a slight downward pressure on the card against the roller. Whenever a hole is encountered on the card, electrical contact is made between the brush and the metal roller under the card. In this way, the code positions on a particular column are sensed by the machine. The resultant electrical impulse may be used to drive counters, one for each code position, which are incremented by one each time a hole is encountered in a particular code position. The electrical impulse may alternatively, or additionally, be used to 'open' one of the output pockets corresponding to the position punched. In this way, both a counting and a sorting facility are provided.

There are 13 output pockets to provide for all 12 code positions and the case where nothing is punched on the column, usually referred to as the 'reject' pocket. Where a card is multi-punched it will normally fall into the pocket corresponding to the code position nearest the bottom edge of the card. If, for example, a card contained a hole in both the 'three' and 'eight' positions, the cards would fall into the output pocket for the 'eight' code. The operator may close any or all of the 12 pockets corresponding to the 12 code positions. This provides the extremely important facility of allowing sorting to take place on selected codes only on a particular column.

For each column on which data are required, the cards are passed through the machine with the brush set to the appropriate column. Figures are copied manually onto sheets, the counters set to zero, and the operation repeated. This may be done on the whole pack or sub-groups as desired. The best known machines are the 082, 083, and 084 made by IBM. These operate at varying speeds from 650 to 2000 cards a minute. A basic point to remember about a counter/sorter is that it can only process one column at a time. In certain cases, tabulators have been used where it is desired to use numbers punched across a field of columns. A tabulator is able to read sets of columns and carry out simple manipulative operations on the number in the different fields. Results are printed onto continuous paper. Instructions are communicated to the machine through wired panels. Usually, a particular panel is permanently wired-up for a particular operation. Tabulators were principally designed for accounting applications, and their use in market research was therefore restricted to specialized fields such as retail audit and other types of panel processing.

The best-known statistical analysis machine was the IBM 101. (There were others which were specially made.) The IBM 101 was able to 'sense' all 80 columns simultaneously. By appropriate wiring of the control panel up to five columns could be read at any one time. At the end of passing the data pack through the machine the results for the five columns concerned were printed out automatically by the machine. The much greater flexibility in logical capability, and the printing feature meant that the machine's output was very much greater than the counter/sorter's. Errors arising from inconsistent manual transcription by the operators on counter/sorters were avoided. Although the form of output was fairly rigid, with ingenious wiring it could be made sufficiently similar to the tables required to make translations to their final form—a manual task—fairly simple.

When mechanical methods became widely available they had numerous important advantages on hand methods. However, with the advent of computers, many of their advantages are no longer relevant. The IBM 101 is no longer manufactured and there are fewer and fewer of the machines around. The same is largely true of tabulators.

The counter/sorter is still found in some organizations. It is extremely useful for checking odd items of data, editing and a variety of other miscellaneous functions. When processing on the counter sorter, however, weighting can only be carried out by either removing some data from over-represented cells or duplicating a sample of the cards in under-represented cells. The cards must be passed through the machine several times, and the resultant figures may require considerable additional manipulation before they can be used by the practitioner. For these and other reasons more and more analysis is done on computers. This is discussed below.

Computers

Computers have not only revolutionized the way in which analysis is done but have had an equally major effect on the form and value of analysis. Whereas mechanical and hand methods meant that data were virtually confined to producing raw numbers and simple percentages, computers enable a variety of other kinds of statistics to be produced. Statistical tests of various kinds can be carried out on an exhaustive scale. They allow rigorous checking and manipulation of the data. At the same time, they have reduced the absolute cost of analysing data. Weighting of data to remove biases due to over- or under-representation of the sample can be carried out more accurately. There are numerous other advantages which is why upwards of 95% of survey analysis is now computer-based.

A computer consists of at least the following devices: facilities for reading punch cards, paper or magnetic tape, a central processing unit (CPU) and an output device such as a line printer on which results will be given. A common additional feature is for the computer to have one or more magnetic disks or tapes which are attached to the CPU and may be used for the storage of data and results. The actual devices vary from one installation to another. Larger installations usually have a greater number of peripheral units as well as bigger and more powerful CPU's.

In brief, for a computer to analyse some data the following is necessary. The data must exist in a form that can be read into the computer. A set of specifications must be prepared which will tell the computer what to do and one or more computer programs must be available which are capable of accepting the specification cards, interpreting them, accepting and processing the data cards, and outputting the desired results. Usually, several programs are required which are linked together to form a comprehensive analysis system, referred to in jargon terms as a 'software package'.

The principal limitation in the use of computers lies in the 'software packages' available. However, with the simplification of programs brought about by the increasing sophistication of high-level programming languages, and the substantial improvements in hardware performance inherent in third generation machines, early difficulties have largely been overcome. Computers can carry out virtually any analysis which the practitioner can conceive.

The actual writing of an appropriate software package is not something with which the survey practitioner need be concerned. This can only be done by a team of computer programmers. Such teams are normally found in computer bureaux or software organizations. Once the package has been written it remains fixed for some time. The user does not need to concern himself with the actual mechanics of the programs but rather with how to use them. To use most packages involves writing specifications on special forms. These are punched on cards which then tell the package concerned what to do.

It is important to distinguish between the writing of a program or package and the writing of a set of specifications to be read by a program or package in processing a particular survey. The latter operation, 'spec writing', is something with which the practitioner may well be concerned.

Most organizations offering analysis facilities are able to offer 'spec writing' as part of their service. It is possible for practitioners to do this themselves with savings in time and cost. The ease or difficulty in using any particular software package depends very much on the way in which the 'specs' have to be written.

The 'specs' will cover such things as labels for tables, rows, and columns, the filter base for each table, the punch card definition in logical form of the rows and columns of each table, the form of output, any editing or rearrangement of the data, etc. Most packages have a wide variety of options which provide considerable flexibility to the user. There are considerable variations in the variety and ease of using software packages for cross-tabulations.

Although a practitioner can, of course, contract processing to whichever computer organization submits the lowest quotation for carrying out the work involved, it pays to have some knowledge of the characteristics of the software packages being used. There are a number of reasons for this. First, some packages are particularly appropriate for some forms of analysis whereas others are not. Computer organizations sometimes quote for jobs

258

for which their software is either completely inappropriate or can only be made appropriate with a greater or lesser amount of reprogramming. Although the job may be done at the original budget (there are many cases where this has involved the computer organization in substantial losses), the execution is likely to be more difficult, and involve the practitioner in substantial additional time in dealing with queries and problems. A knowledge of the characteristics of different packages enables the practitioner to avoid the inappropriate ones. Second, where a practitioner is able to match the way he specifies his analysis to the input requirements of a particular package, there will be a considerable saving in time and costs. Most of the cost savings will come from the improvement in communication. This awareness of the range and capability of particular packages enables the practitioner to exploit their potential much more fully.

Although the nature of the specification cards varies from one package to another, the amount of skill involved in completing them also varies. Some packages will accept specification cards, the format of which is very similar to the way in which the practitioner actually thinks of his analysis requirements. Other packages involve cards containing instructions in, perhaps, a special language. It will often be found that the latter type of package will have more powerful capabilities; on the other hand, the former type is easier to use.

A somewhat obvious point is that any software package is of necessity a compromise between a number of desirable objects, which may to some be incompatible. Efficiency in execution, for example, may be sacrificed to some extent for ease of specification. The software package that is best for everything is more or less an impossible dream. It is very much a case of horses for courses. Simple software packages are right for simple surveys. Small computers are cheaper for small surveys and so on.

Clearly, some judicious shopping will enable the practitioner to gauge for himself which packages to use for the different kinds of project he may be carrying out.

Some of the factors which a user might consider in deciding whether a particular package was suitable for a particular job are the following:

(a) How easy is it to specify the analysis requirements to the specification writer(s)?
(b) Are table, column, and row labels adequate without further annotation?
(c) Does the package have sufficient editing and recoding features to ensure that 'clean' data are produced?
(d) Can multi-card surveys present problems?
(e) Is the layout of the tables sufficiently clear that secondary transcription by typing, etc., is unnecessary?
(f) Are the output options sufficiently flexible to produce data in the form appropriate to the practitioner's need?
(g) Can tables be formed with sufficient flexibility to allow virtually any code or set of codes on any card to appear in a single table?

(h) Can weighting be carried out easily without, for example, having to punch factors for each informant?

(i) Is the package able to cope with the size of the job without numerous re-runs or very long runs?

(j) Do your requirements mean changes to the package, or can they be handled easily within the existing control card procedure?

These are some of the main questions upon which the practitioner himself should be satisfied. There are others, of course, particularly when the processing is atypical in any way.

It is beyond the scope of this chapter to make more than a passing reference to specific software packages. Some of these are discussed below. For fuller information it is really necessary to study the user manuals produced by the proprietors of the packages concerned. This is also necessary because the packages themselves undergo continuous development and up-grading. In selecting companies with software packages, one may consider either an appropriate market research company or a computer bureau.

A number of market research agencies have their own computers, and most of them carry out a considerable amount of work for other agencies or practitioners who require cross-tabulation. Names of such companies may be obtained by reference to AMSO, The Association of Market Survey Organizations. In addition, the Social Science Research Council (SSRC) maintains a register of software packages suitable for survey tabulations. The principal computer bureaux or specialist organizations carrying out market research processing in Great Britain at the moment include CRC, DRS, Denjon, Pritchard Brown and Taylor, and Scicon.

Some of the better-known packages are very briefly commented upon below. Fuller details can be obtained from the relevant manuals. In each case, some guidance is given as to where the package may be used. It is probable that around two thirds of the survey processing in Great Britain use one or other of these packages.

DONOVAN. This package was designed for the IBM 1130 computer which is certainly the most widely-used small computer in market research. The package has been developed over several versions with progressive improvements in ease of setting-up; now available on 360's and 370's.

XTAB. Also designed originally for the 1130. Its principal advantage is the extreme ease in setting-up, and its efficiency in execution. These more than compensate for a number of limitations which the ingenious 'spec' writer can get round by appropriate operation of the data packs beforehand.

SABLE. This package is designed for the ICL 1900 series and is the result of several years development. It has many highly-developed features with powerful editing and recoding abilities. The control cards generate a machine language code which makes the program very fast; currently being written to run on Honeywell 716; (Pritchard Brown and Taylor only).

SAMPLE and STONEWALL. Sample is designed for the CDC 3200 machine. The control cards set up a series of machine language instructions. This makes the package both fast and powerful. Specification writing, however, requires a good deal of skill. Stonewall will produce simple matrices using a control card set-up which can easily be written by the user. It is suitable for the simpler single card surveys; (Computer Projects only).

SPS. SPS is a quick, easy to use system, well within the grasp of most survey practitioners. The package is designed for the XDS Sigma 9 machine and enables interactive processing to be carried out through terminals; (CRC only).

QUANTUM. This package presently operates on a Prime computer. 'Spec writing' requires medium skill, and is usually carried out by the bureau. Its capability is similar to that of SPS. (Denjon only).

Computer Input Requirements

A good deal of discussion has taken place earlier on input data. There are certain aspects of this which need to be borne in mind in relation to computers. First, computers are more sensitive to faults in data and are, at the same time, more accurate in tabulating what is, in fact, there. Thus, the GIGO principle applies. Data cards with errors must be 'cleaned' or the tables will also contain errors. This is particularly important when it is desired to present computer output directly to the final user. The cleaning up operation is likely to involve, among other things, the removal of redundant, erroneous or rogue codes, logic checking with resultant amendments to the data and general sense checking. To ensure 'perfect' output these operations themselves must be carried out by computer. Manual or mechanical editing is seldom good enough. Although this takes extra time at the preparation stage, it is well worthwhile in terms of the time saved at the output stage.

Some packages contain comprehensive editing features. However, it is quite frequent for this to be carried out at a prior stage by special programs. The data are then checked on the computer to ensure that they are 100% correct before the tabulation runs are carried out.

In multi-card surveys it is usually necessary to check that the correct number of cards is present for each informant. Most packages which accept multi-card data will reject invalid or mismatched sets. This can result in a substantial loss of data. Many bureaux have special programs for checking matching and identifying which serial numbers or cards are invalid.

Corrections of this kind are usually done manually, and sometimes involve referring back to original questionnaires. The pack may then be checked again on the computer.

In some bureaux, data are stored for as long as it may be required either on disk or tape. However, in some cases it is stored on card only. In these latter cases great care must be taken to avoid degradation of the data pack through wrecking, mishandling or other causes. The consequences of this are that tables run on separate occasions may well contain differences when they should, in fact, be the same.

Computer Weighting

It is frequently necessary to weigh data to correct for differences in the composition of the sample achieved, and known characteristics of the universe from which it was drawn. If, for example, one found that one's sample contained too many men, most cross-tabulation packages can correct this by assigning separate fractional weights to male and female informants such that the sample which is used for the analysis has the correct composition. It is not easy to do efficiently when using hand or mechanical methods. Usually, it is necessary to specify the desired composition of the sample in terms of the appropriate characteristics. Common ones including age, class, sex, area, etc. A preliminary run is then carried out to determine the actual composition, and from this appropriate factors may be computed. Packages differ in the ways in which weighting is handled. In some cases, it is possible to enter the weights directly; in other cases it is necessary to punch them on to the data cards.

Checking Computer Output

Occasionally, very occasionally, computers themselves make mistakes. When they do so, more often than not the result is obvious and spectacular. However, most errors in computer output arise either because the input data contain errors (referred to above) or because errors have been made in the specifications of the table concerned. It is very rare, especially on a survey of any size, for there to be no errors at all on any of the output. For this reason some kinds of checking should be carried out. How this is done will vary from one organization to another. The procedure outlined below is less than perfect, but rigorous checking procedures are no longer worth the delay they will cause in terms of the increased accuracy which may result. Here are some simple steps:

(a) If any weighting was carried out, calculate what the weighted sample size should have been manually. If the computer gives you another result, there may be something wrong with the weighting. If so, all the tables may be wrong.

(b) Similarly, if the unweighted sample size is markedly different to what you expected, a serious fault may have occurred.

(c) The base figures should then be checked for each of the different base filters for each analysis breakdown. These should add back, where appropriate, to the total sample. It is probable that, if they are correct for the one table with a particular base and breakdown, they will be correct for all other similar tables.

(d) Tables now need to be examined individually for the presence of correct labelling.

(e) The total column should be examined for sense and its addition to 100% (may be slightly different due to rounding off), although this latter check may be done by the computer in some cases.

(f) The number of rejects should be examined. Rejects are informants who qualified for inclusion in the table but for whom no information was found in the data to the question being tabulated. If this number is high it is indicative of an error.

It will be noticed that checking of the data within the table has not been suggested. If the margins, i.e. the base figures and the total column, are checked and correct, then the data within the table will also normally be correct. The elimination of this part of the checking greatly reduces the time involved.

Conclusion

Editing, coding, and data processing are obviously an important part of producing any market research survey. They are largely clerical operations which to a greater or lesser extent make use of modern data processing techniques. The general principles are much the same as those applying to other forms of paper processing. The disciplines necessary in an automated accounting system have much in common with those necessary in market research. Although there is considerable literature on market research or statistical techniques, and also on data processing in general, there is comparatively little literature available on this latter area applicable to market research. It is an area which tends to be taken for granted. In the absence of further reading, attention to detail and common-sense will enable the conscientous practitioner to handle the editing, coding and processing of most kinds of survey.

12. Statistics and significance testing

Paul Harris

Statistics may be defined as 'the collection, analysis and interpretation of numerical data'. As market research is concerned mostly with counting and measuring, it is not surprising that the theory of statistics can play an important part in assisting researchers to collect valid samples of data, and in helping them to draw correct conclusions from those data. The 'collection' aspect of statistics has already been covered in chapters 3 and 4 on experimental design and sampling. In this chapter, the emphasis will be on the 'analysis and interpretation' aspects of statistics dealing mainly with simple descriptive measures calculated from survey data and the testing of hypotheses about those data. The more advanced statistical techniques used for interpreting market research data will be covered in chapter 13. The techniques and significance tests described below are those which have been found most useful in interpreting survey tabulations. This is not an exhaustive list, by any means, and the reader who wishes to know more about statistical analysis in market research may consult the texts given in the references at the end of the book.

Types of Market Research Data

Classified data

This is defined as data which have been collected using only different classifications or categories as the measuring scale. Much of the demographic data collected on market research questionnaires, for example, is of this type, consisting of groups of respondents who fall into one of a number of classifications. Two obvious examples are sex and marital status, where the categories would be:

Sex	Marital status
Male	Single
Female	Married
	Widowed
	Divorced

The numerical data are simply obtained by counting the frequency of occurrence of respondents in each classification. The various classifications used form a type of measurement scale known as a *nominal* scale. The basic property of this weakest form of measurement scale is that items or people that fall into one classification are different in some way from those falling in the other classifications. When the frequency counts for each classification are each divided by a base figure, such as the total number of respondents in the survey, and are multiplied by 100, a percentage is obtained for each classification. A frequency count and a percentage for a number of classifications is one of the most commonly occurring formats of market survey tabulations. The statistical treatment of these counts and percentages will form a large part of this chapter.

Ranked data

Data are often collected by classifications which are not only different, but where some classifications are 'higher' or 'lower' than other classifications in some sense. A common example in market research is where purchasers of various amounts of a product are classified as:

(a) heavy buyers (e.g. over ten packets);
(b) medium buyers (e.g. five to nine packets);
(c) light buyers (e.g. one to four packets).

Another example is where respondents are asked about their attitudes towards a product on semantic scales such as:

(a) very sweet;
(b) sweet;
(c) neither sweet nor bitter;
(d) bitter;
(e) very bitter.

A third example is when respondents are asked to rank a number of products in order of preference, giving classifications of 1st, 2nd, 3rd . . . etc. When the number of products is two this is the often-used 'paired-comparison design'. In all these examples the classifications on the scales have a natural ordering, which distinguishes them from the previously defined classified data. Numerical data are obtained from the count of respondents for each classification and its associated percentage. The natural order of classifications for ranked data gives the researcher more scope in analysing data of this type, which are often referred to as *ordinal* scale data.

265

Measured data

Under this heading are included all data where the scale of measurement consists not of labelled classifications, but real numerical values. Obvious examples are height (in metres), age (in years), and number of packets of 'brand B' bought last week. Measured data include the two types of measurement which are known as *interval* scales and *ratio* scales. In the former, the distance between two positions on the numerical scale is known and is interpretable numerically, and in the latter the ratio of two positions on the scale is independent of the unit of measurement. The ratio scale has the further property that its zero point is known and meaningful. An example of interval measurement is temperature which can be measured on Fahrenheit or centigrade scales. Height is a good example of the use of ratio measurement, where the ratio of two heights is the same, irrespective of whether they are measured in feet and inches or in metres.

A further distinction between types of measured data is that of *discrete* (or *discontinuous*) data and *continuous* data. Discrete data occur when the measurement scale consists of a number of distinct numerical values such as 'the number of times a certain advertisement has been seen in the last month'. The values on the scale must be 0, 1, 2, 3, . . . etc., with intermediate values such as 1.5 being impossible. No such restriction is applicable to continuous data where the measurements may be taken to any number of decimal places, depending only on the accuracy of the measuring instruments being used. In practice, continuous data such as height are usually collected to distinct values such as two decimal places of metres.

Under the heading of measured data are included data obtained from semantic rating scales, to which simple discrete numerical scores have been attached. An example of two such scoring systems commonly used is given below:

	Score	Score
A preferred to B very much	5	+2
A preferred to B a little	4	+1
No preference	3	0
B preferred to A a little	2	−1
B preferred to A very much	1	−2

This practice of taking an ordinal or ranked measuring scale and giving the various classifications a numerical score is widespread in market research. By doing so the researcher is assuming that underlying the semantic scale is a continuous numerical scale which it is not possible to measure accurately, and that the numerical values given correspond approximately to positions on that scale. If such assumptions can be validly made, then a lot more can be done with the data statistically.

Simple Descriptive Statistics

In this section a number of summarizing features of measured data will be given.

Frequency distributions

If data have been collected on the number of 1 kg bags of flour bought by 200 housewives each month, it would be confusing to list all 200 values obtained. It is much better to display the data in the form of a *frequency distribution* as below:

Number of 1 kg bags bought	*Frequency of occurrence* *= no. of housewives buying*
0	12
1	15
2	20
3	40
4	60
5	30
6	15
7	5
8	3
	200

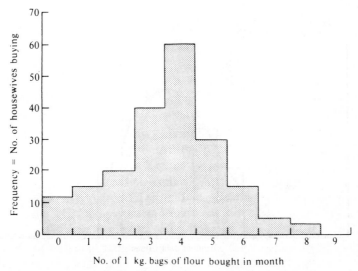

Fig. 12.1 Histogram of frequency distribution of flour purchases.

In this form, the data can be more easily understood and interpreted, especially as this frequency distribution (or 'distribution' as it is often simply called) may be represented pictorially as in Fig. 12.1. This graphical representation of a frequency distribution is known as a *histogram*. In the above example the data are given for a discrete distribution, but these two ways of displaying data are equally useful for continuous data. All one has to do is group the continuous data values into convenient groupings or class intervals and count the number of observations in each class. A number of classes between 8 and 15 is usually adequate. If data on height were collected in metres, part of the frequency distribution might be as follows:

Height (m)	*Frequency = no. of people*
1.51–1.55	20
1.56–1.60	27
1.61–1.65	34
1.66–1.70	46
.	.
.	.
.	.

Continuous data that have been grouped into class intervals may also be represented by a *frequency curve*, which is obtained by drawing a smooth curve through the mid-points of the top of each bar on the histogram. An example of a frequency curve derived from a histogram is shown below in Fig. 12.2.

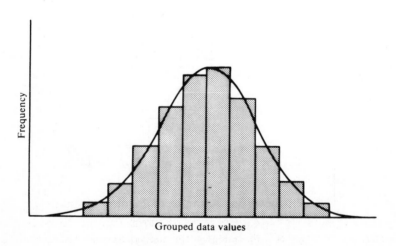

Fig. 12.2 Frequency curve.

The mean, variance, standard deviation and standard error of a distribution

Although the frequency distribution and histogram describe a set of data in simple terms, an even more valuable condensation of the data may be obtained by calculating a single value which summarizes the distribution. Such a value is the *arithmetic mean* or just simply the *mean* of the distribution. It is often referred to as the *average*, but this is not strictly correct as the mean is only one of a number of averages that may be calculated from a distribution. Other averages are the *mode* defined as the data value with the highest frequency, and the *median* defined as the middle value when all the data values are arranged in order of magnitude. To show how to calculate the mean of a distribution the previous data on bags of flour will be used. It is customary to denote the data values by 'x' and the frequency of occurrence by those values by 'f'. The mean, which is usually denoted by $\bar{x}$ (x – bar), is calculated by using the formula

$$\bar{x} = \frac{\sum fx}{\sum f} \qquad \text{where } \sum = \text{the sum of}$$

Putting the formula into words we have—multiply each data value (x) by its associated frequency (f), add up these multiplications and divide their total by sum of the frequencies. This has been done below for the data on flour.

Number of 1 kg bags bought	*Frequency*	
x	f	fx
0	12	0
1	15	15
2	20	40
3	40	120
4	60	240
5	30	150
6	15	90
7	5	35
8	3	24
	$\sum f = 200$	$\sum fx = 714$

$$\bar{x} = \frac{\sum fx}{\sum f} = \frac{714}{200} = 3.57$$

Reference to Fig. 12.1 shows that the value of the mean of the distribution lies near the middle of the data values. Both the median and the mode of this distribution are equal to 4. To calculate the mean of a continuous distribution it is necessary to take the midpoints of the class intervals as the data values

(x). In the height example given above the values would be:

Height (m)	Mid-point	Frequency
	x	f
1.51–1.55	1.53	20
1.56–1.60	1.58	27
1.61–1.65	1.63	34
1.66–1.70	1.68	46
.	.	.
.	.	.
.	.	.

Not only is it useful to have a summarizing value such as a mean for a distribution but it is also of interest to have another value which indicates how much the individual data values are spread around the mean. Such a value is given by a quantity called the *variance* of the distribution, or by the square root of the variance, known as the *standard deviation*. In terms of the data values (x), the frequencies (f) and the mean ($\bar{x}$) they are defined as:

$$\text{Variance} = s^2 = \frac{\sum f(x - \bar{x})^2}{\sum f - 1}$$

$$\text{Standard deviation} = s = \sqrt{\frac{\sum f(x - \bar{x})^2}{\sum f - 1}}$$

The calculation of these two quantities, using the data on bags of flour, is demonstrated below.

Number of 1 kg bags bought	Frequency	$x - \bar{x}$	$(x - \bar{x})^2$	$f(x - \bar{x})^2$
x	f			
0	12	−3.57	12.74	152.88
1	15	−2.57	6.60	99.00
2	20	−1.57	2.46	49.20
3	40	−0.57	0.32	12.80
4	60	0.43	0.18	10.80
5	30	1.43	2.04	61.20
6	15	2.43	5.90	88.50
7	5	3.43	11.76	58.80
8	3	4.43	19.62	58.86
	$\sum f = 200$			$\sum f(x - \bar{x})^2 = 592.04$

$$\text{Variance} = s^2 = \frac{\sum f(x - \bar{x})^2}{\sum f - 1} = \frac{592.04}{199} = 2.98$$

$$\text{Standard deviation} = s = \sqrt{\frac{\sum f(x - \bar{x})^2}{\sum f - 1}} = \sqrt{2.98} = 1.73$$

It is quite usual to replace $\sum f$ by the symbol n, i.e. $n = \sum f$. Figure 12.3 below shows two hypothetical distributions, each with the same mean of $\bar{x} = 5$ units. For distribution A, which has data values ranging from 3 to 7 units, the variance and standard deviation would both be smaller than that for distribution B, where the data values range more widely from zero to 10.

There is a further important statistic that can be calculated from a distribution, namely, the *standard error of the mean*. To explain this term it is necessary to refer back to the theory of random sampling given in chapter 4. Suppose it is known that in a certain town the true average number of persons per household (based on *all* households) is $\bar{X} = 3.12$ with a standard deviation of $S = 1.00$. The values are denoted by capital X and S as they are population values and not sample values. If a random sample of 250 households is selected from the town it would be possible to calculate the mean number of

Fig. 12.3 Frequency distributions of hypothetical data.

persons per household for this sample. Let the mean of this sample be denoted by $\bar{x}_1$. Putting this value to one side, a second random sample of 250 households is selected and the mean ($\bar{x}_2$) is calculated. Similarly, a third sample of 250 is selected, giving $\bar{x}_3$, and so on, until 100 samples have been collected. The resulting 100 values of x may then be grouped into a frequency distribution. In general the 100 values of $\bar{x}$ will all be fairly close to the population mean, $\bar{X} = 3.12$. In fact, their distribution should have a mean, i.e. the mean of all the 100 means, which is indistinguishable or nearly indistinguishable from the value 3.12. Certainly, if all possible samples of 250 households were selected from the town, then the mean of the frequency distribution of all possible sample means would be exactly 3.12 (see page 76 of chapter 4). The distribution of sample means will have a bell-shape distribution, which is known as the *normal distribution*. The standard deviation of the distribution of 100 means may be calculated and it is usually called the *standard error of the mean*. Fortunately, it is not necessary to draw a large number of samples to estimate the standard error, as its value may be calculated from the single sample that is normally selected. If a sample of n members is selected and the standard deviation (s) calculated for some data values (x) then the standard error of the mean ($\bar{x}$) is given by:

$$\text{Standard error } (\bar{x}) = \frac{s}{\sqrt{n}}$$

If the data collected consist of percentages (p) then the statistics defined above take a simple form

		Values for percentages data
mean	$\bar{x}$	p
variance	s^2	pq, where $q = 100 - p$
standard deviation	s	$\sqrt{pq}$
standard error	$\dfrac{s}{\sqrt{n}}$	$\sqrt{\dfrac{pq}{n}}$

Principles of Significance Testing

The market researcher, when interpreting the results of a market survey, has a large number of tables of frequencies and percentages to examine. These results, being based on a sample, will be subject to sampling errors. When the researcher selects two figures for comparison he has to assure himself that any difference between the two figures cannot be explained solely by sampling error. Only then may he validly draw attention to the difference in figures. The *significance test* is a device which enables the researcher to reach a decision objectively in such matters. In this section, the general principles of significance testing will be described. In later sections significance tests for use with various types of market research data will be given.

The null hypothesis and the alternative hypothesis

A significance test is used to decide whether to accept or reject hypotheses concerning the sample data that have been collected. The first step in a significance test is to set up a special hypothesis known as a *null hypothesis* (usually denoted by H_0). It is so called because it is quite often expressed in null or negative terms. A typical one in market research, not in negative terms, would be 'The percentage of men in the population who smoke is $P = 50\%$'. Next, the researcher must define an *alternative hypothesis* (H_1) which may be accepted if the null hypothesis is rejected. The corresponding alternative hypothesis to the null hypothesis stated above might be, 'Percentage P is not equal to 50%'. A significance test based on this alternative hypothesis would be of the type known as a *two-tailed test*, as it states that P may be either higher or lower than 50%. Two examples of alternative hypotheses each of which lead to a separate *one-tailed test* are given below.

(a) P is greater than 50%;
(b) P is less than 50%.

Both of these predict a difference in *one* direction only.

Testing the null hypothesis

The steps employed in conducting a significance test are best explained in the context of an example. In this section the hypothesis concerning the percentage of men who smoke will be tested using the two-tailed alternative hypothesis. To test the validity of the null hypothesis a random sample of n men, e.g. $n = 250$, is selected from the population of all men, and from the data values the statistic to be tested (p_1) is calculated, p_1 being the proportion of men who smoke. This is the result from just one sample. It would be possible in theory, as described in the previous section on the standard error of the mean, to draw all possible samples of size $n = 250$ from the population to produce a large number of estimates $p_1, p_2, p_3, \ldots$ etc. If these estimates were formed into a frequency distribution it would be a normal distribution. If the null hypothesis is true, this distribution, which is called the *sampling distribution of the test statistic*, will have a mean of $P = 50\%$ and a standard error of:

$$\sqrt{\frac{PQ}{n}} = \sqrt{\frac{50(100 - 50)}{250}} = \sqrt{10} = 3.16\%$$

Figure 12.4 shows this particular distribution, from which it can be seen that, if the null hypothesis is true, then a sample value of p_1 lower than 40% or higher than 60% is very unlikely. Of course, it is possible that a sample of $n = 250$ will give $p_1 = 40\%$ even when the null hypothesis of $P = 50\%$ is true;

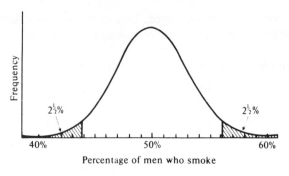

Fig. 12.4 Sampling distribution of a test statistic.

but this would probably not occur. What the researcher has to decide now is where to place cut-off points on this distribution beyond which he is not prepared to accept that the null hypothesis is true but that an alternative hypothesis is true. These cut-off points are normally referred to as critical values in the statistical literature. To assist in this decision a valuable property of the normal distribution may be used. In any normal distribution the area of the distribution outside the limits, arithmetic mean $\pm z$ standard deviations (where z is any number), can be calculated.

Three examples are given below:

(a) only 5% of the area is outside the limits, mean ± 1.96 standard deviations;
(b) only 1% of the area is outside the limits, mean ± 2.58 standard deviations;
(c) only 0.1% of the area is outside the limits, mean ± 3.29 standard deviations.

Tables of the areas of the normal distribution have been calculated and one version is given in Table 12.1. It gives the area of the distribution beyond certain multiples of the standard deviation for one tail of the distribution only. The value corresponding to $z = 1.96$, for example, is 0.025 on one tail and, therefore, as stated above, 0.05 or 5% of the area of the curve is outside 1.96 standard deviations.

Figure 12.4 shows the critical values for the men smokers example, giving the limits outside which 5% of the area of the distribution lies (2½% on each tail). As this is a distribution of a mean, the standard error of the mean must be used in place of the standard deviation to calculate the critical values. These are given by:

$$\text{mean} \pm 1.96 \text{ standard errors} = P\% \pm 1.96 \sqrt{\frac{PQ}{n}}$$

$$= 50\% \pm 1.96 \ (3.16)$$
$$= 50\% \pm 6.20\%$$
$$= 43.80\% \text{ and } 56.20\%$$

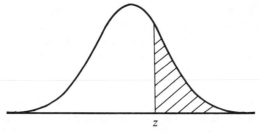

z

Table 12.1   Table of probabilities associated with values as extreme as observed values of z in the normal distribution

The body of the table gives one-tailed probabilities under H_0 of z. The left-hand marginal column gives various values of z to one decimal place. The top row gives various values to the second decimal place. Thus, for example, the one-tailed p of $z \geq 0.11$ or $z \leq -0.11$ is $p = 0.4562$.

z	0.00	0.01	0.02	0.03	0.04	0.05	0.06	0.07	0.08	0.09
0.0	0.5000	0.4960	0.4920	0.4880	0.4840	0.4801	0.4761	0.4721	0.4681	0.4641
0.1	0.4602	0.4562	0.4522	0.4483	0.4443	0.4404	0.4364	0.4325	0.4286	0.4247
0.2	0.4207	0.4168	0.4129	0.4090	0.4052	0.4013	0.3974	0.3936	0.3897	0.3859
0.3	0.3821	0.3783	0.3745	0.3707	0.3669	0.3632	0.3594	0.3557	0.3520	0.3483
0.4	0.3446	0.3409	0.3372	0.3336	0.3300	0.3264	0.3228	0.3192	0.3156	0.3121
0.5	0.3085	0.3050	0.3015	0.2981	0.2946	0.2912	0.2877	0.2843	0.2810	0.2776
0.6	0.2743	0.2709	0.2676	0.2643	0.2611	0.2578	0.2546	0.2514	0.2483	0.2451
0.7	0.2420	0.2389	0.2358	0.2327	0.2296	0.2266	0.2236	0.2206	0.2177	0.2148
0.8	0.2119	0.2090	0.2061	0.2033	0.2005	0.1977	0.1949	0.1922	0.1894	0.1867
0.9	0.1841	0.1814	0.1788	0.1762	0.1736	0.1711	0.1685	0.1660	0.1635	0.1611
1.0	0.1587	0.1562	0.1539	0.1515	0.1492	0.1469	0.1446	0.1423	0.1401	0.1379
1.1	0.1357	0.1335	0.1314	0.1292	0.1271	0.1251	0.1230	0.1210	0.1190	0.1170
1.2	0.1151	0.1131	0.1112	0.1093	0.1075	0.1056	0.1038	0.1020	0.1003	0.0985
1.3	0.0968	0.0951	0.0934	0.0918	0.0901	0.0885	0.0869	0.0853	0.0838	0.0823
1.4	0.0808	0.0793	0.0778	0.0764	0.0749	0.0735	0.0721	0.0708	0.0694	0.0681
1.5	0.0668	0.0655	0.0643	0.0630	0.0618	0.0606	0.0594	0.0582	0.0571	0.0559
1.6	0.0548	0.0537	0.0526	0.0516	0.0505	0.0495	0.0485	0.0475	0.0465	0.0455
1.7	0.0446	0.0436	0.0427	0.0418	0.0409	0.0401	0.0392	0.0384	0.0375	0.0367
1.8	0.0359	0.0351	0.0344	0.0336	0.0329	0.0322	0.0314	0.0307	0.0301	0.0294
1.9	0.0287	0.0281	0.0274	0.0268	0.0262	0.0256	0.0250	0.0244	0.0239	0.0233
2.0	0.0228	0.0222	0.0217	0.0212	0.0207	0.0202	0.0197	0.0192	0.0188	0.0183
2.1	0.0179	0.0174	0.0170	0.0166	0.0162	0.0158	0.0154	0.0150	0.0146	0.0143
2.2	0.0139	0.0136	0.0132	0.0129	0.0125	0.0122	0.0119	0.0116	0.0113	0.0110
2.3	0.0107	0.0104	0.0102	0.0099	0.0096	0.0094	0.0091	0.0089	0.0087	0.0084
2.4	0.0082	0.0080	0.0078	0.0075	0.0073	0.0071	0.0069	0.0068	0.0066	0.0064
2.5	0.0062	0.0060	0.0059	0.0057	0.0055	0.0054	0.0052	0.0051	0.0049	0.0048
2.6	0.0047	0.0045	0.0044	0.0043	0.0041	0.0040	0.0039	0.0038	0.0037	0.0036
2.7	0.0035	0.0034	0.0033	0.0032	0.0031	0.0030	0.0029	0.0028	0.0027	0.0026
2.8	0.0026	0.0025	0.0024	0.0023	0.0023	0.0022	0.0021	0.0021	0.0020	0.0019
2.9	0.0019	0.0018	0.0018	0.0017	0.0016	0.0016	0.0015	0.0015	0.0014	0.0014
3.0	0.0013	0.0013	0.0013	0.0012	0.0012	0.0011	0.0011	0.0011	0.0010	0.0010
3.1	0.0010	0.0009	0.0009	0.0009	0.0008	0.0008	0.0008	0.0008	0.0007	0.0007
3.2	0.0007									
3.3	0.0005									
3.4	0.0003									
3.5	0.00023									
3.6	0.00016									
3.7	0.00011									
3.8	0.00007									
3.9	0.00005									
4.0	0.00003									

The above table is reproduced from *Non-Parametric Statistics for The Behavioural Sciences* by Sidney Siegel by permission of the McGraw-Hill Publishing Co. Ltd, the publishers.
Note: The blanks in the lower part of the table indicate that the values do not differ appreciably from those in the column headed '0.00'.

275

If all possible samples of size $n = 250$, therefore, were drawn from the population and the null hypothesis were true, 5% of these samples would give a value less than 43.80% or greater than 56.20%. If the calculated value of p_1 from the one sample actually selected is outside these two limits, then the null hypothesis is rejected and the alternative hypothesis is accepted. Alternatively, if p_1 is within the limits, then the null hypothesis is accepted. When such a decision is made in practice there is a chance that an error will be made. There is a 5% chance that the null hypothesis may be rejected when, in fact, it is true because the sample just happened to be one of the five per cent of all possible samples that will always fall outside the specified limits. This chosen value of 5% is known as the *significance level* of the test and is often stated in the form $\alpha = 0.05$. In other words, it is often stated as a probability of 5 in 100, i.e. a 1 in 20 chance, that an error will be made. The significance level is often referred to as the *type I error*. Of course, there is nothing to stop the researcher using the 10% or 1%, or any other significance level; it depends on the error he is prepared to accept when making the decision. If the calculated value of the test statistic p_1 obtained from the sample is found to be outside the calculated limits it is said to be *significant* at the chosen level of significance. If it was found from the sample, for example, that 42% of men smoke, this result would be significant as the difference 50 to 42% is greater than 1.96 standard errors, and the null hypothesis that the population percentage is 50% would be rejected.

It is important to note that, although $P = 50\%$ has been rejected, nothing has been said in this significance test as to the true value of P, except that it is different from 50%. In this case the best estimate of P is given by the sample estimate $p_1 = 42\%$. This estimate will be subject to sampling error and it is not possible to state categorically that $P = 42\%$. All that can be done is to give limits known as *confidence limits* within which the true value of P will lie. These limits are based on the areas of the normal distribution and are given by:

$$p_1\% \pm Z\sqrt{\frac{p_1\%(100 - p_1)\%}{n}}$$

When $Z = 1.96$ standard errors, then 95% of the area of the normal distribution is covered by these limits which would then be known as 95% confidence limits. In the present example for sample size $n = 250$ and $p_1 = 42\%$, the 95% limits are given by:

$$42\% \pm 1.96\sqrt{\frac{42 \times 58}{250}}$$

$$42\% \pm 6.12\%$$
$$35.88\% \text{ to } 48.12\%$$

Appendix A gives 95% confidence limits for various sample sizes and a

276

selection of observed percentages. It may be used to give approximate answers to confidence limit problems.

The type I error (or significance level) is not the only error that can be made when doing a significance test. Whereas the type I error is the error of saying a result is significant when it is not, the *type II error* is the error of saying a result is not significant when it is. To explain this new concept the previous null hypothesis H_0 will be tested against the one-tailed alternative hypothesis (H_1) that 'P is greater than 50%'. The assumption will now be made that, unknown to the researcher, in fact the alternative hypothesis is true and that $P = 54\%$ in the population of all men. Just as it is possible to have the sampling distribution for the null hypothesis, so it is also possible to construct a theoretical sampling distribution for when the alternative hypothesis is true. This distribution will also be a normal distribution based on the principle of selecting all possible samples from a population where $P = 54\%$ and its standard error will be given by:

$$\sqrt{\frac{54\%(100-54)\%}{250}} = \sqrt{9.94} = 3.15 \text{ per cent}$$

The sample size is assumed to be $n = 250$ as before and a 5% significance level will be used. Figure 12.5 shows the sampling distribution of samples of $n = 250$ when the null hypothesis (H_0) is true and beneath it is the sampling distribution for samples $n = 250$ when the alternative hypothesis (H_1) is true, and in particular when $P = 54\%$. As the alternative hypothesis only specifies values of P greater than 50%, only the right-hand tail of the null hypothesis sampling distribution is used in the significance test. Table 12.1 of the area of the normal distribution can be used to find the cut-off point, beyond which 5% of this distribution will lie. This value is given by:

$$\text{mean} + 1.645 \text{ standard errors} = 50\% + 1.645\,(3.16\%)$$
$$= 50\% + 5.20\%$$
$$= 55.2 \text{ per cent}$$

If, in the one sample actually selected, it is found that the proportion of men who smoke is $p_1 = 55.2\%$ or greater, then the null hypothesis that $P = 50\%$ in the population is rejected. If p_1 is any value less than 55.2% then there is no reason to doubt the null hypothesis, as 95% of all possible samples will give a result less than 55.2% when the null hypothesis is true. However, if the latter decision is made in the present example where, unknown to the researcher, P is actually equal to 54%, there is a 64.8% chance that the decision will be wrong. This can be seen by referring to the bottom distribution of $P = 54\%$ in Fig. 12.5. The area of the distribution to the left of the significance criterion (55.2%) may be calculated using Table 12.1 of the normal distribution. It is the area shown shaded, and is found to be 64.8%. This chance of error is known as the type II error. It is quite often denoted by β and is sometimes

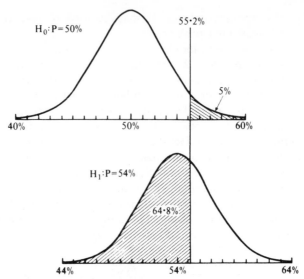

Fig. 12.5 Sampling distributions of the null and alternative hypotheses.

expressed, like the significance level, as a probability. The present example would give $\beta = 0.648$.

If the chances of reaching a correct decision in a significance test are to be high, then both the significance level and the type II error ought to be kept to a minimum. This can be done by increasing the sample size, as this reduces the standard error and the spread of the sampling distributions of the null and alternative hypothesis. To make $\alpha = \beta = 0.05$ in the present example, when testing H_0 against the specific alternative hypothesis that $P = 54\%$, would require a sample size of approximately $n = 1680$.

Some Useful Significance Tests in Market Research

This section will be concerned with giving examples of a number of the most frequently used significance tests in market research. Some tests are more suitable for use on certain types of data than others. For this reason the tests most suited to the three types of data previously defined will be given under those three headings below.

Tests on Classified Data

Testing the difference between two independent percentages

Very often, the researcher wishes to judge whether two independent percentages from different samples are significantly different. He may wish, for

278

example, to know whether a percentage $p_1\%$, based on a random sample of size n_1 selected in 1970, is significantly different from an equivalent percentage $p_2\%$ based on a sample of size n_2 selected in 1968. The null hypothesis is that there is no difference in the percentages and that the two samples were selected from the same population in which the true percentage is $P\%$. The alternative hypothesis is that the two samples come from different populations in which the two percentages P_1 and P_2 are different, giving a two-tailed test. If the null hypothesis is true, then $p_1\%$ and $p_2\%$ are both estimates of $P\%$. To find out whether the difference $p_1\% - p_2\%$ is significant, the standard error of $p_1\% - p_2\%$, when the null hypothesis is true, is needed. This is given by the formula:

$$\text{Standard error } (p_1 - p_2) = \sqrt{p(100 - p)\left[\frac{1}{n_1} + \frac{1}{n_2}\right]}$$

where

$$p = \frac{n_1 p_1 + n_2 p_2}{n_1 + n_2}$$

is the best estimate of the unknown population percentage $P\%$. Tables giving the value of this standard error for various values of n_1, n_2, and p are available[1]. If the difference $p_1 - p_2$ is greater than 1.96 times its standard error then this observed difference can be declared significant at the 5% level. Appendix B may be used to give approximate answers to this problem, It shows for various values of n_1, n_2, and p the differences needed between p_1 and p_2 to be significant at the 5% level.

Example. In 1968 a random sample of $n_1 = 400$ men showed that $p_1 = 42.5\%$ of them regularly read a certain newspaper. Two years later, in a random sample of $n_2 = 200$ men, it was found that $p_2 = 35.0\%$ of them read that newspaper. Is the difference significant or can it be explained as the random fluctuations of sampling? The first step in this test is to calculate:

$$p = \frac{(400 \times 42.5) + (200 \times 35.0)}{400 + 200} = 40.0 \text{ per cent}$$

The standard error of $(p_1 - p_2)$ is then:

$$\text{Standard error } (p_1 - p_2) = \sqrt{40 \times 60[\tfrac{1}{400} + \tfrac{1}{200}]} = 4.24 \text{ per cent}$$

Dividing $p_1 - p_2$ by its standard error gives:

$$\frac{p_1 - p_2}{\text{standard error } (p_1 - p_2)} = \frac{42.5\% - 35.0\%}{4.24\%} = \frac{7.5\%}{4.24\%} = 1.77$$

The observed difference is less than 1.96 times its standard error and, therefore, it is not an unusual value to obtain from the sampling distribution when the null hypothesis is true. Accordingly, the conclusion is reached that

279

these data do not give any reason to reject the null hypothesis that there has been no change in the percentage of men reading the newspaper.

Testing the difference between two correlated percentages

(a) Mutually Exclusive Classifications

Questions to which the respondent may give only *one* of a number of answers occur frequently on market research questionnaires. The analysis of such questions results in a series of percentages adding up to 100% based on a sample of size n. The testing of the difference between two such percentages is complicated by the fact that if one of the percentages goes up, then one or more of the other percentages must go down, as they all must add to 100%. The test differs from the previous one on independent percentages by having a different formula for the standard error:

$$\text{Standard error } (p_1 - p_2) = \sqrt{\frac{1}{n}(p_1 q_1 + p_2 q_2 + 2p_1 p_2)}$$

where

$$q_1 = 100 - p_1$$
$$q_2 = 100 - p_2$$

Example. From a random sample of $n = 400$ housewives the following results were obtained in answer to the question 'Which brand of coffee do you buy most often?':

brand A	$p_1 = 40\%$
brand B	$p_2 = 30\%$
brand C	$p_3 = 12\%$
brand D	$p_4 = 11\%$
no regular brand	$p_5 = 7\%$
	$\overline{100\%}$

The null hypothesis to be tested is that there is no difference between brand A and brand B and that the observed difference in percentages can be explained as sampling variations. The alternative hypothesis is that there is a difference in the percentage share held by these two brands. The standard error of the difference is given by:

$$\text{Standard error } (p_1 - p_2) = \sqrt{\tfrac{1}{400}[(40 \times 60) + (30 \times 70) + 2(40 \times 30)]}$$
$$= 4.15 \text{ per cent}$$

The observed difference $p_1 - p_2 = 10\%$ is 2.41 times this standard error and is significant at the 5% level. The data, therefore, suggest that there is a real difference between these two brands.

280

(b) Overlapping Classifications

With some market research questions the respondent may give more than one answer. The results of analysing such a question will be in the form of a number of percentages adding up to more than 100%, being based on the sample size n. As an example consider the question, 'Which brands of soap did you buy in the last seven days?' The housewives asked this question could possibly have bought more than one brand. To test the difference between two brand percentages a different standard error formula is needed to account for the overlap between brands.

$$\text{Standard error } (p_1 - p_2) = \sqrt{\frac{1}{n}\left[p_1q_1 + p_2q_2 + 2(p_1p_2 - p_{12})\right]}$$

where $p_{12} =$ the overlap proportion, i.e. the proportion buying both brands.

For arithmetical reasons it is best to convert all the percentages in the above standard error formula to proportions when doing the calculation and multiply the answer at the end by 100 to give the standard error as a percentage.

Example.   The following data were obtained from a sample of $n = 2000$ men who were asked which brands of petrol they had used in the previous three months:

brand 1	$p_1 = 25\%$
brand 2	$p_2 = 20\%$
brand 3	$p_3 = 18\%$
brand 4	$p_4 = 18\%$
brand 5	$p_5 = 11\%$
brand 6	$p_6 = 13\%$
brand 7	$p_7 = 12\%$
	$\overline{117\%}$

The difference between brands 1 and 2 is to be tested for significance, the null hypothesis being that there is no difference between the two percentages p_1 and p_2 in the population from which the sample was drawn. The alternative hypothesis is that the two brands have different shares of the market. The survey results also show that $p_{12} = 8\%$ of men had bought both brands 1 and 2 in the previous three months. To calculate the standard error the three relevant percentages, $p_1 = 25\%$, $p_2 = 20\%$ and $p_{12} = 8\%$, are converted to the three proportions 0.25, 0.20, and 0.08 respectively.

Standard error $(p_1 - p_2)$

$$= \sqrt{\tfrac{1}{2000}[(0.25 \times 0.75) + (0.2 \times 0.8) + 2(\{0.25 \times 0.2\} - 0.08)]}$$
$$= 0.0120 = 1.20\%$$

The actual difference $p_1 - p_2 = 25\% - 20\% = 5\%$ is 4.17 times its standard error. The ratio is higher than the value 3.29 needed to be significant at the 0.1% level, and it can be concluded that a real difference exists in the population, from which the sample of $n = 2000$ men was selected.

The Chi-Square Test. Two-way classification tables usually form a prominent part of the results from a market survey. A typical example is given below, based on $n = 650$ housewives.

	Social class			
Purchasing habits	*AB*	*C1*	*C2DE*	Total
Brand A bought most often	35	72	172	279
Brand B bought most often	21	62	164	247
Brand C bought most often	14	26	84	124
Total	70	160	420	650

When both the row classifications and the column classifications are independent, i.e. a respondent can be in only one cell of the table, the differences in the cell frequencies may be tested for significance by using the chi-square test. This test enables one to say whether the observed cell frequencies are in agreement with the frequencies expected when the null hypothesis is true. The formula for computing the test criterion is best explained in terms of an example.

Example. The above data on 650 housewives will be used in this example. The null hypothesis to be tested is that the brand shares are all equal for the three social classes and that differences observed in the above sample data reflect only sampling variation. This unknown distribution of brand shares is best estimated by pooling the data for the three social classes. This is given by the total column in the above table. If the null hypothesis is true then each column (social class grouping) will have its row (brand) frequencies in the same ratio as the total column's row frequencies. It is thus possible to work out an expected frequency for each cell of the table. This may be most easily done by using the following rule. The expected frequency for a given cell is obtained by multiplying its row total by its column total and dividing the result by the grand total. Thus for the cell 'brand A/social class AB' the expected frequency is:

$$E = \frac{279 \times 70}{650} = 30.0$$

The data are reproduced below with each expected frequency (E) being given in brackets next to its observed frequency (O).

Social class

	AB	C1	C2DE	Total
Brand A	35(30.0)	72(68.7)	172(180.3)	279
Brand B	21(26.6)	62(60.8)	164(159.6)	247
Brand C	14(13.4)	26(30.5)	84(80.1)	124
	70	160	420	650

It will be noted that the expected frequencies add down and across to the column and row totals respectively. The next step in the test is to calculate the test criterion:

$$\chi^2 = \Sigma \frac{(O - E)^2}{E}$$

where O denotes observed frequency and E denotes expected frequency and the summation is over all cells of the data. This quantity χ^2 will not have a normally distributed sampling distribution like previously-discussed test statistics. It will be distributed, when the null hypothesis is true, like another well known statistical distribution, the chi-square distribution. The calculation of χ^2 for this example is given below.

O	E	$(O - E)$	$(O - E)^2$	$\dfrac{(O - E)^2}{E}$
35	30.0	5.0	25.00	1.83
21	26.6	-5.6	31.36	1.18
14	13.4	0.6	0.36	0.03
72	68.7	3.3	10.89	0.16
62	60.8	1.2	1.44	0.02
26	30.5	-4.5	20.25	0.66
172	180.3	-8.3	68.89	0.38
164	159.6	4.4	19.36	0.12
84	80.1	3.9	15.21	0.19

$$\chi^2 = \Sigma \frac{(O - E)^2}{E} = \overline{3.57}$$

The chi-square distribution does not have a fixed shape like the normal distribution but takes many forms dependent on a quantity known as its *degrees of freedom*. In the context of a multi-cell table, or contingency table as it is often called, the degrees of freedom are calculated as $df = (r - 1)(c - 1)$ where r is the number of rows and c is the number of columns. In this case $df = (3 - 1)(3 - 1) = 4$. Table 12.2 gives, for various degrees of freedom, the values that χ^2 must attain to be significant at certain levels. For $df =$ four degrees of freedom χ^2 must be 9.49 or greater to be significant at the 5% level. The observed value of $\chi^2 = 3.57$ falls well short of this value, so these data give no evidence to doubt the null hypothesis that purchasing habits are the same for all three social class groupings.

The quantity χ^2 has a distribution like the chi-square distribution only when the expected frequencies (E) are large. How large is a matter of opinion and conflicting advice is often given in statistical texts. For tables with more than one degree of freedom, Cochran[2] suggests that less than 20% of the cells in the table should have expected frequencies less than five and that no cells in the table should have E less than one. If the data do not meet these restrictions, then row and/or column classifications may be combined until the expected frequencies are of sufficient size. The merging of rows or columns must only be done, however, if the resulting classifications are meaningful. The calculation of χ^2 is done using discrete numbers whereas the chi-square distribution is a continuous distribution. If the calculation of χ^2 includes what is known as *Yate's correction for continuity*, then it

Table 12.2   Table of significant values of chi-square*

df	\multicolumn{14}{c}{Probability under H_0 that $X^2 \geq$ chi-square}
	0.99	0.98	0.95	0.90	0.80	0.70	0.50	0.30	0.20	0.10	0.05	0.02	0.01	0.001
1	0.00016	0.00063	0.0039	0.016	0.064	0.15	0.46	1.07	1.64	2.71	3.84	5.41	6.64	10.83
2	0.02	0.04	0.10	0.21	0.45	0.71	1.39	2.41	3.22	4.60	5.99	7.82	9.21	13.82
3	0.12	0.18	0.35	0.58	1.00	1.42	2.37	3.66	4.64	6.25	7.82	9.84	11.34	16.27
4	0.30	0.43	0.71	1.06	1.65	2.20	3.36	4.88	5.99	7.78	9.49	11.67	13.28	18.46
5	0.55	0.75	1.14	1.61	2.34	3.00	4.35	6.06	7.29	9.24	11.07	13.39	15.09	20.52
6	0.87	1.13	1.64	2.20	3.07	3.83	5.35	7.23	8.56	10.64	12.59	15.03	16.81	22.46
7	1.24	1.56	2.17	2.83	3.82	4.67	6.35	8.38	9.80	12.02	14.07	16.62	18.48	24.32
8	1.65	2.03	2.73	3.49	4.59	5.53	7.34	9.52	11.03	13.36	15.51	18.17	20.09	26.12
9	2.09	2.53	3.32	4.17	5.38	6.39	8.34	10.66	12.24	14.68	16.92	19.68	21.67	27.88
10	2.56	3.06	3.94	4.86	6.18	7.27	9.34	11.78	13.44	15.99	18.31	21.16	23.21	29.59
11	3.05	3.61	4.58	5.58	6.99	8.15	10.34	12.90	14.63	17.28	19.68	22.62	24.72	31.26
12	3.57	4.18	5.23	6.30	7.81	9.03	11.34	14.01	15.81	18.55	21.03	24.05	26.22	32.91
13	4.11	4.76	5.89	7.04	8.63	9.93	12.34	15.12	16.98	19.81	22.36	25.47	27.69	34.53
14	4.66	5.37	6.57	7.79	9.47	10.82	13.34	16.22	18.15	21.06	23.68	26.87	29.14	36.12
15	5.23	5.98	7.26	8.55	10.31	11.72	14.34	17.32	19.31	22.31	25.00	28.26	30.58	37.70
16	5.81	6.61	7.96	9.31	11.15	12.62	15.34	18.42	20.46	23.54	26.30	29.63	32.00	39.29
17	6.41	7.26	8.67	10.08	12.00	13.53	16.34	19.51	21.62	24.77	27.59	31.00	33.41	40.75
18	7.02	7.91	9.39	10.86	12.86	14.44	17.34	20.60	22.76	25.99	28.87	32.35	34.80	42.31
19	7.63	8.57	10.12	11.65	13.72	15.35	18.34	21.69	23.90	27.20	30.14	33.69	36.19	43.82
20	8.26	9.24	10.85	12.44	14.58	16.27	19.34	22.78	25.04	28.41	31.41	35.02	37.57	45.32
21	8.90	9.92	11.59	13.24	15.44	17.18	20.34	23.86	26.17	29.62	32.67	36.34	38.93	46.80
22	9.54	10.60	12.34	14.04	16.31	18.10	21.24	24.94	27.30	30.81	33.92	37.66	40.29	48.27
23	10.20	11.29	13.09	14.85	17.19	19.02	22.34	26.02	28.43	32.01	35.17	38.97	41.64	49.73
24	10.86	11.99	13.85	15.66	18.06	19.94	23.34	27.10	29.55	33.20	36.42	40.27	42.98	51.18
25	11.52	12.70	14.61	16.47	18.94	20.87	24.34	28.17	30.68	34.38	37.65	41.57	44.31	52.62
26	12.20	13.41	15.38	17.29	19.82	21.79	25.34	29.25	31.80	35.56	38.88	42.86	45.64	54.05
27	12.88	14.12	16.15	18.11	20.70	22.72	26.34	30.32	32.91	36.74	40.11	44.14	46.96	55.48
28	13.56	14.85	16.93	18.94	21.59	23.65	27.34	31.39	34.03	37.92	41.34	45.42	48.28	56.89
29	14.26	15.57	17.71	19.77	22.48	24.58	28.34	32.46	35.14	39.09	42.56	46.69	49.59	58.30
30	14.95	16.31	18.49	20.60	23.36	25.51	29.34	33.53	36.25	40.26	43.77	47.96	50.89	59.70

* Table 12.2 is abridged from Table IV of Fisher and Yates: *Statistical tables for biological, agricultural, and medical research*, published by Oliver and Boyd Ltd., Edinburgh by permission of the authors and publishers.

approximates much better to the chi-square distribution, especially with small expected frequencies. The correction consists of adding a half to each negative value of $(O - E)$ and subtracting a half from each positive value of $(O - E)$.

In the case of 2×2 two-way classification tables the formula for χ^2 takes a special form. Denoting the four cells of a 2×2 table by the letters a, b, c, d, we have

		Total	
a	b	$a + b$	
c	d	$c + d$	
$a + c$	$b + d$	n	$= a + b + c + d$

The formula for χ^2, including the correction for continuity, then becomes:

$$\chi^2 = \frac{n(|ad - bc| - n/2)^2}{(a + b)(c + d)(a + c)(b + d)} \quad \text{with one degree of freedom}$$

The vertical lines enclosing the expression $ad - bc$ mean that the positive value of the expression must be taken, irrespective of whether it turns out to be positive or negative.

Example. The following data were collected from a random sample of $n = 100$ women.

	Social class		
	ABC1	C2DE	Total
Owners of sewing machines	23	13	36
Non-owners	12	52	64
	35	65	100

The null hypothesis to be tested is that the ownership of sewing machines is at the same level for both social class groupings. The alternative hypothesis is that the ownership levels are different:

$$\chi^2 = \frac{100[|(23)(52) - (13)(12)| - \frac{100}{2}]^2}{(36)(64)(35)(65)} = 18.7$$

Table 12.2 shows that for one degree of freedom the value $\chi^2 = 18.7$ is significant at the 0.1% level, and on the evidence of these data it must be concluded that the ownership levels are different for the two social class groupings. The ownership levels are for ABC1 equal to $p_1 = \frac{23}{35} = 65.7\%$ and for C2DE equal to $p_2 = \frac{13}{65} = 20.0\%$. They have been put in percentage form to indicate that the chi-square test for 2×2 tables is equivalent to the test of two independent percentages given above.

285

McNemar's Test. This test is useful for 2×2 tables where the data have come from matched samples. The term matched samples includes those cases where each respondent in one sample is matched, on a number of criteria, to a respondent in a second sample, and also the case where the same sample of respondents is interviewed twice. The data from such 2×2 tables may often be presented, as below, in a form which might suggest that the ordinary chi-square test is applicable. This example shows the results of interviewing the same sample of respondents twelve months after a previous interview, about ownership of refrigerators.

	Interview 1	*Interview 2*
Refrigerator Owners	a	b
Non-owners	c	d
	$a + c$	$b + d$

It is incorrect to treat the two interviews as two independent samples and do a chi-square test to see whether the proportion of owners has increased or decreased. It is necessary to examine the changes from the first interview to the second.

		First interview		
		Owner	*Non-owner*	*Total*
Second	Owner	e	f	b
interview	Non-owner	g	h	d
	Total	a	c	$n = a + c = b + d$

It is important to notice that all that has been done is to recast the data in a different form. The marginal totals (a, b, c, d) of the 'changes' table correspond to the same values $a, b, c,$ and d in the previous table. To test the null hypothesis that the proportion of owners has neither increased nor decreased it is only necessary to consider the cell values f and g, as these are the only two cells that contribute to any change. If the null hypothesis is true the total number of respondents who change their ownership status will be evenly divided between these two cells. Thus, the expected value E for both these two cells is $(f + g)/2$. Having obtained observed and expected frequencies for these two cells, as given below, the usual formula for χ^2 may now be applied to these data.

	Observed (O)	Expected (E)
Non-owner to owner	f	$\dfrac{f + g}{2}$
Owner to non-owner	g	$\dfrac{f + g}{2}$
Total	$f + g$	

$$\chi^2 = \sum \frac{(O - E)^2}{E}$$

$$\chi^2 = \frac{[f - (f + g)/2]^2}{(f + g)/2} + \frac{[g - (f + g)/2]^2}{(f + g)/2}$$

$$\chi^2 = \frac{(f - g)^2}{f + g} \qquad \text{with one degree of freedom}$$

With a correction for continuity, the formula becomes:

$$\chi^2 = \frac{(|f - g| - 1)^2}{f + g}$$

Table 12.2 of significant values of χ^2 may, therefore, be used to test the validity of the null hypothesis.

Example. A random sample of $n = 500$ motorists are interviewed, before a new advertising campaign for motoring magazine A, to estimate the proportion who regularly read the magazine. The same 500 motorists are re-interviewed some time after the campaign is finished and the following data are obtained.

		First interview		
		Readers	*Non-readers*	Total
Second	Readers	203	66	269
interview	Non-readers	41	190	231
	Total	244	256	500

The null hypothesis is that there has been no change in the readership level, this being tested against the alternative hypothesis that some change has taken place. The test criterion is calculated as:

$$\chi^2 = \frac{(|66 - 41| - 1)^2}{66 + 41} = \frac{(24)^2}{107} = 5.38$$

Reference to Table 12.2 shows that, for one degree of freedom, $\chi^2 = 5.38$ is significant at the 5% level. The data suggest that there has been a real change in the readership percentage for magazine A.

Tests on Ranked Data

Testing rating scales

(a) The Kolmogorov-Smirnov Test For Two Independent Samples

Semantic rating scales are extensively used by market researchers. An example of such a scale would be:

(a) very good quality;
(b) good quality;
(c) neither good nor bad quality;
(d) bad quality;
(e) very bad quality.

This scale represents a non-numerical ranking of the attribute 'quality'. The Kolmogorov-Smirnov test assumes that underlying this scale is a hypothetical numerical measuring scale, to which the five statements approximate. In a later section actual numbers will be attached to each position on such scales, and more powerful statistical tests will be carried out, involving assumptions about the underlying numerical scale.

The Kolmogorov-Smirnov test may be used to compare two sets of percentages on the same rating scale obtained from two independent samples. The test consists of cumulating the percentages for each sample separately, and finding the maximum difference between any two cumulative percentages at any of the positions on the scale. This maximum difference may be compared against known theoretical values to judge its significance.

Example. A random sample of $n_1 = 200$ men and an independent random sample of $n_2 = 200$ women were asked to assess a new brand of sherry in terms of its sweetness/dryness. The results of the test were as follows.

	Men (per cent)	*Women* (per cent)
Very sweet	18.5	15.0
Sweet	22.5	17.5
Neither sweet nor dry	29.0	25.0
Dry	20.0	22.5
Very dry	10.0	20.0

The null hypothesis to be tested is that there is no difference in assessment by men and women, against the alternative hypothesis that there are some differences. This gives a two-tailed test. Denoting the percentages for men by p_1 and for women by p_2 the calculation of the maximum difference D between the cumulated percentages proceeds as below.

p_1	p_2	*Cumulative* $p_1 = A$	*Cumulative* $p_2 = B$	$D = |A - B|$
18.5	15.0	18.5	15.0	3.5
22.5	17.5	41.0	32.5	8.5
29.0	25.0	70.0	57.5	12.5
20.0	22.5	90.0	80.0	10.0
10.0	20.0	100.0	100.0	—

In a two-tailed test the maximum *positive* difference $D = |A - B|$ is taken as the test criterion irrespective of whether the difference is positive or negative. In this example, $D = 12.5$. The significant values of D for two samples of size n_1 and n_2 are shown below. The sample value of D must equal or exceed these values to be significant at a given level.

Significance level (per cent)	Significant value of D $\sqrt{\dfrac{n_1 + n_2}{n_1 n_2}}$ times:
10	122
5	136
1	163
0.1	195

Using the 5% significance level it is calculated that D must equal or exceed the value,

$$D = 136\sqrt{\frac{200 + 200}{200 \times 200}} = 13.6$$

The sample value of $D = 12.5$ is less than this, and therefore these data lead to the conclusion that there is no difference in the assessment of the new sherry by men and women.

For this particular significance test a one-tailed test will also be given, as the significance testing procedure differs from that of a two-tailed test. The null hypothesis will now be tested against the alternative hypothesis that men rate the product sweeter than do women. The calculation of the test statistic D is the same as for the two-tailed test, except that the sign of D in the last column of the above calculations is retained. If A is greater than B, then D is positive, and if B is greater than A then D is negative. The maximum value of D, in the direction predicted by the alternative hypothesis, is taken as the test statistic. In the present example this means considering only *positive* values of D, which would indicate men rating the product sweeter. In the one-tailed test the calculated value of D must be equal to or greater than:

$$\chi^2 = 4D^2\left[\frac{n_1 n_2}{n_1 + n_2}\right]$$

a quantity which has the chi-square distribution with two degrees of freedom, when D is expressed as a proportion and not as a percentage. In the example $D = 12.5\%$ or 0.125 as a proportion and χ^2 is found to be equal to:

$$\chi^2 = 4(0.125)^2\left[\frac{200 \times 200}{200 + 200}\right] = 6.25$$

Table 12.2 of the significance points of the chi-square distribution shows that for two degrees of freedom $\chi^2 = 5.99$ would be significant at the 5% level. The calculated value of $\chi^2 = 6.25$ is greater than this and it may be argued that the data support the alternative hypothesis that men judge the new sherry to be sweeter than do women. This result is different from that obtained previously by using a two-tailed test, and illustrates the point that a one-tailed test is always better at rejecting the null hypothesis than a two-tailed test.

(b) The Sign Test For Two Matched Samples

The 'sign test' may be used in a number of market research contexts, but here it is demonstrated in the situation where two matched samples of respondents rate two items, or where the same sample of respondents rates both items. The results are often presented in survey reports in a form which give the impression that the Kolmogorov-Smirnov test for two independent samples is appropriate. An example of this would be where $n = 200$ men were asked to rate two improved versions, X and Y, of an existing after-shave lotion. The data would probably be presented as below, in terms of frequencies and percentages.

	Version X		*Version Y*	
		per cent		per cent
Like very much	82	(41.0)	50	(25.0)
Like	57	(28.5)	70	(35.0)
Neither like nor dislike	29	(14.5)	40	(20.0)
Dislike	18	(9.0)	30	(15.0)
Dislike very much	14	(7.0)	10	(5.0)
	200	(100.0)	200	(100.0)

As the samples are matched a different approach is needed, which involves presenting one rating analysed by the other in the form of a two-way table. The sign test is then applied to some of the cells of this two-way table.

Example. The data below show the results obtained by analysing version X ratings against version Y ratings in the example on after-shave lotion.

		Rating on version X					
		Like very much	*Like*	*Neither like nor dislike*	*Dislike*	*Dislike very much*	*Total*
	Like very much	20	20	4	4	2	50
Rating	*Like*	30	20	10	5	5	70
on	*Neither*	18	10	8	3	1	40
version Y	*Dislike*	10	7	5	4	4	30
	Dislike very much	4	0	2	2	2	10
	Total	82	57	29	18	14	200

The null hypothesis is that there is no difference in the ratings for the two versions, and this will be tested against the alternative hypothesis that one or other of the two new versions is better liked. If the null hypothesis is true then the number of men rating X more favourably than Y on the scale ought to be the same as the number of men rating Y more favourably than X. Usually those rating X above Y are denoted by a + sign and those rating Y above X by a — sign, and this is how the sign test gets its name. The test consists of comparing the observed numbers rating X above and below Y with their expected frequencies. The test criterion turn out to be identical to the criterion of McNemars test.

	Observed	*Expected*
Number rating X above Y (+)	f	$\dfrac{f + g}{2}$
Number rating X below Y (−)	g	$\dfrac{f + g}{2}$
	$\overline{f + g}$	

$$\chi^2 = \frac{(|f - g| - 1)^2}{f + g} \qquad \text{with one degree of freedom}$$

In the example the number rating X above Y is obtained by summing the frequencies in the lower triangle of the above two-way table and the number rating Y above X is obtained from the sum of the frequencies in the upper triangle. Those men giving equal ratings are not used in the test, but the size of this group should be taken into account when interpreting the result of the significance test. Two summations give $f = 88$ and $g = 58$.

$$\chi^2 = \frac{(|88 - 58| - 1)^2}{88 + 58} = 5.76$$

From Table 12.2 of the chi-square distribution with one degree of freedom it can be seen that a value of 5.76 is significant at the 2% level. The observed differences in the two ratings do not appear to be due to sampling fluctuations, and the data suggest that version X is the better product.

Testing numerical rankings

A technique that is often used in market research, especially in product tests, is for respondents to be shown a number of objects and asked to rank them (1st, 2nd, 3rd, . . . etc.) in order of preference or acceptability. Special methods have been developed to test the significance of the results from data ranked in this way.

(a) Ranking of Two Objects—Paired Comparisons

In paired comparison tests objects are presented in pairs to respondents. The respondent is asked to state which object he prefers, i.e. he ranks them first and second. If more than two objects are to be tested it is possible to arrange that every respondent makes a judgement on all possible pairs. This situation is known as a 'balanced paired comparison experiment' or 'round robin'. In practice, respondents do not always consider all possible pairs of objects but only compare some pairs. Even so, it is possible to arrange that each pair of objects is judged by the same number of respondents. If the number of objects being tested is denoted by t, and n measurements are made on each possible pair, then the total number of possible pairs is given by:

$$\frac{t(t-1)}{2}$$

and the total judgements or rankings will be:

$$\frac{nt(t-1)}{2}$$

When comparing two objects, say A_1 and A_2, a score of one will be given to the preferred object and a score of zero to the object not preferred.

	Object		
	A_1	A_2	
Respondent 1	1	0	A_1 preferred to A_2
Respondent 2	0	1	A_2 preferred to A_1
Respondent 3	1	0	A_1 preferred to A_2
Respondent 4	1	0	A_1 preferred to A_2
	$a_1 = 3$	$a_2 = 1$	

The total score a_i for each of the t objects is used for testing the significance of paired comparison data.

Usually, this type of test is run to determine which objects are preferred overall, and in particular to find the 'best' object. This aim may be accomplished by comparing pairs of scores a_i and a_j on objects A_i and A_j for significant differences. Unfortunately, if the number of objects in the test is large, so is the number of possible pairs and therefore if a large number of significance tests are carried out on the data the probability of obtaining an apparently significant difference just by chance will be quite high. To guard against this the data are examined by an *overall test of significance* to see whether the scores $a_1 \, a_2 \, a_3 \ldots$ etc. as a set are significantly different. The test criterion is given by the expression:

$$D = \frac{4\left[\sum a_i^2 - \dfrac{tn^2(t-1)^2}{4}\right]}{nt}$$

This quantity has the chi-square distribution with $(t - 1)$ degrees of freedom. If this test gives a significant result at the chosen significance level, it indicates that some significant differences between scores exist. Individual pairs of scores may then be tested for significant differences by using the so-called *least significant difference* criterion defined by:

$$m = 1.96 \sqrt{\frac{nt}{2}} + \frac{1}{2}$$

Any pair of scores whose difference is equal to or greater than m may be declared significant at the 5% level. Replacing 1.96 by 2.58 or 3.29 gives equivalent criteria at the 1% and 0.1% levels respectively.

Example. $n = 60$ respondents were asked to do paired comparisons on all possible pairs of $t = 5$ types of biscuit, each respondent making $t(t - 1)/2 = 10$ judgements. The total scores for each biscuit were:

$$a_1 = 132 \qquad a_2 = 102 \qquad a_3 = 178 \qquad a_4 = 48 \qquad a_5 = 140$$

Squaring the scores for each biscuit gives:

$$a_1^2 = 17\,424; \ a_2^2 = 10\,404; \ a_3^2 = 31\,684; \ a_4^2 = 2304; \ a_5^2 = 19\,600$$

Summing these squared scores $\quad \Sigma a_i^2 = 81\,416$

$$D = \frac{4 \left[81\,416 - \dfrac{5(60)^2(4)^2}{4} \right]}{(60)(5)} = 125.55$$

With $t - 1 = 4$ degrees of freedom, Table 12.2 of percentage points of the chi-square distribution shows that at the 0.1% level D has to be 18.46 or greater to be significant. The computed value of $D = 125.55$ is therefore very highly significant and indicates that real differences between biscuits' scores do exist. Using the least significance difference criterion at the 5% significance level the critical value is:

$$m = 1.96 \sqrt{\frac{60 \times 5}{2}} + \frac{1}{2} = 24.51$$

Any difference in scores equal to or greater than 24.51 may be declared significantly different at the 5% level. However, it must be remembered that not too many significance tests should be carried out on the same set of data. Strictly speaking, one ought to test for significance only those pairs which are thought, before the experiment is carried out, to be a comparison of interest and not on pairs of scores which, when inspecting the data, just happen to look as if they might be significant. It is quite likely that the object with the highest score will be significantly different from the one with the lowest score even when the null hypothesis of no differences between any scores, is true. Further analyses on paired comparison data are given by David[3]. Among these is a special version for paired comparisons of a technique known as *analysis of variance*, which will be described later in this chapter. It uses a seven-point rating scale of preferences scored from +3 to −3 and allows for the effect of order of presentation of objects to respondents. This special version of the technique is due to Scheffé and the interested reader may consult his original article[4] for details.

(b) Ranking of Three or More Objects

If a number of objects are to be compared, and the objects have obvious differences, then it is better to get respondents to do an overall ranking of all the objects instead of doing a number of paired comparisons. When t objects have been ranked by n respondents it is possible to test whether there is any agreement between respondents ranking by calculating *Kendall's Coefficient of Concordance* (W) and testing its significance. If significant agreement is found, it is possible to obtain the order of preference or acceptability of the objects. A description of the calculation of W is best done in the context of an example.

Example. A random sample of $n = 100$ housewives are asked to rank $t = 4$ new designs for a breakfast cereal packet. The results of such ranking tests are usually given in the following form:

Cereal packet designs

Rank	A	B	C	D
1	40	10	25	25
2	30	20	40	10
3	20	30	25	25
4	10	40	10	40
	100	100	100	100

A design ranked first is given a score of 1, a design ranked second a score of 2 and so on. First calculate the sum of ranks R for each design:

$$R_A = (40 \times 1) + (30 \times 2) + (20 \times 3) + (10 \times 4) = 200$$

Similarly,

$$R_B = 300; \quad R_C = 220; \quad R_D = 280$$

Then calculate the average sum of ranks, $\bar{R}$:

$$\bar{R} = \frac{200 + 300 + 220 + 280}{4} = 250$$

Next, compute $S = \sum (R_i - \bar{R})^2$

R_i	$R_i - \bar{R}$	$(R_i - \bar{R})^2$
200	-50	2500
300	50	2500
220	-30	900
280	30	900
		$\overline{6800} = S$

S is the sum of squares of the deviations of the individual R_i scores from their average $\bar{R}$. If all respondents were in complete agreement, S would be equal to:

$$S = \frac{n^2(t^3 - t)}{12}$$

Kendall's W is the ratio of the observed value of S to its theoretical counterpart:

$$W = \frac{12S}{n^2(t^3 - t)} = \frac{12 \times 6800}{(100)^2(4^3 - 4)} = 0.136$$

The coefficient W may vary from $W = 0$, when all respondents are ranking at random, to $W = +1$, indicating complete agreement between respondents. To test whether W is significantly different from zero, use has to be made of tables of significant values of a statistical distribution known as the F distribution. Table 12.3 gives the 5% and 1% level values for this distribution, from which it will be seen that two values of degrees of freedom are required to specify significant values of F. It can be shown that a transformation of W given by:

$$F = \frac{(n - 1)W}{1 - W}$$

will have the F distribution with degrees of freedom approximately equal to

$$V_1 = t - 1 \quad \text{and} \quad V_2 = (n - 1)V_1$$

In the example,

$$F = \frac{(100 - 1)0.136}{0.864} = 15.6$$

with $V_1 = 4 - 1 = 3$ and $V_2 = 99 \times 3 = 297$ degrees of freedom. Reference to Table 12.3 of the F distribution reveals that the calculated value of $F = 15.6$ is at least significant at the 1% level. There appears to be a small but real agreement between respondents in their ranking of the new packet designs.

The rank order of acceptability of the new designs is given, when W has been found to be significant, by the individual sum of ranks R_i for each design. A low score indicates a high preference and a high score suggests a low level of acceptability. To test whether one design is ranked significantly higher than another the sign test, previously described, may be used. If design

B is to be compared with design C in the above example, the following two-way table involving the ranks of these two designs must be produced.

Ranking of design B

		1	2	3	4	Total
	1	0	5	10	10	25
Ranking of design C	2	5	0	25	10	40
	3	3	12	0	10	25
	4	2	3	5	0	10
Total		10	20	40	30	100

the number of times C ranked above B $(+) = 70$;
the number of times B ranked above C $(-) = 30$.

$$\chi^2 = \frac{(|70 - 30| - 1)^2}{70 + 30} = 15.21 \text{ with one degree of freedom}$$

Looking up Table 12.2 of the chi-square distribution for one degree of freedom shows that $\chi^2 = 15.21$ is significant at the 0.1% level. Design C is significantly preferred to design B by respondents.

Tests on Measured Data

Testing the difference between the means of two independent samples

A frequent comparison, which is needed when assessing the results of a market research survey, is that between the means of two rating scales, where the scales have been given simple numerical scores. As explained earlier, if one is prepared to assume that the scores represent meaningful values on an underlying continuous distribution, then the test about to be described, which is applicable only to measured data, may be used. As an example of how more than one type of significance test may be used on the same set of data, the data previously used in describing the Kolmogorov-Smirnov test will be examined again for significance. This time a scoring system will be attached to the scale positions, and the frequencies are used in place of the percentages.

Rating on new brand of sherry

	Score	Men	Women
Very Sweet	+2	37	30
Sweet	+1	45	35
Neither Sweet nor Dry	0	58	50
Dry	−1	40	45
Very Dry	−2	20	40
		$n_1 = 200$	$n_2 = 200$

The main assumption being made is that the scoring system is an interval scale and that the numerical distances between the scale positions are valid. The Kolmogorov-Smirnov test makes no such assumption.

To test the difference between two means $\bar{x}_1$ and $\bar{x}_2$ based on two independent samples of size n_1 and n_2 it is necessary to calculate the variance of each set of data. From the two variances $s_1{}^2$ and $s_2{}^2$ the standard error of the difference between two means is calculated as:

$$\text{Standard error } (\bar{x}_1 - \bar{x}_2) = \sqrt{s^2 \left[\frac{n_1 + n_2}{n_1 \times n_2} \right]}$$

where s^2 is a pooled estimate of the variance based on both samples

$$s^2 = \frac{\sum f_1(x_1 - \bar{x}_1)^2 + \sum f_2(x_2 - \bar{x}_2)^2}{(n_1 - 1) + (n_2 - 1)}$$

This average value of the variance is used as this test assumes that the two samples come from populations where the variance is equal. The null hypothesis usually states that there is no difference in the means. If this is true then the quantity:

$$Z = \frac{\bar{x}_1 - \bar{x}_2}{\text{standard error } (\bar{x}_1 - \bar{x}_2)}$$

will have the normal distribution (except when the sample sizes are very small). Tables of the normal distribution may, therefore, be used to test the significance of Z calculated from the two samples.

Example. The data on sherry are used in the example calculations given below. Subscripts 1 and 2 in the formulae refer to the sample of men and women respectively.

Score

$(x_1$ or $x_2)$	f_1	f_2	$f_1 x_1$	$f_2 x_2$	$(x_1 - \bar{x}_1)$	$(x_1 - \bar{x}_1)^2$	$f_1(x_1 - \bar{x}_1)^2$
+2	37	30	74	60	1.805	3.2580	120.5460
+1	45	35	45	35	0.805	0.6480	29.1600
0	58	50	0	0	−0.195	0.0380	2.2040
−1	40	45	−40	−45	−1.195	1.4280	57.1200
−2	20	40	−40	−80	−2.195	4.8180	96.3600
	200	200	39	−30			305.3900

$(x_2 - \bar{x}_2)$	$(x_2 - \bar{x}_2)^2$	$f_2(x_2 - \bar{x}_2)^2$
2.150	4.6225	138.6750
1.150	1.3225	46.2875
0.150	0.0225	1.1250
−0.850	0.7225	32.5125
−1.850	3.4225	136.9000
		355.5000

$$\bar{x}_1 = \frac{\sum f_1 x_1}{n_1} = \frac{39}{200} = 0.195 \qquad \bar{x}_2 = \frac{\sum f_2 x_2}{n_2} = \frac{-30}{200} = -0.150$$

$$s^2 = \frac{305.39 + 355.50}{199 + 199} = 1.661$$

$$\text{Standard error } (\bar{x}_1 - \bar{x}_2) = \sqrt{1.661\left[\frac{200 + 200}{200 \times 200}\right]} = \sqrt{0.01661} = 0.1288$$

$$Z = \frac{\bar{x}_1 - \bar{x}_2}{\text{standard error } (\bar{x}_1 - \bar{x}_2)} = \frac{0.195 - (-0.150)}{0.1288} = 2.68$$

Table 12.1 may be used to determine the significance level obtained by a difference in means which is equal to $Z = 2.68$ standard errors. Such a value is greater than the 2.58 standard errors needed for the result to be significant at the 1% level but less than 3.29 standard errors needed for 0.1% significance. It is actually significant at the 0.74% level. The conclusion which leads from this significance test is that men rate the new sherry to be more sweet than do women.

When scores are attached to the semantic rating scales used in market research and the data are assumed to have the properties of measured data, significance tests such as the one just described may be used to evaluate differences. The gain in doing so may be seen by considering the results of the present significance test on the sherry data along with the analysis of the same data using the Kolmogorov-Smirnov test. This latter test was unable to detect any significant differences between men and women's ratings, whereas the present test between the two means was able to show that a real difference was present. On the debit side the two-means test requires a lot more calculations than does the Kolmogorov-Smirnov test. However, most modern computer programs for survey analysis have facilities for automatically calculating means, variances, standard deviations and standard errors for scales which have been scored.

Testing the difference between the means of two matched samples

When the same sample of respondents rates two separate items, or rates the same item on two separate occasions, the ensuing data are often presented in a form which may suggest that the test for two independent means may be employed. The test, if applied to such matched sample data, would give too few significant results due to the matching. The correct test for this situation will now be described using the data on after-shave lotion previously analysed by means of the sign test. These data consisted of a sample of $n = 200$ men rating two new versions, X and Y, of an existing after-shave lotion, by means of a semantic scale. It will give another example of how ranked data may, if certain assumptions are made, be treated as measured data by attaching a numerical scoring system to the scale positions. The scoring used in the example will be:

	Score
Like very much	5
Like	4
Neither like nor dislike	3
Dislike	2
Dislike very much	1

The matched sample test uses the two-way table, presented previously, of version X's score (denoted by x_1) analysed by the score for version Y (denoted by x_2). From this table the difference in scores, $d = x_1 - x_2$ may be calculated and a frequency distribution of the d value can be formed. If the null hypothesis that there is no difference in the ratings of the two versions is true, then the expected or mean difference score $(\bar{d})$ would be zero, with a standard error of:

$$\text{Standard error } (\bar{d}) = \frac{s_d}{\sqrt{n}}$$

where $s_d =$ the standard deviation of the difference scores,

$$d = x_1 - x_2$$

The null hypothesis that $\bar{d} = 0$ may be tested by calculating the criterion:

$$Z = \frac{\bar{d} - 0}{\text{standard error } (\bar{d})} = \frac{\bar{d}\sqrt{n}}{s_d}$$

Z will follow a normal distribution, when the sample is not too small, and Table 12.1 may be used to evaluate the significance level.

Example. Scoring the two-way table of version X's ratings against the ratings on version Y gives the following table.

		Rating on version X (x_1 score)					Total men
		5	4	3	2	1	
Rating	5	20	20	4	4	2	50
on	4	30	20	10	5	5	70
version Y	3	⑱	10	8	3	1	40
(x_2 score)	2	10	⑦	5	4	4	30
	1	4	0	②	2	2	10
	Total men	82	57	29	18	14	200

From this table a frequency distribution of difference scores is easily obtained; for instance, the score $d = x_1 - x_2 = +2$ is obtained from the cells circled in the above table.

$d = x_1 - x_2$	f	fd	$(d - \bar{d})$	$(d - \bar{d})^2$	$f(d - \bar{d})^2$
$+4$	4	16	3.725	13.876	55.504
$+3$	10	30	2.725	7.426	74.260
$+2$	27	54	1.725	2.976	80.352
$+1$	47	47	0.725	0.526	24.722
0	54	0	-0.275	0.076	4.104
-1	37	-37	-1.275	1.626	60.162
-2	10	-20	-2.275	5.176	51.760
-3	9	-27	-3.275	10.726	96.534
-4	2	-8	-4.275	18.276	36.552
	200	$+55$			483.950

$$\bar{d} = \frac{\sum fd}{\sum f} = \frac{+55}{200} = +0.275$$

$$s_d = \sqrt{\frac{\sum f(d - \bar{d})^2}{\sum f - 1}} = \sqrt{\frac{483.950}{199}} = \sqrt{2.432} = 1.56$$

$$\text{Standard error } (\bar{d}) = \frac{s_d}{\sqrt{n}} = \frac{1.56}{\sqrt{200}} = 0.110$$

$$Z = \frac{\bar{d}}{\text{standard error } (\bar{d})} = \frac{+0.275}{0.110} = 2.50$$

The calculated mean $\bar{d} = 0.275$ is 2.50 standard errors distant from the hypothesized mean of zero. Such a deviation is almost equal to the 2.58 standard errors needed to be significant at the 1% level. It is, in fact, significant at the 1.24% level. The sign test applied to these data gave a result which was just significant at the 2% level according to Table 12.2 of the chi-square distribution.

Testing the difference between the means of three or more independent samples—the analysis of variance

A comparison of arithmetic means from several samples is often required when interpreting survey results. It is not good statistical practice to proceed immediately to carry out a number of individual significance tests on pairs of sample means. It is better first to do an overall test of the null hypothesis that the populations, from which all the samples have been selected, have identical means. The appropriate test for doing this is the F test. To carry out the test it is necessary to use a technique known as *analysis of variance* in which the total variance of all the data values in all the samples is split into two additive parts, that due to variance between samples and that due to variance within samples. The within sample variance in this case is equivalent to the pooled variance used previously, when testing two independent means. When these two parts of the variance, which are called mean squares, have been calculated, their ratio F given by:

$$F = \frac{\text{between samples mean square}}{\text{within samples mean square}}$$

will follow a statistical distribution known as the F distribution, when the null hypothesis is true. Table 12.3, which gives significant values of F, may be used to test whether the between samples mean square is larger than the within samples mean square. If the calculated value of F is found to be significant then it may be concluded that differences between the means exist.

Scale	Score x	Young f_1	Middle-aged f_2	Old f_3
Very bitter	5	21	11	14
Fairly bitter	4	46	29	22
Neither bitter nor sweet	3	37	47	35
Fairly sweet	2	22	18	38
Very sweet	1	12	7	28
		$n_1 = 138$	$n_2 = 112$	$n_3 = 137 \quad n = 387$

Example. Three samples of young men ($n_1 = 138$), middle-aged men ($n_2 = 112$) and old men ($n_3 = 137$) were asked to rate a new beer on a five-point scale of bitterness/sweetness. The results of the test are given above. The total variance has been previously defined as:

$$s^2 = \frac{\sum f(x - \bar{x})^2}{n - 1}$$

The numerator in this expression is known as the total sum of squares, and it is this quantity which is split into two parts, as below:

(a) square all $n = 387$ data values and sum them to give A.

$$A = (5^2 \times 21) + (4^2 \times 46) + \ldots + (1^2 \times 28) = 4132$$

(b) sum all $n = 387$ data values and square this total to give T^2.

$$T^2 = [(5 \times 21) + (4 \times 46) + \ldots + (1 \times 28)]^2 = (1178)^2 = 1\,387\,684$$

(c) divide T^2 by the total sample size n to give the so-called correction factor $C = T^2/n$

$$C = \frac{1\,387\,684}{387} = 3585.75$$

(d) sum the data values for each sample to give T_1, T_2, and T_3

$$T_1 = (5 \times 21) + (4 \times 46) + \ldots + (1 \times 12) = 456$$

similarly: $\qquad T_2 = 355 \qquad T_3 = 367$

Table 12.3 *Significant values*

v_2 \ v_1	5% points of F									
	1	2	3	4	5	6	8	12	24	∞
1	161.4	199.5	215.7	224.6	230.2	234.0	238.9	243.9	249.0	254.3
2	18.51	19.00	19.16	19.25	19.30	19.33	19.37	19.41	19.45	19.50
3	10.13	9.55	9.28	9.12	9.01	8.94	8.84	8.74	8.64	8.53
4	7.71	6.94	6.59	6.39	6.26	6.16	6.04	5.91	5.77	5.63
5	6.61	5.79	5.41	5.19	5.05	4.95	4.82	4.68	4.53	4.36
6	5.99	5.14	4.76	4.53	4.39	4.28	4.15	4.00	3.84	3.67
7	5.59	4.74	4.35	4.12	3.97	3.87	3.73	3.57	3.41	3.23
8	5.32	4.46	4.07	3.84	3.69	3.58	3.44	3.28	3.12	2.93
9	5.12	4.26	3.86	3.63	3.48	3.37	3.23	3.07	2.90	2.71
10	4.96	4.10	3.71	3.48	3.33	3.22	3.07	2.91	2.74	2.54
11	4.84	3.98	3.59	3.36	3.20	3.09	2.95	2.79	2.61	2.40
12	4.75	3.88	3.49	3.26	3.11	3.00	2.85	2.69	2.50	2.30
13	4.67	3.80	3.41	3.18	3.02	2.92	2.77	2.60	2.42	2.21
14	4.60	3.74	3.34	3.11	2.96	2.85	2.70	2.53	2.35	2.13
15	4.54	3.68	3.29	3.06	2.90	2.79	2.64	2.48	2.29	2.07
16	4.49	3.63	3.24	3.01	2.85	2.74	2.59	2.42	2.24	2.01
17	4.45	3.59	3.20	2.96	2.81	2.70	2.55	2.38	2.19	1.96
18	4.41	3.55	3.16	2.93	2.77	2.66	2.51	2.34	2.15	1.92
19	4.38	3.52	3.13	2.90	2.74	2.63	2.48	2.31	2.11	1.88
20	4.35	3.49	3.10	2.87	2.71	2.60	2.45	2.28	2.08	1.84
22	4.30	3.44	3.05	2.82	2.66	2.55	2.40	2.23	2.03	1.78
24	4.26	3.40	3.01	2.78	2.62	2.51	2.36	2.18	1.98	1.73
26	4.22	3.37	2.98	2.74	2.59	2.47	2.32	2.15	1.95	1.69
28	4.20	3.34	2.95	2.71	2.56	2.44	2.29	2.12	1.91	1.65
30	4.17	3.32	2.92	2.69	2.53	2.42	2.27	2.09	1.89	1.62
40	4.08	3.23	2.84	2.61	2.45	2.34	2.18	2.00	1.79	1.51
60	4.00	3.15	2.76	2.52	2.37	2.25	2.10	1.92	1.70	1.39
120	3.92	3.07	2.68	2.45	2.29	2.17	2.02	1.83	1.61	1.25
∞	3.84	2.99	2.60	2.37	2.21	2.09	1.94	1.75	1.52	1.00

Table 12.3 is abridged from Table V of Fisher and Yates: *Statistical Tables for Biological, Agricultural and*

(e) calculate the quantity B given by:

$$B = \frac{T_1^2}{n_1} + \frac{T_2^2}{n_2} + \frac{T_3^2}{n_3} = \frac{(456)^2}{138} + \frac{(355)^2}{112} + \frac{(367)^2}{137} = 3615.13$$

The total sum of squares is given by $A - C = 4132 - 3585.75 = 546.25$.

The between samples sum of squares is given by $B - C$

$$= 3615.13 - 3585.75 = 29.38.$$

The within samples sum of squares is given by $A - B$

$$= 4132 - 3615.13 = 516.87.$$

The calculations are summarized in the following analysis of variance table.

Just as the total sum of squares is divided by total sample size less one $(n - 1 = 386)$ to give the variance, so the between samples mean square is obtained by dividing its sum of squares by the number of samples less one $(3 - 1 = 2)$. These divisors are known as degrees of freedom and, like the sums of squares, are additive. The degrees of freedom for the within samples mean

v_2 \ v_1	1	2	3	4	5	6	8	12	24	∞
					1% points of F					
1	4052	4999	5403	5625	5764	5859	5981	6106	6234	6366
2	98.49	99.00	99.17	99.25	99.30	99.33	99.36	99.42	99.46	99.50
3	34.12	30.81	29.46	28.71	28.24	27.91	27.49	27.05	26.60	26.12
4	21.20	18.00	16.69	15.98	15.52	15.21	14.80	14.37	13.93	13.46
5	16.26	13.27	12.06	11.39	10.97	10.67	10.29	9.89	9.47	9.02
6	13.74	10.92	9.78	9.15	8.75	8.47	8.10	7.72	7.31	6.88
7	12.25	9.55	8.45	7.85	7.46	7.19	6.84	6.47	6.07	5.65
8	11.26	8.65	7.59	7.01	6.63	6.37	6.03	5.67	5.28	4.86
9	10.56	8.02	6.99	6.42	6.06	5.80	5.47	5.11	4.73	4.31
10	10.04	7.56	6.55	5.99	5.64	5.39	5.06	4.71	4.33	3.91
11	9.65	7.20	6.22	5.67	5.32	5.07	4.74	4.40	4.02	3.60
12	9.33	6.93	5.95	5.41	5.06	4.82	4.50	4.16	3.78	3.36
13	9.07	6.70	5.74	5.20	4.86	4.62	4.30	3.96	3.59	3.16
14	8.86	6.51	5.56	5.03	4.69	4.46	4.14	3.80	3.43	3.00
15	8.68	6.36	5.42	4.89	4.56	4.32	4.00	3.67	3.29	2.87
16	8.53	6.23	5.29	4.77	4.44	4.20	3.89	3.55	3.18	2.75
17	8.40	6.11	5.18	4.67	4.34	4.10	3.79	3.45	3.08	2.65
18	8.28	6.01	5.09	4.58	4.25	4.01	3.71	3.37	3.00	2.57
19	8.18	5.93	5.01	4.50	4.17	3.94	3.63	3.30	2.92	2.49
20	8.10	5.85	4.94	4.43	4.10	3.87	3.56	3.23	2.86	2.42
22	7.94	5.72	4.82	4.31	3.99	3.76	3.45	3.12	2.75	2.31
24	7.82	5.61	4.72	4.22	3.90	3.67	3.36	3.03	2.66	2.21
26	7.72	5.53	4.64	4.14	3.82	3.59	3.29	2.96	2.58	2.13
28	7.64	5.45	4.57	4.07	3.75	3.53	3.23	2.90	2.52	2.06
30	7.56	5.39	4.51	4.02	3.70	3.47	3.17	2.84	2.47	2.01
40	7.31	5.18	4.31	3.83	3.51	3.29	2.99	2.66	2.29	1.80
60	7.08	4.98	4.13	3.65	3.34	3.12	2.82	2.50	2.12	1.60
120	6.85	4.79	3.95	3.48	3.17	2.96	2.66	2.34	1.95	1.38
∞	6.64	4.60	3.78	3.32	3.02	2.80	2.51	2.18	1.79	1.00

Medical Research, published by Oliver and Boyd, Ltd., Edinburgh, by permission of the authors and publishers.

Source of variation	Sum of squares	Degrees of freedom	Mean square	F
Between samples (age groups)	29.38	2	14.690	10.91
Within samples	516.87	384	1.346	
Total	546.25	386		

square is, therefore, obtained by difference. If the null hypothesis of equal means is true, the expected value of the ratio of the two mean squares will be $F = 1$. The calculated value of $F = 10.91$ with $V_1 = 2$ and $V_2 = 384$ degrees of freedom may be assessed for significance by referring it to Table 12.3. For $V_1 = 2$ and $V_2 = \infty$, F must exceed 4.60 to be significant at the 1% level. The calculated value $F = 10.91$ is therefore significant and it may be concluded that differences in means do exist between age groups.

After finding a significant value of F, one is now justified in comparing pairs of means for significance using the test for two independent sample means given previously. If the number of samples is large, then so is the number of pairs of means that can be tested, and this leads to some of the comparisons being significant just by chance, as explained in the section on paired comparisons. *Multiple comparison tests* have been developed to overcome this and a good summary of them is given in the book by Snedecor and Cochran[5].

The analysis of variance described above was concerned with data classified in one way only, i.e. by age. Often, data appear in a two-way table, e.g. age by sex, or in multi-way tables. The technique of analysis of variance may be applied to such data to highlight the effects of the various classifications and the interaction between them. A full treatment of this is beyond the scope of this chapter and the reader is referred to chapters 10, 11, 12, and 16 of Snedecor and Cochran[5], the latter chapter giving an account of analysis of variance as applied to percentage data. A related technique to analysis of variance is the *analysis of covariance*. It enables comparisons between classifications to be made using analysis of variance when the effect of an unwanted classification has been eliminated. Details of how to use this technique may be obtained from chapter 14 of Snedecor and Cochran[5].

Some General Points on Significance Testing

Significance tests on small samples

When the data collected are based on small samples, many of the significance tests given in this chapter need modifying or replacing by special alternative tests. As a rough rule it is recommended that, if the sample size is $n = 50$ or larger, the tests given may be all applied without serious error. On this point, it is worth mentioning that the first two tests given for measured data are often referred to as 'the t-test for two independent sample means' and 'the paired t-test for two matched sample means'. This is because the significance test criteria Z, in both cases, will follow a statistical distribution known as the t distribution. This distribution which is applicable for small samples becomes more and more like the shape of the normal distribution as the sample size increases. The convergence may be illustrated by considering the number of standard errors difference that are needed between two means to achieve a 5% significance level. In the case of large samples, where the normal distribution is appropriate, the value is 1.96. For small samples leading to the t distribution, a value of 2.04 is required for $n = 30$ and 2.00 for $n = 60$. This shows that the normal distribution may be used for samples of $n = 50$ or more in such significance tests.

Interpretation of significant results

The fact that a survey result is found, by carrying out a statistical significance test, to be significant often leads to confusion when such a result is presented to people unfamiliar with research methodology. The layman, when told that something is significant, often assumes that the researcher considers the result to be 'important'. As explained in this chapter, such an inference is not necessarily true. In statistical terms, if, for example, a difference between two percentages is declared significant, it simply means that this difference, no matter whether it is a *large* or *small* difference, cannot be explained by sampling errors. With very large samples, where the sampling distributions of the null and alternative hypotheses will have small standard errors, small differences in percentages will be significant. Whether these small differences are important to the researcher and his client depends on the subject matter of the survey, previous survey results and any number of other practical considerations. The example that follows gives some idea in one particular case how small differences in percentages may be viewed. A random sample of 1000 housewives owning washing machine brand A is found to contain 48% who claim to be 'very pleased' with the machine. A further random sample of 1000, who own brand B, contains 56% who are 'very pleased'. The difference in percentages 56% — 48% = 8% is comparatively small and might be regarded as unimportant, even though it is a statistically significant difference. However, if it is known from previous surveys with samples of 1000 that differences between brands of washing machine are always insignificant, then the observed difference may be thought of as being an important finding.

This chapter has been presented in terms of simple random sampling. Most surveys use more complicated sampling methods where the standard errors are usually larger than the standard error formulae given here. The amount by which they are larger is known as the *design factor*. In those cases above where a standard error has been given, this standard error should be increased by the design factor of the survey being analysed, when carrying out a significance test.

On this point about simple random sampling it is difficult to give much advice to users of quota samples. Strictly speaking, it is not possible to calculate sampling errors and, therefore, carry out significance tests on data from quota samples. In practice, researchers quite often assume that the data are as if they had come from a random sample and proceed to carry out significance tests as described above. The limited research that has been done in quota sampling methods indicates that, in some cases, the sampling errors may be higher than for random sampling. For this reason, some researchers increase the standard error by an arbitrary factor such as 1.5 or 2.0 when carrying out significance tests on quota sample data.

Appendix A

The chances are 95 in 100 that the percentage being estimated by the survey lies within a range equal to the observed percentage plus or minus the number of percentage points shown in the table.

Sampling errors on percentages in survey reports

Observed percentage	Sample size						
	100	250	500	750	1000	1500	2000
	±%	±%	±%	±%	±%	±%	±%
50	9.8	6.2	4.4	3.6	3.1	2.5	2.2
40 or 60	9.6	6.1	4.2	3.5	3.0	2.5	2.1
30 or 70	9.0	5.7	4.0	3.3	2.7	2.3	2.0
20 or 80	7.8	5.0	3.5	2.9	2.5	2.0	1.8
10 or 90	5.9	3.7	2.6	2.2	1.9	1.5	1.3

The usual formula for sampling errors of simple random sampling given below, was used in the calculations.

$$\pm 1.96 \sqrt{\frac{P(100 - P)}{n}} \quad \text{where} \quad \begin{array}{l} P = \text{the observed percentage} \\ n = \text{the sample size} \end{array}$$

Appendix B

Significant differences between survey percentages

The following five tables may be used to decide whether observed differences between two survey percentages are statistically significant at the 5% level.

How to use the tables

To compare two percentages $p_1\%$ and $p_2\%$ based on sample sizes of n_1 and n_2 respectively, where n_1 is the smaller sample size:

(a) if the two sample sizes are approximately equal, calculate the average of $p_1\%$ and $p_2\%$

$$p\% = \frac{p_1\% + p_2\%}{2}$$

if the two sample sizes are very different calculate

$$p\% = \frac{n_1 p_1\% + n_2 p_2\%}{n_1 + n_2}$$

(b) look up the table corresponding to $p\%$ (the table closest to $p\%$);

(c) find the cell of the table corresponding to n_1 and n_2, approximately;

(d) the observed difference between the two percentages $p_1\%$ and $p_2\%$ must be equal to or greater than the value given in this cell to be significant at the 5% level.

Example. Is a value of $p_1 = 46\%$ based on a sample of $n_1 = 500$ significantly different from a value $p_2\% = 54\%$ based on a sample of $n_2 = 500$?

As the sample sizes are equal, $p\% = (54\% + 46\%)/2 = 50\%$.

The first table corresponding to $p = 50\%$ shows that for $n_1 = n_2 = 500$ the observed difference must be 6.2% or greater to be significant.

The observed difference of $54 - 46\% = 8\%$ is thus significant.

Differences needed between two percentages around 50% to be significant at the 5% level.

$$p = 50\%$$

Sample size n_2	Sample size n_1						
	100	250	500	750	1000	1500	2000
	%	%	%	%	%	%	%
100	13.8						
250	11.6	8.8					
500	10.7	7.6	6.2				
750	10.4	7.2	5.7	5.1			
1000	10.3	6.9	5.4	4.7	4.4		
1500	10.1	6.7	5.1	4.4	4.0	3.6	
2000	10.0	6.6	4.9	4.2	3.8	3.4	3.1

Differences needed between two percentages around 40 or 60% to be significant at the 5% level.

$$p = 40 \text{ or } 60\%$$

Sample size n_2	Sample size n_1						
	100	250	500	750	1000	1500	2000
	%	%	%	%	%	%	%
100	13.6						
250	11.4	8.6					
500	10.5	7.4	6.1				
750	10.2	7.0	5.5	5.0			
1000	10.1	6.8	5.2	4.6	4.3		
1500	9.9	6.6	5.0	4.3	3.9	3.5	
2000	9.8	6.4	4.8	4.1	3.7	3.3	3.0

Differences needed between two percentages around 30 or 70% to be significant at the 5% level.

$$p = 30 \text{ or } 70\%$$

Sample size n_2	Sample size n_1						
	100	250	500	750	1000	1500	2000
	%	%	%	%	%	%	%
100	12.7						
250	10.6	8.0					
500	9.8	7.0	5.7				
750	9.6	6.6	5.2	4.6			
1000	9.4	6.3	4.9	4.3	4.0		
1500	9.3	6.1	4.6	4.0	3.7	3.3	
2000	9.2	6.0	4.5	3.8	3.5	3.1	2.8

Differences needed between two percentages around 20 or 80% to be significant at the 5% level.

$$p = 20 \text{ or } 80\%$$

Sample size n_2	Sample size n_1						
	100 %	250 %	500 %	750 %	1000 %	1500 %	2000 %
100	11.1						
250	9.3	7.0					
500	8.6	6.1	5.0				
750	8.3	5.7	4.5	4.1			
1000	8.2	5.6	4.3	3.8	3.5		
1500	8.1	5.3	4.1	3.5	3.2	2.9	
2000	8.0	5.3	3.9	3.4	3.0	2.7	2.5

Differences needed between two percentages around 10 or 90% to be significant at the 5% level.

$$p = 10 \text{ or } 90\%$$

Sample size n_2	Sample size n_1						
	100 %	250 %	500 %	750 %	1000 %	1500 %	2000 %
100	8.3						
250	7.0	5.3					
500	6.4	4.5	3.7				
750	6.3	4.3	3.4	3.0			
1000	6.2	4.2	3.2	2.8	2.6		
1500	6.1	4.0	3.0	2.6	2.4	2.2	
2000	6.0	3.9	2.9	2.5	2.3	2.0	1.9

13. Multivariate analysis of market research data

C. Holmes

Marketing is a complex process. It involves the evaluation of many different variables and the ways in which they inter-relate in the marketing 'mix'. In order to try and make sense of a mass of data measured on a sample drawn from a population, more and more reliance is being placed on the use of a variety of statistical techniques. Some of these techniques, such as correlation analysis, are relatively well established; others, such as canonical analysis and cluster analysis, are not so well known, and their potentialities in terms of their problem solving abilities are only just being realized.

Statistical techniques which simultaneously examine the relationships between many variables are known as 'multivariate statistical procedures'. A major contributing factor to the upsurge of interest in this area has largely been due to advancements made in computer technology.

Most multivariate techniques require an immense number of calculations which, whilst not beyond the resources of clerks and adding machines, are more quickly and economically carried out by computer.

It is not my intention in this chapter to dwell at large on the theoretical properties underlying the basis of the varying types of multivariate procedures. The inclusion of statistical and mathematical formulae will be kept to a minimum. References to the appropriate literature will be quoted for the interested reader to pursue at his leisure. The main aim is to present a somewhat simplified overview of a rather complex subject matter in as non-mathematical a manner as possible.

It is useful to consider some of the typical practical problems with which multivariate analysis is concerned. Some may be well known and well documented, others may be of a specialist nature; all are pertinent to the field of market research:

(a) In a survey of television viewing a 'dependent' variable, quantity of viewing, is measured. A hypothesis is formed that this may be predicted by such variables as age, education, readership, etc. *Regression analysis* would assist in the construction of a model to fit the data. Variations in the parameters of the model would enable changes in viewing to be predicted.

(b) In an attitudinal survey about various companies and their products, it is of interest to examine the relationships not only between correlations within the battery of 'company' rating scales and within the battery of 'product' rating scales, but also the relationships between the two data matrices. *Canonical analysis* could provide an insight into the way the two sets of data are inter-related.

(c) Results are available relating salesmen's performances over various activities together with training observations and results. It is required to produce, from these data, criteria to evaluate whether salesmen may be classified into specific groups. The use of *discriminant analysis* will assist in this problem as it attempts to maximize the probability of correct assignment to groups.

(d) From the results of repertory grids a large battery of semantic attitudinal scales is drawn up and administered to a sample of the population of, say 'cake-mix' users. Straightforward correlation analysis is applied to the results but the matrix of correlation coefficients is too large to facilitate an 'understanding' of the data. The researcher seeks to find a certain kind of organization in the data to identify fundamental and meaningful dimensions in the inter-relationships. *Principal components* and *factor analysis* might be used to explore the underlying dimensionality of the data.

(e) A list of a hundred towns (qualifying on certain issues) is drawn up as potentials for test marketing operations. Statistics relating to population, retail sales, readership, etc., are collected. A limited number of towns are required to be representative of national characteristics. In what way can they be chosen? The application of some form of *numerical taxonomy* (*cluster analysis*) might reveal distinct homogeneous sub-groups of towns. The selection of one town from each group would ensure that each stratum is represented in the overall test-marketing mix.

These, then, are just a few examples of marketing problems where the use of multivariate analysis may assist in finding the answers. It must be stressed, however, that the techniques of multivariate analysis are not able to solve problems by themselves. It is not good enough to have masses and masses of doubtful data, consult a textbook for an appropriate technique and feed the lot into a computer. You may be lucky enough to get an answer that 'makes sense', but if the original data are not the 'right' kind of data then you will not get the 'right' kind of answer. In fact, the use of multivariate analysis makes it all the more imperative to consider the hypothesis-making and question-forming stages of the research. To quote Collins[1]: 'Multivariate analysis systems make ever-increasing demands upon the question designer, the

311

question poser and the question answerer. Questionnaires become not only lengthy but extremely monotonous. With so many analysis techniques based upon the search for non-random patterning of responses, boredom is clearly a major problem'.

It is not within the scope of this chapter to dwell at large on issues like these but, nevertheless, they are important and should not be overlooked.

Dependence or Interdependence

So to the actual subject itself. What is multivariate analysis? It is broadly concerned with the *relationships* between sets of dependent variables.

Kendall[2] in a very clear exposition of the subject discerns two main branches of the multivariate tree, and subdivides multivariate analysis into whether we are concerned with dependence or inter-dependence.

Dependence

In this type of problem we are concerned with the way in which one or more dependent variables, often chosen by us or dictated to us by the problem, *depends* on the other (independent) variables. The simplest example of 'dependence' analysis is the regression of one variable on others often in the form:

$$y = a + b_1x_1 + b_2x_2 + \cdots + b_nx_n$$

An often quoted example of a multiple linear regression is the prediction of university degree results from the so-called independent variables (number of 'O'-levels, 'A'-level passes and so on). The phrase, 'so-called independent variables' is a choice one, since they are often genuinely correlated or they are fortuitously correlated in the data sample.

Interdependence

The second branch is that of interdependence: here we are not concerned with any dependent variables, but only with the relationship of a set of variables amongst themselves. No variable is selected to be of special interest. Correlation analysis is a clear example of this part of the subject.

Correlation Analysis

Since multivariate analysis is concerned with the inter-relationships between variables, the starting points of most analyses begin with the way in which the variables correlate (or co-vary) with each other. A useful way of considering the various manipulations that can be carried out on data is to visualize the ends results of a survey in the form of a data matrix (Fig. 13.1).

312

VARIATES (Responses)

		x_1	x_2	x_3			x_i		x_p
	1	x_{11}	x_{21}	x_{31}	$\cdots$		5	$\cdots$	x_{p1}
	2	x_{12}	x_{22}	x_{32}	$\cdots$		4	$\cdots$	x_{p2}
	3	x_{13}	x_{23}	x_{33}			6		$\bullet$
OBSERVATIONS (Respondents)	4	x_{14}	x_{24}	x_{34}			7		$\bullet$
	5	x_{15}	x_{25}	x_{35}			2		$\bullet$
	$\bullet$	$\bullet$	$\bullet$	$\bullet$			$\bullet$		$\bullet$
	$\bullet$	$\bullet$	$\bullet$	$\bullet$			$\bullet$		$\bullet$
	$\bullet$	$\bullet$	$\bullet$	$\bullet$			$\bullet$		$\bullet$
	$\bullet$	$\bullet$	$\bullet$	$\bullet$			$\bullet$		$\bullet$
	$\bullet$	$\bullet$	$\bullet$	$\bullet$			$\bullet$		$\bullet$
	n	x_{1n}	x_{2n}	x_{3n}	$\cdots$		3	$\cdots$	x_{pn}

Fig. 13.1 *Data Matrix:* Generally x_{ij} stands for the jth observation on the ith variable. Thus, the column headed x_i could refer to a rating scale and, as an example, hypothetical ratings are illustrated for respondents.

Whatever the subject matter of the research we can visualize it in this row-by-column tabulation. It is convenient at this stage to look upon the columns as variables and the rows as respondents. By considering each pair of columns separately we can see how each pair of variables correlates.

The most widely used measure of correlation is the Pearson 'product moment coefficient of correlation'. It is a coefficient ranging from -1, through zero, to $+1$ and is a measure of the degree of *linear* association between two variables. We can illustrate varying degrees of correlation by means of a simple scatter diagram (Fig. 13.2). Positive correlation (Fig. 13.2(a)) means that increasing values of variable y are associated with increasing values of variable x and vice-versa. Negative correlation

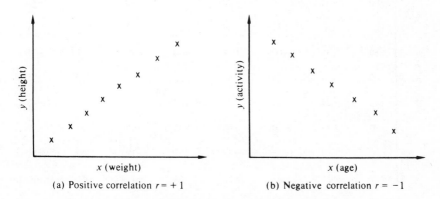

(a) Positive correlation $r = +1$ (b) Negative correlation $r = -1$

Fig. 13.2 Examples of scatter diagrams.

313

(Fig. 13.2(b)) indicates that increasing values of x are associated with decreasing values of y. Zero correlation implies that there is no linear association between the two variables (although there could, of course, be a non-linear relationship). Essentially, Pearson's correlation coefficient, r, between two variables x and y is:

$$r = \frac{\text{covariance } (x \cdot y)}{\sqrt{[\text{variance } (x)][\text{variance } (y)]}}$$

where

$$\text{covariance } (x \cdot y) = \frac{1}{n} \sum (x - \bar{x})(y - \bar{y})$$

and the variances are as defined in chapter 12.

From the data matrix we can calculate the respective correlation coefficients for each pair of variables across all sample members. The resultant correlation matrix (Fig. 13.3) is a useful starter in seeking relationships between variables. A.S.C. Ehrenberg[3] in a robust attack on factor analysts considers that in many cases the 'look at it' approach is equal to the more so-called 'sophisticated' types of analyses. However, it is increasingly difficult to sort out relationships since as the number of variables grows, the number of correlation coefficients increases rapidly. (For n variables, there are $n(c)2 = n(n - 1)/2$ correlation coefficients.)

If variables are highly correlated, it does not follow that the existence of causation is proved. However, if the hypothesis of causation is postulated and a zero or non-significant correlation coefficient is obtained, then the hypothesis may be rejected with a given probability level. Correlation analysis may disprove causation but it can never entirely prove it. Statistical tests may be applied to the resultant correlation coefficients to assist in deciding whether or not the variables show *significant* correlation as opposed

		1	2	3	4	5	6	7	8
	1	100	+31	-50	00	-35	-70	+40	-87
	2	+31	100	+37	-56	+21	+17	+10	-25
	3	-50	+37	100	+34	+40	-70	+25	-37
VARIABLES	4	00	-56	+34	100	-35	+45	+27	-55
	5	-35	+21	+40	-35	100	+05	-97	-43
	6	-70	+17	-70	+45	+05	100	+10	-17
	7	+40	+10	+25	+27	-97	+19	100	+24
	8	-87	-25	-37	-55	-43	-17	+24	100

Fig. 13.3 Example of a correlation matrix (the decimal point has been omitted for the sake of clarity). The 1's in the leading diagonal are conventional.

to purely random (chance) correlation. In general we may test whether:

(a) the correlation coefficient is significantly greater than zero;
(b) the difference between the same correlation coefficient computed from different samples is significant.

In addition to Pearson's product moment correlation coefficient there are a number of 'non-parametric' measures, such as Spearman's rank and Kendall's tau which are often used on data which are not distributed normally, or where the measurement level achieved is only up to an 'ordinal' scale. For details of these and other coefficients the reader is advised to consult Siegel[4].

Principal Components Analysis (PCA)

In the statistical analysis of relationships between variables it is often important that the variables are uncorrelated (orthogonal) with one another. This is particularly true in multiple regression techniques and in the interpretation of factors in factor analysis. The method of principal components analysis is a technique for obtaining new 'artificial' variables which are uncorrelated with one another. It is, therefore, a useful mathematical device as well as being central to the generally accepted method of carrying out factor analysis. Both Kendall[2] and Hope[5] describe the technique mathematically and it is only intended here to describe the mechanics of principal components analysis briefly.

Algebraic Visualization. If one considers the diagonal terms of the covariance matrix (or the standardized correlation matrix with '1's' in the leading diagonal) then the sum of the diagonal terms represents the total variance of the data sample. This total variance can be split up into N latent roots each of which has an eigenvector associated with it. The eigenvectors generate a set of principal components each of which has a variance associated with it equal to its latent root.

Geometric Visualization. Another way of visualizing principal components is to consider the data sample plotted in N-dimensional space. We may, for example, plot measurements made on three variables, say height, weight, and breadth as in Fig. 13.4. The first principal component is directed along the main long axis of the cigar-shaped cluster. Having extracted this component, then the second principal component is along the next longest axial direction of the cluster, orthogonal to the first, and so on.

The main attraction of principal components analysis is that the components are extracted in descending order of the amount of total variance each one accounts for. There are as many components as there are original variables and the sum of the variances of all the principal components equals the sum of the variances of the original variables. In very

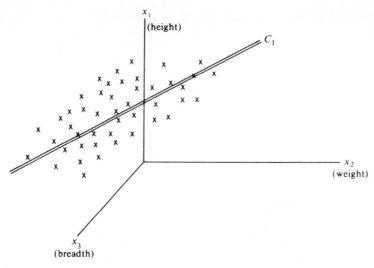

Fig. 13.4 Geometric visualization of the first principal component.

simple terms, we may think of the principal components as weighted combinations of all the original variables. If we start with three variables, X_1, X_2, and X_3, then the three principal components, C_1, C_2, C_3 are given by

$$C_1 = W_{11}X_1 + W_{12}X_2 + W_{13}X_3$$
$$C_2 = W_{21}X_1 + W_{22}X_2 + W_{23}X_3$$
$$C_3 = W_{31}X_1 + W_{32}X_2 + W_{33}X_3$$

where W is a numerical weight determined by the analysis; (they are also termed the 'loadings' of the variables on the components). In practical terms, it is usually found that the first few components account for a large proportion (often in the range 70 to 90%) of the total variance. In certain circumstances the researcher ignores the remaining components in any further analyses and, thus, achieves a significant gain in data-reduction.

Since each component is a weighted combination of the original variables, it is possible to calculate for each person (or object) in the sample a score on each component. Thus, not only does principal components analysis enable us to find out the basic dimensionality of our data, it allows the facilitation of further analyses to be made on scores which are measured on orthogonal dimensions. A practical drawback with principal components analysis is that the components are rarely interpretable in a marketing sense.

Examples of principal components analysis

(a) *Test Market Locations*

Christopher[6] utilized principal components analysis in an attempt to classify towns into homogeneous clusters. Information was collected for 30 towns considered suitable for test marketing operations. A set of mutually independent factors was extracted using principal components analysis and towns were then clustered according to their scores on the factors.

(b) *Classification of Towns*

Moser and Scott[32] classified 164 British towns which in 1951 had populations of 50 000 or over. Four principal components were found to account for 60% of the total variance. The first component itself accounted for 30% of the variance and reflected social class differentiation.

(c) *Stratification of Local Authority Areas*

Holmes[7] similarly carried out experimental work relating to local authority areas in Yorkshire and Humberside. One hundred and forty local authority areas were analysed over seven variables using principal components analysis. Three independent components were found to account for over 70% of the total variance. This exercise was an attempt at optimal stratification for use in the selection of primary sampling units.

Factor Analysis

A concise history and the development of factor analysis may be found in Harman[8]. Factor analysis embraces a set of statistical techniques which seek to analyse the intercorrelations within a set of variables. Developed originally by psychologists—amongst the early pioneers were such distinguished theorists as Spearman, Burt, Kelley, Thurstone, Holzinger and Thomson—factor analysis has gone through a controversial and turbulent history. To quote Cooley and Lohnes[9], 'Each pioneer seemed to feel his procedure was *the* method of factor analysis. Only recently have students of factor analysis begun to see that the different procedures are suitable for different purposes and usually involve different assumptions regarding the nature of human attributes'.

Factor analysis model

Factor analysis is different from principal components analysis (although the latter is often a prerequisite to the former) in that the factor analysis model attempts to describe the data in terms of a model with a number of new variables called 'factors', *less* in number than the original variables. The simplest formulation of the model is that the total variance in the data can be split into two parts, that due to the common factors and that due to residual factors, thus:

total variance (V) = var.(factors) + residual variance

In contrast to the principal components analysis model, the factor analysis model for three variables and two factors may be written mathematically as

$$X_1 = W_{11}F_1 + W_{12}F_2 + d_1R_1$$
$$X_2 = W_{21}F_1 + W_{22}F_2 \qquad + d_2R_2$$
$$X_3 = W_{31}F_1 + W_{32}F_2 \qquad\qquad + d_3R_3$$

where X_1, X_2, X_3 are the original variables; F_1, F_2, are the common factors, R_1, R_2, R_3 are the residual (sometimes known as the unique) factors. The coefficients, W and d are frequently referred to as the loadings. Explained in words, the factor analysis model assumes that each variable may be represented as a linear sum of a number of orthogonal factors, usually less in number than the number of original variables, plus a specific residual factor unique to that variable. In other words, a hypothesis is formed that the total variance of a variable is made up of:

(a) a proportion of variance which the variable shares (or has in common) with other variables;
(b) an amount of residual (unique) variance which is uncorrelated with other variables.

Communality

The proportion of variance that is common to other variables is known as the *communality* of the original variables and is calculated as the sum of the squares of the coefficients (loadings) associated with the m common factors. This estimate of communality, strictly speaking, requires to be inserted in the leading diagonal of the correlation matrix but this cannot be achieved until the factor solution is obtained. This seemingly circular problem is resolved by estimating the communalities, carrying out a trial factor solution, re-adjusting the communality estimates and so on. The most widely used method of estimating communalities is the utilization of the squared multiple correlation between the variable and the remaining $(n - 1)$ variables. It is worth noting that the problem of communalities is only acute in the case of small data matrices. In practice, it has been found that the larger the order of the correlation matrix the less it matters what values appear in the leading diagonal.

The most common methods of obtaining factor solutions are the 'principal factor solution' and the 'maximum likelihood solution'. Neither method will be explained here and the interested are directed to Cooley and Lohnes[9] for the former and Lawley and Maxwell[10] for details of the latter. The principal factor solution, based as it is on principal components analysis, has the important property that it produces factors in order of the amount of variance they explain. The maximum likelihood solution is probably more efficient and does not require any estimation of communalities although the number of factors required has to be stipulated in advance.

How many factors?

The problem of how many factors to extract has plagued factor analysts for many years but with advanced computer technology it is less of a problem today. There are, basically, two criteria for deciding on how many factors to retain:

(a) statistical;
(b) marketing meaningfulness.

Amongst the statistical criteria is the widely adopted Kaiser's[11] rule of retaining factors whose latent roots are greater than one. However, statistical considerations alone are not entirely satisfactory and in most market research studies the meaning and interpretability of the retained factors plays an important part in the decision process. A factor contributing only a small portion of variance may not be statistically important but it may prove a good discriminator for, say, degree of purchase.

Rotation

We now touch upon, what perhaps has caused most controversy in the history of factor analysis, rotation of the factors. The rotation problem arises because of the indeterminancy of factor solutions. It is a mathematical fact that, given a set of correlations between variables, the estimating of the factor equations is fundamentally indeterminate; that is to say that the loading of the variables in the estimating equations may be chosen in an infinite number of ways, consistent with the observed correlations. Over the years, therefore, certain criteria have been established to limit the factor analysis solutions. The accepted criteria in the determination of new reference axes are Thurstone's[12] properties of 'simple structure'. The aim in rotating axes is to enable the factors to be more meaningfully interpretable. Amongst the many proposed solutions, two have stood the test of time, namely Varimax and/or Promax. The Varimax rotation still requires the restriction that the axes are orthogonal (uncorrelated) to one another. Promax, developed by Hendrickson and White[13] is an acceptable extension of Varimax such that the axes are allowed to become non-orthogonal or oblique (correlated). Over several studies, the writer finds that Promax usually gives the same factor structure but is slightly more interpretable. When the factor solution is oblique, knowledge of the degree with which the factors correlate with one another is required. A disadvantage of an oblique solution is that further analysis (such as cluster analysis) may prove to be more difficult to handle. Interpretability is gained at the expense of statistical simplicity.

Factor scores

A 'factor score' may be estimated for each respondent for each factor. These may be averaged for any sub-group in much the same way as ordinary rating

319

scales. Thus, a typical factor analysis may involve 80 rating scales which produce some 10 to 12 dimensions (factors). On each factor we can estimate scores for rated products, brands, services, etc., which together with breakdowns by purchasing behaviour, age, social grade, etc., can provide useful marketing information. Charting methods such as simple 'profile charts' and two and three dimensional maps assist in the interpretation stage. Hill[14] gives clear examples of single and two-dimensional charts whilst Hope[5] devotes a chapter to 'spherical maps'.

Example of factor analysis

Frost[15] gives a clear example of factor analysis applied to seven-point rating scales. 750 television viewers rated 58 statements on two programs they had watched. In total, 61 programs were rated in this way, rotated randomly between the respondents, and the resultant factor analysis gave the following nine factors:

(a) general evaluation;
(b) information;
(c) romance;
(d) violence;
(e) conventionality;
(f) scale of production;
(g) noise/activity;
(h) acceptability;
(i) humour.

As Frost points out, 'It should be noted that, whilst names have been attached to these factors, this has been done simply for ease of reference and that the proper interpretation of a factor is to be found amongst the individual attitude scales which have substantial loadings upon it. Thus, for example, Factor 2 called 'information' in fact describes a dimension of viewer differentiation which has at one end programs which tend to have much scientific interest, which make the viewer think and which convey educational information and which has at the other end programs which contain little scientific interest which encourage the viewer to relax being of a less informative and generally more entertaining type'.

Frost utilized these nine dimensions to compute program attitude ratings covered in the survey. An example in the paper illustrates that programs like 'Man Alive' and 'The Power Game' score highly on the 'information' factor whilst 'Juke Box Jury' 'Black & White Minstrels' and 'The Monkees' are to be found, not surprisingly, at the 'little scientific interest' end. 'These typical results', Frost concluded, 'confirm our original interpretation of this factor as being a dimension which differentiated between educational programs and entertainment programs'.

Numerical Taxonomy

Cluster analysis

An integral part of the analysis of market research surveys is that of *classification*. Traditionally, analysis has been of the uni- or bi-variate kind; i.e., analysis by age, social grade, products bought, etc., and by combination of suchlike variables. Since data are collected for many variables, it seems logical that we should attempt to classify our respondents over many variables. The analytical procedures designed for this purpose of simultaneously assessing respondents over many variables may be subsumed under the heading of 'numerical taxonomy', the principles of which are clearly set out by Sokal and Sneath.[16] The term 'cluster analysis' strictly refers to part of the taxonomic procedure but has come into general usage to mean classification usually in a market segmentation context. Numerical taxonomy has as its objective the classification usually of persons, but not necessarily always so, such that persons within a cluster or group are more alike each other with respect to the measured variables than persons outside the cluster. If definite clusters exist then they may be described in terms of their 'profiles' and utilized as breakdowns in similar fashion to the traditional classification systems such as age within social grade.

Mechanics of numerical taxonomy

Figure 13.5 illustrates the steps required in the taxonomic process. Neither 'sample selection' nor 'measurement' will be dealt with here since they are

Fig. 13.5 Flowchart describing the steps involved in numerical taxonomy as applied to market research.

topics common to all types of multivariate analysis and, in any case, are dealt with elsewhere. Before proceeding to discuss the remaining steps it is worthwhile to reconsider the data matrix (Fig. 13.1) and the possible ways of analysing it. Traditional methods of analysis have always been based on the relationships *between the variables across the respondents*. Analysis of this kind leads to a clustering of variables and is known as 'R-technique'. However, there is another way of looking at the data matrix, and that is to look at the relationships *between respondents across the variables*, known as 'Q-technique'[17].

Coding of characters

Once the information required has been measured on a sample of respondents, a coding operation is required before it is possible to calculate measures of affinity. Basically, there are three different kinds of measurement:

(a) dichotomous characters (1:0 data);
(b) multi-state characters, of a *quantitative* nature;
(c) multi-state characters, of a *qualitative* nature.

The latter type of measurement presents the greatest problems and Sokal and Sneath[16] comment on the potential dangers involved in the coding process.

Calculation of affinities

The next step is to calculate estimates of affinity (similarity) between each pair of respondents so as to form an affinity matrix. The three basic measures available are:

(a) *Similarity Coefficients*

These types of coefficients are mainly used in conjunction with dichotomous measurements (1:0 data). Essentially, a similarity coefficient expresses the number of 'matching' attributes respondents have in relation to the total number of comparisons. A coefficient is calculated for every pair of respondents. Figure 13.6 illustrates how a similarity coefficient may be computed using the familiar 2×2 layout. The most common similarity coefficients range from zero (non-similar) to one for perfect matching. Further examples of similarity coefficients are discussed by Joyce and Channon[17].

(b) *Distance Coefficients*

Measures of distance are based on a geometric model, and in special cases are related to similarity coefficients. The most common distance measurement is:

$$d_{jk} = \left[\frac{\sum (x_{ij} - x_{ik})^2}{N} \right]^{\frac{1}{2}}$$

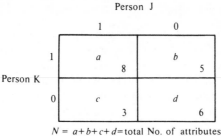

Person J

		1	0
Person K	1	a 8	b 5
	0	c 3	d 6

$N = a+b+c+d =$ total No. of attributes

(a) S_{JK} $\dfrac{a}{a+b+c} = \dfrac{8}{16} = 0\cdot50;$

(b) S_{JK} $\dfrac{a}{N} = \dfrac{8}{22} = 0\cdot36$

Fig. 13.6 Example of the calculation of two different similarity coefficients. The interpretation of the 2 × 2 table is as follows: code 1 for possession of an attribute; 0 for non-possession. Thus, comparing person J to person K in the numerical example—they each match on possessing eight attributes, person K possesses five attributes which person J does not, person J possesses three attributes which person K does not and neither person possesses six similar attributes.

x_{ij} is person j's score on the ith variable and x_{ik} is person k's score on the ith variable, and $N =$ No. of variables.

Figure 13.7 gives a simple two-dimensional illustration of the 'distance' concept. If the respondents are identical as regard to the measured characteristics then the distance between them and, consequently, the coefficient will be zero. The greater the disparity between two persons, the larger will be the distance measurement; thus, distance is complementary to similarity.

Fig. 13.7 Illustration of the calculation of a distance coefficient in two dimensional space.

323

(c) *Correlation Coefficient*

Just as a correlation coefficient between two variables may be calculated, so can a coefficient of correlation between two persons. This is an alternative method to the distance coefficient for handling quantitative data. Inglis and Johnson[18] in a studied paper on the developments in and the analyses of multivariate survey data consider that a distance measurement is often preferable since, conceptually, it measures distances between people more powerfully.

Cluster analysis

Having computed some form of affinity coefficient, the next step is to group together those respondents who are most similar to each other. In a paper read to an MRS course on 'segmentation analysis', Emmett[19] reviewed the new methods of 'clustering' and 'clumping'. Essentially, 'clustering' involves the formation of trial sets of clusters which are continually modified by successive iterations. The 'clumping' methods require the establishment of basic 'clumps', e.g. the two 'nearest' points, which are added to by the addition of nearest neighbours.

An appropriate method of clustering similarity coefficients appears to be that of 'average linkage'[16] whilst Scientific Control Systems Ltd.[20] and Cybernetics Research Consultants Ltd.[21] describe programs in their Users Guide to Cluster Analysis, based on successive iterations from trial solutions which are appropriate when using distance coefficients.

Naming the groups

Once the researcher is satisfied with the cluster solution the resultant groups can be tested for homogeneity using a variety of statistical tests including Holzingers B coefficient. The salient features of each cluster require to be summarized and described in terms of the variables/attributes involved in the analysis. As in factor analysis names may be attached to each cluster for ease of reference but, again, care is required to ensure that any 'shorthand' descriptions used are not later misinterpreted. The charting of simple 'profile charts' is a useful summarizing aid.

Examples of numerical taxonomy

(a) *Political Party—Scientific Control Systems Limited*

Morgan and Purnell[22] report on a cluster analysis using factor scores derived from a battery of attitudinal scales relating to elector's attitudes to political issues. Four factors were obtained and factor scores were estimated for each of 500 electors. A ten-cluster solution was considered to be the most appropriate. Each cluster was 'subjectively' named as follows:

Cluster No.	Name	Sample size
1	High Tory	45
2	Me first	34
3	Whig	36
4	Labour (little England)	70
5	Meritocrat	46
6	Me first (anti-Europe)	57
7	'One nation' Tories	44
8	Left-wing Labour	42
9	Meritocrat (pro-Europe)	43
10	Right-wing Labour	83

One of the aims of this case study was to see whether or not a 'new' political party could be discovered—a position analogous to seeking a new product. A program NEMO seeks to describe the existing products in a market in an n-dimensional product attribute space. The object of the analysis is to look for a point in the space which defines a new product which is as different as possible from existing ones.

(b) *Subjective Clustering of Television Program Similarities*

Several papers in the Journal of the Market Research Society[23] concerned clustering procedures of television programs. An interesting paper by Green, Carmone and Fox[24] described the methodology and application of subjective clustering of television programs. Briefly, this procedure entails respondents sorting into groups various stimuli (television programs). One of the analyses reported is that of respondent configuration. For each pair of respondents a distance measure was computed, based on the degree of agreement in the pair's clustering of programs. The resultant distance maxtrix was submitted to a multi-dimensional scaling program. Whilst the authors report little relationships between the subjective clusters and other certain predictor variables such as demographic and socio-economic variables, the technique is mentioned here as being of particular interest in the area of defining markets and sub-groups in markets.

Multiple Regression Analysis

Multiple regression analysis is a technique for estimating the relationship between one 'dependent' variable and a number of so-called 'independent' variables. Since the technique is concerned with relationship—the way in which the variables are associated with one another—it is not unlike correlation analysis. Indeed, in practice both correlation coefficients and regression equations are generally desired in the same problem. The essential difference is that *regression analysis* is concerned with dependence; one (or more) variable is selected for study and we are concerned to find out whether the magnitude of the variable can be *predicted* from knowledge about the independent variables. *Correlation analysis* is concerned with the degree of association between sets of observations.

Simple linear regression

Let us consider the simplest case of regression, i.e. the way in which one variable may be related (and hence predicted) by another. A useful first step in such a problem is to draw a 'scatter diagram' (see Fig. 13.2). A line of 'best fit' through the points may be drawn visually. If there is a high degree of correlation between the variables then for any given value of x (weight) we can predict the likely value of y (height). Mathematically, we may predict y (height) by the equation;

$$y = a + bx$$

where a is the y-axis intercept and b is the slope of the line. The parameters a and b are known as the regression coefficients and they are chosen so as to minimize the sums of squares of the deviations from the regression line. This method is known as the 'least-squares' method. a is estimated by $\bar{y}$ and b is estimated by:

$$b = \frac{\text{covariance } (x \cdot y)}{\text{var } (x)} \quad \left[\text{or } \frac{\sum xy}{\sum x^2} \text{ when } x \text{ and } y \text{ are standardized} \right]$$

Multiple regression

Mutliple regression analysis is merely an extension of the simple case. Again, there is one dependent variable, but a number of 'independent' variables are used to try and explain the variations of the dependent variable. The addition of more independent variables means that the mathematical model can portray more realistically real life situations. It is rare that only one variable influences another. In a complex marketing situation, variation in sales may be associated with many factors, such as amount spent on advertising, distribution levels, national prosperity, etc.

The linear model for multiple regression is:

$$y = a + b_1 x_1 + b_2 x_2 + \cdots + b_p x_p$$

where x is the independent variable and b the rate of change of the dependent variable y in each of the independent variables when the other independent variables are held constant. They are often called the *partial regression coefficients* and their estimation is carried out in similar fashion to the simple linear regression case. The mathematics is more complicated but the principle is unchanged, i.e. the coefficients are chosen so as to minimize the residual sums of squares. Those interested should consult almost any intermediate

326

statistical textbook for details of the theory and Ferber[25] gives practical examples with detailed worksheets for simple cases. As the number of independent variables increase the computational aspect is considerable. Perhaps the best existing commercial computer programs are those developed by Scientific Controls Systems Ltd. Beale, Kendall and Mann have made very notable contributions to the development of multiple regression. They offer two main alternative programs. One is optimum in that it produces the best possible sets of independent variables. The other is a less expensive procedure which, however, does not guarantee an optimum solution.

Example of multiple regression

Multiple regression is, perhaps, one of the most common statistical techniques used in marketing and yet, unfortunately, few case histories are available in the literature. This is probably because the greatest use of multiple regression is in the sales forecasting area, i.e. given sales data and a set of sales determinants such as economic data, household information, a forecasting model may be set up. The effect of changes in the parameters of such a model may be estimated by regression techniques.

Frank and Boyd[27] studied each of 44 grocery products (the dependent variable) and the way in which the proportion of product purchases related to nine household socio-economic characteristics and five measures of purchasing behaviour (independent variables). They found little association between household socio-economic or total consumption characteristics and *private* brand purchasing. The significant relationships which emerged were the obvious ones, such as households with members that shop in grocery stores with substantial private brand stocks spend a higher percentage of their purchases on private brands.

Canonical Correlation

Canonical correlation procedures are designed to measure simultaneously the relationships between several dependent variables and several independent variables, all measured on the same set of persons (or objects). It is, therefore, a further extension of multiple regression, the main difference being that, whereas in multiple regression we have only one dependent variable, in canonical analysis we have more than one. Canonical analysis works in the following way. The variables are split into two sets, a set of criterion (dependent) variables and a set of predictor (independent) variables. Sets of coefficients are calculated such that the correlation between the weighted sum of the criterion variables has the maximum correlation with the weighted sum of the predictor variables. This equation is the first canonical regression equation. It is analogous to a principal component in that it maximizes correlation and thus facilitates prediction. A second canonical regression line is then found orthogonal to the first and yet has maximum correlation between the two (new) equations. There are as many canonical regression equations as there are variables in the smallest set.

Tests of significance may be applied to the resultant canonical correlations and one hopes that the first few will be large and the remainder negligible. To date the writer knows of only one published example of canonical analysis in a marketing context[26]. It is considered that, as computing facilities become more available, the potentialities of applying canonical analysis to marketing problems will be realized.

Example of canonical correlation

For a detailed discussion of the statistical theory underlying canonical analysis the reader should refer to Cooley and Lohnes[9] who also give an example which uses the technique to test general hypotheses that relate two sets of variables. The example is concerned with a set of seven predictor variables which are scores on scales relating to early home environment, e.g. how close was the respondent to mother and father in childhood. The criterion variables are scores relating to the respondents present orientation towards people, e.g. degree of curiosity expressed towards people. Those interested may consult the reference for actual results. A basic conclusion was that early home environment is related to orientation towards people and that the primary antecedent is early experience of social activities.

Multiple Discriminant Analysis

We are often concerned with the ability to predict a person's response given a set of different measurements about this person. We may wish to predict which car a person will buy from knowledge about his past ownership, his present situation and, say, his attitudes to cars in general. Discriminant analysis and, in general, multiple discriminant analysis is a technique for classifying persons into one group or another given certain information which is correlated with a multichotomous attribute.

In discrimination, the classes are predetermined and we are concerned with allocating a person to one of several classes. In the simplest case, that of two classes, the following example illustrates the technique. Suppose we have two groups of persons, purchasers and non-purchasers, and we have information for each person regarding attitudes, behaviour, socio-economics characteristics, etc. A discriminant function may be calculated by defining a new variable, 'propensity to purchase', as a weighted sum of the attitude, etc., variables. Assume we only have two pieces of attitude information, then we can plot the data as shown in Fig. 13.8. The discriminant function attempts to predict, by considering the weighted score for each person whether or not

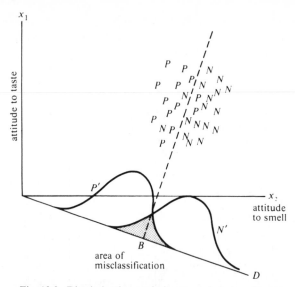

Fig. 13.8 Discrimination analysis: example in two dimensions. Purchasers (P) and non-purchasers (N) are plotted on two dimension x_1 and x_2. A discriminant analysis generates a score (D), based on the two attitude scores. The problem is one of where to draw the boundary (B) so as to minimize the probability of misclassification (shaded area). Predictions may be made for 'new' observations by allocating persons to one or other side of the boundary by considering the score generated by the discriminant function.

he is more likely to be a purchaser or a non-purchaser. The problem is one of drawing the boundary so as to minimize the probability of misclassification.

Sequential Dichotomization Techniques

One of the earliest new classification methods was developed by Belson[28], who was primarily interested in attempting to find the best combination of independent variables which would predict a 'dependent' variable. The 'Belson sort' procedure examined all alternative dichotomizations of a sample to discover those which were significant predictors and then went on to examine in a sequential fashion the best combinations of independent variables. At each stage in the splitting process, chi-square values are calculated to test the predictive performance of the chosen dichotomies (Fig. 13.9).

Example of Belson sort

A recent example where an amended version of the Belson sort procedure was used is JICNARS Reader Categorisation Study[33]. In this study 15

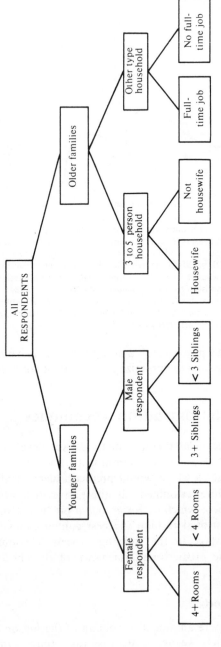

Fig. 13.9 Example of Belson Sort reproduced with permission of Dr W. A. Belson. Matching and Prediction on the Principle of Biological Classification. The criterion variable in this case is the degree to which individuals participate with others in the home, i.e., joint activity. For simplicity's sake further dichotomization has been excluded in the example.

candidate measures were tested as predictors of differences in reading behaviour. Part of the conclusions involved the qualified recommendation of including a question on 'provenance' in the standard questionnaire since this measure increased the proportion of explained variance.

Automatic Interaction Detection

This is a technique for dividing a sample into groups on the basis of demographics or other variables, again splitting on one variable at a time. The method arose because the authors, Sonquist and Morgan[29], were concerned with the inadequacy of simple cross-tabulations to reveal the complex interactions in survey data. It is similar to the Belson sort, splitting on one variable at a time except that the criterion for retaining the discriminating variables is based on analysis of variance. The first predictive variable is that which maximizes the between group variance and minimizes the within group variances.

Thompson[34] has succinctly summarized the differences between A.I.D., and the 'Belson sort' while Willson[35], in a paper devoted to the computational segmentation of multivariate statistics, rightly notes that studies involving A.I.D. are typically concerned with market segmentation. In a brief note, Sampson[36] indicates how A.I.D. may be used as a preliminary to cluster analysis. Those independent variables which account for a high degree of variance on one (or more) criterion variable are chosen as the basis for cluster definition. The writer's own view is that A.I.D. will increasingly be utilized in the preliminary skirmishes researchers have when trying to reduce to sensible proportions large masses of data.

Example of A.I.D.

Assael[37] gives two examples of the use of A.I.D. when other methods such as regression and cross-classification analysis have failed. The first example illustrates how a sample of respondents with a 'usual purchase' level of Brand X is segmented on these key variables; sex, geographical location, educational level, product usage, age, occupation and income. Surprisingly, product usage emerged only at a third iteration and after the fourth some 5% of the sample had a 62% Brand X purchase compared to the sample average of 16.5%.

A second example illustrates a perceptual market segmentation. A sample of 2000 housewives rated the degree with which a beverage satisfied each of thirteen criteria, ranging from 'good tasting' to 'pure ingredients'. The criterion 'restores energy' was the main predictor of the number of family units consumed in a week. A segment comprising 5% of the sample rating the product high on 'restores energy' 'year round drink' and 'easy to prepare' consumed 70.5 units compared to the sample average of 23.3 units.

Non-Metric Multi-Dimensional Scaling (MDS)

The latest developments in multivariate statistics are concerned with the relative low-level degree of measurements achieved in market research data. Much of the data collected by researchers is of the nominal or ordinal kind (non-metric) and, in the past, analysts have indiscriminately applied the techniques described in this chapter which assume the conditions of metric measurement.

Statistical techniques are now available which require only non-metric data and yet yield results which are of metric scaling. These techniques may be subsumed under the heading of 'non-metric multi-dimensional scaling'. The input to a non-metric MDS is typically a ranking in terms of similarity *of all possible pairs* that can be obtained from a set of objects. The underlying statistical logic is that the consideration of all possible pairings *increases* the amount of information available. For example, 20 numbers describe 10 points in two dimensions whereas there are 45 pairings when considering 10 objects taken two at a time. Willson[35] illustrates this concept with the familiar example of the mapping of 11 cities by considering the 55 inter-city distances. A two-dimensional solution is obtained which adequately represents the original rankings. An examination of the derived co-ordinates is sufficient for the dimensions to be recognized geographically, NORTH to SOUTH and WEST to EAST. However, as Willson points out, MDS programs do not purport to reveal the nature of the resultant dimensions. A small-scale study by Doyle and McGee[38] explores the use of non-metric MDS applied to the convenience food market. An interesting paper which would serve as an introduction to this current development is by Neidell.[30] In this paper, Neidell introduces the notion of developing a multi-dimensional attribute space from a uni-dimensional data bank consisting of inter-object non-metric relationships.

Multivariate Analysis: Concluding Remarks

Inevitably this chapter on multivariate analysis can only touch the surface of the subject. It is hoped that the references provided will enable both specialist and non-specialist seeking to widen their knowledge in this complex field to a greater understanding of multi-dimensional space. Increasing use is being made of techniques like factor analysis, multiple regression, and so on, often in inappropriate situations on data that are not amenable to such analyses. The market researcher, faced with such a toolbag of techniques must be familiar enough with the subject to utilize the right techniques. The mathematician/statistician must, likewise, appreciate the research problems and use techniques not for themselves but for their problem-solving capabilities.

The latest developments concerning *non-metric* multi-dimensional scaling are likely to continue with the awareness by analysts of the inadequacy of present-day data input. It is to be hoped that the introduction of 'time-sharing' computers and the advancement of higher level programming languages will enable researchers to utilize multivariate techniques to great advantage. Additionally, Sheth[39] suggests the availability of canned computer programs is a most important factor in the diffusion of multivariate methods.

The initial head-on plunge into new techniques and methodologies is always to be expected. As Green and Frank[31] point out; 'Despite the inevitable misapplication of techniques and over-selling (with the consequent failure to live up to expectations), the fact remains that quantitative and behavioural science are here to stay'. Multivariate analysis as an important sector of quantitative science should not be ignored simply because of its apparent complexities.

Part II. Use of consumer market research

Introduction

The role of market research is to make marketing operations more efficient and profitable, by improving the quality of planning and decision taking. This is the only way in which market research can justify itself. The following chapters, therefore, illustrate how the research tools described earlier are applied to various problems encountered in marketing.

Market research is involved with a very wide range of activities directed towards helping an organization to supply, as efficiently and profitably as possible, goods or services designed so as to satisfy identified consumer needs. These activities cover not only distribution and selling operations but also many aspects of production and, indeed, company policy generally. Market research is certainly not the exclusive preserve of the marketing man. It has increasingly drawn in the laboratory scientist, the production manager, finance and personnel departments, and others. The contributions which follow reflect this broad view of market research.

In planning these chapters we had in mind a structure of the marketing process which explains their sequence. Like all such structures it is greatly over-simplified, but the reader may find it helpful to know the pattern. This is illustrated in Fig. 1, the bracketed figures being the chapter numbers. There are two additional chapters which do not fit so neatly into the pattern: the more specialized but very important field of financial research (chapter 22), and the broader and growing field of international market research (chapter 23).

There are four comments to make about this approach. First, the total material, to be manageable, has to be divided under sub-headings, i.e. chapters. This is inevitable but artificial; and it would be positively dangerous if, in real life, the different problems were treated as though in watertight compartments. A successful brand does *not* consist simply of a formula plus a pack plus a price plus an advertisement plus . . . etc., where each of these elements has been developed in isolation. The whole is (or certainly should be) far greater than the sum of its parts. The various elements of the marketing mix, therefore, have to be interrelated and tested together at various stages. This point is emphasized at several points in these chapters, and is absolutely basic to successful brand marketing.

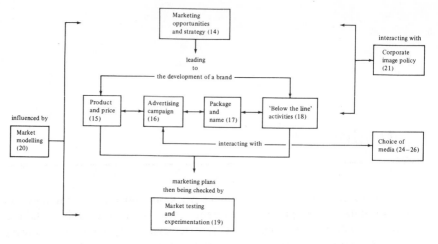

Fig. 1

Second, market research and brand development does not often proceed in a neat and tidy time sequence from a study of market opportunities to the national launch of a new brand. It tends to involve a process of continual re-thinking and adjustment of plans as more information becomes available. The elements of the marketing mix, and sometimes even the brand concept itself, may have to be modified as we progress towards the stage of market testing. This may mean going back on an earlier stage of market research and retesting.

Third, much of the following material is presented in the context of developing a *new* brand. This is the clearest, and in many respects the most comprehensive, method of illustrating the way in which market research is applied. Obviously, a great deal of market research is concerned with *existing* brands, particularly in recycling them to give them a new lease of life in changing and heavily competitive markets. The principles discussed in these chapters apply to such brands also, although not all the steps described will be needed. Probably the major difference is that an existing brand will normally have an established personality or image as far as consumers are concerned. This may sometimes be weak, and quite possibly be one we wish to change, but our research approach must take account of it, for in the market-place the existing image will condition consumers' views about any new developments (product, advertising or other) which we may plan for the brand. As chapter 15 points out, 'blind' testing can be particularly misleading in this context.

Finally, a substantial part, perhaps about a third, of the total expenditure on market research in the UK is devoted to market measurement (retail audits, consumer purchasing panels and barometers of different kinds). This is necessary both for drawing up plans and monitoring progress in existing markets and also to provide certain key background data for investigating

338

possible new markets. Earlier chapters have described these techniques and discussed several of their key applications. The following chapters, therefore, do not make much reference to the more descriptive, background planning aspects of market measurement and similar research, since the latter's value in dealing with various marketing problems should already be clear.

One other general point is worth making. Most of the discussion in these chapters concentrates on the problems of frequently-bought consumer goods. Even so, a lot of what is said applies equally to durable goods and to services, although some of the detailed mechanics of the research have to be adapted to fit the special characteristics of these products.

The chapters on media research call for some additional introductory comments. As Bert DeVos pointed out in the previous edition of this Handbook, there are several important reasons why such research merits a substantial section in a book on market research. Media research is used widely, constantly and intensively and there is considerable similarity of objectives and methods among advertisers and their agencies in the continuous effort to secure maximum value per pound spent in allocating advertising appropriations both between and within media. Similarly, calibration of his audience or readership is the essential basis of any sales effort by a media owner. Accordingly, media research is one of the largest single areas of market research expenditure.

As a result of these factors, media research is (with the possible exception of the political polls) the most visible and generally scrutinized area of market research. Most media research is widely circulated as a direct result of the joint industry committees that have been set up to govern press, television and radio research in Britain; and privately commissioned media research projects are almost invariably published in attempts to convince advertisers and their agents of the particular merits of, say, one publication versus others. Such research is also widely used as a source of basic market data and demographic information and for dividing the country up into realistic marketing areas. Few other types of research come under this type of informed, users' scrutiny. And for this reason the standards achieved tend to set the pace for the market research profession.

Ideally, one would wish for directly comparable techniques for assessing the value of different media, but this has so far eluded both the methodology and the cash resources of the industry. The characteristics of the various media and the differing feasibility of measurement (both technical and financial) have produced quite different ways of calibrating them. This particularly applies to comparisons between press and television. Thus, basic press research is typically based on large, national samples with relatively infrequent reporting periods, compared with small regional samples with weekly reporting of minute-by-minute data in the case of television. However, it is important to avoid the pitfall of assuming that because the research monitoring systems are so dissimilar this necessarily indicates fundamental differences in the way that the respective audiences react to the media.

A general question posed by Bert de Vos was that of the cost efficiency of traditional media research. Are we spending too much on what *can* be measured, as opposed to devoting more time, effort and money on that part of the iceberg beneath the surface? Little work, for example, has been done on inter-media effectiveness compared with the enormous volume of intra-media research. Another important question related to the marginal efficiency of extra-media data in terms of the cost of obtaining it. In the early days of the move from simple circulation data to readership data based on research, the research payoff was manifestly obvious and large in terms of improved advertising efficiency. We now seem to be at a stage in media research where many potential avenues of enquiry, while of considerable theoretical interest, have much less attractive potential in terms of cost effectiveness. Reading intensity measures may be one example. Until recently, the emphasis rested heavily on getting as much data as possible—some would think too many data now that computer processing has made the marginal cost of extra tabulations so low. Possibly the most important step for media research to take over the next decade is therefore to evaluate the uses of the data much more stringently.

This leads us to another broader, but linked, issue. An important development during the last three years or so has been the increasing use of 'econometric' techniques in atempts to measure the sales effectiveness of advertising campaigns—and thus to provide a sounder basis for setting the advertising budget and for allocating this between media, regionally and over time. Such approaches are at present still the subject of considerable argument, although they are gradually gaining wider (if often very qualified) acceptance. The pursuit of this particular Holy Grail is outside the scope of the present book, but there is a growing literature on the subject which the reader can follow up if interested. A good starting point is the set of papers from the ADMAP 9th World Advertising Workshop in Berlin, October 1977, published in ADMAP Volume 14, Nos. 1 and 2 (January and February 1978).

Turning back from the subject of media research to the general field, it is very noticeable that over the last fifteen years or so market research has moved from a stance of *providing information* to one of *solving problems*. This shift reflects not only the raised sights (and ambitions) of researchers themselves but also wider agreement that market research must be directed towards decision taking and marketing action. One aspect of this is that far more research briefs and plans nowadays include not only a discussion of the marketing background to the problem but also a clear statement of the action which will be based on the findings. In the extreme case this can be an action standard of the form, 'If the findings show A, we will take action X; if B, then action Y'. Market research reports in their turn are increasingly concerned with discussing action instead of merely summarizing the information collected, although even now the UK tends to lag behind the USA in this respect.

However, 'problem solving' does not by any means cover all the objectives of market research. Much research is intended to improve the general efficiency of marketing by increasing our *understanding* of the market. 'Understanding' is *not* the same as 'information'. 'Understanding' implies knowledge of both the structure and the dynamics of the market and of the ways in which marketing activities achieve, or fail to achieve, their desired effects. Much of the research described in the following chapters is designed to secure such knowledge. Market research is in the last resort valuable only to the extent it can be used predictively, based on such understanding.

Inevitably, this leads in the direction of model building. Some of these models have relatively limited objectives, e.g. in media selection. More complex ones deal with issues such as consumer decision processes: how *does* a consumer come to choose a particular brand on a given occasion? The major contribution of market research in this area has probably been its emphasis on the value of studying the attitudes and behaviour of consumers *individually*, particularly through panels. This 'micro' approach contrasts with the longer-established 'macro' approaches, as used in econometrics, which involve studying consumers in the mass. The growing importance of the subject is reflected in the inclusion of an additional chapter on modelling in this edition of the Handbook. At this point, it becomes increasingly difficult to draw any clear boundary between market research and disciplines such as operational research.

Another point at which market research tends to cross a boundary is in its concern with information as such. The higher-flying comments of the last paragraphs should not distract attention from this important, if less glamorous, function. In looking at what market research has to offer we must remember that it is one among several sources of data. Within a company, market research information has to be integrated with sales data, trade statistics and much other material. Increasingly, therefore, we have as users to think of total management information systems into which market research data must be fitted. We also have to find better ways of getting the relevant information (and only this) to the right people, at the appropriate time, quickly, clearly and concisely. This is another perspective against which to consider the material discussed in the next chapters.

The fact that market research is not the only source of market knowledge introduces a further issue. Knowledge normally costs money (and time). This is certainly the case with knowledge obtained through research. We should therefore weigh the cost of the additional knowledge to be gained through a particular research project against the pay-off (extra profit) we might expect to obtain as a result of having this knowledge. This is very much more easily said than done. It involves calculations not only of cost and potential pay-off but also of the amounts and different types of risk involved and the probability of different research and marketing outcomes. There is a field of statistics—Decision Theory, based on Bayesian statistics—which attempts to get to grips with this type of problem. So far, very little practical work has been done (rather more in the USA than in the UK) in applying this to the buying of market research. However, the problem is so important that we shall inevitably have to try to use this or some similar approach more effectively during the coming years: reference is made to it in chapter 19.

As market research has developed away from the simple 'nose-counting' of its early days, so the problem of effective communication between market researchers and their clients has also increased. When dealing with the more sophisticated approaches now available (such as those described in chapter 14) the user of research may need to understand at least the principles of quite complex techniques if he is to make good use of their findings. He may, on occasion, even have to rethink his own basic marketing approach, e.g. when considering market segmentation studies. This is a challenge to both researcher and user. The researcher must try to explain his methods and findings simply and directly, avoiding jargon as far as he can, but the user must also build his half of the bridge. He can no longer expect to cope adequately with market research (or with other modern marketing techniques) on the basis of a short briefing plus a skimming of the report's summary of findings. The subject need not be abstruse, except in its most specialized technical aspects, but it has to be worked as if it is to be applied effectively.

The following chapters aim to help with this, although they cannot hope to deal with all aspects of the topics discussed. They will be the more useful if the earlier, more technical chapters have also been studied and if some of the books and articles referred to are subsequently followed up for more detailed information on subjects of interest.

John Downham

14. Segmenting and constructing markets

Tony Lunn

During the past two decades market segmentation has emerged as a central concept in consumer research. It is often defined as a *research technique*, as a type of survey, say, or a method of data analysis: and it has, in fact, been the focal point of major advances in research technology, especially in the field of multi-variate analysis. However, simultaneously with its growth in popularity, segmentation has become a somewhat ambiguous concept, associated with a diversity of analysis techniques, e.g. cluster analysis, sequential dichotomization[1]; with attempts to find new ways of classifying consumers[2]; and with a variety of different kinds of research approach, e.g. market description studies[3], market structure studies[4] and contextual mapping[5]. The position taken in this chapter is that segmentation is more aptly defined in its original sense, namely as an *approach to marketing*. This approach may be summarized as the philosophy whereby products are directed at specific target groups of consumers rather than at the total population, a philosophy that has gained considerable influence in the post war era[6]*.

In a separate publication[7] the author discusses some prominent research issues in market segmentation, and in a recent book[8] Frank, Massy and Wind provide a comprehensive review of methodological and theoretical issues. The purpose here is to outline the present position more from the marketing standpoint, with particular emphasis upon problems and applications. The marketing man is often faced, nowadays, with bewildering volumes of data, gathered from mammoth surveys, and analysed by highly abstruse techniques. There is a danger of both marketing men and researchers

---

* Segmentation is not without its critics: some problems and alternative approaches are referred to later in this chapter.

becoming lost in a forest of complexity; of the former seeking panaceas and, inevitably, becoming disillusioned, and of the latter becoming entranced by methodological niceties. In the present chapter it is hoped to illustrate how even the most sophisticated techniques can have clear and practical applications for both long-term planning and day-to-day decisions.

Given the generality of the segmentation concept, some of the points discussed below are also dealt with elsewhere in the book, usually in greater detail: in particular, see the chapters by Sampson, Morton-Williams and Holmes. The topic has generated a voluminous literature, some of which is listed in the references at the end of the book.

Some Marketing Considerations

General

Segmentation is a new term but an old concept. Manufacturers have long been aware that certain products are bought mainly by certain types of people: gold watches and tonic wines are obvious examples. Again, take the motor car market. A Model T Ford and a vintage Bentley are just as illustrative of market segmentation as are more contemporary cars such as the Ford Capri and the Austin Maxi. Nevertheless, much early segmentation was accidental, i.e. the product was launched with no clear target group in mind, but, by its nature, turned out to attract certain types of people: or, if not accidental, the marketing action was often highly speculative: target groups were based mainly upon intuition, and described rather vaguely in such phrases as 'The modern woman who cares for her children'.

The main difference today is that segmentation policies are pursued more purposefully, and are applied to a wider range of product fields. This development can be attributed to a number of inter-related factors.

As a result of fundamental changes in society, purchasing is becoming more discretionary and less concerned simply with the necessities of daily life. The most important changes for marketing men are the growth of affluence and the rising level of education. These have been accompanied by increasing social mobility and by an erosion of traditional class-determined patterns of behaviour: the typist, like the film star can afford to express her personality through the latest fashions; the factory worker may take his holiday in Greece. As the contraints stemming from low incomes and traditional social values have lessened, so individual patterns of requirements have flourished. The result has been an ever-widening range of consumer tastes and needs for the marketing man to satisfy. Thus, in an era of social change, manufacturers are paying much more attention to consumer differences in their general planning. This consumer-orientation is a matter of necessity in an era of mass production and mass marketing, when the financial penalties of failure to market the right kinds of goods and services can be ruinous.

344

The harsh economic conditions prevailing in the mid 1970's may, if prolonged, lead to changes in consumer needs and other market variables, but they are unlikely to have a fundamental effect upon the trends outlined above. The whole climate of marketing has become much more 'scientific'. The individual entrepreneur is being replaced by teams of specialists; product life-cycles are more carefully planned and monitored; manufacturers are increasingly concerned with maintaining complementary ranges of products within any one area, and also with diversifying into related areas.

The increasing sophistication of technological development in the physical sciences has increasingly been harnessed for the production of consumer goods, e.g. convenience foods, hi-fi radios, disposable clothes. But the resultant new products rarely meet with instant and universal acceptance. Many may be dead ends. To be successful, a new product type usually has to make its appeal, at least initially, to a particular market segment, perhaps broadening its appeal to wider elements of the population as time goes by. Frozen foods are a case in point.

The combination of technological development and mass marketing has meant that basic physical products in certain fields have become almost uniform in composition and scarcely distinguishable by the consumer. As a result, marketing men have sought to establish clearer identities for specific brands, e.g. toilet soaps are given different perfumes and colours, toothpastes special ingredients such as fluoride. These extra product characteristics may well offer to the consumer benefits over and above the basic function of the product. A particular toilet soap may offer cosmetic benefits, a gold fountain pen may act as a status symbol, Scandinavian cutlery may satisfy a need to feel up to date. In some product fields secondary benefits of this kind have become the primary reason for purchase: pop art watches may be valued more as fashion accessories than as time-pieces; the majority of Virginian tobacco cigarettes are indistinguishable on blind product tests, yet often command striking preferences in their branded form. Discussion of this fourth point makes it important to distinguish between at least three levels of segmentation, namely where:

(a) totally different *product types* are produced for different consumer needs, e.g. toothpaste rather than some alternative means of cleaning teeth;
(b) different *product variants* are produced within the same overall types, e.g. special benefits such as fluoride are built in;
(c) different *brands* are produced within the same specific product variant.

A further corollary of mass production has been the neglect of certain minority tastes. These tastes have often been identified in product concept research, and have subsequently formed the basis of new product developments. The growth of delicatessen and health food product ranges provides a contemporary illustration.

Recent years have seen an interdependence between developments in marketing thinking—which have led to demands for more detailed descriptions of consumers—and developments in research techniques, which have themselves opened up wider possibilities for marketing action. At a time when complex data analyses can be carried out with increasing speed and economy by computers, marketing men have much sharper tools at their disposal for the derivation and implementation of segmentation policies.

To summarize the effects of these changes: there has been a growing recognition that consumers may differ in ways that are exploitable by marketing operation, and that to concentrate on producing 'universal products' for the 'average consumer' is to run the risk of missing significant marketing opportunities. Increasingly, therefore, marketing men have become concerned to identify target groups of consumers with distinctive patterns of needs, to develop products with the appropriate benefits, and to promote and distribute these products in optimum ways.

Different types of marketing problem

The segmentation approach to marketing can provide the cornerstone for a company's total planning. It helps to set the basic objectives for the whole marketing operation, and to indicate strategies for implementing these objectives. There are, of course, many different kinds of marketing objectives and strategies, which, in turn, give rise to different types of segmentation problem. It is important to distinguish between these. The particular problem posed will determine the kind of research necessary, including the sort of data that will be most relevant, and the ways in which the data should be analysed. Characteristic types of marketing problem are listed below, and illustrations of research designed to solve them are given later in the chapter.

(a) *Defining the Market*

Consumers do not necessarily perceive the market in the same way as do manufacturers. From the consumer's standpoint, a market may be thought of as a set of products (or brands) which are considered equally suitable for the same need—or set of needs. These products may come from product fields which manufacturers would treat as quite distinct. In a recent project, for instance, it was discovered that the main substitutes for a particular type of frozen food were not rival brands in the field, but two quite different kinds of tinned food on the one hand, and poached eggs on toast on the other. That is, the consumer's product field concept may range quite widely. Moreover, the repertoire of brands he considers suitable for a particular need will not necessarily include all the brands from any one field.

(b) *To Rationalize Policies for Existing Brands and Products*

This problem can be posed at two levels. At one level are questions of optimum strategies for specific brands (or products) marketed by the

346

company. A variety of questions arises, such as how can market share be maintained or improved; how can inroads be made into the position of competitive brands; how best can the brand be protected from competitive activity; and so on. In the light of research, attempts may be made to increase the purchasing of current buyers, to convert buyers of competing brands, or to attract new buyers to the product field.

The second level is discussed under the third objective, namely:

(c) *To Position Ranges of Brands and of Product Varieties*

Where in a given market there are different segments of consumers with differing needs, a company is well advised to market its brands in such a way that in total they satisfy as many as possible of the more important segments, at the same time minimizing direct competition between the company's own brands as far as any one segment is concerned. The same point applies to ranges of product varieties.

(d) *To Identify Gaps in the Market Which Offer New Product Opportunities*

Here the object is to identify consumer segments whose needs (at least in their eyes) are not being adequately met by any existing brand. These needs may be met by launching a totally new brand (or product) or by modifying an existing one.

Underlying all four types of problem is the fundamental issue of competition. Segmentation studies usually include amongst their objectives the location and specification of competition from rival manufacturers. Resultant marketing strategies may, of course, be essentially defensive—particularly in relation to new entries in the market—or more aggressive in nature.

Segmentation and Research Developments

It has been emphasized that segmentation is essentially an approach to marketing rather than a research technique but that it has, nevertheless, stimulated a variety of developments in consumer research. Some of these are discussed below under two main headings: criteria for defining market segments and research methodology. An additional topic is the distinction between consumer and product segmentation. In summary, the former places chief emphasis upon ways in which people can be grouped in terms of their requirements; the latter upon ways in which products can be grouped in terms of the benefits they offer. These have often been represented as rival approaches[9]. They are, however, better viewed as complementary.

For ease of exposition, the following sections on criteria and methodology are written from the standpoint of consumer segmentation: subsequent sections deal with product segmentation and the relationships between the two approaches.

Segmentation criteria

Requirements From Criteria

Market segmentation is disaggregative in nature. To produce a 'universal product' for the 'average consumer' is to run the risk of missing important marketing opportunities. Likewise, for the researcher to represent data in aggregate form rather than analysed by relevant variables is to provide information that may well be misleading. These variables are often referred to as segmentation criteria.

But what types of criteria are relevant? This will depend upon the particular market being examined. There are, however, a number of general considerations determining relevance; namely that criteria should:

(a) discriminate between consumers themselves;
(b) pick out differences in market patterns;
(c) increase the understanding of the market, particularly by indicating consumer needs;
(d) be fully exploitable in practice.

The fourth requirement implies that the criteria should be fully understandable to marketing and advertising men, that they should be the kind of variable that marketing men feel they can influence, that they should be feasible to measure under normal market research circumstances and that they should, if possible, be related to differences in media and shopping habits in order to guide media strategies and distribution policies.

Different Kinds of Criteria

Consumers, and markets, can be described from numerous standpoints. The possibilities of several quite different kinds of variable have been examined in recent years. Those most commonly used in segmentation are outlined below, roughly in the order in which they have attained prominence*.

'Historically, perhaps the first type to exist was *geographic* segmentation. Small manufacturers who wished to limit their investments, or whose distribution channels were not large enough to cover the entire country, segmented the US market, in effect, by selling their products only in certain areas'[10]. Haley's comments apply to many countries other than the US. Indeed, segmentation by region is by no means uncommon even today.

Perhaps the most popular form of segmentation has been in terms of *demographic* characteristics. A comprehensive list can be found in reference 15. They include sex, age, occupation, income, social class and household

---

* For a further discussion, see references 8, 11 and 12.

composition. These charactersistics have become the basic terms in which many marketing men and researchers think about the consumer. This is reasonable up to a point. Demographic variables describe important aspects of people's circumstances which give rise to purchasing needs. They also act as moderators upon the translation of these needs into behaviour, e.g. a low income household may have expensive tastes, but little prospect of indulging them. Moreover, because they have been studied over a long period of time, their relationships with other market factors, such as media patterns, have become well known. They have, however, been subjected to considerable criticism in recent years, mainly through lack of brand discrimination, and because, giving as they do only indirect reflections of consumer needs, they are of limited value in the formulation of marketing strategies. Some of this criticism may be overcome by a more critical and imaginative treatment of demographic criteria, as illustrated by the life cycle concept—a composite of variables such as length of marriage and age of children[14].

The term 'demographic' is itself somewhat ambiguous. And there are a number of additional ways of describing the consumer's background and social environment which may prove valuable for segmentation policies. These include the possession of complementary products. An obvious example is the relationship between the ownership of a refrigerator and frozen food purchasing. For a useful list of such variables, see a paper by Agostini[15].

Recent developments in buyer behaviour theory have emphasized ways in which personal characteristics interact with situational factors. *Situations* relevant to purchasing consumption and the acquisition of information designed to influence these activities are receiving increasing attention. However attempts to develop meaningful taxonomies of situations are still at an early stage[16].

There are many products which either cater for, or are affected by, the consumer's physical attributes, e.g. skin and hair texture; and such characteristics are being increasingly used in segmentation.

The most straightforward way of classifying consumers is in terms of their behaviour, e.g. heaviness of buying in a product field, brand purchasing within product field, different ways of using the same product. For some purposes – e.g. tests assessing formulation changes in an existing product – sample selection and / or data analysis by variables such as user–non user of the product in question may be all that is required. Behavioural segmentation has often been advocated as a simple and logical policy. The 'heavy half' theory popularized by Twedt[17], for instance, argues that, granted that in many product fields 50% of the consumers account for 80% of consumption, these high-volume groups should command maximum marketing effort.

There are, however, two strong arguments against taking this reasoning too far. They are given by Hale[10] and Frank[18]. The former points out that people do not always buy products for the same reasons. Consequently, some heavy buyers may be better prospects than others. The latter points out that, in any case, the heavy half is already the heavy half, and may offer little scope for expansion. This should not be taken to imply that behavioural variables have little part to play in segmentation; on the contrary. Moreover, the increase in our knowledge of buyer behaviour, stemming from the work of Ehrenberg, Kuehn, Massy and others, has considerable value for marketing in general and segmentation in particular. The reader is particularly recommended to Massy *et al.*[19], who provide a highly imaginative treatment of behavioural variables.

Another interesting approach is *backward segmentation*. To summarize, this involves applying techniques such as factor and cluster analysis to purchasing data across a variety of product fields, in the search for patterns of complementary and substitutable products[20]. Three main applications of this approach are to:

(a) stimulate ideas and guide future research;
(b) simplify marketing strategies, e.g. by suggesting common policies of couponing and distribution for related products;
(c) increase understanding by stimulating researchers to question why sets of products group together as they do.

In addition, groupings of consumers in terms of common purchasing and usage characteristics may delineate market segments of value in their own right: they may, for example, describe meaningful 'life-style' segments. Cross-tabulation of these groupings by other variables, such as attitudes, will help to build up profiles to guide marketing action. (See next section.)

The most promising development of the past decade has been segmentation by *psycho-sociological* characteristics. This has been accelerated by advances in psychometrics, which allow such variables to be measured effectively in day-to-day market research projects. Segments identified by this approach have a compelling diagnostic quality. They indicate not only who buys a particular product but also why they buy. Target groups are described in terms of 'real people', and can be immediately appealing to research users—particularly copywriters in their search for appropriate ways of communicating with the target group. Diagnostic advantages can, however, be offset by weak relationships with purchasing and consumption data. It is important, here, to distinguish between different kinds of psycho-sociological characteristics.

When these variables were first introduced to market research the tendency was to use rather general characteristics borrowed from other fields such as clinical psychology. Sometimes total personality inventories—such as the Edwards Personality Preference Schedule—were adopted; sometimes individual traits such as introversion, neuroticism, and inner/outer directedness[2, 8, 19]. Not surprisingly, the results of applying these in market research have proved disappointing. They are at once too abstract and, in many cases, of doubtful relevance to consumer behaviour.

In recent years, the emphasis has shifted towards characteristics more obviously geared towards people in their roles as consumers. Considerable attention has been devoted to the merits of 'life-style' and psychographic variables, typified by the activity, interest and opinion batteries (A.I.O.) pioneered by Wells[21]. Claims and counterclaims about the value of this approach abound in the literature.

A major criticism is that even these batteries are too abstract and lack discriminatory power. The criticism has been particularly severe in relation to the use of broad stereotypes—such as 'The Quiet Family Man', 'The Ethical Highbrow'—derived from carrying out factor and cluster analyses of the total set of items (e.g. ref. 22). In response, some researchers have changed their approach to life-style analysis. Segnit[23], for example, has found more value in clustering people in terms of their purchase and consumption behaviour which are themselves life-style groupings of a kind—and in subsequently deriving diagnostic profiles by cross-analysing the clusters by individual life-style statements. Two recent publications by Wells[21, 24] provide an illuminating view of the life-style area.

The main problem with psycho-sociological classification lies in undue reliance upon generalized characteristics of any kind when attempting to account for specific and widely varying types of choice behaviour. Experience suggests that the most fruitful approach is to derive classifications empirically for the product field in question. The resultant characteristics vary in nature from specific consumer requirements in the product field, such as preference for a strong flavour in a toothpaste, to more general traits, such as traditionalism and economy mindedness.

These latter characteristics have often been found relevant to several different product fields. But it is rare to find a segmentation project where more specific assessments of consumer needs do not play a vital role. See also Haley's work on 'benefit segmentation'[10].

The value of generalized characteristics may well be less for studies of particular markets than in basic research designed to advance our understanding of consumer behaviour. Traits such as propensity to take risks, self-confidence, innovativeness and cognitive style come into this category[25]. In the same context, the author and his colleagues have carried out a project in which over 50 attitude scales derived from specific projects have been brought together in the same questionnaire, which was given to 4000 female respondents. The results were treated by both factor analysis and cluster analysis, and eight groupings were identified, which were labelled.

(1) Young sophisticates (15% of the sample)
(2) Traditional working class (12%)
(3) Cabbages (12%)
(4) Middle age sophisticates (14%)
(5) 'Coronation Street' housewives (19%)
(6) Self-confident (13%)

(7) Homely (10%)

(8) Penny pinchers (10%)

In similar projects, four fundamental theories were found to underlie consumer attitudes and values, namely experimentalism, extroversion, anxiety and involvement. These findings are a valuable back-cloth against which to view more specific action-oriented classifications[12].

Other kinds of socio-psychological variable may be relevant for particular kinds of problem. For instance, empirically derived life-style indices concerning entertaining, interests, division of role in household tasks and family influence on purchasing decisions have helped with long-term product planning[26]; six empirically derived shopper categories, e.g. 'the inefficient extravagent shopper', 'the reluctantly well-organized shopper' have been valuable in work designed to understand the effects of point-of-sale marketing variables[27].

The area of consumer classification is still a centre of active development. Work in buyer behaviour theory (e.g. ref. 25) has suggested a number of criteria worthy of attention, including involvement in the product field, specific self-confidence in brand choice, size of brand repertoire and decision-making styles and strategies.

For a more detailed review see references 8, 11 and 12. Illustrations of the practical application of some of these variables are given later in the chapter.

Changes in approach to deriving criteria

The previous section discusses some of the main criteria used in past and present segmentation research. There have been three main changes in researcher approach to deriving these criteria. First, there has been a move from an essentially *a priori* to an empirical approach. That is to say, through the use of a stage of qualitative exploration (see below under Research Methodology), criteria are increasingly tailor-made for particular markets, rather than imposed on the basis of researchers' preconceptions. Second, there has been an increasing emphasis upon *explanatory* criteria, which provide a direct measurement of consumer needs and motives. Third, there has been a move away from the search for one single kind of variable, a search which dominated much of the early work on segmentation. It has been recognized that purchasing behaviour is determined by a multiplicity of factors, some of them being 'internal' to the consumer such as her specific needs and general attitudes, others being 'external' to the consumer, e.g. her background and circumstances, and the situations in which the product is purchased and used. Consequently, segmentation projects are increasingly concerned with using *multiple* criteria, i.e. with including all kinds of variables that might be relevant to the particular market.

352

Segmentation and research methodology

Marketing problems giving rise to segmentation studies are of different kinds; the nature of the specific problem will determine the methodology to be adopted. There is no best technique, or set of techniques, for all circumstances. It is, nevertheless, possible to map out a broad sequence of stages applicable to many consumer segmentation projects. Four characteristic stages are:

(a) background clarification;
(b) qualitative exploration;
(c) developing measuring instruments;
(d) defining target groups.

This does not mean that all projects must pass inexorably through all four stages or that additional stages may not, on occasion, be appropriate. These four do, however, provide a useful means of categorizing consumer segmentation methodology.

Stage 1. Background Clarification

The first stage in a segmentation project, as in any other major research activity, may be a thorough review of all existing knowledge and assumptions about the market. Most of this will probably consist of desk research. Information reviewed may vary from the findings of past motivation research to purchasing patterns derived from consumer panel records. Prominent issues will probably include:

(a) the nature of the market—is it expanding or contracting?
(b) the number of brands in the market and their respective shares;
(c) any rising or falling trends shown by individual brands;
(d) the proportion of the population buying the product, and the frequency of purchase;
(e) ways in which the product is used.

This information may, in itself, lead to hypotheses about the nature of the market and its basic mechanisms, which will help to guide subsequent research stages. It may also identify distinct behavioural subgroups which will provide a valuable focus for qualitative exploration (see stage 2).

This is a crucial stage with respect to the relationship between client and researcher. Discussions between the two parties can lay the foundation for the mutual understanding which is a prerequisite of a successful segmentation project (see final section of this chapter).

A useful example of how a behavioural analysis can help to set the scene for subsequent research is given by Winkler[28], with reference to the German toilet soap market. One finding reported by Winkler is the close correspondence between behavioural analyses of consumer panel data and consumer ratings of brand similarities. The same point is made by Stefflre[4] and in several recent R.B.L. projects, small-scale analyses of consumer similarity and preference data have provided valuable supplementary indications of market structure. (See also p. 370.)

Stage 2: Qualitative Exploration

This stage is often the cornerstone of the entire segmentation project. It has, however, been neglected all too often in the published literature, and also tends to be devalued by researchers whose particular skills and predilections are towards quantitative methods (see stage 3). The author's position is clear. Having identified, at stage 1, the main behavioural patterns in the market, it is then important to explore the various factors determining or influencing these patterns. Behavioural data may, in themselves, suggest hypotheses, but it is only by a thorough stage of qualitative research that these hypotheses can be fully pursued and amplified.

The techniques of qualitative research have been described by Sampson in chapter 2. Any or all of these may be appropriate to an individual segmentation project. The objectives of this second stage can be summarized as:

(a) to build up a set of hypotheses about the consumer characteristics relevant to purchasing in the market:
(b) to develop a feel for the language used by consumers holding these characteristics, in order to guide the development of attitude scales and other appropriate measuring instruments (see chapter 5).

Qualitative research may not always be carried out as one complete phase. Hypotheses may be progressively refined and developed during successive waves of interviews; some interviews may be carried out on the population at large, others on specific behavioural subgroups of particular relevance to the problem.

Stage 3: Developing Measuring Instruments

Content analysis of the interviews and other procedures used at stage 2 will have provided a set of hypotheses about the main forces relevant to consumer behaviour in the market. The next stage is to express these forces in quantitative form, i.e. to develop appropriate measuring instruments so that they can be applied feasibly in day-to-day market research enquiries. This stage is especially important for psycho-sociological variables. Ways of translating attitude dimensions into sets of statements are discussed in chapter 5. Techniques for analysing the responses to these statements, such as factor analysis, are described in chapter 13. An important issue is that of *how many* factors to extract from a given set of items. There is not necessarily a single best factor solution, and a variety of guides are available to help the researcher to select the best number of factors for the problem in question.

The objectives at this stage are basically three-fold:

(a) to confirm or modify the nature and number of consumer characteristics already hypothesized;
(b) to clarify the meaning of each characteristic in terms of the statements that link together in practice, and also of those that do not;
(c) to produce subsets of statements that will serve as measuring instruments for each characteristic.

Measurement problems are not confined to psycho-sociological variables. Concepts such as income and life-cycle, or behavior in relation to 'prestige products' and 'socially embarrassing' activities, may all involve the creation of special questions and indices. Two illustrations are given below of cases where factor analysis helped to clarify the picture originally provided by qualitative exploration. The first is from a study of the confectionery market, carried out several years ago, where twelve general attitude dimensions had been indicated by the qualitative research, and where sets of statements had been derived for each dimension. There were some 80 statements in all, to which a representative sample of 300 adults responded on a five-point agree/disagree scale. The twelve dimensions were labelled:

(a) sweet-toothedness;
(b) weight consciousness;
(c) conservatism;
(d) extravagance;
(e) compulsive eating;
(f) activity;
(g) gregariousness;
(h) preoccupation with personal appearance;
(i) social self-consciousness;
(j) impatience/impulsiveness;
(k) self-indulgence;
(l) ability to plan ahead.

Responses to the 80 statements were factor analysed. A final solution of eight attitude dimensions was arrived at, comprising 40 statements in total. Basically, the first six dimensions listed above were confirmed. Several of the second six, however, were shown to merge with other dimensions, to produce the following picture:

(a) sweet-toothedness;
(b) weight consciousness;
(c) conservatism;
(d) extravagance;
(e) compulsive eating;
(f) activity;
(g) self-organization;
(h) self-consciousness.

This picture was confirmed in a further factor analysis in a follow-up stage involving a sample of 2000 adults. As will be shown later, the eight dimensions helped to define important market segments.

The second illustration is from a study of general attitudes towards thrift. Initial qualitative exploration had suggested one broad dimension. Twelve statements were drawn up. Factor analysis of these revealed two separate dimensions, namely economy-mindedness and bargain-seeking. Further qualitative research carried out on high and low scorers on each of these two scales indicated that up to five separate attitudes were involved, namely economy-mindedness, extravagance, quality-consciousness, bargain-seeking and price-consciousness. Appropriate statements were derived for each dimension. Factor analysis confirmed the picture but indicated that bargain-seeking and price-consciousness were so closely related as to be scarcely worth separating in practice.

This picture has been confirmed in subsequent factor analyses, and the four separate attitudes to economy have played a valuable part in many segmentation projects.

Stage 4: Defining Target Groups

This stage provides the culmination of the previous three. Having identified the seemingly most relevant variables in the product field, and having developed new measuring instruments where necessary, the objective is now to pinpoint target groups on whom to concentrate maximum marketing effort. A search is made for subgroups of consumers who are as similar as possible to each other in terms of important characteristics, and who are, in the same respects, as different as possible from consumers in other subgroups. The techniques employed here have undergone radical development in recent years, and will undoubtedly advance still further in the future. At the risk of oversimplification, it is possible to distinguish four main historical phases of development in this area:

(a) simple cross-tabulations;
(b) regression-type techniques;
(c) sequential dichotomization;
(d) cluster analysis.

In the first, researchers simply examined cross-tabulations between pairs of variables, e.g. the tendency to go on a packaged holiday to Europe would be analysed separately by age, social class, income, adventurousness, and so on. This approach is most appropriate when only a few variables are being analysed. Take the position in the UK floor polish market a few years ago. There were two main product types: wax polish, a long-established product which, amongst other characteristics, demanded considerable effort on the part of the user; liquid, no-rub polish, a relative newcomer, and very much a

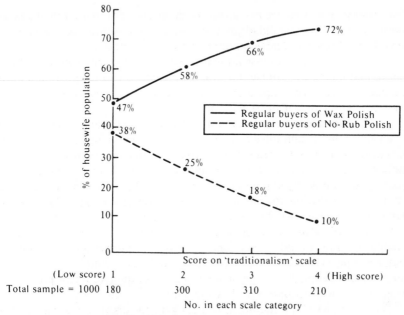

Fig. 14.1 Score on traditionalism scale.

labour-saving product. In recent years, wax polish had been on the decline, and liquid on the ascendancy.

The client had a brand in each type. He wondered whether the position of his wax brand might be improved by giving it more of the characteristics of a no-rub polish. No help had come from analyses by demographic variables, which failed to show any differentiation between buyers of the two types. However, a scale measuring the extent to which women are traditional or modern minded in their approach to housework was developed specially for this market. As shown in Fig. 14.1 this scale neatly segmented the market, clearly discriminating between buyers of the two types of polish. In the light of further analyses of the traditionalism scale, the client reversed the previous policy decision for his wax brand. Instead, through changes in both product characteristics and advertising themes, he further emphasized its current characteristics. Likewise, he re-emphasized the labour-saving and other characteristics of his liquid brand. The wax brand subsequently increased its share, and maintained its sales volume despite the continuing decline of this market, and the liquid brand improved its share in the other market, which continued to expand. Moreover, an attempt by a competitor to launch a brand combining the characteristics of the two product types was a failure.

Cross-tabulations run into difficulties when several segmentation criteria are important. Take the packaged holiday case referred to earlier. Let us assume that there was a marked positive relationship with adventurousness and income. An inference might then be made about the existence of a target group for this kind of holiday amongst, say, highly adventurous people with a high level of income. The inference is, however, invalid. It can only be made through carrying out a cross-tabulation, with the two characteristics interlaced; and there is, of course, for practical reasons, a strict upper limit to the number of such cross-tabulations that is feasible, especially when three or more variables appear to be relevant.

There has been a growing awareness that consumer behaviour is determined by a multiplicity of factors, some combining to precipitate or reinforce it, others to deter it and, consequently, of the need to analyse behaviour in terms of multiple characteristics. This led to the second phase, namely the popularity of multiple regression, multiple discriminant function, canonical correlation and similar techniques (see reference 1). This was the kind of approach used by Massy *et al.* in their study of the relationship between purchasing and personality variables[19]. However even these techniques fail to take adequate account of interactions amongst the independent variables. In the packaged holiday example, for instance, adventurous people with high incomes may have quite different preferences from adventurous people with low incomes.

The third phase has attempted to deal with the disadvantages of the first two, i.e. by taking into account interaction, and by examining 'automatically' a large series of cross-tabulations. The approach referred to is sequential dichotomization (see reference 1) exemplified by the AID programs developed by Sonquist and Morgan[29]. An illustration of successful application by the author is quoted below. It should be emphasized that the technique is appropriate for only certain segmentation problems. It is most relevant where the objective is to explain *one* particular variable, say heaviness of purchasing, in the product field.

There are many problems where this would prove too constricting, where, for instance, the objective is to examine the basic need structure in the market, or to define target groups from among the most important consumer characteristics, *without* gearing these groups to one particular variable. Here the collection of techniques known as cluster or profile analysis (see reference 1) are more relevant. These constitute the fourth phase of development.

The search for target groups may well be carried out on the data collected at stage 3, i.e. where a sample of between 150 and 300 respondents will be interviewed with the main purpose of developing attitude scales, etc. It is, however, more customary to use a large and fully representative sample. The size and nature of the sample will be determined by the sorts of consideration discussed in chapter 4.

Let us assume, for simplicity, that the data collected on our full-scale sample are of five kinds:

(a) demographics;

(b) specific consumer needs in the product field:
(c) specific attitudes to the various brands in the market, i.e. brand image data;
(d) more general values and attitudes;
(e) consumer behaviour such as brand purchasing and usage.

In the light of the above, it is unlikely that cross-tabulations or regression techniques will be used, at least initially, but a decision will have to be made between sequential dichotomization and cluster analysis.

An instance where the former method seemed more appropriate was in the confectionery project referred to on p. 355. The main marketing problem posed had been to provide a description of current purchasing in the product field, with a view to guiding strategies for reinforcing existing buyers, and suggesting ideas for new product development. The sample of 2000 respondents was roughly divided into two equal halves on the basis of heaviness of purchasing in the field. An AID analysis was run, using all independent variables considered relevant. Ten clear subgroups of consumers were identified. Only three will be described here. The first, which contained 12% of the sample, contained 85% heavy buyers and 15% light buyers, compared with 50—50 in the total sample. It was defined in terms of four main characteristics:

(a) sweet-toothedness;
(b) low conservatism;
(c) highly compulsive eaters;
(d) D.E. social class.

It portrayed the typical buyer of the product in question and was used by marketing and advertising men to reinforce current purchasing. The group turned out to have distinguishing habits of buying the product at certain types of outlet, a finding which guided distribution policy.

By contrast, a second group, consisting of 11% of the sample, had a very low propensity to purchase, namely 21-79. The defining characteristics of this group—low sweet—toothedness, low activity, older respondents without children—indicated that it was unlikely to respond to marketing action, and should, therefore, not be given special attention.

Particularly interesting was a third group, comprising 20% of the total sample, which had a buying propensity of 55-45. Some of the characteristics of this group, e.g. their low sweet-toothedness, strongly deterred them from purchasing; other characteristics, e.g. the fact that that they were predominantly young married couples with children, and of D.E. social class, were factors which might be expected to encourage purchase. This was a group sufficiently large to be of interest from the marketing point of view; and analysis of their requirements guided the development of a totally new confectionery product which, among its other characteristics, was designed to be less sweet than other variants in this sector of the product field.

For many segmentation problems, however, cluster analysis is a more appropriate means of treating the data, at least initially. A key decision to be made then concerns which variables should be included in the cluster analysis itself, and which should be used subsequently in building up profiles of the groups obtained. Various positions have been adopted by different researchers.

One extreme approach is to cluster respondents in terms of all available data, including behavioural variables and attitudes towards brands. This approach, although comprehensive, may lead to difficulties in interpretation: the groups produced may be something of a hotchpotch, rather than clearly delineated descriptions of people. The second extreme involves clustering respondents only on data directly representing specific consumer needs. This has the advantage of clarity and precision, but may often be too limited.

Several years of experience with cluster analysis suggest that it is difficult to lay down hard and fast rules. There is no single, absolute way of looking at a market. In some recent segmentation projects guided by the author, data have been cluster-analysed more than once, using different variables, e.g. specific needs only the first time, general attitudes the second and both sets of data the third time. On each occasion fresh and valuable light has been thrown upon the market. Much depends upon the purpose of the study. For instance, where the main objective is guidance concerning the *physical* development of existing products, specific consumer needs are probably most suitable; where *advertising* themes are sought, or insights for new product concepts, more general attitude variables assume greater importance.

With the above provisos, a sound general principle is to omit behavioural and brand image data from the cluster analysis, and to concentrate upon characteristics describing the consumer and his circumstances, e.g. general attitudes and values, specific needs, and demographic variables; and to select any variables of this kind which exploratory work has indicated will interact with each other to influence behaviour.

A number of detailed but important methodological issues surround the choice and treatment of input data for cluster analysis. A major issue is whether the same analysis can include continuous, e.g. general attitude, non-continuous, e.g. sex, and categorical, e.g. age, data. There are theoretical grounds for assuming that the inclusion of data of such different kinds will produce distorted results; in particular, that the categorical data will swamp the remainder, and play an artificially high part in cluster formation[30]. This issue has been tested out in several unpublished studies in which cluster analyses have been run under different conditions: the results suggested that this fear is not realized in practice. Other issues include the question of whether the variables should be allowed to be correlated, whether they should be normalized to zero mean unit variance, and whether individual items should be given different weights.

It was pointed out above, in referring to input data, that there is no unique way of looking at a market. This also applies to the number of groups that should be extracted from cluster analysis. In fact, most methods allow us to inspect a *range* of cluster solutions. They either start with each individual respondent, progressively combining those who are most similar, until, say, only two groups of respondents remain; or they start with the total sample and break it down into progressively smaller subgroups. The issue of selecting the optimum set of subgroups can prove a taxing one for researchers. A number of criteria can be brought to bear on the problem. First, *size*; there is a limit to the number of groups which marketing men can seriously consider: moreover, once a cluster contains less than a certain minimum proportion of respondents, it ceases to be of marketing interest. The minimum proportion acceptable will vary with the product field; for instance, 5% of the population of cigarette smokers is an acceptable level, whereas 5% of the owners of dishwashers is not. Second, *Homogeneity*; that is, at certain levels of generality, clusters may become too diffuse. Criteria have been suggested (e.g. ref. 31) for assessing the tightness or compactness of clusters. These can be at each level of a cluster solution. Third, *meaningfulness*; inspection of a range of cluster solutions usually leads one to reject several on grounds of interpretability. They just don't ring true; they are not describing real people. Fourth, *discrimination*; the most valuable cluster solution is generally considered to be that which discriminates consumer behaviour most sharply. This is true up to a point, but clusters which do not distinguish between current purchasing patterns may indicate sets of needs currently uncatered for. That is, they may indicate marketing opportunity groups.

Cluster analysis provides a convenient means of describing subgroups of consumers in terms of shared characteristics. But these groupings are not fixed entities with rigid boundaries. They are relative, not absolute. Products directed at one particular group may be expected to attract sales from other adjacent groups—those which are most similar to it in terms of key characteristics. Furthermore, within a given cluster, individuals will usually vary in their strength of membership: some will be central, hard-core members; others will be more peripheral. It is not uncommon to find certain respondents who are so peripheral to all clusters that they are better removed from the anlysis altogether and treated as non-classifiable. In a recent study of a specialist market, cluster analysis of the total sample proved hard to interpret, but a very clear set of groups was revealed once 25% of the sample, all outliers, had been removed from the analysis.

In the context of the relativity of clusters, it should also be pointed out that cluster membership may change over time, either because the clusters themselves change, e.g. different combinations of needs become relevant, as happened to the UK detergent market after the launch of enzyme products; or individuals themselves may change, perhaps developing different needs with changes in their background circumstances.

Despite the usual proprietorial constraints, published examples are starting to appear. Heller[32] describes a project where consumers in the automobile market were grouped in terms of both relatively general attitudes:

(a) attitudes towards travel;
(b) social activities and mobility;
(c) attitudes towards highway safety;
(d) liberalism—conservatism;
(e) self-image;
(f) attitudes towards automobile buying and maintenance;
(g) driving habits and patterns;

and more specific consumer requirements from automobiles:

(a) styling;
(b) size;
(c) economy;
(d) driving characteristics;
(e) special features;
(f) prestige factors.

Four groupings were produced. First, a group of consumers who like to travel a lot in their car and are generally safe drivers. They take good care of their car and they are not at all economy minded. They require large cars and are not overly concerned about style, power or speed. Second, a group which does not like to travel a lot by car. They are socially active and fairly reckless, being unconcerned about safety, care of their car and conservative behaviour. They desire a car that is stylish, and has power and speed. Third, a group which tends to be socially inactive, conservative and economy oriented. They are unconcerned about automotive styling, power, speed or the size of their car. Fourth, a group of drivers who are primarily interested in a conservative car that is expensive but stylish, powerful, fast and roomy. Their view of travel is neutral, they are neither socially active nor inactive and they care little about their car or about safety.

Sherak[33] quotes a detailed description of consumer segments in the American beer market, based on such variables as benefits to be found in the 'ideal' beer, e.g. quality, prestige, smoothness, youthful image, mildness, robustness, dryness; and also more general personal characteristics, e.g. gregariousness, self-consciousness, price-orientation, masculinity. Nine clusters were identified, three of which he labelled 'the sociables', 'the rugged individualists' and 'light beer drinkers'.

The definitions of groupings such as these are based in part on the variables included in the cluster analysis, in part on additional personal characteristics against which the clusters are cross-analysed, and which provide extra profile data. These data may be obtained in successive stages, as illustrated below.

Some recent research in a motor-product market clustered 1000 respondents in terms of five types of variables—general attitudes, specific

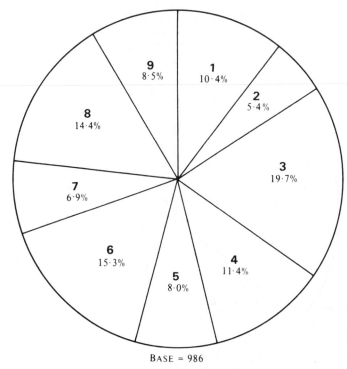

BASE = 986

Fig. 14.2 The nine clusters.

needs, demographic variables, description of car, and behaviour in relation
to the product in question. Nine clusters were produced. Figure 14.2 indicates
the proportion of respondents coming into each cluster. Unfortunately, it is
not possible to publish descriptions of the clusters.

The main purpose of the study was to show where the client's brands were
positioned *vis-a-vis* competitive brands, in order to suggest both aggressive
and defensive advertising strategies, and to indicate gaps for a new brand
launch. The first cross-analysis gave brand shares for each cluster.
Substantial brand discrimination was obtained (see, e.g., Figs. 14.3 and
14.4). This information in itself suggested a number of marketing and
advertising strategies. Further analyses incorporating brand image data
sharpened the picture of the structure of the market, including the strengths
and weaknesses of the various brands within each cluster.

The next step was to attempt to determine the relative importance of the
consumer needs indicated to be salient to the particular decision. It has
increasingly been recognized by researchers that consumer needs are not all
equally important for brand choice. Relative importance cannot be obtained
directly from analysis of cluster characteristics alone. These characteristics
only show the extent to which members of the cluster deviate from the general
population. Techniques for this purpose are still under development.

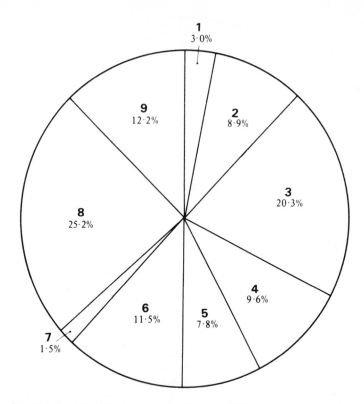

Fig. 14.3 Brand 'A' (Base = those claiming Brand 'A' as usual brand = 270).

The one employed in this project was the St. James Model, developed in the UK by Hendrickson, which uses the 'ideal' brand, product or service as a yardstick against which to evaluate assessments of actual brands etc[34]. Its use in the motorist project quoted here was of considerable value in indicating which particular aspects should be given prime marketing effort within each cluster. One result of the total study was that the client's two existing brands were more clearly directed towards different clusters, in each case by reinforcing the appeal to one cluster, and aiming the brand at an adjacent cluster with many similar needs. In addition, a new brand launch was aimed at two clusters in which no existing brand had established a dominant position.

The research approach outlined so far will have helped marketing men decide which clusters should be regarded as target groups. The purchasing and brand image profiles of different clusters will have played a major part in this; so will the hypotheses developed at the behavioural classification and qualitative exploration stages. An acid test, however, is the likely *responsiveness* of the various clusters to proposed marketing and advertising strategies. The importance of assessing responsiveness has been recognized by researchers for some time[35]; but the step has often been neglected in practice.

364

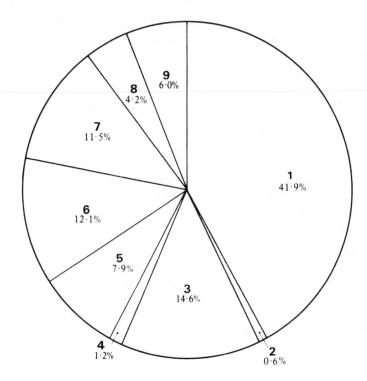

Fig. 14.4 Brand 'B' (Base = those claiming Brand 'B' as usual brand = 165).

One way of proceeding is to include items designed to assess consumers'
reactions to specific product concepts in the main questionnaire of the
segmentation project: another is to include such items in follow-up questionnaires, perhaps using postal methods (e.g. ref. 33).

Subsequent marketing action

Properly carried out, the stages outlined above will provide a comprehensive
background picture of the market. In some cases, this is regarded as the end
of the story. In fact, it is really the beginning. The target groups that have
been identified should form the basis of subsequent marketing strategies.
They may in themselves lead to the generation of *new product concepts*. One
example is the case of the non-sweet confectionery product referred to earlier.
Another is provided by Moss[36]:

    Let's take an example of the way research has helped us to spot a
marketing opportunity.

    When we examined the usership of Fish Fingers, we found that the
housewives who were the heaviest buyers were mainly of a particular
type. They tended to be very conservative in their food purchasing

habits; they were very concerned about the nourishment or goodness value of food; and they tended to be down the market in terms of social status.

But there was another large group of housewives, in many ways similar, but who were much more willing to experiment with new products, and were much less concerned about the nourishment value of food.

To them, tastiness was all important. Compared with the first group, these people tended to be either light or non-users of Fish Fingers. The research seemed to suggest that there was an opportunity to sell the second group an entirely new and novel fish product—a product that was very tasty but concerned itself less with nourishment value. This seemed likely at first to get a high level of trial, because we would be appealing particularly to the experimentalists.

The result was the launch of Crispy Cod Fries in the UK.

In addition, these groups should now figure at the centre of research designed to test the effectiveness of marketing strategies. It is the ratings, attitudes and preferences of the target group that matter, not those of the population in general. This applies to product concept tests, product tests, advertising copy tests, brand image research, media research, and so on.

Product segmentation

The discussion so far has concentrated on consumer segmentation, with particular reference to the identification of target groups. During recent years researchers have paid increasing attention to a different, if related, concept, sometimes known as product segmentation.

Barnett[9] gives a useful account of issues which stimulated early developments in this area, although he does, in the author's opinion, adopt a rather extreme position.

Barnett begins by discussing some traditional consumer segmentation criteria, e.g. demographic and personality variables, points out that none of these, individually, has shown much success in brand discrimination and goes on to argue that researchers should concentrate instead on deriving product-field-specific criteria by which consumers themselves distinguish between brands and products. He then goes on to imply that researchers should turn away from grouping consumers and should, instead, confine their efforts to grouping brands and products. Here the argument breaks down. Barnett's critique of traditional approaches is just as effectively answered by the developments in consumer segmentation outlined above, namely, that the criteria elicited should be relevant to the product field in question, and that techniques such as cluster analysis should be used to deal with the multiple influences on consumer behaviour. It is just as valuable to cluster consumers in terms of their requirements from product-field-specific variables as it is to cluster products in terms of the extent to which they are perceived to satisfy these requirements. The criticism being made here is not of the value of clustering products, which is, in fact, illustrated below, but of the extreme position exemplified by Barnett's paper. A more balanced view is that both consumer and product segmentation are valuable, often for different kinds of marketing problem. The former is important for questions about the kind of consumer who should be appealed to. It can throw light upon brand positioning through examining which brands are bought by the same types of people and can also indicate new product opportunities by identifying clusters of consumers whose pattern of needs is not currently being closely matched by existing products.

Product segmentation, too, can identify gaps for new product opportunities. Another application is market definition. Consumers do not always perceive markets in the same way as do manufacturers. Consequently, it is important, for market planning, to establish which brands and products are seen as substitutable. Manufacturers can then check which brands or products are competing with each other and in what respects, and whether there are any sections of the market where they might usefully reposition a brand—either to attack competition, or to fill a current gap.

Product segmentation has been the subject of several different methodological approaches. Three main categories are outlined below. For a fuller description and a critical appraisal see Beazley[37]. The first is a logical extension of traditional brand-image research. The basic methodology closely resembles that used for consumer segmentation as described above, and has been labelled the *factor/cluster approach*. Consumers are asked to rate brands or products along a series of double-ended scales, e.g.

Soothes the skin . . . . . . irritates the skin
Makes you feel more feminine . . . . . . doesn't make you feel more feminine

Preferably, the phraseology of these scales, like those used in consumer segmentation, will be based on qualitative research (stage 2 above). In many cases, individual scales will have been selected, by factor analysis or similar procedures (stage 3), as instances of underlying attitude dimensions, such as medication or cosmetic-benefit.

The simplest analysis is to compare the various brands or products along each factor, e.g. set of highly correlated scales, separately. The 'ideal' brand, say, for a particular usage occasion, may be used as a yardstick, as below.

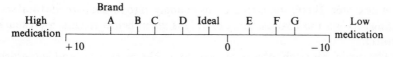

This step can provide valuable diagnostic information in its own right. It is more illuminating, however, to compare brand ratings on pairs of factors. Where feasible, each pairing is examined in turn. Figure 14.5 gives an illustration. This second step portrays a series of 'contextual maps' of the

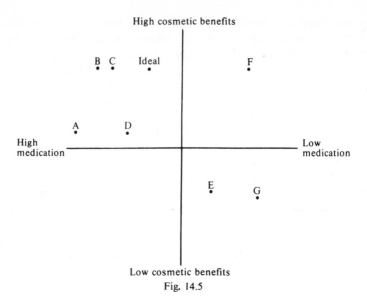

High cosmetic benefits

B C   Ideal   F

A   D

High   Low
medication   medication

E   G

Low cosmetic benefits
Fig. 14.5

product field, which provide:

(a) an indication of which brands are competitive in the sense that consumers perceive them as closely substitutable—in this case, brands **B** and **C**;

(b) market gaps, in that no brands are judged by consumers to provide this particular combination of characteristics—in this case the combination of high medication and low cosmetic benefits.

If products have been rated on a small number of factors, say three or four, it is relatively easy to examine contextual maps for all possible pairs. In many projects, however, more factors will have been included; quite often more than ten. Here, it is no longer feasible to inspect all the maps. A further problem is that each pairing deals with only part of the total information. Full knowledge about both substitutability and gaps can come only from a procedure which attemps to examine data from several factors simultaneously.

A next step, therefore, is to use cluster analysis to summarize the total set of ratings for all the brands. An example is given below from a food market project.

The main research objective was to guide marketing and advertising planning by showing how each of the client's products fitted into the wider context of all the products competing for the housewife's attention at certain meal occasions. Some twenty products were selected as characteristic of the meal occasion in question; most were manufactured products but others were

368

home produced alternatives; some were essentially 'hot-served' products, others 'cold'; some were fruit-based, others savoury. Ninety scales were elicited (stage 2) and reduced to twelve factors (stage 3), using a pilot sample of 300 housewives. A sample of 1000 housewives rated the twenty products on the twelve scales. The cluster analysis progressively combined the twenty products into two main groupings. Each grouping, from the nineteen product solution to the two, was examined for its defining characteristics.

The four-cluster solution was judged to be the most meaningful, and was also the most compact statistically (see Consumer Segmentation above). One finding was that four out of the five client products came into the same cluster, a grouping which was, on the whole, assessed rather unfavourably by consumers. Several leads, in both product development and advertising terms, were obtained for repositioning two of the client's existing products, and for launching two totally new products.

An extension of this approach has been described by Morgan and Purnell[38], who have developed a computer program which searches for gaps in the total brand space. It also attempts to assess the viability of possible new products by examining how many people would be attracted by particular product concepts, and from which existing products they would gain market share.

The second main approach to product segmentation has been labelled the *brand associations/pattern analysis method*. In many ways similar to the first, it is marked both by a relatively simple means of data collection and by a certain novelty in data analysis. In summary, respondents are not asked to rate brands along attitude scales—instead they are presented with a matrix of brands and attributes, and asked to specify simply which of the nominated brands they believe to be associated with each of the listed attributes.

Patterns of responses can be examined from a number of standpoints. For example, taking each attribute in turn, it may emerge that:

(a) No brands are associated—this may imply that the attribute is irrelevant, at least at present.
(b) One brand only is associated—i.e. the attribute is unique to that brand.
(c) Several brands are associated—i.e. the attribute is unique to that sub-set of brands.
(d) All brands are associated—i.e. the attribute is not differentiating between brands.

These data can then be treated by cluster analysis in which either attributes, brands or respondents can be the basis for seeking homogeneous groupings. For a practical case history see a paper by Buckle and Hughes-Hallett[39].

The third main approach makes use of non-metric multi-dimensional scaling. Descriptions and applications of this branch of methodology have been extensively documented (see ref. 1). A distinctive feature is the derivation of maps of brands and product relationships directly from respondents' assessments of the degree of brand similarities—and from respondents' preference judgements—rather than by using attribute data. Attribute dimensions characterizing the market are subsequently inferred from the ways in which the brands and products are grouped together. This procedure for identifying attribute dimensions has sometimes been attacked, on the grounds that it relies too much on the subjective interpretation of the researcher. One means of answering this criticism is to include attribute data in the questionnaire and to derive attribute profiles of the obtained clusters. This approach is also closely related to consumer segmentation: consumers can be clustered in terms of the 'points of view' they hold about brands and products on the market derived from similarity and preference data.

Practical experience suggests that all three types of product segmentation yield broadly similar results. Beazley[37] suggests several criteria for choosing between them on particular occasions. For instance, the factor/cluster method is most appropriate for major, comprehensive market investigations: the brand association/pattern analysis method is a valuable, intermediate method when economy and ease of communication are of the essence: non-metric methods are valuable exploratory tools for hypothesis formulation, especially where consumers may have difficulty in verbalizing their attitudes.

Linking Consumer and Product Segmentation

Like many aspects of research, consumer and product segmentation are better regarded as complementary rather than competitive. Each can throw light on a different aspect of the market. An illustration of this was provided by a recent study of the food market. The research involved the four stages of consumer segmentation described above, as well as product segmentation, in which the various brands in the market were clustered in terms of empirically derived attribute ratings. Two findings of the consumer segmentation were of particular interest. First, research failed to confirm certain strongly-held marketing convictions. It was assumed that the market was roughly divided into nourishment and economy segments, and that consumers would be grouped accordingly. Cluster analysis on specific consumer requirements failed to find any evidence of this. A number of clusters were, in fact, identified, but they had very different characteristics to those hypothesized by the marketing team; moreover, they did not show any distinctive patterns of brand usage. Second, when the cluster analysis was re-run with the addition of more general attitudes, a much clearer picture emerged. The clusters were more readily identifiable as 'real people', and showed pronounced discrimination between current brands. This illustrates the value of characteristics additional to product specific requirements, a point ignored by some researchers. The nature of these clusters, combined with an assessment of the relative importance of the product attributes, formed the basis of the re-launch of two existing client brands and stimulated thinking for two possible new brands. It is worth adding that the two re-launched brands achieved significant differences in product, pack and copy tests, within the target clusters and in terms of the attitude dimensions selected as most important.

Returning to the first point, the product segmentation did, in fact, confirm the marketing presuppositions in one respect. The twelve brands in the market grouped together into two clusters, one a mainly nourishment cluster, and the other a mainly economic one, defined in each case by distinctive attribute ratings. The point of this comparison is that the manufacturers had been successful in their policies: brands in this market were perceived in the intended ways; but their success had not had a full marketing pay-off, for the benefits conveyed did not correspond to consumer needs as revealed by the consumer segmentation analysis.

The whole area of linking consumer and product segmentation presents an important challenge to researchers. One means of attempting this is to super-impose actual and ideal brand clusters in the same spatial representation. Examples can be found in publications by Sherak[33] and Green et al. (e.g. ref. 40). Another means is to carry out product clustering *within* previously established consumer segments.

Some General Research Issues

A few comments of a more general nature before leaving this section on methodology. Although in itself a relatively simple concept, segmentation has been the focus of some highly sophisticated research developments. Some of the techniques such as factor and cluster analysis and the various non-metric procedures are now widely used in consumer research; their strengths and weaknesses are well known.

This wealth of different approaches may sometimes lead to a certain feeling of arbitrariness; to a fear that quite different marketing inferences might have been drawn had other techniques been used. But, as was pointed out earlier in the chapter, different techniques have different properties and underlying models, and should, strictly speaking, only be applied to problems and data which meet the assumptions of these models. It is often possible to cross-check the results of any one technique by the use of another, e.g. by the combined use of qualitative and quantitative methods in attitude research[3, 41].

Different marketing problems require different types of analysis technique. Here the writer echoes the warning given by Holmes in chapter 13 about the dangers of standard packages. The marketing man should be wary of the researcher who encounters him armed with an all-purpose set of segmentation procedures.

The very complexity of segmentation methodology can lead to a total rejection by marketing men in favour of a much more simple approach. One school of thought, for instance, confines research for new product development to the following three stages:

(a) group discussions;
(b) the development of new concepts in the light of these group discussions;
(c) an assessment, on a national sample, of the proportions of the population responding favourably to each concept.

Such an approach may sometimes be justified, for instance if budgets are tight; but the marketing man should be aware that he is adopting a rudimentary, hit and miss approach. For his medium term strategic planning he will derive much more value from identifying consumer groups of varying potential defined by the needs they are seeking to fulfil by purchasing in the product field, and also from the richer assessment of the competitive situation which a segmentation study provides. Moreover, it is important to regard projects of the kind described in this chapter as contributing towards banks of data which can be used for re-analysis on several occasions. This is not to deny that there will be occasions when projects which are relatively modest in scale will be adequate. Increasing use of the brand association method referred to above reflects a concern to use simple methodology where this can be justified.

A more specific research issue concerns the *ideal brand* concept. This has been referred to several times in this chapter. It is widely used as an anchor point on semantic differential scales, and as an index of specific consumer requirements; for instance, as illustrated on page 368), respondents can be asked to rate not only particular brands but also 'the ideal brand' in terms say of cosmetic properties. Many researchers hold considerable misgivings about this concept. It is thought to be rather artificial and prone to ambiguity — what exactly does the respondent understand by an 'ideal' brand, something purely fanciful or something highly desirable but 'realistic'? There are many product fields where a respondent might be expected to have several ideals, according to the mood or usage occasion: for instance, would it be helpful or meaningful to ask a woman to conceptualize her ideal dress?

In practice, however, the concept often appears to work well, especially where use is made of appropriate scenarios. For instance, women might be asked about their ideal dress for a formal occasion, for going shopping, and so on. The ideal should, however, only be used in contexts where it is meaningful, and care should be taken in the interview to provide a precise, operational definition to the respondent, thus minimizing dangers of ambiguity. Furthermore, it is better regarded as a reference point indicating consumer needs on specific attributes, rather than as a general concept in itself. That is, we are not asking consumers to describe their 'ideal' brand in a total sense.

This chapter has emphasized the need for an empirical approach to market segmentation studies. It is equally important that these projects should be guided by appropriate theories and models of consumer behaviour, especially those which deal with decision processes in a dynamic manner.

372

A segmentation study can only provide a snapshot of the market at any one period of time. For a full understanding, and for effective marketing action, we require a consideration of the changes that take place over time. Some relevant insights can be found in the work of Howard and Sheth[25] and Nicosia[42].

Conclusion

There is still considerable scope for improvement in segmentation methodology. In some respects it has already outrun the practical value being derived by marketing and advertising men. This final section summarizes some problems arising from—or inhibiting—the application of this type of project.

There is still a basic suspicion by some marketing men of the whole segmentation philosophy. To focus upon specific target groups seems to imply a deliberate rejection of certain sections of the market. To a certain extent this is a question of facing up to the issues raised earlier under 'Some Marketing Considerations'. Consumers do have different needs, and there is more to be gained from identifying and catering for these needs than from ignoring them. Moreover, as pointed out elsewhere, segmentation is not always a matter of focusing down. Certain products may start with a minority appeal, and steadily capture sales from large sections of the population. In this context, the author has already suggested 'market construction' as a more positive term from the marketing standpoint one, which does more justice to the range of marketing activity than can stem from a 'segmentation' project. Hence the title of this chapter. From the research standpoint, 'market description' or 'market structure' might be preferred to the term segmentation.

To illustrate the potential superiority of the segmentation approach, consider three alternative approaches to market planning, listed by Sheth[43]. First, *planned obsolescence*, which is more of a technology-orientated concept. The fundamental assumption is to introduce new products according to technological programs, by stimulating additional demand in the market place. 'Innovate or perish' is the watchword. Second, *aggregate modelling* of market responses, where it is assumed that the market place is composed of homogeneous customers who deviate from the average response only in terms of the law of statistical error. Third is the concept of *market variety*, which takes essentially a short-term approach. It is argued that a company is better off simply to produce a large variety of the same product or service, market them equally, and let the market place decide which variety is most desired by the consumers.

Some of the early segmentation studies produced disappointing results. Little discrimination was achieved at brand level, or even, at times, at product level. The picture has improved considerably with the incorporation of less

373

restricted input data and more appropriate analysis techniques. At the same time, there are circumstances where it would be unrealistic to expect clear-cut results. For instance, consumers may be largely homogeneous in terms of determinant needs in the market; there may be considerable overlap in brand purchasing (although it must be remembered that quite different motivations may underlie similar purchasing behaviour); where involvement in the product field is low purchasing may be more a matter of chance or of easily changed habit than of strongly motivated habit or conviction; and finally, there may have been little systematic marketing or advertising policy in the past in terms of either established or even hypothesized consumer needs.

Given the volume and complexity of segmentation research findings, a particular strain is placed upon client credibility and client-researcher relationships. Undoubtedly, it is important for marketing and advertising men to be involved in and committed to a segmentation project from the outset, to understand its possibilities and limitations, and to specify the problems they expect it to illuminate. It cannot be emphasized too often or too strongly that a client should commission a problem-solving project, not a set of techniques. Ideally, close liaison between client and researcher will be maintained throughout the project, and special attention will be given by the researcher to the ways in which the data are presented and communicated. A variety of devices can be brought to bear here[44]. Effective use can also be made of cartoons, pen-portraits, and other visual aids. The company research officer has a crucial role to play, as described by Hill in a paper which also gives several valuable examples of the practical value of segmentation research[5].

Media constraints still present a problem. Some marketing people feel that segmentation projects are only of value where the target groups identified have distinctive readership or viewing patterns, thus laying the foundation for differential media scheduling. This is a somewhat extreme position. Absence of distinctive media profiles does not lessen the purchasing potential of a target group, or its value in product development and copy formulation. Research on selective perception suggests that consumers will respond to information that is congruent with their needs and filter out that which is not. At the same time, media problems undoubtedly help marketing men to extract the fullest possible value from research.

Discovering distinctive media profiles is complicated by the recent trends in segmentation criteria described earlier in this chapter. In the days when demographic variables formed the major criteria it was relatively easy to find corresponding media profiles, but these chances have lessened as target group definitions have become increasingly tailor-made for specific markets. However, the discovery of fundamental psychological or life-style variables, relevant to a wide range of product fields, is emerging as a strong possibility, and would open up promising avenues for media.

There are still issues to be resolved in identifying target groups quickly and cheaply in everyday market research projects, where there is little opportunity for extensive batteries of questions. Methods currently under experimentation include asking respondents to allocate themselves to pen portrait profiles, based on cluster analysis descriptions, and the use of shortened batteries of attitude scales.

Finally, the question of change. It was pointed out in the previous section that a segmentation project produces a static picture. There is, however, a need to be aware of and to anticipate market changes. This may be helped both by the use of motivational variables as segmentation criteria, and by reference to theories and models of buyer behaviour. The crucial point is to recognize that target group profiles are not fixed for all time. Markets evolve naturally: they may also be changed by manufacturers. Segmentation and construction projects can indicate some of the means for achieving this.

Postscript

The first edition of this chapter was prepared in 1971, when large-scale market structure studies were enjoying a boom, and their potential was still being explored. Some seven years later it is possible to bring a fresh perspective to the scene. Many more such projects have been carried out and a fuller assessment can be made of benefits and problems associated with their design and execution and with the implementation of their findings. In particular, the author has been associated with a major, unpublished review for a multinational corporation of market structure projects from several European countries.

The picture is an encouraging one. In all cases examined in the review, marketing men volunteered the information that the benefits derived more than justified the time and expenditure involved. In some cases the findings were held to have contributed to substantial gains in market share, in others to arresting an anticipated decline in share in the light of fierce competition. All the facets of marketing strategy discussed above have been influenced, to a greater or lesser extent in different projects.

In certain cases, the results of a single project carried out five years or more previously were held to have influenced marketing thinking to the present day. The minimal benefit claimed was an enriched understanding of consumer and market behaviour, which was held to be of value in itself.

At the same time this particular review highlighted a number of extraneous factors which influence the extent to which 'good' research is related to market-place 'success'. There is not a simple one-to-one relationship because, to quote:

(i) Marketing decisions are frequently complex and depend on many factors other than research (e.g. competitive activity, production considerations, financial considerations, marketing judgement, etc.). *Similarly marketing success is a function of complex circumstances, in particular the nature and effects of competitive activity.*

(ii) The personnel involved in the commissioning, execution and application of research change jobs with such frequency that the situation is often encountered in which *a study will not be used by the same people* (e.g. marketing or advertising executives) *who initiated* it. This may be an obstacle to realizing the full effectiveness of a research study.

(iii) Marketing decisions based on previous research are not necessarily pretested in order to establish whether the solution is consistent with the recommendation—this could result in inexplicable differences between forecast and observed effects in the market-place.

These factors are not, of course, confined to market structure studies although they are especially applicable to them.

Moreover, seven years further experience has led to certain changes of emphasis. Perhaps the major one has been towards simpler, smaller-scale projects with a more flexible and discriminating approach towards methodology. Large-scale market structure studies, involving extensive batteries of attitude statements and the combined use of several types of multivariate analysis, will continue to play their part. But they will be carried out less frequently and more purposefully—for instance where there is reason to believe that the basic patterns of the market have undergone a pronounced change.

Their value will be as periodic base-line studies, to be supplemented by small-scale surveys, designed to monitor specific aspects of marketing activity. Both sets of data will be appropriate to feed into Management Information Systems, and to feature in attempts to stimulate and forecast future patterns and opportunities, as described in chapter 20.

15. Research for new product development

Colin Greenhalgh

It would be convenient, not only for the purposes of this chapter but also for marketing companies generally, if new products were developed by a logical step-by-step approach—by surmounting a succession of hurdles which remained constant from product to product, so that new product development could be 'learned by rote'. The facts, of course, are quite the opposite. The majority of new products are developed by a series of fairly unordered steps, the order and the degree of attention paid to each varying from company to company and from project to project.

There are many reasons for this lack of formality. Principal amongst these are:

(a) the large contribution which is undoubtedly made by sheer creativity to most new products which have much chance of success;
(b) the interaction of all the elements in the total 'marketing mix' (product, price, pack, name, advertising, etc.);
(c) the cost and timescale pressures which are ever present in most competitive situations.

Nevertheless, despite the difficulty of pursuing a thoroughly logical procedure, in practice it is well to have one constantly in mind, to avoid going too far off the charted course. This chapter, therefore, is written in terms of such a formal structure, though it is recognized that, once studied, this may well often have to be amended in the face of practical difficulties.

Coverage

Many of the steps in a new product program are ones in which market research has no part to play. Several publications are available to take the reader through all these stages (refs. 1–6 are some relevant sources). We are concentrating here on the contribution of consumer research to new product development, and are only describing those other, non-research, elements to the extent to which it is necessary to put the whole into context.

There is a stage at the very start of any new product program which can be described as 'selecting the product field'. This is not covered here for a variety of reasons. Firstly because, rightly or wrongly, many companies are in one product field (or a small number), feel themselves constrained to stay within those product fields and, as a matter of policy, work at new product introductions in each of them concurrently—so there is no problem of selection. Secondly, where a pre-selection stage *is* necessary it usually rests on considerations of company capabilities—such as finance, technology, the sales force—and familiarity, backed by market-size and market-trend information of the desk research and sales research type. And thirdly, insofar as *ad hoc* consumer research does play a part in this fundamental decision to 'look at' a particular product field, this can come about in many and varied ways which are rather outside the scope of this chapter, ranging from small-scale group discussions and structured usership and attitude surveys, to long-term social trends research. (See chapters 2, 8, 9 and 10 of this book, and the general bibliography at the end of the book, if further reading on this particular use of consumer research is required.)

This chapter is also essentially restricted to low price, pre-packed and branded consumer goods (colloquially 'cheap things bought often'). In other words, even within the context of consumer goods, it excludes specific discussion of durables and services. The major contribution of market research to new product development has, so far, undoubtedly been in this area of consumer non-durables, but marketers and researchers working in the area of durables, services (and even industrial goods) will certainly find much of relevance here and will, no doubt, amend and adapt the techniques described when necessary.

Finally, the research contributions described in this chapter stop short of the market-place (whether national, test market or mini-test market) because these later stages are dealt with in chapter 19. It also precludes detailed discussion of elements of the marketing mix except the central ones of new product concepts, new products themselves and their price. This is not to say that the other necessary elements—packaging, name, advertising, etc.—are less crucial to ultimate success, but that they also are covered elsewhere, in chapters 16 and 17.

Why New Products?

It is, perhaps, worthwhile dwelling for one moment on why new product development is so important in the first place, and why so much market research effort is devoted to this particular end-use.

Mass-marketed products undoubtedly go through a life cycle*. The exact shape of the life cycle is irrelevant; its length is certainly very variable from product to product, but it is almost axiomatic that any product will eventually start to decline in the face of competition, advancing technology and changing consumer needs. Various devices can be resorted to to postpone the effects of this decline on profits, e.g. a cut in advertising or increase in price. Such devices, however, are generally self-defeating in the long run. More promising is 're-cycling', i.e. finding and promoting new uses for the product, attacking new segments of the market, or straight product improvements designed to hold up sales in the face of the inevitable life cycle. Even re-cycling, however, will wear thin in the long run and profits will start to decline.

It follows that most companies need to develop new products regularly, so as to phase in their profit contributions as those on existing products start to decline. The new products which are developed may be new brands in an existing product group, they may be 'new, new products', of which the like has never been seen before, or they may be range extensions, companion brands to existing company products. Which of these they turn out to be is for the new product program, allied with the necessary research, to determine.

It is for these reasons, though—that the changing demands of consumers, allied with the spur of competition, technological change and the urge to grow, forces innovation on most companies—that new product development is so vitally important to the prosperity and, even, survival of most companies.

Generating New Product Concepts

While 'product concept' is a term which is often used at the initial 'ideas' stage of a new product program, there is no universally accepted definition of what a concept is. One definition which has been used elsewhere is 'A description in words of a product: the vocabulary employed should be non-evaluative and descriptive'. This would not seem to cover all cases, however. For one thing, many concepts (particularly in the non-durable consumer goods markets which we are considering here) cannot be adequately conveyed in *non-evaluative* words, if they can be conveyed in words at all. These are the concepts which depend not so much on what the end product looks like or what it does but on the way people feel about it. The justification for a new toilet soap, for instance, may be, 'A soap which contains an

---

* King[2] has argued forcefully—and justifiably—that most companies market much more than products; they market brands. It is, strictly, *brands* which go through a life cycle and we ought really to talk of new *brand* development: however the use of the word 'product' to embrace 'brand' is so ingrained that we propose to continue to use it in this sense in this chapter.

ingredient which will eliminate blemishes and restore the skin's natural soft-ness'. It may be that a more profitable concept, however, is that of 'A soap which makes you feel young again!'

The most important characteristic of successful concepts is probably that they are based on the *consumer's* point of view, that they express what consumer benefits will be offered, what consumer needs will be satisfied, even if this means they cannot be expressed in words at all! Perhaps a fairer defini-tion, if a definition is needed at all, would be that a concept expresses the 'essentials of the product idea—that collection of consumer benefits by which it differs from other available products and which are believed to be essential to its portrayal to enable it to achieve its desired position in its target market'.

Where do new product ideas come from?

The majority of new product ideas are generated in one or more of the follow-ing ways[6,7]. The task of consumer research is to take its appropriate place amongst these different sources:

(a) creative flair;
(b) R & D (Research & Development) breakthroughs;
(c) deliberate search procedures:
   (i) non-consumer based,
   (ii) consumer based;
(d) deliberate invention:
   (i) non-consumer based,
   (ii) consumer based.

While there is only sketchy evidence (see below) on the relative effectiveness of these different sources in generating *successful* product ideas, it is likely that the continuing growth of the marketing philosophy throughout industry will result in an increasing proportion of new product ideas being directly consumer based. Therefore, while all these sources will be briefly described in this section, the particular contribution of consumer research will be stressed.

Creative Flair

Marketing men, advertising agency people—particularly those in 'creative' jobs—salesmen, laboratory workers—all are likely to think of new product ideas out of the blue—'I wonder what consumers would think if we gave them ...?' This creative flair is not, however, necessarily accidental and it can be cultivated and stimulated in various ways. One of these is deliberately to expose such people to consumers and to relevant consumer research. If a copywriter attends group discussions on an existing product group, it exposes him to the possibility that a chance remark may suggest the germ of a new idea. If an R & D scientist reads the detailed results of a product test, it increases the chances that he will spot a new way of satisfying a minority segment of the market.

Doing consumer research at all—almost any type of consumer research—exposes the lively minds of marketing, advertising and technical people to consumers' behaviour, attitudes, needs and aspirations and increases the chances of a *relevant* creative breakthrough.

R and D Breakthroughs

Another fruitful source of new product ideas may certainly be investment in R & D. Sometimes, though rarely in the type of packaged consumer goods which we are considering here, these ideas are the result of basic research in the natural sciences; more often they come from the accidental or deliberate application of well-known technologies and processes in new areas.

The major contribution of consumer research is probably in keeping the R & D technologists, and those who direct their efforts, constantly aware of consumers' needs. In this way the company's R & D effort can be directed into the potentially most rewarding areas and ideas for new product breakthroughs, when they occur, will be more readily recognized.

Deliberate Searches

These are broadly of two types. Those which are:

(a) conducted amongst and about consumers and are therefore, to a greater or lesser extent, consumer research based;
(b) not amongst and about consumers.

We will take the latter (historically the more usual) first.

Non-consumer based searchers

These differ in kind from 'flair' and 'breakthroughs', in that there is a conscious effort to go out and look for possibilities, not to wait for them to arrive 'out of the blue'. Such searches include:

(a) routine vetting of the home market for new entrants to copy, or improve on;
(b) perhaps more productively—similar observation of overseas markets;
(c) routine observation of the home market for potential growth areas;
(d) reading of technical periodicals and journals (and those of consumer testing organizations);
(e) regular searches of the register of patent applications;
(f) morphological, gap and spectrum analysis (e.g. see ref. 3 and ref. 8).

(The latter has much in common with gap analysis based on consumer attitude surveys (see below). In this context, however, it refers to a conscious search for gaps in product technology rather than in consumers' perceived images of products.)

Consumer-based searches

Probably the cheapest and simplest search procedure amongst consumers is the regular vetting of correspondence on existing products; though, in truth, new product ideas from this source will generally be very unformed and needing astute recognition and nurturing.

In the area of more formal and *research* based attempts to find new product ideas, the first is quite straightforward. It is simply to read previous qualitative and quantitative research (usership and attitude studies, product tests, advertising tests, etc.), very comprehensively and with a very detailed eye, in a conscious attempt to look for openings via, for instance, likes and dislikes of existing products[2,9]. As with many procedures, some researchers and commentators have proposed that this type of search is likely to be much more productive if it is set into a formal framework. For instance, Tauber[10] suggests the use of a 'problem inventory'. He lists 134 possible problem areas for consumers in food and drink markets, e.g. physiological (weight / hunger / thirst), sensory (taste / appearance), buying and usage (portability / spoilage), psychological / social (eating alone / self-image) etc. By reviewing the standing of existing products against this checklist—and such a review is likely to lean heavily on previous consumer research—then the chances of finding an opening for something new must be enhanced. However, the odds are that, if consumer research is to be increasingly productive in generating new product ideas, it will be through 'tailor made' studies. Four techniques are worth describing.

Qualitative Research[10]

This involves the use of group discussions and individual depth interviews to explore consumers' behaviour, attitudes and needs in the selected product group or need-area (see chapter 2). (The expression 'need-area' is used here and later, in preference to 'market', because in really forward-looking cases no recognizable selection of brands or products may as yet be on sale for that purpose.) Being qualitative, the research can be comprehensive and reasonably exhaustive and, in this way, unsatisfied needs and aspirations can be looked for. Once found, these needs can become the starting-point for a deliberate attempt at new concept invention.

The reasons for using qualitative research are (a) that, at this stage, we are only searching for possible ideas, not evaluating their potential, and (b) that most of the markets we shall be looking at are already highly developed—latent needs will be lurking beneath the surface, to be patiently winkled out, by discursive questioning. 'Qualitative' research, however, is not necessarily synonymous with 'small scale' research. If our marketing criteria are such that we are prepared to look for latent needs in a very small segment of the total market, then we may well have to employ substantial sample sizes, minimizing the cost of researching the interesting segment by filtering out the remainder at an earlier stage of the recruiting procedure—as long as we know in advance how the potentially interesting segment will be defined!

A development of qualitative research which has sometimes been used for suggesting new product ideas is 'action studies'[6,12]. These generally take the form of very detailed studies of consumers' behaviour in a need-area of interest to the manufacturer. A panel of women, for instance, might keep a detailed diary of their use of toiletry and cosmetic products over a period, or a sample of housewives might be filmed throughout a working day in their kitchens. These records can be used to draw conclusions about possible needs or, more productively, they can be used as recall aids when informants are subsequently interviewed in depth about their feelings and frustrations at each point in the 'action'. These are merely devices to increase the chances of latent needs being recognized; any other productive or cost-effective device is open to the researcher at this ideas generating stage (providing, of course, it complies with the accepted professional and ethical standards).

Quantitative, Structured Research

This is the next logical progression in the use of research to look for possible new product ideas. If the company has no, or inadequate, previous research in a market or need-area in which it is currently interested, then it might consider it worth its while to specially commission usership and attitude studies, product tests on existing brands and so on. Then, of course, to use these as previously described, to sift and search for new product possibilities. Kuehn and Day[13] in particular describe how product tests can be used this way. However, such specially commissioned research may be something of an exception and a luxury *for this basic, inventive purpose*. (It must be clearly distinguished from the very frequent use of market surveys *after* the product idea is available, to optimize the way in which the new product is to be marketed.) Structured consumer research may be productive of product ideas if one needs it for other purposes anyway and, obviously, it is then very cost-effective. But if one wishes to specially commission research to generate new ideas, then the odds are that qualitative research will be more productive, £ for £, than larger yet, inevitably, more circumscribed structured research.

Gap Analysis of Existing Products

There are several variants on consumer-based gap analysis[14,19]. In general, a representative sample of consumers in a broadly defined target group is interviewed about existing products in a broadly defined market. ('Broadly defined', in both cases, because the end-product of this whole search procedure may well be a concept which has the potential to attract new types of users to the product group. Such a concept may be at, or beyond, the fringe of existing products and existing consumers.) The vital information collected in these interviews is consumers' perception of the existing products along relevant attitudinal dimensions, i.e. their 'image' of each product relative to the others (see chapter 14). Appropriate multivariate techniques are used to analyse this image data and to 'look for gaps' (see chapter 13). These gaps are empty spaces in the multi-dimensional attitude space, where no existing product represents a particular set of attitudinal characteristics as seen by a significant segment of the population covered. Such gaps in the attitude space represent potential areas for the positioning of a new product with significant appeal. They *are* only potential areas at this stage, because such a procedure inevitably throws up obvious but impractical gaps (e.g. a cheaper product than any existing brand, but using only the highest quality ingredients), and 'nonsense' gaps (an expensive product using poor quality ingredients). Such gaps are thrown up simply because no manufacturer is able (or would be foolish enough) to market such a product: their existence is no great disadvantage in the research because they can easily be eliminated on sight.

Since most consumer markets have a substantial number of relevant attitudinal dimensions, certainly if they are sufficiently broadly defined, such a gap analysis will often throw up a large number of attitudinal gaps. Each of these could, if wished, be subjected to the next (evaluation) stage of the new product program, but the available gap analysis techniques often have built-in devices for ranking the gaps in approximate order of their potential[15,16,20] so that the least interesting can be passed over without further ado.

Market Segmentation

Market segmentation[21,22] can perhaps, be conveniently visualized as multi-dimensional mapping of consumers, rather than of products. (See chapter 14.) Data about the market of interest are collected from a large and representative sample of the possible target group, very much as above. There tends, however, to be a greater emphasis on descriptive information about the consumers themselves; demographic, personality, behaviour in the relevant need-area, and attitudes to the need-area itself. Appropriate multivariate techniques enable the consumers to be clustered into groups which are homogeneous within themselves, but as different from each other as possible, in terms of the descriptive and attitudinal data collected about them. Simple tabulation of existing product-use and attitudes for each of these clusters can now help to identify significant segments of consumers who appear to have a (possibly latent) unsatisfied need. Examples are quoted in the literature; one such might be, say, 'Elderly women who worry about their health, who believe that a particular ailment can be cured and not just relieved, but also believe that existing remedies might not be entirely safe'. If, in addition, a high proportion of this hypothetical segment currently uses no proprietary medicine (or has very fragmented brand-use—another way of saying their needs appear not to be very effectively met by currently available products), then they would appear to present the necessary potential for a possible new product.

By drawing an 'Identi-kit picture' of potential market segments, such a technique clearly goes a long way to suggesting possible product concepts which might attract those segments.

Deliberate Invention

The final option is to move from techniques which are designed to search for possible *openings* (which a minimum of deduction must then fill) to those which actively set out to *invent* the product idea itself. As before, the more usual of these are not basically consumer based. Others, possibly insignificant at this time, do derive from consumer research techniques, though in truth the dividing line between searching and inventing can become very hazy here.

Non-consumer-based invention

Perhaps the three most common attempts at deliberate invention are:

(a) asking R & D people, inside or outside the company, to 'invent something';
(b) suggestion schemes amongst employees;
(c) 'brain-storming' amongst employees and other groups.

A development of the latter is 'synectics'[23]. This is a form of high-powered brain-storming which brings together experts from several different, and apparently unrelated, disciplines and, by making them aware of the nature of the creative process, attempts to turn them into highly original inventors. Synectics has not been much used in the marketing of everyday products (whose success does not often depend on the solution of difficult technical problems) but it is a technique which may well be adapted to such areas as time goes by.

Consumer-based invention

Getting consumers themselves to invent products is by no means easy. Attempts which have been made tend to be qualitative in nature and in scale. At their simplest they involve brain-storming in a group discussion context. All the evidence, however, is that consumers are not very productive or inventive when being handled in this way. Various approaches have been tried to get over this reticence: one manufacturer[24], for instance, is reported to have tackled it by what he calls 'reverse brainstorming', that is by putting the emphasis in his groups on the discussion of problems with existing products. Others clearly do the same, while giving their technique different names. But,

385

of course, this is likely to generate ideas only for functionally new products, and even its proponents do not claim that such a technique will result in consumers actually *inventing* something new.

A few practitioners have attempted to go rather further and to apply such knowledge as we have about creative processes to ordinary consumers—even to try the full synectics approach. From their attempts, they claim to have at least learnt how to *encourage* inventiveness in consumers; for instance, Sampson[25] says that the principal lessons are:

(a) not to expect consumers to spell out potential new products in all their detail, but to get ideas to the prototype stage where they can be recognized and carried forward by experts;
(b) to allow much more time than for conventional group discussions, and even to hold repeat sessions (as, of course, happens with synectics);
(c) to have materials and props available, rather than expecting informants to discuss too much in the abstract;
(d) not to hope for much *technical* inventiveness from ordinary consumers, even in a synectics environment.

Conclusions on This Stage: Generating Concepts

These, then, are the principal sources which have generally been used to generate new product ideas. It is for the individual manufacturer to decide how comprehensive he can afford to be in setting up such facilities. In doing so, however, he should remember two things. The first is that, despite what the future may hold, the vast majority of new product ideas do not at present, derive from specially commissioned consumer research. The author has, in fact, demonstrated elsewhere[7] that, at least for supermarket-type products, about 40% of new products introduced in Britain in 1970 were claimed to have derived from some form of market-searching (including accidental 'one-offs' as well as planned investigations), about 25% from consumer research (half specially commissioned and half already on file), about 15% from R & D, with the balance from other sources. There was a suggestion that market-searching might be responsible for an even higher share of *successful* new products (50%) at the expense both of consumer research and the other sources. The principal contribution of consumer research is to act as a catalyst, to prompt creativity, and to help the recognition of valuable ideas when they are otherwise suggested.

The second thing is that none of the above procedures can produce a unique or 'best' new concept in a particular product area. Several of these procedures, e.g. searches, gap analysis, will almost certainly produce several different ideas. It is the principal function of the next stage to evaluate concepts and to sort the more promising from the less promising.

Evaluating and Developing New Product Concepts

When new product concepts have been generated, by whatever means, they need to be:

(a) evaluated;
(b) developed.

'Evaluation', in its turn, has two meanings. First, assuming there is more than one possible concept to pursue, putting them into a likely order of interest, so that the available management time, R & D expense and financial investment (which are never unlimited) can be devoted to the most promising ideas. Second, determining whether the best, or the only one, of these concepts deserve time and money put against them at all.

Then, these new concepts need 'developing', because no product idea will be complete and optimal in every respect as it comes straight off the 'ideas production line'. It will need rounding-out: some aspects to be pronounced, others to be suppressed or amended, before it stands a good chance of success in the market-place. The marketing man will also need guidance, at an early stage, about which segments of the total available market appear to offer the easiest target including, for instance, which competing products might be most profitably attacked; and which concept will best complement, rather than compete with, existing company products. Such 'diagnostic' information is all part of the development of the new product concept, before the manufacturer gets down to the serious job of specifying the physical product, its packaging, advertising and other detailed elements of the marketing mix.

Initial screening

The first stage of the evaluation process has, again, little or nothing to do with consumers or consumer research. It is the stage of 'initial screening'[1,6,26,27]. Is the potential new product compatible with the company's strategic aims? Is it compatible with its financial objectives? Is it compatible with company know-how? Are there any legal constraints to its marketing? Is it compatible with plans for the sales force?, and so on. While this initial screening is a vital stage in weeding out concepts which never could lead to marketable products *for this company at this time*, it does not generally involve consumer research and is not, therefore, expanded on here.

Evaluating new product concepts

After initial screening, new product concepts are generally evaluated in the context of a 'concept test'; but bearing in mind that what is required is often just 'a steer'—a rough idea for the marketing man whether he should recommend going on or not—consumer research can sometimes help in quicker and cheaper ways. A very simple behavioural check (perhaps two or three questions on an omnibus survey) can, maybe, demonstrate that the available market is nothing like big enough to support the potential new product at a level which would be acceptable to the manufacturer[4]. (A typical example might be a new medicine, where a simple check might demonstrate that the number of sufferers in the market could never support a product which was compatible with the company's financial objectives.) In rejecting a potential new product on these grounds, however, it is vital to ensure that there is no question of a blinkered approach; that there is no possibility of stretching the proposed product to encompass more interesting and extensive end-uses.

Concept testing[28]

Useful though a simple usership check, or even a full usership and attitude survey into the existing market, may be in its own right—for general 'orientation' throughout the whole of the development program—the majority of new product concepts will *not* be amenable to go—no go evaluation in such a quick and easy way; some form of concept test will generally be called for.

Concept tests provide guidance in all four of the areas listed above:

(a) which of these ideas looks most interesting?
(b) does it (do they) warrant further investment of time and money?
(c) in what ways can it (they) be further developed?
(d) which segments of the market look most interesting to aim for?

If these are the *aims* of concept testing, however, a discussion of particular *techniques* must embrace the following main headings:

(a) in what form the concepts are exposed;
(b) to whom;
(c) where;
(d) in what particular research design;
(e) what questions are asked.

How are the Concepts Exposed?

The expression of the concept(s) to be tested can vary, at one extreme, from simple oral statements (sometimes tape recorded for uniformity from interview to interview) through written statements ('words on cards') and line drawings, to dummy packs and mock advertisements (press or video-taped television). If there is no heavy investment involved, or if a 'cribbed' product will do, the dummy pack might even contain a close approximation to the real product, as it is envisaged at this stage. It goes without saying that this is an ideal way to express the physical elements of the concept if it is possible.

It is widely argued (the 'holistic' argument, as opposed to the 'atomistic'[29,30]) that the saleability of a product depends so much on the *interaction* between different elements of the total marketing mix, that the nearer we can get to testing 'the whole thing' the less likely we are to make errors in predicting the success or failure of new concepts. However, carried to its logical conclusion the holistic approach introduces three major difficulties into the research design:

(a) any testing short of the market-place (with real advertising, real media, actual retail outlets, point-of-sale material etc.,) may produce wrong answers;
(b) component parts of the marketing mix cannot be developed and tested independently;
(c) *every* element in the marketing mix must be optimally executed before *anything* can be tested.

In other words, the holistic approach would argue that the concept itself cannot be evaluated until all the other elements of the marketing mix have been optimally developed and yet, if *anything* needs to be changed after this initial evaluation, then *everything else* might have to be changed and re-evaluated because of their interactions.

While such a thoroughgoing holistic approach is never seriously com-mended, there would seem to be fairly wide agreement that the diametrically opposed atomistic approach can lead to serious errors, certainly in products where the 'communication' elements are likely to play a large part. The most practical approach would seem to be to build into the concept testing stage those elements which are necessary to convey the proposed new product idea adequately (bearing in mind its possible novelty and uniqueness) and seem likely to interact significantly. And to leave out those which, on judgment, are unlikely to interact to any significant extent. This would suggest that the concept test should often include:

(a) the emotional aura surrounding the product, as well as its functional claims;
(b) the creative execution up to a fairly advanced stage;
(c) its expression in the chosen main medium;
(d) and (very possibly) its proposed name, price, etc.

This would argue, in such cases, for expressing the concept in a fairly finished advertisement[2]. In other cases, we can probably get near enough by using a mock pack alone and, in rare cases, a new product idea may be so functional that 'words on cards' will be adequate. No hard and fast rule can be laid down. Much depends on the perceived risk in missing out some elements of the marketing mix which could significantly affect consumers' evaluation of the proposed new product, against the costs and time involved in building these other elements into the initial concept testing stage.

To Whom is the Test Administered?

Quite simply, the test should be administered to a representative sample of the target market. This should be defined as those consumers (leaving aside the possible value of pre-tests on other relevant groups, e.g. retailers) who are likely to have any part in affecting the purchase decision: it would probably, for instance, include the users of many day-to-day products as well as the housewife purchasers. The target market should certainly not be defined too restrictively, however. Bearing in mind that one of the objectives of most concept tests is to provide guidance on how the product might be developed, and on which segments of the market it will mostly appeal to[22], it is highly desirable to include in the sample all consumers who could be in the market for the proposed product—perhaps in an amended and improved version. (Then, of course, it becomes necessary to analyse the results by relevant characteristics of the testers—particularly current behaviour and attitudes to this need-area—to establish the acceptability of the concept to different segments, their likes and dislikes and so on.)

It is increasingly suggested that the definition of the target group, for recruitment to concept (and other) pre-tests, should employ attitudinal characteristics, as well as demographic and behavioural characteristics, e.g. see ref. 31 and chapter 14 of this book. In theory this is obviously desirable, provided—as so often in this particular area of marketing—(a) we already have relevant attitude definitions as a result of previous research in this market, or (b) the commitment to the project is such that the time and cost of refining the target group in this way makes sense, and (c) we do not allow it to restrict our vision of how the concept might be re-positioned and re-targeted *as a result of the test.*

Some researchers believe that in-depth, qualitative concept testing[32] on small samples is likely to be more helpful than straightforward quantitative testing, certainly for diagnostic purposes if not for quantitative evaluation, and, indeed, there is often a strong case for both. For such tests, the participants are often recruited purposively and they might comprise, for instance, heavy users of the product group, recent brand switchers, known innovators, extreme acceptors and extreme rejectors of the new concept, without too much regard to strict representative sampling.

Where is the Test Administered?

Usually this is 'in-home' (sometimes by post) but the use of video-taped commercials to express the concept often necessitates 'in-theatre' testing (very much as for pre-testing advertisements themselves)[33]; and 'in-depth' qualitative testing often implies the use of group discussions in a typical discussion room.

In What Research Design?

If there is only one concept to be evaluated then there is little problem about research design: it has to be monadic (with rare exceptions (see below)). It is well to remember, however, that no known method of concept testing can forecast the absolute viability of a new product idea, i.e. whether or not it will make a profit, nor even what level of sales it is likely to achieve. Therefore, the only reliable uses of monadic test designs for *evaluative purposes* are to ask:

(a) is the idea so utterly rejected by testers that it is highly unlikely to be viable at all (even to a minority segment)? (In truth, however, this is a very rare finding for any sensible idea which has passed initial screening);
(b) how does it compare with other concepts which have also been tested monadically in the past? (This implies really comparing like with like, in a comparable research design, with comparable questions.)

If there were plenty of such comparable cases from the past which had subsequently been marketed, then we would have 'normative' data to set the latest concept against; but it is unlikely that much normative data of this type exists. Individual manufacturers may have accumulated such norms for particular product groups but, in general, it is not possible for most concept testers to refer to past data and to say 'This new concept achieves such-and-such a score, therefore the product should sell so much'.

However, if several new product ideas are to be evaluated at the same time, then it is possible to use well-known research designs such as matched monadic tests, paired comparisons, complete ranking, etc. (see chapter 3), with a reasonable degree of confidence. It goes without saying that such tests should still be trying to compare like with reasonable like. Indeed, as with all tests, concept testing is probably on safest ground when it is trying to choose between alternative *treatments* of the same basic idea, different creative claims, different end-uses, different prices etc.[33], than between different basic ideas.

In this context, particular attention may be drawn to the 'trade-off' approach with has been described by Johnson[35] and Westwood *et al.*[35]. This is essentially comparative, testers being asked to choose between concepts which, as in other forms of factorial design testing, contain all combinations of the relevant product attributes at different levels (or, in complex cases, a balanced sub-set of all possible combinations). An example might be, say, a new paper tissue which could come in any one of three different colours, several different sizes and different thicknesses, but some of these combinations might need to cost more than others. The trade-off approach would not only predict the winning combination of these attributes but would also estimate how much consumers value changes in one attribute against changes in the others—in other words, to what extent they are prepared to 'trade-off' size against thickness, colour against size, and all of these against price. Such an approach clearly provides understanding, flexibility and (hopefully) validity to the evaluation of alternative treatments of the same basic concept. Equally clearly, it is always likely to be on safer ground when dealing with the rational, factual elements of a new product idea than with the intangibles—say the everyday or special-occasion positioning of the paper tissues—which are difficult to communicate easily and unambiguously.

Occasionally, new concepts are tested against existing marketed products.

Theoretically, this does build in the necessary point of reference to predict an approximate level of sales in the market-place, but such a procedure is obviously of less certain value if the existing product is known to testers; like is not, then, being compared with like. It could, however, be of real value in those rare cases where the test can be conducted amongst a universe to whom the existing product is itself new: e.g. the existing product may still be in test market, so that it can be used as a new concept but with a known level of sales, in other parts of the country. The trade-off approach could be particularly valuable here and Westwood describes (admittedly for a more functional, industrial product) how hypothetical developments of *competitors'* products can be built in, to deduce this manufacturer's best strategy under conditions of uncertainty about other brands' intentions.

What Questions Are Asked?

The questions that are asked in a concept test, as in any piece of research, depend on the marketer's informational needs. But there are pitfalls to be avoided in thinking that concept tests are more definitive than (given our present knowledge) they can be.

For the evaluative aspects of concept tests it is certainly necessary to ask one (or more) questions which will provide a measure of 'overall accepta-bility', an index of saleability. Such questions can range from simple rating questions, 'How would you describe this product: excellent/very good/good?'; through propensity to purchase, 'How likely are you to buy this product at 15p?'; to mock purchasing situations, 'Would you like to buy a pack for 15p?' A danger to avoid, however, is that of rejecting the concept because of the stated price at which it was put into the test. Price is, after all, one element of the marketing mix and the proposed new product may well be marketable at other prices, something which could be tested by putting alternative prices into the test.

The most important point about such questions, even those of a mock purchase nature, is that they cannot be used blithely to predict sales. Any test is a highly artificial, heightened situation and quite unlike real life. Therefore, their major use must be for comparative purposes and, for this, they should be as comparable as possible from test to test within a given product group.

In the case of straightforward comparative testing, particularly paired comparisons, rankings, etc., the problem of meaningful questions is eased. Any sensible questioning technique would probably be acceptable, e.g. 'Which of these products would you be most interested in trying?', and the usual arguments for using the most *discriminating* questions would apply. Some commentators, however, go further and claim that this sort of simplistic question is always likely to provide invalid data—even for compara-tive purposes. Iuso[32], for instance, believes that concepts should be assessed by trained researchers working from 'discursive reactions', i.e. semi-structured interviews. Tauber[36], correctly emphasizing that 'adoption includes a sense of product commitment', believes we should measure importance and involvement. And Twedt[37] is specific that this can be done by 'tri-variant analysis', i.e. by rating the desirability of the claim $\times$ its exclusiveness $\times$ its believability. It is another area where it would be nice to have concrete *evidence* that the more sophisticated approaches are actually more valid (i.e. more likely to lead to profitable products) than the simpler ones.

The diagnostic questions which can be asked in a concept test are of almost infinite variety. Typical questionnaires have much in common with those of advertisement testing, i.e. in studying:

(a) comprehension of the new concept;
(b) perception of its attributes (particularly its differences from existing products);
(c) its believability (as a possible new product);
(d) its perceived advantages and disadvantages, again with particular reference to existing products;
(e) its ratings on relevant specific attribute scales, to establish its strong and weak points;
(f) what situations it might be used in;
(g) how often/how much at a time;
(h) which existing products it might replace;
(i) what sort of people it might appeal to.

One would say that it is in these *diagnostic* areas that qualitative concept testing mainly comes into its own and ingenious techniques are often used for learning how best to develop the new product idea. Typical examples are 'creative group discussions' and 'word-of-mouth chains', in which successive informants pass on the idea to each other in their own words, and discuss it together, their conversations being tape-recorded and subsequently analysed. This is sometimes found to provide new insights into the most promising appeals of the potential new product. And, of course, if this diagnostic evidence is to be used constructively to *develop* the new concept, it must be ploughed back and re-evaluated. Quite often, this results in a feedback procedure—test, evaluate, diagnose, develop, re-test[2]—with the marketing man 'carrying on a dialogue' with his potential consumers.

Another method of evaluating new product concepts

Some variants in concept testing[18,20] depend less on asking consumers directly what they think of the possible new concepts, and more on asking them to provide ratings relative to existing brands and, sometimes, relative to an 'ideal' product. They are rated along the image dimensions which are known to be relevant in their market: indeed, such techniques are often directly derived from the gap analysis which may have invented the new concepts in the first place.

The alternative concepts are now evaluated by their nearness, in the image space, to the ideal product and/or to their distance from existing brands in the market. The number and the characteristics of the consumers they could hope to attract are deduced by the relative distance between each concept and each existing product in the image space. One particularly interesting example of such a linked invention and concept test—the invention of a new political party—has been written up by Morgan and Purnell[9].

A Postscript

It is probably worthwhile to stress three final points. The first is that concept testing has never been *proved*, at least in any general sense, to provide a *valid* technique for predicting the success (even the relative success) of new product ideas. It has this, however, in common with most other techniques in the market researcher's battery in the present stage of our knowledge. Many researchers would claim that, because of the complexity of the real marketplace and the interaction of content and execution (particularly in advertising) concept testing never will be completely validated.

Second, despite one or two interesting experiments in extended-use concept tests and, for instance, Tauber's attempts to measure 'commitment'[36], current methods mostly depend on 'first-time interest'. The long-term success of most products undoubtedly depends on their ability to generate repeat purchase and this, in its turn, must be due to something more than simple propensity to try. Perhaps 'first-time interest' *is* highly correlated with 'long-term persuasiveness' but some evidence to this effect would be consoling.

Third, these limitations are probably well known to most users of concept tests. Generally their problem is to 'screen out' obvious failures from a wealth of possible new product concepts, certainly if they are using really productive sources for new ideas. They want to avoid putting more time and money than is absolutely necessary against too many concepts which are going to be failures anyway, no matter how well they are handled by R & D, advertising etc., and, despite the lack of evidence, they feel confident that concept testing does effectively screen out most of the real failures—even if, occasionally, a baby may be thrown away with the bathwater.

Evaluating and Developing New Products

In our idealized model of the new product process we have, at this stage, an idea (or ideas) which we believe to have potential saleability but which must be *developed* into a physical product before there is anything available to test. This first stage of development will tend to be in the laboratory, the R & D chemists, engineers, designers turning an agreed blueprint, based on the concept testing stage, into something physical.

Business analysis

This laboratory development is often an expensive process, in terms of both management time and out-of-pocket expenditure. For this reason, a full 'business analysis' is often undertaken at this stage of the program[1-6]. The marketing man has the benefit of a fully developed product concept and is to turn this into a complete business proposition—forecast sales, cost of goods, advertising, selling and other marketing costs (and, therefore, anticipated profit), proposed channels for distribution, advertising strategy, etc. Only on agreement of this business analysis can he expect to get top management approval to invest in physical product development and maybe, even then, only after they have considered external influences such as future legislation.

Product testing[38-40]

Once there is a physical product to 'evaluate' and 'develop', the almost invariable way of tackling this is by product testing. As with most types of research the exact boundaries of product testing are somewhat vaguely determined but, as a working definition, we can say that a representative sample of the target group will be exposed to the physical product under more-or-less controlled conditions, will use it under more-or-less realistic circumstances, and will then express their opinions about it in a more-or-less structured way.

A great deal of what has been said of concept testing is entirely analogous here. Product testing, too, has two basically different purposes:

(a) to evaluate;
(b) to develop.

However, there *are* differences in emphasis which often affect research design. At this stage of the program, the manufacturer will generally have focussed onto one or a very limited number of new product concepts. Everything up to this point (initial screening, concept testing, business analysis) will have served to weed out many non-runners so that projects which are still under serious consideration at this stage are probably *intended* to be put on sale (even if only in a test market).

'Evaluation', then, is generally to help decide whether or not to proceed with a project at all, rather than to compare and rank basically different products; in other words, to help to make simple go/no-go/amend decisions.

'Development' still has the purpose of rounding-out, determining the strengths and weaknesses of the prototype product, amending and adjusting its weak points and (unless the concept testing stage managed to do it exactly—which would be unusual) determining which segments of the market are best attacked. Often, too, it is aimed to provide R & D guidance as much as marketing guidance: not only to *suggest* changes in physical characteristics but to *choose* between alternatives—different strengths, flavours, perfumes, colours, shapes. The manufacturer's aim is to market the optimum combination of product attributes (compatible with manufacturing costs) and, as such, product testing is frequently a dialogue between the consumer and the R & D man, albeit via the marketing man. In summary, then, the areas in which product tests provide guidance are:

(a) does the potential new product (now in its physical form) live up to its concept, which has already been shown to be potentially saleable?;
(b) does it warrant further investment of time and money?;
(c) which of several alternative treatments is likely to be most successful?;
(d) in what ways can it be further improved?;
(e) (if there is still any doubt) which segments of the market look most interesting to aim for?

As for concept testing, discussion of particular product testing techniques must embrace the following main headings:

(a) in what form the product is exposed;
(b) to whom;
(c) with what instructions;
(d) where;
(e) in what particular research design;
(f) what questions are asked.

How are the Products Exposed?

For the major purpose of evaluation, it is highly desirable that the product itself be tested in a reasonably complete form under reasonably realistic conditions. But we are really involved in the holistic *v.* atomistic dilemma again—whether a product can be correctly evaluated unless it is surrounded by *all* the other elements in the total marketing mix, including specifically the communications elements.

Again, there is no categoric solution to this dilemma, though it would still seem that a thorough-going atomistic approach could lead to serious errors in some cases, e.g. the packaging of many day-to-day products certainly contributes a great deal to their acceptability to consumers, both in practical and aesthetic terms. It is quite likely that a test product placed in an unsuitable and unpleasing package would be misleadingly assessed by testers, no matter how acceptable they found the product itself.

On the other hand, it is also true that many of the elements of the total marketing mix cannot be faithfully reproduced except in the real market-place. The only sensible solution would seem to be much as for concept testing, namely to build into the test those elements which are necessary to convey the product and its performance adequately (bearing in mind its possible novelty and uniqueness) and seem likely to interact significantly[40].

As a broad generalization, then, the elements which it is often found necessary to put into the test include a reasonable approximation to the final packaging, and enough copy (on the package and/or contained in accompanying material) to make clear the benefits which will be claimed for the product. This copy will, of course, itself be based on the development concept from the preceding concept testing stages. As the product itself moves from the 'functional' towards the 'emotional', e.g. from a staple food towards a luxury cosmetic, so the creative execution of the claims becomes of greater significance in expressing the product benefits. It may become necessary to execute a finished pack design, to accompany the test product with a mock advertisement, even to give it the aura of a suggested price, in order to be confident that the product has a realistic chance to 'express its point of view' in the test.

Conversely, if the communications elements become overwhelmingly important, it may be that the product itself becomes almost an irrelevancy—any competent formulation, e.g. an exact copy of an existing brand, may perform as well as any other. In extreme cases, there might even be a case for getting the communications elements right, by concept, advertisement, name and pack testing, and then going straight into the market-place without product testing at all.

A particular problem in deciding what to include in the test is whether to use the proposed brand name or not, whether to test 'blind' or 'branded'. Bearing in mind that we are considering potential new products here, and not accepted brands, it is probable that in many cases the name serves a relatively unimportant part in 'expressing' the product and has little interaction with other elements of the marketing mix, so that it is not generally essential to include it. Having said which, it is generally difficult to convey the other creative elements *without* a name. Since the name itself costs very little to develop, it will frequently be included as a peg to hang the package and mock advertisements on. In some cases, indeed, judgement may suggest that the name *is* an important conditioning element in its own right and then it is essential that it be included if consumer acceptability is to be reliably assessed. The most obvious example is where the new product is an extension to an existing, familiar brand range. Perhaps the manufacturer's name is more often important in this respect than the proposed brand name itself.

Testing for 'development' purposes, or for R & D guidance, may result in different conclusions about how the product is exposed. For example, we may have established that a potential new product is sufficiently well evaluated to be worth putting into a test market. Before that crucial step, however, we will normally want to develop the optimum formulation including, say, finding the colour which is most consonant with our proposed gentleness claim. We *could* continue to test alternative colours accompanied with copy claims which say 'gentleness' and then establish which colour produces the highest overall acceptability of the test product. It is equally valid, however, and is often more discriminating, to test the alternative colours without any promotional claims but asking the testers (amongst other things) which they found to be most gentle.

To Whom is the Test Administered?

Again, the test should be administered to a representative sample of the target market. However, it may now be possible to specify the target market in rather more specific terms; that, indeed, was probably one of the objectives of the previous concept testing stage. Care should still be taken, however, not to recruit too restrictively for fear of eliminating potential consumers who would find the product acceptable if it were amended in accordance with their opinions as expressed in the test. Testing is often to provide guidance on which segments of the market the product will appeal to most, *including* consumers who might become users if it were amended in certain ways.

Unlike concept testing, in most cases there is probably little point in testing a new product, in use, on people who are expected to be purchasers but not users, e.g. on housewives who buy for their husbands. The original concept and its presentation may well be highly relevant to such purchasers but the performance of the product *in use* probably is not (except at second-hand).

With What Test Instructions?

The instructions to testers should say, simply but unambiguously, what they are expected to do with the product. Therefore, they generally embrace the essence of the instructions which will accompany the marketed product, *less* any unnecessary 'blurb' but *plus* any additional clarification for the purpose of the test itself. For instance, the marketed product may eventually say 'Whenever you feel jaded and under the weather, a teaspoonful of delicious X, stirred into a glass of cold water, will give you that get-up-and-go feeling'. The comparable product test instructions will probably say something like 'Use this product whenever you feel a little tired and would like a refreshing drink during the next week. Please try, in any case, to take it at least once during that time. To prepare, stir one teaspoonful into a glass of cold water'.

There is one particular trap to avoid in writing product test instructions. Testers are generally very co-operative and will try to do just what they are asked. If one of the developmental objects of the test is to encourage experimentation and provide information on different ways testers find of using the product (different end-uses, different modes of preparation) then they should be clearly invited in the instructions to experiment. For instance, in the example above, by adding statements such as 'Stir one teaspoonful, or more or less according to taste, into a glass of cold water'; 'Use it also on other occasions when you feel like a drink'. Otherwise, the test will stand in danger of simply demonstrating that the product was used as specified in the test instructions and consumers in the real market-place will probably not feel so constrained.

For some developmental purposes, particularly for choosing the optimum treatment of one factor in the new product, a full in-use test is not always judged necessary. It may be that a 'sniff test' is adequate for choosing a perfume, a 'look-and-handle test' for choosing a shape and a 'taste test' for choosing a flavour[40]. While advising caution in the use of such truncated tests—the physical attributes of a product can interact substantially and 'snap judgements' may sometimes be misleading—such tests clearly simplify the instructions which are given to testers, simply to 'please smell this' or 'please taste this'.

The length of time over which participants in full in-use tests should be invited to use the products is, however, a problem too. The pressures are often to produce a result quickly. Against this should be set the fact that many products are used infrequently 'in real life', or take some time to use up, while opinions can and do change after continued trials. A flavour or perfume which was initially acceptable can pall after repeated exposure. Yet all the evidence is that the majority of successful products depend for their long term health on achieving adequate repeat purchase over several years. Certainly, it must be a danger to base important decisions about a potential new product on an unrealistically short test period and, if in doubt, the researcher should always veer towards extending the period rather than curtailing it, even if this means providing a supply of samples for each individual.

One interesting application of extended-use tests—'controlled consumer choice'—is to place several packs of the test product (and, if relevant, another existing product) after the short-term re-call interview and then, at a later date, to observe how much has actually been used up when the pressure of a short-term test is off. This, it is suggested[12], can provide a worthwhile estimate of the off-take the test product might achieve in the market-place, other things (shop distribution, advertising, etc.) being equal.

Where is the Test Administered?

In-use tests are almost always administered in-home, unless there is something very specific to the product which makes this inappropriate. Even products which are used out of the home (handbag cosmetics, alcoholic drinks, etc.) are generally placed and testers reinterviewed in their homes, because this is the most efficient way to contact and re-interview a representative sample of testers.

It is not unusual, however, for in-use product tests to be conducted by post, since relatively simple questionnaires are often involved. Some organizations have standing panels specifically recruited to test products by post in this way[40]. Since the panel members get an element of practice in completing tests, and appreciate the supply of test products, response rates can be much higher than with other postal research. However, since conditioning is a latent problem with all panels, product testing panels are probably particularly well-suited for developmental purposes, choosing between alternatives, etc., but should be used with caution for absolute evaluation.

Sniff, look and handle, and flavour tests are often conducted, for economy, in a 'hall test' situation, where a sample of testers is invited into a test room, e.g. a church hall, an advertisement testing theatre or a specially equipped test van, and exposed to the test on production line principles. Apart from the limited exposure to the test products in these circumstances, however, we must bear in mind that it is an artificially controlled exposure, fixed as to time of day, methods of preparation, etc., and this could possibly be a distorting influence. On the whole, such hall tests should probably be restricted to screening tests, to eliminate the obvious failures amongst a number of alternatives.

In What Research Design?

Once again, we must distinguish between evaluation and development. For the former, we shall be attempting to put a measure to the likely success of a single test product. All that was said above about monadic concept tests will, therefore, apply here, and particularly the lack of normative data for projecting results to the market-place[40]. Penny *et al.* have shown in a comprehensive paper[40] which discusses many of the different aspects of product testing techniques—often with evidence to support particular procedures—that monadic rating scores do correlate quite well with subsequent market-place performance *within one particular food market where product quality is believed to be important.* This gives rise to the hope that the development of norms for different product groups (or need-areas) might be valid, but the task is clearly formidable for individual companies. However, unless a product is really 'new, new' it can more often be tested against an existing brand. Whilst it is difficult to take an existing product and express its basic *concept* in truly 'blind' form (except in the rare case where it is still only on sale in part of the country), it is much easier to repack a competitive *product* so that this does effectively become 'blind'. Provided the product itself does not have peculiarly recognizable physical characteristics then 'like' will reasonably well be being compared with 'like' and we shall have *some* sort of benchmark against which to judge the test results.

Having settled on a suitable benchmark of this type (or more than one, if that is possible, to increase the reliability with which the results can be interpreted), then paired comparisons or complete ranking can generally be used for establishing relative preferences. Sometimes, however (see below), it is desirable or necessary to use matched monadic designs despite their lower sensitivity.

Turning to research designs for developmental purposes, simple diagnostic information—strong points, weak points, suggestions for improvement—are a natural by-product of all test designs and are simply a function of asking relevant questions about each test product. To choose, however, between different treatments of one or more factors in the product calls for careful consideration of research design.

First, this is one of the few cases where we usually are testing like with like in most relevant respects. Even if the different treatments would be given different creative support, this can be built into the test design with supporting pack material or mock advertisements. Therefore, the relative evaluation of one variant against another probably does reliably predict relative market-place performance.

Second, paired and other side-by-side comparisons are generally more discriminating for a given research expenditure than matched monadic tests. This is the case both statistically, in the sense that sampling errors are reduced by making the comparisons within each tester rather than between sub-samples, and psychologically, in the sense that a tester can often express a preference when he would give identical scores on independent rating scales.

Some researchers argue that paired comparisons ought *never* to be used, because products are used monadically in real life. While this argument is important in relation to evaluation testing, it would not seem to be a particular cause for concern in development testing. Most testing of the latter type is only to determine the *direction* of preferences (which variant is most preferred, which next, etc.) and it must be rare for the test design actually to reverse the direction of a preference[40].

Occasionally, paired comparisons do have drawbacks peculiar to the product under test or to the particular circumstances and objectives of the test. It may not be possible, for instance, at least within a sensible timescale, to test two alternatives on an equal footing. The first medicine may cure the ailment, so that there is no opportunity to test the second realistically. The first application of a cleaning product may remove the dirt for good. Even if the use of the first test product does not make the second irrelevant, it may so affect the condition of the test material that the second cannot be tested under comparable conditions. Ingenuity can sometimes overcome these difficulties, for instance by dividing the test material into two and using one product on each half. In some cases, however, there are no ingenious solutions to such problems and then a matched monadic design—or a 'sequential monadic' with a long enough gap between testing and rating the two products—is inevitable.

Sometimes, too, particularly in tests which involve several elements of the 'marketing mix', the researcher will judge that there is something inherent in the alternatives to be tested which could make paired comparisons invalid. This is usually because of the danger of consumers being too 'sensitive' or too 'rational' in the test situation. As an extreme example: a 'marketing mix' test which included a statement of alternative retail prices might tempt consumers to choose the more expensive product in a paired comparison situation ('because it must be better quality') where, in a monadic situation, therefore being oblivious of the price differential, they might choose the cheaper (because, in truth, they judged it to be better value). Similar situations could arise with other elements of the marketing mix, e.g. with particular product claims which lend themselves to a degree of rationality or sensitivity on the testers' part which *would not exist* in the actual marketing situation.

No *general* rules about this can be laid down. The researcher must be on his guard to recommend paired comparisons or complete ranking, for their greater sensitivity, where they are practicable and are not likely to distort the results, but to recommend a matched monadic design where one tester cannot sensibly use more than one test product or where a multi-product design might actually distort the results as they would relate to 'real life'.

It should go without saying that, whatever research design is chosen as appropriate for a particular test, full use should be made of the principles of experimental design (see chapter 3) to get the maximum information for a given research expenditure. If several different factors in a product are to be explored, say colour, flavour and perfume, it is not only more cost-effective to test all the variants at once in a factorial design, but information can be obtained which might not otherwise be available. Information on the interactions between the different factors—flavour and perfume, perhaps—allows the optimum *combination* of these to be marketed and not a simple addition which might be less than optimum.

What Questions are Asked?

The form of the questionnaire for most product tests follows fairly uniform lines. There is usually a measure of overall acceptability which, in the case of monadic tests, will be similar to those used in concept testing, described earlier. Just as with concept tests, and in the absence of norms of the type described by Penny[40], the answers to such questions cannot be used directly to predict sales. Their major use is, again, for comparative purposes, to choose between alternative variants, or against an existing brand for normative data. As before, they should be made as comparable as possible from test to test within a given product group.

Side-by-side testing—paired comparisons and ranking tests—eases the problem of designing sensitive and reliable questions and any sensible comparative questioning technique is likely to be acceptable. 'Which product did you prefer?' is probably as sensitive and valid as anything, but some researchers prefer to bring the decision nearer to the market-place by asking, for instance, 'Which of these products would you be most likely to buy for 12p?'. Unless there is likely to be an *interaction* between the variants being tested and the price at which they might be sold, it seems unlikely that such a device adds anything to the validity of the test.

However, mock purchase situations are sometimes introduced further into the test design. Since the long-term health of most products depends on their level of sustainable repeat purchase, an offer is made to sell another pack (or packs) of the product at the end of the in-use test*. The reasoning is that the proportion of testers who do purchase will approximate to the proportion

---

* The Code of Conduct of the (British) Market Research Society is generally interpreted to mean that no money must actually change hands. This can be achieved by telling the respondent, immediately after the purchase decision has been made, that he or she will in fact be given the product *free*.

who will repeat purchase in the long-run in the market-place. This is an ingenious and promising use of product tests which comes very close to mini-test marketing (see chapter 19), but it has again to be admitted that there is, as yet, very little published evidence that such tests do, in fact predict subsequent market place performance.

As well as appropriate overall acceptability questions, most product tests also ask diagnostic questions of the type 'Why did you prefer that product? What did you like about it? What did you think were its good points? Was there anything you disliked about it? Any other way in which it could be improved?', and so on. There will also usually be preference or ratings questions, as appropriate, on specific attributes of the test product(s), 'Which of the two products did you prefer for its flavour?' or 'How would you rate this product for its flavour—excellent/very good, etc?'. These, too, will sometimes be followed by more specifically diagnostic questions, 'Why did you prefer that one for its flavour?'. As a matter of questionnaire design, note that Brown and Millward[41] have contended, with some evidence, that there are definite advantages in asking other evaluative and diagnostic questions before overall ratings. This appears to increase the discrimination between products (in other words, to improve the chance of picking the 'winners' from the 'losers') on the very reasonable grounds, as they claim, that to do otherwise is to ask testers to give the verdict before the evidence!

While the specific attribute questions can prove of great value in suggesting where to look for product improvements and even, in some cases, for determining 'the winner', like many other measures they must be treated with caution. Some effort will have to be made to attach relative importance weights to the different attributes asked about. This may have been attempted at an earlier stage of the new product program, as part of the basic market survey or of preliminary qualitative research. On a quantified scale, the St. James's or Fishbein models may have been employed (see chapter 3) or Twedt's tri-variant approach[37]. The discursive nature of qualitative research is often thought to be more conducive to the reliable attribution of import-ances (see chapter 2) and some support the use of projective tech-niques—though their interpretation has the disadvantage of being very personal to the individual researcher[32]. The attribution of importance weights may also be built-in to the product test design itself but, often, it must be based on nothing more sophisticated than asking informants about the relative importance of each attribute to them.

It is also obvious that large 'halo effects' exist in product testing. The test variant which is preferred overall will often also be preferred on every individual attribute, including those on which it does not, in fact, differ from the other variants. In the present stage of our knowledge, the most defensible procedure to isolate the effects of different attributes on overall evaluation, should it be necessary, is to build the different treatments of these attributes into a factorial test design in the first place.

A different problem to do with specific attribute questions is that of semantics. It is very important to ensure, for instance, so far as possible, that the attributes described in the questionnaire mean the same thing to typical consumers as they do to R & D technologists and others. Much has been written about the necessity for prior qualitative research into the relevant semantics and reference should be made to the relevant paper[42].

The final questions, as with concept testing, will often deal with the way consumers perceive this particular new product—what situations it might be used in, how much at a time, etc. These can obviously be catered for as appropriate within each specific test.

Three Final Comments on Product Testing

What has been described so far has been, on the whole, quantitative product testing, i.e. the design of tests in which numbers can reliably be attached to the results. *Qualitative* product testing can also be very valuable. Sometimes this is conducted on independent samples of testers; sometimes on the same testers, say those who expressed extreme favour or disfavour with the new product in a quantitative test. In either case, the test procedures are much the same, except that sample sizes are generally much smaller (for cost reasons) and the final interview is much more discursive and unstructured. Such qualitative testing can prove valuable for gaining insights into product performance which more structured tests cannot do, and for suggesting product and creative leads which might not otherwise have been forthcoming.

Sometimes, the concept testing and product testing stages are collapsed into one, by placing a test product with the sample of consumers who have just carried out the concept test. While such a procedure can save research costs it can also have limitations and potential dangers. Diagnostic leads from the concept test obviously cannot be taken into account in designing the test product itself. It also follows that the test product must be exposed in the context of the original 'unrefined' concept, without the benefit of any improvements in presentation which might have resulted from a prior concept test. There is everything to be said for testing a new product in the context of its claims but two separate stages of concept and product testing would seem to be both safer and more productive.

Just as with concept testing, and most other aspects of new product development, successful projects are always likely to result from feedback—the willingness to test, evaluate, diagnose, develop and re-test. For this reason, some commentators (e.g. refs. 2 and 43) recommend starting off with small-scale, possibly qualitative, tests (even 'workshop' tests, where the communication elements—prototype advertisements, etc.—may be inserted and amended as testers react to them), gradually working up to larger and more structured tests as certainty grows that the project is on the right lines.

Pricing New Products

As stressed earlier, the product itself is only one element, although a vital one, in the total marketing mix. Development and testing techniques for the more important of the other elements—name, packaging, advertising—are described in chapters 16 and 17. There is one element, however, which is so vital to the whole *business proposition* that it must be considered almost as basic as the concept and the product itself; namely, its price. Indeed, so basic is price that it will almost certainly have been built into the early evaluation, concept and business analysis, because it is only by converting anticipated sales into approximate revenue that management could evaluate the whole project at that stage. However, despite the fact that an approximate unit price must have been in mind at a very early stage of the project, there will probably be a need later in the development process to refine and firm up on this price.

How is price determined?[44-45]

Techniques for determining an optimum retail price ahead of actual marketing are probably sketchier than for any other element of the marketing mix. (Controlled experiments to choose between a number of alternative prices can be conducted in the market-place (see chapter 19) but we are only concerned here with what can be done before actually putting the product on sale, even on a 'mini' scale.) As a result, retail prices are very often determined as a fixed mark-up on the cost of goods (or cost of sales)[16]. Such a procedure, however, though it may limit the possibility of loss, is unlikely to result in an optimally profitable price. There is certainly evidence that a 'just' price, from the consumer's point of view, has little relationship to the manufacturer's costs and, indeed, why should it when these costs are generally not known to consumers?

An examination of the ruling price structure

When a new product is going into an existing market, or even into peripheral competition with existing products, its price must bear *some* relationship to competition. Exactly what relationship is up to the manufacturer to decide in the light of his marketing strategy. He may have decided, on judgement or, better still, in the light of his research into the existing market, that he wishes his new product to be seen as relatively premium-priced. Then an examination of existing brands, their retail prices and brand shares, will obviously help to set his own lower limit. (Also, clearly, vice versa if his intention is to be seen as relatively cut-price.)

Occasionally, the manufacturer may feel that the ruling price structure determines his own price exactly; perhaps all brands sell at one price and he cannot afford to be different.

Such an examination still, to some extent, begs the question because the decision, to be seen as premium-priced, cut-price or average-priced is, in itself, a pricing decision, and *marginal* differences in price thereafter can affect volume off-take and profit significantly. Therefore, the manufacturer of a new product would usually like assistance in determining its price fairly exactly, not in the sort of broad range which an examination of the ruling price structure generally affords. What assistance, then, *can* research provide?

Propensity to purchase

Price questions are often asked as an integral part of concept and product tests[3,6], as indicated earlier in this chapter. Generally, they are of the type 'What do you think you would be prepared to pay for a 4 oz size of this product?' or 'Do you think you would buy a 4 oz size of this product for 25p?'. Sometimes, too, they are asked as rating questions; 'How likely would you be to buy a 4 oz size of this product for 25p; very likely, fairly likely?', etc.

It is dangerous, however, to apply the answers to such questions, as they stand, directly to 'real life'. Consumers probably tend spontaneously to understate the price at which a new product will subsequently establish itself in the market-place; in other words, a smaller proportion tends to nominate the market price than will actually become regular purchasers at that price. Yet, perversely, when the question is asked the other way the evidence is that a much *greater* proportion tend to claim to be interested at a nominated price than ultimately do buy regularly at that price.

In order to get over these difficulties, some researchers have, as described above, used actual selling situations at the end of product tests (and even at the end of concept tests) by offering to sell another pack to the tester: what would certainly improve predictions from test situations to real life would be reliable normative data to build into an 'aiming-off' formula. While some companies and some researchers may claim to have such a formula it is safe to say that there are none generally available which have been validated for a wide variety of product groups. Predictions based on such formulae will usually need, therefore, to be treated with great caution.

Propensity to purchase questions (and mock selling situations) are probably on safer ground when they are simply intended to choose between two or more alternatives. In such cases it is obviously nonsensical to ask testers whether they would rather purchase a given product for 25p or 30p; matched samples faced with the alternative prices is the appropriate research design to use. Clearly, such tests are much more reliable for predicting which price is likely to sell more and which less than in attaching precise magnitudes to the difference, but even if this only eliminates some options before market testing, it may prove to be very worthwhile. It also goes without saying that the nearer the test product can be to an 'as marketed' situation (including its packaging and advertising) the more reliable such a test is likely to be, since price undoubtedly creates an 'image' of its own which may well interact with other elements in the mix.

Developments of Propensity to Purchase

Gabor and Granger[46,47] have suggested two developments on simple 'propensities to purchase'. In the first variant, which is said to be more relevant to completely new products, a representative sample of the target group is shown a sample of the proposed product either in illustrative, conceptual form or, better, in its physical form. Each tester is asked whether or not he would be prepared to buy at each of a range of prices, up to about nine in number, from one which is obviously too high to one which is obviously too low, asked in random order. For those prices at which he would not buy, he is also asked why: because it appears too expensive, or because it is too cheap to trust? (though a more recent paper based on their work[48] suggests that this supplementary question is redundant and that the 'buy-response' curve can be deduced simply from willingness to buy or not—which seems to take us back to the simpler approaches described above). The summation of these data over the total sample gives the proportion prepared to buy at each discrete point within the range and, from this, appropriate pay-off calculations can be attempted.

In the second variant, which is said to be more relevant to a new entrant in an existing product group, each tester is asked what would be the most he would be prepared to pay, and the least, before he would begin to suspect the quality of the product. A cumulative calculation then enables the demand curve to be calculated at all points between the most and the least that any tester says he would pay.

These extensions of simple propensity to purchase do not avoid all the difficulties referred to earlier, but obviously provide more comprehensive data for choosing between all possible prices and, since they produce a continuous curve, certainly demonstrate which particular price *ought* to be optimal. They also demonstrate the sharp peaks and plateau-edges which are typical of 'natural' and 'threshold' prices and the plateaux which occur between prices. Whether or not the demand curve as it stands is truly predictive of the market-place for potential new products, there must be a strong presumption that such *patterns* have some relevance to reality, i.e. that sharp troughs should be avoided, that it is more profitable to price at the expensive end of a plateau rather than just 'over the edge', on its down-slope. This, at least, may enable the manufacturer to find a localized optimum price when the range has already been limited in other ways, e.g. by the cost of goods or ruling price structure[48].

One important limitation of all such pricing techniques must, however, be stressed. A new product with an innovatory formulation or communication elements could markedly change consumers' expectations of, and judgements about, what constitutes a suitable price in a particular product field. The techniques referred to above tend, in the main, to provide answers based on the current market price structure, and (especially at the concept stage) do not easily cope with innovations which may upset this*.

Re-Cycling

As indicated at the beginning of this chapter, a process which frequently goes on in parallel to new product development is the re-cycling of existing brands, i.e. the attempt to prolong their profitable life by finding new uses, attacking new segments of the market, reinforcing existing appeals or incorporating new ones, and generally combating competitive and other market changes. This may involve making product and pack improvements, using more persuasive advertising claims, altering the price, and other marketing activities.

Of course, devices such as these designed to increase or maintain profits are the *constant* preoccupation of marketing men, but we are concerned here with something more than a new copy line, a revamped pack design, a revised trade price structure or increased advertising expenditure. Recycling, to warrant the title, implies a significant change in what is on offer *in the consumer's terms*, together with a thoroughgoing examination of all the other elements of the marketing mix to ensure that they optimize on that change, whatever it is. The really significant change, therefore, will generally be in the product itself (or, occasionally, in its packaging where this is an important element of the product) and/or in its creative claims and 'positioning'. An example of the former would be the development of instant coffees into their accelerated freeze-dried form; of the latter, the repositioning of foot-soaking salts as a general bath additive†.

Similarities with new product development

Expressed in this way it is clear that re-cycling has a very great deal in common with new product development. Every product, even an accepted brand, has a 'concept': to re-cycle, it may be necessary to *generate* a new concept for the brand, to *evaluate* and *develop* this new concept, and then to *evaluate* and *develop* the product itself in the context of this concept.

The first really major difference between re-cycling and new product

---

* There must, too, be difficulties in interpretation at a time of rapid inflation — which will be more of an issue at some times, and in some markets, than others.

† We are also concerned with something more than the substitution of ingredients, or change in manufacturing processes, for simple cost-saving reasons. This may be a very effective way to revitalize profits, and it certainly calls for careful product testing[49,50]. But it probably does not represent a discernible product improvement in the consumer's eyes.

development, however, is that some of these stages may not be appropriate in any given case and they may, therefore, be eliminated. It may, for instance, be decided that the basic concept (and all that this implies in creative treatment) should be unaltered. What is really required is a radical product improvement. Maybe what was the 'whitest' washing powder is now only 'white' compared with its competitors—then we might go straight to the product development and product testing stages.

Maybe the product itself cannot easily, or economically, be reformulated; what is needed is that it should be repositioned. Then it will be necessary to generate, test and develop a new concept for the brand, and although the product itself will almost certainly need to be *evaluated* in the context of its proposed new concept, product development will be irrelevant.

What is needed from the marketing man and the researcher is that they think of their re-cycled brand *as though* it were a completely new project, eliminating only those stages in our idealized program which are clearly inappropriate or unnecessary.

Branded and blind tests

There are, however, two other major differences between re-cycling and new products. One is that, as far as the consumer is concerned, existing brands already have a wealth of associations from the full range of marketing elements which have been deployed in their support: pack, name, price, advertising, promotion, etc. Since it will be impossible to divorce the re-cycled product from these associations it will often prove not only desirable but also necessary to carry out concept and product tests in a 'branded' rather than a 'blind' form.

The principle for the researcher to remember is basically the same as that for new products. If the new element being tested—concept or product—is likely to interact with other existing elements of the marketing mix (and in this case it most often is) then these other elements should be introduced into the test. At the very least this frequently involves the introduction of the brand name because of all its prior associations.

Research design

The other major difference is that of research design. Re-cycling of an brand implies that there is almost always a built-in 'norm', namely the brand as it is now. Instead, therefore, of often having great problems in evaluating the proposed new concept or new product in any absolute sense, this becomes comparatively easy; it can be evaluated against its current self. Many more of the tests in such a program will, therefore, be paired comparisons or (in the circumstances described earlier) matched monadic tests against the current brand. Even if such a norm does not permit a prediction of absolute consumer off-take it does help in making a reasonably reliable 'more–less–or about the same' projection. Such testing does not, of course, necessarily remove the requirement also to test against competition; we will often still need to check that improvements to our own brand have gone sufficiently far to match, and preferably beat, the competitor's brand.

Companion brands

One special case of re-cycling is that of range or variety extensions or companion products, in which increased sales and profits are derived not from the existing product (though that may well benefit in the process) but by adding new products under the umbrella of the same brand name.

Companion brand development has so much in common with completely new brands that the test program outlined above may well be adopted in its entirety. There are, perhaps, two special considerations. In the first place, the brand name, with all its associations with the existing product, is vital. In this respect, the companion brand is in much the same position as the recycled product and its correct evaluation by consumers may well depend on the use of branded tests. Second, the introduction of a companion brand may well have a 'kick-back' effect—either good or bad—on the parent product. It is highly desirable to try, through research, to anticipate this effect, because of the importance of the existing product; the techniques for doing so are not appropriate to this chapter but are, indeed, very much akin to those of advertising research on existing brands.

Conclusion

The outline program described in this chapter has been very much idealized. Apart from the fact that several important elements of the marketing mix have been left to elsewhere in this book, a new product program will rarely be so logically pursued 'in real life'. At the simplest the whole program will often *start* with a product—from R & D or from overseas—rather than starting with a search for product ideas. The structure of the program can, however, easily be adapted. The important thing is to appreciate the two underlying functions which all of this research is designed to perform.

The first is to *understand* consumers better, in their total relationship to the proposed new product. This basic understanding, aided by any existing research, acts as a general 'orientation' and constantly conditions the activities to do with the development of a new product, in directions which are favourable rather than unfavourable.

The second underlying function is to provide a series of checks, along the line, that all the elements of the marketing mix are satisfying the original concept, and the 'blueprint' which was derived from it, in a *consistent* way. Even if the whole research program cannot be 'holistic', it is certainly desirable that each element is pulling in the same direction, towards the ideal specification rather than (perhaps unwittingly) away from it. In other words, a program of research and testing acts like a compass on a strange journey, a constant source of reference that the new product is not straying too far away from its intended path.

16. Advertising research

Mark Lovell

Introduction

This chapter examines research into *advertising*. Although media researchers regard much of their work as 'advertising research', media research generally is left to the next section. Anyone engaged in advertising research presupposes that there is, in fact, something about advertising that *can* be studied, and is worth studying. From time to time, in a given instance, he may question either assumption. Researchers who have limited contact with advertising research often voice these questions, critically, for various reasons.

Given the total amount of money spent on advertising, it must, logically, pay people handsomely to conduct research into it, but attempts to hold various factors under experimental control, in order to isolate the effects of advertising, prompt two lines of argument against this.

First, that a campaign should influence the consumer's mind, in the face of heavy competition for attention, is important, but we are unlikely to know *how* important it is, relative to other factors. Why not simply judge that the direction of the advertising is right, examine the expected advertising/sales ratio to find a reasonable level of pressure, and assume that all will go more or less according to plan? Why try to calculate what may be incalculable?

Second, markets change, as to consumers, products, needs, and interests, but the advertising scene in a product field can change more quickly, more dramatically than anything else. This tends to make advertising research data *historical*. Does it do any more, then, than satisfy academic curiosity?

Advertising researchers have been known to touch the extremes of confidence and despair. Assurances have been given from time to time that a particular technique, or interpreter, has been proved beyond reasonable doubt to provide utterly reliable indications of advertising effectiveness. This has applied to pre-tests and post-tests alike, but no sooner has the new sun appeared over the horizon than clouds of doubt have blotted it out. There is then a reaction, which can be summed up in the words by Peat and De Vos as a statement of 'Murphy's Law': 'If something can go wrong with advertising research, it will'. Someone with a new technique, then, appears little better off than a huckster preparing bottles of cure-all medicine in his cellars.

A presentation of advertising research results can sometimes be notable for this individual feature: cynical eyebrows are raised not only at explanations of what preliminary depth interviews suggest but also at percentages indicating differences of 'shifts' based on respectably-sized samples. The terms of reference are suspect; the context of the interview is suspect; the questions are suspect; the analysis is suspect; the people, even, are suspect.

Why cannot the research world develop, agree, and validate set procedures for advertising research? Advertisers, and some advertising agencies, have oft⌐n demanded this. It is good that they do so. The result is progress, up to a point. To expect a complete answer, however, is unrealistic. *Why* this should be so, is important. Formalization of advertising research is difficult because:

(a) advertising itself works in different ways—*or* achieves a range of effects with varying degrees of emphasis;
(b) the marketing context within which advertising is expected to work is itself variable—between brands and products and over time;
(c) the demands placed on advertising research vary, according to the interest of the parties concerned;
(d) the relevance of certain survey data (whether collected in a pre-test or in a campaign evaluation study) to the end results of advertising is a matter of dispute.

These factors need to be looked at separately, before proceeding to techniques.

Advertising theory

The case has often been put that anyone who is doing research into advertising must consider, first of all, how advertising works; i.e. he must have some theory or model in his mind, and his research activity should be consistent with that theory. It seems, on the surface, a sensible requirement.

There have been several attempts to systematize advertising theory. Step-wise models have been constructed, like these:

$$AIDA—Attention$$
$$Interest$$
$$Desire$$
$$Action$$

What AIDA suggests is that advertising works by including each of these four effects in sequence.

A slightly more complex scheme was put forward by Colley in the early 'sixties';

DAGMAR = Defining Advertising Goals
for Measured Advertising
Results

The steps up which advertising was expected to take the consumer corresponded to:

Awareness	*Comprehension*	*Conviction*	*Action*
(of existence of brand or product)	(of what the product is, and will do)	(mental preparedness to purchase)	

It seems straightforward. A consumer needs first to be made aware of the brand and what it is; then there is understanding of its advantages, its characteristics; 'conviction' is a matter of persuasion that the brand delivers these goods and that he wants them; 'action' speaks for itself.

The big problem is that step-wise models of this kind do not take time and experience into account. Various studies, particularly of buyer profile and buying pattern data, have pointed to one main finding—that much advertising effort that can be judged to be successful succeeds by virtue of marginally increasing the frequency of purchase of the brand among consumers who already have experience of it. A further finding is that attitude changes are not necessarily measurable when this advertising effect occurs. There are situations, in fact, where the progression shown in Fig. 16.1 seems to be more likely. In this situation, it may be very difficult to observe

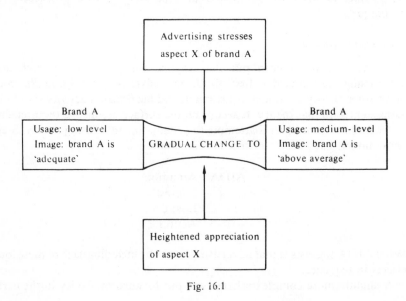

Fig. 16.1

414

subtle differences in attitude until after the increased usage has developed into a strong trend of which the consumer is conscious.

There are, of course, special cases, such as product launches, or when advertising is being put behind a near-dormant brand for the first time, that make DAGMAR seem much more realistic. Here, advertising must develop awareness, understanding of what is special about the brand, and so forth, but even then, the various stages of a DAGMAR progression may happen all at once; and the item 'conviction' in an impulse purchase will be something very elusive by contrast with a consumer durable buying situation. Time, competition and other marketing support make advertising seem even more complex in its ways than any of the above models suggest.

Time   Advertising input is rarely, if ever, separate from a stream of past and future activity. Reactions to a new campaign are conditioned by past advertising.

Competition.   A competitive market means competitive advertising. One brand's claims are not judged in limbo. There is *other* advertising, *other* promotion.

Other Marketing Support.   If a campaign succeeds in sales terms—how far was it the work of a banded offer, or the advertising that told people about it? (This point is expanded below.)

In our present state of knowledge, there is no reason why a particular advertising theory should be regarded as central to all or even most advertising research. There are, in fact, good reasons why only a very flexible theory could be regarded as allowing for many different cases. This makes the experienced researcher more likely to be eclectic than systematic.

The marketing context

The point has been made above that advertising does not happen in a vacuum. Special provision may have to be made to study other influences, in parallel with the analysis of how a particular 'above the line' campaign has performed. The success or otherwise, for example, of that campaign may be affected by the extent to which promises about a reformulation of the brand are borne out by experience of it. Copy tests combined with product tests may be one means, before the event, of seeing that results are in line with expectations raised. During and after the campaign, comparisons between trialists and non-trialists may be necessary. This argues a need to choose or adapt advertising research techniques according to the circumstances of the market. Even where standard methods are used, judgement may have to be applied as to what the resulting figures mean. This applies both to the question of whether a particular score is 'good' or 'bad' and to the problem of disentangling the elements that have produced such a score.

Sometimes the purpose of an advertising research study seems to undergo changes as it moves from planning to presentation. This has encouraged some researchers to analyse the motives behind particular tests. Here is a list of possible reasons, any number of which may be operative when a research brief is delivered:

(a) information about advertising that is developed; about possible improvements to advertising; about the market (as a substitute for formal consumer research);
(b) justification to make sure one's judgement has been right;
(c) conformity e.g. because the managing director is expecting it to be done;
(d) litigation to settle an argument;
(e) in search of a weapon to use against the agency.

The interesting section is 'information'. It is enough to recognize the others when they occur.

Information is required by different people at different stages. In the early stages of creative development, the value of advertising research lies mainly in providing the creative team with indications of advantages and disadvantages in particular approaches and in presenting data about consumers' comments on the product field, the brand, past advertising, etc., that helps the team *create* approaches.

When finished advertising is being pre-tested, most clients will want some indication of its absolute value. The account executive may want the same. A choice may have to be made—in which case all parties will want research that is sensitive enough to discriminate between reactions to alternative advertisements. The creative team will be interested in evaluation but will usually want to know more about *why* a particular effect has been achieved.

When a campaign is being tested in the field, other specialist needs may have to be catered for. Whoever is responsible for marketing and media planning will be concerned to know what sort of response function data are available. That is to say, how many exposures to the advertising are required to get the consumer to register, understand, or buy something?

The emphasis put on special information needs in advertising research will vary according to the nature of the individuals involved, and the efficiency of the communications that connect them. Not everyone will see the same value in the data he is given. The researcher must be aware of how this affects his brief, and plan accordingly.

Relevance of advertising research measures

A great deal, still, has to be taken on trust. Commonsense suggests that, if after heavy advertising pressure there is still no demonstrable awareness of a new brand's name, something is likely to be wrong with the creative content; but if there is moderate awareness, how much *latent* awareness is there that may be raised to the surface by sight of the product at point of sale? How good are question and answer methods at uncovering the amount and the value of material that has been registered as a result of advertising?

There is a lot of evidence, from psychologists as well as from market researchers, to suggest that the deeper you dig the more you will find. Dig deeper, then; but the more intensive the interview, the smaller are the chances that it will be administered in a standard way.

Awareness data should be treated as symptoms, not achievements in themselves. Those claiming they first learned about a newly launched brand when they saw it on display might or might not have noticed it if advertising had not helped. A new campaign for a well-known brand may, paradoxically, remind some consumers of previous advertising, a question mark against figures for 'claimed' and 'proved' advertising recall alike. Irrespective of what may be the most sensitive or the fairest way to gauge awareness and recall, it has been claimed by some that neither of these measures has much relevance anyway. When advertising is very successful indeed, awareness is usually high along with most other measures. At the other extreme, one of the features of a dead loss is lack of any evidence that anyone has noticed the campaign. Between the extremes, however, recall data can mean practically anything. For a fuller exposition see Lovell and Lannon[1].

Some attempts have been made to observe what kind of measure, in pre-tests or in post-tests, have results that correlate well with sales change data in test markets, where other marketing factors can be kept more or less constant. The most sensitive and stable measures and the best predictors are those which prove to be the most useful *on average*. They will not be appropriate in every case[2].

The more that is known about question forms and interview situations, the greater the choice seems to be for the individual who is planning and interpreting a particular advertising study.

Who Does What

If standardization is suspect, the responsibility for briefing, planning, and making sure that what gets presented in the end is what people need to know, quite apart from being accurate, is all the greater. The past decade can be looked upon as one in which individual advertising research experts have evolved, who adapt and choose from the techniques available. This is a move away from a more technique-oriented era, in which advertising researchers tended to be made use of by organizations who had pet systems. It is also very different, however, from what might be called the 'age of the wizards', in the fifties, when advertising research was often the province of an intuitive virtuoso whose analogies were drawn from Viennese consulting rooms. The advertising researcher today knows that there are various kinds of evidence, which can be gathered in different ways, and he judges their relevance and importance according to marketing circumstances. He can be found in four

Table 16.1   Communication in advertising research

Advertising agency	
A Research executive	is responsible for day-to-day communication with creative team. Plans internal work, to B's brief. Plans formal work jointly with D (or E); and with F (or G) as required, by agreement with D (or E).
B Creative team	asks A for help; gets answers from A, and (by arrangement) from F and G.
C Account executive	observes that communications are working. Combines with B and E to deliver brief for formal pre-tests, and post-testing.
Advertiser	
D Research executive	liaises with A to ensure advertising research fits without duplication into overall research programme. Discusses with A plans and results; commissioning work from F and G; presentations to C and E.
E Brand manager	draws on D's advice for briefing input; for considering interpretation of results.
Independent research consultant	
F	may be retained by A or D, either continuously or 'ad hoc'. He may do planning; perform small-scale work; provide objective assessment of large-scale work.
Research agency	
G Advertising research specialist	as F; but conducts large-scale work as well.

places:

(a) in an advertising agency;
(b) in a research agency;
(c) in an advertiser's research department;
(d) on his own, as an independent consultant.

The proportion on the client side (the third category) is growing, only slowly. The biggest increase has been in the fourth category. This analysis is important because it has an effect on communications, which are crucial if advertising research is to be meaningful, understood, and acted upon.

A communications system is suggested in Table 16.1. It works, but it is expensive, in that it demands the presence of certain people whose time is valuable. It may, of course, save time and money in the long run. Alternatives can be worked out by doubling-up certain of the functions.

Several large advertising agencies have developed 'creative workshops', whose prime purpose is to apply research in such a way that it actively helps creative people to develop campaigns. Sometimes a creative team actually commissions such work. Usually, it has at least got direct access to the researcher. Close involvement by the creative team often leads to a sequence of qualitative studies, rather than one single job, as the creative team gains and elaborates new ideas from the research.

Problem Analysis

A careful distinction often needs to be drawn between two things:

(a) creative strategy,   the effects that advertising is intended to have on the consumer;

(b) creative tactics, how the creative team intends a specific advertisement to work.

Failure to observe the differences between these two is often at the root of any frustration that follows a presentation of copy test results. It also thickens the blanket of fog that may surround the advertising component in a test market study.

An example of this difference is afforded by a television campaign for Cadbury's Whole Nut. The *strategy* included, as one of the basic advertising aims, that the brand should be made distinctive, differentiated from other chocolate bars in a desirable way. Since the confectionery market is kaleidoscopic, the need for a clear-cut identity is particularly important. But the identity has to be relevant to confectionery eaters, as well as sharply defined.

A campaign was developed (see Fig. 16.2) in which the creative *tactic* was to dramatize the unique product feature of Whole Nut: the fact that it contains entire hazel nuts, not the results of chopping or grinding. This was achieved creatively by introducing a zany recognition scene into certain ordinary situations, where sudden observation of a bar lends a protagonist to exclaim 'Nuts! Who-ole Hazel Nuts! Cadbury's take 'em and they cover them with chocolate!' in a chant which is vaguely reminiscent of a Harry Belafonte number.

The first pre-testing work on this campaign, which has run successfully for several years, was concerned with the reactions of the target to the first film—*in terms of its execution of the tactical principle*. This was *not* a test of the advertising strategy. What was at stake was the question whether, when shown in a reel of other commercials, it established clear awareness of Whole Nut; and whether people were made to react positively towards the product, by accepting its unique feature as well as by appreciating the fun.

Further pre-testing, on follow-up ideas for further commercials, revealed that some of them were more powerful than others in securing the right balance of tactical effects. It helped the creative team to find that those situations which included an element of conflict between the participants (before the Whole Nut recognition moment) had a stronger result in terms of dramatizing the product and its benefit.

Research into the evaluation of the campaign was a very different matter. Here the brief was, basically, to investigate the links between the advertising and sales; and to analyse how far the evidence here was consistent with efficient execution of the strategy. Audit data from test areas showed the extent of sales increases that accompanied the advertising. Consumer data showed the extent to which, for example, chocolate bar buyers showed awareness and recognition above the level of other competing campaigns.

The point of the example is to underline that certain aspects of the campaign evaluation brief *could* have been put into the pre-test brief. This might have shown, for example, that, after exposure to this film, very few

Fig. 16.2

were prepared to regard Whole Nut very differently from the way they looked at it before. This is because with a well-known brand the response to advertising must be understood to be gradual. A good campaign *could* have come under suspicion; an irrelevant part of a pre-test *could* have condemned it to be jettisoned.

Pre-testing—At Different Stages

A pre-test may happen once in the development of a campaign or there may be a pre-testing program. There may be cases where preliminary work on rough creative material is ruled out because of a conviction that the kind of advertising envisaged demands finished or near-finished treatment if it is to have any appreciable effect on the consumer. A similar case can be made out against testing at an early stage on the grounds that reactions to rough material may be misleading. The two arguments are not quite the same. When this happens, the campaign may be discussed with the advertising researcher who is required to give his views, based on other research or experience of the brand, of the campaign's likely success. This may be useful or not, depending on the people concerned: but it should be recognized that it is discussion, *not* research.

The preliminary stages of a pre-test program are often explorations of basically different advertising approaches. The term 'concept test' is some times used in this context, except by those who have taken a public stand against formalized concept testing, in which case they may use other phrases to describe the same thing.

The problems of concept testing are very real. The main ones can be stated briefly. The essence of a concept may be easy to describe, logically, on a plain piece of card but it may seem very bald; it may provoke the response 'So what?' among the same people who would react positively to an emotionally-loaded presentation of it. How, then, do you interpret the 'So what?' Any attempt to present concepts in forms that approximate to advertising, on the other hand, may lead to difficulties in disentangling response to the concept and response to the treatment. There is both the difficulty of deciding what constitutes a meaningful but undistracting illustration to the claim, and the difficulty of avoiding an interview situation where the informant has clear-cut but misguided ideas that his job is to improve advertising.

Nevertheless, many find it useful to put a rough advertising treatment in front of some consumers and analyse their reactions in order to assess the viability of an advertising platform or approach. The data are, perhaps, no different from any other advertising research data, in that they require interpretation to sort out what influences are at work. There is a question of degree of obscurity, however: this makes it more often a matter for qualitative research, and for psychologists, than for using a pre-coded questionnaire. Disagreement among advertising researchers is often, therefore, about the value of certain people, e.g. 'Is X *really* objective?', rather than about techniques.

Some believe that concept research is of most use when the primary features of the possible campaigns are rational, rather than emotional. The point here is that the strength of an effective rational theme is more likely to be apparent despite crude representation, since it depends on logic. An emotional theme may depend on the suspension of logic, and it may only be by use of elaborate professional treatment that the right mood for this can be established. (Of course, very little advertising is *entirely* rational or *entirely* emotional.)

A second limiting point sometimes made is that valuable negative information is more likely to emerge from concept testing than any meaningful indication of the degree to which an idea may be a good one. That is to say, concept testing is allowed the credit for pointing out what probably won't work, and saying why; but sorting out the good from the average is another matter. This is the territory of opinion. Practitioners will disagree about how positive, as well as about how sensitive or accurate, concept test work can be.

The development of an advertising campaign for National Benzole petrol is a case in point. In 1968, a new campaign was prepared with the purposes of projecting National as a big, dynamic brand, a technological leader in tune with modern idiom, having a recognizable style of its own. Any number of advertising platforms, in theory, could achieve this. In practice, the limitations imposed by the nature of the target market, by the need to avoid territory pre-empted by other brands, by the need to demonstrate consistency of tone with past advertising and by what is permissible as a claim for differentiating a petrol brand from others; are severe. The advertising concept for National needed to be new, distinctive, re-echoing past success, making desirable points, and above suspicion; all at once. The task of advertising concept research was, therefore, as much one of suggesting *how* a concept might best be developed, as *whether* it should be encouraged at all. Figure 16.3 shows three press ad layouts. There were tested in parallel with pilot film material to investigate the concept. 'National is the Motorway Petrol' ought, basically, to make an association. Was this association, in which the fastest, most modern, most technically admired means of road travel was pre-empted for the brand, desirable, noteworthy and without danger? What possible aspects of the association were likely to work hardest for National?

Layout A shows an attempt to provide a technological background to the motorway claim. Layout B shows a 'human interest' approach in stressing that the 'motorway petrol' is right irrespective of the road, picking up a commonly experienced motoring situation. Layout C makes a dramatic, if imprecise announcement of the 'motorway' theme.

Consumer reactions in group discussions suggested that, despite criticism of certain aspects of motorways, motorists admired them and acknowledged

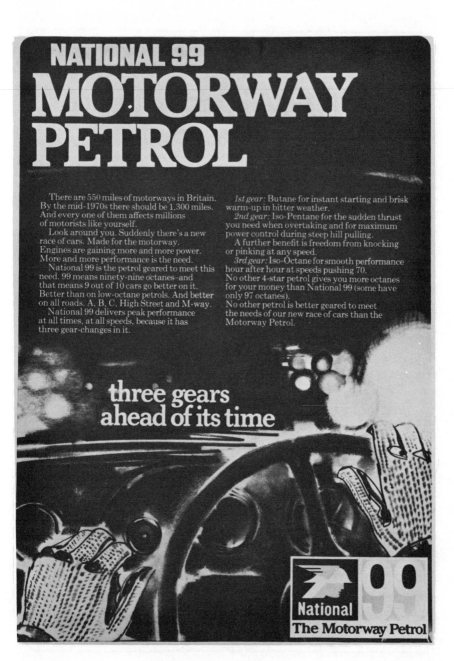

Fig. 16.3A
Reproduced with permission of Leo Burnett Ltd.

Fig. 16.3B
Reproduced with permission of Leo Burnett Ltd.

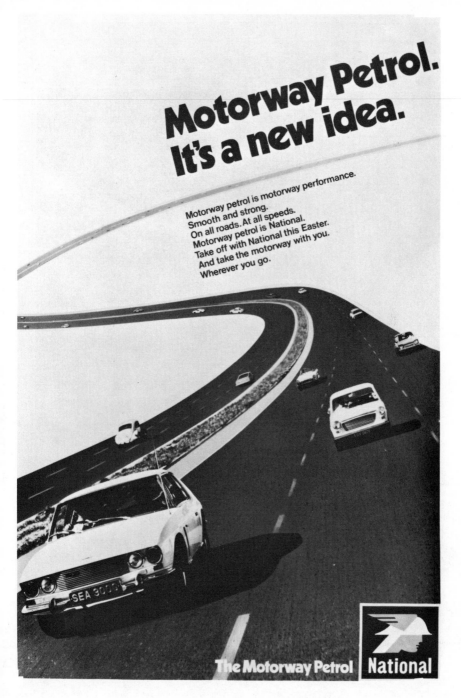

Fig. 16.3C
Reproduced with permission of Leo Burnett Ltd.

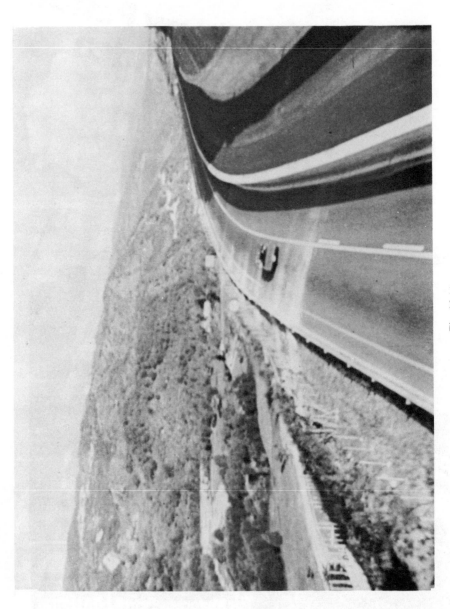

Fig. 16.4A
Reproduced with permission of Leo Burnett Ltd.

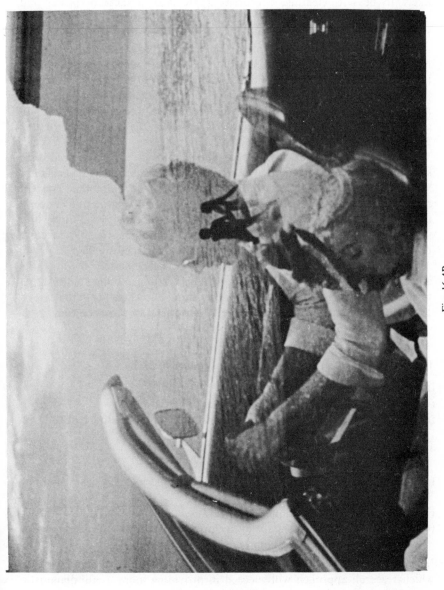

Fig. 16.4B

Reproduced with permission of Leo Burnett Ltd.

their superiority and necessity, but the argument attempted in Layout A aroused suspicion. Building the campaign around one octane rating (99) was also limiting. Further concept work suggested that *any* logical approach was likely to be self-defeating. Motorists appreciated a sense of power and 'motorway performance' that appealed to them in Layout C. If they were not made to work it out, they did not query it. The attempt to widen the motorway theme in Layout B merely achieved bathos. This underlined the importance of capitalizing on the dynamic aspects of motorways, to achieve interest and meaningful association. Concessions to normality were resented.

Television commercials were created and produced with the concept research in mind. Figure 16.4 shows stills from these films, which aimed at an emotional rather than a rational declaration of the superiority of 'the Motorway Petrol'.

Subsequent research showed that the campaign had registered very strongly with the target market; and that National buyers, in particular, spoke of 'the Motorway Petrol'. This illustrates the point that concept research must be directed towards development opportunities of a concept, in order to aid judgement about the viability of the concept itself. Putting up a sheet of paper with 'National is the Motorway Petrol' on it would have put research informants into an intolerable situation if asked to react to it.

Once a campaign theme has been established—tested or not—the advertising material developed from it may be tested in any state of finish. At this point it is worth observing that advertising researchers (as in the case of product development research) incline to either end of this spectrum:

Holistic ——————————— Atomistic

The more 'holistic' they are, the more likely they will be to:

(a) test only finished material;
(b) test campaigns, rather than individual advertisements;
(c) examine specific elements using techniques that allow breadth of expression of consumer reactions.

The more 'atomistic' they are, the more often they will:

(a) test individual advertisements, as individual queries arise, using material in any state of finish;
(b) test headlines, illustrations, other details;
(c) examine specific elements using techniques that allow precise reflection of effect of those elements in consumer reactions.

It is not necessarily *bad* to be more one than the other. It is a matter of dispute which research approach will succeed in providing more useful diagnostic data that can help improve creative work. Possibly, however, it is easier to observe cases where a holistic approach allows greater insight into the real business of advertising than it is to see where an atomistic approach has a clear advantage. Questions of detail, e.g. which of several recipes attract sufficient interest to warrant including in a food advertisement, tend to be those at which the atomist shines.

Pre-testing Techniques

Several techniques are common to market research in general. The depth interview, group discussion, the use of structured questionnaires, are all involved in advertising research, but scarcely need separate comment here. This chapter will concentrate only on features of such basic tools that require specific attention in the advertising context.

For convenience, techniques for testing television commercials will be covered separately from press and other media. There are first, however, some considerations which apply in all cases. These are stressed, because they show exactly why it is impossible to expect anything like absolute truth from any of the techniques outlined here. Figure 16.5 shows the relationships between the actual situation—consumers (C^1) actually exposed to real

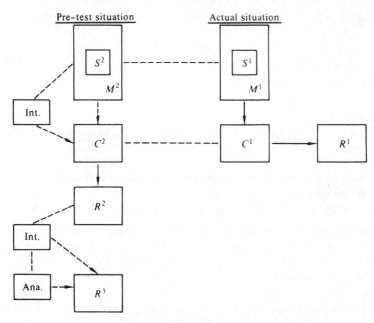

Fig. 16.5

Note: The point at issue in pre-testing is the extent to which R^3 is an aid towards calculating R^1. This figure shows the influences and possible differences, that can make the relationship between R^3 and R^1 uncertain.

C^2 is a sample selected to be representative of C^1. S^2 is advertising that may be in any state of finish. M^2 could be a theatre test, or a folder, etc... Int. (interviewer) is an important component of the exposure to test advertisements. Both Int. and Ana. (Analyst) mediate the direct response to S^2, (which is R^2) and record and/or interpret it as R^3.

advertising (S^1) in its media context (M^1), and reacting to it (R^1)—and the pre-test. Any broken line indicates a relationship that will vary in closeness; a broken arrow shows that there is an influence by one factor on another, that also varies in nature and strength.

It is rather unlikely that the pre-test result will show *how* successful the advertising will prove, but what one can demand from pre-testing is direction, with a rough indication of extent—other things being equal.

Television Commercial Tests

The first problem in a TV commercial test is to choose the form in which the material can best be shown; and what equipment to use to expose it to a sample of informants. Filmed storyboards are usually preferable to showing the raw storyboards themselves, in that they give a sense of what the medium is all about. La Belle Courier machines or Sony equipment can be used to show cheaply assembled photographs with a synchronized audio-tape to individual informants, or to groups, quickly and economically. For finished commercials, 35 mm equipment is expensive and difficult to use in a private home. Much more convenient is videotape, or—easier still—VCR, which only require the insertion of a cassette in the right compartment.

Once the question of equipment is solved, the place needs to be chosen. The alternatives are, for the most part:

(a) a theatre (or large hall) in which large audiences can be exposed to the commercial;
(b) a room in a studio or agency, allowing use of permanent equipment and special features, e.g. videotape recording of a group discussion in progress;
(c) a room in a private house, to which informants are invited;
(d) a mobile unit (test van);
(e) informants' own homes, using easily portable equipment (e.g. VCR).

A number of research companies have developed systems for testing television commercials, in theatres or halls, but anyone can organize his own theatre tests, using a fieldwork agency to recruit an audience and to supply projector and projectionist.

What happens at a theatre test depends on the kind of interview situation and questions favoured by the research agency or the executive who is organizing the test. It also depends on the degree of flexibility with which the test is approached.

The sample size has an influence on what can be done. Small audiences of, say, 12 to 50 have been split up into groups, after exposure to the commercials, and separate group discussions in separate rooms conducted. Alternatively, this size of audience can be considered a 'large group', in which informants use self-completion questionnaires, and are then led by an interviewer into discussion. When there is disagreement, the interviewer can ask the informants to write down their personal views or to give a show of hands or to use Votometer machines.

Some research companies have theatre test systems in which standard questions are used nearly every time, with a number of 'slots' allowed for specific questions that refer directly to aspects of one test commercial. By analysing the results of many such tests, norms have been developed against which the scores achieved by individual test commercials can be compared. Because some types of commercial perform better than others on certain measures, and because the target market varies in the precision with which it is defined, e.g. 'analgesic users' as opposed to 'all adults', norms can be built up for product fields, or market segments, and used for comparison as well. Most companies nowadays favour having a range of standard measures within each test. Those who buy tests of this kind appreciate the fact that there is a combination of the standard and the specific. Comparison with the norms they see as supplying a perspective against which to examine individual features of the commercial.

Critics will be found to say that a norm has, in fact, little relevance. This is because the commercials for a product field may have been made for products at very different points in their life cycle, and with very different creative aims in mind, both at the strategic and the tactical level. How far any standard question can be relevant to many such aims is a matter for conjecture. The average of different commercials' scores is unlikely to be *more* relevant.

Many advertising researchers at this point in time are likely to be suspicious of any comparisons against norms, except in those cases where the question seems to measure something that coincides precisely with a creative aim and where the brand's own past commercials have contributed most of the normative data. This avoids the problem of nobody knowing when they are comparing like with like.

The search for a single measure that discriminates infallibly between commercials in terms of their overall selling effectiveness has long occupied the minds of researchers. The ground is strewn with the remains of systems that have been promoted on this basis. There is no reason whatever why such a measure should exist anyway; the problems of relating R^3 to R^1 (see Fig. 16.5) suggest that evaluation must be complex, and must be relative to a specific advertising context.

One alternative to standard questions for quantified pre-tests has been to make use of brand image batteries. This can mean administering attitude scales before and after exposure to the commercial. The scales may be established in advance, separately, for each product field (sometimes for each brand) as being those which are critical for choice between brands. Comparison between the rating scales before and after exposure can be both evaluative and diagnostic. Objections to this practice centre on the question of how attitude formation *really* happens. Attitudes to well-established brands, in particular, are unlikely to change after one 30-second commercial. When informants react to scales the second time round, they may mislead by trying to be helpful.

Brand image questions can be useful in pre-tests, more so for lesser known brands, but comparison ought to be between measures taken on separate, matched samples, which is expensive.

Many of the measures used in theatre tests are dependent on recall; or on informants' verbalized explanations of what has been shown to them; e.g.: 'What did the advertisement say about brand A?' or 'What was the main point that the advertisement was trying to get across?'

Answers to this kind of question certainly have a significance, but one which varies with the advertisement being tested and which requires interpretation. Recall *as such* has been shown to bear little relationship to advertising success, but the *kind* of recall may be important. Such questions are dependent, to some extent, on informants' ability to verbalize their impressions. Some people are more articulate than others, or more imaginative. The nature of the target market, and samples drawn from it, obviously affects the answers that result; but so does the nature of the advertisements. Jingles, slogans, with obvious meanings, are easily repeatable, but consumers may well be deriving the desired information and emotional colour from a television commercial that lacks these recall aids without being able to put these into the neat, elegant language of the creative *rationale*.

Several techniques have been developed to avoid this kind of problem. In one of these, informants are asked to note down what were the main thoughts that occurred to them while they saw each separate section of a commercial. Analysis shows whether the thought processes that the creative team imagined would be set in motion were, in fact, forthcoming. Supplementary questions check on whether informants agree that they were given a particular communication, or not. The technique involves showing the commercials in small 'reminder' sections, as well as in their complete form. This yields a mass of diagnostic data, but criticisms are made that the way of showing commercials in pieces is so unnatural that reactions to them among the audience are suspect. In a sense, this is a development of a very simple research situation, whereby spontaneous reactions to a commercial shown to a small audience are noted, probed and analysed in detail.

Some theatre test operators have maintained that the large screen required in most theatres gives a false impression of how a commercial will appear on most people's television sets with normal size screens. There are no published data on this point, but theoretically a close-up of, say, an eating shot on a large screen might detract from the appeal of a food commercial. Occasionally minor details that are unobtrusive on a small screen seem to make a stronger impression on a large one.

Some theatre test operators are opposed to using large screens, since these tend to alter the balance of visual input that the informant receives. There are good grounds for this. Most try to use TV monitors, nowadays, and distribute them around a hall if necessary.

The question whether to test in colour or in black and white has entered a critical phase in the UK. Approximately 35% of households had colour TV in the summer of 1975, and the growth rate had declined. Some commercials gain immeasurably from being seen in colour: but the majority of the target market will still only see them in black and white. The ideal solution is to split the test between those who normally view in colour and those receiving black and white—showing the test commercial to each half in the form to which they are accustomed. This costs more, but makes for a more thorough answer.

Theatre tests organized for quantified research have been criticized for the unrepresentativeness of the samples who appear there. A considerable proportion, varying according to incentive, of those who are invited refuse to come. An extension of this point is that those people who *do* attend may be rather unsociable people, who ordinarily have little evening life. The kind of products and commercials that appeal to them may be atypical. Day-time interviewing in a hall by a busy shopping precinct can avoid this.

Taking the test to the people is the obvious alternative to invitation to a theatre. Mobile units, which can go to any suburb they please to pick up any kind of sample, have an obvious appeal from this point of view. A large number of small-scale sessions can be held in them throughout the day, so that the system bears economic comparison with theatre tests. The measures applied may be exactly the same. The differences are mainly a matter of interview atmosphere and the fact that there can be closer supervision.

Private houses are sometimes preferred for television commercial tests, because this is closer to normal viewing conditions; but trying to achieve greater reality in this way is an expensive business unless one limits oneself to small-scale qualitative work.

Distrust of the meaning of question-and-answer has driven some researchers to want physiological measures. These may be applied in a theatre, or a mobile unit, but they are mainly used in laboratories. Their basic purpose is to provide objective indications, that are not subject to interpretation, of the extent to which an informant is emotionally aroused by a commercial. Either the total effect of the whole commercial is observed or the separate effects of the constituent parts as well.

The psychogalvanometer, which provides a measure of the sweat response—an autonomic indicator of emotional arousal—is the tool most often used. In the US an eye camera was developed to measure pupil dilation, another autonomic indicator. The latter, it was argued forcibly for some years, was superior to similar devices for two main reasons—sensitivity and direction. Very precise, minute measurements make it possible to have fine discrimination between reactions to successive parts of a commercial. At the same time, the *nature* of this particular response encouraged some to consider that it showed direction, i.e. not just emotional arousal was being

433

measured, but *desirable* reaction which could be related to likelihood of purchase behaviour. A bigger response to brand A's pack, after exposure to a commercial, suggested to them that the consumer was wanting to see more of it (with pupils dilated) because he was now more in favour of buying it. Efforts to substantiate this suggest that whatever diagnostic value the tool may have the evaluative promise that it held out has not really been fulfilled.

Physiological psychologists have noted that different people react emotionally in different unconscious ways, e.g. some turn white with anger, others red. A polygraph is an instrument developed to account for this by taking a range of arousal measures, including galvanic skin response and pupil dilation. The costs are, needless to say, very considerable. It seems likely to remain a matter more for experiment than for consistent commercial use.

More recently, experiments have been made with a machine that measures the tension in the eyebrow while people observe commercials. It seems unduly pessimistic to assume this had to go the way of the eye observation camera, but we still seem to be a long way from a physiological technique in which one is entirely confident, and which seems to be useful and economic in most pre-testing circumstances.

An alternative objective measure is to test on a large scale, near a supermarket, and offer informants money-off coupons which can only be used there. A matched control panel needs to be interviewed. Even with fast-moving consumer goods, such a test can be very slow, and very insensitive. Unexpected re-interview with commercial test informants, or signing them up for diary panels, might be more fruitful avenues.

An on-air pre-test demands small, localized operations if it is not to be a contradiction in terms. In the UK (as opposed to the USA) it is impossible to have subdivisions that are smaller than a television area, *or* that extend over space where overlap is ruled out, e.g. Dover transmitter. On-air pre-tests can be arranged in Border Television Areas, where only a small, but reasonably representative, section of the population will be exposed to the test commercial. Consumer research services are available for evaluation.

On-air tests, e.g. 24-hour recall, together with Starch tests, or reading and noting tests for print media, have tended to be more popular in the USA than in Europe. They take place, by definition, after a finished film has been developed. It is therefore too late to make radical alterations to it economically. The counter argument is that it is useful to apply to all finished products, rather like a quality control screening. It also has appeal to those who want a realistic exposure situation rather than employing a test where the respondents' attention is artificially focused. There are elaborate procedures for determining who, and how many, constitute the potential audience for a particular screening of a particular commercial, and then measuring its recall. Recall of ads is not above criticism (as explained above) as a criterion of effectiveness. But the method appeals to advertisers who aim as a basic rule to communicate simple, easily verbalized sales points.

Another standard form of testing that is sometimes used for finished commercials is to arrange a situation in which some kind of pre-post attitude shift is measured. The technique first advocated by Horace Schwerin, of finding out how many more people expressed a preference for the test brand after exposure to a test commercial compared with before exposure, is now used as one of a number of measures by Audience Studies Inc. in the USA. As a rough quality control mechanism for isolating a commercial that seems remarkably poor or remarkably good, it has its appeal. Some research work has however demonstrated that in practice there is a rather worrying amount of 'random' switching of choices in this test situation, and it is very difficult to establish a correlation between sales effectiveness with this measure. But this is not the only type of pre-post measure. Specific attitude changes are also studied. It is important to accept that since in many types of test the respondents often are aware, at least in part, of what they are doing, the attitude shift is in fact a communication measure. That is to say, it shows how many people have taken the point that they are being told a product is (e.g.) more healthy, and are prepared to play this back. This is particularly so where the *same sample* is used for the pre and the post measurements. Alternatively, a *parallel sample* can be used, as a control: this parallel sample is *not* exposed to the test commercial. Another possibility is to have a *baseline sample*, as a reference point for the attitudes to the brand of the population at large, against which comparisons with test samples can be made. None of these methods is in fact perfect. To use the same sample for pre and post is somewhat obviously artificial: people do not undertake the same task twice without at least some of them having an idea of what they are doing. Where a baseline sample is used, there is the problem of allowing for changes, over time, which may be affecting the population at large. But using separate parallel samples means that there are problems of sample matching to be overcome and that shifts have to be larger if statistical significance is to be read into them. Although they give one better experimental control they also tend to be expensive. Nevertheless, this latter procedure is the one to be recommended where possible.

Press Advertising Tests

There is a problem of definition of pre-testing that tends to occur more when press advertisements are being discussed. What, exactly, constitutes a 'pre-test' as opposed to a 'post-test'?

The standpoint taken here is that 'pre-testing' may include any situation in which a deliberately restricted proportion of the target population is exposed to the advertising. This includes cases where a magazine or newspaper actually appears, with the advertisement inside it, provided this is on a restricted scale. (The point here is that a check of advertising is being carried out prior to putting the bulk of media expenditure behind it.)

Folder test

Probably the most frequently-used technique of pre-testing a press advertisement is to expose the sample of informants to an advertisement included in a folder containing control advertisements. The classical version of this is described below, but in passing it should be mentioned that there are several variations. The first of these is where specially prepared copies of magazines are used for the same purpose as the folder. The main advantage claimed for this procedure is that the advertisement appears in a natural, rather than a contrived, context. It also becomes possible for the informant to consider the advertisement in a more realistic situation, e.g. the magazine may be substituted for his normal magazine in a particular week, when it is left to be read at home for a period of time before the second interview. Another variation is where a folder, as such, is not used but a number of advertisements are shown to the informant, divorced from the media context, and the informant's reactions are observed.

In a sense, these two variations represent a deliberate movement in opposite directions: towards greater realism in the research situation, and away from it, in order to concentrate attention on particular items. The advantages of either approach are matters of dispute. Some claim that greater realism in the research situation allows for greater meaningfulness in informants' response. Others argue that realism is illusory in the context of advertising research, because getting insight into likely reactions to advertisements depends, to some extent, on focusing attention.

A typical folder test will proceed as follows. Informants are allowed to look through a folder containing press advertisements. Included among them is a test advertisement. The folder should preferably be not too bulky, so it can be flicked through easily and the state of finish of all the advertisements should be roughly similar. It is sometimes claimed that only advertisements of comparable size or nature (black and white with black and white, or colour with colour, etc.) should appear in the folder. In fact, this seems less important than that the kind of advertisement included should be calculated to have roughly comparable appeal in terms of subject matter and style to the target group. At the same time, it is obviously undesirable to have all the control advertisements in black and white, and only the test advertisement in colour. At this stage, the informants should not realize which is the test advertisement. Sometimes the interviewer will be instructed to pay attention to the amount of time spent looking at each advertisement. Occasionally, a time limit is imposed for looking at each advertisement but this procedure has been known, on occasions, to unnerve informants. Allowing the informant to browse through *ad lib* seems better practice. The folder is then withdrawn, and informants are asked a variety of questions, usually designed to elicit evidence of 'impact', 'involvement', 'interest', and the like. These questions are often favoured: 'We have only time to talk about two or three of these advertisements. Which would you prefer to discuss?', or, 'People sometimes like to turn back to a particular advertisement and have a closer look at it. Do you feel that about any of these? Which?' The questionnaire may often proceed: 'Which products can you remember seeing advertised here? Can you remember the brand name?'

The importance and relevance of these and other questions depends very much on which aspects of the advertisement are being researched, and what they are intended to do. This is particularly to be borne in mind when considering questions about the message received, e.g. 'What was the main point of the advertisement for . . . ?'

A check list of adjectives is sometimes offered to the informant. This aims at getting evidence of the *kind* of message received, and the way in which it has been received. Informants may be asked, for example, to choose from a list including 'attractive', 'childish', etc. In themselves, the choices of adjective may be puzzling, bearing in mind that different people read words differently; therefore, reasons for choice of adjectives are often probed.

At some point in the interview, some kind of recall question, demanding playback of detail, is often included. The extent, or often the nature, of the recall of details may not in itself tell very much. It may, however, indicate the degree to which, in the short term, an advertisement tends to dominate attention or to be swamped by other advertising. It can also suggest which features of an advertisement are dominant; but careful interpretation is needed here, because some features may be simply easier to describe than others.

Coupon response

Arrangements can be made for advertisements to be included in local media, or in restricted issues of national media, in order to check how the advertising would work *in situ*. As opposed to relying on consumer research to show what the results are, behavioural measures can be used. The main ones in this group are:

(a) coupon response—redemption at local shops;
(b) coupon response—sent to advertiser/agency;
(c) 'hidden offer'.

These measures are valuable only to the extent that the behaviour itself is the result that the creative work is designed to achieve. It is easy to visualize a short-term effect being contrived, possibly among consumers outside the target, which risks cheapening expectations of the products among the best long-term prospects.

The total number of people who send in coupons from couponed advertisements may give an impression of precision in advertising evaluation that is entirely illusory. Where durables or services are concerned, it is the total number of conversions that is of interest. It is one thing to encourage twice as many to send in coupons for a brochure or a salesman's visit; it is another to do so without leading to disappointment. Relying on conversion data makes the assumption that the brochure and the salesman are standard items, with a fixed value. This may not be true.

When coupon response is a matter of detaching a coupon and handing it over as part-payment for the brand, certain other considerations apply. Some housewives collect coupons of this kind, as a matter of principle. They are continuously defraying the costs of their basic household purchases. In the shops they need to get the brand name right, but beyond this, they are simply thinking in terms of commodity. Further, if premium pricing means anything for a brand, this technique may affect the brand image particularly badly. There is also the question of 'malredemption' whereby retailers accept coupons indiscriminately, without strict reference to the brands concerned.

'Hidden offers' are said to provide evidence that consumers have really penetrated as far as the body copy. (A coupon, of course, may just have been seen as a coupon.) Insofar as the consumer must have read deep into the advertisement in order to know that the offer exists, and how to get it, this is a fair assumption; but the principle that some people are more likely than others to be 'offer-hunters' is still an influence on results.

There is one variation that should be mentioned, i.e. research that is organized into much department store advertising, without often being described as bargains available at the time, can be varied so that they include different combinations of bargains. Some combinations are then proved to be better at getting people into the store to make a purchase.

Some have found that these measures distinguish better between *media* than between the advertisements themselves. This is an important consideration for interpretation. All these measures are best regarded as telling part, but not all, of the story. Qualitative research among matched groups of coupon senders—those who are converted into buyers and those who are not—can often indicate far more about the advertisement's *role* and *how* the advertisement played it.

Laboratory methods

The equipment used to make physiological measurements discussed under 'Television Commercial Tests' (p. 430) is used for testing press advertisements too. The same comments apply. Tachistoscopes are also used to determine the thresholds at which features of one or more press advertisements are registered. Two points can be of interest here—the degree of legibility, or recognition that the advertisement is for brand 'A', and the *order* in which certain features are recognized.

There are few things as unlike real media contexts as a tachistoscope, which is a large box used for exposing material for small, controlled periods of time. If it suggests or confirms, however, that an advertisement is not communicating identity, or a basic point, efficiently, then its evidence needs to be considered alongside data from more 'natural' sources.

438

The eye movement camera (as opposed to the eye observation camera used for measuring pupil dilation) is capable of showing *how* people look at advertisements. It traces the path taken by the eye when it passes over a printed page. Some media owners have found it useful as an indicator of how people read magazines, but consistent use on individual advertisements seems unlikely, outside special experimental programs.

Post-testing

There is little point in describing all the pitfalls to be avoided in consumer surveys, which are covered elsewhere. Essentially, post-testing tends to be a matter of finding out, by means of *ad hoc* consumer survey work, what effects of advertising can be found among consumers. For anyone to want to do this, he must have good reasons for supposing that other, simpler steps that could be taken will not give all the information necessary. These simpler steps include:

(a) counting sales changes, retail audit;
(b) coupon return analysis;
(c) playback from sales force;
(d) consumer audit;
(e) standardized post-test services.

Sales data, in the final analysis, must be relevant, but the point has already been made that advertising is one of many things contributing to sales and that the relationship between these factors is more likely to be dynamic than additive. It is like testing fertilizer by observing whether the flowers come up big and strong from a packet of seeds. If the results are good, perhaps the product (the seeds) is so good that advertising (fertilizer) is scarcely necessary. Comparision with what happened last year, with a different fertilizer, is difficult, because the weather conditions may have been different. The metaphor can be extended indefinitely.

Coupon returns have their limitations, which have been discussed in the previous section. The opinions of the sales force are subject to remarkable bias.

Consumer audit data are a half-way house between retail audit work and sample surveys. The Television Consumer Audit in this country is organized in such a way that there is objective recording of purchases made, among large, representative samples. This audit of purchases can be broken down by area, or looked at over time, depending on how the examination of advertising effect is required. Several research agencies offer broadly similar services.

Analysis of any changes in user profile and brand switching can be made and these can be related to probability of advertising exposure. For the latter special questions may be required. Data on price paid and promotion up-take can be collected, which give an idea of below the line influence. This kind of information goes considerably further than simply counting the cases that leave the factory but it still gives no indication as to what may be going on in the consumer's mind, to the brand's advantage or disadvantage, as a result of advertising. A campaign may compare well or badly with *competitive efforts.* Unless consumers are interviewed, we cannot know. This gap, it has been claimed, can be filled by standardized post-test services, such as 'reading and noting' studies—press—and 24-hour recall studies—television. In fact, they are, in the author's view, quite inadequate for anything but a very superficial reading. This argument is based on experience, as well as on what have been shown to be the severe limitations of recall data apparent from the literature.

Very often the worst aspect about planning a post-test for the researcher is matching the practical need for speedy information to aid forward planning, and the likelihood of getting meaningful results while the campaign is still new. The timing of a post-test must take into account:

(a) How much advertising pressure is being put behind the brand—in absolute terms and in relation to competitive activity?
(b) Over what period is the money being spent?
(c) When was there advertising behind the brand before? At what level? On the same theme?
(d) How far is advertising trying to introduce a new thought, about new or generally reformulated products? How far is it a matter of trying to amend the image of a well entrenched product, which has near commodity status?
(e) What is the repurchase rate for the product?

All these points, which are obviously inter-related,can decide whether a clear picture is likely to emerge from survey work done earlier or later. Most researchers tend to advise later research. They do so for a number of reasons. They are less sanguine, as a rule, about the chances of consumers really seeing a product in a new light, when that product has already been around a long time. They also prefer to judge a campaign once they have seen how appreciation of the product in use ties in with expectations derived from advertising; for this it helps if time has been allowed for a repurchase rate to establish itself. The classical approach is to conduct identical checks before and after a campaign appears. This allows one to evaluate how much progress has been made. There are problems, however, in that several factors may not be the same, before and after the campaign break. The product may be seasonal or dependent on epidemic conditions, etc. The sales force activity may be heightened by the campaign. Competitors may have started to retaliate. This makes it desirable, in some cases, to have a control area, as below.

	Pre-campaign	*After campaign break*
Test area	Check 1^A	Check 2^A
Control area	Check 1^B	Check 2^B

Some prefer to take the rest of the country as the 'control' on the principle that a particular control area may be rendered unsuitable half-way through the test, by competitive activity.

Sometimes, no pre-check is possible, because the decision to post-test comes too late. In this case, a control area is most desirable. Long-term effects, or campaign wear-out, can be studied by repeating post-checks.

What to measure? Recall measures will certainly figure among what is measured, although relatively uncomplicated things such as purchase, and the presence of the brand in the pantry, etc., can also be covered. These question areas are sometimes useful:

(a) brand saliency (first mentions of brand when product field is mentioned);
(b) spontaneous awareness (any mentions of brand);
(c) prompted awareness (recognition of brand);
(d) trial and repurchase (for new brands);
(e) purchase and frequency of purchase (established brands);
(f) spontaneous awareness of advertising;
(g) prompted awareness of advertising;
(h) detailed recall of advertising;
(i) impressions of the advertising;
(j) brand image questions;
(k) attitudes to purchase (possibly using 'constant sum' technique);
(l) media exposure data.

A long questionnaire already, and no mention has yet been made of specific questions that may be important to establish the penetration of a particular

Fig. 16.6

campaign, e.g. 'How does brand A compare for price against brand B? Is it more, or less expensive, do you think?', where an economy platform has been used. The optimum question order must be expected to vary.

Some of the questions above, it has been suggested, are better indicators than others that a campaign has succeeded, or is succeeding, in increasing sales—'brand saliency', 'spontaneous advertising awareness', and 'constant sum' have support here, e.g. Axelrod[2]. Certain useful cross-analyses stick out a mile. Ability to recall advertising detail can be usefully crossed with trial, repurchase, and intentions to purchase. 'Brand image' can be crossed with 'frequency of purchase' groups. The value of this is fairly obvious.

A lot can also be done with media exposure data. Given analyses of media questions a series of cells can be built up as follows:

Likelihood of advertising experience:

	Very high	*High*	*Medium*	*Medium/ Light*	*Light/ None*
Definition:					
Television	Watches ITV every night	Watches ITV 4–5 nights a week	Etc.	Etc.	Etc.
Press	Reads daily two out of three publications on schedule	Reads daily one publication on schedule; occasionally sees others	Etc.	Etc.	Etc.

These groups can be considered separately on such questions as 'brand saliency', 'advertising awareness', etc. Figure 16.6 shows two very simple examples of the value of this. The example assumes that 'brand saliency' is a crucial measure as it may be for a fragmented market. Brand A has achieved no significant increase in brand saliency, given that heavier ITV viewers were very much aware of it already. Both the media choice and the creative content need to be critically examined. Brand B has fared better. The fact that the response function seems to be linear could be important. Briefly, this suggests that the *more* advertising received, the *greater* the effect. One implication could be that greater advertising pressure would be useful.

The story is still incomplete, however. Large-scale quantified work usually yields hypotheses about advertising effects, e.g. 'Those who were exposed to the advertising message were made aware of the brand, but not of its advantages; this is reflected in disinclination to purchase it'. The paradox of advertising research is that one is often forced, then, to go below the surface and examine hypotheses by means of qualitative work. Campaign evaluation studies can often be considered as establishing which sub-groups need intensive interviewing. This stands much conventional market research procedure on its head but advertising research is territory where the practitioner needs to develop and follow his own rules.

Two further approaches to campaign evaluation deserve attention. The first is to have a continuous survey checking on a brand's performance. This makes use of measures that relate to the effect that advertising is supposed to have on long-term promotional objectives. The second involves having panels that are set up on a permanent basis, in which there is built-in experimental control over media exposure. Both systems lend themselves to syndicated services, because of the high costs.

Most large research agencies nowadays offer a continuous survey (or one that is repeated at regular, frequent intervals). Some of these are specifically angled towards advertising post-tests, but most omnibus surveys can be adapted to a similar purpose.

It is often useful to observe the progress of a brand's advertising penetration, compared with other brands' performances, and broken out by usage and media exposure groups. Standardization of interviews means it is easier to note significant changes over time.

To be satisfied with standardization presupposes that one is confident that certain questions, repeated every few months, will continue to get at reactions to a brand's advertising in the most meaningful way, despite campaign changes, and possibly altered strategy. For some brands, in some situations, this may, almost, be the case, but to understand what a specific campaign is achieving, it is usually necessary to add specific questions. The same argument can be applied to the standardization of the sample.

While many advertisers will find it easier and cheaper to buy into a continuous survey, say twice a year, to get data of this kind on brand saliency, awareness, comprehension of messages, brand image, and so forth, a larger advertiser with a number of brands often reaches a different solution. This is to buy fieldwork direct, at appropriate intervals, from a fieldwork agency. The sample will be structured to suit his purposes, and there is no risk of 'interference' from questions on other advertisers' product fields.

There is another approach to campaign evaluation in the USA—the AdLab—which has attracted the interest and hopes of advertising researchers for some years. Unfortunately it has never been established in Europe; and it must be admitted that even in the USA it has not become as popular as classical area tests. It is also somewhat expensive to administer, and demands more time to measure results than many advertisers can afford. The system involves setting up matched panels of homes within the *same* geographical area and controlling their reception of advertising (e.g. with a split cable for commercial television reception). The effects of exposing comparable groups of homes to alternative advertising can then be measured. The system is described further on pages 487–488. The principle seems above criticism, provided there is accurate panel matching (in terms of shopping behaviour and access to different outlets) and provided the test area is reasonably typical. Control of media exposures will never be perfect so long as people visit each other, but this is a minor problem.

American experience suggests that a lot of time is needed before getting clear-cut trends, whether it is advertising pressure or scheduling or campaign content that is the subject of the test. Nevertheless, many European advertisers and researchers would probably appreciate having a similar realistic campaign evaluation opportunity available—if it did not cost too much and if it could aid judgment sufficiently quickly.

Advertising Research Program

There is no perfect advertising research program, but here is an example of one, taken from work done to re-launch Silvikrin Shampoo in the UK in 1966–8, which introduces many of the points made in this chapter.

In 1968 Silvikrin Shampoo was re-launched as a range of shampoos based on natural ingredients, called 'The New Naturals'. The outline of research is given below.

(a)	Summer 1966	Concept of 'New Naturals' tested on small scale in group discussions.
(b)	Winter 1966	Reactions to 'New Naturals' concept (adapted since summer, 1966) tested on larger scale, in parallel with tests of optimum balance of shampoo variants, names and packs.
		(1967. Product and packaging development.)
(c)	Winter 1967/8	Tests of four advertising approaches for the 'New Naturals' introduction.
(d)	Spring 1968	In light of the above, two press advertisements in finished form. (One 15-second announcement commercial was also prepared, using the features that came out best in winter 1967/8.) These press ads were tested on a small scale.
(e)	Summer 1968	Tested on a large scale, in a folder test, against other toiletry and cosmetic advertising.
		Autumn 1968. Advertising broke (national launch). Mainly press and television in support.
(f)	Autumn 1968/70	Tests of further individual press advertisments, featuring each shampoo variant separately. Mostly small-scale, to check for negatives and appropriateness to specific hair types; occasional larger-scale tests to check the strength of the continuing campaign.
(g)	Spring 1969	Large-scale national usage and penetration study, checking inter-relationships of: brand use; advertising awareness; understanding of 'New Naturals' theme; appreciation of 'New Naturals' theme; media exposure.

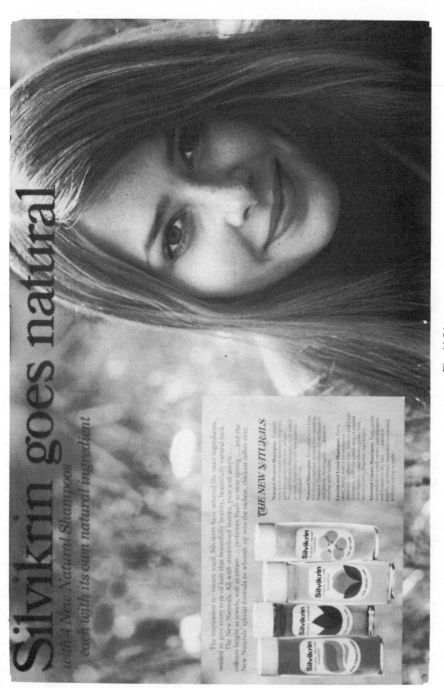

Fig. 16.7A

Fig. 16.7B
Reproduced with permission of Leo Burnett Ltd.

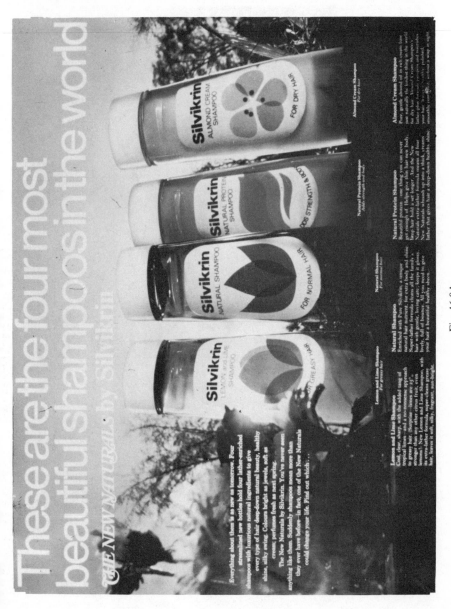

Fig. 16.8A

Reproduced with permission of Leo Burnett Ltd.

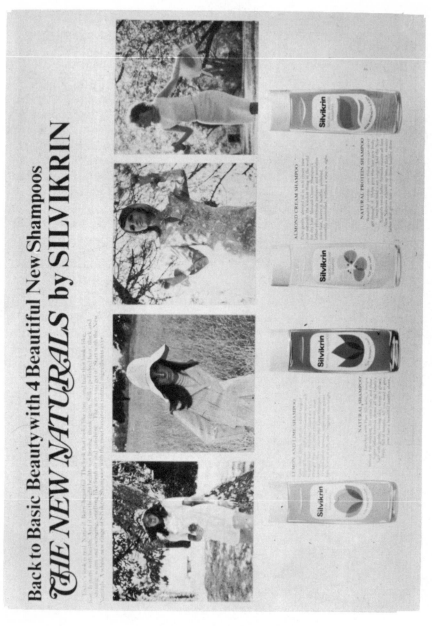

Fig. 16.8B
Reproduced with permission of Leo Burnett Ltd

448

The length of time spanned by this whole program is a function of the fact that the re-launch involved a re-vamping of the whole brand. The right formulations, colours, bottles, and names for each of the four Silvikrin variants—'Natural', 'Protein', 'Lemon and Lime', and 'Almond Cream'—had to be developed in parallel. As the creative work was developed, it had to take into account any new turn taken in the presentation of the range.

The first stage showed that the idea of the 'New Naturals', as a means of reintroducing a well-known brand, was arresting, intriguing, and pleasing to the target market. The natural ingredients featured seemed to carry considerable promise, and were consistent with the brand image idea, 'beauty through health' (see original concept board in Fig. 16.7). The work in the winter of 1966 (b) confirmed this impression. It also showed which names, colours, packs were consistent with the promise of the 'New Naturals' theme, and which were not.

The 'Natural' theme inspired four creative routes, one of which is illustrated in Fig. 16.7. Of these, one featured a headline 'Once Upon a Time', recalling the days of childhood when hair was naturally attractive. This had significant negatives for some women, who saw it as a reminder of advancing years, and was abandoned; but the one illustrated in Fig. 16.7 'Silvikrin Goes Natural', combined emotional arousal with communication and appreciation. The other two were workmanlike, rather than inspired.

Figure 16.8 shows the two advertisements that were tested at (d) and (e). Both were significantly more likely to arouse comment, interest, and remarks suggesting relevance to consumer need than the other advertisements tested in the folders at (e). Further, they succeeded in securing the attention and enthusiasm of both the younger and the older parts of the target market, which earlier creative work had never quite succeeded in achieving. The sales results of the re-launch thoroughly vindicated the whole operation. The close inter-relationship of all factors in the marketing mix made it extremely difficult to apportion results to causes. (Note that the original concept research was as much product concept as advertising concept research.) The comparison of awareness, usage and media exposure in the post-campaign evaluation at (g), however, showed that advertising must have played a considerable part.

17. Packaging research and name testing

William Schlackman and David Chittenden*

The Package

Clearly, the package has many different functions to fulfil. It is a key vehicle in the passage of a product from the manufactured state to the point of consumption. As such, it has to contain the product physically, protect it from contamination or degradation, stand up to transportation and storage by the trade, present the product to the consumer, allow consumer transportation and storage, allow the product to be dispensed (and perhaps resealed) whenever needed, and stimulate repurchase—to name a few major functions only; and it has to do all this at low cost and in a way which allows of easy disposal and minimal wastage.

All of these functions require creative consideration and are simultaneously subject to research techniques. Some of these are laboratory tests. For example, tests of the physical properties of a package and its materials, e.g. degree of resistance to heat or pressure, or interaction of any kind with the product contained, form a first step in screening a pack for acceptability. Such tests are normally conducted in laboratory conditions by manufacturers, packaging companies, or (in Great Britain) by organizations such as the Packaging Industry Research Association.

Having passed such laboratory tests, a pack may yet be liable to fail in the customer's hands. In particular, packs offering easy opening and/or resealing are subject to misinterpretation and misuse by the customer; the development of Metal Box's highly successful ring-pull cans provides many examples of this, and of the type of research needed to understand the problem—the provision of real packaging to the customer for his experimentation either, as in this case, under observation, or for subsequent investigation by questionnaire procedures.

---

* In the first edition of the Consumer Market Research Handbook, this chapter was written by William Schlackman and John Dillon.

Nevertheless it is probably true to say that most controversy and the greatest opportunity for packaging design arises in terms of the way in which it presents the product—first to the retailer, and more importantly to the consumer. As James Pilditch has said in his book 'The Silent Salesman'*, with the growth of self service and self-selection 'The package as salesman, ... is the connecting link between company and consumer . . . . The final step, from shelf to shopping basket, depends on the package.'

The research methods outlined in this chapter are concerned primarily, therefore, with assessing the performance of existing or alternative new packaging in terms of sales and marketing criteria, so as to optimize acceptance at the retailer and consumer levels, and specifically to ensure that the packaging effectively presents the product it contains.

Retailers

With regard to retailers there are many functional considerations one should determine through research during the design planning stage. There is much evidence to suggest that if a package fails to meet the retailer's needs he will behave in such a way that distribution of the product will be severely inhibited. He may not display the product or he may discourage consumers from making a purchase, or he may simply not carry the product because its packaging creates too many problems for him.

There are a number of general characteristics to be borne in mind but, ultimately, one might usefully survey a representative cross-section of retailers to discover their requirements. Broadly speaking, we may conceive of a number of research areas which we shall put in terms of questions:

(a) What kind of package will be most convenient for retailers to stock and maintain in an orderly fashion?
(b) What kind of package will minimize the expensive cost of handling?
(c) What kind of package will minimize breakage and pilferage?
(d) What sizes and shapes will fit into his display arrangements, and in conjunction with this, what kinds of point-of-purchase display racks and assistance will be welcomed?
(e) What kind of package does the retailer have faith in from the viewpoint of what he thinks consumers will buy?
(f) With what types of packs currently on the market has he experienced difficulty?
(g) What are his personal preferences and how do these influence his buying practices?

---

* Revised Edition 1973, Published by Business Books.

Before one designs a package which will meet the needs at this stage of the distribution process, one should have the answers to these questions. A successful deodorant package, for example, which was selling well met with retailer resistance because it occupied too much space on the display counters. The result was that retailers only displayed a small number of packages. Because it was a good turnover item, the customers frequently missed it on the counters. Changing the package size enabled the company to have more packages displayed and, at the same time, satisfied the retailers.

The Consumer

Although the research questions and methods on the wholesaler and retailer level present certain complexities, the most challenging question to be answered by far—and certainly the most critical—is the role of the package as it relates to consumer behaviour. *The package is not simply a functional carrier of the product but is intrinsically continuous with the meanings the consumer attaches to the product.* The package design is a key factor influencing the image of the product and brand. As in the case of retailers, it is first necessary to determine, preferably through careful investigation, what the package will be required to do at this stage of the distribution process. Here, one must know:

(a) Will the package be sold on a self-service basis or not?
(b) Will it act as a container for the product within the home or simply be discarded?
(c) Is the product an impulse item or a planned purchase?
(d) In what units do consumers prefer to buy?
(e) Where is the package kept in the home—on the table, in a store bin, etc.?
(f) What are the brand imagery requirements in selling the brand?

These are a few of the simple questions that should be examined with regard to designing a good package for consumers, for how the consumer will buy and use the product will dictate the design direction. The responsibility of the market researcher in the early stage is to provide the designers with this type of basic information.

At this point it is useful to bear in mind that researchers cannot create designs. Research should not be a design function. Attempts at using research as a way of getting consumers to give specific design concepts have almost always failed. During the criterion stage of research the researcher should provide the designers with a comprehensive and sensitive understanding of the problem so that the designers can maximize their ingenuity in solving the problem. Research can never be a substitute for creative effort. In a study for a hosiery manufacturer, for example, it was found that the brand was rarely displayed on a self-merchandising shelf, but that consumers frequently saved the package for storage of personal items. In conjunction with this, it was also found that in shopping for this product the first contact the consumer had was with the inner wrapper of the package when offered before her eyes by the sales assistant. This indicated two important directions for design. It:

(a) was relatively unimportant to have an 'impact' design (rapid recognition) but it was most important that the package have a pleasing feminine quality which would look attractive in a lady's boudoir;

(b) pointed to the need of having a luxurious transfer design on the inner wrapping because that was the first thing the consumer saw at the point of purchase; her first judgement of the product was influenced by the tissue sheet on the inside.

In a study for a large producer of eyedrops, it was found that frequent users of the product usually carried it in a glove compartment or in handbags but the pack was awkward and many women thought it was inconvenient and unattractive. A new single unit package dispenser was developed which was also attractive.

In the past, drug manufacturers—particularly of vitamin pills—found that the packaging which was used frequently created reluctance to use it at meal times due to the old-fashioned medicinal-looking containers. One manufacturer created a completely new design for the various nutritive supplements he sold. The bottles were made to look like attractive condiment jars. Housewives enjoyed keeping them not in the medicine chest but on the table with flowers and salt shakers. Such a redesign created more interest in the product.

The brief examples given above illustrate how the package can be a powerful selling tool. The packet can contribute to overcoming barriers to product consumption and provide greater satisfaction in use. In this planning area the role of the market researcher is critical. By thoroughly understanding the dynamics of the 'consumer/product' interaction he can provide the designer with directions which will enable the creative people to produce packages which will effectively help the marketing of the product. Often, in these research areas, statistical procedures of study are not required. Understanding derived through qualitative research procedures is sufficient.

The marketing performance characteristics of a package require serious attention. Here, we should think in terms of three dimensions of importance in the marketing process as it relates to the package, the:

(a) *subjective mental* features as a vehicle of communication with the consumer;

(b) *functional* features of the package as it meets both the retailers' needs and the needs of the consumer;

(c) *visual* structure—speed and clarity of perception.

The package and the unplanned purchase

Self-service and effective packaging, both interdependent developments of recent years, have opened up a new type of selling phenomenon. This change has expanded markets and drastically changed merchandising concepts. We refer to the whole area of the unplanned purchase. This is sometimes referred to as the impulse sale. Actually, only a fraction of the unplanned purchases are purely impulse, in the sense that no apparent need for the product exists but that which is nurtured at the point of sale. Most unplanned purchases are purchases made where the consumer is reminded of a need for the product by seeing the package at the point of sale. Unplanned purchases account for a substantial proportion of buying in some product fields, although of all the unplanned purchases only a minor part are based solely on impulse.

Today, stores with a wide variety of merchandise (particularly super-markets distributing with self-service techniques) encourage the consumer to shop without a prescribed list for purchase. One survey found that only 9% of shoppers tested actually had a written shopping list with them. Most of the shoppers stated that they usually walk through the aisles and get what they 'need'. (This word 'need' should be put in clearly labelled quotation marks.) This suggests that, in assessing the features of importance for research on a package, one should know the extent to which it is an impulse item.

Subjective Mental Factors

The package projects the brand image. People buy products for the promise of the gratifications offered and *these gratifications are not simply physical but emotional and social as well.*

The package, seen as clothing for the product, must communicate in visual symbols the promise that what is within the container will fulfil these satisfactions. In order to do this, it is first necessary to know the buying habits, usage patterns, attitudes, and motives of consumers with regard to the product and brand. Once this is done, one is in a position to establish the criteria on which the designer can fruitfully start to work.

The package is one vehicle in the marketing and advertising program. In a sense, design planning research is not significantly different from research in these broader areas of marketing and advertising, although its focus may be somewhat different.

The most critical consideration is the degree to which the package activates purchase behaviour. If, for example, you are selling ice cream and you want to create an aura of 'abundance' and 'traditional qualities', it would be necessary to measure the degree to which the package does, in fact, induce this image. By using motivational procedures which include depth interviews and projective tests it is possible with a relatively high degree of accuracy to determine the image projected by the package. An example relates to a brand of dandruff remover. Here, it was found that, although women were the most frequent users and invariably those who bought the product, men used the product as well. However, the package being used was extremely feminine and many potential male users were reluctant to use the brand. With these factors in mind, the company dropped the use of a flower pattern but

454

retained all the other design elements. This made the package less feminine and tended to make the product less cosmetic in its appearance. This simple change resulted in increased usage by men while, at the same time, holding its female users. The symbolic cues of a package can influence judgements about the taste and other physical characteristics of a product. It can also suggest the character of the product, who uses it and, sometimes, when the product would be used. In this way the packet can define the psychological character of the brand. Since the consumption of products in our culture satisfies not only physical requirements but also psycho-social needs, correct manipulation of the symbolic cues can help to create consumer satisfactions and make a major contribution to the marketing effort. Most of the packaging research done today concentrates on this aspect of a pack's performance. A number of examples of how this can be done usefully are given below.

Concept Association Tests.   The most common procedure used to deal with this aspect of the problem is what might be described as the 'Concept Association Test'. This is a projective test procedure in which the respondent links concepts with the packet. There are a number of versions that can be used in research terms but the principle is usually the same, depending to some extent on the context of the research. In a nondirective-type interview, for example, there would be little structure. The respondent might simply be asked to free associate to the packet, i.e. simply relay all the thoughts that come to mind as he/she looks at the packet or in slightly more structured form to *imagine*:

(a) the kind of product that would be in the packet;
(b) the kind of people who might use it or not use it;
(c) where the product might be used and seen;
(d) types of shops in which it would be sold.

Still within the framework of an unstructured interview the respondent may be required to make up a story involving the stimulus pack, or make-believe that the pack is a person and describe what sort of person the pack would be. All these procedures are projective in nature and based on associative procedures. This type of research principle is easily extended to quantitative surveys.

In either case (whether at the qualitative or quantitative stage) it is important not to concentrate solely upon the evaluative ('I like it') or aesthetic ('It looks pretty') aspects of the pack, but upon the way in which it works to project desirable imagery and associations on behalf of the product it contains.

While in an unstructured interview such associations may be produced by nondirective questioning, the requirement of the quantitative interview that every respondent be asked the same question in the same way leads one to produce a series of statements dealing with aspects of the product, its qualities, and likely appeal to its different types of user. Each such statement can then be considered by the respondent before she is asked to express *her* view:

(a) by applying that statement (e.g. 'This would be a good quality product') to as many as it seems appropriate of several brands on display before her; or
(b) by checking the most appropriate answer from a series (e.g. agree strongly, think I agree, think I disagree, disagree strongly) in relation to *one particular* product.

In the first of these cases, where a statement can be applied to as many or as few of the products displayed as the respondent thinks appropriate, a matched sample is required for each alternative design as it is compared with competition. Since the competitors have a well-established image the results of this test may be biased against the new design (an unknown compared to a known, etc.). This research design done monadically, however, is nevertheless useful in that we emerge with a score for each design against its normal competition and the relative imagery effectiveness of the designs can be seen. One answers the question 'Given the image we want to create which one of the proposed designs does best against competition?'.

However, this exercise may prove fruitless if there is very little difference between the packs in terms of their ability to convey different ideas about or associations with the product. It is still a valid research exercise to attempt to find aspects of differentiation between the packs in aesthetic or projected imagery terms; and the next alternative therefore would be to display *all* the test packs, *again* asking respondents to apply a series of statements to as many of the pack/product combinations as they think appropriate. It is particularly important in this case not to ask for a single 'forced choice' response since this is liable to distort responses in what is already an artificial situation in that the consumer will never be confronted in the market place with all the designs to be tested in the research.

It should also be born in mind that in this forced 'head-on' comparison situation there is a tendency for any pack which is very different from the others to attract to itself a great deal of both favourable and unfavourable imagery precisely because it is different from the rest; and if this is foreseen as likely to occur then it is advisable to set up the 'head-on' comparisons using a paired comparison design, e.g. AB, AC, AD, BC, BD, CD, if four different test packs are to compared

A further refinement increasing the precision of the data from such head-on comparisons would use a simple scaling technique, the respondent being asked to consider only one pack/product combination at a time, and to indicate her agreement or disagreement with each statement read out by the interviewer by checking the answer category closest to her own view (e.g. 'Think I agree' or 'Strongly disagree'). Such a technique is, however, more exhaustive in its demands on the respondent, and will only yield more sensitive data provided the number of scales and the complexity of their verbal cues are kept under strict control, so as to avoid respondent irritation, boredom, or actual termination of the interview.

It should be noted, however, that the scaling and association tests described above serve only to provide information on the acceptability of the imagery produced by each pack without giving any idea (except by inference) of 'why'. In order to provide such diagnostic data within the context of the association test procedures it is necessary to adopt further probing questioning techniques in relation to the test pack, using phraseology such as 'What is it about (NAME TEST PACK) which makes you say it is . . . (READ OUT STATEMENT PREVIOUSLY APPLIED TO TEST PACK)?'

The Pseudo-product Test Procedure. As mentioned earlier, experience has shown that the symbolic cues on a pack design will influence the perception of the product. This is especially true in the case of food and other such products involving ingestion. This is an important phenomenon in the marketing of such products, since reliance on blind product tests alone does not reveal how the packaging will influence the consumers' judgement of the product. In these instances the pseudo-product test procedure is ideally suited to evaluating symbolic influences on product judgement. The method consists of either double placement or sequential placements of the *same product* but in alternative pack designs. Allowing respondents to act as their own control, i.e. by testing and comparing more than one pack, is somewhat more efficient than the monadic design for this purpose because the use of one sample to provide data on both pack/product combinations undergoing test allows a smaller sample size to provide the same efficiency. For example, a difference occurring between the views of a representative sample of 400 respondents on one product (in pack A) and the same product (in pack B), when both products have been exposed to the same sample, is more likely to be statistically significant than the same difference occurring between two separately interviewed samples of 400 respondents, each of which has been exposed *either* to pack A *or* to pack B, but not to both.

Since the manufacturer usually has a clear idea of the desirable characteristics for the product and as he knows which sectors of the market the product is aimed at, the dimensions for measurement are normally predetermined. A simple illustration is from a beverage study where two alternative labels were studied. A sample of 200 who were drinkers of the beverage were recruited. These were people drinking normally a mild version of the beverage. The client who was not currently a producer of such a version wanted to launch a new brand into this section of the market. The problem was to indicate which of two alternative labels would be most appropriate.

The same product formulation was presented in two differently labelled bottles 'M'–'L' (it was a simultaneous double placement test). Respondents were instructed to use one bottle first and, on completion, to use the second bottle. This sequential instruction was rotated from respondent to respondent in 'M'–'L'—'L'–'M' order. Respondents were simply told that they should consume the product and that the interviewer would return in four days and ask them some questions about their experience.

The results from pseudo-product tests are often dramatic, as in this case. Consumers experience differences where chemically and physiologically no differences could possibly exist. Here are some results from the pack test.

	'L'	'M'	Don't know	'N' = 200 Total (%)
Product found most acceptable	20	75	5	100
Product which was mild	25	65	10	100
Product most bitter	70	28	2	100

This very brief abstract illustrates a clear difference in the perceptions of the same product presented with two varying labels. Version 'M' moves the product more effectively in the direction of the marketing intention than does 'L'.

Functional Considerations

Another trend in recent years relates to the entire concept of convenience in marketing. Functional innovations in packaging which facilitate actual product usage are welcomed by consumers. Consumers are learning to expect effective, convenient packaging from manufacturers and when they do not get it they may express hostility toward the brand. In your own experience as a consumer, think of all the times you had difficulty opening a can or bottle. Try to remember how aggravated you got. Then multiply your experience by thousands and you can easily realize the sales effects such experiences can create for a given manufacturer.

The familiar closure problem, however, is only one of the many in the area of usage. Consider such things as: slippery glass bottles that break in the bathroom while shaving, bulky bottles, and cartons that cannot be easily disposed of and bottles which are cumbersome to use.

Packages which overcome such problems are attractive to consumers. Packages which go beyond problem solving and make it even easier for the consumer become an even more important brand differential. Through research in the usage pattern area, it is possible to locate such consumer difficulties and even uncover new directions which will facilitate usage. One familiar example is crushproof 'flip-top boxes' for cigarettes which have been well received in the UK because of their functional characteristics.

Measuring Functional Considerations Using Placement Tests. The functional features of a pack are best studied under in-use conditions. This research is best presented in a way which avoids any concentration on the pack as such by the respondent at the time of placement and usage. A useful procedure is to conduct a sequential pseudo-product test research design.

The product is kept constant while the package construction varies in each placement. Unlabelled packets are used to eliminate 'symbolic interference' and brand bias.

Example. This study comprised a package construction test for a hand-rolling tobacco, in which two alternative types of construction were compared. These are referred to, for convenience, by the code letters 'R' and 'T'. These two packs were tested upon a total of 200 men who smoked brand 'Y' as their usual brand. The two packs were placed with informants, separately and in sequence, with the placement order rotated; informants were allowed two days to smoke the tobacco, and then were called upon and interviewed to find their reactions. At the end of the test, when the informants had tried both packs, they were asked to express a preference between them, and to give reasons for this. This emerged as follows.

	$N = 200$
Preferences between the packs	%
Prefer pack 'R'	31
Prefer pack 'T'	68

There was no difference in these preferences when one considered the size of pack normally bought by the informants; over the range half-ounce, one-ounce, and two-ounce usual pack, there was the same pattern of preference.

When asked the *reason* for their preferences, the informants replied as follows.

*Reasons for pack preferences**
Bases = informants who preferred each pack.

	Prefer 'R'	*Prefer 'T'*
	%	%
Just like it, for no particular reason	2	4
Easier to open	7	43
Easier to get at the tobacco	4	31
Better sealed	26	2
Easier to reseal	9	6
Keeps the tobacco fresh	42	10
A stronger pack	19	8
Easier to use	0	9

These comments on the reason for preferring one pack or the other centred upon two aspects of the packs, *convenience* and *protection*. The informants seemed mainly concerned with either one or the other of these aspects: those

---

* Open-ended question—does not add up to 100%.

who were convenience-oriented preferred pack 'T' and those who were protection-oriented preferred pack 'R'.

Measuring the Visual Factors

With the increasing importance of self-service merchandizing, creating pack displays which will easily be singled out by the consumer has become an important criterion in packaging success. However, measuring this dimension in a meaningful way is difficult. And the methodology involved in such studies is somewhat complex and difficult to handle.

One primary aim in this phase of research is to establish the extent to which a pack will 'stand-out' in a visual display. There are other 'identification' factors such as legibility and brand recognition. These latter factors are of significance but they should not be confused with the problem of 'stand-out', as they often are.

Now, let us look at the sequence of visual events occurring as a prospective buyer first sees a retailer's display of products. For the sake of simplicity, we will imagine that the viewer has her eyes closed, and we will examine the sequence as she opens her eyes and thereafter.

The viewer is suddenly bombarded by the light coming from the total display. At that moment, each item is competing with each other item in the display for the viewer's attention. Where the viewer's attention goes is influenced by several factors. However, it is possible to control for a number of these factors in the test situation so that the critical factor—the effective contrast between each item and its background, i.e. other items in the display—is the one measured by the test.

Let us call this immediate, attention-capturing stage 'visual stage 1'. What happens next? The viewer's eye will stay on the item which has now caught her attention for an indefinite time, during which her brain (at least) will begin and continue to process the information transmitted by the pack; and then her eye may move to another item in the display. Let us call the stage at which she is *processing* the information transmitted by the first item to which her eye has moved 'visual stage 2' and the later event(s) 'visual stage 3'. This is a simplified model of the situation for the purposes of our argument. We can summarize the sequence as follows.

Visual stage 1: viewer's attention goes to one item in the display;

Visual stage 2: viewer processes the information transmitted by that item;

Visual stage 3: further events occur.

In stand-out research we are trying to measure *simply what happens at visual stage 1*, i.e. how well the test pack competes with its competitors in terms of catching the viewer's attention.

It may be noted that *as visual stage 2 progresses* the viewer will begin to be able to identify the brand, the manufacturer, the (projected) product characteristics, etc., and she will be reacting to what we might call the imagery properties (of the pack, the brand, as described elsewhere). Using questions relating to brand identification as a measure thus presupposes *both* visual stages 1 and 2. Since in most tachistoscopic* measures the respondent is required to report what she saw, these do not adequately measure 'stand-out' as it has here been defined. To measure stand-out it has been found that a 'find time' method is most useful. It has several advantages in addition to its relevance; for example, it avoids certain procedural problems and it is sensitive. However, tachistoscopes are usefully employed when visual stage 2 information represents the research objective. The most common instance of this is when one wants to establish the ease of brand identification.

Another device which has sometimes been used for packaging research is the eye camera, measuring where the eye is focussed from moment to moment. However, this has proved to be of little value in market research generally, and its application in the area of packaging has similarly been discouraging. There are three main problems associated with its use: first, where the eye is fixated does not reliably indicate what the person is in fact perceiving; second, the equipment tends to be cumbersome to use (and unpopular with respondents); third, data analysis is time-consuming and costly.

The Find Time Procedure.   The procedure is a variation on what is known as 'disjunctive reaction time'. In essence, the respondent has to search for an item in each of a series of displays, knowing that it will sometimes be in a given display, and sometimes not. If she finds it, she gives one response; as soon as she decides that it is not there, she gives an alternative response (which is normally ignored, but which could also be taken into account). One is measuring how long it takes to find a pack when it is there. Prior to the main task each respondent should be tested for normal vision (with glasses if worn), and undertakes a practice run in an unrelated product area and series of displays.

Let us say there are two test variants, 'A1' and 'A2'. These might be two (competitive) current packs, a current design and a proposed new design, or two possible designs for a new product. The type of display should correspond to the actual market environment—gondolas, counter tops, counter units, dump bins, display stands, window displays, etc. Also, two or more different types of display, e.g. supermarket gondola plus chemist's counter top, can be used in the one series.

Although the number is arbitrary a frequent pattern is, for any one test series, to use six displays with a given test item *present* (in six different

---

* A tachistoscope is a mechanical or electronic device for exposing stimuli (packs, advertisements, etc.) to a viewer for strictly controlled (brief) periods of time.

positions, with detailed control over the pack adjacencies from display to display) plus three displays with the given test item *absent*. A separate closely matched group of, say, 50 people will see each different test series (on nine displays). One series will differ from the other only in respect of the *test variant* which appears (in six out of the nine displays).

After screening and the practice run, each respondent (individually) is shown her particular test item and is allowed to familiarize herself with it as she wishes, and she has it in front of her during the rest of the session. She is instructed to press a small response-key (situated immediately beneath her fingers) as soon as she sees the test item in any display *or* as soon as she decides that it is not present in any display (speed *and* accuracy both being emphasized). She is then asked to state whether the test item was present or absent from the display.

Each display is projected by means of a pre-loaded, pre-focused, automatic projector (the order of test item present/absent being determined by the experimenter in advance), which is electronically linked with a timer, and the response key. Exposure time continues from the start of the projection (which starts the timer) until the response key is pressed, stopping the timer. Having recorded the reaction time (or 'find time' as it is often called) and reset the timer, the start button is pressed to start the next display (and the clock).

The data derived from the test consist first of records of whether the respondent said 'Yes' or 'No' on each occasion, indicating that she believed the test item was present in or absent from that display; and secondly of the time taken for her to reach that decision on each occasion. If there are nine slides in the series, six of which have the test item present, a sample size of 50 will provide 300 opportunities for respondents to be right in saying the test item is present; while there are a corresponding 150 opportunities (3 per respondent) for them to be right in saying that the test item is *not* present.

In the course of the series of tests conducted since 1971 various measures have been taken to increase the level of accuracy of response (brand presence or absence correctly reported) so that the expected normal performance of any given sample is 95% or better; and, where this is achieved, direct comparison of the mean reaction times or 'final' times of the total samples is appropriate, the statistical significance of any differences registered between packs or products being calculated by use of a *t*-test procedure.

Where this figure is considerably reduced, however, it is necessary first to consider whether the interview conditions have affected results in some way; and if not, what other causes there may be. Clearly, if one particular pack continually fails to be identified as present (when it should be), one strong hypothesis must be that it has little visual impact. If it is often said to be present when it is not, in fact the most appropriate hypothesis may well be that there is some other pack which is continually being mistaken for it in the display situation — in other words the problem is confusion not lack of impact.

Occasionally, however, series of displays are tested in which accuracy of response is very low indeed, either because the pack styles adopted by most products in the display are very similar to one another, with the test pack following a similar path; or because the problem is not of variety identification where the only visual cues to identification have intentionally been subordinated to other pack design requirements. In such cases more attention has to be paid to the relative performance of each pack in establishing a minimal level of correct identification, and speed becomes less relevant.

Stand-out testing of this type would normally be preceded by a photographic survey of retail outlets to confirm for an existing test product the most representative positions and types of display, the number of end or front facings normally found, the products most often displayed alongside it, and the lighting levels in which the pack will have to make its impact. In the case of a new product, a similar investigation among its potential competition at the retail outlet is desirable.

Whether or not such a photographic survey is undertaken, however, the displays represented in the stand-out test should be as realistic as possible especially in terms of the likely number and disposition of test and competitive packs. Within this context, it is possible to set up a more complex series of tests specially adapted to the investigation of ease of identification of individual varieties within a range (for example, by the use of colour coding, symbols, or emphasis upon the written word); or to problems of confusion with a competitor's packaging.

Example of 'Stand-out' Problem. The aim in this research was to assess two variations of a new pack design for a confectionery product in terms of stand-out effectiveness relative to the current pack. The research involved the use of the find time technique. The test material comprised:

(a) variation 1 of a new pack;
(b) variation 2 of a new pack;
(c) the current pack 'P'.

Table 17.1 *Stand-out results*

Packs	Mean reaction times	t-test value	Significance level		Accuracy levels Pack present	Pack absent
'V2' Current 'P'	1.77 s 1.59 s	1.99	Not significant	Current 'P'	98%	97%
'V1' Current 'P'	1.98 s 1.59 s	3.71	P < 0.001	V1	96%	96%
'V2' 'V1'	1.77 s 1.98 s	2.05	P < 0.05	V2	94%	97%

The total sample of 150 respondents was split into three quota-matched subsamples of 50 respondents each, corresponding to the three test items. After visual screening, and a full practice run, each respondent was given the test pack appropriate to her sub-sample. She was then shown, sequentially, a series of nine slides showing displays of confectionery items. In six of these displays the test pack was present and in the other three displays it was *not* present. The respondent was required to press a response key, according to whether or not she found the test item present in the display. The length of time taken to find the test pack when it *was* present comprised the data for this research, summarized in Table 17.1. The 'V2' packet was thus significantly better in stand-out than 'V1' at the five per cent level. However, there was no significant difference between 'V2'and the current pack, which was also significantly better than 'VI' at the 0.1% level.

Perhaps the central virtue of the stand-out test, apart from its sensitivity in terms of discrimination between test items, lies in the fact that it appears to overcome the familiarity bias found in all tachistoscopic tests—which nevertheless remain the most appropriate way of measuring communication of product type, brand name, and other detailed elements within a total pack design.

Example of Identification Problem. The aim of the research was to provide some measurement of the:

(a) visibility of a rectangular panel introduced onto the main display face of a frozen food brand package;
(b) relative visibility and legibility of the various components of the message contained within that panel.

The method employed in the research was a tachistoscopic procedure (sample size 36) in which each respondent was first familiarized with the normal current carton, i.e. one *not* bearing the panel which was the subject of the research. The woman was given the carton to hold and study, and the major design elements of the pack were pointed out to her. The respondent was then told that she was about to be shown a similar pack 'for just a very short space of time' and would be asked to say if she saw anything on that pack which was in any way different from the carton she just studied. The test pack, bearing the rectangular panel, was then exposed to the respondent in a series of controlled-time exposures, by means of a mirror tachistoscope. Eight progressively longer controlled-time exposures were used, ranging from 10 ms ($\frac{1}{100}$ of a second) to 2000 ms (2 s). After each exposure the respondent was asked to say what, if any, difference she saw in the test pack, compared with the initial prompt pack, and her responses were recorded verbatim. Responses were probed to ensure that maximum available data emerged after each exposure. If, at the conclusion of the full series of eight controlled-time tests, the respondent had not fully verbalized the message contained on the panel, the test pack was exposed to her for such a period of time as was necessary for her to do so. This constitutes the ninth (infinity) trial on the table of results included in Table 17.2.

The panel introduced onto the display face of the test pack contained the

Table 17.   Summary of responses.   Trial at which design component/element first mentioned

Sample base: 36

Trial No.	Controlled time exposure	Design Component Code (see key below)						
		A	B	C	D	E	F	G
		No.	No.	No.	No.	No.	No.	No.
1	10 ms	—	—	—	—	—	—	—
2	20 ms	1	—	—	—	—	—	—
3	50 ms	4	—	1	2	—	—	—
4	100 ms	9	2	—	2	—	—	—
5	200 ms	12	8	3	3	—	—	—
6	500 ms	5	8	6	3	—	—	—
7	1000 ms	1	6	3	6	4	8	—
8	2000 ms	—	3	1	3	12	4	11
9	infinity	—	—	—	—	—	—	25
Total responses on each design component		32	27	14	19	16	12	36
Median score—in trials		4.17	5.44	5.5	5.83	7.66	6.75	—

Key to coding of design components:
Noting of, reference to . . .
A difference from prompt pack/panel mentioned
B design motif in panel, i.e., stylized flower
C red/red lettering in panel
D blue/blue lettering in panel
E actual phrase 'Free Gifts'
F actual slogan
G identification/verbalization of total message

message 'Free Gifts' in red lettering and a slogan in blue lettering. It also contained a central stylized flower design motif. The results are shown in Table 17.2. Of the total sample of 36 respondents, 32 (89%), registered their awareness of the test panel, by shape, position on pack, etc., as not having been present in the prompt pack. The most readily noticed and remarked feature of the panel was its stylized flower design motif. Rather more respondents registered awareness of some blue lettering in the panel than those mentioning the red lettering (although these produced essentially the same median score related to speed of perception). However, rather more respondents deciphered the red rather than the blue lettering, as a prelude to verbalizing the total message, even though they did so somewhat more slowly. Only about 30% of the entire sample of respondents were able to decipher the *total* message at the maximum operable time exposure of two seconds.

In summary the findings of this research suggested that, although the test panel, as a total unit, made its presence known widely and promptly, its ability to communicate a message was relatively poor within the terms of normal tachistoscopic procedures. Within the panel, the stylized flower design motif appeared to be the most visible and, therefore, the dominant element. The blue lettering appeared to be more *visible* than the red in this particular design context, but less *legible*. (However, this last point must be considered in the light of the longer phrase and, perhaps, less familiar words involved in the blue print, compared with the simpler 'Free Gifts' in red.)

Name Testing

Is testing a name really a worthwhile exercise? Some marketing men have disputed this point on the grounds that any name given advertising backing can be made effective. And many examples of names meaningless in themselves can be cited where the brands in fact are highly successful. In some cases the names themselves would on the surface appear to be detrimental in marketing terms.

One may conclude from this that in all probability the name itself is not a key factor in marketing. Success might be achieved without it. Yet an ineffective name or one which is inappropriate represents a significant handicap at least in the early stages of a brand's marketing life. Assuming that other factors in the product mix are right an inappropriate name places a burden on the total effort while one that communicates effectively will facilitate the marketing process.

The criteria for an effective name

The manner in which we research the name problem is to some extent conditioned by the criteria by which we are to judge its value. One might usefully delineate two types of criteria:

(a) general;
(b) specific.

General Criteria

Here we may list a number of factors one would ideally like in any brand name:

(a) easy to pronounce;
(b) suggestive of the product class;
(c) easy to recognize quickly;
(d) easy to recall;
(e) not spontaneously associated with negative ideas;
(f) not associated with other products;
(g) not previously registered by another company.

Specific Criteria

Specific criteria are those dimensions one would like to communicate by the name in terms of the way in which one intends to position the brand within the market. Such ideas are usually related to the findings of previous market surveys and, more especially, the findings from motivational types of studies. Hence, for example, in a study for a shampoo manufacturer who wanted to position a brand in the cosmetic shampoo side of the market, in addition to the general criteria cited he wanted the name to suggest *beauty, softness, lightness, romance,* and *luxury*.

In sharp contrast, a washing machine manufacturer wanted to suggest *durability, engineering quality, speed, modernity*, and *reliability*.

Methods of researching the problem

As a rule, research itself is not effective in generating specific names for testing. However, background research does provide specific criterion information which is useful to the marketing executives and advertising agencies in their efforts at building up a preliminary list of names.

In our experience, one usually starts with a very long list of possible names which as a rule is too exhaustive to test. Hence, short-listing procedures are required. More often than not this step is conducted on the basis of judgment, though there is no reason, budget allowing, why the names should not be short-listed by means of a simple open-ended word association test for the entire list. At this point, it is as well to check-out the short list to ensure that no name is submitted to further testing which has previously been registered by a competitor or another company. A good deal of money and effort can be spent only to find at the end of it all that prior registration makes it impossible to use the winning name.

Testing the Short List

Pronunciation. Respondents can be asked to read aloud from a printed list the various names. Two features of the act can be usefully observed. First, the relative ease or difficulty the respondent encounters in saying the name aloud. Second, an indication can be made by the interviewer as to where the accent falls. Ideally, one likes a name which will usually be asked for in the same way.

Association Tests

One of the most useful procedures in name testing is the use of free association. The procedure consists of simply saying the name aloud to the respondent and asking him to give you all the thoughts and ideas that occur to him. Experience suggests that it is a good idea first to give the respondent a few words not related to the test by way of practice trials. Practice trials are important in that they familiarize the respondent with the task and serve as a learning experience for an act which many ordinary people find unusual. A further useful preliminary procedure is to give examples of what you want the respondent to do. Hence a typical introduction to the question might be, 'I'm going to say a number of words to you one at a time. After each word I say I want you to tell me the first word or thought that pops into your mind; for example, if I say 'hot' you might say 'cold'; if I say 'sweet' you might say 'bitter'. Alright, now when I say ———— what pops into your mind?' (It is at this point that the trial or warm-up words are introduced.)

Two types of information should be recorded. First, though less important, is the amount of time (using a stopwatch) that the respondent takes in responding. Second, the actual verbatim response.

An analysis of the time it takes to respond may be significant. An average response time is worked out for the entire list. This is compared with the mean time for each name. If a name yields a time factor which is significantly larger than average it gives reason for concern because very slow reaction times are usually indicative of blocking or emotional complexes of an unconscious nature. However, by far the most important feature of this part of the test is the content analysis. Here one can determine the extent to which the name induces:

(a) positive/negative tendencies;
(b) imagery which may be related or unrelated;
(c) spontaneous product expectancies if such emerge.

In this type of research, rotation of name presentation from respondent to respondent is particularly important, since it is known that the responses to some extent will be influenced by the previous stimuli.

After eliciting spontaneous associations to the names we have found it useful to get respondents to anticipate the kind of product that each name might represent. Here it is best to start with open-ended procedures, e.g. 'Some of the words I've read out to you are in fact names for products. Now for each name I read out to you could you try to guess what product or products it might be a name for?'. After a question on product anticipation using open-ended procedures one might repeat the question requiring the respondent to select from a list the product that each name might represent. (It is as well to point out to the respondent that he can use the same product on the list more than once if he so desires.)

Anticipated imagery

By far the most important aspect in name research is to establish the kind of imagery that the name in itself will elicit in terms of the specific criteria discussed previously. A multiple choice type of association test similar to the procedure used for packaging research might be employed. The respondent would be given a printed list of the brand names and asked to say to which of the names a series of statements (read out by the interviewer) most applied. Analysis of these data will give the researcher and client a good indication of the extent to which the test names will contribute to the desired imagery profile for the brand.

The Common Requirements for Successful Name and Packaging Research

There are a number of similarities between the performance required of an appropriate brand name and an appropriate package. In both cases there is need for functional excellence. The chosen name must be easy to read and to pronounce. The chosen pack must be capable of containing and protecting the product, and of allowing it to be extracted as necessary. And it must also have visual impact.

In addition, however, it is essential for both to perform well in terms of projecting desirable and appropriate associations and imagery in relation to the product and its use in certain circumstances or by certain types of people; and these associations and imagery *must* be consistent with what is required by the total marketing plan of which these two elements form parts. It follows, therefore, that the first step in setting up research in either format is to establish precisely what marketing objectives and strategy have been decided upon.

18. Research on 'below the line' expenditure

Martin Simmons

This chapter deals with the contribution of research, both in the planning and evaluation, of 'below the line' activity. Any definition of 'below the line' assumes a false dichotomy since many promotions are dependent on media advertising. This would be so, for example, when reduced offers are backed by national press advertising. In the current context 'below the line' expenditure is defined to include the following, whether or not they are supported by media advertising:

(a) any in-store promotional activity to the consumer such as premium offers, reduced price offers, stamps and coupons, competitions and banded packs;
(b) any trade incentives or discounts to the retailer;
(c) all display material whether in support of specific promotions or not;
(d) any point-of-scale aids such as leaflets, brochures, store demonstrations;
(e) any direct promotion to the consumer such as couponing or free samples.

Expenditure on items such as sales force incentive schemes and sponsorships is excluded for the purpose of this chapter.

The Growth of 'Below the Line' Expenditure

There are three trends in British retailing which have placed increasing emphasis on 'below the line' activity. The first is the development of self-service techniques, especially in the grocery trade. Self-service retailing now accounts for 90% of grocery turnover and is becoming increasingly important in other retail outlets such as chemists, confectioners, hardware stores and off-licences. Any self-service operation lends itself naturally to 'below the line' activity. The manufacturer has to ensure that his goods are noticed and subsequently purchased. The second trend is the increasing concentration of retail trade into a smaller number of outlets, about 2% of stores accounting for over one-third of the grocery trade. Manufacturers spend vast sums of money to secure a favourable position at the point-of-sale, particularly at these key outlets. The third trend is the ever-increasing range of brands from which the consumer has to choose. To identify his brand from the competition, the manufacturer resorts to varied forms of promotion as well as media advertising.

There are no validated figures for the size, in monetary terms, of 'below the line' activity but the growth has been substantial in the last decade. If all 'below the line' activity is included, expenditure now probably exceeds that of media advertising.

Planning 'Below the Line' Activity

The problems facing an advertiser in planning his 'below the line' activity can be classified into four broad categories:

(a) *Budget allocation*—he has to decide for, possibly, a range of products on the optimum allocation of limited resources. What part of his promotional expenditure should be made on television, press, and other media and what part should be spent 'below the line'?
(b) *Setting promotional objectives*—what exactly is the aim of the promotional activity? It is necessary to distinguish between retail objectives which can be regarded as 'intermediate' such as increasing shelf space, and final consumer objectives which are 'ultimate' in the sense of actual sales?
(c) *Pre-testing*—the next problem involves pre-testing the promotional plan in order to evaluate its likely success, or which of several possible tactics should be adopted. In practice, this normally means pre-testing the components of the promotional plan, i.e. the individual promotions.
(d) *Post-assessment*—having decided on a certain level and form of 'below the line' expenditure, how effective has this been? The manufacturer will want to assess whether or not his objectives have been achieved.

The allocation of budgets for 'below the line' expenditure is often not planned on any scientific basis. Because of the difficulty of creating a marked division above and below the line, there is a tendency to consider an overall promotional budget. Then portions are hived off for 'below the line' activity as and when needed. This philosophy is encouraged by the reluctance of some advertising agents to fit 'below the line' into their services and functions.

Budget allocation and the setting of promotional objectives for 'below the line' activity are inseparably linked, and equally liable to neglect in forward planning. Many marketing executives would have difficulty if asked to define exactly what a specific promotion is designed to achieve. It can be argued that the aim of any promotional activity is to increase sales, either short-term or long-term. The advantage of more precise objectives is that they can determine the most appropriate promotional techniques to be used. Some examples of possible promotional objectives and techniques are shown below.

Promotional objective	*Technique*
(a) To encourage consumer trial of a new product or pack size.	Product sampling.
(b) To clear old stock prior to brand re-launch or main promotional campaign.	Consumer offer, e.g., plastic daffodils for two packs.
(c) To widen retail distribution prior to commencement of media advertising.	Trade discounts.
(d) To obtain prime display position in key outlets.	Trade bonusing backed by special display units.
(e) To maintain display space in key outlets.	Self-liquidating consumer offer.
(f) To encourage consumer purchasing across a range of, e.g., soup flavours.	Money-back consumer offer, e.g., 20p postal order for five packs of different flavours.
(g) To emphasize a new variety, e.g., a flavour of soup.	As above, requiring two of the packs to be of the new flavour.
(h) To combat competitive pressure; blocking the competition.	Price cuts.
(i) To stimulate repeat purchasing.	On-pack coupon, i.e., money off on next purchase.
(j) To widen consumer interest in a brand.	Competition.

The Contribution of Research

While many stages of marketing activity are scientifically planned and researched, the influences on consumer purchasing have been widely neglected at perhaps the most vital point of all, the point of sale. A survey on point of sale, carried out in 1966 by Industrial Facts and Forecasting on behalf of Abbey Goodman Display Limited revealed that fewer than one company in ten has ever assessed point-of-sale effectiveness on a systematic basis; more than a decade later the situation has hardly changed. Relatively little research is being conducted on promotional activity despite the fact that 'below the line' expenditure now exceeds traditional media expenditure. Decisions still tend to be based on experience, competitive activity, and hunch. Some reasons for the slow development of research into promotional activity are:

(a) lack of clear promotional objectives to measure;
(b) vested interests; i.e. those with the function of promotional planning at advertiser and agency level resisting the entry of research into a traditionally creative area;
(c) the *ad hoc* nature of many aspects of promotional activity which does not allow for long-term conclusions to be drawn for future promotional planning;
(d) the apparent limitations of time and confidentiality when pre-testing any parts of a promotional plan. This is due to the tight schedules (or lack of forward planning) operating and the fear of any 'leak' to the competition.

There are also doubts about the validity of research on promotional activity coupled with the failure of research agencies to develop and convincingly market appropriate techniques. These techniques, their applications and their limitations are described under the following headings:

(a) budget allocation;
(b) pre-testing;
(c) post-assessment.

Research: budget allocation

The problem here is what part of advertising expenditure should be made 'below the line' or, more specifically, on point-of-sale activities. Research has contributed very little to this decision and certainly no available technique can give an exact figure for the appropriation to be allocated to point-of-sale activities. The decision is clearly not a simple matter of statistics. Media advertising is often an important strategic weapon to use with retailers to gain distribution. Also point-of-sale advertising can act as a reminder of a message previously got across by other media. We are back to the extreme difficulty of introducing an artificial line between media and other promotional activity. Nevertheless, a premise which is gaining acceptance is that point-of-sale activities should be concentrated on product groups where the impulse sector is high. That is where the brand, and often the product purchased, is decided inside the store. Research can contribute by assessing the magnitude of the impulse sector. Shoppers can be interviewed before and immediately after purchase.

The expenditure on a product can then be divided into four sectors:

(a) *Specifically planned*—product and brand known before the shopper arrives at the store;
(b) *Substituted*—specifically planned but brand substituted in the store;

(c) *Generally planned*—the shopper knew the product, but not the brand, before arriving at the store;

(d) *Unplanned*—the shopper had no intention of buying the product when arriving at the store.

This information establishes the relative influence on the purchase of store factors. Research conducted by the Gallup Poll in conjunction with the Association of Point of Sale Advertising showed the level of impulse purchasing across a range of products illustrated in Table 18.1. A limitation of this method is that it can only be applied to 'quick-moving' product categories, otherwise the expense of interviewing shoppers at the retail outlets is prohibitively expensive. For less frequently purchased products, research methods, relying on a reconstruction of buying behaviour at a single-call interview can be used to establish the importance of impulse buying. Before deciding how much to spend at the point of sale, it seems relevant for a manufacturer at least to find out what part of brand expenditure is decided there. This information can only be used as a broad guideline, indicating whether more attention is warranted to 'below the line' activities in a particular market or not. It can be used to avoid the situation where 60% of consumer brand decision is made at the point-of-sale, and 15% of the promotional budget is spent 'below the line' and vice versa.

Another consideration on budget allocation is whether the brand is growing, static or declining. With a growing brand, promotions have an element of investment in encouraging trial and, thereafter, repurchase. With

Table 18.1

	Product expenditure	Specifically planned	Substituted	Generally planned	Unplanned	Impulse sector
Breakfast cereals	100	52	19	13	16	48
Brown bread	100	38	10	24	28	62
Butter	100	65	13	13	9	35
Cakes and pastries	100	17	4	37	42	83
Canned cat food	100	61	11	17	11	39
Canned dog food	100	62	9	18	11	38
Canned milk pudding	100	45	6	17	32	55
Canned soup	100	55	10	12	23	45
Chocolate confectionery	100	16	5	29	50	84
Frozen foods:						
Burgers	100	45	5	11	39	55
Fish fillets	100	43	5	24	28	57
Fish fingers	100	43	7	21	29	57
Green beans	100	45	5	18	32	55
Mousse	100	39	2	16	43	61
Peas	100	61	4	18	17	39
Instant coffee	100	59	9	12	20	41
Instant milk powder	100	60	4	5	31	40
Margarine	100	73	6	10	11	27
Meat and vegetable extract	100	48	8	6	38	52
Paper handkerchiefs	100	18	20	25	37	82
Paper kitchen towels	100	48	12	23	17	52
Soft tissue toilet rolls	100	33	9	29	28	67
Tea (not tea bags)	100	70	8	9	13	30

static or declining brands, this is unlikely to be true and promotions may have to justify themselves in terms of short-term payoff. A further factor determining 'below the line' expenditure is the marketing situation. Again, there is an investment element in a new product launch or a major product relaunch, compared with the continuing activities connected with an ongoing brand.

Research pre-testing

There are various techniques which exist for pre-testing either with the consumer or the retail store the likely success of promotional activity. These tests can be carried out on a wide variety of materials ranging from verbal concepts to actual examples of the promotion. These techniques can be classified into:

(a) group discussions;
(b) hall tests;
(c) van tests;
(d) mini-van tests;
(e) postal and door-to-door tests;
(f) pre-testing the advertising of promotions;
(g) in-store tests.

The first six of these methods are consumer based for the very good reason that they tend to be easy, quick and cheap to operate. They are designed to give a reliable indication of the relative levels of likely consumer acceptance of a given set of promotional ideas or propositions. This may be further divided into two parts; first, which is the most likely to succeed of a list of possible ideas; and second, how successful is the best one likely to be.

Group discussions. Before considering any kind of quantitative research, a company will often make use of group discussions with their likely target group to test concepts and ideas. Groups may be used to:

(a) glean ideas for promotions which could warrant further consideration and research;
(b) assess which of several promotional ideas should be pursued, and which should be discounted as completely unacceptable.

Group discussions should be used only as a first filter and never interpreted as a final quantified result.

Hall Tests. Hall tests can be used to sort out which one is the most likely to succeed out of several similar possibilities. The hall test would usually be employed to pre-test such offers as free gifts, extra-size packs, on and in-pack premiums, and with-pack premiums. The methodology usually involves bringing a sample of target consumers into a hall or theatre and asking them to rate alternative offers in rank order. Briefly, the procedure of hall tests to pre-screen promotional items is as follows: a ranking of, say, six possible items, consumers are invited to take part at the hall on a particular day; the interviewers ask the respondents which items they like best, which second best and so on, and which they would not be interested in at all. The sample size is usually 100 to 150, which is sufficient to indicate the favourably and unfavourably considered. In the items to be tested it is advisable to include a control item, an item that has performed well in the past and, consequently, will give a relative measure of success and failure. The following points need to be built in to the test for the results to be of value:

(a) a maximum of eight items—large numbers would confuse the housewife and produce distorted ranking;
(b) the items to be tested should be of a similar cost to give the company a basis for decision;
(c) items should be of a similar nature—gimmicky items should not be tested against practical ones. Although the housewife may prefer the gimmicky items, she will be reluctant to admit so in the interview situation;
(d) only certain types of promotional ideas may be tested in the hall test. Money-off offers, for instance, will always be ranked the highest alongside other ideas.

The hall test may also be used effectively to test differing designs of the same proposed offer, e.g. drinking glasses or table mats.

Van Tests.   In this instance a motorized caravan can be parked in a busy shopping area. Respondents would then be invited into the van to take part in similar tests to those carried out in hall tests. The advantage over the hall test for this technique is that larger samples of respondents can be obtained for the same field costs.

Mini-van Tests.   A more sophisticated method was pioneered by Research Bureau Ltd. Promoted items are sold through vans calling at homes and the extent of buying each item is recorded to assess their likely success. The mini-van sets out to provide as closely as possible an actual retail sales situation within which promotions can be tested. To that extent, it is similar to store testing.

Postal and Door-to-Door Tests.   The postal method consists of a panel of consumers to which the promotional offer is sent by post. It is then possible to assess the likely success of an offer or the relative success of offers by recording the extent to which the panel members buy the offer or offers. Information would also be collected on the types of consumers who are liable to take up a particular offer. This type of test does not necessarily have to be carried out by post. It is possible, for example, to place by distributing door to door and then measure the effects of couponing, sampling, etc., by recording returns or by re-interview.

Pre-testing the Advertising of Promotions.   It is useful before embarking on a large-scale promotion to pre-test supporting advertising and display material which may have an effect on the success or failure of a promotion. The aim of this is two-fold.

(a) Is the advertising and what it has to say readily understood?
(b) Is the approach attracting the target consumers?

Tests can be carried out with consumers to assess these aims and can check whether the advertising is likely to have an adverse effect on the brand's image, even though it may persuade people to buy in the short-term. These tests may involve using the same pre-testing techniques as for ordinary display advertising (referred to in another chapter).

In-store Tests.   In-store tests are offered by a number of research companies in this country. The in-store test is a natural progression from hall tests and van tests, in that the items for offer that did well in these tests may now be put on the market-place. This will provide a useful indicator in a realistic situation of likely market sales. There are two main methods which can be employed both based on the technique of retail auditing:

(a) two panels of stores, one with the promotion or particular activity that is béing tested and the other panel as a control. The success of the promoted item is measured by the sales achieved compared with the control item;
(b) alternatively, the two items (promoted and control item) are rotated within the same panel of stores. This reduces any error which may arise from using two matching panels. The disadvantage is the extra administrative work involved in switching the items so that both are tested in the same store within the test period.

In-store tests, unlike hall tests, can also be used to assess the effect of price changes, different shelf space allocations, changes in display material and variations in display position. The tests can involve a particular promotional activity versus no promotion, e.g. a banded pack tested against the normal marketing situation. Or they can involve an assessment of two possible promotions, e.g. two different self liquidators, or $1\frac{1}{2}$p off tested against 1p off normal price. Most forms of promotional activity can be tested in-store but there are certain limits. It is not possible to take account, in the pre-test situation, of promotions which, when they go national, are going to get media backing. The test, if carried out, cannot measure the influence of television or press support. It is also difficult to pre-test competitions and contests, since this involves giving away the prizes which can result in an expensive piece of research. Additionally, the main practical problem in these tests is to ensure that all other variables are controlled throughout its duration. It is essential that each test item is examined in exactly equal competitive situations. To achieve this, complex designs have been developed using, for example, Latin squares. These are more complicated to administer but achieve a tighter control of outside variables.

Research: post-assessment

The case for not assessing the effect of promotional activity is that it cannot be measured quantitatively because there exist in the market-place too many other variables which are difficult to isolate. This is a somewhat defeatist attitude emphasizing the problems and dismissing any possible solutions. Provided the objectives are clearly defined, measures can be found to assess their achievement. Outside variables may blur any assessment but allowance can be made for them, where necessary, in the interpretation.

Rather than have no assessment of promotional activity, it is preferable to develop research techniques whilst recognizing their uses and limitations. As in pre-testing of promotional activity the research methods are retail and consumer based.

Store Checks. Measures of effectiveness obtained from store checks can include:

(a) penetration achieved by the promoted product in the retail outlet, i.e. the number of stores handling the product;
(b) shelf space achieved by the promoted product in relation to competitive brands;
(c) penetration of display material; and its type and position.

All these statistics are relevant to a manufacturer who wants to assess his return on point-of-sale investment.

Retail Audits. All the above data can be obtained from retail audits. Additionally, sales data are collected from retail audits providing accurate information over specific time periods. However, identifying the sale of promoted items is generally very difficult because the timing of the retail checks may not fit in with the promotional activity, while competing promotions may overlap.

Consumer Research. Consumer research on aspects of 'below-the-line' activity must not be considered as an alternative to retail research. The retail research can be used effectively to answer a number of important questions on distribution, sales and stock cover but it provides no information about the target audience. It then becomes necessary to research the important questions of, for instance, who are the buyers taking up the promotion?, are they existing or new buyers?, will they or have they repeated their purchase of this brand or product?, is there an increase in the rate of buying per buyer resulting from the promotion?, how did buyers come to take up the promotion in the first place?, does the promotion affect the shopper's attitude towards the brand? These are some of the numerous questions that the manufacturer will ask when planning his promotional strategy and the consumer techniques available at the present time can, and do, provide some of the answers.

Consumer Panels. The consumer panel is one of the more important methods of obtaining the relevant data and has a great advantage over other methods in that the information is continuous over time. Parfitt and McGloughlin[2] described the use of consumer panels in evaluating promotional activity. They state that the consumer panel is valuable for three basic reasons.

(a) It measures consumer purchasing behaviour accurately and sensitively.
(b) It measures this on a continuous basis to gain information over time.
(c) It is possible to ascertain accurate information on when purchases are made.

They also outline the practical difficulties involved which may obscure the relationship between promotional activity and sales. Again, three factors are basically involved:

(a) Consumer purchasing behaviour is extremely complex in that individual rates of buying a product may change continuously in what appears a relatively static market.
(b) Competitive activity may have a blurring effect and, for one brand, individual promotions can and do overlap with each other. This makes it more difficult to isolate the effect of a particular promotion.
(c) The objective of a promotion, as in advertising, may not be to increase sales in the short-term but rather to maintain a share or halt a declining share of the market.

It may be necessary to measure the extent of repeat purchasing some time after the promotion to establish whether the initial purchase has been followed up by a repeat purchase, and the relationship of repeat buying by 'new' buyers to those original buyers already using the brand. This can be observed from consumer panel data. The model developed by Ehrenberg and Goodhardt[3] is based on a theoretical framework. Basically, it states that in a 'stationary' market the average rate of buying per buyer is constant. The model takes actual sales and predicts what would have happened without the promotion. The difference is the effect of the promotion. As Barnes, McDonald and Tuck[4] point out, the limitation of this method is that it can only be applied in 'stationary' markets, and in a market undergoing change a control panel would be needed. One advantage of this method is that it eliminates the necessity of controlled experiments and consequently reduces the expense.

Impulse Buying.   The share that a brand achieves of impulse purchases is largely determined by its point-of-sale activities—its retail distribution, shelf space, display, pricing and other promotional activities[5]. One measure, therefore, of the success of these activities is the share taken by a brand of impulse purchases in the product category. Expenditure on a product group can be segmented as described earlier. We can look at the brand's position in the two broad sectors of the market—the planned sector and the impulse sector where the brand is decided in the store; for example, a brand may have a 24% share of the impulse sector. This can be taken as a bench mark *prior* to promotional activity; and a similar look can be taken at the market at a later date to assess the brand share of impulse purchases *after* the promotional campaign. The advantage of this technique is that it removes the planned sector, which is largely dictated by media advertising, from any evaluation. This argument is rather tenuous in markets where promotional activity is supported by media advertising.

Appraisal and Limitations of these Techniques

Pre-testing

Qualitative and quantitative research should be regarded as a means, despite their limitations, of reducing the risk of failure. Relatively small expenditure on research, prior to embarking on the expense of the promotional campaign, can enhance the likelihood of success. The consumer and retail pre-tests are complementary rather than competitive in the sense that ideas and offers that have been successfully screened in group discussions, hall tests and van tests may then be tested in stores. The limitations of consumer pre-tests are:

(a) The methods do not measure accurately what is likely quantitatively to take place in the actual market situation. They cover preferences and attitudes but should not be used to forecast potential sales.
(b) They cannot be used for certain types of promotional activity, e.g. price changes, display positions, shelf space allocation, etc.

The limitations of in-store pre-tests are:

(a) They are difficult to control.
(b) They tell you nothing about the consumer, e.g. whether the promotion is attracting new buyers or people who would have bought the item anyway. This limitation can sometimes be overcome by linking in-store consumer interviews to the test.
(c) There is also a limit to the type of promotional activity that can be tested, as described earlier.

Despite these limitations, the present pre-test methods do go a long way in helping the manufacturer to assess the likely success or failure of promotional activity. It is a small price to pay for what could turn out to be an expensive failure.

Post-assessment

The main problem in any post-assessment of promotional activity is that of isolating all other variables such as seasonal effect and competitor activity. Controls can sometimes be set up but these are normally expensive and not always appropriate. The practical answer to this problem is to deal with outside variables in the interpretation of the results, making due allowances according to the particular circumstances.

The retail audit has limitations:

(a) The timing of a retail audit, e.g. bi-monthly, may not fit in with the promotional activity. Promotions often last only two to four weeks.
(b) Retail audits are highly organized and inflexible. It may be impractical or expensive to adapt an ongoing service to the specific needs of promotional assessment.
(c) Retail audits provide no information about the consumer, e.g. on repeat buying behaviour.

Consumer panels do not provide information on certain in-store activity, e.g.:

(a) retail distribution;
(b) display penetration;
(c) the penetration achieved by a promotion.

The objectives of the promotional activity and the criteria for success must, therefore, be defined. The criteria taken determine whether retail checks, consumer panels or both are appropriate to measure the effect.

Future Development

The contribution of research to 'below-the-line' planning and evaluation has not progressed in recent years mainly because of the resistances outlined earlier. Investment in new research techniques has been at a low ebb in the 1970's either because the demand is not apparent or because research companies are unwilling to invest in order to stimulate a possible latent demand. Possibilities that still remain to be explored are as follows.

Shelf Space Allocation. What is the relationship between shelf space and brand share? It would be very useful for a manufacturer or a retailer to be able to assess what shelf space he requires to achieve a target level of sales. The evidence of some work carried out suggests that in high-impulse markets shelf space tends to equate with brand share or, putting it very simply, to get

20% brand share you need 20% of shelf space. In low-impulse markets however, e.g. margarine, a high brand share can be achieved with a relatively low share of shelf space. In such markets, consumer brand loyalty is high and impulse purchasing is low. The shopper knows what she wants before she gets to the store and the manufacturer must get his brand across at that stage. In the store, the manufacturer does not necessarily require shelf space exactly pro rata to brand share provided his brand is currently one of the leaders. Shelf space allocation requires a great deal of researching and could be rewarding.

Data Bank. Another important question (the answer to which depends upon the particular situation at the time and also the creative aspect) is what type of promotion seems to work best for particular objectives in a particular product field. If a sufficient backlog of information were available about different types of promotional activity in different product fields, it would be possible to draw some useful conclusions about what type of promotion seems to achieve a particular objective best.

Trade Reaction. Research can also help to avoid waste by getting trade reaction to a new promotion at an early state. Many promotions have failed, not because of lack of appeal to the consumer, but because the trade would not accept them. Too often this is found out when large sums of money have already been spent.

With the growth of promotions 'tailor made' for specific major multiple retailers, the most fruitful area for research development would appear to be an independent research means of testing trade reaction at chief buyer level to their suppliers. Promotional activity would be one of many aspects of trade relations that could be monitored.

19. Market testing and experimentation

John Davis

One major function of market research is to provide a feedback of information from the market to the manufacturer or distributor. This information shows the state the market is in as a result of the marketing strategies currently being applied to the various competing brands. Taken together with other relevant data, such as the observations and impressions of the executives concerned, this provides the basis on which the company can take its decisions about continuing or changing the strategies for its existing brands, or developing strategies for new brands.

As long as the possible alternative strategies remain mostly within the company's existing field of experience, the likely outcome of changing from one strategy to another can sometimes be assessed sufficiently accurately for the purpose of making a decision *without* conducting extensive additional research. It may be possible to base the decision on judgment alone, but more often it will be necessary to supplement this by various types of pre-testing research. However, problems can still arise even where the company knows the field well and, once it moves outside its existing range of experience, pre-testing is very unlikely to provide a sufficient guide to the likely results of introducing a given change into the market. The company will then need to carry out some form of market testing or experimentation in order to gain the additional experience required to make its marketing decisions, in some cases merely to form an initial assessment of whether a project is worth carrying further; in other cases major planning and investment decisions may depend on the results. Some may be concerned with comparing the relative effects of two or more alternative courses of action open to a company, others only with assessing the effects of a single proposed course of action. Projections of the scale of effects in a wider market may be required, or merely a 'better, no-change, worse' result. A whole new product and its marketing plan may be involved in a test-launch, or only a single factor in the marketing mix of an existing product.

The difference between this type of experimentation and the various forms of pre-testing is that the changes and innovations are generally introduced into the market through the normal channels of communication or distribution—through normal advertising media and retail stores. Any effects are then measured among a population who have been exposed to the media and who have made their preference and purchasing decisions in the normal way. Experimenting under these conditions is generally expensive, and there is a marked rise in costs as a project moves out of the pre-testing stage into a marketing experiment. As a result of this step in costs, a number of attempts have been made to provide 'mini-testing' marketing facilities which, while sacrificing some of the benefits of full-scale testing, provide the means of obtaining some key information and measurements at much lower costs. One development has been the establishment of panels of housewives who are visited by a mobile shop or van and from which they can make purchases of a range of foods and household products. By calling on the same housewives regularly through time and recording their purchases on each occasion, details of their buying patterns, and any alterations in them through an experimental change or innovation, can be built up. Hence, for a comparatively small outlay on stocks and research a manufacturer can gain information on such key factors as the rate of repurchase among triers of a new product. While the results may not be adequate to provide a firm forecast for the total market, they will indicate whether the project is worth proceeding with in its present form, either through immediate introduction or through more extensive testing in the market. Similar limited testing facilities are also available among retail outlets, special panels of stores being set up in which to experiment with new products, pricing, etc.

The remainder of this chapter is concerned with the principles and problems of the more general larger-scale forms of marketing experiments, but as will be seen later, considerations of the costs and risks involved may frequently indicate the advisability of moving through some form of initial exploration before becoming committed to a major experiment.

Practicability of Testing

With some projects a company may not have the option of testing in the market, since production or other constraints may preclude the possibility of introducing the proposed changes into only some parts of a market in advance of a total market decision. It may, for example, be impossible to produce a new product in quanties sufficient to supply a test area without building a plant capable of producing on a national basis; or of adapting the style or design of an existing product without changing the whole output. It may be impossible, because of overlapping and interlocking channels of distribution, to vary trade terms or prices within test areas without serious repercussions on the total market, and so on.

484

The competitive situation in a market may frequently inhibit any experimentation, because this will reveal company planning or product formulation. Competitors may then react and, if the time necessary to take counter-activity or even copy the product is short, be the first to launch on the wider market. In any case, much of the experience to be gained from an experiment by one company can be frequently acquired by competitors if they merely observe and measure the effects for themselves. One advantage of some forms of mini-testing referred to above is that they preclude competitive access to the results.

If such problems cannot be overcome then the possibilities of mounting specific experiments do not exist. For the purposes of this chapter, however, it is assumed that an experiment is not precluded by such constraints.

Definition of the Problem

Seldom is the initial request for an experiment or test framed in a way that can lead to an effective plan. Frequently a great deal of questioning has to be done to establish the proper objectives of the experiment, and to quantify them sufficiently to determine such factors as the scale of the experiment or the precision required in the results. A client, for example, recently asked for help in designing an experiment to see whether a proposed display stand would be worth introducing into stores. The first question was whether the experiment was to cover the rate of trade acceptance and use of the stand, and possibly its life expectancy, or whether it should only cover the in-store effect of the stand when it was there. This is a vital planning question, since an experiment of the first type would have involved normal distribution through the sales force, large numbers of the stands, and heavy expenditure on display checks and store audits. The second type of experiment could have been carried out, in this market, with two matched panels of 20 stores and 20 display stands, and for a modest expenditure on auditing. The question had not previously been considered explicitly by the group concerned, and discussion immediately showed that some members were expecting only an in-store test, others the wider experiment.

A major problem area concerns the precision and type of results required and the uses to which they are to be put. A simple feasibility study to assess whether some project holds sufficient promise for further limited investment in it should not be allowed to become large or elaborate. At the other end of the scale, an experimental launch from which estimates are to be made of the likely effects in a wider market must be mounted with a great deal of careful planning, executed under properly managed conditions and measured in ways which will provide the required data. Dangers frequently arise when a modest experiment, designed perhaps merely to assess certain aspects of a complex situation, is then expected to provide forecasts for which it was not originally intended.

Examination of Existing Experience

Given that any experiment is a means of gaining experience, before any experiment is undertaken the question should be posed whether additional experience is necessary in order to arrive at an adequate decision. Because of the costs involved in a major marketing experiment, it should only be considered as a last resort when all other means of reaching a firm decision have failed. Consequently, before an experiment is started a rigorous reassessment of all available data and experience should be made, including the subjective assessments of those who know the market, to establish the range of the possible profits or losses which might arise from the marketing activity under consideration. Not infrequently this rigorous assessment based on existing experience shows that the entire range of possible results is profitable, or that the entire range is uprofitable. The latter result must mean that testing the project in its present form will be a waste of time and resources which would be better spent on some other activity. The former result (that all outcomes of the project would be profitable) should lead to immediate marketing without testing if the proposed course of action can only take one form, but there may still remain a need for experimenting if there is scope for variations in the project which would lead to different levels of profitability. If the optimum level cannot be prejudged but there are marked differences between the optimum level and other levels, further investigation of the value of experimenting is needed. If a manufacturer of a packaged product, for example, is considering whether or not to add a 3 lb pack above his existing range of sizes, and all assessments of the outcome are profitable, there is no point in an experiment. If, however, he is considering the more open question of introducing a new larger pack which could take one of a range of sizes, there might still be a case for experimenting in the market to get as near as possible to the most profitable new size.

Where the expected range of possible outcomes shows that some will be profitable but some will lead to losses, the company has three options. First, introduce the course of action fully into the market in the hope of success, but with the risk of losses. Experience is then gained after the events. Second, experiment by introducing the proposed course of action into one or more small parts of the proposed market, thus limiting the risks while experience is acquired, but at some cost. These costs may well include the loss of profits through delaying the introduction of a beneficial change into the wider market or the losses through the sacrifice of any lead time the company has achieved or even pre-emption by a competitor. Third, postpone or shelve the project, thus avoiding the risk of direct losses through failure, but accepting the risks that profits are being forgone through delay, and may be lost altogether through pre-emption.

At this stage we assume a decision to test, and examine some of the problems involved.

Types of Experimental Design

Basically, the normal principles of experimental design as described by Rothman in chapter 3 apply to marketing experiments, although there are frequently some practical limitations which prevent the full application of some more complex designs. Hence, experimental designs tend to be simple 'before and after' or 'side-by-side' designs, and generally without replication, so that each treatment and control appears only in a single area.

In 'before and after' experiments the relevant results are measured in the selected area before and after the introduction of the innovation or change, and comparisons are made between the readings. Since other conditions in the market may cause changes beyond those due to the experiment itself, a control area (in which the experimental measurements are made but no experimental action is taken) is normally needed to arrive at a sound interpretation of the results. Hence, even simple 'before and after' experiments tend to become comparative or 'side-by-side' experiments anyway. Not infrequently a control area can be found among marketing areas already being measured and analysed in normal continuous research.

Comparative tests, where the relative merits of two or more different 'treatments' are to be assessed, call for designs in which the treatments can be run side by side in different areas although there is no need for the selected areas to be contiguous. To avoid wrong conclusions a control area free of any experimental stimulus is again needed, as one recent set of results showed. Here, the introduction of two experimental methods of promotion into separate areas was followed by uniform increases in sales of about 10%. Without further information the conclusion would have appeared to be that the introduction of either method into the market would be beneficial. Fortunately, a control was used, because this showed a rise in sales of the same magnitude but without any experimental stimulus. Some other factor, in this case probably the weather, was affecting the market, and this could only be detected, at least in the short-run, by the inclusion of a control area in the design of the experiment.

Because the individual areas used in experiments, whether towns, television areas or other units, may vary in their initial pre-test states and in their reactions to an experiment, the ideal design of any type calls for the placing of each experimental treatment in a number of areas. This is particularly so in comparative tests. However, in the great majority of marketing experiments such replication of the design is not administratively or financially possible, and operations are limited to single areas. This is a condition which generally has to be accepted—although every opportunity should be taken to use multi-area designs—but it should never be forgotten. To some extent, and given adequate background data, some of the risks involved in single-area tests can be reduced in the later stages leading to forecasts (referred to later in this chapter) but this again is only a poor substitute for proper multi-area testing.

An alternative method of attempting to overcome the problems posed by the variability of sales or other factors between areas has been to create facilities for mounting some types of test with the different treatments, or treatment and control, within the *same* geographic area or market. The method is particularly applicable to experimenting with different advertising campaigns or media schedules, and much of the early development was undertaken by the Advertising Laboratory which operated in Milwaukee up to 1971. There, by split-running and then controlling the distribution of the local newspaper within its distribution area, and (more importantly) by using an electronic device known as a 'muter' to cut out reception of certain television commercials in selected households, matched panels of households or people living close together in the same general environment could be subjected to different advertising campaigns or schedules. Any effects on purchasing patterns could then be measured, and they would be free of any inherent 'between-area' difference.

The Milwaukee Ad-Lab suffered from two limitations basic to any system using muters. First the muters have to be attached to the television sets in homes willing to participate in the research. The costs limit the sizes of the panels which can be established, and the only people who are subject to the changes in the television advertising are those in panel homes. Hence the number of respondents available for research is limited, and data collection is normally restricted to the use of purchase diaries. Second, the muters can only mute the transmitted commercial to prevent it being seen or heard by selected households; there can be no substitution of an alternative signal, whether an alternative commercial or something else, and the screen is merely left blank for the duration of the suppressed commercial. Exposure to different campaigns in different samples of homes can therefore only be brought about by selective suppression of different commercials within a master schedule which in most cases involves booking more airtime in total. This introduces a number of logistical and other problems.

A more flexible system free from the limitations of the muter has been developed in other cities in the USA, making use of the Community Antenna Television (CATV) systems and their associated cables distributing the incoming signal to sets in homes. Here it was realized that if, instead of the normal single cable system linking homes to the antenna, a double or split cable was used, alternate blocks or individual homes within an area could be fed from each. By introducing appropriate switchgear and signal generators into the system it was possible to feed different schedules or different campaigns into homes on a chequer-board pattern throughout a city.

488

Measurements of results could then be made with a sufficient reservoir of people for any combinations of diary panel research or successive surveys on independent samples of the population.

So far, for a number of reasons, including legal problems, these methods are not available in the UK although several possibilities have been discussed and investigated. It is however still to be hoped that these difficulties can be overcome, because in appropriate circumstances the facility of being able to run two different schedules or campaigns within the same community affords a more powerful experimental design than the use of geographically separate areas.

The Scale of Experiments

Three main sets of factors operate to determine the appropriate scale for an experiment. These are the physical requirements to mount the experiment at all, the research requirements to provide adequate measurements, and the risks and costs of success or failure.

Physical requirements include such factors as availability of advertising media, the use of administratively coherent sales or depot areas, or that the experimental areas shall absorb a given proportion of capacity if production or packaging lines have to be modified to provide the necessary materal. Such factors may place either upper or lower limits to the scale of an experiment, and may, on occasion, rule out the possibility of an experiment of the desired type. Thus, an experimental launch heavily dependent on television advertising may not be possible if available production facilities could only supply a few dozen stores.

The *research requirements* will set lower limits to the scale in terms of the number of areas needed and the populations of consumers or stores within them. Hence, they will depend on the extent to which the market varies between areas, on the current or expected levels of distribution and consumer usage, the magnitude of any expected changes or results, and the precision with which the results are to be measured.

Where the research requirements call for experimentation on a scale above the limits set by the physical factors, then the experiment must either be abandoned or its objectives modified. On the other hand, the research need not, and often should not, cover the whole area into which the experimental stimulus is introduced; e.g., in test-launching a new product using television in the area covered by a single transmitter, it will normally be considered necessary to allow—if not impossible to prevent—distribution of the product to extend to the limits of transmission. If, then, research measurements are carried out over the whole transmission area, and this includes some overlap areas, the results will be diluted through the inclusion of outer areas in which the advertising is not achieving full impact. Hence, the research should be limited to the primary area, however far distribution may be carried.

489

The *risks and costs* of success or failure seldom receive the attention they merit in planning the scale of an experiment. The costs of research usually receive some attention, and they can normally be estimated in advance from quotations, whether for *ad hoc* work or for the use of the increasing number of packaged facilities. Such costs tend to depend far more on the design of the experiment than on the scale or the size of the areas used.

There are two other sets of possible costs, one of which will have been incurred by the end of the experiment (although in certain cases the costs may prove negligible). If the experiment leads to the project being introduced into the wider market, then there may have been some *loss of profits* during the period in which the project was held back from the main market awaiting the test results and a decision. This is not inevitable, e.g. when a test launch is carried out using pilot plant production and where the timing of the main launch depends on the completion of production facilities already under construction irrespective of the test; but whenever the introduction into a market of a profitable project is held back by the decision to test, there will be some loss of profits chargeable against the costs of the test. Taking time to test projects which are profitable always costs profits; but these opportunity costs can be reduced by carrying out the experiment, and thus avoiding this loss of profits, in a wider area.

Conversely, if the test results lead to the project being abandoned there will generally be *pull-out costs*. In some cases, such as in a test of a revised television schedule which has not affected media or production costs and which has failed to move the market share away from the line it would normally have followed, these may be insignificant. However, if the same experiment had led to a fall in market share, there would have been some loss of profits during the test and for such time afterwards as it took the market share to recover, plus the costs of any additional efforts put into the area to aid recovery. With test launches that fail, there may be considerable losses on plant and equipment, on materials and labour, and such costs as cleaning-up operations and uplifting stock in the areas used. These pull-out costs can be reduced by keeping the size of the experimental areas as *small* as other requirements permit.

It follows that, where the project is believed to have a high probability of succeeding, the ultimate costs of testing may be reduced by allowing the sizes of the areas used to increase. Where a project is believed to have a high probability of failure the area involved should be kept to a minimum or key factors in the situation tested first on some more limited basis.

In some cases a rolling launch, in which the project is introduced through time into successive marketing areas across the country, may be the appropriate form for an 'experiment'. A company may be certain of gaining a profit, for example, from a new product if production is geared to the right level. Underproduction may kill the market, overproduction may kill the profit, and there may be a wide range between the available estimates of the upper and lower limits of potential sales. In these circumstances, if other

490

factors are favourable, a logical plan would be to install capacity to meet the lowest estimated total sales level, and to launch in a part of the market which could still be adequately supplied if the highest level of demand was reached. Treatment of this area as an experiment would then provide the data for planning any necessary expansion of production as the product was 'rolled-out' into the remainder of the market. As a corollary to this, if for other reasons concerned with production, manpower, cash-flow or whatever, a rolling launch is imposed on the marketing planning then, again, the patterns of development in the initial areas should be researched in the same way as for a test launch, to provide bases for forecasting and indications of failings or weaknesses in the marketing processes.

The Selection of Areas

The problem of selecting areas to be used in marketing experiments presents some difficulties. In an ideal situation the major market would be divided into areas on some suitable basis, and an adequate number of areas for use in the experiment and the control would be drawn at random. Unfortunately, this ideal method can seldom, if ever, be applied to marketing experiments for two major reasons. The first is that many of the areas which would appear as natural sub-units of the market are for one reason or another not suitable for particular experiments, e.g. in any experiment using television advertising in the UK the natural sub-units of the market tend to be the respective areas covered by the various program contractors. Some of these serve too large a part of the population to be generally economic as test areas, and they may put too large a slice of the market at risk in the event of a failure. Other areas may exhibit other characteristics which would make them unsuitable for use in particular tests. Consequently, only three or four may remain which can be classified as suitable. When towns are considered as test areas, a number may be rejected as too large or too small, or possess other features deemed unsatisfactory; the number remaining can again be very small.

The second reason is that random selection of the single areas within which most testing is conducted, or even two or three areas in exceptional cases, is too 'chancy' to be acceptable. The selection of only one or two areas at random for a test to be carried out only once does not allow the chance factors in random sampling to operate effectively. Hence, it becomes preferable to sample on a purposive basis, selecting each area for what it is known to be or to contain.

Logically, this leads to attempts to select areas for use in experiments and controls which are typical of the wider market, and which reflect within themselves the major characteristics of the wider market. This can be extended, where more than a single area is used, to selecting one typical of the north, one typical of the south, one hard-water area and one soft, and so on. In practice, however, it is doubtful whether there is a completely typical area in any market, because even after the usual comparisons have been made on demographic or economic bases it may still be found that particular relevant market parameters differ in the area from any 'national' pattern. Normally, then, the most that can be done is to ensure that the areas finally selected for an experiment are not widely atypical, and then to cope with moderate degrees of atypicality through more sophisticated methods of interpretation and projection.

In some situations where there is a choice between a number of areas, such as towns of medium size, some form of cluster analysis may be useful (see chapter 13). This has been used to divide towns into groups with similar characteristics, and one set of such clusters has been devised and published by Christopher[1]. If, then, a spread of towns is required to provide a range of results from a single set of experimental conditions introduced into a range of different environments, this can be achieved by selection from as many of the different groups as the resources permit. On the other hand, when comparing two or more alternative projects, or selecting pairs of towns for experimental and control use, selection is made *within* the groups.

A wide range of test market research and other facilities is offered by media owners in the UK, sometimes at specially favourable rates to users of the media concerned. Lists of such facilities available are published from time to time by the media owners themselves, by trade journals and advertising agencies.

Timing

Many tests and experiments suffer from being run over too short a time. Often, this is a condition imposed by other considerations, but not infrequently it arises from an inadequate appreciation of the time which may be needed for a project to produce an effect on the market at all or, having produced one, to reach a stable level. Where a new product is introduced into a market or where some additional activity is added to an existing marketing program, it is frequently found that sales will move to an initial level from which they subsequently decline before stabilizing. If, then, the experiment or the measurements associated with it are discontinued prematurely the final readings will still be above the stable level and misleading results may be obtained. An analysis of 141 test markets in the UK and USA, for example, carried out by the AC Nielsen Co., suggests that, after the first six months of testing, the chance of adequately predicting the final test market share (achieved at the end of 12 to 18 months) is only about 1 in 2. This rises to about 2 in 3 after eight months of testing. In the opposite situation, where some factor is being removed from a marketing program or is being diminished, such as the advertising appropriation or the frequency of representatives' calls, there can be an inertia effect, and the market can continue unchanged for some considerable time before any movement can be observed. In one case there was an interval of fifteen months between the complete withdrawal of advertising for an established brand and any fall in market share in the test areas.

When both sets of factors may occur together, as in experiments where one type of activity is substituted for another, extreme care is needed in interpretation and in deciding when an experiment can be terminated. If the benefits of introducing the new type of activity appear quickly and before any detrimental effects from removing the old activity, sales or other measures will show a rise irrespective of the real strengths of the two activities. Conversely, if removing the current activity leads quickly to a detrimental effect but it takes time for the effects of the new activity to appear, early sets of measurements will show falls from the previous level. In either case, the initial results may be seriously misleading and time must be allowed for the position to stabilize. In the ideal situation, apart from using a suitable area as a control in which the existing activity will continue unchanged, a further area should be utilized in which the existing activity is removed and not replaced by the new one, in order to observe the decay of the current activity effect. This, however, may be too drastic a solution to be acceptable.

Apart from endeavouring to ensure that adequate time is allowed for experimentation, two further points relating to the time factor should be considered during the planning and execution of the research. The first is concerned with saving time by making provision for projections from the early results to provide estimates of the way the market is likely to move in subsequent periods. For consumer goods, such projections are based on analyses of the build-up of penetration of the product concerned (either from scratch in the case of a new product or from base levels for existing products) and of the repeat buying patterns among buyers of the product concerned. For details the reader is referred to chapter 8.

The second point is that the experiment and its associated research and measurement should continue in the test areas after any decision to introduce the project into a wider area is taken. Then some warning will be obtained should any detrimental movement occur in the market at a later stage, and appropriate action can be initiated. There is also a supplementary benefit from such a procedure, in that the experimental areas may then be used for further experiments for which they are uniquely suitable, such as testing the second year's advertising for a new product in an area which has already completed its first year, or in testing other forms of follow-up activity.

Projections, Predictions, and Forecasts

The problem of converting the results observed in an experiment in a limited area into a assessment of what can be expected to happen if the project is introduced into the wider market is one of the most critical in marketing experimentation.

There is a range of experiments in which it may not be a vital concern, as in early feasibility studies of a new project or in some forms of pilot marketing where the emphasis is on ensuring that the more mechanical aspects of an operation will work efficiently. Even in those cases, however, where the development of wider market estimates may not have been part of the original brief, demands for some form of estimate will almost inevitably be made at later stages in the operation. In other cases the development of estimates of the likely effects of introducing the proposed course of action into a wider market is a prime requirement.

It is useful to differentiate between projection and prediction, and between the results of these processes and a forecast.

Projections are essentially simple means of obtaining estimates from test results. A brand share of $x\%$ in a test launch is merely projected to an estimate that $x\%$ of the wider market will be obtained; a rise in sales of y points as a result of an experimental promotion is projected to a rise of y points nationally, and so on. Straight projection is easy, but highly fallible, because there is an underlying assumption that 'all other things' will remain equal. Almost inevitably differences will be found between test areas and the wider market in such factors as demographic characteristics and the size of the target group, the existing penetration and rates of consumption of the product group, market shares of existing brands, shop populations, media coverage and so forth. These and other factors will tend to render the simple processes of projection inaccurate.

Predictions are the result of more complex series of calculations, in which some attempt is made to take account of the factors which vary between the test area and the wider market. An attempt is made to construct a 'model' of the situation in the experimental area from the relationships found between the level of sales, or whatever criterion is being used, and the other market factors such as the demographic structure of the population, the store population, the shares held by competing brands before and after the experiment and so forth. Once these relationships are established in the test area, then predictions of the likely results in a wider market can be calculated by inserting the wider market values of the other factors into the relationships. One simple model which has proved useful is based on calculations of the proportionate changes in existing brand shares before and after a test launch. The predicted new brand share is then calculated by applying these proportionate changes to the wider market shares held by the existing brands and subtracting from 100%.

If x_0, y_0 are the market shares held by brands X, Y in the test area prior to the test; x_1, x_1 are the test area brand shares after the test; X_0, Y_0 are the wider market shares of X, Y, when the new brand is introduced there; then T, the expected wider market share of the test brand, is given by:

$$T = 100 - \left(\frac{x_1}{x_0} \cdot X_0 + \frac{y_1}{y_0} \cdot Y_0 + \cdots \right) \%$$

Normally, only simple models can be built up from the results of a single experiment because data to quantify many of the possible relationships are lacking. Where, however, a company has been able to bring together larger amounts of data, either from experiments or from observations in the main market, and to establish relationships between the main marketing factors and the levels of sales, the resulting marketing models can be invaluable not only in the interpretation of the results but in the planning stages of experiments as well.

A *forecast* should be developed from the projections or predictions as a joint effort between the research team and the marketing team involved. At this stage the whole history of the experiment should be reviewed and allowance made in the forecast so far as possible for any factors which may have detracted from the integrity of the experiment—difficulties in maintaining supplies, the effects of competitive activity, problems with major multiple organizations and so forth. Beyond this, there may be elements in the situation whose effects are wholly 'unpredictable' however sophisticated a model may be used, such as knowledge that a new competitive product is to be launched, and allowances for such factors can only be made at this final stage of turning projections or predictions into forecasts.

One point which is often overlooked in forecasting from the effects of test launches or other experiments is that a time element should be incorporated. This is because the forecast needed for the main operation should be pitched at some point in the future, while the information on which it is based is inevitably historic. Failure to take due note of time trends has led to significant differences between projections and results in the past, and the need to have information on movements outside the test area, in other parts of the main market, calls for the establishment and measurement of a control—a factor which is often left out of the design of experimental launches.

It follows that, since results from test areas may not be related to the results likely to occur in a wider market by a simple relationship, comparisons between the results of different strategies tested in separate areas should only be made after forecasting to a national level. There is always the risk that, if comparisons are made between raw area results, different conclusions may be drawn. The only safe procedure is to produce forecasts from each individually before comparing the results, in order to remove as far as possible any specific area influences.

Establishing the Appropriate Test Conditions

The application of experience gained in experiments to wider markets or at later periods depends for its justification on the experience being valid. To be valid the experience must, among other things, have been generated under appropriate conditions, and setting up such appropriate conditions is probably one of the more difficult aspects of many marketing experiments.

In bald terms, the object of experiments is to create in a small area a prescribed set of conditions. In a full-scale experiment this normally means establishing as nearly as possible the conditions under which the project will be introduced into a wider market, in order to measure the effects. In the most complex case of an experimental launch this involves introducing the proposed product with the proposed advertising material used in the proposed media, and backed by promotions, offers, the activities of the sales force and any other factors at appropriate levels. If the experiment is to succeed it is necessary to look at each of these factors carefully to see precisely what is needed in the test areas and what can be achieved.

With the physical factors, such as the product or the pack, achieving comparability with what will be marketed on a wider scale may not be difficult—although it is not always easy. The product from a pilot plant may differ in some ways from the product which will eventually come off the main production line. An imported product used in anticipation of setting up a production line domestically may differ in its formulation, in the nature of the ingredients, in the form of packaging, or even only in the fact that it may bear the name of the country of origin, but any of these factors could be significant in affecting results achieved.

With advertising and promotion, the material to be used in the wider market may already be available for use in the test area, although even here the media selection problems may make changes necessary. The increase in split run facilities among newspapers and of tipping-in and other facilities among magazines is reducing the extent of such problems, but they still exist for many experiments and should always be looked for. With television advertising the problem appears simple, but this is deceptive and it is a good example of how an apparently simple solution to the problems arising in experiments can be damaging.

Consider an experimental launch in which television is the only form of advertising and the national appropriation has been set at £300 000 for the first six months. The problem is to assess the advertising appropriate to a test area containing, say, 5% of the population. One approach is to put 5% of the appropriation into the test area but this, of course, will take no account of variations in 'costs per thousand' between stations. A second approach is to put into the test area the national schedule of advertising which would be run in the event of a wider launch. However, because of the ways in which companies allocate their budgets after taking account of differences in card rates and other conditions between television areas, there may not be a 'national' schedule as such but only a series of differing area schedules. If there *is* a national schedule, or if an approximation to one can be constructed, this achieves comparability between the test area and the expected national pattern in terms of transmitted advertising—but still not necessarily the national pattern in terms of received advertising or opportunities to see.

There appear to be quite marked differences between viewing habits in different parts of the country so that to attempt to set up a pattern of received advertising which will be 'typical' it is necessary to consider the reach and frequency schedule which is being aimed at on a national basis, and to reproduce this in the test area.

Even if comparability is achieved on this basis it may still leave problems unsolved, because of the relationship between the advertising for the experimental brand in the test area and advertising for brands already existing in the market. If there are area variations in the weights of advertising generated by competition it is quite possible that, whereas on a national basis the effort put behind the new product X may leave it below the effort put behind existing product A but above that for existing product B, variations in spending by A and B between areas may provide a quite different set of relationships in the test area. The main point is that a very detailed approach to the establishment of the appropriate experimental conditions is needed, not only in the media field but in others as well, both in an attempt to set up an appropriate set of test conditions, and also in order to know how far the conditions actually achieved may depart from the ideal and may need to be specifically allowed for in forecasting.

Beyond setting up the appropriate conditions at the beginning of an experiment, it is necessary to maintain them during its life. This involves such factors as ensuring that the sales effort is not unduly augmented either by the activities of the personnel normally working in the area, or by the attention or the visits paid to an area by head office personnel, acting on the best of motives of gaining experience but possibly influencing the experiment in some way at the same time. Hence, rigid discipline must be maintained over any company activities which might impinge on the experimental results.

Outside the company other factors may come into operation. The general effects of exogenous factors should have been catered for by setting up an adequate system of control areas in designing the experiment. Beyond this, however, competition may introduce counter activities into the test area which may affect the results. To maintain the integrity of the experiment, these activities must be carefully monitored and appropriate action taken. If, for example, a new launch is countered in the test area by increased advertising or other activity on the part of competitors, this may, in fact, enhance the value of the test operation if it is the type of activity which is to be expected on a wider scale in a wider launch. Further, if in the wider launch plan a contingency reserve has been set aside for use should such counter activity develop, then it is logical to use similar appropriate resources in the test area for this purpose.

However, if the counter activity mounted by competitors is specifically aimed at wrecking the test, such as flooding the area with coupons or samples or advertising on a scale which could not be supported nationally, then it may be necessary to abandon any hope of obtaining a projectable result from the test area, and to proceed as seems best with more limited objectives; for example, competitive couponing or sampling may have so distorted the market that any immediate estimate of brand share is unlikely to be valid but it may still be possible to gain a great deal of useful information from the test. Valid data may still be obtainable on the extent of awareness of the new product, the comprehension of the content of the advertising, the types of people who have bought and, in particular, the repeat buying patterns of those who have tried the new product at all. Some of these measures may have become suspect as a result of the competitive activity but almost certainly something can be gained from any test, whatever the interference, and any opportunities of gaining useful information should be taken rather than allow the whole operation to be written off.

This raises a point on the advisability of attempting to interfere in tests run by other manufacturers. In general, it would appear that far more is gained by watching and measuring the test oneself, and possibly using it in order to test any logical counter activities, rather than by becoming involved in a wrecking exercise.

The Cost-effectiveness of Experimenting

While there are numerous cases where hindsight shows that prior experimentation would have enabled a company to avoid losses incurred in launching some unsuccessful project, there are also many examples to be found where experiments were needlessly undertaken with a subsequent increase in costs or loss of profits. One large company, since taken over by another, for years prided itself that it never took a major decision without proper experimentation, and time after time it lost heavily because competitors had pre-empted the market by the time the experiments were completed. The problem of whether a particular experiment will justify the full range of costs involved is therefore vital.

The first requirement is for the likely range of outcomes of launching the project to be assessed in the light of existing knowledge and experience, together with assessments of the probabilities of the various outcomes occurring. Some such assessments are normally made anyway in considering a new project, although few take the process as far as attaching probabilities to the outcomes. This, however, is easily achieved by, in effect, carrying out an opinion survey among executives who know the project and the market, and deriving mean assessments of the probabilities, weighted perhaps to allow for different degrees of experience (or different weights of authority).

The outcomes normally need to be assessed in terms of profits or losses. In some cases, any effects resulting from the project will be immediate and of short duration, such as with a short-term promotion in a market with little brand loyalty. The effects will appear within a limited period and there will be little carry-over into the future, and there is little difficulty in putting a profit figure onto any set of market conditions which may arise. At the other extreme, if the project is one of launching a new brand which may be expected to have a life of some years ahead of it, it may be preferable to discount future profits in some way to provide figures of current net worth.

Where the assessed range of outcomes shows some probabilities of profits and some of losses if the project is put directly into the market, the first point to consider is the size of the maximum loss and its assessed probability of occurrence. If the loss is one which the company, the marketing group, or the executives within it, could not survive, then the only logical options open are to 'test' or 'abandon', irrespective of all other factors. If the maximum loss would not be crippling in this way, then all three options of 'launch now', 'test', or 'abandon' are still open and further calculation is required.

The next stage is to consider whether a test operation would lead to a more precise assessment of the range of outcomes, allowing for the problems of measurement and forecasting. Measurements can be made more precise by increasing sample sizes at a cost, and forecasts can be made more firm by increasing the number of areas into which the experiment is introduced, but again at a price. If the original assessments of possible outcomes were based on solid information and experience, the range may already be so narrow that further testing may do little to provide additional information. On the other hand, if existing experience is sketchy and the possible range of outcomes developed is wide, then even a simple experiment may help in refining the estimates of outcomes.

The problem of balancing the costs and the benefits of market testing is one of Bayesian Statistics, and a full discussion is beyond the scope of this chapter. For the general theory readers should consult Schlaifer[2], and for an application to market experiments, Davis[3].

In essence, the procedure involves balancing the costs against the improvement in the probability of avoiding losses or of gaining profits, as a result of testing. Hence, apart from the estimated outcomes and their probabilities, calculations of the costs already mentioned are needed, and some estimate of the accuracy likely to be attained by the possible methods of testing and forecasting. In many cases, where experimentation could proceed at more than one level, separate calculations need to be made covering the various options open to the company.

If the whole range of assessed outcomes is profitable two situations arise. On the one hand, if the investment required to introduce the project will remain flexible and can be adjusted to meet the market requirements as they develop, then clearly there is no point in incurring the costs of a separate test operation. An immediate launch, nationally or on a rolling base, is logical. On the other hand, if there are severe penalties involved should planning and investment proceed on a level which is not subsequently matched by market performance—even though that performance in itself would have been profitable had it been properly planned for—then testing may be called for. Thus, an achievement of selling 400 000 cases of a product a year in a market may be profitable if the whole planning was on the basis of achieving that level, but it may prove to be *un*profitable if the original planning and investment was based on achieving a level of 800 000 cases. This is a further complication which can be brought into the calculations if required.

Exploratory Experiments

In the past, it has probably been true to say that most market experiments have been carried out to secure information relating to some specific immediate problem—whether a new product will gain a viable share of a market, a new campaign will increase sales, changes in an appropriation will be profitable, and so forth. With many aspects of marketing this is the only way in which experiments can be conducted at all, because until the new product has been formulated and its marketing mix agreed, or until a new campaign has been developed or a new pack designed, there is nothing to experiment with. On the other hand, there are some areas of marketing in which useful experience can be gained through exploratory experiments at almost any time and added to the company's fund of knowledge for future use. Such areas include the level of the advertising appropriation, the way it is allocated between media, the ways in which it is scheduled; the representative journey cycles and the frequencies of calling on customers of various types; the effects of display bonuses and so forth. With these factors it is not necessary to wait until a particular decision has to be taken before beginning to collect experience by introducing planned changes into different parts of the market and measuring their effects. This type of experimentation becomes more important if the company is attempting to build marketing models, when all too frequently it is found that some factors which may well have a bearing on sales or profitability has hitherto been running at a steady level so that no information can be gained about the effects of variations from a study of past data. In these fields, then, it is possible to anticipate needs for experience and to carry out a comparatively inexpensive program of experiments accumulating the information through time, either in order to increase the running efficiency of an operation or to be able to provide more specific data when faced with future problems.

Collecting Data

Linked with this is the idea that whenever any changes are made in the way a product is being marketed—whether in limited areas or on a total market basis—as much relevant information as possible should be collected. In general, most marketing experiments suffer from a lack of resources applied to the collection of data. The results of test launches, appropriation tests, campaign tests, and so on, too often tend to be assessed only in terms of

500

changes in retail sales measured through some form of store panel. Such measurements may be adequate to answer the immediate direct question of whether the test produces beneficial results or not, but they fail to cover two other vital aspects.

The first is that if the experiment does not generate an improved level of sales or profitability then unless the failure is due to some in-store conditions, such as a lack of distribution, there will be no information to show where the marketing process broke down. If, for example, in an experimental launch only store audit data have been collected, there will be no means of diagnosing many possible causes of failure—or even of detecting weaknesses in a project which is in most respects successful. There will be no way of knowing whether the advertising failed to achieve attention or to create awareness; whether awareness was created but interest in the product did not develop; or even whether adequate numbers of the population did, in fact, buy the product but did not repeat their purchases. Thus, even though some of these measures may not be needed in order to assess the profitability of the project they are vital in any attempt at diagnosing weaknesses or causes of failure.

Second, in a more general way, the lack of this type of information, whether collected during experiments or when changes are introduced into wider markets, means that our knowledge of marketing is more restricted than it need be. There is, for example, little information about the way in which awareness of a new product or of a new advertising campaign develops. Too often, research in this area is merely confined to a single *ad hoc* survey some weeks or months after the launch which will then show some existing single measure of awareness. There will, however, be no indication of whether the level found has only just been reached, whether it was reached some time earlier and has merely been held since, or whether the level has been higher in the past and is now declining. It is also then difficult to assess whether the achieved level is a satisfactory one or not. Increasing the amount of research to collect this information will, of course, involve additional expenditure in most cases, but this need not be unduly high. Against this the benefit of being able to plan future launch advertising against a more secure knowledge of the way in which awareness develops could well lead to significant increases in the efficiency of such operations.

Any collection of additional data beyond that necessary to assess and interpret the results of the particular experiment must, however, be done within the context of the experiment itself. Attempts to use or modify an experiment being run for a specific purpose, in order to test some other quite different factor at the same time, must normally be resisted. The bits and pieces tacked on are likely to jeopardize the main experiment. However, arranging for a more comprehensive set of measurements to be made within the context of the experiment should normally enhance the value of the results as well as adding to the company's fund of experience.

Summary

To sum up: marketing experiments need to be carefully designed and measured in order to answer the questions being posed—and this applies whether the experiments relate to immediate problems or are being mounted in order to gain long term experience. Before embarking on any experiment, four basic questions should be answered:

(a) Is it possible to get the information required in this experiment from any other source, such as re-analysis of existing data, comparisons with other markets, or the accumulated experience of the company?
(b) Given what is already known about this situation, will an experiment add to that experience in a way which will lead to a better-based decision?
(c) Will the benefit expected from the better decision be sufficient to cover the costs of the experiment, taking account of the full range of costs which may be incurred?
(d) If this experiment is run can it be used as a source of other useful information and experience?

When an experiment or test is to be run, four major considerations should be covered as far as is possible:

(a) The experiment should, wherever possible, be conducted in more than a single area.
(b) The integrity of the experiment must be established and maintained, and all decisions relating to the way it is handled operationally must be made in the light of the objectives and needs of the experimental situation.
(c) Adequate time should be allowed for the effects of the changes to be developed and to reach stable levels.
(d) An adequate amount of measurement should be undertaken, not merely to provide measures of performance, but also to provide for diagnosis of the causes of weaknesses or failure and to increase the general understanding of the market.

20. Consumer modelling

Tony Lunn

Introduction

Modelling is a diverse and complex area. It is also a controversial one. For over two decades, researchers have developed and adapted models of widely differing kinds, ranging from econometric systems designed to forecast changes at the global market level, to theories about individual consumer decision processes. There has been considerable activity and enthusiasm, especially amongst marketing academics, but also amongst a number of research practitioners and marketing managers.

On the other hand, many researchers and marketing men have reacted with either indifference or scepticism. Models have been condemned as too complicated, both conceptually and methodologically; as necessitating long and costly procedures of data collection and analysis; as being difficult to implement; and as irrelevant for practical decision making. These criticisms have stimulated protagonists of the modelling approach to pay more attention to building usable models and to finding ways of getting models used. An increasing number of successful case histories have been reported in the literature, although it has been suggested in a recent review article[1] that these are still outnumbered by projects where apparently little or no practical application has ensued.

The purpose of this chapter is to draw attention to some major issues in the area. Space restrictions do not permit anything approaching a comprehensive overview and the writer has, in fact, summarized the state of the art in other publications[2,3]. For the most part points are made in outline rather than in detail. Fuller discussion can be found in the references. Particularly relevant are references 4–7.

The chapter is complementary to that by Rothman in this Handbook (chapter 3), which is written from a more mathematical standpoint. Primary emphasis is given here to certain models of individual choice behaviour, which have received increasing attention from researchers in recent years. Allied to developments in computer simulation, these are already demonstrating considerable potential as tools for management decision making. The earlier part of the chapter deals mainly with issues at a general level: the latter part gives illustrations from two successful published case histories.

Definitions

The term 'model' covers a multiplicity of constructs, some of which, it has been alleged[9], have little in common except that they share the same label! However, there would be general acceptance for the definition given by Zaltman[10], namely that 'A model is a simplified but organized and meaningful representation of an actual system or process'. It specifies both the key elements in a system—such as consumer beliefs, situational factors and purchasing behaviour—and the relationships between these elements. It is a replica of the real world and not the real world itself: it is simplified in that usually only a sub-set of the total pool of possible elements is incorporated—those critical to the nature and objective of the model in question. Where the phenomenon under investigation is relatively complex, as is the case with market and consumer behaviour, it becomes especially important to ensure that an adequate number of variables are included without, as a result, producing models that are too unwieldy to be of practical value.

A more colloquial definition has been suggested by the writer and his colleagues[11]. To quote:

> Models may be regarded as essentially views of how things work. As such, we all use models all the time. In everyday life we need models in order to act at all, and effective models in order to act successfully—in preparing a meal, catching a train, etc. Likewise, every market research project implies a model or series of models of one kind or another. We assume that our questions reflect phenomena in the real world; that the variables we cross-analyse are linked in a meaningful way, that our questions and analyses have relevance to the problem in hand. All of these assumptions imply models—views of how consumers operate and how they are affected by marketing action.

The same point holds for managers in their planning and implementation of marketing strategies. It cannot be emphasized too strongly that even the most unsympathetic critics of formal models in practice base their management decisions upon implicit models, which may well be totally misleading. As discussed more fully elsewhere[11], a particularly important function of a modelling exercise is to make explicit the implicit assumptions held about market structure by both marketing men and researchers, thereby enabling these assumptions to be criticized, tested and developed.

The Value and Role of Models

The function of marketing models has been discussed extensively in the literature[2, 8, 12]. Particularly important considerations are that models are valuable in:

1. Providing an improved *understanding* of how particular markets—or markets in general—work, of how consumers arrive at purchasing decisions, and of ways in which these decisions may be influenced by marketing action.
2. Enabling better *predictions* to be made of the nature of future market structures. This refers both to circumstances outside the direct control of marketing management but also, and more importantly, to the likely outcome of alternative marketing strategies—re-launching an existing brand with a revised formulation, putting more expenditure into below-the-line promotional activity, etc. The main benefit here is to enable management to ask 'what if' questions—e.g. what would be the effect of repositioning a minority brand in a certain way?—whilst avoiding the time, expense and practical problems associated with traditional research approaches such as experiments and test markets[9].

   For this purpose, models take the form of quantitative representations of market forces translated into computer programs. These can be thought of as 'artificial worlds', which are intended to provide an accurate reflection of key elements of the real-life situation. The manager can use these 'artificial worlds' in order to simulate the effects of different courses of action. Simulation is essentially a process of imitation. A detailed exposition of computer simulation procedures can be found in reference 9, which also discusses their claimed advantages compared with traditional research procedures. Practical illustrations are given later in this chapter.
3. Helping to *integrate* the plethora of disparate concepts and findings which exist both in market research generally, and also within the information systems of individual marketing companies.
4. Indicating gaps in our knowledge of market structures, thereby helping to *generate* relevant basic research projects; likewise models help to indicate gaps in the knowledge about particular markets, thereby guiding the commissioning and implementation of specific market studies.
5. Improving *communication* between researchers and marketing management, partly by establishing a common language in which research planning and findings can be linked to management decisions.

6. Improving *specific research projects* by identifying the kind of data required and ways in which these data can be operationalized, and by indicating the most relevant analysis techniques.

Typologies of Models

Several researchers have advanced typologies of models as a basis for comparison and evaluation, e.g. refs. 13, 14 and 15. Some major categories are outlined below:

Micro — macro

This distinction refers to the level at which the market is considered during the model-building process. A *macro*-model focuses upon the market at a global level and treats it as a total system. An example would be an econometric model which aims to predict market share as a function of differential weights of advertising expenditure.

In a *micro*-model every unit is treated separately: as an example, the characteristics and responses of consumers are examined on an individual basis. These individual responses can then be aggregated either to form subgroups of consumers sharing common characteristics or to produce an average response for the total sample. For instance, the likely market share of a new product could be forecast by aggregating the reactions of individual consumers.

Statistical — behavioural

In a *statistical* model, market behaviour is represented as a mathematical function of the variables included which, in turn, are often selected by statistical procedures such as regression analysis. The consumer is usually treated as a 'black box', the mechanics of which are not explored. Stochastic forecasting models are typical examples[5].

In a *behavioural* model the aim is to illuminate the mechanisms within the 'consumer black box'. The model may be based upon knowledge or assumptions about consumer behaviour and choice processes, and will typically incorporate theory drawn from the behavioural sciences.

In contrasting these two approaches, Nicosia[16] draws attention to their limitations when pursued separately. Statistical models tend both to make sweeping assumptions about behavioural processes and also to contain a somewhat parsimonious number of variables. Behavioural models, by contrast, sacrifice formal precision to richness of content and may, as a result, be regarded as too insubstantial as a basis for decision making. Nicosia argues strongly for 'substantive models' which combine the two approaches.

Low, medium or high level

This classification refers to the simplicity or complexity of a model's coverage. *Low level* models take a relatively simple standpoint and concentrate upon a restricted facet of the market picture, for example a rule by which consumers process information about alternative products.

High level models take a comprehensive standpoint, and delineate both a full range of marketing stimuli, and the various ways in which these might influence market behaviour, e.g. ref. 2. There are, of course, models which operate at an intermediate level. For a discussion of the pros and cons of these approaches see ref. 3.

Generalized or ad hoc

A *generalized* model is one which is considered to encompass processes sufficiently common for the model to be applied, almost as it stands, to a large variety of problems and situations. Until recently most models in the literature were of this kind.

In contrast, *ad hoc* models are tailor-made to deal with specific problems and market situations. While unique in their totality they may well contain generalized sub-components also to be found in other *ad hoc* models. For instance, the Trade-off model is a common feature of the two very different *ad hoc* models described later in the chapter.

Descriptive — diagnostic — predictive

Some models are essentially *descriptive*, in that they are concerned primarily with providing descriptions rather than explanations of market behaviour. An example is the work of Ehrenberg[17] who, in analysing purchasing data, has identified simple general rules or laws such as the Logarithmic Series Distribution. 'Starting without any formalized preconceptions of how or why people behave or feel as they do, the emphasis is on inter-relating simple empirical patterns, in cases where these are known to hold under wide ranges of observed conditions'. Interest is in both the laws themselves and in deviations from them: the latter are regarded as cases where special marketing action may be called for.

There is a grey area between description and explanation. As descriptions become more detailed and sophisticated, so a model becomes more *diagnostic* in nature and provides explanation of the phenomenon of interest. Many models, especially behavioural ones, are essentially diagnostic.

Prediction of how markets will react under specified circumstances is also a feature of many models. This is certainly the case for econometric models[5] and is increasingly so for the consumer choice models which are described later in the chapter.

Theoretical Bases for Consumer Models

As mentioned in the previous section, behavioural models in particular are characterized by an explicit theoretical basis. In fact, few consumer models are totally devoid of some kind of conceptual foundation. The writer has discussed this area in detail elsewhere[2], and there is only space here for a few brief comments concerning aspects especially relevant to current developments in modelling.

For the most part, theory has been drawn or adapted from the behavioural sciences. The potential of many different approaches has been explored. Many of these have dealt with states and processes *internal* to the consumer; for instance, those dealing with motivation, attitudes, learning and perception. These theories throw light on issues such as how people develop needs for different product characteristics, how they evaluate alternative products in terms of these needs, how information about products is acquired, structured and stored, and how predispositions towards buying different products are developed and changed. To quote just one instance, the work of social psychologists such as Rosenberg and Fishbein has been incorporated in a variety of multi-attribute models, as reviewed by Wilkie and Pessemier[18].

Attention has also been devoted to theories concerned with *external* influences upon the consumer, such as his reference groups, the situations under which he buys and consumes various products and the nature of family decision making. These external factors have two main kinds of influence. Firstly, they help to formulate consumer states such as awareness, needs, attitudes and buying intentions. Secondly, they help to mediate or modify the translation of predispositions into actual behaviour. For instance, a housewife may herself be highly inclined towards exotic foods, but may buy other foods instead because of her husband's traditional tastes.

Much model building is concerned with representing the consumer in his social environment. And, increasingly, the importance has been recognized of incorporating theories dealing with both internal and external factors. At a specific level, the work of Fishbein[19], with its emphasis upon social normative beliefs, has been implemented here. At a more global level, so have the *comprehensive* theories, such as those of Howard and Sheth[12], Engel *et al.*[20] and Nicosia[21].

Comprehensive theories are an especially important development. They represent the emergence of buyer behaviour as a discipline in its own right[22,23]. Somewhat ambitiously, they aim to integrate a number of social science theories purportedly relevant to consumer behaviour, as well as the findings of published empirical studies. As a result, they tend to be too complex to provide a direct basis for consumer modelling, but indirectly they have considerable practical value, indicating ideas and concepts which might be embodied in particular projects. One example is the concept of evoked set[12]. This distinguishes those brands in a product field which a consumer would consider buying from those of which he is either not aware or would not consider. The size and nature of the evoked set may vary over time according to factors such as experience and confidence.

Another important feature of comprehensive theories has been their dynamic property. This is manifested in Nicosia's argument for shifting the emphasis away from the purchasing act itself, and towards the decision processes which both precede and follow this act. As he points out, 'the act of purchasing is only one component of a complex, on-going process of decision-making—a process of many interactions amongst many variables over time'[21].

One of the most influential recent developments upon modelling has been the *information theory* approach to buyer behaviour, e.g. refs. 24, 25 and 26. To quote:

> Information Processing Theory is concerned with the mind and the way it is organized. It postulates that people think and make decisions by processing information according to some mental structures. The information will be certain cues or stimuli received from the person's environment and stored in memory as verbal concepts. The structures comprise fundamental processes that in the end result in some observed behaviour[25].

The information theory approach is concerned with ways in which consumers acquire and process information and how they use this information in making purchasing decisions. It has provided a fresh perspective for understanding existing research findings, and has also been the starting point for new conceptualizations[26].

An important development deriving from information theory has been the identification and operationalization of different types of decision rule used by consumers in their handling of cues about alternative brands, products and services. Many models have assumed that consumers normally use a compensatory rule; that is, they will choose brands which are perceived to have the best overall balance of favoured characteristics across all attributes. In some of these models, attributes have been weighted for importance in arriving at an assessment of purchasing probabilities.

Increasingly, alternative rules have been identified, and applied in consumer modelling probjects. For example:

(a) a *threshold* rule, where brands are eliminated from further consideration when they are perceived to have unacceptable characteristics or an insufficient score on favoured characteristics;
(b) a *disjunctive* rule, where a brand with a single overwhelming advantage is chosen;
(c) a *lexicographical* rule, where the brand most perceived to demonstrate an advantage on a sub-set of key attributes, considered in order of importance, is chosen;
(d) a *trade-off* rule, where the basic contention is that consumers are not

as a rule faced with alternatives which they can meaningfully judge against some hypothetical ideal. Instead they usually have to choose between a series of imperfect options: and to obtain a desired level of a particular product quality (say efficiency) they will have to sacrifice, i.e. trade-off, a certain level of some other product quality (say, gentleness).

There has been much discussion in the published literature of the relative merits of different decision rules, the circumstances under which they are most appropriate, and the ways in which they may be used by consumers in the same choice situation either sequentially or in combination[27,28,29,30].

Some Obstacles Inhibiting Application

There is a striking contrast between the large number of models that have been built over the years, and the small number of practical applications. Little[31] gives four main reasons why models have not been used more widely:

1. Relatively few models have been built which accurately reflect the marketing manager's approach to achieving his objectives.
2. The data required by a particular model may be unavailable or difficult and expensive to generate.
3. Researchers have been too prone to describe models either in terms of mathematical equations or abstruse socio-psychological concepts, or both. One result has been poor communication between researchers and management, and experience suggests that a model which is poorly communicated or understood will not be used by the managers for whom it is intended.
4. The necessity for a model to concentrate on the important elements in a system rather than attempt to be fully comprehensive has not always been understood or agreed to by marketing management.

Additional reasons include lack of management support, which may stem from several reasons, including emotional antipathy, a sincere disbelief in models, or unwillingness to commit the required level of investment.

Various attempts have been made to overcome these obstacles. An especially promising one involves the building of *micro-analytical behavioural simulation models*. Detailed description can be found in several recent publications, e.g. refs. 9 and 32.

Micro-Analytical Behavioural Simulation Models

Some chief characteristics are:

1. Mathematical representations of market behaviour are avoided whenever possible, except when working with a company where decision makers

themselves have a strong mathematical background, and tend to conceptualize their market in such terms.

2. Micro rather than macro models are preferred, because the latter are usually of a mathematical nature.

3. Consequently the modelling activity is concentrated at the level of the individual consumer. This tends to lead to more realistic models and to improved communication.

4. Greater emphasis is placed upon behavioural than upon statistical representation.

5. The modelling activity incorporates at least three kinds of data source, namely:

   (a) *management perspectives*, obtained by a 'structuring process' (see below),

   (b) *behavioural sciences*, i.e. knowledge, concepts and theories of the kind referred to in the previous section are adopted where relevant to the objectives of the model;

   (c) *empirical data*, as appropriate.

   In each modelling project an attempt is made to strike the optimum balance between these various sources.

6. The temptation is avoided of attempting to build, at the outset, large-scale models encompassing all aspects of consumers' reactions to marketing activities. Instead, a sequential approach is adopted in which the model is built up, stage by stage, in a sequence determined by company priorities.

   A valuable strategy is to begin with a 'core' model, such as a representation of the central consumer decision process. Extra sub-models are progressively added which are relevant to the project in question (e.g. modules representing advertising or point-of-sales factors).

7. Attempts are made to obtain a high degree of involvement from the managers in the marketing company at every stage in the development process. This increases the possibility of securing a degree of understanding and acceptance of the model which will provide the key to its effective implementation.

   One means of generating the involvement is through the 'structuring' process discussed by Palmer[33]. Basically, this consists of managers and researchers working closely together in order to elaborate a picture of the market which is consistent with the manager's view of the environment and is relevant to the problem in hand. It is not intended that either managers or researchers should impose their respective pictures on the market; rather, this picture should evolve from discussion.

8. The emphasis upon involvement has important consequences for the organization of modelling projects. A valuable procedure is to set up a task force with members drawn from relevant sources: e.g. marketing management, research laboratories, advertising agencies, research suppliers. The task force will be in charge of managing the project; it will

define the problems to be solved and the model's objectives; it will set up priorities and criteria for assessing the results at each stage.

Stages in the Model Building Process

Each modelling project should proceed at its own pace, depending upon the problem in question and prevailing circumstances. A characteristic series of steps is outlined below. Brief illustrations are given from a project carried out jointly by Philips, Floeilampenfabrieken and RBL in the UK dry shaver market, which is reported in detail in reference 32.

Problem definition

Modelling is a problem-oriented activity, and obvious first steps are to clarify both the problem to be solved and the objectives of the model. A task force should be established at the earliest moment, and criteria agreed for evaluating the results of each stage of the project. In the dry shaver study, a project team was established with members drawn from the initiating company's headquarters, the research agency, and outside consultants. Some objectives are mentioned in the next sub-section.

Developing a macrostructure

The next stage is the development of an overall representation of all relevant elements in the market and their interrelationships. At first this 'macro-structure' would be highly descriptive and qualitative: it can be progessively refined in the light of experience and research findings. The objective is to provide task force members with a common language, and to ensure that they share a common perception of the main issues involved.

In the dry shaver project, the macrostructure represented the flow of information available to consumers, and the role of this information at various stages in the buying process. Various elements in the decision-making situation were specified, each of which could be the subject of a sub-model.

1. *Wet/Dry Choice Model:* representing the factors which influence whether an individual will become a customer in the dry (electric) shaver market or in the wet-shaving market.
2. *Pre-store Choice Model:* representing the interplay of brand awareness, beliefs about brands, and the individual's value system in the development of purchasing dispositions, prior to active shopping.
3. *In-Store Model:* representing those distributional and point-of-sale factors which may interact with 'pre-store choice' dispositions in the determination of actual choice.
4. *Retailer Model:* representing the attitudes and requirements of the retailer and how these influence stocking, display and sales activities.

512

5. *Theme Advertising Model:* representing the content and delivery of advertising messages.
6. *Gift Model:* representing that part of total buying which arises from the purchase of electric shavers to be given as unsolicited (i.e. non-requested) gifts.

These elements are represented in diagrammatic form to show the inter-relationship between the separate parts (Fig. 20.1).

Where several elements can be identified, priorities will have to be established over where to concentrate initial effort. In the dry shaver study the 'Pre Store Choice' area was selected, mainly because it was judged to hold most immediate benefit to the company in making various marketing and advertising decisions. Objectives for this sub-model were set—e.g. 'To identify when an existing brand or type is approaching the limit of its appeal to consumers, i.e. has been bought or considered by all who value its attributes'—and a flow chart was produced to represent its main characteristics (Fig. 20.2).

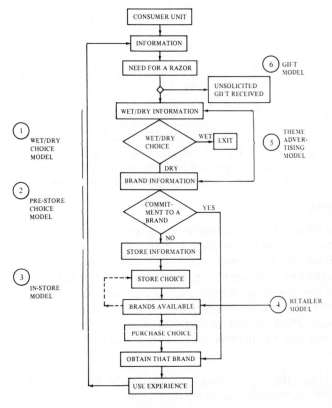

Fig. 20.1   The macrostructure. Source: Gunter and Beazley[32].

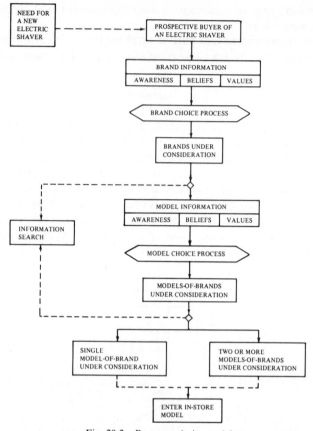

Fig. 20.2   Pre-store choice model.

Source: Gunter and Beazley[32]. *Note:* The broken lines connect the pre-store choice model with the other elements in the macrostructure.

Operationalization

The next stage is to operationalize the various elements within the structure. For instance, in the shaver project, measuring instruments were developed for variables such as awareness, beliefs and values, and for the various decision rules hypothesized to be relevant to consumer choice in this area, for example the threshold, disjunctive, lexicographic and compensatory rules referred to earlier in this chapter. Exploratory research conducted during a preliminary phase of this project had suggested that consumer decision-making was based in the product field upon a combination of these rules. To quote:

> In effect the brand choice model can be thought of as asking the following sequence of questions:
>
> (i)   Which brands is the respondent aware of?

(ii) Do any brands have completely unacceptable attributes (i.e. Threshold Rule)? If so, reject them.

(iii) Does any brand have a unique advantage on any important attribute (i.e. Disjunctive Rule)? If so, accept it as the predicted choice.

(iv) Are any remaining brands inferior on any particular important attributes (i.e. Lexicographic Rule)? If so, reject them.

(v) What is the total utility associated with the characteristics of each remaining brand (i.e. Compensatory Rule)? Select brand with most utility[32].

Validation

Models will be used by management only if they are comprehensible and relevant to decision-making. In addition they should have face validity; that is, they should provide a representation of the market that makes sense to the managers concerned. However there is also a need for validity of a more stringent kind, namely that models should provide accurate representation of the markets under investigation in particular cases. A thorough review of issues involved in the validation of marketing models is given by Faivre and Sanchez[34], who describe a case history of a relatively complex model where there was an impressively high goodness of fit between results predicted by the model and those observed in the market place: the variables on which comparisons were based included awareness, attitude measures and market shares.

Validation of the dry shaver model was also encouraging. Three basic forms were used:

1. comparison of the model's prediction with measures of purchasing intention. Correct predictions were obtained for over 90% of respondents;

2. comparison of the model's prediction with individual consumers' measured reactions to a set of new shaver concepts, obtained on a re-interview of the original sample. A satisfactory brand choice was obtained from about 75% of individual respondents;

3. 'Process validity' where, through the analysis of questions answered by the original sample but not used in building the model, comparisons were made between the choice processes used by individuals as suggested by the model and as perceived by the respondents themselves.

Applications

Consumer models of the kind discussed above have already begun to demonstrate their value for management decision making. Two aspects are dealt with below, namely explanation and prediction.

An example of their *explanatory* power lies in the illumination of the choice processes adopted by individual consumers. For instance, it is possible to identify how many respondents reject each brand on threshold characteristics, and which attributes lead to a brand being rejected in this way; likewise, for people who choose each brand, it is possible to identify how many make disjunctive, lexicographic and compensatory choices, and also to indicate the determinant attitudes. Moreover, it is possible to classify consumers in terms of the way in which they use different combinations of these rules.

Their *predictive* power lies in the mechanism they offer marketing management to estimate the effects of alternative strategies. The procedure is for the marketing man to formulate 'what if' questions and for answers to be obtained through computer simulation. Typical 'what if' questions (from ref. 32) include:

1. What formulation changes, effectively communicated, would increase the frequency with which our brand is selected?
2. What attributes should be stressed in our advertising?
3. What are the characteristics (attitudinal, demographic, behavioural, media, etc.) of the people who are likely to be attracted by a new strategy?
4. Does our current advertising platform have continuing potential, or is there a case for a new one?
5. What is the likely effect on brand choice of our competitor's change in his advertising positioning?
6. What would be the most effective response to protect our brand from competitive activity?
7. Which combination of attributes would be the strongest basis for a new brand? from where would a new brand, of a given specification, attract its customers?

Simulation can take place at both micro and macro levels. The description of the dry shaver case provides illustrations of both. Computer print-out is obtained under both the pre-simulation and simulation conditions. Firstly, at the *micro* level it was shown how, for instance, a particular respondent would currently choose a Ronson razor, given his perceptions of the various brands available. The print-out also showed how this decision was a function of the threshold and disjunctive rules, and which attitudes appeared to be determinant. It was then assumed that marketing action could change his perceptions of the brands in terms of a certain key attribute. Given this assumption, a simulation run showed that he would now choose a Philishave. The print-out also indicated that, under the changed conditions, he would use four decision rules in sequence, namely threshold, disjunctive, lexicographic and compensatory.

At the *macro* level, effects of marketing action are provided by aggregating the total set of individual results. One means of showing these is by a brand switching matrix, as in Fig. 20.3 below.

In this example Philishave seems capable of achieving an 8% increase in brand choice if a particular attribute can be effectively communicated and if other factors are constant. It would appear, however, that 4% of this increase

Brand Choice Pre-Simulation		Post Simulation					
		Philips	Philishave	Boots	Remington	Ronson	Braun
Philips	21	17	4	—	—	—	—
Philishave	30	—	30	—	—	—	—
Boots	4	—	—	4	—	—	—
Remington	21	—	—	—	21	—	—
Ronson	12	—	2	—	—	10	—
Braun	12	—	2	—	—	—	10
	100%	17	38	4	21	10	10

Fig. 20.3 Shaver brand switching matrix. Source: Gunter and Beazley[32].

would come from the Philips brand, thus giving only a 4% increase in the combined share of Philips and Philishave.

The results of macro simulations may also be represented in terms of brand choice percentages. An illustration can be found in a case history from the office equipment market, described in references 11 and 35. In this case the trade-off model was the main method employed.

This latter project was designed to guide the manufacturer's future new product development. His plans were to enter a sub-market which, although highly developed by competitors, was new for him—his dominance lay in other sub-markets.

Following comprehensive discussions of the basis for modelling with the client, it was decided that the structure should represent a world where each customer possessed full and accurate knowledge about all competitive products in the market place, and made logical choices between them on the basis of their abilities to satisfy his requirements. The simulation model was to be designed so that the product planner could specify a possible future market in terms of the features of both his own products and those of his envisaged competition.

The manufacturer used the model to assist in a wide range of decisions. The common theme across these was that he was always checking the sales implications of a new product idea in a specified market configuration. To quote:

> To take an example, at one stage in his planning, the manufacturer was pursuing an idea we will call product X. He felt that he would not be able to make that product available immediately and that, by the time he would be ready to launch, his competitors might well have developed products A, B, C and D.
>
> In order to check the viability of product X, he firstly simulated a

market composed of products A, B, C and D, with the following results:

	Simulated brand share %
Product A	52
Product B	4
Product C	33
Product D	10

Having observed that product A and, to a lesser extent, C would dominate this market in formulation terms, he then simulated the market again — this time with product X also included:

	Simulated brand share %
Product A	30
Product B	3
Product C	16
Product D	8
Product X	43

These results suggested that product X was a very promising idea—it appeared to have the potential for becoming the dominant product in this market.

The manager next questioned his assumptions about future market developments, and decided to investigate what might happen if manufacturers developed products B and D into the superior formulations N and P. When product X was entered into this market, the following results were achieved:

	Simulated brand share %
Product A	28
Product N	20
Product C	13
Product P	25
Product X	14

Thus he could see that product X would be very susceptible to developments in B and D, and looked for formulation changes he could make to counter such developments. He tried out various changes which could readily be engineered in practice, and eventually discovered a reformulation of X which could perform relatively well in this market:

| | *Simulated brand share* |
	%
Product A	27
Product N	12
Product C	15
Product P	21
Product X Mk 1	25

The planner continued the investigation of product X after this fashion by looking at a range of other possible future developments, seeing the potential of X MK 1 when competing in these contexts, and investigating ways of increasing its competitive appeal when necessary.

This example shows the way the manufacturer is able to build his planning decisions around a structure incorporating the trade-off model. By, on the one hand, identifying ways of competing successfully in a range of possible market configurations and, on the other hand, monitoring market developments as they occur, he is able to take a very flexible approach to his product planning. Having initiated and evaluated a series of product plans at this point in time, he also knows how to modify some of their objectives in the light of market developments. And, as the competitive developments become clearer, he learns which of his own developments are likely to prove most effective and which could be shelved. Should any unexpected changes occur in the competitive structure of the market, he can immediately check out their implications by simulating their effect.

Conclusions

Micro behavioural modelling is still in an early phase of development. It has been applied in an increasing number of projects during the mid-1970's and has, in the process, undergone considerable modification since the early exposition by Faivre[9]. It is no longer viewed as a uniform procedure with fixed, clearly delineated stages. Rather it has become a more flexible approach offering a range of options, any or all of which may be adapted according to the nature of the marketing problem. Consumer modelling studies may be complex or simple, large or small scale, expensive or inexpensive. They may be explicitly initiated and designed as modelling exercises: or they may be incorporated within, and extend from, conventional pieces of research. These characteristics of flexibility and versatility are discussed in Lunn and Blackston[36]. Some major points from this paper are summarized below:

(1) Trade-Off can be used in small-scale or qualitative studies as a valuable means of elucidating particular aspects of consumer needs and priorities or providing supplementary information.

(2) Large-scale, quantitative studies—of the kind described in chapter 14 of this book—may involve simple Trade-Off application as a means of lending greater precision to the assessment of consumer needs and priorities.

(3) Such studies (i.e. 1 and 2 above) readily lend themselves to computer simulation. Sometimes, simulation may be planned at the outset of the project. It may, however, be implemented at a later stage. That is, computer simulation may be considered to be a relevant extra process, in the light of the initial data analyses and / or the subsequent development of marketing planning.

(4) Other choice rules—see the previous sections of this chapter—may be introduced, which in combination with Trade-Off can lead to a closer imitation of individuals' choice processes. This opens the way to the development of a fuller simulation model which will lend itself to being addressed by a wider range of 'what if' questions.

(5) Achieving the required degree of verisimilitude in modelling complex market processes may involve the development of two or more sub-models—each reflecting a particular aspect of the market (see p. 512).

(6) Whatever the degree of simplicity or complexity, modelling projects usually involve additional commitments of management time and of research expenditure. These may not always be justified and, in common with other research techniques, modelling should only be used where a clear pay off can be anticipated. Already, however, modelling is emerging as a cost-effective tool. This is exemplified both in the greater precision offered for a relatively small additional expense, and also in the way in which, through the use of simulation, the original data can be re-worked time and again, often as an alternative to the collection of additional data.

Two points by way of conclusion. First, there are a number of issues in micro behavioural modelling which require basic methodological development. For instance, when using Trade-Off, there is the question of whether to present data in pair-wise or full concept form (e.g. ref. 37); and also the point that adding utilities assumes that there is little or no interaction between the various product features being assessed. At a more general level, this total approach to modelling might appear best suited to markets where product benefits are tangible rather than emotional and where the consumer decision process operates at a conscious and rational level. However, recent applications indicate that such problems can be surmounted (e.g. ref. 36), and the interested reader is recommended to publications such as the JMR and JCR for additional contributions.

Second, despite the emphasis in the present chapter upon one aspect of modelling, it is not intended to decry the value of alternative approaches, especially econometric models (e.g. ref. 5), which are more appropriate for tackling problems of a more global nature.

21. Corporate image research

Robert M. Worcester

Corporate research encompasses all aspects of research conducted among publics of importance to the corporation, company or organization in the direct role other than as customers. Consumers are obviously the primary target of marketing research, but there are many other publics of importance to the corporation. Industrial customers, while not included as such in this handbook, are of prime importance to a company selling industrial products. The financial community, including shareholders, are another important audience; financial relations research is covered in the next chapter.

There are other publics of importance as well. Employees are perhaps the most important, but the general public are becoming increasingly influential as 'consumerists' (as opposed to consumers) and are for this reason a vital audience to be researched. The general public may also be a source of potential recruits. Opinion leaders, senior civil servants, the press, students, people living around manufacturing plants, suppliers, and trade union officials: all impinge on corporate actions to a greater or lesser degree. In the complex world in which we live, it is likely that a prudent senior manager will demand to know as much as he can about the attitudes and behaviour of those he wishes to influence and so corporate research will be demanded. It is for this reason, and because it is likely that (while corporate research is perhaps out of the mainstream of the average market research manager's usual activity) the company's market research manager is the one to whom public relations will turn for a study amongst the general public and personnel will turn for assistance on an employee attitude study, as will others for research into their areas of interest.

In succeeding sections this chapter defines and puts into perspective the role of corporate image research and discusses research among a number of the other publics of importance.

Over the last three decades, a great deal of research has been carried out into the images of companies, institutions, products and brands. It may be said that generally there are four major categories of image influences. There is *the image of the product class* as a whole, *the image of the brand* as opposed to other brands within the product class, *the image of users* of the brand, and *the corporate image* of the company that stands behind the brand[1]. Of course, there are other influences at work on image as well, such as the time and place that the product or service might be useful.

Research has shown that the crucial image influences sometimes occur in one of these dimensions and sometimes in another. This situation varies from product class to product class, brand to brand and company to company. Substantial variance also occurs during the life-cycle of a product of some manufacturers; witness the prominence given the corporate identity of Proctor and Gamble during the first eighteen months of their new product introductions in America.

The product class image is that collection of image attributes shared by all the brands of a particular product class, such as motor vehicles, cigarettes, textiles or a certain sort of machine tool. Every class and product exists for a reason, meets certain needs and desires, plays a certain role in the lives of its users, is associated with certain kinds of people and competes directly or indirectly with other product classes in various ways, most often for disposable income, increasingly frequently for leisure time.

Brand images are the unique characteristics of a brand that distinguish it from others. These include how, and how well, the brand is seen as fulfilling the functions of the product class, its appearance and style, package, price, and the degree to which it is believed to be economical and of good value.

Alan Brien's comment in Punch some time ago related brand images to the third category of image, the brand user image. He said:

> When I was a boy, men would talk about their cigarettes as they now talk about their cars. Brand loyalty was as strong as class loyalty and the two were often linked. Park Drive, de Reske, Black Cat, Balkan Sobranie, Passing Clouds—they were clues in a detective story. It was possible to deduce the sex, the income, the accent, even the favourite fantasies of the last person to dump a fag in your ashtray just by reading off its name. For a gent to be discovered smoking Woodbines was as suspicious as a tramp lighting up a fresh cigar[2].

Especially when there are few clear and demonstrable functional differences among brands, brand user images can be crucial to a brand's success.

The fourth source of image is that of the corporation or other institution that stands behind the product or service. This includes the company's general familiarity and favourability and many specific corporate image attributes that can be categorized as relating to product reputation, customer relations, employer role, ethical reputation, and others.

In 1967, David Lowe Watson set out a theory of advertising based on the concept of a set of relationships between the buyer, the 'personality' of the brand, and the 'personality' of the seller, or company[3]. This theory, he suggested, is more useful than standard advertising theories because it can satisfactorily account for a number of discrepancies between existing theory and empirical observations.

Lowe Watson provided a model that distinguished three key factors involved in effective advertising: a customer's image of the company, his image of the product, and his perception of the advertising. He said that the company image is related to advertising effectiveness and this underscores the concept of 'total communication' which includes the coordination of policy in every part of the company's communications activity, advertising, sales promotion, packaging, product planning, public relations, and corporate identification. He concluded that the advertiser who can build up a strong and favourable relationship with his customers will establish a fund of goodwill from which he can derive future benefits. These benefits include not only a greater readiness on the part of the customer to pay attention to his advertising, and a predisposition to put a favourable interpretation on the message received but also a favourable attitude toward the product itself and expectation of satisfactory product performance and a greater willingness to try a new product.

The late Leo Burnett was quoted as saying 'We feel that proliferation of brands and mergers have brought on a growing need for corporate advertising. No brand can be given the support it needs and corporate identity is becoming more important as a seal of approval'[4]; and in speaking about industrial purchasing, William Paterson of Tube Investments said 'The reputation of the company is an important factor and it is in this area that subjective decisions tend to be made'[5].

Definition of Corporate Image

What is a corporate image? Corporate image may be defined as 'the net result of the interaction of all experiences, impressions, beliefs, feelings and knowledge people have about a company'. The sources of image are extensive. These include the product, its packaging, both product and corporate advertising, distribution, and promotion patterns. Also, all the other manifestations of its communications, such as its letterhead, brochures, public relations, the impressions left by the company's employees and salesmen, its factories, offices, lorries and the activities of the industry in which the company operates, frequently have important effects on the corporate image. Opinions of other people and messages from competing companies also play an important role in forming a person's image of a company.

The Role of the Corporate Image

A strong corporate image influences the predisposition to buy a company's products, speak favourably of it, believe its statements, apply for a job with it,

	Agree	Disagree
'I never buy products made by companies I have never heard of'	33% (37%)	55% (53%)
'New brands on the market are usually improvements on the old established brands'	37% (37%)	47% (41%)
'Old established companies make the best products'	51% (48%)	30% (32%)
'A company that has a good reputation would not sell poor products'	65% (75%)	25% (16%)

Fig. 21.1 MORI Cooperative Corporate Image Study, Autumn 1975. National Probability Sample of 1875 Adults in Great Britain. (1969 figures in brackets.)

and the like. It is important for industrial goods companies with listed shares. It is important to companies seeking highly technical staff in a tight staff availability situation. It is important to a consumer goods company whose very life is dependent on successful new product introductions. Just how important it is to a consumer goods company is illustrated by recent findings that show that a sizable proportion of the British public are less than enthusiastic about any new product, and yet still show faith and trust in companies they feel they know well—in spite of decreased confidence over the past six years that 'A company that has a good reputation would not sell poor products' (Fig. 21.1).

And how important a company's reputation is to a housewife's propensity to try new products is shown by research which found women 14% more

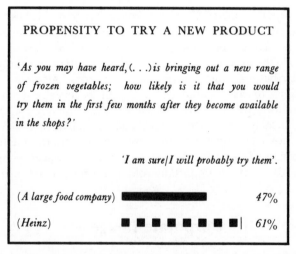

Fig. 21.2 Split sample of 1072 adult women in Great Britain. National Probability Sample. MORI Cooperative Corporate Image Study, Spring, 1970.

likely to try a new product from 'Heinz' than from 'a large (unspecified) food company' (Fig. 21.2).

The Context of Corporate Reputations

The detailed image profile of a company or organization as seen by external publics can best be understood within the perspective of overall attitudes

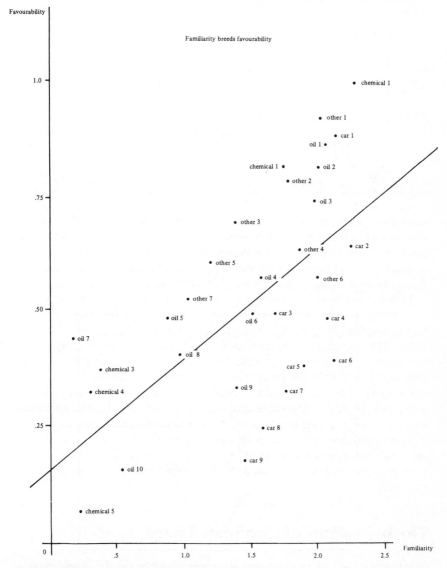

Fig. 21.3 MORI, 3761 interviews, National Probability Sample of all adults in Great Britain, Cooperative Corporate Image Study, Autumn 1975.

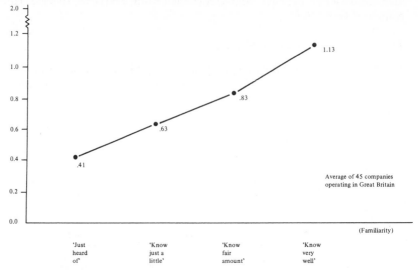

(Favourability) Companies are *usually* most highly regarded by those who know them best.

2.0

1.2

1.13

1.0

0.8
.83

0.6
.63

0.4
.41

Average of 45 companies
operating in Great Britain

0.2

0.0

(Familiarity)

| 'Just
heard
of' | 'Know
just a
little' | 'Know
fair
amount' | 'Know
very
well' |

Fig. 21.4 MORI, 3761 interviews, National Probability Sample of all adults in Great Britain, Cooperative Corporate Image Study, Autumn 1975.

towards business; atttitudes towards specific industries, not only the industry in which the client is involved but other industries as well; and then towards the client company versus its competitors and in the context of many companies, some better known and some less well known. Images cannot be measured in a vacuum. All images are relative and must be comparative.

That favourability increases with familiarity is an important finding indeed to a company with a low level of public awareness. Companies are most highly regarded by those that know them best. The scatter graph (Fig. 21.3) shows the correlation between familiarity (on the horizontal axis) and favourability (on the vertical axis) and also illustrates clearly how the car companies in Britain are going through a particularly bad patch (excepting car company 1 which happens to be Rolls-Royce Motors). The car companies as a group are well below the 'line of best fit' which is the graphic representation of the general rule that 'familiarity breeds favourability, not contempt'.

This correlation is shown in another way in Fig. 21.4, which shows that across 45 companies studied in 1975 there is an almost straight-line relationship between how *well* a company is known and how favourably it is regarded.

The Ingredients of Corporate Image

What goes to make up a good corporate image? When the British public were asked 'Which two or three things do you consider most important to know about a company in order to judge its reputation?' about a third talked in terms of the company's reputation as a good employer and being fair to its employees. A third also spoke about the standard and quality and reliability of its products. About 10% talked about good service to public and customers, honesty, reliability, price of goods, reasonable and competitive pricing, the company's management, and its financial stability.

Image and Behaviour

In this chapter a number of examples are introduced to suggest links between image and behaviour. The research methodology for relating variables that conceivably control overt behaviour to one another has been considerably developed in the last decade. This is one of the basic problems to which corporate image research is addressed and some progress along experimental lines of analysis has been achieved.

Variables which were related to behaviour included data on ratings of the company's products, support for public relations platform objectives, corporate symbol recognition, data on recent purchases of the company's products and recommendation of the company's products to others. Multiple regression analysis techniques were used to rank corporate image measures and other variables in terms of their relationship to action. The most closely related image measurement to recent purchases of the company's brands was not the company's product reputation image as might have been supposed but the customer treatment image. The same image dimensions related to those who had recommended the company's products. On the other hand, willingness to listen to a company spokesman on an issue was most closely associated with having a favourable attitude towards big business.

The actions people take with respect to a company depend on far more than whether or not they like or dislike the company. Yet, complex and subconscious as a person's feelings and beliefs about a company may be, they can often be synthesized into ranked data that may be examined statistically. Images differ from company to company in important ways. While they are undoubtedly rooted in general value systems, each company has its own strengths and weaknesses among various segments of the population. With objectively measured knowledge of corporate strengths and weaknesses, companies can organize their efforts in appropriate directions, capitalizing on their strengths and, where possible, identifying and taking steps to correct their weaknesses.

One of the most useful findings from a study of corporate image is where the facts of the situation contradict the image. One large, very well known and well respected British company has a price earnings ratio far below where its management believes it ought to be. In fact, it is well diversified and reasonably profitable company. Yet nine out of ten AB British men think of it as selling only one product and that product is traditionally a low profit item.

Thus, the company has a blueprint for communications action based on objective knowledge of the facts, *as seen through the eyes of the shareholding public*.

Measuring the Effectiveness of Corporate Advertising

A number of companies augment their product advertising with corporate campaigns designed to benefit the company as a whole. In doing so they are attempting to do considerably more than just sell their products (though a laudable ambition in, and of, itself). When one is trying to build a corporate reputation the results are sometimes subtle and often have a wide effect.

For example, in 1975, Woolworth launched the 'That's the wonder of Woolworth' campaign, principally on television. One per cent of the general public attributed 'That's the wonder of . . .' to Woolworth before the campaign broke, seven months later the figure had rocketed to 64%. In conjunction with this, awareness of the range of goods stocked increased and respondents were visiting Woolworth stores more frequently.

Research in another case showed television to be a very powerful medium for putting across corporate communications. In a campaign for Philips in 1973-4-5, which centred around the slogan 'Simply years ahead', television and the press were used equally during the first year of advertising, but by the last of the three annual campaigns this had been changed to 100% television. Research showed that television was much more forceful in getting across the message.

Figure 21.5 shows how Philips, over a period of time, built up and sustained its slogan awareness. At the same time it also demonstrated the value of ICI's image building over the years. Although 'Simply years ahead' is unconnected with ICI, 17% of the respondents initially associated the slogan with ICI. It took considerable effort to overtake ICI as the 'natural' recipient of a slogan awareness such as Philips'. Also vividly shown is the effect of repeated exposure on television versus the effect of national press advertising in the first two years of the campaign.

Several years ago Trust Houses Forte built a campaign around the slogan 'The biggest smile in Europe', which was designed to show THF as a large, British-based company offering good service in several different fields. The success of this campaign could be seen from the results of a pre-post corporate image survey in the Thames Television area which also showed how their reputation had increased, particularly as an employer and in the quality of their management[6].

ICI has for many years believed in developing and maintaining a good corporate image. Its 'Pathfinder' campaign on television together with press followed years of steady effort in press advertising, a well developed public relations effort, and generally good corporate activities in providing good products, having low-key product advertising (e.g. the Dulux dog), treating

528

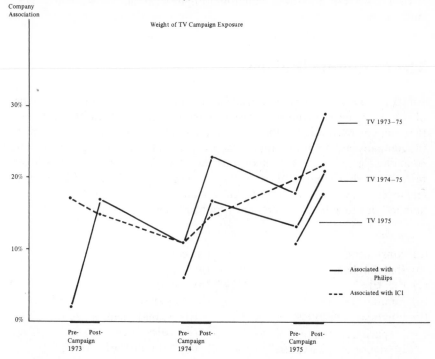

Awareness of 'Simply Years Ahead' 1973–1975

Company Association

Weight of TV Campaign Exposure

TV 1973–75

TV 1974–75

TV 1975

Associated with Philips

Associated with ICI

30%

20%

10%

0%

Pre- Post-
Campaign
1973

Pre- Post-
Campaign
1974

Pre- Post-
Campaign
1975

Fig. 21.5 MORI, National Probability Samples of approx. 2000 adults in Great Britain.

its employees well and generally behaving in many ways as a good corporate citizen. The success of its policies is tracked regularly by a series of studies among publics of importance to the company, but the 'flagship' of their research program is an annual measure of the general public's image of ICI. One analysis of interest examined in 1976 was the effect on the public of living in an 'ICI area', defined as areas in which ICI has a physical presence such as a manufacturing plant or chemical works. This analysis showed that there is a substantial and measurable difference in attitudes to ICI between those who

Response	ICI areas−non-ICI areas %
Say they 'know' ICI well	+8
'Favourable' towards ICI	+6
Think ICI shows an interest in people as well as profits	+6
Think ICI have excellent benefits for employees	+12
Think ICI is fair in the wages they pay	+19
Think ICI have good relations in communities where they operate	+7
Think ICI makes too big a profit	−9

Fig. 21.6 MORI. 149 respondents in 'ICI areas', 758 respondents in 'Non-ICI areas'. Great Britain, Autumn 1975.

live in 'ICI Areas' and those who don't. Figure 21.6 illustrates a few of these differences.

The Corporate 'Publics'

Any company has a number of masters who must be served. The prime public of concern to every manager is the customer. Certainly without the customer the company must fail; but there are a number of other groups without which the company could not live, much less prosper, and chief among these are the company's employees. Yet there must be literally thousands of consumer research studies conducted each year for every study conducted amongst employees, or even, if the truth be known, amongst *all* of the other corporate 'publics' put together. The company 'publics' generally include:

(a) consumers;
(b) shareholders;
(c) the 'City';
(d) opinion leaders;
(e) potential employees;
    (i)   parliamentarians;
    (ii) senior civil servants;
    (iii) local government officials;
    (iv) trade union officials;
    (v) press;

(f) community;
(g) suppliers;
(h) the 'trade';
(i) employees
    (i)   management;
    (ii) sales force;
    (iii) administrative staff;
    (iv) scientists and engineers;
    (v) production workers.

Consumers

Much that has been said above relates to work with consumers, yet so often, as Lowe Watson has pointed out, the relationship the consumer feels with a company is overlooked or ignored.

There is considerable variability in the image influences that determine the brand commitment of the consumer. Each product field differs in the way in which brands are discerned and in the criteria that consumers use to compare brands. Conducting corporate image research to determine the effect of an image on a brand, the researcher seeks to determine the image of the company that stands behind the brand as differentiated from the companies that provide other brands.

As Pilditch put it in his excellent book, 'Communication by Design',

> The pertinent question is not when to adopt the brand policy, but how to see this in corporate terms. In the soap business, the archetypal product or brand structure, an important change is taking place.

Marketing men have thought in the past that the brand name was the important thing to get across. They felt that the company making the brand was unimportant, and didn't help sell the product. Who cares who makes Tide as long as Tide has what the shoppers want?

This view is now less strongly held. In front of the author now is a bottle of Square Deal Quix. Which is the brand name? In a prominent place it states: "A Lever Product—guaranteed". Below it is written: "Lever quality and performance guaranteed or your money back" . . .

A corporation needs to become well known in the interests of attracting shareholders and employees, and developing good relations generally. Three points emerge. First, the relationship between brand and corporate identity is being reassessed. Second, the requirements of a corporate identity are different from those of a brand. This difference must be understood and preserved, and the problem of relating the two will then be much easier to solve. Third, relationships must vary to suit the situation, particularly the comparative strength of brand name to corporate name, the ubiquity of the corporate name, and the appropriateness of the product to the corporate identity[7].

Another use is in product compatibility research. This type of study determines whether a new product is compatible with the company's existing image. Where it is not, different brand names are often used so that these names will *not* be identified with the company. Where it is, the company can use the corporate name to help sell the product. Research can help determine the compatibility of prospective new products with established brand and corporate names.

Corporate image research may also be used to uncover new products people think are compatible with an established corporate name which may not be those that management expects. Consumers judge product compatibility from a personal point of view that may differ drastically from that of the manufacturer. The manufacturer may reason that he should keep within his special areas of manufacturing competence. Consumers may see this in a different light entirely.

Shareholders and the 'City'

These groups are receiving increasing attention from companies in recent years. While consumer research techniques in the main apply, there are special problems one may encounter in researching these publics. The next chapter is devoted to financial relations research.

Opinion leaders

Much misleading work has been done in the name of opinion leader research in the past. Many studies of AB men have purported to represent opinion leaders' opinions. Yet for all the work that has been done in this area, none has shown that there is any constant segment of the public that can truly be termed 'opinion leaders'. Other studies have been conducted with parliamentarians, the press, with business executives, and even with clergy, in the belief that they are in a position to mould public opinion: *so they are* but what is most often forgotten is that this ability to mould public opinion varies enormously, depending on the subject. The big businessman, for instance, may wield enormous influence among his contacts when he recommends an industrial product, or a share to buy; he may also influence the son of a friend seeking career advice; but it is unlikely his word on washing powders or washing machines, or even for whom to vote, would swing much weight, for the thing that is often overlooked in this sort of study is the selective perceptions of those led, and selective indeed they are.

Precise sample selection and careful attention to ensure full and comprehensive interviews (nearly always personal if to be most useful) is of prime importance. A key is the thought that the most valuable image study, probably by a factor of ten, is the second one, after the facts have been obtained from a first study and action has been taken based on the facts uncovered. It is necessary to structure the study so it may be replicated a year or two hence. This requires a sample construction that will enable comparisons to be made and more attention to sampling than 'ten of those and twenty of those'.

Potential employees

Potential employees generally fall into three categories: managers, staff and workers. In each category there are a number of factors that affect the two elements of successful recruitment, attracting appropriate applicants and convincing the desired applicants to 'sign up'. Factors potential employees consider important to know about a company, media they value and remuneration expectations may be researched. Hundreds of thousands of pounds are spent each year on recruitment activities, yet the amount of research to improve the effectiveness of recruiting is practically nil.

Community studies

Consumers, employees, potential employees, opinion leaders, a prime source of shareholders, suppliers, and others gather in the community in which the company is located. Some companies have looked at residents of these local areas as a separate audience to be researched. Especially interesting to factory managers and other executives concerned with community relations are social issues and the concept of corporate citizenship. Do the townspeople regard the company's offices and factories as assets or liabilities? Is the company blamed for pollution? Is the company regarded as a good place to work? If not, why not? These and many other areas of general interest become especially relevant in communities in which the company is a major force.

Suppliers

Another audience of importance often overlooked is the company's suppliers. A few companies have realized that if they can help their suppliers serve them more economically and effectively, the company will itself reap rewards in lower prices, better delivery and service, and generally more effective purchasing.

The 'Trade'

Other important, but also often overlooked, links in the chain are the company's distributors, dealers, or agents. These are, to many companies, the only contact with consumers, and yet often go unresearched. Within the trade, corporate image—dealer relations, delivery practices, payment policies and the like—are very important and sometimes the key to success or failure. This is a group usually easily, if not inexpensively, researched. As in any 'image' study, it is most valuable done periodically, so that the effect of changes that occur can be reliably measured over time.

Employees

And finally, employees. How much 'upward communication' is there? Management attention is overwhelmingly devoted to telling employees what to do and rarely listens to what employees, at all levels, think about the company and how it can be made more effective. As a letter to the Editor of the Financial Times: put it,

> However much it spends on the introduction of modern management techniques and up-to-date equipment and machinery, a company still depends for its success in the end on recruiting and holding sufficient staff of the right calibre at all levels from the boardroom to the shop floor. In these days, this can be a difficult enough process without the added drawback of a poor employer image. Anyone who has had anything to do with the operation of confidential reply or box number services must be able to compile a list of firms to which candidates frequently request their applications should not be forwarded. In the closer knit professional groups, a whisper on the grapevine can mean death to successful recruitment. How many companies even take the trouble to find out what their employees think about them—as employers? The attitude survey technique is still too little used. Perhaps some employers prefer not to know just how bad their image is. Sometimes, no doubt, the bad employer's image is a deserved one in which case the remedy lies elsewhere than in improved communications; but employers who take more trouble in talking (by word of mouth or in print) to their employees in a language they can understand, who take pains not to create mystery where none exists, will find the rewards in

terms of improved recruitment and reduced staff turnover are well worth the trust and effort.

Still too few companies have made employee attitude measurements a regular aspect of their research program.

How to do it

Corporate images don't exist in a vacuum; they are affected by the company's activities, its industry's image and by information from competing companies. All images are comparative; therefore, wherever possible, and this means in most studies of corporate 'publics', one must study a company's image in the context of other companies. This, in the case of image studies of 'publics' outside the company itself, leads to the development of cooperative studies and the dual advantage of the reduction in the demands made on the public under study and the price to the client.

There are such surveys conducted by a number of market research organizations. These include semi-annual surveys of corporate image amongst the general public and annual corporate image surveys amongst AB men and final-year male undergraduates in universities. Also, technical staff recruitment surveys are undertaken periodically, as are various trade surveys. Employee attitude studies are more difficult in that comparative studies are impossible (except of course over time) without access to data collected from a cross-section of other studies and few agencies have done enough work in this area in the UK to provide a sufficiently broad data base of 'normative' information.

As there are a number of special considerations as to the methodology of internal studies, it may be useful to devote a few paragraphs to how employee attitude studies are carried out. Further reference to this type of work is found in a recent article in Delta Review[9].

The goal of an employee attitude survey is to produce an accurate and detailed picture of employee satisfactions as well as their dissatisfactions, their knowledge and understanding of the company and its operations, any 'road blocks' which may be limiting employee productivity, reactions to company communications and the like.

It is important, whenever possible, to have access to previous studies which have developed data on important aspects of employee attitudes and thinking. These accumulated results can serve as norms against which to judge survey results in any given company.

In order to develop the necessary understanding of the specific company's employee relations practices and objectives, to discuss current operating problems and to explore employees' ideas as to 'what the survey really should cover', the research agency normally conducts preliminary interviews with members of management and representatives of all groups to be surveyed.

534

Depending on such factors as the geographical dispersion, levels to be included, the number of employees who can be taken off the job for the survey and the budget available for obtaining and processing the data, the procedure may be as follows.

Ideally, survey all employees—a survey based on 100% coverage takes maximum advantage of the morale-building potential of employee attitude research. It also permits detailed analysis of results department by department or unit by unit and an analysis of the thinking of small groups of employees whose functions or problems may be deemed especially important. If a census is not possible, all employees at a single location, of like job classification, should participate in the survey. If half are sampled, the half that are selected tend to say 'Why pick on me?' and the half that are left out say 'Don't my opinions count?'.

Alternatively, if a representative sample of employees is surveyed, the sample can be so planned that an adequate number of interviews is obtained from both supervisory and non-supervisory employees and that enough interviews are taken in major departments to permit separate analysis of the results for key employee groups.

Some employee surveys have been very satisfactorily carried out by mail. In 1975 a ten-country employee attitude survey was carried out among salesmen, service engineers and managers from a large multinational company. A response rate of 75% overall was achieved while response rates from individual countries ranged from 65% to 91%.

The following list suggests possible questioning areas that might be considered:

(a) How is the company regarded as a place to work?
(b) How do employees regard their supervisors?
(c) What do employees think of the employee benefits provided for them?
(d) How do employees evaluate the various methods of communication used by the company?
(e) What is the attitude toward promotion practices and policies?
(f) How do employees feel about job security?
(g) How do employees appraise working conditions?
(h) What is the extent of employees' knowledge of important economic facts?
(i) What is the appraisal of the management of the company?

In addition to this type of question, the survey should include some questions that give employees the opportunity to say, in their own words, whatever is on their minds.

Also included on the questionnaire are background questions designed to permit analysis of replies of various groups of employees. Frequently, special tabulations are made by departments, sex, length of service, occupation, location, etc. This detailed type of analysis enables the company to isolate

535

sources of dissatisfaction wherever they exist. Results are reported only for groups of employees, of course, not for individuals.

Conclusion

Corporate research differs from most other forms of market research being carried out here today because it is at the same time both tactical and strategic. It is geared both to finding out gaps between the facts as they are and as people believe them to be—immediately actionable—and to pointing the way for the future.

Corporate research can take many forms among the 'publics' under research. Corporate research can be carried out with all 'publics' of interest to a corporation, all 'publics' having influence over its destiny, including consumers, employees, potential employees, the plant community, parliamentarians, opinion leaders, shareholders, and so on.

The importance of the corporate image is just beginning to be felt here. It will become even more important in the future than it is today. It is the responsibility of research to help management to understand and measure its importance and effect on the future.

22. Market research in the financial field

Michael Burrows

Financial research may be most simply defined as 'all market research survey work concerned with matters affecting the financial community'. For a variety of reasons, some practical and some emotional, the financial community made comparatively little use of market research until recently. However, the situation is changing rapidly, as the City itself is changing, in response to the increasing influence of the 'professional investors' (the insurance companies' investment managers, etc.) and the brokers' investment analysts, whose success depends largely on the quality of their own research activities. There is also, among insurance companies, unit trusts and merchant bankers, a growing awareness of, and interest in, new marketing methods—often involving a more direct approach to the public or to potential customers, the development of new services, and the need for more effective advertising and promotional campaigns. Moreover, the financial community is being subjected to the constant pressures of increasing costs and growing competition which, as in industry, encourages the growth of larger units, which in turn need a more 'professional' management structure. Against this background, it is not surprising to find that financial research is a growing segment of the market research business, continually throwing up new problems and new opportunities.

Research Problems

The range of problems that may be encountered in the field of financial research may be divided into three broad categories, as follows.

First, factors affecting the portfolio investment decisions of both professional and private shareholders including, for example:

(a) how investment managers judge the 'quality of management' in a company, and the 'personality of the chief executive'; or what influences private shareholders to invest in government stocks, unit trusts, building societies or the shares of individual public companies;

(b) factual data about individual companies or sectors of industry for use by investment analysts. This is usually a very different type of work, more akin to industrial research than the problems described in the above paragraph which are, perhaps, of a more fundamental, qualitative, attitudinal nature. Problems may be concerned primarily with long-term forecasts of the demand for industrial products, the degree of competition and the prospects for profit, the scope for rationalization or mergers, the import/export situation, and, perhaps most important, brand share data which may indicate which companies are on the up and which are failing;

(c) the collection and analysis of market research data for general forecasting purposes, in order to confirm or modify statistical forecasts in accordance with the degree of optimism existing among consumers or in industry, changes in consumers' attitudes towards spending and saving and towards the different savings media, i.e. the Building Societies, the clearing banks and the TSB, and unit trusts, etc.

Second, factors affecting the use made of the services offered by City firms concerned with banking, insurance, or brokerage, e.g. what influences a public company to use one bank rather than another? Why do the institutional investors use one stockbroker rather than another? Why do people use one insurance company or invest in one unit trust rather than another, and how can they best be influenced to change?

Third, corporate communications including:

(a) factors affecting the 'image' of a company. In all matters affecting finance a firm's reputation and standing is of prime importance and, indeed, a company's continued existence may depend upon its reputation if it becomes involved in a disputed takeover bid. One may be concerned with either an industrial company's reputation in the City, or a bank's reputation in industry, or even a foreign bank's reputation with other banks in the City from which it may expect its business to come;

(b) readership and advertising research insofar as it affects the financial community, e.g. what do stockbrokers read in the train on their way to the City, and before the market opens? Who reads the Chairmen's statements advertised in the press? How best can one reach private shareholders or investment managers during a takeover bid?

It is, of course, always easier to delineate problems than to solve them, and the rest of this chapter is concerned with, first, a discussion of some of the problems common to most financial research surveys, including sampling, contact and interviewing, quantitative and qualitative analyses; and then more specific notes on recent developments and some of the major issues encountered in each of the three fields of research outlined above.

538

Sampling

The sampling problem is usually unique to each survey, but there are certain basic works of reference which should provide at least the basis of a sampling frame, although they may each have their limitations, as explained in the paragraphs that follow.

First, the *Stock Exchange Yearbook* contains a formidable list of institutions—banks, insurance companies, etc.—but many of them are quite small offices of foreign banks, and must have only limited investment interests. There are probably only about 175 to 300 effective institutional investors (including the insurance companies, pension funds, investment and unit trusts, merchant banks, etc.) and their identification is mainly dependent upon personal knowledge. The *Stock Exchange Yearbook* does not, however, provide a list of stockbrokers.

Second, *Crawfords Directory of City Connections* lists the major stock-broking firms, with some indication of size given by the number of listed companies which principally consult them. Crawfords also gives lists of companies and their primary stockbrokers and merchant banks. The Directory is updated every six months.

Third, in many surveys, particularly those concerned with takeover bids and 'financial' corporate image studies, the views of the 20 City editors of the major daily, evening, Sunday and weekly journals may be of prime importance because of their persuasive influence upon influential City opinion, particularly their morning and evening 'captive' train readership audiences.

Fourth, *The Financial Times Acturaries' Index* includes 625 major British public companies, conveniently divided into 41 groups and sub-groups, such as building materials, breweries and banks, etc. Together, these firms account for 80% of the market value of all British quoted companies and about 60% of UK manufacturing capacity. Its main limitation is that the major subsidiaries of foreign firms, such as Ford, IBM and Alcan, etc., are excluded, as are the major private companies such as Rubery Owen and Pilkington's. The 'Times 1000' gives details of the largest 1000 companies operating in Britain, including subsidiaries of those owned abroad.

Finally, for the larger universes, as in industrial surveys, one may go to Dun and Bradstreet's *Guide to Key British Enterprises*, which lists the largest 15 000 firms, or to Kompass, which includes most firms with more than 50 employees and those who are members of the CBI.

The names and addresses of all private shareholders are, of course, listed in Companies House, and for a small fee a representative sample may be compiled. This is useful in the case of a takeover bid when there is a need to interview the shareholders of a particular company, but if the requirement is to interview shareholders—or unit trust holders—in general, it is usually cheaper to ask an identifying question on a continuous omnibus survey, with a view to re-interviewing an appropriate sample in a second-phase operation.

Contact and Interviewing

Respondents in the financial community are usually as busy and brusque as any in industry, and probably less willing to suffer fools gladly. However, if the subject interests them, and if the interviewer is well-briefed and intelligent, they can be more courteous, better informed and more helpful than most people.

During a recent survey among senior investment managers, a response rate of 90% was obtained, which is better than one would expect from either an average group of housewives or AB class men as a whole. The subject was of particular interest to them, but the markets were quite busy and this response rate was much better than anticipated. The questionnaire guide had been carefully designed, and piloted, to keep the interview down to 40 minutes, which was thought to be the limit of a busy man's tolerance, but in fact many of the discussions ran on to 90 minutes, and even two hours, in spite of explicit instructions to interviewers to 'get out before they became a bore'.

In these situations the quality and character of the interviewer is of fundamental importance, and there is persuasive evidence that, even in the City, an intelligent, mature, and experienced female is far superior to a male! It seems that, in the City as elsewhere, men tend to judge men instantly, instinctively and usually unflatteringly—'a young demo' 'a drunken has-been' or a 'retired colonel', etc.—and respondents become quickly bored. By contrast, an intelligent woman who has had previous experience in commerce may listen more sensitively, probe more delicately and record what she hears more objectively, perhaps because she has fewer preconceived opinions. Good male interviewers can be very good but they are not easy to find or to keep, as interviewers, for long.

The danger in financial research, as in the industrial field, is that the very small number of potential respondents will become over-interviewed, and permanently alienated by over-persistent, ill-briefed, dull interviewers struggling through a long, highly structured questionnaire more suitably designed for pet-food purchasers.

There are certain situations, such as takeover bids, where it is quite unnecessary to waste respondents' time with lengthy personal interviews. City people are accustomed to doing much of their business by telephone, and are usually quite ready to spend ten minutes discussing the factors affecting a particular bid situation, or the effect of a recent counter-offer: but it is often helpful if respondents have met the interviewer previously, or at least have been interviewed, without antagonism, by the research agency on some previous occasion.

540

Whom to Interview

Perhaps the major problem in any survey concerned with City services, such as banking, is deciding whom to interview (as in many industrial research surveys). One may, for example, telephone a large company and ask to speak to 'the person who takes the responsibility for export trade insurance matters': eventually one should get through to an export manager or an insurance manager or perhaps a shipping manager, depending on the firm's organization and job titles (no two firms seem to call the man doing the same job by the same title: or if they have the same title their responsibility and status may vary enormously from company to company). However, one's problems are then by no means at an end, because the person who takes important day-to-day decisions about insurance or shipping problems may not be the person who takes the responsibility for a major change of policy: this could well become a boardroom decision, powerfully affected by the views of the finance director or the company secretary (whose responsibilities and status may again vary considerably from company to company).

One solution is to interview the person contacted by telephone, then to ask who else might be concerned with a major policy change of the type outlined, and then who might finally decide if there was a conflict of opinion within the company on the subject. This final referral is probably as near to the decision maker in that company as one can get, and a final five minute interview with him, if it can be arranged, is often of the greatest value.

Quantitative and Qualitative Analyses

Most clients in the financial field are numerate by nature, and they tend to be more impressed by percentages than by qualitative comment and interpretation; therefore, in spite of the comparatively small universe, it is usually desirable to interview at least 100 respondents, which allows perhaps two or three breakdowns; for example London versus The Rest; those aged under 45 versus the over-45's; large, medium, and small scale stockbrokers (according to number of partners or investment analysts), etc. In theory there might seem to be a large standard error involved in small samples, but in practice 100 interviews may cover a substantial part of the total universe involved, so that the problem is less than it appears.

In order to provide a sensible statistical framework for analysis, it may be necessary to evolve a simple code list—sometimes merely 'favourable', 'unfavourable', 'mixed', 'indecisive/no comment'—upon which answers can be quickly and cheaply coded, punched, and run through the computer to provide a quantified framework for an essentially qualitative analysis of opinions and facts influencing investment decisions, etc. The questionnaire guide must, however, also be designed so that at least the main points of any significant answers can be recorded by the interviewer, so that a research executive can subsequently go through the interview notes and pick out quotations which illustrate, qualitatively, the tenor of respondents' replies and the emphasis with which they express their preferences or prejudices. This is a task that requires considerable skill, experience and patience: the best interviewers' work can be reduced to platitudes by an unimaginative commentator, or worse still biased by an injudicious selection of quotations. In this sense, the success or failure of most surveys may depend ultimately upon the quality of the commentator, and the skill and patience with which he 'de-briefs' his interviewers.

Private Shareholders

During takeover bid situations, or as part of the development, or assessment, of a corporate communication program, it may be desirable to interview a sample of shareholders. These will fall into three groups: institutional investors, whom we have already dealt with, nominee shareholdings, which are 'cloaked' holdings whose real identity can not be unravelled by a market research company, and private shareholders.

The names and addresses of these latter can be obtained either from Companies' House or, if one has access, from the Company's own Registrar, who can normally make available computer printout lists, and printed address labels. The problem is that private shareholders may live in widely dispersed areas, but they do tend to be elderly and to live in the main retirement areas and the up-market commuter areas (including Hampstead and Fulham). Most shareholders have telephones, but elderly ladies do not interview well on the telephone, and unless the questionnaire is kept very short and simple, it becomes necessary to conduct time-consuming and expensive personal interviews, often during the evening in order to contact a proper proportion of working executives.

Relevant Research Work

Development problems

Factors Affecting Investors' Decisions

As regards institutional investors two surveys have been published: *the GEC bid for AEI* (published by J. Walter Thompson) and *Professional Investor* (published by the 'Investors Chronicle').

The 'GEC bid' survey was conducted about two months after the event, and was mainly concerned with the factors influencing institutional investors to support one firm rather than the other, and to enquire into City readership habits. One of the most interesting tables, which may merit reproduction yet again, showed the four major factors influencing investment decisions to be:

Factor rated as important:	Stock-brokers	Institutional investors	Private shareholders
Quality of management team	36%	35%	38%
Profit potential (over next two years)	31%	25%	53%
Profit record (over past five years)	11%	25%	36%
Personality of chief executive	20%	12%	27%

To the numerate, such a table may have a certain plausibility, but in fact the argument tends to go round in a circle. 'How do you estimate future profits'? Partly at least by reference to past profits. 'How do you judge the quality of management'? Partly at least by the past profit record. Similarly, 'How do you judge the quality of the chief executive'? Again, quite frequently, by his profit record—'Arnie Weinstock must be good: look at his record'. The last few years, and months, however, have seen several examples of men with a brilliant record who have made a miscalculation or over-reached themselves and been unhorsed as a result. A research man must feel instinctively that some more objective criteria could, or should, be developed which would at least give some early warning signals when matters were going astray, or the chief executives were moving from the 'dynamic' category to the 'eccentric' or 'megalomanic' classification.

In a rather different field, a series of unpublished surveys has been conducted recently into factors affecting attitudes towards savings in the various media ranging from building societies to the banks and unit trusts. It is clear that most people look for 'security' and a 'reasonable' rate of interest, and they are reluctant to invest in things they 'do not understand', which often includes stocks and shares, unit trusts and complicated insurance policies.

Part of the building societies' success in attracting funds can of course be attributed to the fact that they open the way to home ownership, and the prospects of capital gains and tax relief that are associated with that happy state, but they also benefit from the feeling of security, permanence and familiarity engendered by their High Street presence (where they have probably been established since you first passed them in your pram!). But much more research needs to be done before one can fully explain why the building societies pull on so much more private money than the banks, or unit trusts or the Stock Exchange—and whether their present success will be any more enduring than the 1960's equity cult.

Special problems arise when conducting research during an actual take-over situation, when the usual problem is to identify the major factors affecting the outcome and to monitor changes of opinion as they occur, almost from day to day, in a variety of different audiences.

Thus, in one major bid 'battle' one research company (BMRB) was asked to launch seven separate surveys in seven days among financial editors, stockbrokers, and institutional investors, bank managers, shareholders, customers, university appointment boards, and the company's own staff. Daily reports were supplied each day at about 5 p.m. for consideration that evening and at the following morning's executive committee meeting.

On another occasion the research company was asked to interview 20 shareholders a day (in practice it was usually each evening): the results were telephoned in on the following morning, hand tabulated, commented on, printed and delivered each day at 5 p.m., so that the results of bids, counterbids, and press conferences could be monitored day by day. Within 48 hours a sample of 40 was available, which built up at a rate of 20 a day, until the next phase of the 'battle' was signalled by a new bid or counterbid.

The most surprising result of such surveys is the general antipathy among small private shareholders to takeover bidders, who are often described as 'brash', 'arrogant', 'conceited', 'young' men. This may of course be attributable to the fact that in a typical British 'blue chip' company, 65% of the shareholders may be over 55, 60% women; 40% may have held their shares for over 10 years, and probably a third have had the shares 'left' or given to them. Even so it is surprising to find how reluctant many shareholders are to see 'their' company taken over, despite the financial benefits that they stand to gain.

Factual data for investment analysts

Comparatively little research is as yet commissioned by investment analysts, who usually prefer to collect their own data and to visit companies themselves. In some ways this is surprising, because market research agencies are generally much closer to the consumer and service industries than is the City, and usually have a great deal of background information and library facilities at their disposal which few broking firms could equal. Firms in the consumer and service industries do of course account for about one-third of the 500 in *The Financial Times Actuaries Index*. However, at least two major syndicated services deserve mention. The first is Taylor Nelson's 'business opinions' survey, from which some of the major results are printed monthly, in statistical form, in *The Financial Times*: but in addition monthly reports are circulated, on a confidential basis, to a limited number of stockbrokers and financial institutions. These are based on interviews conducted at regular intervals at a senior management level and designed primarily to pick up changes in management attitudes, from industry to industry, from company to company, and from year to year. Changing attitudes may be signalled by a variety of signs ranging from a change of managing director to the appointment of a finance director, the rationalization of production facilities (and an improved turnover/personnel ratio), the introduction of management consultants, or a change of advertising agents (in the case of consumer goods). Or they may be more directly reflected in growing optimism or pessimism in the company's prospects, changes in its methods of distribution (particularly overseas), changes in the product mix, etc.

On a larger scale—and more closely concerned with financial services and consumer goods industries—is BMRB's 'Target Group Index'. This is based on an annual analysis of 25 000 self-completion questionnaires (with a simplified mid-term marketing report). It covers investment media, i.e. building society investment and the ownership of stocks and shares, unit trusts and government savings, etc., and the use made of financial services, such as insurance, banking, credit cards, as well as some 112 consumer product fields including food, drink, household goods, cosmetics and medicines. All the data about product purchasing and the usage of financial services are analysed by the usual demographics (class, age, region, etc.) and by TV and newspaper readership habits, so the information can be used in two ways.

First, one can see what kind of people are investing in the different savings media, how they are changing from year to year, and through which TV station and publication they can be most readily reached. Secondly, from the investment analysts' point of view, one can see in which product fields demand is increasing, or decreasing, and which brands are expanding and which are contracting. Brands can then be indexed to companies, so that one can see at a glance how a company like Boots is faring across a range of product fields. Ideally, a company should have an expanding share of a number of expanding markets: a firm can, of course, lose money expanding a market share, but, in the longer term, it is almost impossible to increase profits while losing out in a major market (vide BLMC). In the consumer-goods field one can, of course, also check advertising expenditure, materials and labour costs, and other major variables in costs, so one should be able to assess the trend of UK profits—at least well enough to question a company's chairman with pertinency.

Research data for forecasting purposes

Since 1958 the CBI and its predecessor the FBI have been producing reports on businessmen's current experience and expectations over the whole range of manufacturing activity. The full reports are now produced quarterly, with interim notes monthly. The results are widely reported in the press and are taken into account by government departments, economists and industrialists (references to the survey's predictive value are to be found in *Applied Economics* August 1969, *CBI Review* 1974 and *NIES Review* August 1975)[6, 7, 8].

A 'business opinion' survey has also been conducted by the Taylor Nelson Group since 1966, and is reported monthly in *The Financial Times*. It is based on the views of about 30 industrialists each month, representing the firms listed in *The Financial Times Actuaries Index* of 500 major public companies. Experiments illustrating its predictive value were reported to the 10th CIRET conference in Brussels in September 1970.

In the field of consumer durables the Gallup Poll have been collecting data on 'intentions to purchase' durables and the attitudes of consumers to the economy over the period 1959–1975. An Index of Consumer Confidence is derived with the aid of a principal component analysis from five attitudinal questions. The Index is incorporated into an econometric model and is shown to have a useful predictive value up to six to nine months ahead. References to this study were included the EEC reports to the 12th CIRET Conference at Stockholm in June 1975, and in *Konsum und Qualitat des Lebens* 1974.

BMRB has also been following the work done in Michigan University, interviewing a nationally representative sample of 1000 adults a month and asking them basically whether they feel better or worse off than 12 months previously; whether they expect economic conditions to improve or worsen in future; and whether they think it a good, or not a good, time to buy durables. Now that the series has been running since 1970, some useful predictive developments are appearing: experimental work is being conducted at a number of universities, including Warwick, Edinburgh and Exeter and was reported upon at a symposium in the City in April 1975 and at the Montreux ESOMAR Congress in September 1975.

Echoing Gilbert and Sullivan it can be said that 'A forecaster's lot is not a happy one', but one is persuaded that further research along these lines is merited, and that the 'areas of uncertainty' are being steadily diminished as a result of the continuous research work being undertaken by a variety of academic and commercial organizations.

Research into Services Provided by the Financial Community

The City and other financial centres in Britain provide a wide range of services including banking, insurance, brokerage, merchanting of all kinds and money management. An intricate network of agents, brokers, bankers and discount houses had developed over centuries which makes the City of London in many ways unique. Some have better adapted to changing conditions than others; but attempts to alter established methods in advance of demand can cause difficulties.

An example of this was an attempt to alter established insurance procedures for containerized traffic. There is general agreement that containerization reduces pilferage and damage to goods in transit, and it seemed logical to offer a standard rate of insurance for such traffic; but this was calculated to be higher than existing rates for large companies with a good insurance record, and there was a loss of flexibility which caused the scheme to be shelved. This is the type of problem that can be surveyed by a competent agency with an experienced research staff, but most City firms would probably still be reluctant to entrust such a problem to a non-City research agency, for fear of alienating potential clients by wasting their time with superficial questions. They can only be reassured, over a period of time, by competent, and constructive research work conscientiously undertaken.

In recent years NOP Market Research has conducted major syndicated surveys based on random samples of 80 000 personal interviews. These cover both savings habits and private investment patterns.

Corporate Communications

Major developments have been taking place in the field of corporate communications during the last few years, as more companies have come to appreciate that their reputation, or 'image', is of prime importance in all matters affecting finance and that the continued existence of the company (and the career prospects of its senior executives) may be at hazard if the firm becomes involved in a takeover bid. A sound 'corporate image' will, of course, also greatly assist the marketing staff to sell more goods and introduce new products, the personnel department to recruit and retain managers and staff at reasonable salaries, as well as all those who have dealings with the government, local authorities, the unions and the press, over matters ranging from planning permission to pollution. This aspect of the problem is dealt with at greater length in chapter 21.

As regards a company's 'corporate image' in the City, a very great deal depends upon its profit record, which, as was explained earlier (in connection with the 'GEC bid' report), powerfully influences the City's views on a company's future earnings, the quality of its management and the effectiveness of its chief executive. It follows that the main determinant of a company's reputation in financial circles is its profit (or loss) figures, but companies do also have a powerful opportunity to communicate with professional and private investors through the medium of the annual chairman's statement and by discussions with individual stockbrokers and merchant bankers.

A recent survey showed that a surprisingly large proportion of company directors felt it quite wrong that a firm should try to influence its share price on the stock market, which, it was said, was quite irrelevant to the proper conduct of the company's business. In many cases stockbrokers' visits were regarded as a nuisance, and primary factors governing the drafting of the chairman's annual statement were that nothing should be given away to competitors and that no leverage should be given to the executive staff, the unions, suppliers, customers, the DTI or the DFT to expect higher bonuses or pay, or better bargains or lower prices, etc. Such negative attitudes, however, may be counter-productive, because there is some evidence that private shareholders, at least, and some advisers including bank managers and solicitors and stockbrokers, are instinctively attracted towards companies like Marks and Spencer, Beechams, and Boots, which have established a reputation for quality and sensitivity to public opinion. Indeed, it can be argued that it is only companies that have established a reputation for social responsibility that can steadily raise their prices and their profits without public outcry and government interference and this could be of increasing importance in the years ahead, as governments struggle to control wage-cost inflation and rising unemployment by an intensification of prices-and-incomes policies.

It follows that if a company has a policy for developing and projecting its 'image', then it should also assess the effectiveness of that policy by regularly measuring its own standing and reputation against that of its major competitors, or comparably sized firms, in the financial field as well as in the spheres of customer relationships, personnel recruitment, etc.

Readership and advertising research

Financial advertising varies enormously in scale and content from the announcement of company results and the chairman's statement to 'offer' and unit trust advertisements and corporate advertising beamed at the financial community. It is necessary to discuss each in turn because they differ so widely. As regards chairmen's statements a great deal of research still needs to be done. It used to be traditional for the chairmen of major companies, particularly the banks, to print their statement in full in the leading financial journals. Insofar as these statements were often the company's considered views on the state of the country's economy this was, and still is, useful, because in paid space a chairman's views cannot be distorted, edited or ignored. However, in recent years, it has become customary for some companies to limit their annual advertisement to a few headlines covering profits, major changes and prospects. One may argue that this more commercial approach may have gone too far, and that a valuable promotional opportunity may often be being discarded too lightly, often, it seems, because the advertising and drafting of the chairman's statement is the responsibility of the company secretary rather than, say, the advertising manager or a director concerned with marketing or sales who might take a broader view of the issues involved.

The research problem is not only to identify the various target audiences for statements of this kind but also to determine how best they may be influenced. A basic difficulty is that one part of the audience is highly numerate and is basically interested only in the profit and turnover figures, analysed in as much detail as possible, and the prospects, preferably expressed in numerate terms; but the wider audience, ranging from Members of Parliament to elderly private shareholders and employees, may not be very numerate and they primarily want to be reassured, or persuaded that they are concerned with a company which is large, but humane; profitable, technically advanced and efficiently run but socially responsible (not surprisingly, survey results show that, under such headings, Marks and Spencer, ICI and Sainsbury rate very well with all sections of the community).

Turning to 'offers' (company prospectuses, etc.) and unit trust advertising, one is immediately restricted by the legal requirements, which are largely responsible for the tone and format of those formidable advertisements which fill the City pages when the market is rising, but perhaps market research could, and should, be used to test the effectiveness of such advertising and the relative impact of advertising and direct mail.

In the case of unit trust advertising, in particular, the case for further research work seems persuasive, because only about 20% of their income is derived from the 'instant response' to City page advertising, i.e. the money received within days in direct response to a unit trust advertisement. The bulk of their money therefore comes from regular weekly or monthly payments, often linked with an insurance policy or via a bank, perhaps influenced by the 'point-of-sale' material available in most banks.

Further research might well show that more promotion or more advertising in the popular dailies and the women's weeklies could substantially increase this market, particularly if rational arguments could be developed for investing when the market is historically low rather than pulling in the money as the market rises to a peak (thereby inevitably creating groups of dissatisfied customers soured by any subsequent market fall).

The whole subject of unit trust advertising was discussed quite fully at the Advertising Association Conference in May 1970, and again at the Unitholder's second conference on 'Unit Trust and Money Management' (June, 1970) and at the ESOMAR "Financial and Banking" seminar at Versailles in January, 1975. At present only about 5% of all adults hold unit trusts, as compared with 39% who have Premium Bonds and 29% who have a National Savings Bank account: the differences are large, and seem certain to attract more research and analysis.

The third area for research in this field is more concerned with conventional readership or 'reading and noting' studies. Readership surveys are probably the most rigorously controlled of all market research work done: an effective survey will almost certainly require the imprimatur of the IPA, who will need to be satisfied that a survey has been based upon a statistically valid sampling frame and the use of the exact JICNARS phraseology (see chapter 24) to ensure comparability with other surveys. However, stockbrokers and investment managers tend to read, or look at, a very large number of publications, and therefore the JICNARS questions need to be supplemented by questions about the relative 'authoritativeness' attributed to each journal read, and also about reading habits. Is a paper bought privately or by the firm? Is it read at home, on the train or in the office? Is it read early in the day or, perhaps, days later on an office circulation list?

The 'GEC bid' report drew particular attention to the importance of morning train readership and the influence that certain commentators, notably 'Lex' in *The Financial Times*, have upon morning investment conferences and opening prices, even if they form only the basis for discussion between partners or brokers and investment managers. Two quotations from that report may illustrate the point: 'I have 25 minutes in the train: I allow five for idle chatter and 20 for the FT'; 'I would sack any analyst who had not read Lex by the time the market opened'.

Conclusions

Financial research covers a wide range of subjects—none of which have been adequately investigated as yet: indeed, very little had been done at all until the late 1960's, but there is every reason to believe that the demand for such work will grow rapidly in the future as investors, the City institutions and the brokers become more professionalized and better able to handle—and put to profitable use—the flow of information that can be fed to them.

23. International market research

John Downham

International Research can be defined as research carried out in a country other than that of the sponsor. For the purpose of this chapter, this means research conducted outside the UK on behalf of UK-based organizations.

This covers a very wide variety of situations. At one extreme, the sponsor may be interested in whether or not he should move into some market with which in the past he has had no dealings of any kind. At the other extreme, he may already have a substantial local operation—agency, associate or even branch—active in the market concerned, but nevertheless wishes for reasons of international policy himself to carry out research there. On a different dimension, international research may be concerned with a single country exclusively; or with several countries simultaneously, or in sequence; or even with research carried out regularly across a number of countries on a more or less continuous basis. International research thus comes in many different shapes and sizes. It is *not* synonymous with 'export' market research, or with 'multinational' studies—although both these types of activity form part of the total.

This chapter looks at a number of the key issues which are encountered in such research. Certain of the issues are peculiar to the international field. Many of the problems are, however, to be found in national or domestic research also, although on the international front they tend to appear on a larger scale and sometimes in a rather different guise.

The Development of International Market Research

The development of market research generally is bound up with, and depends on, the development of modern marketing methods. The same is even more true of international market research. Although international *trade* pre-dates history, international *marketing* in any full sense is a very recent development indeed. Systematic and scientific international research did not really get underway until the 1950's, the breakthrough coming during the 1960's. For a long time the majority of such research was sponsored by the larger multinational companies, particularly American, British and a few Continental firms operating in fields such as consumer durables, detergents, food, oil, pharmaceuticals and tobacco. A great part of this work was in fact carried out for local rather than international planning purposes, since many even of the multinationals have only recently marketed brands on a genuinely international (and internationally researched) basis.

It is worth emphasizing that the growth of international manufacturing and service organizations does not in itself necessarily lead to an equivalent growth in international research. The majority of marketing planning and operating decisions are still carried out at national rather than international level. As a result most market research work is also commissioned at national level. International surveys form a relatively small proportion of all the market research carried out, even for the international companies[8].

As Keegan[17] has pointed out, there is a range of different strategies possible in multinational marketing:

1. The same (or virtually the same) product can be sold in different countries, using the same advertising approach—he cites Coca Cola as an example.
2. The same product may be sold, but using a different advertising approach in different countries—an example being the outboard motor business.
3. The product offered may differ in some way but be sold with the same advertising approach—the example quoted being Esso petrol.
4. Both product and advertising may be varied to suit the needs of the local market—for example, Nescafé.
5. Finally, in the extreme case the company may market completely different product concepts and formulations, differently advertised, in different countries.

These alternative strategies may of course be associated with differing degrees of centralization or decentralization in the company concerned. Multinational research policies vary all the way from completely standardized approaches and methods, centrally specified, to complete independence of the local branches to decide what to research and how to do it. Whatever the situation in this respect, the requirements for international research as such are likely to be quite different (in both amount and type) from one strategy to another. Any discussion of international research approaches and case histories thus makes sense only when it is related to the sponsoring company's strategy and operating methods[16].

Problems of International Research

One basic difficulty of much international research is the element of *unfamiliarity*[30]. Compared with his home market, the sponsor may know relatively little about the characteristics of the country and its people, the local customs and ways of life, the market structure and marketing methods, etc. He may know even less about the possibilities and problems of carrying out research in the country. This situation can lead to uncertainty and insecurity on the one hand, and the danger of false assumptions and conclusions on the other. The sponsor will, if he is wise, realize the need for even more help and careful pre-planning than in the case of domestic research.

Even for a company experienced in international marketing and research, however, there are still many additional hazards. The first is the vastly greater problem of *communication*. This is not just a question of different languages, although these undoubtedly complicate the issue. Nor is it due only to geographical distance, although this may add to the time, difficulties and cost involved in setting up the research. More basic problems stem from differences in customs, ways of thought and experience between different cultures, in addition to the more obvious range of local market differences, which can complicate and confuse the planning of a research project. It is easy to fall into the trap of assuming that someone from another country is working to the same (unspecified) assumptions as yourself, or is using words in the same way, when this is not the case. A shake of the head, or the word 'yes', mean different things in different cultures: it is even easier for misunderstandings to arise with the more subtle issues of research design and logic.

Further problems arise in connection with the *organization and administration* of international research, sometimes at long range. In the case of multinational projects, there is the issue of which research organization(s) to select and how to coordinate their work. Even where only one country is involved, how do we best ensure that the research on the spot is adequately set up and efficiently carried out? Effective control of an international research project is liable to be much more difficult than that of a national project.

Further difficulties sometimes arise from the *nature of the client company* itself. It has already been pointed out that international companies vary greatly in their international management style. The degree of centralization or decentralization is likely to affect the way research is initiated, planned and carried through. It may be difficult for a highly decentralized organization to arrange for closely comparable multinational research, given widely varying interests and requirements of its local operations. Conversely, there are sometimes occasions on which the regional or international headquarters wishes to carry out research without directly involving its local operators in the project—where for example the findings of the research are concerned with confidential international planning, diversification issues, etc. Problems of these kinds at best complicate, and can at worst stultify, effective international research.

All these problems, and others, are normally in addition to—or at least a magnified version of—the kinds of research problems discussed in other chapters. They must of course not be overstressed. It is perfectly possible to carry out effective market research in most countries of the world, given adequate planning. Adequate planning does, however, mean full awareness of the difficulties which are likely to be encountered, knowledge of how these are most likely to be overcome, and acceptance of the fact that certain kinds of research information cannot practicably be obtained in certain countries for cost, technical or other reasons. Before turning to the practical issues of how to set about international market research in ways which minimize these problems, we should therefore first look more closely at some of the problems themselves.

Market Differences

The problem of unfamiliarity referred to above reflects many different factors. Most of these are obvious ones, although some of their effects may not be. Certain operate even *within* the UK—witness Allen's book on 'British Tastes'[1]: as researchers we ignore at our peril differences in vocabulary between North and South, or the more fundamental cultural differences between (say) the Home Counties and the mining areas. On the international scene such differences are, however, magnified many times. The fact that we are probably more likely to anticipate them in international research does not mean that it is easy to deal with them when they turn up.

Language

This obviously can produce considerable complications for market research, especially where a number of different languages are used within the same country. It causes problems in the wording (translation) of questionnaires, in the organization of fieldwork and in the analysis of open-ended questions. We therefore have to decide, for example, how far we should attempt to cover all the different language groups in a given survey. Unless we are concerned with some specialized study of, say, crofting we can usually afford to exclude Gaelic speakers from a study of the UK market. But in the case of Switzerland, for example, should we ignore the minority of Italian speakers living in the Ticino region? In the Republic of South Africa, most general market studies will be involved with both Afrikaans and English; but how many of the Black African languages ought we to use in order to cover the key sectors of this increasingly important part of the total market? Worst of all, probably, how many of the fourteen key languages is it necessary to use for a national survey in India? The fact that in a number of countries one particular language—Swahili in parts of Africa, Bahasa in Indonesia, or even on occasion English—acts as some kind of *lingua franca* does not really offer a solution. Except in the very simplest forms of research, or research among special groups, effective interviewing involves using the language normally spoken in the home by the person we wish to interview. We are unlikely to get the right information on (for example) attitudes towards different products if the housewife is having to express herself in a tongue which is not her customary one.

Fieldwork is the most critical part of any international survey. The problem of language also enters into other key sectors of the research project, however—most obviously when it comes to communication between the client and the local research agency which will carry out the survey in the country concerned. In the best of all possible worlds, the client or his research representative will be fluent in the key local language, so that all discussions with the local researchers are carried out in the latter's language. A number of international market research organizations quite rightly make an important point of this. However, we ignore reality if we try to make this a rule of operation. It is a fact of life that sometimes researchers in other countries will speak English much better than we can speak their own language. This is generally true of, for example, Scandinavia. It is almost invariably true of Japan. There can be no universally valid principle of operation here. The only possible approach is a pragmatic one—but one where we take every precaution to make sure that misunderstandings do not arise.

Ethnic differences

To some extent this point is associated with the last one: different ethnic groups often speak different languages. This is certainly not always the case, however, and anyway may well not be the most important difference between ethnic groups. Obvious major examples are the differences between white and black groups within the USA, or between the various regions of Brazil. Such differences are often reflected in consumer habits and attitudes, especially in food, and need to be very carefully considered when planning research in a foreign market. They may call for different interviewing approaches, and often for different interviewers.

Religion

This factor also can radically affect a range of habits and attitudes, most obviously again with food and drink. Differences with respect to the use of meat and alcohol are very clear as between Christians, Muslims and Hindus. There are many more subtle differences, however, which carry through into various aspects of lifestyle. These may be reflected in differing attitudes towards newer or more 'permissive' patterns of thought and behaviour, as well as in such aspects as the differing roles of men and women. The Reformation in Europe had effects which can still be traced in differences between consumers in (for example) different parts of Germany, despite the generally declining influence of religion on everday life in Western Society during the last half-century.

Social structure

In developed 'western' markets we are accustomed to talk in marketing terms of ABs, C1s etc., as being appropriate target groups for specific products or services. It is extremely dangerous to attempt to translate socio-economic concepts of this kind to other types of society. Even within Europe it can be misleading, especially if we take the UK as our model. Insofar as there is a class structure at all, that in Sweden certainly does not parallel that in the UK. Various attempts over many years to reach a generally agreed and consistent set of social class definitions in Europe have on the whole been unsuccessful. In countries outside Europe the kinds of definition used in the UK bear even less relationship to local social structures. In many countries there is no substantial middle class in the British sense, and it may be necessary (as in India or other parts of Asia) to classify households by factors such as the sources of income, ownership of land, life-style ('traditional' or not), etc. This again affects the design and analysis of surveys.

Culture and tradition

To some extent the preceding headings already cover cultural differences. There are, however, many other aspects of local cultures which can affect marketing. International studies of certain markets in Latin countries which ignored the 'machismo' factor would be incomplete. 'Face' is an important consideration to take into account in both the content and the manner of market research—and not just in the Far East. The role and significance of 'gifting' is a key element in many markets: perfume or jewellery in Western countries, but much more apparently mundane products such as toilet soap in Japan. Examples of such cultural differences are easily multiplied.

Literacy

Even in parts of Europe, literacy levels may be well below 100%. Official statistics are likely to be particularly misleading in this connection. Often the definition of 'literacy' implies no more than the ability to sign one's name. For marketing and research communication in written form to be effective, very much more than this is required. Visual aids, let alone self-completion questionnaires of various kinds, do not work well unless people have reasonable facility in reading. This problem is much more acute outside Europe. It obviously reduces our research options, particularly for techniques such as diary panels and postal product testing panels.

Income patterns

Differing levels of average per capita income clearly influence the kinds and amounts of goods and services bought by the local population. In planning research, equally important considerations are the pattern of income *distribution* and also the ways in which incomes are *earned*. Much wider variations in income between the top and the bottom of the economic scale frequently mean much more variability in buying behaviour—and consequently additional sampling problems. Another important issue is the difference between urban and rural populations. In many parts of the Third World some of the rural population may hardly be in the cash economy at all—or if they are, only at certain times of the year. In such countries the geographical spread and particularly the timing of research must take these points into account. In East Africa, for example, some sections of the rural population do most of their buying of many products during limited periods which vary from one part of the country to another, depending upon the harvesting and sale of the particular type of cash crop grown in the area.

Geography and climate

Air conditioners and fur coats are clearly products which are likely to have different market potentials varying with the climate. There are many other less obvious but nevertheless fundamental differences resulting from geography which have a profound effect on marketing—and therefore research—possibilities. Such variations very often do not conform to political frontiers. Within Europe a good example would be the 'olive oil frontier'. The availability of oil in Mediterranean Europe as a medium for cooking, and the greater difficulties of producing and marketing butter in hot countries, mean that there are major differences not merely in the cooking oil/butter/margarine markets themselves but in a whole wide range of cooking and eating habits also, within as well as between countries. The planning of multi-country research in particular is often affected by such differences—not just of latitude but also of altitude, soil, water hardness and many other factors—which cut right across the pattern of national boundaries.

Institutional factors

Differing types of market background in different countries frequently call for changes in the research approach. For example, consumers' needs in personal and clothes washing are often similar over broad regions of the world, but the ways in which these needs are met can be considerably affected by factors such as the nature of the local washing facilities available—domestic water supplies, heating arrangements, the ownership of washing machines of different kinds, the predominant use of baths or showers, etc. Even within Europe a research approach and questionnaire which is appropriate to measure clothes washing habits in the UK may need a number of modifications to make it equally suitable for Scandinavia (with communal laundry rooms in apartment blocks) or for Switzerland (with differently programmed washing machines).

Distribution

Distribution channels vary greatly from one country to the next: the rapid development of hypermarkets in France, and of discount stores in Germany, has led to a different shopping situation in these countries compared with the past and with many other countries in Europe. The degree of concentration of the grocery trade also varies enormously. Differing emphasis on competition through pricing, convenience in location or facilities, credit terms offered, etc., all affect the ways in which people carry out their shopping.

Media and advertising

The level of literacy is only one factor which affects the relative importance of different media in different countries. Commercial television does not exist at all in some countries (for example, Sweden) even though in general television tends to be the dominant medium in most advanced—and even many of the developing—economies. The quality and geographical spread of press media vary enormously, especially the relative importance of national and regional newspapers. The quality of advertising agency facilities is highly variable. And so on. Such differences affect not only the way in which consumers learn about products, but also the *nature* of the information and impressions they receive.

Legislation and regulation

The rules within which marketing operates vary from country to country. Legislation relating to fair trading issues, pricing, different types of promotional activities, the content of advertising, labelling, date-stamping, the sales of drugs and a hundred and one other marketing activities are still far from harmonized even within the EEC. Alongside the law as such there is a growing body of 'voluntary' codes, restrictions and procedures which affect the ways in which marketing operates. International research into (say) a possible advertising campaign for a food product based on a health claim could very quickly go off the rails if it failed to take account of local differences in formal and informal regulations of these kinds.

This list of differences between markets is only illustrative, and far from comprehensive (see also ref. 21). While it indicates some of the ways in which marketing has to adapt to local situations, its purpose here is to emphasize how many different issues are liable to influence the design and carrying out of marketing research internationally. All the factors mentioned can, and do, affect the design of a research project. They should, of course, be very much part of the stock-in-trade of an international market researcher. They call for considerable local knowledge and awareness of where the (often hidden) differences may lie. Much more extensive examples, including case-histories, are quoted in the literature—see for instance the papers by Berent[2] and Rusby[28].

Differences in Market Research

Market differences of the kinds referred to all influence the design and carrying out of international research projects. There are a number of other factors which even more directly affect the possibilities for market research and the way in which it is handled. These include the following.

1. *Differences in the basic data* available for use in designing the sample of people to interview. Some countries have better basic data than the UK, many have much worse. Quota sampling may be quite adequate for many commercial research purposes in the UK; but in certain other parts of the world—particularly in developing countries—it is virtually impossible to design an adequate quota sample, either because the necessary data about the relevant population characteristics cannot be obtained or because the structure of the population is in any case such as to defeat appropriate quota setting. In such cases some form of random or quasi-random sampling is called for. Even here the necessary information, for example suitable maps, may not be easily available. It is generally possible to find some way round these problems, but to do so often involves considerable ingenuity and improvization, together with a good local knowledge of where and how appropriate help might be obtained.

2. *Local legislation or social customs* which may make it difficult to obtain interviews, particularly among certain sectors of the population. Sometimes the researcher will run into problems in trying to interview people living in 'protected' upper- and middle-class housing blocks or in areas where entry is restricted. In some countries it is necessary to obtain central or local official authorization to carry out research at all—in Indonesia this may have to be obtained at three different levels before interviewing can start. It is essential for the researcher to know about such problems in advance, and how they may best be solved, in order to avoid gaps and delays (or worse) in carrying out the research.

3. *It may be necessary to use different types of interviewer.* For example, many UK research organizations tend to be wary of employing students as interviewers except for certain special types of project, on the grounds that they may be too much a 'floating population' which does not repay the effort of training, or may not have the right motivation for the work, etc. In some other countries, however, there may be few suitable alternatives to using students, whose position is in any case very different to that of students in countries like the UK. Travel and accommodation problems (sometimes even physical dangers) mean that it is preferable to use men as interviewers in some countries, especially in rural areas. On the other hand it can be impossible for men to interview women in some Muslim cultures. Our choice of potential

interviewers is very often severely limited by such problems of education levels, ethnic groupings, mobility, etc. It is important therefore not to export UK views and prejudices about the kinds of people who make suitable interviewers into quite different cultural situations.

4. *The interview situation* itself may differ radically. The possibilities for postal surveys or for telephone interviewing obviously vary enormously from country to country, even within the 'developed' world, depending on the efficiency of postal services, literacy levels, etc. The personal interview situation will also differ. In many countries it is much more difficult to obtain privacy for an interview, and at the extreme (for example among rural communities in developing countries) a personal interview frequently takes on the characteristics of a group interview session.

5. *People may also react quite differently* to the interview situation. In Western societies interviews are generally accepted as a familiar and normal situation in which interviewer and informant can interact on reasonably level terms, and on the whole with sufficient frankness. This is certainly not the case in many countries where market research—indeed, any kind of contact with people from outside the local community—is relatively unknown and where the conventions of social intercourse may be quite different. Question-and-answer interaction with a stranger can seem strange, even uncomfortable or threatening. Depending upon the local culture, informants may turn out to be more or less frank than would be the case in the UK. In the Far East politeness and 'face' can be dominant elements in the interview situation. In a country such as Nigeria, on the other hand, it may be possible even on fairly personal issues to get an uninhibited response which would surprise many interviewers in this country. Local differences in cultural or social customs may also affect the handling of other forms of research. Informants in a discussion group situation can behave differently. Even more than in the UK, certain topics may turn out to be taboo; members of the group may be less inclined to disagree with other members; they may try harder to give the socially acceptable or most 'favourable' answer; etc. This is certainly not always the case, however. The only possible generalization is that it is impossible to generalize: once again, there is no substitute for close familiarity with the local culture.

6. *Linked with the last point is the fact that in some countries interviews may need to be much shorter* if we are to avoid the danger of respondents mentally—if not physically—withdrawing from the interview. This too requires awareness and sensitivity on the part of the researcher since the innate politeness of many cultures towards a stranger means that the more obvious signs of interview breakdown are not apparent.

7. Another problem that must be watched for in this context is that in some cultures people are simply not accustomed to *thinking in abstract or conceptual terms*—a fact which makes it more difficult to carry out attitude research, for example brand image surveys. A typical example is the greater difficulty which may be found in obtaining images of brands which the informant has not personally tried—a frequent and quite natural response being 'I have not tried it and so I don't know what it is like'. While such problems are by no means restricted to overseas markets, they are often more acute there.

8. In a slightly different context, it is notoriously more difficult in many countries abroad to obtain information on matters relating to people's finances. This is particularly a problem in attempting to organize retail audits: not only may traders not be accustomed to keeping efficient records, they have for taxation reasons a very marked antipathy to *any* kind of record-keeping.

These are examples of differences between countries which affect the mechanics of carrying out research. In addition, *market research organizations* themselves differ tremendously from country to country. Clearly technical knowhow and experience are likely to be less in countries where market research is a more recent and still relatively limited activity. Apart from this, the standards of professional conduct also vary. While in a number of countries market research standards are as high as in the UK, in many they are not. It is often necessary to look very much more closely into the quality of fieldwork, and at field control and supervision procedures; editing, coding and analysis work may be less systematic and accurate; confidentiality of the project is liable to be more of a problem; and 'cutting corners'—whether deliberately or unwittingly—needs to be carefully watched for.

Finally, and partly reflecting the previous points, the *costs of market research* vary sharply between countries. Despite the inflation of recent years the charges for research in the UK are still lower than in most other countries. The additional work involved in organizing and controlling an international market research project means that in any case extra expenses are involved. Apart from this consideration, however, the on-the-spot costs of carrying out a given piece of research in certain Continental countries can be up to twice or three times the equivalent costs in the UK—sometimes more. Even in many developing countries where in the past market research costs used to be low—mainly because of relatively low salaries—charges have been rising steadily, in many cases to European levels. This is one further factor calling for additional thought and care in planning international research, and putting an extra premium on skill and experience in finding economical answers to the various other problems described earlier.

Standardization and Comparability in International Marketing and Market Research

From what has been said so far it might seem that the scope for standard approaches and methods is extremely limited in both marketing and market research. The various national or regional differences outlined above should certainly lead us to be cautious in transferring ideas and techniques from one country to another without checking how they may be affected by factors of these kinds. There is, however, no need to become obsessed by the differences. In practice a considerable degree of standardization is often possible.

Any discussion of the principles, procedures and problems of international marketing falls far outside the scope of this chapter. However, some indication of the extent to which standardization is occurring internationally is given in an article[29] by Sorenson and Wiechmann. This study was based on about 100 interviews with executives from 27 major multinational companies in the food, soft drink, soap-detergent-toiletries and cosmetics industries, and refers to marketing operations in Europe and the USA. Figures quoted in the article provide an index of the degree of standardization of marketing decisions relating to a number of different elements in the marketing programme. This index is based on the degree of similarity for the individual marketing mix elements for each of a number of products across a series of pairs of countries in which they are marketed. For a full description of how the index was arrived at, and a commentary on the findings, the reader is referred to the original article. Some key figures are shown in Fig. 23.1.

Index of standardization of marketing decisions

	high	moderate	low
Product characteristics	81%	4%	15%
Brand name	93%	–	7%
Packaging	75%	5%	20%
Retail price	56%	14%	30%
Basic advertising message	71%	6%	20%
Creative expression	62%	4%	34%
Sales promotion	56%	11%	33%
Media allocation	43%	10%	47%
Role of sales force	74%	10%	15%
Management of sales force	72%	10%	17%
Role of middlemen	80%	7%	13%
Type of retail outlet	59%	7%	34%

Fig. 23.1   (Based on products marketed by 27 multinational companies, each product being marketed in 3 to 5 different countries in USA/Europe. Source: Sorenson and Wiechmann.)

Even allowing for inevitable imprecision in the concept of 'standardization', it is clear that for many marketing activities the companies investigated look to a fairly high degree of standardization across these markets.

The Sorenson and Wiechmann study shows that the differences between market conditions in different countries should not be over-emphasized, at least in the case of developed markets. The article argues that many marketing programs are standardized in spite of significant differences in these conditions, and that 'a widespread rule in multinational companies seems to be: When in doubt, modify only those parts that *must* be modified because of insurmountable barriers to standardization'. Among the reasons why companies would follow such a policy, the authors suggest that:

1. To people at the centre, standardization may well appear a much simpler and more straightforward approach than the need to deal with innumerable permutations of programs for different countries. It is also easier to monitor and control. (This point is clearly linked to the degree of centralization of company operations referred to earlier.)
2. Standardization can sometimes lead to significant savings in the design of products and of their advertising and promotion. While, as the authors comment, it is not very often that this argument is backed up with hard facts, it is certainly true in principle that the relatively scarce and expensive resources of technical research and top level creativity will yield a bigger pay-off the more they can be exploited internationally.
3. Standardized marketing programs may lead to more economical use of local man-power (and, it might be added, can simplify international training and transfer of staff).
4. There is a general feeling that if a successful marketing formula has been found in one country the sensible thing is to try to transfer and exploit it elsewhere rather than laboriously work out a new solution for each new country.

Against these arguments there are plenty of examples where a relatively unsophisticated and uninformed approach to standardizing international marketing has led to disaster. The authors refer to the example of three US food companies in their earlier attempts to break into the UK and subsequently the Continental markets. The conclusion they draw is that:

'The experiences of these three companies lead us to believe that managements of multinationals should give high priority to developing their ability to conduct *systematic cross-border analysis*, if they are not already doing so. Such analysis can help management avoid the mistake of standardizing when markets are significantly different. At the same time, systematic cross-border analysis can help avoid the mistake of excessive custom-tailoring when markets are sufficiently similar to make standardized programs feasible.'

This is the classic argument for taking the international view of international research; and it is not confined to multinational companies. From the market research point of view, it implies starting from the position that international research should be handled similarly in different countries *unless* there is good evidence in a particular case to show that local variations are needed. Against this is the strongly held view which emphasizes the many differences between countries and the over-riding importance of very carefully tailoring research techniques to the local market situation. The latter approach concentrates on the end-result of the research—the interpretation of the information provided—as ultimately the only issue where full comparability is likely to be critical.

The problem of what international 'comparability' really means has been usefully discussed by Day[5]. He argues that in practice comparability in research is important only insofar as it 'allows or facilitates *marketing* decisions to be reached for the *totality* of countries under consideration'; that comparability may be either 'direct' (i.e. using very similar research methods in the different countries) or 'indirect' (using different approaches in order to achieve essentially the same marketing objective); and which type of comparability should be sought in any given case depends on:

(a) the freedom of marketing action possible in the individual markets;
(b) the type of research under consideration;
(c) the degree of homogeneity or heterogeneity between the marketing situations in the different countries.

This distinction between the need for *comparable information* and *standard research methods* assumes that for the purposes of international planning the user of research is mainly interested in having *findings* which are comparable, and he should not be unduly concerned if varying methods are used in different countries in order to obtain these. More than this, given the kinds of differences between countries discussed earlier in this chapter, we sometimes *have* to use differing research approaches if we are to get genuinely comparable data. For example, using the identical questionnaire in different countries can in practice produce information which is *not* comparable.

All this is true. There is no point in pursuing standardization merely for the sake of standardization if this runs us into other problems. A key argument of this chapter is precisely that the researcher has to be especially alert to the risks of miscommunication, and the possible need to adapt his approach, when working internationally. The validity of the local information obviously must not be sacrificed to a simple-minded pursuit of standard techniques and (even more) of standard questionnaires. Good examples of the possible dangers are to be found in papers such as the one by Berent[2].

This said, the more exaggerated versions of these arguments considerably over-stress the need for local adaptations to take priority over the use of standard approaches. Some arguments based on the mystique of local research know-how are not always entirely disinterested. They are also not the whole story. There are in fact several very strong arguments in favour of the standardization of research methods wherever possible:

1. The use of standard approaches can *save time and money* internationally (as they do nationally), especially at the project briefing and design stages.
2. They *simplify life for the user* of the research—whether he is trying directly to compare research findings from different countries or is moving from one country to another during the course of his work. If the research methods used are similar, it will be much easier for him both to discuss research proposals and also to absorb the background to the findings.
3. Marketing people are not necessarily closely interested in—or do not have sufficient time for—the more esoteric aspects of market research technology. They feel *greater confidence* in using research findings based on standard approaches, provided of course that the latter are soundly designed.
4. The *international training and transfer* of market researchers is simplified by the use of standard methods.
5. There are in any case certain types of information where *absolute uniformity* internationally is essential and where this can only be obtained by rigorously standard approaches in the field. A good example is the kind of data required for technical development work, such as information on the detailed routines followed in clothes washing.

One particular issue raised by Day in the article quoted is worth returning to, in pointing to difficulties for research arising from the fact that markets themselves are heterogeneous. He gives as an example the problem of designing an international research project to help in a marketing decision as to whether or not it would be a viable proposition to introduce an international brand into three adjacent markets which differ fundamentally in the stages of development reached, but which would be supplied from one (new) factory. In one market the type of product under consideration is already well established, with many well known brands; in the second market the product type has only just been introduced, with one or two brands in the process of trying to establish themselves; and in the third market the product type is as yet completely unknown. What international research, he very reasonably asks, could give us 'comparable' information in this situation? The question asked in fact underlines not so much the risks of trying to use standard research approaches internationally as the much more general danger of trying to answer quite different problems with the same approach. It is as vital (but often much more difficult) with an international research project to define our problem clearly in each country in order to establish what research is relevant as it is in the case of a domestic project.

It is also important to point out that the problem of comparability is not confined to surveys which are explicitly 'multi-country'. It is often just as important in the case of a survey carried out in a single country where the results may at some time in the future need to be compared with findings from equivalent surveys in other countries.

To sum up this section, comparing and interpreting research data from different countries is already sufficiently complicated without also having to make allowances for variations in the techniques used. The assumption that the soundest market research approach to a given problem could be reached by first examining it from each national viewpoint involved may in many cases be theoretically correct. In real life it is often inefficient and even unpractical. For most problems it is better to start from a well planned international approach—preferably one which has been piloted already in one or more countries—and then to modify this for other countries *only if* good evidence is produced for doing so. The stress here should be on the word 'evidence'—market research is no freer than other disciplines from prejudices of the 'not-invented-here' type or from anecdotal evidence and folklore of the kind 'someone tried it once some years ago and it didn't work'.

Which Countries Should We Research?

Often there is no choice in this—the answer is dictated by the marketing problem. On other occasions, however, there may be quite a long list of possible countries of interest. The question then is how to select the most appropriate ones to research. This is typically the case, for example, with a firm which is seriously planning to export on a significant scale for the first time.

There are several approaches which can be considered before starting any new and more extensive research:

1. The different markets can be ranked in order of potential importance to the company. 'Desk research' on production, imports and exports, consumption, income trends, etc., can often be used for this purpose. The approach is similar in many respects to desk research in the domestic market, although the sources of information will be different: the reader is referred back to chapter 1 and its comments on the international scene. (Another useful article is one by Foreman (in ref. 15), which also quotes various sources of information.) Such classification and ranking of countries can sometimes involve quite extensive sets of data[7, 18] and more sophisticated forms of statistical technique such as regression or cluster analysis; but relatively simple and straightforward approaches are likely to be quite adequate in most cases.
2. It may be possible to categorize countries into groups or clusters, each of which has various characteristics (economic, social, marketing) in common which differentiate it from another group. Thus the Scandinavian countries, or certain of the Latin countries, are sometimes held to share important characteristics which mean that research findings for one member of the group can up to a point be projected to the others. Research can then be concentrated on a 'typical' or key member of the

group. This can be a dangerous procedure without further evidence to support it—as the Scandinavians themselves are the first to point out, the national character and customs of Denmark, Norway and Sweden are far from identical. Nevertheless, there are certain criteria which can provide a valid basis for categorizing countries into groups along such lines. Dependence upon different types of food grains (rice, wheat, etc.); different methods of cooking (margarine, butter, olive oil, ghee, etc.); different types of clothes washing facilities (front-loading automatic machines, twin-tubs, tanque, bowl, etc.)—these and similar criteria have been used to categorize countries or regions in this way, along with the other more conventional variables such as per capita income or consumption levels.

It is worth stressing again that such groupings often do not follow national boundaries. In some respects northern Germany differs more from southern Germany than it does from other northern countries; while the 'olive oil line' mentioned earlier sharply distinguishes southern from northern France and for many purposes puts it into a different group. An overall national average is always a dangerous statistic, and this context is no exception.

3. Many attempts have also been made to classify countries on the basis of whether in any given field of activity they are trend setters (innovators or early adopters of new market developments) or come towards the tail of the new developments queue. It is naturally very tempting to try to find the international equivalent of 'what Manchester thinks today, London thinks tomorrow'. For many types of new product innovation in the affluent society, it used to be assumed that North America would lead the way, with Northern Europe (particularly Sweden) following and providing a bridge for the diffusion of new ideas to other less prosperous or more conservative parts of Europe. While it is true that a great deal of marketing innovation has in the past occurred in the USA, it is certainly not correct that diffusion of different new ideas follows more or less similar geographical paths internationally. Any international market research program founded on such a premise is likely to produce misleading results.

Whether or not different countries are grouped or ranked in some such way before starting on a full-scale study, there are two alternative strategies which can then be pursued in actually carrying out multi-country projects. Both strategies have their obvious advantages and disadvantages, and sometimes it is possible to combine elements of each.

The first strategy is to follow a *selective* (or *sequential*) approach. Although from time to time particular countries, e.g. Belgium, have been put forward as suitable test markets for a much wider group of countries, for most research problems it is extremely unlikely that any single test country can be found which is sufficiently representative to provide an adequate

567

answer internationally. It is however often very sensible to carry out a major international project in only a few key countries (perhaps 3-4) at the outset, either simultaneously or in sequence—the results being looked at partly from the point of view of projecting them to other similar countries but also as a form of sensitivity analysis: what important elements in the situation are likely to vary in practice between different countries, in what directions and how far? Depending on these findings, the decision can then be made whether or not to extend the research to additional countries, and which ones.

The second strategy is to start by carrying out relatively limited *broad spectrum* research over a larger number of countries, before going into any of the individual countries in detail. Such research can be limited in one or both of two ways. It can confine itself to a restricted set of key questions asked of reasonably large national samples, perhaps using omnibus surveys, in order to get a 'first feel' of the major dimensions of the problem and the likely extent of differences between countries. Or it can be a more intensive survey carried out on a total international sample which is large enough to provide the opportunities for more detailed analysis and understanding of the sample as a whole, but where the individual national sub-samples are too small to provide anything more than first rough indications of differences between countries. In either case further research can be carried out subsequently to complete the picture in more detail for some or all of the countries previously 'dipped into', depending on the findings of the first stage.

A very different way of looking at the problems of where to research is illustrated by the concept of various 'international cultures' which have been identified for marketing and research purposes. Major city/smaller city/rural life styles are an example of one such trans-national concept. Another is that of the typical teenager (with international tastes in clothing, pop music, etc.). A third is that of the international businessman and traveller. For certain research purposes such international strata may be perfectly valid, although it is obviously unwise to assume that they are not also strongly affected by purely national or local factors. Where such strata exist, it could well be useful to direct market research at such groups right across countries rather than set out to conduct a series of separate national surveys. This would of course argue for a multi-national study early on, and so indicate a different research approach to that involved in selecting certain key or representative countries. Even in cases of an international target group of this type, however, it is usually necessary to take some measure of the differences between countries for the purpose of marketing decision and action.

Preliminary Steps

Once we have decided that we want to research a particular market in a given country, what steps are then involved? Many of these are naturally similar to those we would take in researching a UK market, and the following comments therefore concentrate on points where there are more likely to be some differences.

First, and most obviously, we should pull together any relevant *published or otherwise available information* there may be which bears upon the market we are studying. This may already have been done in the course of selecting which country to research, but probably not in great depth. We can commission a research agency to carry out this work for us; or set out to collect as much data as possible for ourselves. Chapter 1 has described the possibilities open to us. A considerable and growing volume of published information on different markets in different countries has become available in recent years—some of it for a fee, much of it free. In addition to the more obvious government statistics on population, production, trade, etc., in many countries other data (e.g. consumer budgets) may be available from official surveys on request where it is not formally published. Other likely sources of information include international organizations of many kinds, university departments, banks, media organizations, etc. The standard warnings about using such data apply, and even more strongly in the case of data relating to foreign countries. It is essential to establish how, and on what basis, the data were collected, and what definitions were used. It is not possible to use data published even by reputable international agencies without very carefully reading the small print, and even then it is unwise to assume that figures which appear to be comparable in fact necessarily are[33]. Also it is sensible to remember that sometimes governments or other bodies have an interest in presenting information in a particular light, which can mislead the unwary. Retail price indices are notorious for this, but even fundamental data such as the population census are not immune in some countries. Wherever possible it is advisable to check such figures with people who know the country and its statistics well and who can warn if there are liable to be serious inaccuracies or distortions in the data.

It is also worth checking at this stage whether there are any *syndicated market research services* available on subscription which could provide all or at least some of the information required. There is a growing number of such services, especially in the more developed markets—some of them run on a continuous or periodic basis, others 'one-off' jobs. An alternative approach is to buy questions in *omnibus surveys* (see chapter 9), which are now available in most parts of the world. It is generally possible to track down the major services of these kinds with the help of an international agency (market research or advertising) or a body such as the British Overseas Trade Board. There are also directories of these services published by organizations such as the UK Market Research Society or the BOTB itself[14]—although since the situation is constantly changing these directories inevitably find it difficult to be completely up-to-date or comprehensive. Once again it is necessary to sound a loud warning note. Some of the syndicated services on offer are technically inadequate, at least for certain purposes; and before subscribing it is important to check the detailed specifications of the study, and also wherever possible its likely accuracy either with other subscribers or by asking for a few sample figures which can be cross-checked with other information. Failing these possibilities, it is worth trying at least to get an informed and objective opinion of the technical competence and general reputation of the agency producing the service. Above all beware of syndicated services which promise the earth at a bargain basement price. Sound work costs money, even on a shared basis, and if the price quoted looks commercially unsound this can be evidence of corner-cutting in assembling the information. The argument that 'We can't lose, after all it costs so little' simply does not hold water: inaccurate or misleading information may cost you a great deal of money in terms of a wrong decision based on it.

Setting-up the Research

The preliminary background work completed, how should we organize any new research needed? There are basically four main ways in which a client can arrange for a research project in a foreign country:

1. He can—using his head office staff or his local branch or associates—directly organize and control the necessary fieldwork and other facilities in the country concerned ('do-it-yourself' research).
2. He or his associates can select a local research agency to carry out the work.
3. He can commission the UK member of an international research chain to organize the project through its local branch or affiliate.
4. He can commission a UK market research company or consultant to control the project on his behalf, either (a) sub-contracting the on-the-spot work to a local agency in the country concerned or (b) itself organizing the necessary field and other facilities for the job.

There are a number of possible variations around these main themes.

Not all these options are available in every case. Some clients do not have the resources or skills themselves to arrange for an international project. Many countries around the world still do not have adequate (or perhaps any) local market research agencies, so that it is necessary for someone to go in from outside on each occasion in order to set up the facilities. Even where the client does have appropriate internal market research resources and some familiarity with international research, it is sometimes more convenient or more efficient to work with an outside research supplier based in his home country or in a regional centre.

The pros and cons of the different routes have been debated on public platforms almost *ad nauseam*, and the alternative cases made out at length by sometimes not-entirely-disinterested protagonists. It is not intended to replay all the arguments here, and the reader is referred to the literature (e.g. refs. 15, 16 and 26). Among the more important questions which a client needs to consider in choosing his best course of action, however, are:

1. How can he most effectively shorten the length of the communication chain, and minimize the risks of miscommunication between the research user, the research planner, the questionnaire designer and the field front-line (both down the chain and back up again)—and how are any language hurdles best crossed?
2. Which course will make for the most effective contact with local research personnel, tapping their skills and local knowledge of the market?
3. How can the necessary local facilities—especially fieldwork—be most effectively and efficiently selected/controlled/evaluated?
4. How can comparability between countries best be insured?
5. How can time delays be minimized?
6. What are the alternative *total* costs? (For example, planning and coordination by a UK agency mean money on top of the on-the-spot costs, but so will the additional efforts of client head office staff in dealing with a series of local agencies.)

In answering such questions there are a few considerations worth mentioning among the many others. First, even though at first sight it may not seem the most cost-efficient solution it may be well worthwhile on many more important and complex jobs for the client to incur the cost and time penalties of himself travelling to the countries involved in order to benefit from the additional local knowledge gained, the direct contact with and feedback from the local researchers, and improved communications generally: third-hand impressions at long-range do not often give a real 'gut understanding' of the market situation.

Second, when is a chain a chain (or perhaps, how long is a chain)? Some international research chains have a common ownership, standard international systems and research methods, international training and exchange of personnel, tightly organized briefing and control methods across countries; others have relatively loose affiliation arrangements, changing membership, little direct personal contact, limited standardization in their approaches. The first are not *necessarily* better than the second, but they are certainly different—and the client needs to understand the facts of the situation.

Third, research agencies which work on the principle of having no fixed affiliations but of 'selecting the most appropriate local agency for the particular job' often seem to have a good case going for them (e.g. ref. 3). The strength of a chain is that of its weakest links; few if any chains are equally strong in all their links for every type of job. This is particularly true in qualitative and 'industrial' research. On the other hand, the 'horses-for-courses' approach may at times just be a case of making a virtue out of necessity.

It is quite impossible to generalize about what is likely to be the best solution in any given case. Apart from reading and considering the arguments put forward in the literature, the most sensible procedure is to talk to a number of different research suppliers and users and where appropriate apply their international experience to your problem; and to seek such disinterested advice as you can find.

Choosing a Local Market Research Agency

If an international project is being handled through a UK market research company, the latter will normally be responsible for selecting suitable local agencies. If, however, the client is involved in choosing the local agency, he is faced with the question of how best to appraise the various available alternatives.

In many respects the problem is similar to that of selecting an agency for research in the home market, and this chapter does not set to deal with this in detail. (For anyone who wishes to follow up this issue, there is an exhaustive checklist approach suggested by Mayer[25]; other advice and suggestions are contained in publications by Marsh[24], ISBA[31], the Market Research Society[23] and IMRA[10].) Lists of research agencies operating in various countries abroad are contained in several of the references already quoted, and in directories published by the Market Research Society[13] and by ESOMAR[22]. Further information and advice can be obtained from the British Overseas Trade Board and also from the local professional associations listed in the Market Research Society Yearbook.

Although similar principles apply, the difficulties of choosing a research agency in an overseas country are likely to be considerably more acute than in selecting a UK agency. Unless the client himself has a good understanding of what is involved in carrying out sound market research, and is fully aware of the pitfalls and shortcomings which may lie beneath an imposing commercial veneer, he would be well advised to seek UK professional help in making his selection. There are however a number of checkpoints which it is often useful to have in mind in looking at a potential overseas research supplier. For example:

1. Does it belong to any international market research chain or group? If it does, there is then the possibility of checking further with the chain headquarters or local UK representative about the particular experience, skills and other aspects of the local company.
2. Which clients (particularly international ones) has it worked for during the last two years? And which has it worked for *regularly*? There may be an opportunity to check with such clients for their experience. The fact of working regularly for larger or more sophisticated clients provides some evidence of the standing of the research agency—although it is necessary to check what kinds of work it has carried out for such clients.

3. What is known in the UK about the agency? Some information may be available through the Market Research Society, or from other British companies operating in that part of the world.
4. How long has the agency been in business as a market research company? Is market research its *only* business? What is its financial standing? Newly formed companies, and ones offering a range of non-research facilities such as 'marketing consultancy', 'import agency facilities', etc., need additional probing since market research may be just an occasional side-line.
5. Does it belong to any group of companies with other interests outside the market research field? If so, which—and how independently does it operate? In some cases there may be links with other types of commercial organization which could pose problems of competing interests or lack of objectivity (e.g. sales agences or media).
6. Are there any possible conflicts of interests with other existing clients?
7. Does it in its work conform to accepted Codes of Standards and Practice in market research (for example the joint ICC/ESOMAR International Code)? In particular, what guarantees can it give of confidentiality?
8. What experience does the agency have of tackling the *type* of market research problem under study? Some companies specialize only in certain fields of research, or at least have had little or no practical operating experience in many fields they may claim to cover.
9. What procedures does the agency follow in drawing up and submitting research proposals? What form of reporting does it normally use—is an example available? What language(s) will the research proposals and reports be written in?
10. What is the system of payment expected—in instalments or on the completion of the project?

In addition to questions of these kinds about the agency and its general methods of working, it is naturally important to check the qualifications and experience of the key members of staff—and particularly of the research executive who would be handling the particular project. Apart from the fact that the level of technical research skill varies considerably between countries, especially outside Europe, language difficulties and/or a lack of *marketing* knowhow can lead to problems in research design and interpretation. It is also vital to check certain of the research facilities operated by the agency—in particular its field organization. The latter is often the weakest link in the whole operation. What are the qualifications and training of the fieldworkers; what supervision procedures are carried out (and can they be checked by the client); can the client meet the fieldworkers and see them in action? On the office side, is it possible for the client to see how much, and what kinds of, editing and checking of questionnaires is carried out, and the control procedures used at the analysis stage?

This summary list of checkpoints should not be regarded as

comprehensive—or as necessarily essential in every case. In the case of international research, however, checks of these kinds are likely to be more necessary than they are when commissioning research in the UK.

Some Further Considerations in Organizing International Research

The operating conditions for market research vary so much in different parts of the world that it is impossible sensibly to discuss in a single chapter the detailed aspects of how to carry out research in other countries. The kinds of local factor which affect the design and conduct of surveys have been referred to earlier. Dealing with them efficiently and effectively calls for experience, determination and imagination; but in an increasing number of countries around the world—not just in the main developed markets—research is now sufficiently well-established for the major local problems to have been identified and solutions found.

As far as technical issues are concerned, it is inevitably a question of steering a course between underrating local differences and over-reacting to them. We should not automatically accept an 'it won't work here' opinion without checking the evidence for this assertion, whether or not the view comes from a local researcher. Much received wisdom of this kind is based on quite inadequate or out-of-date information. Conversely, it is clearly dangerous to assume that a particular research approach or technique used successfully elsewhere will work in a new country without carefully checking it out first. The fact that interviewers succeed in obtaining answers and completing the questionnaire does *not* indicate that these answers are meaningful or valid. The most difficult field for international research is that of attitude measurement.

Techniques and standards differ widely between countries. The concepts we are trying to measure are not always easily defined, and may well vary greatly but in unknown ways between different cultures; the measuring devices we use are often not very precise or robust, and may sometimes themselves be culture-specific; and the problems of language and semantics are at their most acute. Some work has been done to get to grips with such problems (e.g. ref. 6), but qualitative work generally is a minefield for those inexperienced in international research.

Without plunging into the detailed aspects of research in particular countries, there are certain general points which it is again worth underlining in connection with international research projects. The first is *the crucial importance of precise communication*—especially in briefing the local agency. There is much more scope for misunderstandings to occur than in the case of UK research. Where some at least of the communication between client and local research agency is indirect or at long range all details of the research approach and methods must be clearly set down and agreed on paper. It is safer to go into possibly too much detail than to take anything for granted: research experience and practices differ from country to country and it is essential that any underlying assumptions are brought out into the open. Quite apart from affecting the efficiency with which the research is carried out, such breakdowns in communication often lead to unfortunate arguments over the costing of international research projects.

A second requirement, particularly with multi-country projects, is the need for *firm coordination*. There must be a clear and generally recognized central point of responsibility for decisions affecting the design and conduct of the research if comparability is to be achieved, and time and money not wasted. It is especially important that the respective roles, contributions and involvement of the centre and of the local units—in *both* client and research organizations—is agreed from the outset. Confusion about this is a frequent cause of delay and even friction.

Among other issues which are peculiar to international research, and which need particularly to be watched, are the following:

1. Who is to be responsible for any *translation* work involved, and how will this be paid for? This can be a major item in certain types of research, especially qualitative work involving group discussions and/or extended individual interviews. Is such material going to be digested and analysed by local staff in the local language(s), so that only the final report needs to be prepared in English; or is it (also) going to be necessary to translate the basic questionnaires and transcripts into English, so that they can be read and if necessary worked on in the UK? The author has come across cases where translation charges have added 50% to the basic cost of carrying out the study; and if several countries are involved this could be a major consideration in the original design of the research project.

2. Is the *analysis of the data collected* to be carried out locally or in the UK? The likely advantages of the latter are in helping to ensure comparability of the analyses (and their layout) across different countries; in the existence of better computer facilities and programs compared with certain other countries; in providing further checks centrally upon the quality of the data; and on occasions it can be cheaper. Against these arguments, central analysis adds to some of the logistical problems. It is often expensive to ship all the original field material back to the UK and may be dangerous. There are too many examples of such material being lost in transit, temporarily or even permanently, and usually it is safer to copy any basic information of this kind before despatching it—which also can cost a lot of money. If on the other hand the information is part-processed, on to punchcards or tapes, we have to be confident that the local processor can provide a reasonably clean and accurate job, otherwise additional time, money and frustration will be involved before the final tabulations can be carried out.

3. How is the actual *report* to be prepared? Should this be written back at

base in the UK, by the agency actually carrying out the research in the country concerned, or by some combination of the two? A case can be made out for each of these courses, depending on the nature of the study. Where a number of countries are involved in the same project, there is certainly a strong argument for an overall report to be prepared centrally. Conversely, even where the main analysis and reporting is being handled centrally and not in the individual country or countries concerned, it is foolish to forego the opportunity of potentially valuable local comment on the data collected. The organization actually carrying out the fieldwork will in most cases be well placed to suggest why particular findings come out the way they do; and a local research agency of any insight and experience will be able to contribute usefully to the interpretation of findings. It is generally sensible at least to invite their comments on any central interpretation of the local research results in those cases where they are not asked themselves to prepare a full report.

4. How much will the *total bill* be—and *how will it be paid*? Which currency will payment be in, at what rate of exchange? Are there any arrangements for inflation-proofing or hedging against currency fluctuations? It is very easy to leave out of account certain types of local tax, costs of international transfers, etc., or to overlook the importance of cost or currency adjustment clauses.

This by no means exhausts all the problems and 'tricks of the trade' which arise in planning and carrying out international market research: the reader who is interested in going further should consult the references at the end of this book, and the additional follow-up suggestions contained in some of those.

The Export Marketing Research Scheme

This final brief section might equally well have figured earlier in the text but helps to end the chapter on a practical note of encouragement. One factor deterring some companies from carrying out international research is obviously cost. It was pointed out that market research abroad will tend to be more expensive than the equivalent job in the UK. One possible way of keeping costs down has already been mentioned—that of buying into syndicated research or omnibus surveys. In addition, however, the British Overseas Trade Board has since 1969 given financial help to British exporters wishing to carry out research in overseas markets.

Full details about the scheme can be obtained from the BOTB, which publishes a descriptive leaflet and guidance notes for firms likely to be interested[4.11]. Apart from advising firms on ways of carrying out research in overseas markets, the BOTB will in approved cases provide direct financial support. For agreed projects this can cover up to $33^1/_3\%$ of the costs of

576

research where it is carried out by an individual company, up to 50% in the case of joint research by two or more unconnected firms, and up to $66^2/_3\%$ for research carried out by trade associations. While most projects so supported are individual *ad hoc* studies carried out through a research agency, the BOTB is in suitable cases prepared to support the purchase of syndicated multi-client studies and also research carried out by 'in-house' researchers belonging to the client firm itself. In certain circumstances financial support can be provided over the first year for a firm wishing to set up an appropriate export market research department of its own.

Where a grant is being sought the BOTB naturally needs to be given full information about the research brief and proposal, and to be able subsequently to check that the work has been carried out to the required professional standards, but the project is treated as entirely confidential to the organization commissioning it. Projects supported in this way now number several hundred per year.

24. Print media research

Michael Brown

This chapter is concerned with research into print media in the sense of newspapers and magazines, whether aimed at a wide, general audience or a narrower, more specialized one. This introductory section comprises, first, a brief review of the several purposes to which research in this area is put and, second, a synopsis of the order and content of the other parts of the chapter.

Media research is often interpreted as being synonymous with audience measurement, particularly in the case of newspapers and magazines, and, further, as providing data solely of relevance to advertising agencies or, in some cases, for direct use by the advertisers whose accounts they handle. Both of these concepts are oversimplifications. From the point of view of the advertiser or his agency, the requirement from research into any medium is to provide information that will assist both in choice between media—between newspapers and magazines, for example, or between magazines and television—and as regards intra-media choice; the selection, for instance, of individual advertising vehicles, such as the *Daily Express* or *Woman's Own*. The criterion of both inter- and intra-media choice will be, at base, one of cost-effectiveness: a relation between the price of using a particular advertising medium and the 'effects' of the campaign concerned, however defined.

The contribution of media choice itself to the overall variation in effectiveness, from campaign to campaign, is a matter of opinion and contention, rather than one of fact; some authors[1] would rate the creative content of advertising ten times as important a factor as media selection. However, insofar as the media element is certainly not completely negligible, one factor of obvious relevance to effectiveness is the size and nature of the audience delivered by an advertising schedule. At the same time, to enumerate the audience that has opportunity to come into contact with advertisements is far from providing a complete assessment of a campaign's likely results. There are thus many other aspects of 'effectiveness' beyond audience size and composition and some of these fall into the proper area of media research.

Turning to the publisher's viewpoint, the advertisement department of a

578

newspaper or magazine will, in common with the advertiser and agency, require from print media research data on audiences and other criteria of effectiveness; the difference in application of the results is the self-evident one that the publisher will be seeking to demonstrate a competitive advantage for his vehicle *vis-à-vis* others, both generally and in relation to the particular marketing and advertising briefs of a potential client. However, the publisher has also other interests, since he is operating in a situation of joint supply in two markets: not only is he selling advertising space or a potential audience, but also his actual newspaper or magazine to readers. He thus requires marketing research, in all its aspects, which treats the publication as being just as much a 'product' as any other one. Under this heading may be included investigation of readers' preference for and reaction to editorial material—a particular form, relevant to media, of 'product content' research.

Within the total area of media research, there are thus a number of measurement requirements, some overlapping, from advertisers, agencies and media owners. The next section of this chapter covers audience measurement; after consideration of the relevant concepts, research methods and problems in the measurement of issue, page and advertisement audiences are discussed. The section ends with a review of the sub-groups identified in audience research—demographic, attitudinal and behavioural, including, under the latter heading, audience breakdowns by product/brand purchasing and the research requirements of 'single source' and integrated data.

The third section turns to the use of audience measurement and other data as input to computer programs designed either to construct print media schedules or forecast their performance on certain prespecified criteria. The objectives, broad lines of development, advantages, and limitations of such programs are described, but full, mathematical treatment of methods is outside the scope of the section.

In the fourth section, criteria of newspaper and magazine advertising effectiveness other than audience measurements are discussed. Requirements and difficulties peculiar to media research are highlighted, fuller treatment of relevant techniques being provided in other chapters.

The final section deals with the applications of market and marketing research to print media as a product field and to individual newspapers and magazines as 'brands', rather than as advertising vehicles or providers of audiences.

Audience Measurement

Audience concepts

Given that the overall requirement in the implementation of any advertising brief is to achieve optimum cost-effectiveness, a sub-objective is to select advertising vehicles in such a way that the size and nature of the audience, and the pattern of their opportunities for contact with the advertisements is 'best', on some agreed set of criteria. There thus exists a need for audience measurement, so that the performance of alternative schedules, on these criteria, may be evaluated; but before dealing with the practical problems involved, it is necessary to consider what is implied by 'audience'.

Issue audience may be defined as the number and kinds of individuals that come into contact with either a specific issue of a given newspaper or magazine or with the 'average' issue. People counted within the issue audience are often referred to, loosely, as 'readers' and their total is frequently labelled the 'readership' of the publication concerned. Further, being an issue reader is said to provide an 'opportunity to see' (ots) an advertisement carried by the issue. Any definition of issue audience is essentially an operational one, as will be seen below; but irrespective of the exact definition selected, it will not reflect differences, within the total issue readership, between individuals and occasions as regards the amount that is read or looked at *within* the issue. A narrower definition thus exists of the *page* (or double-page spread) *audience* as comprising the number of people who look at anything on a page or spread, or on the 'average' one.

Being counted within the page audience obviously confers on an individual a higher probability of contact with an actual advertisement than does merely being a member of the issue audience. However, it is possible to refine the concept yet further and define, as falling within the *advertisement audience*, those people who have contact with the ad itself.

The main points to note from the brief discussion of audience concepts above are two: there exists a hierarchy of increasingly narrow definitions; but at each level—whether issue, page, or advertisement—the interpretation of 'contact' is not an unambiguous one.

Issue audience

Having dealt briefly with basic audience concepts, attention is now turned to the practical problems of issue audience measurement. The simplification is first made below of assuming a 'black and white' division between those individuals who are and are not issue readers. The refinement of recognizing probabilities of issue contact other than 0 or 1 is introduced later.

Average Issue Readership

Although the audience for a specific issue of a newspaper or magazine can be and sometimes is measured, by far the more frequent research objective is to provide an unbiased estimate of the audience for the average issue of the vehicle. Meeting this requirement raises two essential problems: defining 'readership', in the sense of contact with an issue, and selecting an appropriate data-collection method.

As already noted, *any* definition of issue readership is operational; there is no absolute standard against which it may be assessed whether a person is or is not a reader. As an example, the National Readership Survey takes a reader to be a respondent who claims to have read or looked at any copy of the newspaper or magazine concerned, anywhere, within a period equal to the publication interval of the title prior to the date of interview. (That is to say, a reader has to have seen a daily paper on the day before the date of interview, a Sunday paper or a weekly magazine within the seven days ending on the day before the interview, and so on.)

Three points within this NRS definition serve to illustrate the contention that 'readership' is not an absolute concept. First, a respondent qualifies as a reader irrespective of the proportion of an issue they have seen at all and of whether they have read intently or merely glanced. In fact, people labelled as 'readers' in the NRS sense do have a high probability of having looked at the average page within an issue, as experimental work preceding the 1968 Survey[2] shows; but it is possible to count within the average issue audience only those with some 'proved' level of 'within the issue' reading intensity.

Second, the NRS definition allows readership of current and outdated issues to count equally; but it is possible, if it is relevant to the application of the research, to consider only those reading occasions that occur within some set interval of an issue going on sale producing, naturally, a numerically different estimate of average issue audience.

Third, NRS readers are not necessarily those who actually purchased the newspaper or magazine—they may equally be people, within or beyond the purchaser's household, to whom the issue was passed on; nor, to be counted within the average issue audience, must they have read the issue concerned at home or in some other, specified, circumstances. Clearly, audience definitions may be framed which take a different view on these points.

Turning to research techniques relevant to average issue audience measurement, a first, major choice lies between recall and recognition methods. The National Readership Survey approach is basically to rely on respondents' recall of newspaper or magazine reading occasions. Whilst this method allows, amongst other advantages, standardized questions to be asked, within one survey, regarding a large number of titles, it also has deficiencies. For a number of reasons, underclaiming, overclaiming, and the displacement in time of a reading occasion in the respondent's mind all occur; evidence from Belson's work[3] is to be noted. However, the biases resulting from faulty recall of reading behaviour may often be within acceptable limits. If recall is to be used, the further question arises of whether it should be prompted and, if so, to what degree. The NRS utilizes, as prompts, reproductions (reduced in size) of publications' mastheads, i.e. their titles, in the type style used on the cover or front page. However, there are many examples of average issue readership measurement using other forms of prompt—including just the names of the newspapers and magazines, whether shown to the respondent or only read out—or none at all. Formal evidence of the effect on the level readership claims from varying the style of recall aid is very limited. Completely open, unprompted questioning, however, certainly tends to result in underclaiming of issue contact, particularly for titles which the respondent sees infrequently or irregularly. Recognition methods provide a complete contrast to relying on people's recall of previous reading behaviour. In their typical form (as more widely used in the US than in Europe or the UK), they involve showing the respondent an issue of the publication concerned and asking them to glance through it before stating whether they have looked at it before the interview.

While it may appear that recognition-based readership claims will be more reliable than those based on recall, the former technique brings its own drawbacks. Its demand on interview time and on the amount of material physically to be carried by the interviewer are considerable; these problems are only partly alleviated by using, in place of complete issues, 'stripped-down' ones containing, hopefully, just sufficient pages for the respondent to be able to say, unambiguously, whether they have looked into it previously. Further, the age of issue to be used is not simple to determine. If it is very recent, the audience it will accumulate, through the mechanism of pass-on readership, may not have 'grown' to its limit by the time of the survey. If, on the other hand, an 'old' issue is used in an attempt to circumvent this problem, respondents will have increased difficulty in saying definitely that they have or have not read it some time ago.

In parallel with the choice between recall and recognition approaches, there are options of average issue readership measurement via personal interviews, telephone contact and self-administered questionnaire. Whilst readership research has, very largely, grown up in a face-to-face personal interview setting, there is a growing volume of evidence that satisfactory estimates can be obtained from self-administered questionnaires; comparisons between NRS results and those from the Target Group Index[4] provide an example. At the same time, once questioning is beyond an interviewer's direct control, there may be problems in adequately conveying to a respondent the precise definition of 'readership' that is being employed; in what prompts may be used; or in controlling the order in which the respondent answers similar questions on different publications. This last point is important since, from personal interview data at least, there is evidence that estimates of average issue readership depend on the position of the publication within the interview sequence.

Readership measurement by telephone interviewing is by no means impossible, although this particular data-collection technique has had limited use in the media area in the UK. Apart from sampling problems imposed by the low absolute penetration of telephone ownership and its skewness, it would not be easy to maintain respondent interest throughout a lengthy, largely repetitive readership covering many newspapers and magazines. Further, prompting is self-evidently limited to verbal naming of titles.

Turning to another dimension of research design, the majority of readership surveys tend to provide either 'one-off' estimates or regularly published reports, in the latter case derived from fresh samples on each occasion. However, panel techniques may also be employed[5].

It is beyond the scope of this chapter to consider at length the numerous special problems that may apply in specific cases of issue readership measurement. However, a note must be added regarding publication with narrow and specialized audiences. Here, in the interests of sampling economy, it is not uncommon practice to obtain self-completed data on a sample drawn from a magazine's list of subscribers, or to insert a questionnaire in all copies of a particular issue. Whilst there is nothing intrinsically wrong in a well conducted readership survey by mail—given that, with or without follow-up, a satisfactory response rate can be obtained—the characteristics of readers who choose to return a questionnaire inserted in the actual publication can often be markedly different from those of its total audience. Further, pass-on readership clearly cannot be directly measured in any 'one copy, one questionnaire' design.

As a final point in relation to average issue audience measurement, it is to be noted that, non-response errors apart, the particular National Readership Survey method cannot produce a completely unbiased estimate. This situation arises through the phenomena of 'replicated' and 'parallel' readership. Respectively, these are the cases where one person reads a given issue within each of two or more different publication intervals; and where one person, within one publication interval, looks at two or more different issues (a publication interval being the time span from one publication date for a given title to the next one). Replicated readership leads to overestimation of average issue readership; in effect, two or more reading events by the person concerned each have a chance of being 'counted' when, in fact, only one issue and one reader is involved. Parallel readership, by contrast, tends to bias a readership estimate downwards. Two or more contacts with different issues are involved, but they will be counted as one only.

The net effect of these biases may not be large and their elimination, while possible, would involve a much more complex research approach. A very complex research approach, one of the first UK attempts, is seen in the Odham's work on women's magazines[6]. A very full treatment of the replicated and parallel readership problem is provided by the published papers submitted for the Thomson 1962 awards[7].

Reading Frequency

The discussion, in the section above, of issue audience measurement has been on the basis of an oversimplified assumption that a given individual is either in or out of an audience; that is to say, the picture has been one of a population divided on a black and white basis into 'readers' and 'non-readers' of this or that publication. In fact, of course, the situation includes shades of grey. For a particular newspaper or magazine, there will be a group of people who, to all intents and purposes, never come into contact with it; another set of people who see virtually every issue; and, in between, those who are irregular readers to a greater or lesser degree.

The probability that an individual has of contact with the 'average' issue has come to be known colloquially as his or her *reading frequency* for the title concerned. The importance of measuring reading frequency lies in the fact that readership research results are used not only to forecast the potential audience for one insertion in one issue but, more generally, to investigate the full pattern of contacts arising from a schedule of several insertions in one or more publications. This pattern will depend intimately on the reading frequencies involved. Consider, say, five issues of one magazine, having an average issue audience of one million. On the simplifying assumption of there existing only 'readers' and 'non-readers', each of the million will see five issues and the remainder of the population none. On the more realistic model of issue-contact probabilities other than zero or one occurring, somewhat more than one million people will read at least one issue, because the audience from issue to issue will not comprise always exactly the same individuals. On the other hand, the average number of issues read, amongst those who see any, will now be less than five.

There are at least three distinguishable approaches to reading frequency measurement. First, consistent questions on issue readership can be repeated twice or more to the same individuals in a panel context. As previously discussed, this will normally involve a self-administered questionnaire depending on respondents' recollections of historical reading occasions. Recognition of distinct issues will not normally be involved. Note, therefore, that it will not in general be known whether a given individual's claim, for example, of two reading events in relation to two successive publication intervals relates to the two issues respectively current in these periods, to some other two issues or, indeed, to the same issue. The panel approach to reading frequency estimation has, in practice, been little employed in the UK outside the work by Attwood. A much fuller consideration of its possibilities and limitations than is given here is provided by the Thomson award papers[8] on the general problem of panel use in audience measurement.

As a second method, recognition can be relied on: a respondent can be asked, in a single interview research design, which of each of a number of issues of a newspaper or magazine they have seen. The previous comments on the limitations of the recognition method apply here also, in particular the sheer logistics of the interviewer carrying several issues of each of a number of titles.

Third, and most commonly, as regards UK or European practice, a reader may be asked, in effect, to make a subjective estimate of their usual reading frequency. In the National Readership Survey, for example, with the aid of a prompt card, a respondent is asked which of a number of illustrative frequencies best apply to their usual behaviour; for a daily newspaper, the choices provided are between 6, 5, 4, 3, 2, 1, 'less than 1' and no issues, out of 6. In France and several other countries, a verbal scale rather than a numerical one is employed, e.g. a person may be asked whether he sees 'every issue' of a title or reads it 'fairly often', 'occasionally' or 'never'.

The difference between the use of a numerical and a verbal scale is not so great as may at first appear. The intention in both instances is to segment the population in such a way that within-group differences in true frequency of issue-contact are smaller than between-groups ones. Responses to a verbal scale have, clearly, to be given a quantitative meaning; but so, in fact, have those on a numerical scale. Answers here cannot be taken at face value; individuals, generally speaking, tend to *over*estimate their reading frequency, so that a claim to see 'six issues out of six' implies, in fact, a probability of contact with the average issue not of one but of some smaller number.

In the NRS case, the scale of reading frequency is 'calibrated' by use of the data on average issue readership obtained in the same interview; e.g., if, for some weekly magazine or Sunday newspaper, 90% of those claiming to see four out of four issues actually qualify as 'average issue readers' on the definition used, then the *adult probability*, as it is termed, for this group will be taken as 0.9. It will be noted that there is an implicit assumption that the true reading frequency is the same for all respondents making a given frequency claim. The developmental work behind the NRS scale and its application are fully dealt with by Corlett[9].

It is equally possible, of course, to give numerical values to each position on some frequency of reading scale by research quite separate from the readership survey in which the scale is to be employed; e.g., a verbal scale might be put to the individuals providing readership data on a panel.

As noted earlier, the practical application of reading frequency data involved using it to forecast the pattern of contacts over several issues and publications. With panel data, individuals' claims of issue contact in successive periods may be used directly for this purpose, assuming only that the pattern of claimed reading actually observed is stable over time. With NRS-type information—providing, in essence, average probabilities for groups of individuals—further assumptions are involved, principally that successive issue contacts for a given individual are independent events. Given such an assumption then if, say, the adult probability for some group and title is 0.6, the Binomial Theorem can be employed to calculate distributions such as:

Number of issues read	Probability
3 out of 3	$1 \times (0.6)^3$
2 out of 3	$3 \times (0.6)^2 \times (1.0 - 0.6)$
1 out of 3	$3 \times (0.6) \times (1.0 - 0.6)^2$
0 out of 3	$(1 - 0.6)^3$

To obtain the forecast pattern of issue contacts resulting from a schedule, calculations of the above type would have to be performed, person by person, for each newspaper or magazine involved and the results then accumulated. Clearly, this is a time-consuming process, even in computer terms. A number of mathematical techniques have thus been developed which approximate, with adequate accuracy, the results of a full binomial expansion.

A full treatment of these short-cut approaches to obtaining a frequency distribution of issue contacts is beyond the scope of this chapter. However, it is to be noted that there are calculation techniques which achieve the same objective without the use of frequency of reading data at all, utilizing, typically, only average issue readership figures and the degrees of audience overlap between publications taken two or three at a time. The best known formulae of this type are attributed to Metheringham[10]. An improved version of his original technique is utilized in one of the UK sets of computer-media programs[11].

Spread, page and advertisement audiences

If an individual qualifies as a reader of the average issue, or of a particular issue, of a newspaper or magazine, this clearly confers on him a better chance of contact with an actual advertisement in that issue than would be the case if he were outside the audience for the publication. However, only wide limits can be set on the probability of such ad contact actually occurring: even if they see an issue, some people will read more of its contents, some less. Given that the media selection objective is essentially to put an advertisement economically before a relevant group of people, a more refined measurement than issue audience seems desirable. Exactly the same two basic problems occur here as have already been noted in relation to issue audience: selecting a workable operational definition that is sensible in relation to the basic concept; and devising the best technique for measuring an audience against this definition. It is convenient to consider these problems first in relation to the audience for a particular page of newspaper or magazine.

Conceptually, the audience for a page comprises those individuals for whom, at some time, the page was in their perceptual field, i.e. those who were in a position to perceive some particular item on it or, colloquially, had 'open eyes in front of the page'. Unfortunately, it is extremely difficult to frame an *operational* definition, suitable for large-scale audience measurement use, which well mirrors this concept. On the one hand, evidence may be sought merely that a given page in a publication has been opened, using the 'glue-spot technique', first introduced many years ago[12]. Here, a small spot of glue, hopefully imperceptible to the reader, fixes together each pair of pages near their edge. Copies specially prepared in this way are placed with a sample of people and collected again after a period. A person is then counted within the audience for a pair of pages if the glue seal between them is found to have been broken. Setting aside the practical difficulties of neither making the glue spot so weak as likely to be broken accidentally nor so strong as to interfere with normal reading behaviour, the technique is clearly more suited to limited-scale use. It is artificial to the extent that the respondent will be receiving the copy to be measured in an 'abnormal' way. It is necessary to check that the issue has only been handled by the respondent between placement and recall interviews. Finally, and most importantly, the evidence is, literally, of a pair of pages having been opened—whether or not as a prelude to the reader giving attention to anything on them is not known just from the glue-spot break.

On the other hand, far more complex observational techniques may be employed; e.g., it is possible to take a continuous record on film of a respondent in a reading situation—unavoidably, a somewhat artificial one—that can show not only which pages were opened and for how long but also the direction of gaze in relation to the page. Equipment for this purpose, originally developed in Germany, is currently in use in the UK by the British Market Research Bureau. The technique is known as the Direct Eye Movement Observation System (DEMOS) and is referred to again below.

Whilst it may be possible, by such approaches, to obtain relatively direct evidence of page contact, on a small scale or under 'laboratory' conditions, survey measurement of page audience has, in practice, come largely to rely on an operational definition where a respondent is counted as within the audience if, on their own report, they have looked at one or more items on the page in question. For this purpose, unprompted *recall* is little used; to ask a respondent, without the use of any recall aids at all, what items they remember having read or looked at will produce generally low scores and ambiguous data, in view of the peripheral importance to the reader of many reading events. Instead, *recognition* is largely employed. In Gallup's Field Readership Index, for example, having established that respondents claim to have seen a particular issue at all, they are taken through it page by page and asked to indicate each item—whether editorial or advertisement, text or illustration—that they have previously looked at. *Page traffic* is then defined at the proportion of the issue audience claiming one or more items on the page in question.

There is little doubt that, unavoidably, the recognition approach leads to some bias in page audience estimation. In the interview situation, there may be strong internal pressures on a respondent to report, even if it can be recalled, not exactly what he or she did when previously looking at the issue—which is the answer sought—but what they think they did or think they 'ought' to have done. Faced with a dominant item on a page which now seems unavoidable to the eye, it is not easy to say 'I didn't look at it'. Equally, reading some items may seem less socially desirable to the respondent than other ones; comic strips (or, for that matter, advertisements) as against leading articles. To this extent, to deduce page contact from *claimed* self-exposure to an item on it is far from straightforward.

There is another approach to page audience measurement, distinct from the recognition technique just discussed. Here, a respondent is presented with some form of scale indicating degrees of thorough or less thorough reading within the issue of a particular title and asked to choose that scale position which best describes their own behaviour. The scale itself can take a number of forms. In the National Readership Survey, a pictorial scale is currently in use. It was employed for some years; however, many other formulations are possible. People might be asked, for example, how many pages out of ten they look at on average or, in verbal rather than numerical terms, whether they read 'all' of an issue, 'most', 'some' or 'little'. Some of these alternatives were investigated in the developmental research preceding the introduction of the NRS scale[13], while their relationship to page audience and that of some other, indirect, measures of issue reading 'intensity' has also been reported[14].

Irrespective of the exact form of scale employed, this technique will require actual numerical values of probability of contact with the average page to be ascribed to each scale position, if the data are to be of practical use in choosing between print media vehicles in planning schedules. In the National Readership Survey case, the scale of reading intensity was 'calibrated' (so far for groups of publications only rather than individual titles) by taking a page traffic measurement amongst people opting for each of the scale positions, but using a postal survey rather than personal interview approach[15].

It will be seen that there is an important difference between deriving page audience data from claims of what was read or looked at previously and using a scaling approach of the type just described. The former is applicable to one or more specific issues; the latter can use questions phrased in relation to a respondent's 'usual' behaviour. This raises a basic problem in the application of the data, if it is desired to forecast the probability of contact between a given person and the 'average' page in a particular publication: it is likely that not only will people differ between themselves in the amount they 'usually' read of this newspaper or that magazine, but also that, for any one reader and title, the amount they look at will vary from issue to issue, dependent on content and reading circumstances.

So far, the discussion of this section has been entirely in terms of *page* audience. However, the various measurement methods touched on can equally well produce data in relation to the double-page spread formed by two facing pages; and operational definitions of 'spread audience' follow naturally from those for 'pages'. Indeed, it has been strongly argued that the spread is the more natural unit in relation to audience measurement, in the sense that it is difficult to imagine a reader having no opportunity to perceive an item on a given page if the evidence is that they have focused some attention on the facing one. In fact, the validity of this argument may be seen very much to depend on definitions of 'reading' and 'attention'. All too little is known about the mechanisms of perceptual organization of complex stimuli as applied to newspaper and magazine pages. However, it does seem likely that a large amount of scanning—probably subliminal—will be involved before the eye fixes on this or that item. Thus, everything on a double-page spread may have been 'seen' in a subconscious sense; but the items later

588

reported—quite honestly—as 'looked at' may be far fewer. This point brings one directly to the final topic of this section—measurement of audiences not for issues or spreads or pages, but for advertisements themselves.

It is to be stressed immediately that this subject lies on the borderline of 'media research' in the sense taken throughout this chapter. *Post facto*, the number and sorts of people whose knowledge, attitudes or opinions have been modified by anything transferred to them from a particular advertisement will heavily depend on its content—its product or brand subject, the ideas the advertisement expresses and the way it expresses them. This variation of advertisement audience with ad content is not the province of media research. There are, however, a number of 'media' variables which *are* relevant at this level. An advertisement's size, absolutely or relative to the page; its position on the page; the position of the page in the issue; whether the page is left- or right-hand; whether the ad faces or is amongst other advertisements; whether it is surrounded by a margin or 'bled' to the edge of the page; and whether it is in monochrome or colour are all characteristics which may, in principle at least, affect the size of an advertisement's audience and render it distinguishable from the audience for the page on which it appears.

Conceptual and operational definitions offer even more difficulty at this stage than before. In terms of '*opportunity* to see', the advertisement audience is virtually equivalent to that for the page carrying it; refinement must invoke some idea of communication. Whilst the principle may be to count only within the ad audience those potentially affected by it, the practice is far more difficult; what cut-off point of behaviour in relation to the advertisement should be taken, and how is unbiased evidence of this behaviour then to be obtained?

In practice, methods already mentioned are the ones in use. Unaided recall of advertisements read can be employed. For an exhaustive treatment of comparisons of recall and recognition results, the reader is referred to the Advertising Research Foundation's Printed Advertisement Rating Methods (PARM) study[16]. Regarding recognition methods themselves, the Field Readership Index referred to above has the measurement of claimed readership of individual advertisements as a prime objective, its page traffic results being a byproduct. Here, reported ad contact is researched at three levels, respondents being categorized on whether they claim to have 'noted' the advertisement, to have 'read most' of its text and to have registered the brand name concerned.

As already noted, claims regarding previous advertisement reading behaviour are not unbiased, and the work reported by Fletcher[17] with the DEMOS equipment well illustrates the difficulties.

In conclusion, it is to be stressed that the techniques currently in use for measuring contact with advertisements have primarily been developed for assessing the apparent, comparative effectiveness of the ads themselves, as influenced by their content and its creative expression. Quite apart from the difficulties of definition and technique, considerable reprocessing of the data is needed to render it of relevance to media decisions; e.g., noting scores from many individual advertisements may be examined to see if the effects of such factors as ad size may be partialled out. Considerable work in the UK by the now-dissolved Agencies Research Consortium, reported by Twyman[18], had as its objective the development of more immediately 'media-oriented' ad audience research, but did not lead to basic changes of the recognition method.

Audience classification

A Rationale of Audience Breakdowns

In the preceding sections, the concentration has been on the measurement of total audience—whether for the average issue, a page or an advertisement. However, the sub-groups which are to be examined within this total are of considerable importance; and their identification may call for considerably more than gathering straightforward 'classification' data in the usual sense of that term.

There are two basic concepts which underlie the need for audience breakdowns. First, people differ between themselves in their value as prospects to a given advertiser. This leads to a search for criteria which meaningfully segment the population both as regards their actual or potential purchasing behaviour and also in respect of their contact with media and vehicles.

Second, the effectiveness of a particular campaign may be thought to depend—holding creative content constant—on the vehicle which carries it. This variation, again, may derive from the characteristics of the audience and their interaction with the newspaper or magazine.

Demographic Classification

The most commonly occurring audience breakdowns utilize demographic criteria, including sex, age, socio-economic class, marital status, household size and composition, employment status, and geographical area. The collection of data on these criteria does not call for special comment here, except in two cases.

The objective of any socio-economic classification is to group individuals in a clear-cut and unambiguous manner into segments which may be expected to display differing patterns of consumption of goods and services. Such an objective is difficult to meet in practice. A simple, robust, reproducible coding framework for social class is hard to find. The categories developed by the National Readership Survey are based on employment, combining basic data on job-type with information on size of firm and status within it. Reasonably stable results are produced but the method is still criticized. These difficulties, combined with the limited discrimination between socio-economic classes in purchasing behaviour in many fields may lead to a decline in the use of the criterion.

Regarding age, there is a school of thought that favours replacing age group classification with stages in the life cycle. However, there has yet been little if any move in this direction as regards day by day audience classification practice in the UK. The greater utility of the 'life-cycle' segmentation in relation to purchasing behaviour has also been questioned.

Attitudinal Classification

The demographic breakdowns of print media audiences covered briefly above have, as their basic objective, the identification of population sub-groups with varying actual or potential behaviour in the market-place. However, on turning to attitudinal classification of audiences, both of the two distinct concepts noted in the beginning of this section are relevant. On the one hand, brand or product-oriented attitudes of members of the audience of a newspaper or magazine may be measured. Such criteria may yield a more meaningful segmentation of the population than demographics alone can provide, in terms of 'value as prospects' for a given campaign; and it will be desired to ascertain media coverage within the attitudinally defined segments.

Within the last few years, there have been considerable advances both in quantitative attitudinal measurement techniques for market research purposes and in market segmentation methods based on such data. Despite this progress, however, there has been very limited introduction, so far, of attitudinal classification into print media research, at least as regards syndicated or other generally available work as distinct from private surveys. One likely reason is that, quite apart from many remaining difficulties on the prediction of *future* purchasing behaviour from measurement of attitudes, in the cases where some success has been achieved by an advertiser in developing measures of demonstrable relevance to his market, the scales in question will have tended to be specific rather than general. By contrast, the objective of much print media research is to provide market-actionable data to a wide variety of users, operating in many different product fields. Few attitudinal scales are likely both to be general enough to offer 'something for everybody' yet also 'sharp' enough to provide actionable data in specific marketing and advertising planning instances. There may be exceptions: conservatism versus experimentalism (as affecting behaviour towards new brands) or attitudes to price may be cases in point. The Target Group Index[19] provides instances of including general attitudinal, as well as demographic, audience classification.

There is, in fact another consideration relevant to classification of audiences in attitudinal terms. Such data can certainly provide a 'richer' portrait of an audience group; and 'pen portraits' of this or that set of readers are to be welcomed in a situation where media selection decisions, increasingly, jointly involve both creative considerations and viewpoints equally with 'traditional' media department opinions.

So far, the attitudinal measurements discussed have been market-oriented; but, quite separately, attitudes to vehicles—to newspaper and magazines themselves—are measured. The thought here is that, in addition to behavioural aspects of the interaction between a reader and a print-media vehicle, what the audience thinks of and feels towards the publication is of importance to the likely effect on them of advertising it carries.

The classification of audiences according to the 'image' the medium or vehicle presents to them is, again, limited at present to isolated cases rather than being general practice. Examples of measurement of perceptions of newspapers or magazines on such dimensions as their prestige, sophistication and modernity are provided by the work of the National Magazine Company[20], the Evening Newspaper Advertising Bureau[21] and *TV Times*[22].

One particular instance of 'attitudes to media' has received quite considerable attention, though more in Europe than the UK. It argues in favour of a generalized dimension of a reader's 'involvement' with a newspaper or magazine and thus of the importance they attach to it; an example is provided in research by Gallup for the *Reader's Digest*[23]. A common question format here is to ask how vital it would be to a reader if he or she could not obtain a particular title—the so-called 'regret at loss' question. A related idea is to classify readers according to their claimed strength of interest in each of a number of product areas and activities, on the argument that the higher their interest in a given subject the better prospect a person is for advertising on that topic.

In conclusion, it seems a reasonable assumption that readers hold definable attitudes towards print media vehicles, largely (though not wholly) determined by their perceptions of the contents of the various publications. Whether, as a result, the editorial environment in which an advertisement appears has a material bearing on its effectiveness is, at present, a more debatable point. Research in support of this contention—and thus justifying attitudes-to-media classification—is limited. Experiments by Winnick[24] are often cited but, as Broadbent[25] has pointed out, the evidence they provide is not strong.

Behavioural Classification

Just as in the previous section, there are two separate aspects to the classification of members of an audience in terms of behaviour. On the one hand, measurement of a person's behaviour towards a particular newspaper or magazine may be used as an indicator of the likely effectiveness of an advertisement it contains. On the other hand, the 'behaviour' in question may be in the market-place and of importance in grading people as more or less valuable advertising targets.

Under the first of these headings, the dividing line between attitudes to media vehicles and behaviour towards the same publications is a narrow one; e.g., measures of a person's 'involvement' with a particular magazine or newspaper, or of the importance they attach to it, or of their interest in its editorial contents will correlate highly with many of the behavioural criteria dealt with below. A danger to be avoided, therefore, in media research design and the application of its results, is the use of a number of audience classifications as if they each provided independent evidence of vehicles' values when, in fact, their information is largely redundant.

Apart from actual criteria of issue, page, or ad contact, dealt with above, a common behavioural measure is of claimed time spent reading, usually in relation to the 'average' issue and thus asked about in terms of habitual behaviour. Whilst usually seen as an indicator of probability of advertisement exposure, reading time is equally a likely correlate of the importance the reader attaches to the title and thus, possibly, of the degree to which its editorial authority 'rubs-off' on advertisements.

Adding another dimension to people's reading behaviour is a measurement of the number of separate occasions a particular issue is looked at. (This criterion is to be distinguished from reading frequency, where the concept is one of regularity of contact taken across *different* issues.) Apart from observational techniques—impracticable economically and otherwise on other than a small scale—readers' recall of their previous reading behaviour must be relied on. This in turn normally limits research to the measurement of the number of different dates on which a particular issue was looked at—a variable that has come to be known as 'reading days' from the first, American, research on the subject. UK examples of investigating issue reading occasions are provided in work by *Radio Times*[26] and *TV Times*[27].

Next, the reading locale may be measured by asking, for example, whether the newspaper or magazine concerned was read 'at home', 'during a journey to work', 'at work', and so on. Similarly, the time of day when reading took place may be questioned. The common rationale in both cases is that the circumstances surrounding a reading event, such as the degree of distraction or relaxation or concurrent preoccupations of the reader are of likely relevance to the effectiveness of advertising in general or of a particular campaign carried by a vehicle.

Finally in this list of aspects of behaviour towards a newspaper or magazine, audience members may be classified according to how they acquire it: whether it is delivered to their home and if so whether wholly or mainly for them or for some other member of their household; or, if not delivered, whether copies are personally purchased by a respondent or passed on to him or her.

Data of this kind have relevance for circulation marketing problems of a publication treated as a 'brand', discussed later in this chapter. In the present context, the justification of the measure is again that being a 'primary' reader of a publication is likely to be a correlate of a person's general attitude to it and thus of the effect on him of advertising it contains.

The above paragraphs have listed various aspects of people's behaviour towards newspapers and magazines that may identify meaningful audience sub-groups. In a print media survey, it will also be common practice to collect at least relatively simple data on respondents' contact with other media, such as television, radio or the cinema. The objective here is not so much to provide audience estimates in their own right (which may better be achieved by research techniques tailored to the task) but again to allow breakdowns of the readership of publications which are relevant to print media selection, e.g. to demonstrate the penetration of a particular magazine amongst those who view little commercial television.

Turning, now, to the other area of behavioural classification of audiences mentioned at the head of this section, demographic and attitudinal measurements noted earlier provide indirect evidence of whether a reader is a better or worse prospect from an advertiser's viewpoint, as regards their present or prospective purchasing behaviour. Self-evidently, readers may also be classified directly in terms of what they buy. This subject of integrated data (integrated in the sense of providing both media contact and purchasing behaviour information on the same individual) is a wide one and only a few salient points can be covered here.

First, the two sets of information can literally both be measured on each of a sample of individuals, in which case the data are not only integrated but also 'single source'. Alternatively, separate media and market research can be conducted and the data then 'married'. This technique depends on locating a set of classification criteria, common to the two surveys which, collectively, correlate highly either with behaviour towards media or towards products and brands. On this basis, appropriate purchasing characteristics can, for example, be ascribed to each individual in the other, media survey. Examples of single-source data are provided by BMRB's Target Group Index operating both in the UK and the USA—and by their US competitor, Simmons. Integrated data obtained by 'marriage' have not been largely developed in Britain, but in France Agostini has undertaken considerable work[28].

Next, as regards single-source data, the number of technique alternatives is large. In principle, at least, any appropriate audience measurement method can be linked to any one of several approaches to collecting purchasing data, including single contact versus continuous (panel) reporting and personal interview versus self-completion questionnaires.

Third and last, the limitations as well as apparent advantages of integrated data are to be recognized. Being able to classify media survey respondents in terms of their purchasing behaviour does not of itself solve previously existing problems of whether vehicles should be so selected as to reach heavy or light buyers of a product, buyers or non-buyers of a brand. Again, readers' purchasing behaviour may often be inferred with adequate accuracy on the basis of indirect classifications, e.g. demographic ones, although by no means always so[29]. Fine distinctions between newspapers and magazines in terms of the buying behaviour of their respective audiences may, in practice, be swamped by gross difference in their advertising rates, as largely dictated by the sizes of their total audiences.

594

Schedule Construction and Evaluation Programs

Program types and objectives

In parallel with the refinement of audience measurement methods, a notable feature of the media research scene in the last decade has been the development and application of computer programs which take as their input, partly or wholly, the data discussed in earlier sections of this chapter. Whilst such programs are usable, in principle, in relation to any measured advertising medium, in practice they have related most frequently to newspapers and magazines and therefore should be briefly covered here, although the subject is by now a wide one, with a very considerable literature.

Media programs may be divided according to objective into two groups. First, *evaluation programs* take as input an existing schedule or schedules of insertions in a number of vehicles and provide, as output, measures of schedule performance—notably full data on the pattern of contacts that should be produced and indices of the 'effectiveness' of this pattern.

Construction programs by contrast have, as input, audience data and much other information and produce an actual schedule on the basis of given instructions and assumptions. The term 'optimization' (of schedule selection) has been and is still often applied to these routines. It is more accurate to regard them as producing, within stated constraints, a selection of vehicles and numbers of insertions in each of them which is 'best', if at all, only under the assumptions made. Further, the schedule can often be guaranteed to be no more than 'very close to the best', for technical reasons of the programming method employed.

In the next section, the input requirements and calculation methods of these programs are described, in bare outline only. No detailed comparisons between programs are drawn, but several general reviews are available[30, 31, 32, 33]. A later section turns to some consideration of the advantages and limitations of their use.

Methods

It is convenient to consider first schedule construction programs, although it is to be stressed that evaluation routines are, almost certainly, finding wider day by day use at present, at least in the UK.

The first input requirement is a list of *candidate vehicles* from amongst which a schedule is to be selected. Different programs will accept lists of varying lengths. For each vehicle, the cost of the size or sizes of insertion associated with it is to be specified. Some programs are able to take series discounts into consideration. The audience data included in the input will usually relate to issue contact, often but not invariably in the form of reading frequencies. It is required for each population sub-group to which the program is instructed to ascribe a different 'value'. Unless the schedule is to be constructed on the assumption that all people are equal in their worth as prospects for the advertising concerned, a full set of *market weights* is to be specified, comprising the relative values—whether based on assumption or measurement—of each type of individual to be separately considered by the program. Such groups may be identified by any classification covered by the audience research data used, but are most commonly demographic ones. Some programs require the user to specify weights separately for each criterion he nominates—to say, for example, that upper social class individuals are twice as valuable to him as lower class ones and that, separately, younger people should carry three times the weight of older ones. Other input formats may call for weights for groups identified by interlaced criteria; thus, for instance, a figure might be attached to mothers with children under 16 living in the south east and to other mutually exclusive groups similarly defined.

Quite separately from market weights, most construction program inputs will allow the optional use of *media weights*, which are quantitative expressions of the varying values the program user attaches to a contact between one individual and the different vehicles within the candidate list. In the calculations the computer subsequently performs, these media weights are almost always treated mathematically as probabilities; but in fact they may reflect either of two different concepts.

On the one hand, a media weight may express the probability of advertisement contact (or, at least, of opportunity of such contact) conditional on contact with an issue of the vehicle. Clearly, data on page traffic, or its correlates such as time spent reading, could be utilized to provide weights in this sense. On the other hand, a media weight may be an attempt to express a judgement on the relative strength of impact delivered to a reader by exposure to an advertisement in one vehicle rather than another; e.g., it might be felt that the editorial authority of some magazines was greater than others, that this 'rubbed off' on their advertising and, therefore, that the former should be given higher media weights.

Data input requirements are completed by a statement of the budget available for the schedule to be constructed—some programs will call for a single figure, others a range—and by a set of constraints which limit the pattern of insertions the program may choose. These may be partly 'environmental' in the sense that, for example, if a rule of 'one insertion per issue' is being followed and the schedule period is a year, the computer must be instructed that there are only 52 issues of a weekly magazine available for selection; or constraints may again reflect purely the program user's wishes that, say, no more than half of the total budget is to be expended in one media group.

Given the type of input data outlined above, the objective of a construction program is then to arrive at a schedule which is permissible within the constraints laid down and is also 'best', in some sense, amongst all feasible alternatives. This simple statement of the problem raises three basic issues:

what criterion is to be nominated, against which any given schedule may be evaluated? How is this evaluation to be achieved in practice? And how is the program to arrive at a candidate schedule for evaluation?

The type of criterion most commonly adopted is the weighted number of contacts a schedule delivers for given expenditure. The weighting involved comprises the varying values of individuals as advertising prospects, as expressed in market weights; the differing worth of contacts effected by this vehicle against that one, or media weights; and, usually, a third weighting expressing a view that successive contacts with a given individual are not of uniform value. This last-mentioned set of weights is termed, collectively, a *response function:* a numerical expression of the marginal or cumulative value of the first, second, third . . . contact with a given individual. It may be in-built into a program; or it may be variable at the user's choice and form part of the required input. Different response functions may be chosen to reflect viewpoints that the first, tenth, and hundredth impact are of just the same value; that several impacts are necessary to gain any effect at all but that, beyond this critical point, nothing is added by further ones; that cumulative effect rises slowly at first with number of contacts, then more rapidly and later tails off once more; or that early impacts in a series are the relatively most forceful, diminishing returns then applying.

In evaluating any given schedule against such a criterion of market, media, and response function weighted impacts, a program's central task is to calculate a frequency distribution of issue contacts—to calculate the numbers of people, in total or within relevant sub-categories, seeing varying numbers of issues. Here two basic approaches are possible. First, the program can consider each individual in a population (or, more strictly, each member of a sample of that population) in relation to each vehicle concerned and 'decide' on the basis of the data provided (reading frequency information, for example) whether a contact will or will not occur. This *simulation* approach may use up much program running time where a large sample and many vehicles are involved. Alternatively, a program may estimate a distribution of contacts, through the use of appropriate formulae, by considering reading patterns for the population or group as a whole, rather than one by one; this technique has come to be known as the '*formula*' approach.

Turning to the third essential problem, even given a meaningful criterion on which schedules' values can be compared and a calculation method for such evaluation, a program has still to arrive at a feasible schedule in the first place; and, even given the very high calculation speeds which attain, it will not be economically practicable to generate and evaluate every one of the myriad alternative sets of vehicles and numbers of insertions that derive from even a short candidate list.

A common approach is to build up the 'best' schedule in a series of steps. Such a *stepwise* program first ranks candidate vehicles on a value for money basis, comparing market and media weighted audiences with costs; selects the most economical; examines the value-weighted patterns of contacts formed by this first insertion combined with each possible addition to it; again makes a choice on value against cost; and so continues until the budget is exhausted.

Any form of such a procedure is properly subject to the criticism that it cannot be guaranteed to produce a schedule which is optimum. However, the shortfall is likely to be small and can be further reduced by refinements which allow the deletion of insertions as well as their addition or permit the program, in effect, to 'look back' and compare, in terms of value, the point it has currently reached with branches of its path that it rejected earlier.

The discussion of this section has, so far, been entirely in terms of schedule construction programs, but it will be seen that the essential problems of evaluating an existing schedule have also been covered. The calculation of a frequency distribution of contacts, together with the application of market, media, and, probably, response function weights are, on the one hand, intermediate stages in most 'optimization' routines but are equally the core of evaluation programs.

Advantages and limitations in program use

The period which saw the first introduction of computer programs for the construction or evaluation of print media schedules was characterized by considerable over-claiming of resultant benefits; but subsequently and currently, the gains from the use of the computer remain hotly debated. This section summarizes some few points on both sides of the argument. A longer and very balanced review is provided by Broadbent[34].

It is unquestionable that computer use permits fast, numerically accurate comparative consideration of far more schedules, permissible within the budgetary and other constraints, than could ever be reviewed by manual means within economic time and cost limits. Equally, a program may 'consider' simultaneously a large number of factors held to be relevant to a schedule's value. However, the program of itself adds nothing to the logic of its constructor. What factors are to be considered and how they are to be traded off the one against the other must be specified in its instructions. There is no genie in the hardware bottle, only a totally obedient, incredibly fast-working slave. Further, 'garbage in, garbage out' is no empty truism. If the logic of the program's construction or the quality of the input data are indefensible, so will be the output. Even so, the availability of only limited data is no argument against using sophisticated analysis techniques on it.

The two areas of input information most frequently criticized are media weights and response functions. It is properly said that, in relation both to the contribution of vehicle environment to advertisement impact and to the marginal effect of successive impacts, judgement must currently largely stand in for knowledge.

On the first of these areas, if any 'qualitative' factor, beyond intrinsically quantitative audience and cost data, would be taken into account in selection of advertising vehicles by non-computer means, it seems hardly logical to ignore it when writing a program. At the same time, the hard task has to be undertaken of turning generalized 'feelings' about relative media value into overt, quantified judgements the computer can note.

As regards response functions, the advent of the computer has merely given a name to a problem existing long previously. Every hand-constructed schedule for which reaching many people was traded-off, to some purposeful degree, against contacting a smaller audience more frequently concealed an opinion on the planner's part regarding the relationship between cumulative number of impacts and cumulative 'effect'.

In relation of both these areas of 'doubtful' input, it is to be noted that computer use allows—and should ideally always include—investigation of the effect on the schedule constructed or evaluated of varying the assumptions that have been made. Such sensitivity analysis cannot answer the question of whether this media weight or that response function, assigned on judgement, is 'right' or 'wrong'; but it can indicate, quickly and relatively inexpensively, how critically dependent a particular media decision is or is not on some unmeasured factor.

Finally, there are those who are happier only to use the computer to evaluate, rather than to construct schedules and who, further, stop short at weighted distributions of impacts; they point out the uncertainties of whether (for mathematical reasons) a strictly 'optimum' schedule can be arrived at, and stress the non-knowledge regarding response functions. The counter-arguments are that a handful of trial schedules constructed outside the computer can, equally, not be guaranteed to contain the 'best', or even 'nearly best', one possible; and that two or more tables of the numbers of people subject to varying levels of contact can only be compared when, for example, '70% receiving eight opportunities to see' and '60% with 10 ots each' can be put on a common denominator. This reduction to common coinage involves, inevitably, a response function concept.

Measuring Print Media Effectiveness

Media effect and content effect

This section is concerned with the measurement of the effectiveness, as advertising vehicles, of media at large and newspapers or magazines in particular.

Taking a mass media advertising campaign as a whole, it is neither theoretically desirable nor practically possible to separate its effect (however 'effect' is defined) as between contributions from the content of the campaign—the advertising theme and its creative expression—and from the media in which that content appears.

On the theoretical point, the contributions to effectiveness of advertising content and media vehicles are unlikely to be straightforwardly additive; they will interact. Even holding advertised brand and audience constant, a given medium or set of vehicles may be more effective carrying one campaign than another. Hence, any concept of a fixed 'pecking order' of media effects, irrespective of mode of advertising use, is somewhat sterile.

On the practical point, media effectiveness cannot be measured *in vacuo;* an actual campaign, or advertising created for test purposes, must enter into the research. The ability then to generalize from one particular set of circumstances to the intrinsic, forecastable value of the medium under test is limited by a total lack of any comprehensive model of 'how advertising works'.

These somewhat pessimistic comments are intended to point up some overall limitations of media effectiveness measurement. The following paragraphs firstly review criteria of 'effect' and then comment on some aspects of research design and method. These are not explored in depth since many of the relevant points are covered in other chapters of this handbook.

Effectiveness criteria

One half of the problem of media effectiveness research is the question 'what to measure?' There exists a continuum of variables which may be utilized. In one direction this runs from data which are relatively easy and inexpensive to collect to more complex and more costly measurements. Unfortunately, however, the ranking of measures in terms of relevance runs in the opposite direction.

At the one extreme lies a measurement of consumers' purchases or of retail sales. Given that the objective of advertising, and thus of the use of some particular medium or vehicle, is to increase or maintain sales, there is no doubt here of relevance. (The admitted fact that achieved sales will depend on many other factors besides advertising complicates research design and interpretation but is not, *per se*, a reason for measuring achievement against some other criterion only.) However, accurate purchases or sales measurement is costly. Manufacturers' deliveries may, occasionally, be an adequate substitute, given no complications of alternative distribution channels, varying stock levels or inability to break out delivery figures just for the area required.

Midway in the continuum lie measures of attitudes to the brand advertised and of their change. Research costs *may* be lower than for sales' measurement, although very considerable developmental work may be involved if relevant attitudinal dimensions have to be established from scratch and scales for their measurement built up and tested. The major question is, however, of relevance, since the link between attitudinal change and subsequent purchasing behaviour is far from unequivocally established.

Questions in the general area of communications effects are the easiest to formulate and probably the least expensive to administer; they include recall and recognition of product, brand name, attributes and copy points. Unfortunately, an individual's knowledge of an advertised brand or its campaign is but tenuously connected to his behaviour towards it in the market-place. The relevance of communications measures is thus considered the lowest of those here mentioned.

Effectiveness research design

In parallel with the choice of criterion measure discussed above, research into media effectiveness can be conducted under controlled 'laboratory' conditions, at some cost, unavoidably, of realism, or in the field. The latter alternative subdivides according to whether data are collected in parallel with an ongoing advertising campaign or whether a special pattern of exposure is imposed for experimental purposes.

'Laboratory'-scale research may constrain costs and allow at least some of the many unwanted, confounding variables to be controlled. It will typically involve exposing relatively small samples of individuals to advertising in the vehicle or vehicles under test and taking measures on these people of the chosen 'effect' variable. A simple 'before and after' measurement approach is often used but more complex experimental designs may be introduced. An example of this general category of media research is provided in work by the *Daily Mirror* aiming to demonstrate its effectiveness relative to that of television[35].

The main limitations of 'laboratory' work are two-fold. First, the conditions of exposure to the media vehicles concerned and of contact with the test advertising are often far different from those naturally occurring and, if a comparison of widely dissimilar media is involved, the bias thus introduced regarding their relative 'effectiveness' may not easily be assessed. Second, the measures that may be taken obviously stop short of any actual expression of brand preference in the market-place.

Turning to field research, one approach to effectiveness measurement in the context of a normal, ongoing campaign is to monitor both levels of exposure and 'effect' amongst the same sample of individuals. At the analysis stage, weight of purchasing of the advertised brand of changes in attitudes towards it, for example, may then be compared as between a sub-sample with low numbers of ots and a group exposed to many issues. Whilst some success has been reported with such a method[36], there is a major danger to be avoided in confusing correlation with causation when interpreting the results. Even if high levels of 'effect' are found to be associated with high exposure, it is quite possible for some third variable to be responsible, which predicates both 'effect' and exposure. More commonly, the advertising plan will be tailored to research requirements. The simplest design will be to run a press schedule in one area only, and to take measurements of the chosen variable(s) before and after the advertising period. The problem of other uncontrolled factors also affecting the observed difference between the 'before' and 'after' readings leads naturally to the addition of parallel research in another control area, in which there is no advertising. This device cannot, however, solve the problem completely; in general, neither will it be known what other factors it is important to take account of, nor in practice will it be possible to select two areas which are comparable in all aspects tl.ought likely to be relevant. More complex experimental designs may, therefore, be sought (as discussed in chapter 3), using several areas and allowing statistical estimation of the contributory effects of the actual media being researched, of between-area differences, of time effects, and residual factors. An example of an elaborate experimental project, aiming to compare the effectiveness of magazines and television, is provided in American work by General Foods[37].

Another practical problem in the application of experimental designs to print media effectiveness measurement is that the regions available will be dictated by the areas in which part or all of the circulation of a newspaper falls, which may not be ideal, in size or nature, on research grounds. (It is to be noted that experiments *are* possible with national media since, increasingly, regional editions are available as a regular facility or by special arrangement.)

One alternative to using naturally occurring circulation areas for experimental purposes is to so arrange matters that, amongst two otherwise comparable samples, one receives copies of a publication containing a test advertisement and the other sees issues which are apparently similar but do not, in fact, carry the campaign. The method of achieving this result will depend on the realism demanded and the level of permissible costs: an extra advertisement may just be 'tipped-in' or, at much greater trouble and expense, a whole section of four or more pages may be 'doctored'. Whilst unwanted inter-personal and inter-regional differences may thus be eliminated, it will be administratively extremely difficult to supply specially prepared copies through normal trade channels. The artificiality may have to be accepted of having respondents receive the test publication other than by the delivery to the home or purchase at a newsagent as would normally be the case.

Finally, the use of coupons or keyed write-in addresses as a means of evaluating media vehicles is to be noted. The analysis only of enquiries resulting in actual sales may be preferable to looking just at total enquiries received by the advertiser. Clearly, a *media* comparison properly results only from the use of the same couponed or keyed advertisement in two or more newspapers or magazines. Note that, as in virtually all attempts to evaluate media effectiveness under 'real-life' conditions, the overall level of coupon response actually derives from the combined effect of many factors, including the size and nature of the issue audience, intensity of reading within the issue, the contents of the advertisement itself and interaction between vehicle and ad.

This section has provided a very brief overview of some approaches to print media effectiveness assessment. A useful further summary of American methods and case-histories has been published by the National Industrial Conference Board[38].

Circulation Marketing Research

Introduction

The research problems and methods discussed so far in this chapter have been concerned almost entirely with newspapers and magazines viewed as advertising vehicles. However, as already noted, a publisher is often operating in a situation of joint supply. He derives income not only from offering an audience, or opportunities for advertisement contact, but also from selling actual copies to readers. Clearly, the relative importance of the two markets will vary from case to case. At the one extreme, a free sheet or controlled circulation magazine depends entirely on advertisement revenue. At the other there are periodicals (although few, if any, now, in the consumer area) carrying no advertising and deriving all income from copy sales. In practice, in the UK at least, less research effort is devoted to publications as 'brands' in their own right than as advertising vehicles; but some mention is to be made of the techniques relevant to the former.

Note that the concept of a newspaper or magazine as a 'brand' is often questioned, on the argument that 'product content' is entirely variable from issue to issue. However, a publication is unquestionably seen by its readers as a continuing entity: and those needs which a title seeks to satisfy are no more impermanent than for other fields.

Circulation market measurement

Nearly all newspapers and magazines provide a figure of their net sales. Often, this will be one endorsed by the Audit Bureau of Circulation (ABC), a body calling for sales returns in a set format and carrying out spot-checks of publishers' internal auditing procedures. ABC figures usually relate to a net sales' average struck over all publishing days in a six months' period; monthly data are also published, in arrears. Some publishers not in membership of the ABC will appoint their own auditors to produce net sales figures, or offer merely a 'publishers statement' of their sales. Audited circulations lie somewhere between ex-factory sales data for other product fields and a true, unbiased estimate of net consumer offtake. They do take into account not only the quantities of copies supplied to the trade, but also the numbers unsold and returned for credit. However, in the UK at present, newspapers are *not*, in general, supplied ex-publisher on a 'sale or return' (SOR) basis; and whether SOR applies to a magazine, either as a permanent feature or a limited period, will vary from case to case.

There is a further complication to audited circulation figures. Even if SOR applies, the promptness and speed with which unsold copies are returned through the trade channels will vary. However, an audited figure for a given period will be based on ex-publisher supplies for that month or months and on returned copies recorded in that same period, but representing outdated issues of varying age. Thus the audited figure may well provide a biased estimate of short-term variations in net consumer offtake. The problem can, of course, be overcome, at some trouble and expense, by sorting returned copies according to their cover date.

It is to be noted that ABC and similar figures provide, in this country, total sales data only. The parallel American returns go into considerable detail on geographical and other breakdowns.

Seeking fuller information on sales to, or purchases by, the final consumer of newspapers and magazines, there are at present no continuous, generally available measurement services analogous to those for many other product fields. However, techniques employed in other areas can be applied—with some modifications—and are in use by some publishers on a limited or experimental basis.

Purchase data can be derived both from single-contact surveys (either using personal interviews or self-administered questionnaires) or by panel techniques. Two problem areas are to be noted. First, the casual, irregular purchase of a particular title will not be a highly memorable event to a respondent. Second, publications are acquired through more than one channel. Separate questioning may be required to cover copies received on direct subscription from a publisher (of negligible proportions in the UK, save for some few magazines); copies delivered to a household by a newsagent; copies purchased at a retail outlet—whether newsagent, station bookstall, other type of shop or street vendor; and copies passed on by an initial purchaser to someone else. Loose questioning can lead to copies in this last category erroneously being counted more than once.

Retail audits are also possible with, again, some special problems attaching to newspapers or magazines as product fields. Street sales will be unmeasured if the universe sampled is only of newsagents and bookstalls. Newsagents' normal recording of 'deliveries' may need to be specially supplemented, particularly where they receive supplies not only from wholesalers but also by publishers' representatives 'filling-in' their additional requirements. Far more than in other product fields, 'outdated stock'—yesterday's newspapers, for example—are waste and will normally be disposed of unrecorded. Finally, if sales data are required issue by issue, the audit period becomes as short as a week or a day for some publications, which would clearly lead to astronomical costs if a normal stock-check approach were used. However, self-completion of a questionnaire by the retailer may be employed.

Research for publication launches

Formal test marketing of a major new newspaper or consumer magazine hardly ever takes place. Editorial, production and distribution economics are such that 'first copy' costs are high and pilot-scale production hardly feasible. This is not to say, of course, that 'dummy' issues are not produced, both for early circulation to advertisers and agencies and, sometimes, to gauge reaction to a new title from the wholesale and retail trade. Short of full-scale test marketing, however, the publisher can apply much of the methodology of other areas of consumer research to measuring prospective demand before committing himself to a new publication. An example is provided by research for Thomson Regional Newspapers[39].

'Product' and pricing research

The individual newspaper or magazine, as much as any other brand, has definable 'product content' in the shape of the news, comment, fiction, and features it carries. The actual items vary from issue to issue, but the satisfied reader is, nonetheless, buying a mix with a consistent shape imposed on it by editorial policy. Systematic product content research is relatively little applied to print media; a strong journalistic tradition makes more for a producer-oriented outlook than a marketing one. However, relevant evidence can be obtained.

Post facto investigation of claimed readership of individual items, discussed above, points to their apparent relative interest to different segments of a publication's readership. Reasons for an individual pursuing this item but ignoring that one can be probed by direct questioning, with the usual caveats that some degree of rationalization will be unavoidable. More elaborately, a market segmentation approach can be applied to mapping the consumer needs that print media satisfy.

The 'make-up' of a newspaper or magazine—the style and arrangement of its content on and through its pages—is in many ways the analogue of packaging in other fields. Again, research techniques used in other areas may be applied to measure the legibility of a particular typeface or the brand image conveyed by a magazine's cover design. Examples of research in this area that are generally available are few; some have been summarized by the American Newspaper Publishers Association Foundation[40].

Finally, in this section, the special problems of pricing research may be mentioned. For British newspapers and magazines, resale price maintenance is the invariable rule so that experimental manipulation of cover prices for research purposes is not practicable; questioning on readers' attitudes to present or prospective prices must be relied on. The limitation is perhaps not a critical one, since print media do not occupy an essential 'price-market', nor is pricing used as an aggressive marketing weapon, being largely determined, at least for newspapers, on a 'cost-plus' basis.

25. Television media research

W. A. Twyman

This chapter concentrates on the measurement of aspects of television which are an aid to its commercial use as an advertising medium. Many of the principles involved are, of course, similar to those applying to other aspects, such as the public service role of television.

The types of television media research that are usable, and the particular methods that are relevant and valid, depend largely on the conditions under which television advertisements are transmitted, and on how they are bought and sold. The relevance and validity of research systems and methodology can be affected by local conditions and, since experimentation is costly, it is desirable to separate generalizations from the peculiarities of particular conditions.

The relevant factors which affect choice of methodology are listed below.

How commercial advertising is screened:

(a) as part of a sponsored program, e.g. USA;
(b) isolated commercials, e.g. USA;
(c) as part of a short break of several advertisements, e.g. USA, UK;
(d) as part of a longer block of advertisements, e.g. Germany;
(e) within short pieces of entertainment material, e.g. Italy (Carousella).

These alternatives vary along the dimensions of how much they are separated from programming, how predictable is their timing, and the extent of the total period of advertising requiring attention.

Control of the timing of advertisements by advertisers. The alternatives include combinations of the following:

(a) to the nearest minute including position in break;
(b) to a break within a program;
(c) as part of a sponsored program;
(d) within broad time segments;
(e) day of transmission;

(f) week or longer period of transmission;

(g) as part of blocks with time roughly specified;

(h) as part of block with time unspecified.

The relevant dimension here is how much control the advertiser has over the placing of his advertising. This determines the degree of precision in audience measurement which is usable.

The commercial conditions under which advertising space is bought

(a) with competition for the best timing/blocks or packages;

(b) by allocation in a sellers market.

In considering a research design for any particular circumstance therefore, the conditions should be analysed from the check lists above and the following questions answered:

(a) Are the precision and complexity of the data to be produced optimal for the possible use of the research?

(b) Is the supporting evidence on the validity of the proposed methodology relevant to the particular conditions?

The former question can be carried further into an analysis of whether any efficiency arising from a greater complexity of data offsets its greater cost. This is hard to determine by experimentation when a position of considerable data complexity exists because it then becomes difficult to simulate decision making with simpler data.

Television Advertising Conditions in the UK

In the UK there are currently three TV services, Independent Television (ITV) carrying advertising and administered by the Independent Broadcasting Authority (IBA) through its appointed contractors, and two non-commercial services operated by the British Broadcasting Corporation (BBC). The legal bases of these two bodies end in 1979. In 1977 the 'Committee on the Future of Broadcasting', chaired by Lord Annan, has made its report, but by mid-1978 no government proposals have yet been put forward. The committee has recommended the setting up of a fourth channel, only when adequate funds are available, to be run by an Open Broadcasting Authority. This channel has been suggested as 'a test-bed for experiment' and the Authority would not so much originate the programs itself as act as a 'publisher' for a variety of sources. Financial considerations may, however, affect the implementation of this recommendation.

ITV program companies are financed by the sale of advertising time in breaks containing several commercials, within and between programs but separated from the programming material. Advertising time is sold in a variety of ways but the majority is bought on a spot-by-spot basis with potential control on timing to a specific break, subject to competition, which is considerable.

This system has hitherto led to requirements for recording of specific commercial audiences using continuous panels which also allow the coverage and frequency of exposure to whole schedules over time to be measured. Regional panels vary in size to be the more accurate where most money is at stake. Currently this requirement is met by a meter/diary panel system operated through a single industry contract awarded by JICTAR (Joint Industry Committee for Television Advertising Research). The BBC have operated an entirely independent research system based on daily 24-hour-recall interviewing using quota sampling.

Following recommendations in the Annan Report, the BBC and ITCA (Independent Television Companies Association) have at mid-1978 announced their agreement to cooperate in research and a formal structure for this is being set up.

Audience research in the UK has been summarized historically elsewhere[2] and also critically evaluated[3] and subjected to regular development[4]. Television audience data are also collected in various ways within other research systems in the UK which are reviewed in an IPA publication[5].

The Measurement of TV Set Ownership, Station Reception and Definition of Station Areas

Purpose of the data

The measurement of set ownership and reception arises in two types of situation. There is the research problem of defining the media sources to which an individual or household is potentially exposed. This may be necessary for a number of reasons, e.g. in order to relate media exposure potential to other aspects of behaviour, or merely as a sample stratification control.

The second situation is that of defining the coverage of a television station. This also involves measuring the reception potential of individuals and households but may involve the further stage of making judgements about populations of individuals, such as administrative districts.

An ITV station is created by the allocation of one or more transmitters to a program company which is then responsible for both programming and collecting revenue by the sale of television advertising time. Elsewhere these functions may be separated. The coverage of the station is one basis of selling time and its definition an important research problem.

There are three aspects of defining a station's coverage:

(a) fixing the potential audience for a station. This means measuring the number of people or households effectively receiving the station and their characteristics;

(b) defining the areas to be sampled for audience measurement. Theoretically, there need be no geographical limits. Since coverage of a station generally does have geographical limits and because of marketing needs, it has been usual to associate the media measurement with a formally defined area;

(c) defining the area effectively covered by the station. This can be used for various marketing purposes such as retail distribution of the advertiser's brand in a regional campaign.

These three functions could be satisfied by three different definitions. Potential audience could be independent of area while audience measurement could be limited to an area of dense reception and the marketing area based on another criterion. JICTAR has published only one 'official' set of ITV areas (overlapping), but advertisers have also published a set of non-overlapping areas.

The potential audience for an ITV area is limited to a count within that area. This same area is sampled for the viewing research panels. This common solution to the three functions has created some strains. Some advertisers feel that the boundaries overlap too much for distribution purposes and devise their own different marketing areas, sometimes from their own research. These problems barely exist for the BBC which is not concerned with marketing products and basically operates national TV services. The importance of area definitions will vary between countries according to geography and how stations operate.

Asking the respondent

In an 'out of home' interview an individual can be asked whether his household has a TV set and which stations can be received. How reliably this can be reported depends on the confusability of local stations, by name or programming. An alternative approach where there is risk of confusion is to ask about the availability of programs unique to individual stations.

Interviewer-assessed reception

At a home interview, interviewers can inspect the switched-on TV set. The respondent can switch between known stations to demonstrate the household's range of stations and the interviewer can search for any others, perhaps unknown to the household. Trained interviewers can apply a quality of reception scale for each station. These can be based on technical standards available from broadcast authorities but are not always easy to apply and reception can vary by time and season. An alternative approach is to ask the respondents to assess their own satisfaction with the picture for each available station using an appropriate scale. While this is not an objective measure of quality, it is likely to be predictive of behaviour. A check in the UK has shown that, for comparisons between alternative stations, the subjective preference scale ranks them similarly to an objective picture scale.

The difference lies on the general level accorded; some people are readily satisfied, others are hypercritical. The choice of approach can therefore depend upon the purpose of collecing the data.

Respondent-assessed picture quality

The respondent is asked to conduct the same kind of investigation as the interviewer would, if necessary by telephone or post. Checks between postal and interviewer assessments showed no overall biases and as noted above scales of satisfaction with reception can be used discriminatingly by respondents. The success of this approach, however, may be dependent on the degree of station choice complexity and as this increases some validation is advisable.

Interviewer check on respondent-assessed channel preferences

An interviewer calling on a household may check the reception capabilities of the set and then ask the respondent questions about his viewing habits. This is concerned with the problem of respondent classification rather than just reception measurement. This extension has been regarded as particularly important in relation to the situation where several stations with similar programs can be received. If one station were strongly preferred, there could be arguments for counting that home as 'belonging' to one station's potential audience and not to the others.

One JICTAR study examined the viewing records of panel homes receiving two ITV stations. These were checked against their answers to the question 'Out of every 10 hours watching ITV how many hours would you and your family watch each of the ITV transmitters?'. (This form of question contrasts with that on the UK National Readership Survey which, after asking whether ITV is received on more than one channel number on the set, then reads 'Which ITV station do you (generally) watch if you are watching ITV?')

The conclusions from the JICTAR study were that classifying viewers as belonging to one ITV station, when in fact they receive two, is not meaningful for about 40% of households, because they view both. A forced choice question hides this fact, although the station viewed a majority of times can be identified reliably in 80% of cases if an interviewer asks the question while checking the set. Questioning away from the set relies on memory of station or channel number identification and becomes increasingly unreliable with increasing complexity.

Measuring viewing habits

Having established that a television set can receive more than one station, any audience measurement technique can be applied to establish which stations are viewed by the household. This can then be used as a basis for classifying the household as 'belonging' to one or more stations. This procedure is clearly more elaborate and expensive than asking questions. To be useful, such a procedure would have to be quick, possibly measuring a week's viewing by diary or aided recall. Such a sampling of viewing may give an atypical result for some households although, in another context, Buck & West[6] have shown that total ITV viewing weight is consistent for four out of five consecutive weeks. Comparisons have not been made for choice between ITV stations.

Overall comments

Measuring a household's reception capability is reasonably unambiguous if carried out by a competent interviewer checking the television set, although there may be difficulties when new reception possibilities are involved. Greater complexity of choice makes it difficult to measure reception possibilities without either the interviewer or the respondent checking the set.

For some purposes there may be a need to classify a respondent in terms of stations habitually viewed rather than available to view. It will probably not be possible to allocate all households to just one station; some who receive two will view both about equally.

Possible approaches to household classification are asking a viewing allocation question or measuring a sample period of viewing using a single respondent from the household. Both would correctly show some households as 'belonging' to more than one station and both would probably involve some inaccuracies of classification for the remainder. These shortcomings have to be evaluated in the light of the purpose of classification.

Defining television areas

A station area can be defined by a list of its smaller population units, such as administrative districts. Defining an area involves making decisions about possible districts, accepting or rejecting them on criteria which have tended to be based on the proportion of homes effectively covered by a station.

The current JICTAR criterion for defining an ITV station area is to include a district if 15% or more of the households have sets capable of receiving that station whether by direct transmission or by relay. Station areas overlap because a district may have 15% of homes receiving each of two or more ITV stations.

Definition of Areas by Minimum Signal Strength Boundaries

For technical purposes authorities responsible for transmitters publish maps showing a contour defining the extent of a certain level of measured signal strength. How far this corresponds to a true reception boundary depends on alignment of aerials which in turn is affected by the history of services available to the area. Ideally this approach should be tried first since it is far cheaper than conducting surveys.

Use of a Sequential Sampling Approach to Measurement for Reception Criterion

A sequential sampling procedure has been used for determining whether or not a district qualifies for inclusion within an area boundary. This has involved surveying an initial minimum sample, usually 50. If the percentage of reception found can be regarded as above or below the criterion percentage at a pre-set level of confidence, the decision to include or exclude the district is taken. Otherwise, further samples are interviewed until the decision can be made at the pre-set level of confidence. This ensures considerable savings in sample sizes for districts with very high or low densities of reception. This method can only be used where the sole object of the survey is to make a decision about including a district rather than measure its absolute density of reception.

System of data collection

A television station is likely to require basic data describing the size and characteristics of its potential audiences and other features of its area. Often these data can be supplied from existing data sources by adding questions like those discussed above on TV reception. Otherwise it may be necessary to run special surveys for this purpose. The possible functions of such surveys covering the catchment area of a TV station can be:

(a) to define the extent of reception of various TV stations in that area;
(b) to describe the characteristics of the station potential audience including demographics, exposure to other media and various marketing data as required;
(c) to provide targets for quota weighting or stratification purposes for other samples such as regular audience measurement surveys or panels;
(d) to provide a master sample from which TV panels can be selected.

Such surveys are called establishment surveys and in the UK have generally been conducted annually using a subsample of an existing survey source with adequate regional coverage (the AGB Home Audit)[5].

If signal strength definitions cannot be used to define station areas, 'boundary surveys' using the techniques discussed above will have to be used. These tend to be expensive since decisions have to be made about many small districts accumulating to a large sample. Since these are usually peripheral to the main urban areas, the possibility of combining this research with any other is remote, unless a large national sample is available.

Where the object of such a survey is to record change in viewing possibilities, pilot or preliminary work is necessary to check that the change has occurred and that the situation is stable. Guidance may be obtained from television dealers who are closely concerned with the problem.

Many data sources incorporate some form of measurement of potential exposure to television stations and can use differing approaches. When comparing between sources therefore, it cannot be assumed that a 'TV station viewer' always means the same thing.

612

Techniques and Sources of Measurement for Broad Viewing Habits or Average Media Exposure Probabilities

In long-term planning of advertising campaigns, having identified those people who form the target market it is necessary to establish which are the media vehicles by which they are most economically reached. This is often done by a narrowing down process: deciding whether to use television, radio and/or press; which broad categories; and, finally, which specific vehicles. Computerized media selection models[8] could enable decisions to be made across a mass of vehicles in different media together, were it not for the lack of knowledge about the relative values of different kinds of media exposure. Such lack of knowledge also presents an equal problem for the stage-by-stage approach, but the greater opportunity for making personal judgements may make this a more efficient way of using unquantified experience and certainly more reassuringly conceals lack of fundamental knowledge about media values.

Either approach generates a need for data about an individual which represents a prediction about his behaviour in terms relatable to his probability of exposure to the medium. It is likely that the more computerized the media selection process, the more precisely defined in terms of vehicle (i.e. timing in the case of television) the media exposure probablity will have to be expressed.

The biggest television research effort often goes into a ratings service which obtains a continuous historical record of an individual's viewing. This continuous record can be condensed into probabilities of viewing the medium, defined with any level of precision; within a week, within an evening, within a certain time class, or within a program. Limitations are cost, the need for access to the basic data, and the fact that often a restricted range of information is available about the individuals on the panel, mainly basic demographic characteristics.

Data about purchasing habits are frequently used to define marketing opportunities and target groups. The question of how to reach these target groups then leads to simplified media measurements on product surveys and consumer panels. One solution is that detailed media and detailed product data could all be collected from a 'single-source' or easily integrable system[9].

The following section discusses methods of obtaining broader estimates of probability of exposure to television other than by collecting a detailed historical record of all viewing. These measures can be used to link product and media data or as a stratification control in surveys where television exposure may be relevant, and in studies where the aim is to relate probability of exposure to the medium to some other attitudinal or behavioural variable.

Derivation from detailed viewing records

If detailed viewing records are available, which is likely to be from a TV panel, viewing probabilities can be computed for a class of individuals for a single viewing occasion or for a single individual averaged over a number of possible occasions, e.g. viewing three weeks out of four on Monday at 7 p.m. gives a probability of 0.75 for that individual. Looking at a number of similar individuals gives a further average and a distribution of probabilities, by putting TV panel basic data tapes through a computer. No purchasing or other media data will be known about the individuals. It is, however, possible to combine viewing data like this with other forms of data via demographic characteristics using various data marriage systems[10,11].

It is also possible to obtain detailed viewing records for a short time period from respondents for whom purchasing or other information is available. Television diaries for a single week's viewing, for example, are sometimes completed by housewives in ITV homes on the Attwood Consumer Panels. On the TCA Panels a seven-day aided-recall survey is sometimes carried out on panel housewives. These techniques are discussed in the section below dealing with the measurement of audiences for time segments, programs, and advertisements. In both examples the data obtained are used almost exclusively to classify housewives into the three viewing categories; heavy, medium and light ITV viewers. This kind of intermittent collection of viewing records precludes the use of meters and generally less is known about their validity. It is arguable that if only broad classifications are used these may be accurate enough even though the precise details of viewing might be a fault. Some findings reported by Buck and Taylor[12] suggest that seven-day aided-recall as used by the TCA gives classifications as consistent as JICTAR data whilst producing overall higher levels of viewing.

The use of questioning techniques for collection of exposure probabilities

This approach involves asking about usual viewing to time periods in the form of frequency claims. The precision with which the time periods are defined can vary from bookable segments through to very broad general claims. Generally, 'frequency of usual exposure' measurements in media research involve overclaiming for the more memorable and habit-based media. Respondents omit the exceptions to what they regard as their usual pattern and claim the intended, idealized or perhaps just simplified pattern of behaviour. This means that, to convert a frequency claim to a probability, some calibration of the scales against actual viewing habits will be necessary. Typical findings would be that a frequency of claim of 'three times out of every five' did not represent a probability of 0.6 but perhaps more like 0.45.

A set of questions which has been used and calibrated by CESP in France (and which can easily be adapted or extended) is of the following form, with the scale presented on a card for each relevant time segment.

'Normally do you personally view even if not at home between mid-day and one-thirty' . . .

Every day
Nearly every day
Once or twice a week
Once or twice a month
Hardly ever
Never

This question can be asked for television as a whole and/or for each station segment by segment. With a calibration study, probabilities can then be attached for each respondent to each segment and station asked about.

The use of questioning techniques for general classification by weight of viewing

Media research often employs classification of viewers into broad categories such as 'heavy', 'medium' and 'light' viewers. These are basically simplified probabilities of exposure. Such categories can be based on taking more detailed actual viewing records or exposure probabilities and analysing them into broader groups. A typical approach would be to take the sample of individuals under study, arrange them in rank order of amount of viewing or exposure probabilities, and then divide the ranked list into equal thirds, quarters or fifths, etc., according to the number of categories involved.

A widely used approach is to ask a series of three questions which can be multiplied together to give an index of viewing.

Question one: How often do you watch television these days?

The respondent indicates whether it is nearer to seven days, six, five, three or four, one or two, or less often per week.

Question two: On a day when you watch, for about how many hours on average do you watch television?

The respondent selects an answer from scale running from 'none', 'over one and up to two', 'over two up to three', etc., to 'over nine'.

Question three: About how many hours out of every ten that you watch television would you say that you watched ITV?

The respondent replies on a similar scale to question two with a zero and ten positions.

There are two ways of analysing the answers. One involves a response guide from which looking up the combination of answers given will lead to a viewer classification; this method enables instant classification. It is the approach used on the National Readership Survey which classifies viewers into five categories, plus non-viewers. JICTAR multiplies out answers to the questions, thereby creating an indicator of ITV viewing hours followed by a rank ordering of respondents and a division defining heavy, medium and light ITV viewers. The values of the indicator figures occurring at the boundaries between categories can be used in subsequent surveys (subject to rechecking or adjustment for seasonality) to provide instant categorizations of individual respondents if the interviewer multiplies out the answers.

These two approaches can be calibrated to give similar classifications.

A general problem is the validity and durability of viewers' assessments of their own broad viewing habits. Classifications as above can fall short of absolute validity because:

respondents cannot adequately summarize their current behaviour in these, or perhaps any, terms;

viewing habits are unstable and change with time.

This is one aspect of the important issue of the capacity of respondents to summarize normal media behaviour. JICTAR investigated this by comparing the answers to broad habit questions given by viewing panel members with their actual viewing recorded in the panel[13].

One JICTAR investigation compared answers at a sign-up in January 1973 with subsequent average actual viewing levels from four weeks distributed through 1974. This ensured that a single unusual week would not dominate the results and also gave opportunity for the passage of time to have affected usual habits. To check whether changes with time were responsible for any difference or whether 'usual' habits cannot be reported accurately anyway, the questions were also asked again in mid-1974. A further line of investigation was based on the idea that the answers, being in this instance given by the housewife about her own viewing, might inevitably be inaccurate because her viewing was affected by the viewing habits of other members of the household. This led to the consideration that the procedure might be improved by using questions about total household viewing (i.e. set usage). The results are summarized in the table of correlations in Table 25.1.

The conclusions were:

(a) Housewife ITV viewing is very closely related to household ITV viewing; there were no very light housewife ITV viewers in very heavy ITV viewing homes.
(b) Answers at mid-year were better predictors of viewing in that year than answers from early in the previous year. This showed that viewing habits change and people are to some degree aware of the changed levels.
(c) None of the approaches to questioning gave a correlation with actual viewing better than 0.6. This shows that there are limitations to peoples'

Table 25.1 *Correlations between ITV weight of viewing estimates asked of the housewife and actual levels of ITV viewing*

	Household actual viewing 1974	Housewife actual viewing 1974	Household questions new 1974	Housewife questions new 1974	Housewife questions est. survey Jan. 1973
Household actual viewing 1974	1.00				
Housewife actual viewing 1974	0.88	1.00			
Household questions new 1974	0.51	0.47	1.00		
Housewife questions new 1974	0.46	0.58	0.74	1.00	
Housewife questions est. survey Jan. 1973	0.42	0.43	0.42	0.44	1.00

capacity to report their *usual* viewing levels and proportion of channel choice. There was some suggestion that housewives had a tendency relatively to underestimate their own viewing and overestimate their household's viewing.

(d) A major feature of the findings, not shown by the correlations however, was that radical reversals between usual claims and actual viewing were very rare. Virtually no very light ITV viewers claimed to be heavy or vice versa, although there is no reason why this could not have occurred validly, given the passage of time.

It is known from other work that individuals are stable in their tendencies to be heavy or light ITV viewers. It appears that this is also accurately reported. What is less stable and must also be open to more distorted reporting is the finer detail of viewing habits. Even when questioned concurrently people do not accurately identify their exact viewing levels even in rank order terms.

The conclusions are that it may not be possible to measure usual viewing habits any more precisely than through something which correlates across respondents at about 0.6–0.7 with actual viewing, although it is worth experimenting with new forms of questioning in a national context. Later JICTAR experiments have found similar correlations with actual viewing from questions based on regularity of viewing particular time segments or programs.

Terms like heavy, medium or light viewers are widely used in media

617

surveys. There are a variety of definitions, and when trying to understand results or compare between surveys it is worth checking the basis of the classification system:

(a) whether it relates to viewing for a single station or total television viewing;
(b) whether it is based on actual viewing records or usual-habits questions;
(c) for which period the classification data were obtained and to which period the classifications are being applied;
(d) whether they are individual or household classifications;
(e) the exact method by which the classification is derived from the original consumer data.

The Measurement of Audiences for Time Segments, Programs and Advertisements

Regular data on the size of actual audiences are widely collected for both advertising and programming purposes. The emphasis here is for advertising purposes but the total range of methodology common to both is considered and the two sets of needs do not usually dictate different research approaches.

Although the concept of audience size sounds unambiguous there is a problem in deciding how to define an individual as part of the audience for a transmission. Does the individual simply have to be in the room with the set on, or should some attempt be made to include *attention* in the definition? How much of the piece of transmission does the individual have to have 'viewed' (however defined) in order to count as being in the audience? Techniques for defining an audience vary, leading to problems of non-comparability of data.

It is generally felt that standard audience measurement techniques such as the meter-diary system are measuring something close to 'presence in the room with the set on'. To probe further into behavioural attention requires special questioning. This has generated a class of 'attention studies' which have been experimental rather than regular sources of data collection[14, 15].

Units of measurement can be *time-based*, expressed in minutes, quarter hours, or averages of separate minute readings, or *content-based*, covering commercials, breaks, programs, or parts of programs. Sometimes, the technique determines this basis, as with meters which must measure by time, but some techniques can be adapted to cover any unit. Within a single unit of measurement the quantity criterion may vary both intentionally and in the way a viewer interprets instructions. The most commonly used approach is to ask viewers to count themselves as viewing if they cover more than half a quarter-hour program. On this basis, measured audience levels disregard brief absences from the room.

Such absences could, however, cover some commercials under a quarter-hour or broader-based measurement system. This has led to a sub-class of audience measurement work concerned with establishing presence levels

618

during commercial breaks and seeking to relate these to conventionally measured quarter-hour data[15].

The requirement for program data can be met by any of the methods mentioned. A minute-by-minute record shows both the detailed pattern of response to the program and can provide a meaningful average. Similarly, quarter-hour data can show some changes during the program. Direct measurements in program units lead to various definitions however, such as 'seeing any at all' (a cumulative audience), 'seeing more than half' of either the whole program or of each of various discriminable parts. Again when comparisons are made between surveys exact definitions should be checked.

Techniques of measuring audiences for time segments, programs and advertisments

Interviewing: Coincidental

This technique is generally regarded as the most artefact-free and is therefore used as an expensive yardstick in validation studies.

It can be based either upon personal or telephone interviewing; the approach will depend on national audience characteristics. The use of telephone interviewing depends on the extent of telephone coverage, and personal interviewing upon ease of access to households during evening viewing. Where both techniques are viable the choice will probably be made on economic criteria unless any special interviewing requirement can affect the decision.

The coincidental technique makes a measurement of viewing at a given time by calling at a home and asking whether the individual (and perhaps other household members) had the set on and were viewing at that exact time. It is clearly an expensive technique; one interview yielding a measurement for just an instant of television transmission time. There is also a major problem for the technique in that it is not considered reasonable to knock on doors after about 9.30 p.m. This again makes for use of the technique for methodological purposes rather than routine data collection.

It is obviously efficient to keep evening interviews short and to maximize the number of effective calls an interviewer can make. This inevitably means clustering, which should be done as carefully as possible.

It may be worthwhile to split the survey into two stages. At the first enumeration stage, by day, a sample of households is interviewed to establish those which can receive the appropriate television stations, and the household demographic details. The second call can be confined to the true universe for the study and questioning limited to 'who was viewing what'. It is possible to conduct about eight of these interviews per hour. Clearly, the home should not be forewarned at the first interview that a later check will be made.

There is a problem about the exact time period an interview covers. Unless all interviewers are issued with special watches it is difficult to keep to precise timing. This makes it a difficult technique to use in relation to commercials if time alone is to be relied upon with no reference made to what is on the screen. Time control is more precise in telephone calling.

There is a choice as to whether actual viewing is questioned, or just presence in a TV room. If respondents are asked about other activities, such as reading or ironing, as in attention studies, they may give answers which cover, say, five minutes, since these activities may be discontinuous.

A decision has to be made on how to treat refusals and non-contacts. Refusals at a second stage are rare if previously contacted respondents are interviewed. Ignoring refusals equates their behaviour with co-operators. An ARF study in the USA[16] found that refusals on a one-stage survey had different (lower) viewing levels than co-operators but this may not be a general rule.

Non-contacts, or a sample of them, can be called back on the following day to check whether they were out, or viewing and not answering the door, which often happens. In a recent study it appeared that around one-third of households not answering the door were actually viewing. This can be measured on a sub-sample and total figures adjusted accordingly, but the greater the incidence, the less the value of the coincidental data.

The problems of coincidental interviewing and practical solutions are well displayed in industry studies by TAM[17] the IPA[18] and JICTAR[19]. Coincidental interviewing by telephone is the norm in the USA and hitherto little used in the UK, where the level of telephone ownership has been relatively low enough to be thought to bias samples in relation to television viewing. This position is likely to change.

The absolute accuracy of normal telephone coincidental interviewing in the USA was challenged in CONTAM Study No. 4[20] where it was found to underestimate ratings slightly. This study showed that results could vary with training and supervision of interviewers, procedural rules for dealing with contact difficulties, and rules for interpreting non-contacts. Telephone interviewing is increasing in the UK and other countries as the proportion of telephone ownership increases. The basic question is whether, in general, telephone owners differ in viewing behaviour from demographically similar non-owners. If they do not, then telephone interviewing would be possible if some means could be found for obtaining, economically, samples balanced to match the television universe.

Interviewing: Near Coincidental

This approach consists of making what is almost a normal coincidental interview and questioning back over the recent viewing periods. Interviews covering the last hour of viewing conducted during evening viewing time have been used by LPE[21] and TAM[22]. A version of this technique was developed in an industry study by BMRB for the IPA and ISBA[23, 18] and JICTAR[19] where the objective was to measure presence in commercial breaks. The difficulty of

Thursday 13th June 1968

Fig. 25.1 The interview obtaining near-coincidental data.

precise timing was overcome by scheduling calls just after a commercial break, checking at the interview that the break had just occurred, and then effectively carrying out aided recall over the previous three commercial breaks and intervening programming. This procedure is best illustrated diagrammatically as in Fig. 25.1.

The validity of this approach depends upon the care with which the interview is conducted and the form of questioning. In a 1968 study there were no significant differences between results for the same break or program and the viewing levels reported checked with the current meter diary panel data. A similar study in 1974 with slightly less uniformity in fieldwork, however, showed small differences occurring with time[19]. These differences were not great enough to invalidate all uses of the data, and the technique remains viable for some purposes. A small survey using a version of this technique, without the program prompts, found big differences in quality of data back over an hour[24].

The approach seems to depend very much on the interviewer creating a re-construction of a programming sequence in the respondent's mind and thereby making a behavioural rather than an attitudinal measurement.

The telephone approach is still relatively costly and, as with personal interviewing, cannot be used late in the evening.

Interviewing: Recall: Aided and Unaided, Next Day and Seven Day

A variety of media research problems are approached through various kinds of recall techniques.

(1) *Day-after recall* (DAR) of specific commercials is used as a kind of on-air advertising testing procedure and, according to circumstances, may be used

621

to measure attention and communication aspects of the advertisement. This is really concerned with a dimension of advertising effectiveness.

(2) *Next-day aided recall* has been used in some experimental studies to measure the behaviour of audiences to television advertisements. A London Press Exchange[21] next-morning-recall technique showed a program sheet with competing ITV and BBC programs laid out side-by-side on a time scale, the ITV list showing where the commercial breaks came. Respondents indicated which programs they had viewed and were then taken through the list with careful probing as to when they started and stopped and whether they saw the commercial breaks. After rating their liking for the programs, they were then asked what their behaviour had been at the time of each commercial break, classified into a number of possible activities. The LPE study compared results from the next-day recall technique with those from similar questions asked of a different sample on the actual evening most recent hour of viewing. Housewives in the morning recalled consistently less activity during breaks than those asked in the evening. The various kinds of activities were reported in similar proportions from evening or morning. Men, however, reported slightly more activity during commercials in the morning and there were some noticeable but non-significant differences in the kinds of activity reported. Despite the optimism of the LPE reports these and other differences between next morning recall and same evening recall suggests that more methodological work would be needed before findings from 'next morning data' could be interpreted with confidence.

(3) Another technique used in the LPE studies was based on the ability of program viewers to identify commercials that had appeared from a list containing three commercials shown and three not shown in a particular break. This yields measures of correct responses for true and for false commercials and a 'no decision' score.

Results from the technique were also compared from evening and morning interviews. There were more 'no decision' responses from next-morning data but, of the decisions made, the proportions correct were mostly similarly related to factors like time, reported viewing behaviour and interest in programme, whether from evening or morning interviews. The use of these recognition procedures in relation to commercials seem promising but has not had the necessary methodological development since the LPE studies.

(4) *'Next-day aided recall'* designed to cover all transmission times in a comprehensive service measuring audience size is used by the BBC[25]. Interviewers ask first about yesterday's radio listening and then about television viewing. Television viewing is probed from a list of programs and starting times for available services shown side by side. A program is counted as viewed if the viewer claims to have seen more than half of it. A quota sample is interviewed in public places or at home.

A version of 'next-day aided recall' tested in the TAM Comparison Survey[17] used simplified displays of programs taken from the program magazines printed out side by side in the questionnaire. The respondent was taken through the program and viewing recorded on the questionnaire by quarter hours. This technique, using a random sample, was close to the coincidental results in the TAM Comparison Survey in peak time but significantly under-reported in early time (5.30 p.m. to 7 p.m.). This result has been interpreted as suggesting that a technique relying on memory may be less accurate when covering periods of low attention or less distinctive programs.

Little has been published comparing BBC aided-recall data with JICTAR meter-diary data. Comparisons between overall station share of audience have shown the two systems moving in parallel on a trend basis but with a gap between the absolute figures generating public controversy, partly attributable to definitional differences. Larger discrepancies between the two systems have appeared for public events shown on both channels, or where programming was similar on both channels. This may be a particularly difficult situation for program-prompted recall techniques to handle, since here program titles can be a source of confusion rather than an aid.

(5) '*Seven-day aided recall*' is one of the most economical techniques in that a whole week's viewing is collected at a single interview. Each informant is taken back over program aids such as the program magazines or some derivation from them and questioned more closely about exact timing. The viewing record can be completed by the interviewer in terms of quarter hours or half hours viewed. This technique was used by Granada Television in 1959–60, studied in the TAM Comparison Survey 1961, and used by Marplan for JICTAR 1962–4 to produce data on more demographic groups than the meter-diary service. The technique has been used intermittently with TCA panels to establish housewife weight of viewing classifications. The technique has been surrounded by controversy, heated because seven-day aided recall appeared to offer a cheaper alternative to more expensive industry services and arising from the possibility of interpreting limited validation evidence in alternative ways.

Extensive, if somewhat perplexing, discussion of seven-day recall is given by Ehrenberg[3, 26]. Evidence and interpretation from various sources is conflicting. It is reasonable to conclude that the data need not weaken over the seven days as the recall period gets longer, but that the technique does report relatively low-levels of viewing in early time and off-peak time generally. The suggestion of over-reporting in peak time depends on whether one expects exact correspondence with coincidental interviewing. The technique has produced slightly different deviations from the JICTAR meter-diary data on different groups of surveys, suggesting sensitivity to small variations in procedure.

A recall aid, discussed by Simmons[27], with considerable potential for methodological work is a series of story-boards which can show the progress of transmissions through programs and breaks.

Meter Recording of Set Switching

The most comprehensive form of meter is a device which, fitted to a television set, records with precise timing the channel to which the set is tuned when switched on.

Such a meter needs to be capable of recording an increasing number of channels, to be adaptable to changing structure of television sets (particularly in relation to switching and tuning), and to be robust and attractive. The meter used in the JICTAR systems is AGB's SETMETER (Fig. 25.2) which records on a tape each switching occasion and its time. Other meters are used internationally, for instance the INTOMETER in use in Holland where a signal within the station's transmission signal is recorded by the meter if received.

Designing, developing and mass producing trouble-free meters is a costly capital investment with design the least of the problems. No doubt meters will

Fig. 25.2   (Reproduced with the permission of AGB Ltd.)

become smaller but they are unlikely to become cheaper. Other areas of development include methods for collecting and processing recorded data. Earlier meters produced spools of track-marked tapes which had to be collected weekly by interviewers. More recent versions have tapes or tape cassettes which can be removed by the housewife, posted by her, and read automatically.

The most recent development is the meter which transmits records via some on-line facility. The on-line meter panel with ratings accumulating instantaneously at some central point was piloted in various countries in the late fifties. TAM and Nielsen both developed such systems, but the high cost appeared not to be commercially worthwhile to potential subscribers. More recent developments include meters from which accumulated data can be collected by line on a daily basis. A line collection system is operational in Germany after many initial problems and this is used by Nielsen in the USA[28].

A recurring problem with all new meter developments is that a system has to be bought initially on the basis of a small proportion of operational equipment. It is unlikely that a research company can speculatively incur full capital costs for an unsponsored research system. However, moving from working prototypes to a full operational system involving some degree of mass production seems invariably to lead to mechanical problems for which it is difficult to allow. New meters therefore tend to have considerable initial operational 'teething' troubles.

Meters have had a double role in audience research methodology:

(a) to produce a precise time record of the channels to which the set is tuned. There are two components—the timing of switching and the identification of the channel;

(b) as a monitoring device used in conjunction with diaries. This also works in two ways—the 'on' and 'off' records serve as a check against diary keeping and the presence of the meter has a psychological incentive value in that the household knows that some check is being made. The set switching record, by relieving diary keepers of the need to identify the channel viewed, thereby lightens the respondent load.

A recent development, operational in Germany and shortly to operate in the Irish Republic (developed by Attwoods), is the meter which incorporates the diary function by means of a push button for each household member. Viewing presence by an individual is registered by pressing the individual's button and passes directly onto the meter record.

The records of set switching which meters produce can make them usable on their own, providing 'audiences' expressed only in terms of sets tuned. The graphs currently produced under the JICTAR system are in this form. Set switching data are, in fact, one useful way of looking at audiences because that is where the main variation arises.

Meters eliminate virtually all possible sources of error in recording set switching. The only possible bias that might be created is that panel members know the correct time, but the clock faces could be eliminated if this seemed important. Meters discussed in this section so far do not include devices which merely record total set usage which is only of use as a partial monitoring device for diaries. These include the Nielsen/TAM Recordimeter and AGB's Metrilog used in the Channel Islands.

TV Diaries: Fully Monitored

These are diaries used with meters where the meter records set-switching and channel. The individual records only viewing and has no need to identify the channel. If the individual completes the records totally from imagination or fading memory the disparity with the meter record is immediately noticed and an interviewer can call. In the JICTAR system the diaries are read by machine and their data checked against and incorporated with meter records within the computer. This kind of system checked well against coincidental interviewing in the TAM Comparison Survey[17]. It is the only validated technique which must be immune to problems from the increasing complexity of services available since the respondent does not record *what* he is viewing, only *when* he is viewing.

JICTAR diaries have separate pages for each individual in the household and for guests and cover each quarter hour of transmission. The diaries for the household are posted weekly with the meter tape.

Individuals ideally mark their diaries when they start and finish viewing sessions filling in the quarter hours in between. In practice, they may well fill in their diaries more in arrears than that, although grosser malpractices should be minimized by being part of a monitored supervised panel.

An advanced form of metered diary is where individuals indicate their presence by pressing a button which records directly onto a meter tape. A difficulty is that if the respondent realizes that he has been viewing for half an hour without pressing the button, he cannot correct the error. A system has been piloted in the UK, and another is operational in Germany as part of the line-based data collection system. Any memory lapses can be taken care of by use of a supplementary diary where 'missed' viewing can be recorded. This record has the disadvantage of not being available 'on-line' and thereby seems to diminish the advantage of daily available data. However, it is claimed that coincidental validation checks have indicated that the percentage of buttons correctly pressed is very high and that the supplementary diaries may be unnecessary.

An issue with diary panels is whether the diaries are kept by all individual panel members or on a one-person-per-household basis. A cost accuracy trade-off is involved. It is undoubtedly cheaper (and vastly so if meters are used) to collect data on an 'all persons' basis. However, the TAM Comparison Survey 1961 showed that because of the high correlations between the viewing of household members, the accuracy of the data from, say, 500 adults in 250 households is hardly greater than that from 250 adults in 250 households. The number of household units really represents the effective sample size for groups represented more than once per household. For other audience composition breakdowns, where there is rarely more than one per household, there is not likely to be any loss of sampling efficiency through collecting data from all persons in a household. The loss of efficiency applies to groups like adults, individuals or children.

TV Diaries: Partially Monitored

Diaries can be used in conjunction with devices like the Recordimeter or Metrilog which record total set usage in coded form which the respondent notes down. This provides a check on his other recording good enough to indicate serious malpractice in diary-keeping, and the incentive value probably improves upon this. This kind of technique was closest to coincidental interviewing in the simple two-channel situation in the TAM Comparison Survey. It requires that individuals record which channel the set is tuned to as well as when they are viewing, usually by quarter hours. New problems may arise as reception possibilities become more numerous and difficult to distinguish. Whilst it seems likely that panel members could be trained to record channel accurately, further validation would be advisable before using the technique more widely in a multi-channel situation. One set of diaries will be required for each television set in the home.

TV Diaries: Unmonitored

Unmonitored diaries are potentially the cheapest form of audience research, particularly if they can be used by mail. Diaries can take a variety of forms. Somehow, the respondent must indicate the channel viewed and minimally the start and finish times of viewing sessions. Some possible formats include:

(a) *Time-Scale Diaries.* The channel to which the set is tuned can be recorded on one scale with further columns to be marked by individuals present; or individuals may indicate channel by the column used. Basically these diaries would be like the successful Recordimeter diaries without the Recordimeter. All entries are recorded on grids representing time units, usually quarter hours.

Time-based diaries were used on the AMP's survey[29] and the results correlated reasonably closely to those from metered diaries. A more recent unpublished study has also shown unmonitored time-based diaries corresponding reasonably closely with meter diary results[30].

A risk associated with unmonitored diaries is potential confusion of the channel viewed, and can be a problem if diaries are filled in retrospectively. The error patterns, if this occurred, are likely to be something like those for aided recall, possibly slight overclaiming on well known and established programs or viewing times, and confusion at times where program titles are not unambiguously discriminable between channels.

(b) *Start and Finish Time Diaries.* This form of diary has been used in the USA by ARB[31] and experimentally in the UK by AGB. The respondent records the start and finish times of viewing sessions, i.e. when the set is turned *to* and *from* a channel, the name of which is entered in another column. Individuals present are recorded in separate columns. Data from the ARB system in the USA has in the past correlated well with the Nielsen meter/diary data[32,33]. In the UK, a sample of 100 homes who had this form of diary, and a meter which they believed to be faulty, showed that they could keep accurate set switching records. It is possible, though, that the meter was still acting as a motivator.

This form of diary apparently gives minute-by-minute data although probably misses brief absences, and it has succeeded in US multi-channel conditions. Further validation may be necessary in other national conditions.

(c) *Program Diaries.*   Diaries can be used which show the timing and titles of programs for alternative services and require respondents to mark those which they view. The programs can be split up into several parts. This form of diary is undoubtedly attractive to the respondent providing as it does a miniature viewing guide. There are likely to be some considerable administrative problems, however, in producing such diaries with accurate programming information. However efficiently this is managed, there will inevitably be some last-minute changes and these create considerable confusion about the meaning of the data at times when they occur, because not all respondents will manage to obey instructions to enter program changes.

A variant on the purely program diary is the program break diary where validity has been substantially investigated in the UK[18,4]. At one time, this seemed the most economical and promising technique for establishing *presence* in commercial breaks with possible extensions to cover *attention*.

Program and break diaries had been used at TAM[22] and BMRB[34] and produced very meaningful-looking results showing how the pattern of viewing varied between programs and breaks. This technique, using the format shown in Fig. 25.3, was subjected to a rigorous program of validation through an industry group[23,18]. The pilot stages involved the identification of certain 'wrong-looking' completion syndromes, with later evening calls on those homes to see how they were keeping their diaries. This established a number of patterns which had to be rejected, some arising from completion in advance as well as the more conventional completion in arrears.

On the main study the diary results were checked against coincidental data. Surprisingly, in view of the success of other unmonitored diaries, the viewing levels recorded by the diary were much too high compared with coincidental data which were also in line with metered diary results. Furthermore, many of the most interesting findings from this kind of diary appeared to be artifacts. Whether such a diary could succeed if monitored by a meter and with greater training and supervision of respondents is untested.

Errors likely to occur with program diaries therefore include overestimation, particularly of well-known regularly viewed programs. This is similar to overclaiming on most frequency of media exposure claims and suggests some influence of usual or intended behaviour, in turn implying some completion in arrears. The role of the program diary as a program guide should also be considered in relation to possible effects on viewing. Further sources of error are likely to arise at times when program titles can be readily confused between channels and where program titles are obscure.

Observation Techniques

Viewing behaviour can be investigated by the use of observers present in the television room and recording the behaviour of others present. Such techniques are obviously not appropriate for the regular collection of large amounts of data, but suitable for experimental studies investigating patterns of viewing behaviour in greater depth than conventional measurement techniques. The use of observers can vary considerably as to the degree of awareness and obtrusiveness generated. One study by RBL for Lintas[35] placed selected interviewers in the homes of a recruited sample of households for two consecutive evenings. Useful information was obtained about family activities and attitudes to viewing, although clearly there must have been some influence upon the behaviour observed. By contrast a very well conducted American study by Steiner[36] used a wide range of college students to observe their own families and, by careful training, obtained quantifiable data with a negligible level of obtrusiveness. Other studies in the USA have used students in this way[37] and have included the recording of exposure to individual advertisements in press and television as well as the detail of conditions of exposure[38]. In the UK, the TAM experiment with program break diaries[22] required other members of a household to keep a diary about the housewife where this was possible, although otherwise she completed it herself. There is a wide range of approaches to observation studies and the major problem is achieving a representative sample. Their unique advantage is that they can get a closer and more objective record of behaviour in relation to advertising exposure than can be obtained by direct reporting from an individual. The observation approach has considerable potential, therefore, for gaining understanding of the true meaning of more conventionally reported measurement.

Cameras

Cameras can be used with a television set to take pictures of the viewing audience and the screen itself via a mirror. This can be arranged to occur either programmed by a timing device or triggered by some transmitted signal. It could thus cover commercial breaks, or rather fractions of them because a picture covers a very short exposure time compared with most television measurements.

A major problem with the technique is clearly low co-operation rates and the probability that typicality of behaviour is affected even if the camera has a

Office use   16.1 17.4 18.1

1.   Have you viewed any of these television stations during this part of the evening in your own home?

NORTHERN ITV	Yes	✓	BBC 1	Yes	✓
	No			No	
OTHER ITV	Yes		BBC 2	Yes	
	No	✓		No	✓

2.   If you do view any television at home during this part of the evening, please complete the diary below, placing a tick in one of the five columns (A, B, C, D or E) for each program part and commercial break listed.

BBC 1

HAVE YOU VIEWED ON BBC 1:—

		A	B	C	D	E	Office Use
		All	Most	About half	Not much	None	
4.40	Jackanory					✓	20.
4.55	Deputy Dawg					✓	21.
5.15	Tom Tom					✓	22.
5.20	All Change					✓	23.
5.45	The Magic Roundabout					✓	24.
5.50	The News	✓					25.
5.55	Look North	✓					26.
6.15	Whicker's World			✓			27.
7.05	Z Cars					✓	28.

BBC 2

HAVE YOU VIEWED ON BBC 2:—

		A	B	C	D	E	Office Use
		All	Most	About half	Not much	None	
7.05	Bonjour Francoise					✓	33.

privacy switch-off device. A further problem is interpretation of pictures. They relate to a very short period of time and certainly it is almost impossible to assess level of attention from them. People adopt a wide range of postures during attentive behaviour which overlap with the postures of inattentive behaviour. The camera can record unambiguously presence versus absence at an instant, and this may have some methodological value. An account is given of some experimental work in the USA by Allen[39] which records no new findings other than the nature of audience composition compared with set ratings.

Detectors: External.   Detection machinery is capable of registering that the television set is on from outside a house. The technique has been used by the

NORTHERN ITV

HAVE YOU VIEWED ON NORTHERN ITV:—

	A All	B Most	C About half	D Not much	E None	Office Use
4.40 Thunderbirds Part 1					✓	41.
Commercial Break					✓	42.
Thunderbirds Part 2					✓	43.
5.05 Felix The Cat					✓	44.
5.10 World Of Life					✓	45.
Commercial Break					✓	46.
5.20 Come Here Often Part 1					✓	47.
Commercial Break					✓	48.
Come Here Often Part 2					✓	49.
Commercial Break					✓	50.
5.55 News					✓	51.
6.05 Northern News					✓	52.
Commercial Break					✓	53.
6.10 New Faces					✓	54.
Commercial Break					✓	55.
6.30 All Our Yesterdays			✓			56.
Commercial Break		✓				57.
7.00 Turn Of Fate Part 1	✓					58.
Commercial Break				✓		59.
Turn Of Fate Part 2	✓					60.
Commercial Break	✓					61.

Fig. 25.3   A program/break diary.

ARF in the USA as a means of establishing whether refusals and non-contacts in a coincidental survey had their television sets switched on[16]. The machine used had limitations in that it could only be used unambiguously for detached houses. This would seem to be a technique with a clear but limited methodological potentiality. Since detection must take about as long as a personal coincidental interview, it is also not likely to be any cheaper than that technique.

Detectors: Internal.   It is technologically possible to operate some kind of electronic counters in the television room which would either count and record numbers present or even identify individuals if they could be persuaded to carry some electronically identifiable object. This kind of development would obviously require capital investment and there might be problems of respondent co-operation. No experiments of this kind yet appear on record, although various designs exist.

The Validity of Television Audience Research Techniques

It is unfortunate that techniques which have never been subjected to any validation test are used with more confidence than those which have been tested and found to have some minor faults.

Tests which compare results from a technique under test with some specially set up 'objective' measure are somewhat rare, although data are sometimes compared between techniques without a control measure. The conventional yardstick for television viewing is the coincidental interview, personal or telephone, which asks people at an exact moment what they are doing in relation to television viewing. While this seems a very clear-cut yardstick, it presents some problems of interpretation. The following issues need to be taken account of in comparing coincidental results with those from other techniques:

(a) whether the techniques as used are sampling the same populations and, if not, whether that should or should not form an element in the comparative test.

(b) whether at the coincidental interview respondents can correctly report the channel viewed. (In a recent UK study it appeared that about 10% of the sample could give the wrong channel unless prompted with program titles.)

(c) how non-replies should be treated. In a UK winter evening personal coincidental study a substantial proportion of non-replies were found at follow-up to have been in and watching television. If this problem is likely, some kind of call-back on non-replies will be necessary. For telephone coincidental checking the conclusions of the US CONTAM study apply[26].

(d) is the coincidental measure definitionally comparable with the measure to be checked against it?

In the UK, the largest validation study was the TAM Comparison Survey[17] sponsored by an industry committee. This was, in many ways, a model of planning and covered coincidental interviewing, TAM meter monitored diaries, Recordimeter-monitored diaries, 'one-day' and 'seven-day aided recall', all on sample sizes of 500 households for each quarter hour comparison.

The recall methods showed under-reporting in early evening. For peak time, all the techniques deviated in the same direction, i.e. slightly above the coincidental level, but recall slightly more than diary methods. If comparisons are made with the coincidental survey, the recall methods show most significant differences; the interpretation made in the report. If the main techniques are compared among themselves, there are few significant differences between them; the interpretation offered by Ehrenberg[26].

Logically, being averages of instantaneous readings and, therefore, depleted by brief absences, coincidental ratings should be lower than those from other techniques which are based on seeing more than half of the units measured and consequently are not depleted by brief absences. The results of all techniques should have been higher than those for coincidental interviews by an unknown amount and they were indeed higher for peak time. This leaves as the major finding that recall techniques were under-reporting in early evening and had a tendency to report higher for better known programs with clear titles compared with lesser known or ambiguous program titles. Data from meter-monitored and partially unmonitored diaries were subsequently validated by the coincidental survey. There are further adjustments which can be made to the data to cover definition differences[40].

All this illustrates the difficulty of establishing validity even with a large, expensive and well planned study. A further limitation in this study was that, because of the enormous commitment of coincidental interviewing (500 interviews per quarter hour added up to nearly 9000 interviews per evening), only three evenings could be covered between 5.30 p.m. and 9.30 p.m. It so happened that ITV ratings graphs on those evenings were fairly smooth and no exceptional programs were screened. Thus, nothing could be discovered about the techniques in relation to late evening, sharply changing audience levels, or unusual programs. Other gaps included children's viewing, since the TAM Comparison Survey covered only adults. Most techniques are used with children, sometimes with adults reporting for them. The validity of some of these procedures seems unlikely for the youngest age groups and little checking ever seems to be done on media measurements among children.

A further UK validation study was the IPA and ISBA Television Audience Presence Research in 1968 carried out by BMRB[18]. Many of the findings have already been mentioned. This study, concerned with more detailed measurements than normal ratings research, supported near-coincidental interviewing and largely invalidated the program-break diaries. This result is a salutary one for market researchers because the data from the invalidated technique had a lot of 'face validity', i.e. they supported widely held views. The truth, if that is what was established, was much less interesting. For this study, too, there could well be some alternative interpretation of the coincidental findings.

Both this and a further UK study in 1974[19] confirmed that coincidental interview data broadly validated the standard meter/diary measurement. This is essentially a validation not of the technique alone, but the technique as operating within a system of long-term panels.

In the USA, a program of validation was conducted for CONTAM[26,32], an industry group representing broadcasters. There were four studies. The first showed sampling theory applied to audience measurement which, although enjoyable, seemed to be a large hammer to crack an opened nut. The second compared Nielsen meter panel data and ARB diary sample data and found them basically in agreement. This implied that there were no conditioning effects on the Nielsen panel and no other mechanical fieldwork errors unless they cancelled out. The third demonstrated a bias in audience size-estimates because of non-cooperation, discussed below. The fourth examined the telephone coincidental technique and has already been discussed. Some smaller scale validation studies are reported by Simmons[27].

The Bureau of Broadcast Measurement (BBM) in Canada conducted an extensive development and validation program for short-term diaries. For some time they operated a research system using a *postal, one-week, combined radio-and-television* diary. The Quantity Control Test published in 1973[41] compared diary sample results with a telephone coincidental check on another sample who were also sent diaries, enabling a comparison to be made between the coincidental ratings of diary co-operators and non-co-operators. The diary data from the coincidental sample was found to be affected by the telephone call in that it appeared to lower the diary TV ratings while not affecting radio.

The coincidental results showed that, in total, television viewing was correctly diary-reported but that this was because cooperators were very slightly lighter viewers than non-cooperators but overclaimed their viewing by 7%. Paradoxically the diary radio results, also correct overall, seemed to come from underclaiming by heavier listeners. These results must be viewed against national conditions but the most crucial points to note are that the diary followed telephone contact and the percentage of the population keeping diaries was around 30–35%. Since that time the BBM has carried out further development work and validation in relation to both single media and two media diaries. The findings were published in 1975[42]. They included reports on intensive interviews with people to whom diaries had been sent about their reasons for non-response; and on interviews with people about their mode of keeping different forms of diary. The principal errors for television were failure to keep diaries up-to-date, failure to indicate viewing if not interested in a program and incorrect recording of parts of programs. There was also some confusion about the definition of viewing (but not so extensive as confusion about the meaning of radio listening). For the dual-media diary there were more respondent problems overall, but radio appeared to suffer more than television.

In 1975 another comparison study was carried out of single- and dual-media diaries against a benchmark of telephone coincidental interviewing on an independent sample. A further coincidental check was carried out upon people sent diaries some weeks after their diary keeping was over, which again enabled a comparison to be made between responders and non-responders. The single-media diaries achieved a higher return (about 35—40%) than the dual-media diary (about 25—30%).

The coincidental survey measured exposure to television (and radio) at four levels at the moment of call, 'aware of TV set on', 'being in the same room', 'noticing what was on the set' and 'paying attention to what was on'. The 'TV only' diary gave viewing levels corresponding to being in the room while the set was on; 'dual-media' diary was closer to the 'noticing' level, although there was less difference at peak times. Share was distributed similarly across the techniques. There were no significant differences in the subsequent coincidental measure between levels of TV viewing of responders and non-responders. The results were interpreted as 'calibrating' the TV-only diary as corresponding to 'presence in the room', and single media diaries have been adopted. Because two survey results produce the same level for different measurements, it cannot be concluded one measurement means the same as the other, but the findings provide a basis for taking action, and at least set up a hypothesis as to the meaning of different diary measurements. Results of this kind depend very much on the conditions under which they are obtained and while the methodological insights from this program are valuable, the findings cannot be universally generalized. An interesting side observation, however, was that television audience measurement seemed fairly robust, relative to the technique used, and radio audience measurement much more sensitive.

Large scale methodological and validation studies are expensive and are sometimes suspect if they are produced from a single source with a vested interest. For both these reasons they are often co-operative efforts across a variety of advertising and media interests. Even the best studies raise some problems of interpretation and absolute validity is largely a myth. In practice, many techniques are either accepted on 'face validity', which can be dangerous, or because their results compare well with those of other techniques which may have some validation support. Emphasis has been laid here upon limited knowledge of the validity of many of these techniques. Validity, however, is often a relative matter and more is known about techniques in television audience research than in most areas of market research and the methodological problems to be solved are slightly easier.

Panel controls, sample design, and special problems in television audience research

The running of panels and designing of samples are topics dealt with else-where in this book. The present discussion concerns some problems particularly related to television research.

(a) *Short- vs. Long-Term Panels*

The general suitability of TV panels for measuring change is reviewed by Buck, Sherwood and Twyman 1975[13]. Very different practical issues of operation arise, according to the length of panel operated. There are two major differences between any panel and an interviewer-administered questionnaire:

(i)   the load on the respondent is greater, involving some degree of continuing commitment;
(ii) the respondent has to work mostly unsupervised by the interviewer.

There is a wide range of techniques, and major differences can arise from:

(i) length of commitment (ranging from days to years);
(ii) frequency of recording;
(iii) onerousness of the task;
(iv) degree of interviewer instruction and contact;
(v) feedback and supervisory checking.

When panel operations are reported, the results often ignore the need to consider conclusions separately for different kinds of panel. This produces apparently conflicting results which are resolvable if the *kind* of panel under discussion is taken into account. A particular source of differing conclusions is the distinction between short- and long-term panels, which can be radically different research approaches.

For long-term panels:

(i) the respondent can have extensive training over a period of time in carrying out the recording task; but
(ii) the task must not be so onerous that the respondent cannot keep repeating it over a long term; and
(iii) the research must not affect the behaviour under study.

For short-term panels:

(i) normally, by definition, there is little training 'on the job'; training is normally by advance instruction;
(ii) respondents can be motivated to carry out a more extensive task for a brief period of time;
(iii) after the panel task is completed, questions can be asked of the respondent which, while potentially affecting future behaviour, can still usefully relate to an immediately past period of reported behaviour.

Clearly both approaches have their uses in particular situations, but they are approached rather differently. For long-term panels, the aim is initially to check upon and improve quality of reporting and subsequently to maintain this and avoid conditioning. For short-term panels, the aim is to get correct reporting from the beginning and to avoid an initial artificial response while recognizing that it may not be possible to maintain this level of responding. Successful long term panel operations check that training in a running-in period improves quality of reporting; successful short-term panels check that the first week is not atypical. Only by recognizing these essential differences can findings supporting the benefits of a training period for long term panels be reconciled with these showing no difference between the first and subsequent weeks for medium or short-term panels.

(b) *Conditioning and Running-in for Long- to Medium-Term Panels*

What little evidence there is suggests that conditioning is not a problem with meter-diary systems. Newly recruited Recordimeter samples gave similar results to existing TAMmeter panels and both matched the coincidental results[17]. Similarly, long running Nielsen panels gave similar results to fresh ARB samples in CONTAM[32]. A Nielsen study[43] and a number of *ad hoc* survey results which match panel data also confirm these findings.

Some published work by JICTAR in the UK[19] examined the relationship between the viewers-per-set reported by samples of meter-diary members after they had been on a panel one, two and three years, compared with matched samples of newly recruited members. After panel membership of a year viewers-per-set became about 5% higher than for new members. It was not possible to trace the cause of this or to establish which was right, but the result does set a limit to about 5% for any possible conditioning effects on long-term panels under these conditions.

Related to conditioning is the question of running-in periods for diarists. *A priori* it could be rationalized that diaries are kept most conscientiously when people are fresh to the task and they then tire; *or* that people have to learn to fill in diaries and are best after a running-in period; *or* that people behave atypically at first and then settle down. The evidence is scanty and conflicting. Unmonitored diaries run by BMRB[44] and Research Services for AMPS[29] showed consistency over their first 12 and eight weeks respectively. This was taken as evidence against the need for running-in periods. JICTAR experience has been that monitored diary results on long-running panels are sensitive to contact with interviewers and instructions; for example, in relation to the recording of guest viewing. The high levels obtained by IPA/ISBA program/break diaries also support the view that diarists are more sensitive to format and procedures than had been believed. The only deduction one can make from a mixture of evidence is that individual cases need testing.

(c) *Fatigue in Short-Term Panels*

Short-term diaries represent a very different task for the respondent who is asked for a brief, once-and-for-all effort with no training on the job. Everything then depends on the clarity of the original instructions with less of a commitment and no chance for a correct diary-keeping habit to have been created. There is some suggestion from the BBM work[42] that, even with a one-week diary, the accuracy of recording can change; there was relatively higher reporting at the beginning of the week, declining a little at the end.

(d) *Co-operation Biases, Panel Controls and Stratifications*

A number of studies in the USA[32,43,45] have shown that cooperators in samples and panels view television more than non-cooperators; the amount varies with study and cooperation rate. The effect may be partly compensated for by substitution procedures involving stratification controls. The Canadian work reviewed above, at rather lower response rates, did not suggest a significant cooperation bias for television[41] with a dual-media diary. With the TV-only diary, however, and a slightly higher response rate there was a non-significant tendency for the diary cooperators to be heavier viewers[42].

JICTAR has adopted a stratification procedure which applies a control by weight-of-viewing classification. On establishment surveys, respondent housewives are asked the questions discussed on page 615 and divided into equal 'heavy', 'medium' and 'light' ITV viewing thirds. Recruitment to the viewing panels is equally divided between these thirds. At the initial sign-up of the AGB panels it was found that response rate increased with viewing-weight classification. Overall it varied between 65 per cent to 75 per cent of households originally selected for the AGB Home Audit. It was possible to compare viewing level results on the panel, with the viewing control operating, against what would have happened without the viewing control. For one area it seemed that ratings would have been some five per cent higher without the control. Table 25.2 shows how demographically similar groups viewed more in the initial sign-up group without the weight of viewing control than in the final balanced panel with the weight of viewing control. Other ITV areas examined showed less effect but in the same direction.

It was shown earlier, on page 617, that the weight of viewing classifications have only limited correlation with viewing. This section demonstrates how even an imperfect measure can be useful. Even an irrelevant stratification, correctly applied, cannot be harmful[46]. These results of controlling a panel by a direct forecast of what it is supposed to be measuring seem to be a promising approach to panel control where there may be a cooperation bias. In JICTAR panels normal demographic controls are applied (for a full list see JICTAR[17]) marginally and interlaced.

The BBC reported[47] that terminal education age was associated with ITV and BBC preferences, which suggests some measure of education as an appropriate control. Other stratification controls used by JICTAR include reception capabilities and geographical location in relation to ITV areas.

There may be value in some form of multivariate analysis of television viewing which would group people by the similarities in certain aspects of their viewing behaviour and provide other data about the groups. This might

Table 25.2   ITV viewing hours with and without weight of viewing control
(week ending 24 November, 1968: Midlands Area)

	With/without children		Social class		No. in household			Age of housewife		
	with	without	ABC1	C3DE	1–2	3	3	−35	35–64	65+
S/U (without control) Total	19.3	18.5	14.1	20.5	16.8	21.2	19.7	17.9	20.2	17.0
balanced panel	18.9	17.1	13.3	19.6	15.1	20.1	19.4	17.7	18.9	15.9

Source: JICTAR/AGB

establish either groups of people or factors which were as meaningful as the heavy viewing syndrome and which could be used as a basis for stratification controls, perhaps in place of some of the less effective demographic controls.

With panels there is not only the problem of bias in sign-up but bias in drop-out. With the JICTAR panels after some initial drop-out from heavier viewers the regular pattern appears to follow sign-up bias, and lighter viewers drop out more frequently.

(e) *Aspects of Accuracy*

Sample surveys and panels can be used very differently in relation to the accuracy of what is measured. Repeated surveys on independent samples, say for different months, can be added together to provide average data over a period of months. This means that, while monthly trends can be followed on the broad sample categories, with the addition of samples much smaller breakdowns can be analysed on an average basis.

The use of panels very often results in smaller samples on grounds of cost and they are generally used for following trends on broad audience categories. There are a number of ways in which panels can be used which mitigate the *prima facie* limitations of sample size. For the measurement of trends panels give greater statistical efficiency, as discussed in Buck, Sherwood and Twyman[13]. Basically, the sampling error of an observed change between two measurements is a function of the sampling error of each of the measurements reduced by a term which reflects the association between them. The variances of two measurements X_1 and X_2 and the difference between them have the following relationship.

$$\text{Variance } (X_1 - X_2) = \text{Variance } X_1 + \text{Variance } X_2 - 2 \text{ Covariance } (X_1 X_2)$$

Panel data can further be used to examine the sources of change as well as its size.

The association between readings reduces variance when measuring change. When *averaging* data, however, there is less efficiency than when samples are independent. Indeed the general tendency is to treat all data from panels, single readings or averages, as if their variance was simply that implied by the basic panel size. In the case of averages this is not true because different readings from the same sample are not wholly correlated and are to some extent independent readings. Averages over a number of times or days have lower variances than a single reading.

An empirical study of the sampling errors associated with averages from panels was published in 1974 by Arbitron in the USA[48]. A way of expressing their findings is in terms of the total sample size implied by the size of the variance associated with an average. This can be expressed as a multiplying factor termed the Statistical Efficiency Value. A Statistical Efficiency Value of 4.0 for an average would mean that the sampling error or variance for that average was equivalent to that associated with a single reading from a panel size four times as large as the actual panel. For that average, therefore, the panel sample is performing as if it was four times as large as it actually is.

The level of Statistical Efficiency for an average depended on the audience sub-group. The empirical efficiencies quoted by Arbitron ranged up to about 3 for averages based on 30 quarter hours and up to about 18 for averages based on 420 quarter hours. Some Statistical Efficiencies quoted for single reading were well below one. This showed that, for some sub-groups of individuals who may be grouped with more than one per household, in households where there are any, the effective panel size for single readings is much lower than the actual panel size. A similar conclusion was reached in the UK TAM Comparison Survey[17] where adults, of whom there are often two or more per household, had an effective sample size of about the same as the number of households. In other words the variance of data from 200 adults in 100 households would be about the same as that from a random sample of 100 adults in 100 households.

Thus panels and surveys which interview more than one individual per household may lose statistical efficiency if there is a correlation between the individuals behaviour within households—as there is with television viewing. The small sizes of panels can be offset for averages because there is not a complete correlation between viewing at all times and the gains in statistical efficiency from broad averaging can be very large. A cumulative audience is not an average and has the sampling error of a single reading even where it is a cumulative audience over many scattered times and days.

Systems of Research

The demand for media research is often regular, leading to the creation of a total system of research which can comprise any or all of the following elements:

(i) research to define the boundaries of station reception;
(ii) research to measure the size and nature of potential audiences to stations: these are likely to be sample surveys. They can be easily integrated with other research, and they can serve as an address bank for panel recruitment;
(iii) regular measurements of TV audiences: this can be through regular sample surveys, or a continuously or intermittently reporting panel;
(iv) a data bank for special analysis.

In the UK, there have been two such systems. One is a national daily survey by the BBC which interviews a quota sample of 2250 individuals aged five years and over. Interviewing is by aided recall about the previous day's viewing. Daily reports are issued internally but are not generally published; a weekly bulletin summarizes the main trends in viewing and findings of special interest. Results can be cumulative over long periods to give a large sample base for average data. The BBC also measures audience reactions to programs, and commissions *ad hoc* studies on a variety of topics. A description of systems and methods is published by the BBC[25].

The other system is operated by JICTAR, which is a committee representing program companies, advertisers and advertising agencies with various other subscribers. JICTAR puts its research out to tender and awards a contract to a research company for a panel system, currently using meters and diaries. Boundary surveys are conducted when necessary. Establishment surveys with regional samples from 5000 down to 1000 households have been integrated with another large national random probability sample. The panels are recruited from the establishment survey sample and matched to audience characteristics found on those surveys. The area net viewing panels range in size from 350 households, nearly 1000 people, down to 100 households and about 300 people. A surplus of some further 15% is maintained to allow for unavailability of records. Panel households post in a tape from the meter each week together with daily viewing diaries for the week from all household members aged four and over. Interviewers call for diary education if necessary, and at least every six weeks. Weekly reports start appearing within a week following the receipt of records and are published to subscribers. Program and quarter-hour audiences are shown. For commercial breaks, costs per thousand homes, adults, housewives, men, women and children are compared with the previous four week average. All commercials shown are listed chronologically with their audiences, and by brands in product groups. Thrice-yearly reports show quarter-hour data for more detailed audience composition groups. Data are also supplied to users on tapes and special analysis facilities are available to subscribers. The most frequently used special analyses show the coverage and frequency of viewing by a target group for schedules of spot times usually covering several weeks. These are based on the continuous week-to-week records of the individual panel members.

A fuller description of the JICTAR system is available in the JICTAR Reference Manual[7] and has been summarized by Sherwood[49]. JICTAR carries out only audience size measurements and relevant methodological studies. Studies of audience appreciation and reactions to programs are carried out by individual program companies, the Independent Broadcasting Authority and the BBC.

In other countries large scale measurement systems for commercial television services are usually co-operative efforts either syndicated or industry organized. Where non-commercial television systems exist, research is usually commissioned by a single broadcasting authority. There has been a tendency for non-commercial systems to use recall techniques and commercial systems to use diaries—in the latter case probably because of a greater interest in short term trends and the ability to accumulate audiences over schedules.

The Measurement of Responses to Television Viewing

Purpose of the data

An advertiser initiates transmission of advertisements to increase his profits above what they would have been without advertising. He may think that this will be achieved through some intermediate and more readily measurable sub-goals such as attention to his advertisements, the communication and under-standing of his advertising message, retention of certain facts, the change of certain attitudes and the formation of 'intentions to buy' his brand. While it is likely that advertising can *sometimes* work this way it is clear that it does not *always* work this way. Nevertheless, this is the easiest way to study advertising effects and, appropriate or not, advertisers sometimes adopt this approach. Advertisers may also attempt the more difficult task of relating sales to media exposure.

Those making and screening programs have complex aims according to the basis of their legal franchises. In simplified terms these aims amount to satisfying certain audience requirements for entertainment, news, informa-tion, education, and special personal interests.

Defining these requirements in terms of who has them, how important they are and how they might be met for different people, is such an overwhelming task that it has largely discouraged attempts at comprehensive research. If requirements can be deduced from other research, or merely hypothesized, in terms such as entertainment, information, etc., then respondents can be asked to score programs on scales based on these 'requirements'. This gives some impression of the way in which programs are being received. The simplest form of this research is to apply a single scale of liking to all programs. Thereafter one can progress from a few to many scales. It is also possible to simplify the problems by creating a program typology[50] and a viewer typology[51]. The whole area is, of course, an application of the methodology of attitude research fully discussed elsewhere in this book. Only some special points of relevance to television are discussed here.

In addition to checking how far programs meet general requirements, there may be occasions when a study in greater depth is needed on the impact of a specific program or series. This may be to check achievement of the detailed aims of the program-maker, such as the comprehensibility of a documentary and the communication of certain information.

The advertiser, too, may have an interest in program research because he feels it will enable him to predict where the highest target audiences are or because he believes that attitude to programs influences reception of advertising material.

Responses to television are also of interest to those other than originators of programs and advertisements such as sociologists, psychologists, educationalists and politicians. All that has been discussed so far could be of interest to this group. Additionally, they may be concerned with broader problems, such as the effects on beliefs, attitudes and behaviour within the community, which go beyond the programs and products advertised. The influence of the media on violence is a much discussed example. Social scientists are also interested in establishing general principles of communication. While most of this work is outside the scope of this chapter, it is suggested that, viewed selectively, it has considerable heuristic value for the development of media and advertising research. There are, therefore, three reasons why this section deals with a vastly complicated and interesting area only briefly:

(a) this area is really only bordering on that covered by the definition of media research adopted for this book;
(b) the methodology is not peculiar to television and is therefore discussed elsewhere in this book;
(c) much of the research in this area is unpublished and the total volume is smaller than for research into audience size and media exposure.

The response to advertising

Aspects of Advertising to be Studied

There are a number of decisions which an advertiser has to make about using the medium which can be broadly classified under the headings of 'content, volume, and patterning'.

Content is usually studied for individual commercials in the form of some pre- or post-testing of a specific advertisement. Most advertising research in the form of pre-testing examines responses to single advertisements. How much money an advertiser should spend is a question which cannot be answered directly by research. Ideally, a market model should be capable of showing the return in profits for money spent on advertising. In practice, budgets are fixed in a variety of ways as discussed by Broadbent[52].

Return for advertising money could be deduced if the average response of an individual to each possible number of exposures were known, together with the number of individuals likely to see each number of exposures. This amounts to combining an absolute response function and the expected frequency of exposure distribution. Once an advertising budget is fixed, even a relative response function (one that shows the relative value of each number of exposures) would be useful. Unfortunately, it has proved difficult to establish even relative response functions and some assumptions have to be made on limited evidence. This area has been thoroughly reviewed by Broadbent[52,53].

A closely related problem is that of choosing between ways of using the medium in terms of the way spots are patterned in time. Are they more effective close together or spaced, for example? A further aspect of advertising strategy is the length of advertisement to be used. Both choices depend on establishing the factors which change the nature of the response function. They could be solved independently of establishing the response functions if the effects of patterning or spot length are simple and do not interact with repetition.

Studies of all aspects of advertising effectiveness have common problems relating to experimental design. Theoretical designs for evaluating the effects of mass communication have been critically reviewed by Haskins in an Advertising Research Foundation Monograph[54].

Measuring Sales

Evaluation of alternative advertising strategies in terms of sales is, in practice, exceedingly difficult. There are a number of approaches, only some of which will be mentioned briefly here.

(a) *Using Historical Consumer Panel Data.* Consumer panels yield purchasing data all the time. It is, therefore, possible to try to relate sales volumes or brand shares to concurrent or past advertising expenditure by regression analyses. A program of research for the BBTA[55] suggested that different models are necessary for different markets. Even a model with some general applicability across markets would not necessarily sort out the causality in the relationship.

(b) *In-market Experiments.* An advertiser can vary his advertising strategy either between different time periods in the same area or different areas in the same time period. The problems here are lack of controlled identical conditions in the two periods or areas, and uncertainty concerning over what period the effects should be measured. For these reasons, the results of such experiments are often inconclusive and advertisers seldom publish them. Segnit and Broadbent[56] give one case history and show how understanding of this kind of experiment can be improved by using consumer surveys where the respondent's media exposure was estimated as well as purchasing behaviour and awareness. An example of a model being used to assess in-market the difference in sales between two alternative TV commercials is given by Bloom, Jay and Twyman[57].

(c) *Advertising Laboratory Experiments.* The best controlled design reviewed by Haskins[54] is what he called the 'controlled field experiment'. This is the situation where purchasing is measurable in as near to real-life conditions as possible for two matched populations identical in every way except in the advertising input they receive. In the USA this has been achieved for television, by having alternative cables serving two panels in the same district their input differing only in respect to the advertising experiments, or by use of muting devices which block out some part of the advertising transmissions on either panel, leaving a blank screen. Experience with the surviving system in the USA was reviewed by Adler and Kuehn[58].

This approach can be used theoretically to study alternative contents, volumes of advertising, and length or patterning strategies. A major limitation on the approach is that it can be used only for effects big enough to show above the noise level of the sampling error of economically viable panels. Another problem is in deciding over what period to study the advertising effects. It appears, from what little has been published so far, that findings are likely to be specific to marketing situations and therefore cannot be immediately reduced into the simplest rules like 'always cluster spots'. No form of this kind of experimental system has yet started in the UK. Despite the difficulties mentioned, it does appear to be potentially the most powerful design for studying response to advertising.

Measuring Intermediate Advertising Effects

(a) *In-home, On-air.* Measurements of attention triggered by individual advertisements in-home are not really attempted. Recall, measuring the combined result of attention, understanding and retention, is used following on-air transmissions. Similarly, the progressive effectiveness of campaigns is often judged by a sequence of measures of awareness, attitudes or 'intentions to buy'. If these measures are acceptable they can be used in any time-period or area experiment with advertising strategies, and in an advertising laboratory situation.

(b) *Out-of-home Testing.* The majority of pre-testing is conducted in theatres, coaches and testing centres. This provides control over exposure conditions at the expense of realism. The passive privacy of the normal home viewing is exchanged for an involved, forced-attention, observed situation. In these conditions only intermediate measures can be used unless respondents are drawn from a panel or followed-up afterwards. These forms of advertising research are discussed in chapter 8.

Measuring General Responses to Advertising

Advertisers have concentrated on studying the effects of individual commercials and have seldom looked at overall attitudes to advertising. An exception is a group of studies published by the IPA[59] which included a comparison of attitudes to press and television advertising, reactions of audiences under different survey conditions, and data from a variety of analyses derived from theatre testing a large number of commercials.

The response to programs

Deducing Reactions from Audience Size

It is easy to assume that, because many people watch a program, it must be enjoyed more than a program seen by fewer people. A similar deduction may be made that people watch the kind of programs they like. These hypotheses are weak. The mismatch between what people like and what they view arises from the following reasons:

(a) people cannot watch all the programs they would like to very much because:

    (i)   other people determine what is viewed;

    (ii) the programs may not be on at convenient times;

    (iii) the programs may clash with something equally liked on another channel:

(b) people sometimes watch programs they like less because:

    (i)   other people determine what is viewed:

    (ii) they may just want to watch television and there is nothing on any channel which particularly appeals to them;

    (iii) they follow or precede ones they like.

Deductions can be made from ratings research about the popularity of programs, but they are likely to be in very general terms. These factors have also generated the lack of patterning found in the actual viewing of individuals investigated extensively by Ehrenberg and his collaborators[60].

Measuring Reactions to Programs

(a) *TVQ.* During 1964, TAM introduced an approach to measuring simple audience reaction, based on a service operating in the USA, TVQ. The TVQ system used postal questionnaires with lists of programs against which people indicated whether they were familiar with the program and how they rated it on a five-point verbal scale—'one of my favourites', 'very good', 'good', 'fair', 'poor'. Such data helped to explain ratings but were not such a strong predictor as had been hoped, probably due to the reasons for the liking and viewing mismatch suggested above. The data nevertheless represented a measure of enjoyment independent of ratings which could be of use to the programmer. It was suggested that one universal liking scale was not appropriate to the different kinds of programs screened. In practice people do see programs, apart from news broadcasts, as part of a continuous stream of material rather than separate categories. The TVQ service ran for several years and was bought by the ITA and by several program companies and for an experimental period by some advertising agencies.

(b) *The IBA Research Program.* The IBA (then the ITA) commissioned a program of exploratory research in 1967–8 ending in a pilot panel operation in London for a limited period. This was fully described by Frost[61]. The research program started by seeking the terms in which viewers described programs using the Repertory Grid technique (Kelly triads). The constructs obtained were converted into seven-point semantic differential scales. These were then applied to programs by another sample and the results factor-analysed. This yielded nine factors upon which any program could be rated. A program typology was then built up by cluster analysis. Following this pilot work a further large-scale pilot study, covering three areas over six months, was commissioned by the ITA and ITV program companies from a consortium, Television Opinion Panel Ltd. (TOP). A variation on the earlier procedure was used to establish eleven factors and a general evaluation factor. Programs were again clustered and the importance of factors within cluster determined in some cases. Panels of 300 in each of the three areas then reported fortnightly by mail on the programs they chose to view. The data covered an appreciation index for all programs, detailed factor scales for a limited list, spontaneous comments and, occasionally, special questions.

More recently the IBA has operated a less complex audience appreciation service for ITV, measuring programs on all stations by rotation using intermittently reporting panels of adults keeping self-completion diaries.

A full discussion of TOP and some examples of its applications to program scheduling was published by Haldane[62]. Another approach to forming a program typology is given by Kirsch and Banks[63] and a viewer typology, in terms of programs liked, by Rothman and Rauta[51].

(c) *BBC Research.* The BBC has collected audience reaction data from a 'viewing panel'. This comprises some 2000 people recruited from those interviewed on the daily listening and viewing survey who report weekly by postal questionnaire. Respondents are asked to comment only on programmes seen in the normal course of viewing. The questionnaire covers both detailed aspects of the program's content and evaluations on a number of dimensions such as 'funny-unfunny', 'entertaining-boring'. This service is described by the BBC in a booklet[25].

(d) *Other Research.* The BBC, ITV program companies, and the ITA all carry out surveys concerned with aspects of individual programs or classes of program. These are seldom published but do not represent any unique methodological problems. Similar data are obtained in most countries.

One point which should be emphasised is the need to talk about programs in the viewers' terms. Viewers cannot be relied upon to understand classifications such as 'ITV play' which are obvious to program planners and market researchers.

Measuring the Understanding of Television Programs and their Immediate Effects

A program originator may wish to establish how far his program has been understood and whether it achieves some particular aim. A range of techniques is open to him including group discussion and survey interviews. This was thoroughly discussed with case histories by Belson[64].

Measuring what people require from television

This question can be approached on a number of levels. At the general level, establishing the interests and habits and knowledge of the population provides background material for program planning. Studies of this kind are again reviewed by Belson[64], and a large-scale study was published by the BBC[65].

Reaction to existing programs can also provide some guidance as to needs but it may be difficult to generate new ideas this way. Emmett[66] discussing this problem quotes Galbraith on a related area: '. . . only a few goods serve needs that are made known to the individual by the palpable discomfort that is felt in their absence'. This is true of television programs and means that it is very difficult to get people to report directly what they want in terms other than existing programs. In an approach used by the IBA (described on p. 608) viewers' own constructs for programs were elicited by triadic interviews. It must then be assumed that a person's constructs reflect his requirements and the scales then developed are at least related to requirements. The concept of the ideal program in various categories can be used[62]. If viewer typologies are formed then requirement groups can be identified[51]. The problem of translating these data into policy decisions is a formidable one and some very exploratory suggestions are made by Emmett[66]. A related series of studies in the USA was reported by Steiner[36].

At the most detailed level, research may be needed for planning a particular program or series which is intended to communicate certain facts or attitudes. Belson[64] reviews techniques and case histories.

In the USA a modification of TVQ technique has been used on new program ideas by the Home Testing Institute[67]. One might expect this to be the more meaningful the more the programs tested resembled existing programs.

Response to programs in relation to advertising

An advertiser would be interested in any program reaction data which could be used as a basis for predicting ratings. It is probable that no reaction data would do this perfectly because of factors affecting viewing other than an individual's preference, i.e. timing, competition and other people.

There is evidence that attitudes to the surrounding program context are correlated with some measures of commercial effectiveness. There may be different principles at work with program sponsorship, where the attitude to a program may represent an attitude message-source relevant to the advertising, compared with spot advertising, where commercials are clearly unrelated to the programs and seen as separate from them[59]. With spot advertising it seems likely that the mediating link between a positive attitude to a program and response to its commercials is reduced competing activity or even increased probability of staying with the set during the break, rather than any kind of editorial mood association. The source of the effect remains to be demonstrated. That there is an effect, although sometimes a weak one, is shown by studies by TAM[22] and Unilever[68] while a number of American studies are briefly mentioned by Bogart[69] and some recent data reported by Corlett and Richardson[70]. Generally, those viewers liking a program show higher levels of behavioural attention and/or recall than those viewers liking it less.

A review of context effects by Twyman[71] also includes some recent JICTAR evidence that brief absences by the stable (non-switching) TV audience do not seem to vary in extent from program to program in UK conditions.

Establishing principles of communication and studying the social effects of television

This title covers the general body of 'mass communications research'. It is really outside the boundaries of media research in the sense used here. Nevertheless, advertising media researchers may well be able to learn from this work. There are many reviews including those in the Annual Review of Communication Research and in De Sola Pool and Schramm[72].

Findings and application of television research in the UK with methodological implications

While the subject of this chapter is media research rather than findings about media, certain of these findings do have implications for research methodology. Not all are covered by occasional comments in the previous sections and some principal issues are summarized here.

The nature of audiences to single transmissions

The main output of audience size research comprises the ratings for individual transmission times. In the UK the following pattern has been broadly true up to now but may change with any increase in the complexity of services available. Ratings for viewers may be broken into two components: sets switched on (from meters) and viewers-per-set (from diaries). The total of sets switched on to all channels combined is generally consistent for a given time of day, day of week and season, and appears to be based largely on social habit. The number of sets switched to an individual channel, however, varies with the programming competition. Within the evening, sudden changes in audience level can occur at times of program change. The quarter hour viewers-per-set factors are much more consistent for time of day and less dependent on programming.

Regularities in the data lead to the question of whether so much need be collected. Ehrenberg[3] has questioned the value of minute by minute and continuous data. Continuing work by JICTAR[73] has investigated whether viewers-per-set factors could be obtained intermittently and applied to continuous set data. In all these cases evaluating the effects of small decreases in accuracy is difficult for the reasons outlined at the beginning of this chapter. The findings, largely unpublished, may become of more importance if other factors, such as rising costs or the need for combination with other research, lead to changes in the research system. Although audience composition data are collected continuously, viewing patterns by sub-groups are now published by JICTAR less frequently. This follows evidence that sub-groups are not particularly selective in their viewing. Some unpublished analyses carried out by the IPA showed a very high correlation between the ordering of the 'best' advertising breaks whether these were defined in terms of cost per thousand for broad audience categories (e.g. men), small demographic groups (e.g. men aged 16 to 24) or purchasing groups (e.g. men who buy aperitifs). Similar conclusions were published by the Five Agencies Study Group[74] although some possible exceptions were found on AMPS data[75, 76] TAM studies of the viewing patterns of 'heavy', 'medium' and 'light' viewing housewives[77] also showed little difference between the lists of programs viewed most by each group. The implications are that television is a relatively unselective medium and that advertising schedules can usually be planned on the viewing habits of the main audience. This conclusion can be reached too readily because of the difficulty of isolating small but useful effects in a mass of data full of large effects. There may be more exceptions to non-selectivity in British television viewing than have yet been discovered.

The nature of viewing to groups of transmissions

A widespread use of the continuous records obtained from a panel system is in special analyses showing the coverage and frequency of viewing distribution obtained across the target audience group by a schedule of spots. This kind of data reflects the nature of viewing habits over time.

Ehrenberg and Goodhardt[78, 79] extensively analysed the duplication of viewing between pairs of transmissions. Their findings include a duplication law which suggests that all pairs combine in the same way unless the transmissions are adjacent or nearly so. This implies that viewing is not systematic and dependent upon strong personal preferences, but random. Having viewed one program, a viewer is no more likely to view any one other program more than another unless it is the next or next but one in time. This conclusion also holds good in the USA and the work is carefully summarized in Ehrenberg, Goodhardt and Collins[60].

This lack of selectivity probably arises because the viewer's own preferences are obscured by components of his viewing arising from other sources mentioned earlier. Certainly individuals have program preferences and feel that they are exercising selectivity, as shown by Piepe, Emerson and Lannon[80] in their work on class differences in relation to television. Non-selectivity does make coverage and frequency data relatively easy to predict in most cases. It is possible to estimate the data from formulae[81] and tables[82] given information such as the number of spots in the schedule and the ratings they achieve. Studies in support of this finding are discussed by Ehrenberg and Twyman[3, 83]. An internationally tested model is reported by Hulks and Thomas[84].

Apart from really exceptional and very rare changes in program schedules, coverage and frequency data could probably be obtained, as adequately as response functions can utilize, from summaries of past analyses or intermittently collected data.

Some findings on media strategy

Results from advertising laboratories[58] show that one strategy may be appropriate for one brand situation and the reverse for another.

Findings on repetition have been reviewed by Broadbent[52] under discussion of the response functions and elsewhere. There is also a useful discussion of this work by Bogart[69] (see his chapter 8), and a review from BBDO in the USA[85].

In addition to advertising laboratories and other field studies there are also findings based on physiological measurements taken over a series of advertisement presentations. Some of the work was reported by Grass[86] and further discussed by Krugman[87, 88]. It is suggested that the physiological aspects of response to commercials may not be so closely related to their effectiveness as this work implies. They may reflect habituation to the physical stimuli of the advertisement but learning or persuasion may still continue.

Findings on the effectiveness of spot lengths also vary between studies and also according to whether recall or attitude change has been taken as the measure of effectiveness.

Reviewing American evidence, Bogart[69], in his chapter 7, finds that the 30-second length generates most recall per second. A study in the UK reported by Treasure and Joyce[59], using pretesting conditions, shows a greater shift in the gift choice measure, the shorter the commercial. This may reflect the kinds of shorter commercials available or a distorted relationship between this kind of testing and 'real life'. The present lack of knowledge about response to various possible advertising strategies makes it difficult to use coverage and frequency analyses with any degree of confidence. Probably the most constructive approach to their interpretation is that suggested by Broadbent[52].

Behaviour while watching television

Observations of viewers reported by Steiner[36] represent the most detailed attempt to study what happens when people view commercials. Krugman[88] has attempted to extend this further into studying their thinking about commercials while viewing.

In the UK, the findings on *presence* in breaks are most relevant to the existing continuous services. The LPE study[21] showed that more program-viewing housewives were missing from breaks early in the evening than later on. The IPA/ISBA and later JICTAR studies conflict with this, showing virtually no time effects for presence in breaks, and some evidence for no program effects. There was little difference between centre and end breaks for adults but more housewives were missing in end breaks. An overall level of absence in breaks of around 20% appears in both American and UK studies. Program audiences are based on seeing more than half of the program so that an unknown proportion of viewers will also be missing from program audiences for short time periods. Recent UK evidence suggests that much of the commercial audience loss is associated with the timing of set switching between programs. Where there is a metered measurement of set switching, therefore, the unrecorded audience loss at breaks may be considerably less than the 20% found with other techniques.

The apparent absence of variability in the proportion of program audiences present during breaks suggests that such data need be collected only infrequently. The hypothesized absence of program effects does, however, need further checking, before it is generalized. If there were even small real program effects on presence in commercial breaks, then this could weaken the meaningfulness of regular audience measurements as an indicator of commercial audiences.

Studies, including unpublished data from the IPA/ISBA[18], generally agree that behavioural *attention* levels rise from early to peak time although relatively little is known about late-night viewing. Evidence for the importance of behavioural attention rests solely on its correlation with higher levels of recall. There is evidence of programming effects particularly in relation to program interest or liking from studies by LPE[21], JWT[34], and TAM[22]. Work by BMRB has shown that indications of attention-level additional to time effects can be deduced from frequency of viewing or loyalty to television programs[70]. This approach may offer the greatest accessibility to the concept of attention since it can be deduced from regular audience measurement rather than by expensive coincidental surveying.

The use of media selection models

Computers are widely used for special analyses such as the assessment of schedules in terms of coverage and frequency of viewing. There are also programs designed to build, from research data, optimal schedules to certain criteria. Optimization programs are now relatively little used in the UK, having shown little advantage over skilled schedule construction. The primary television research input for these programs is a collection of viewing records or probabilities for individuals together with their classification information. To select an optimal television schedule involves choosing a response function, or putting a value on each number of advertisement exposures. Other adjustments which might be made include weighting individuals according to their expected market value and perhaps also applying weights to viewing at certain times to take account of hypothesized attentional effects. If a multi-media schedule is to be selected, it is necessary, having chosen advertisement sizes for each medium, to allocate weights to the different types of media exposure. On current knowledge it is virtually impossible to do this satisfactorily.

The use of computer media selection models has been mostly developed by press media owners for the press rather than television. In practice, the problems of time availability and short term buying and last-minute adjustments of timing make a computer selected television schedule only relevant in relation to the broad characteristics of the schedule structure. If time availability were also on the computer, and schedule selections quickly available, these models could be more used in television planning and perhaps even as an aid to buying decisions. Discussion of computer schedule selection models can be found in Broadbent[89.52].

Prediction, feedback and reported value

Arguably, the major advertising function of audience research is to enable predictions to be made about future ratings so that the best time may be bought. Various studies of prediction by UK advertising agencies have been reported[84.83].

Longer-term predictions are limited by programming knowledge. In the short term, predictions are likely to represent a summary of past data combined with estimates of program popularity. The latter, where successful, have usually been based on subjective experience rather than programming research but there is possible room for the development of more formalized program research for use in prediction systems.

Another role for audience research is that it provides feedback to those striving to buy the best television time, so that actions which improve cost per thousand are subsequently reinforced. While this is true to a limited extent, it should be noted that this feedback is entirely in audience research terms and depends on the validity of these terms. It also means that computerization of this function should be possible.

Finally, research is said to provide a record of value for each spot bought. This provides a basis for negotiation between buyers and sellers and an index of success as between agency and advertiser. It is difficult to say what this value amounts to in practice and how much it would be diminished if this activity were based on other than continuous data.

A possible trend in research requirements would be an increasing emphasis on prediction rather than the other research roles, if, through computerization, it becomes easier to assess the pay-off of alternative research systems in terms of time-buying efficiency.

Future Developments with Implications for Television Research

Sources of change

Changes in advertising media research are likely to arise from changes in:

(a) the structure of media;
(b) the marketing of products;
(c) methods of buying and selling media;
(d) research methodology;
(e) the economics of research.

(a) *The Structure of Media*

The structure of television in any country can change with new legislation, the building of new stations and the reorganization of existing ones. In the UK the organization of TV research is to be changed to allow cooperation between ITV and BBC. Size and regionality of stations is an important factor in the requirements for research. Technical developments with implications for the medium include those where the television set is used for something other than direct reception of transmissions, such as the recording of transmissions, the playing back of recorded transmissions, private or commercial, and the use of the TV monitor for other forms of information, reception or even games. These are all available commercially but have had little impact so far. In the long run, they might create some new minor media as well as directly affecting the television medium. Also, the introduction of new media forms, e.g. commercial radio, can have its effect.

(b) *The Marketing of Products*

Changes in the degree of segmentation which manufacturers look for in markets and the advent of new classes of manufacturer pursuing different types of market on television can all lead to changes in research requirements. This can be in terms of the relative interest in the mass market versus the smaller market segments, the latter leading to more interest in selectivity within the television medium. The degree of selectivity available from television is likely to depend heavily on the fragmentation of services available. It is difficult for monolithic services to achieve selectivity of response even with programs of highly segmented appeal. Clearly the size of market which can be selected effectively with a medium has an effect on the form of measurement and size of samples required. Such things as the banning of advertising cigarettes also have their effects.

(c) *Methods of Buying and Selling Media and Evaluating Research*

Television research systems depend a lot on the sales structure of television and vice versa. If selling methods change, so does the appropriate research. However, it is still buying methodology that seems to be most influential. Here, one trend (which has now slowed) is towards computerization. Starting with the use of computers both for accountancy and for theoretical exercises in media selection this could ultimately lead to total buying and selling systems being operated on computers. This would involve storing availability, allocation rules and research data. Exercise of media skills would lie in the choice of forms of stating advertising aims and the development of programs for achieving the consequent requirements.

Such systems would tend to impose the form of data requirements although much of their content would depend on the other factors discussed in this section.

One side-effect of greater computerization of media transactions is that alternative forms of research could be systematically evaluated to see what effect on decisions they have. At present this is difficult because a human system cannot forget its past experience for the purposes of an evaluation exercise and only rather artificial decision-simulating analyses are possible.

(d) *Research Methodology and the Economics of Research*

These two elements cannot be considered in isolation. Much depends on how rich a medium television is in the future and how costly research becomes. A decline in the value of the money available for television research can bring simpler data collection methods despite the potential availability of more sophisticated techniques. There has always been a strong presumption that research (and its use) brings a return for the money it costs. There may be greater pressure for evaluating this under economic stress.

There is room for development in meter techniques. They could get smaller and less obtrusive and suitable for portables or even radios. The meter could become personal and record proximity to a television set. People-detectors and identifiers linked to a meter are another possibility. Cost and value for money considerations are likely to inhibit these developments.

The growth of telephone ownership will enable more countries to use telephone interviewing which is widely used for media surveys in the USA and Canada, some European countries and elsewhere (e.g. New Zealand). The associated developments of facilities for transmitting data by line could extend the use of instantaneous or stored line data collection systems, already in use in the USA and Germany. Such systems were pioneered in the UK by Nielsen and TAM in the early 1960's but failed mainly because the value of speed was not considered great enough to offset the cost. Instantaneous audience measurement has also been attempted through the monitoring of cable television services but depends on the extent of such services to achieve representativeness and still requires some measurement of individual viewing.

The increasing complexity and cost of product and media research has led to suggestions for more attempts to integrate various research systems, syndicated or financed on an industry basis[5, 9]. There are additional arguments based on the value of obtaining product and media data from the same source. This is clearly a development which could affect the nature of the television research system as a whole and, possibly, influence the techniques used. The capacity and willingness to move in this direction will vary between countries according to both economic pressures and the strength of the entrepreneurial spirit in research.

26. Radio, outdoor and cinema research

Frank Teer

The attention of the media researcher is not unnaturally concentrated on the two main advertising media. Relatively little attention is given in the UK to the cinema, radio and posters as subjects for audience research, and the reasons are not hard to find. In advertising expenditure terms they are minor media. Together, in 1976 they accounted for about 9% of £814 million spent on display advertising and less than a quarter of the expenditure on television advertising alone. The 1976 figures were: Posters and Transport Advertising £43m, Cinema £8m and Radio £21m. Commercial radio is of course a relatively new medium, and the 1976 figure was 3½ times that for 1974.

As advertising media, they are very different in terms of the nature of the advertising presented and the quality of exposure offered. The creative opportunities of the cinema, with colour, sound, movement and a large screen, contrast with the limited message which can be transmitted in a poster advertisement. Radio, standing between the two, calls for special creative attention because of its total dependence on the aural sense. In terms of the quality of exposure delivered by each medium, the same contrast can be observed. The considerable absorption of the cinema audience is at one end of the attention spectrum, with posters at the other, the poster audience being almost totally 'casual'. Radio listening falls some way between the two. Often it does not claim the undivided attention of its audience, who may be working, driving, even reading, while listening. On the other hand, for some members of the audience there may be a very close and direct link between the presenter and the listener, offering very special opportunities to an advertiser.

Although so different in kind, these media have two very important characteristics in common as vehicles for advertising. First, they are used by national advertisers mainly as support media to press and television campaigns. This is true of all three for different reasons. *Cinema* offers an opportunity to reach population sub-groups who are relatively under-exposed to other forms of advertising: for example, young, unmarried people aged 16–24. *Radio* offers relatively low-cost repetition of an advertising message. *Posters* provide high coverage of the population and high repetition, both of which can be concentrated near the point of purchase. All three media lend themselves to selective area campaigns. Blanket national or regional coverage is not obligatory. Advertisers with localized interest such as retailers, garages, etc., can make particularly effective use of the media, confining their expenditure purely to their areas of operation.

The role given to advertising in these media and the total sums expended on them affect the type and amount of research undertaken. The advertiser requires information about the audience before deciding to spend money on the medium, but the information he can expect must necessarily be restricted.

As with press and television, audience research should enable the advertiser to predict the size and nature of the audience to a series of advertisements. The advertiser wants to know how many people will see at least one advertisement in a campaign (its cover), and how many times on average each member of the audience is likely to see an advertisement (repetition). This information, ideally, should be available for target groups, defined either in demographic or product usership terms, but at least he will require to know the nature of the audience as a whole in demographic terms.

Radio Audience Research

We are concerned only with research into the audiences of stations which carry advertising. Until the advent of Independent Local Radio in 1972, UK research into these radio audiences had been relatively spasmodic; before then the only commercial radio programs received in the UK were those transmitted from abroad. A brief review of that research does, however, give an overview of the main research alternatives available to the audience researcher.

Radio Luxembourg has been transmitting commercial radio to the UK since 1946 and carrying out survey research into its audience since 1952. These surveys have been based on personal interviews with 2000 or more individuals for each day's listening surveyed. The questionnaire generally covers claimed listening to programs on the day before the interview and also broader claims for the previous week. Recently, the questionnaire has been augmented to include an attempt to measure the recall of the previous evening's advertising. The surveys are undertaken on a number of days a year to measure seasonal variations in listening and from the data collected advertisers can estimate the size and nature of the audience at different times of the day and at different seasons of the year[1].

Surveys of this type, which measure listening over the preceding 24 hours (24-hour recall surveys), provide useful data for the advertiser. They measure the characteristics of the audience for any given time-period and can be used to estimate the total audience for any given time-spot, and, thus, the cost per thousand members of the target audience reached by that spot.

Because the detailed listening data extend only over a 24-hour period, direct survey evidence of cumulative cover and repetition (or *reach* and *frequency* in commercial radio jargon) over a long time period cannot be directly adduced from the survey data. However, the cumulative audience and the amount of repetition delivered by a radio advertising campaign can be estimated from 24-hour data if these are combined with limited questions on listening frequency. American experience based on work carried out by Westinghouse Broadcasting indicates that these estimates can be refined to a considerable degree of accuracy[2].

Because 24-hour recall surveys do not provide direct measurements of cumulative cover some users have favoured the diary as a method of collecting radio audience data. In November 1968 Radio Luxembourg used a seven-day diary to collect listening data[3]. In this technique, which is also extensively used in the United States and elsewhere, a sample of the general public are asked to keep a record of their radio listening, television viewing and newspaper reading over a seven-day time-period. This record then gives the researcher direct evidence on the question of cumulative cover.

During the 'pirate' radio period in the mid-1960's, when unlicenced stations operated from off-shore bases (mainly on ships moored outside national waters), the radio research undertaken fell into two distinct types. In the first place, the stations obtained, through 'omnibus' surveys, weekly audience figures based on questions such as 'Did you listen at all during the last seven days?' and 'When did you last listen?'. Weekly audience figures of this kind were little more than station popularity polls and were used to reinforce the station's claims that they had a wide and interested audience. They were not particularly useful as media research. Consequently, the 'pirates' later undertook 24-hour recall surveys similar to the Luxembourg surveys and on one occasion used a seven-day diary.

Other methods of collecting radio audience data, in particular the telephone interview, which has been used extensively in the USA, have not found favour in the UK. Because of the relatively low incidence of telephone ownership (only about 60% of homes have a telephone) and the extent of 'out-of-home' radio listening, there has been considerable doubt about the usefulness of telephone surveys. The method employed in the USA is to use a coincidental check whereby the interviewer telephones a random sample of homes at specified times and asks whether the radio is switched on and, if so, the station to which it is tuned and also who is listening. Without a further increase in the penetration of telephone ownership, it is unlikely that this method would be used for general radio research in the UK, except possibly for certain minority interest groups, such as high-income groups, investors, etc.

659

Methodology

The objective of radio audience research is the same as any other media research—to estimate the opportunities to hear an advertisement or series of advertisements; this with a view to establishing the cost efficiency of the medium, a particular station or a specific schedule of advertisements. There are a number of measurement problems peculiar to radio which have to be considered in appraising the two main alternative approaches of 24-hour recall and personal diary.

Station identification

If a listener is to be asked to record or recall his listening behaviour there is a presumption that he is always aware of the name of the station to which he is listening. When there are a number of alternative stations with a similar format this presumption may not be completely valid. Some indication of the extent of this problem is shown by a small scale pilot conducted by National Opinion Polls in the latter days of 'pirate' radio in 1966. This pilot consisted of a simple coincidental check in which interviewers called at homes and enquired if the radio was switched on and whether the respondent was listening to it. If the answer to both questions was 'yes', the interviewers went on to ask to which station the radio was tuned. Having recorded this, the interviewer then checked the set to determine whether it was, in fact, tuned to that station. This is a simple check of simultaneous recall. Out of 322 listeners interviewed, about 10% gave incorrect answers on the question of station. In the case of those who said they were listening to a commercial station, 18% incorrectly identified the station. Of those who said they were listening to a BBC broadcast, about 5% were incorrect. This experiment was very limited in scope and neither investigated the causes of confusion nor the methods required to minimize it. It goes no further than to demonstrate that station identification is a problem and it was a significantly greater problem for commercial stations of the 'pop pirate' type than it was for BBC stations (as they were then).

The casualness of the event

There is a widespread view that much radio listening, especially to 'pop' stations, is casual in nature—that the radio does not demand the same degree of undivided attention as press or television. This seems to be borne out by the extent to which radio listening occurs while other activities are in progress. There is, therefore, some doubt whether this type of event can be recalled accurately 24 hours later or whenever the panel member fills in his or her diary. Memory cannot readily be jogged because program lists consisting almost entirely of names of disc jockeys or program presenters are unlikely to be adequate recall aids.

It is possible that one of the advantages of the diary may lie in taking some of the casualness from this 'event'. Because panel members know that they have to record their listening, they will pay greater attention to it in terms of taking note of the station to which they are tuned and mentally noting the time.

The location of the event

Because of the portability of the transistor radio, listening can take place almost anywhere inside and outside the home. The radio audience is an extremely mobile one. In addition, because the radio is often used as background, it can be played at work or in a car. Although most radio listening does in fact take place in the home, a substantial amount of it occurs outside the home.

In recent diary-based surveys carried out on behalf of the Association of Independent Radio Contractors, Research Surveys of Great Britain have found that of all listening to radio roughly one-fifth takes place outside the home. The proportion recorded in the surveys varies from area to area within the range of 16–23%. This is a substantial proportion of total listening and much of it is to radios not belonging to or tuned in by the listener, making further difficulties of recall and/or diary keeping.

These special difficulties serve to highlight some of the questions which need to be answered before opting conclusively for one measurement technique or the other. The problem is further confounded because the 24-hour recall method and the diary are subject to a considerable number of possible approaches—using quota or random samples, personal, postal or telephone interview, including or excluding measurements of other media, etc. That the chosen method should have validity seems to be accepted as a guiding principle but attempts at validation have proved inconclusive.

Validity requires that the chosen technique reliably reflects the 'real' audience. In using measures which depend on an individual's recall of an event, that measure may not reflect the true audience because of the frailty of memory. Listening occasions may be forgotten and the audience is consequently understated. If a diary method is used, individuals participating in the survey know that they have to record their listening and are likely to pay greater attention to it but diary-keeping could condition panel members into adopting a listening pattern (especially in the short term) which is not 'normal'. This could be either for prestige reasons or to make their own diary-keeping simpler. The act of completing a diary may make them more radio conscious than previously and this might result in an overestimate of the actual audience.

As there are no independent audience data against which measurements of the above type can be checked, the only method of validating the information is the coincidental check. This technique requires that the methods being tested are put into operation simultaneously and an independent measure of the audience is taken by a method which is known to be valid. The coincidental check, which is a valid measure, requires that the radio listening of a large sample of individuals be checked at specific moments in time by observation. If a large enough sample of individuals is contacted at a precise point in time and a note taken of the station to which the individual is listening (if any), a reliable and valid estimate of the listening level at that time can be made. This was the method used by Television Audience Measurement Limited in the comparison surveys undertaken in the early days of commercial television[4].

The need to validate measurement for all listening imposes considerable problems in designing suitable coincidental checking techniques. We have to cover listening in private households, in work places, motor cars, as well as in public places. It is not impossible to devise a coincidental check to cover the audience at home and at work. The former would follow the television pattern and the latter would require sampling work places and determining whether any radios are being played, to which stations they are tuned, and what proportion of employees are listening to them at given moments in time. Listening out of doors is more difficult because the population of any outdoor location is constantly changing.

It may, however, be possible simply to sample listeners, not to determine the absolute level of listening but to check that the relative listening to each station is correctly recorded in diaries or 24-hour recall. It would be extremely difficult to validate listening in motor cars though a possible answer would be to check motorists as they stop, e.g. for petrol. Surveys have indeed been undertaken in the USA and elsewhere which have required interviewing motorists stopped at traffic signals to check their listening behaviour.

A number of validation surveys have been carried out in the United States and Canada:

1. the ARB—RKO Radio Experiment[5];
2. ARMS—All Radio Methodology Study[6];
3. a Report on the BBM Tests of Revised and Single-Media Diaries February 1974[7];
4. Polyphase[8].

The RKO survey concluded that multi-media diaries agreed with 'standard' and the radio-only diaries over-reported by a factor of two. ARMS concluded that radio-only diaries and personal recall came closest to 'standard'. The Canadian BBM study showed television and radio diaries came closest to 'standard'. In all of these cases telephone coincidental checks were used as the standard measurement (a measure which of course validates only 'in-home' listening). The Polyphase survey was an exploratory study rather than a validation exercise, but it did demonstrate that radio research was highly sensitive to bias through non-response and in particular that low response rates tended to produce inflated listening figures.

The inconclusiveness of this work is, perhaps, not surprising in view of the enormous variations in approach and the somewhat erratic quality of the sampling methods used for much radio research. One is tempted to conclude that either of the basic methods (diary or recall) will approach to standard if it is implemented with good sampling, interviewing and the appropriate memory and identification aids.

In those parts of the world where radio research is undertaken with any degree of regularity the diary approach has generally found favour. The main reasons for the success of the diary have less to do with validity than economy. From the point of view of data yield the seven-day diary is a much more cost-efficient vehicle for data collection than a 24-hour recall study. Clearly if a sample of individuals completes a diary for a seven-day period the researcher collects seven times the amount of information compared with a 24-hour recall survey with the same sample size. Furthermore, the longer-term nature of the diary makes it simpler to produce evidence of the cumulative audience to more than one commercial.

UK research

The commencement of local commercial radio in the UK in 1972 led to considerable speculation about the type of research which would be undertaken. This speculation ran along two quite distinct and widely separated lines. On the one hand there was a belief that the local stations would not be able, or prepared, to finance expensive media research in their broadcasting areas. On the other hand, many advertisers and agencies were concerned that a formalized system for radio research should be implemented and that this system should be able to produce estimates of the cumulative audience and therefore include estimates of listening behaviour over a long time-period, e.g. seven days.

Initially, the independent stations produced audience estimates by a variety of techniques ranging from popularity polls to diaries but during 1974 the Association of Independent Radio Contractors (AIRC) decided to establish a common method for audience research. They sought the guidance of advertisers and advertising agencies on survey methods and this led to the establishment of a Joint Industry Committee for Radio Audience Research (JICRAR). This committee recommended the adoption of diary research in the broadcasting area of each station.

AIRC issued a specification for this research which called for:

1. the use of radio-only diaries covering a seven-day time-period;
2. recording of listening to all radio—BBC and commercial;
3. random samples of 1000 or 800 individuals in each area;
4. personal placement and collection of diaries by interviewers;
5. response rates of 65% or more;
6. the collection of listening behaviour quarter-hour by quarter-hour (with the exception of the night hours of midnight to 6 a.m. when half-hourly information was thought to be acceptable);

DAYTIME 5.00 a.m.–4.00 p.m. Wednesday		BRMB Radio	Radio Luxembourg	BBC Radio 1	BBC Radio 2	BBC Radio 3	BBC Radio 4	BBC Radio Birmingham	Listened at home	Listened elsewhere
		1	2	3	4	5	6	7	X	A
01	5.00– 5.30									
02	5.30– 6.00									
03	6.00– 6.15									
04	6.15– 6.30									
05	6.30– 6.45									
06	6.45– 7.00									
07	7.00– 7.15									
08	7.15– 7.30									
09	7.30– 7.45									
10	7.45– 8.00									
11	8.00– 8.15									
12	8.15– 8.30									
13	8.30– 8.45									
14	8.45– 9.00									
15	9.00– 9.15									
16	9.15– 9.30									
17	9.30– 9.45									
18	9.45–10.00									
19	10.00–10.15									
20	10.15–10.30									
21	10.30–10.45									
22	10.45–11.00									
23	11.00–11.15									
24	11.15–11.30									
25	11.30–11.45									
26	11.45–12.00									
27	12.00–12.15									
28	12.15–12.30									
29	12.30–12.45									
30	12.45– 1.00									
31	1.00– 1.15									
32	1.15– 1.30									
33	1.30– 1.45									
34	1.45– 2.00									
35	2.00– 2.15									
36	2.15– 2.30									
37	2.30– 2.45									
38	2.45– 3.00									
39	3.00– 3.15									
40	3.15– 3.30									
41	3.30– 3.45									
42	3.45– 4.00									

Have you recorded ALL your listening for today?

EVENING 4.00 p.m.–5.00 a.m. Wednesday		BRMB Radio	Radio Luxembourg	BBC Radio 1	BBC Radio 2	BBC Radio 3	BBC Radio 4	BBC Radio Birmingham	Listened at home	Listened elsewhere
		1	2	3	4	5	6	7	X	A
43	4.00– 4.15									
44	4.15– 4.30									
45	4.30– 4.45									
46	4.45– 5.00									
47	5.00– 5.15									
48	5.15– 5.30									
49	5.30– 5.45									
50	5.45– 6.00									
51	6.00– 6.15									
52	6.15– 6.30									
53	6.30– 6.45									
54	6.45– 7.00									
55	7.00– 7.15									
56	7.15– 7.30									
57	7.30– 7.45									
58	7.45– 8.00									
59	8.00– 8.15									
60	8.15– 8.30									
61	8.30– 8.45									
62	8.45– 9.00									
63	9.00– 9.15									
64	9.15– 9.30									
65	9.30– 9.45									
66	9.45–10.00									
67	10.00–10.15									
68	10.15–10.30									
69	10.30–10.45									
70	10.45–11.00									
71	11.00–11.15									
72	11.15–11.30									
73	11.30–11.45									
74	11.45–12.00									
75	12.00–12.30									
76	12.30– 1.00									
77	1.00– 1.30									
78	1.30– 2.00									
79	2.00– 2.30									
80	2.30– 3.00									
81	3.00– 3.30									
82	3.30– 4.00									
83	4.00– 4.30									
84	4.30– 5.00									

Please check ALL today's records for accuracy.

Fig. 26.1

7. the collection by personal interview, at the diary placement stage, of information about exposure to other media and broad radio listening claims.

Subsequently, in October 1974, a contract for this research was placed by the Association of Independent Radio Contractors with Research Surveys of Great Britain, since when a series of surveys has been carried out in accordance with the specification[9].

In these surveys the station's broadcasting area has been defined by reference to the IBA's one millivolt contour line delineating the VHF area. As the stations broadcast on both VHF and medium wave, this area is clearly smaller than the area which the stations cover through their medium wave signal. Consequently, in a number of surveys the basic sample in the VHF area has been supplemented by additional samples in a wider and more loosely defined area.

With the exception of this question of area coverage the JICRAR surveys have been conducted to a standard format. The diary used is designed to be carried in a pocket or handbag and those pages on which listening behaviour is recorded conform to the example shown in Fig. 26.1. To avoid bias there are two versions of the diary for each area: one lists BBC stations first, the other lists the independent stations first. Half of the sample receives each type of diary.

As an aid to station identification the diary contains a description of the program content of each station (see Fig. 26.2). In order to encourage cooperation from individuals who claim not to listen to the radio the diary contains a general information page which is not used in the analysis of results but requests information about radio listening and other activities in each day of the week.

Radio Stations

BRMB Radio 261m, 1151 KHz, Med. wave and 94.8 MHz VHF (in Stereo). The Midlands commercial radio station. Popular music, sport, local news and information with advertisements.

Radio Luxembourg 208m, 1439 KHz Med. wave. Commercial "POP" music station with advertisements.

BBC Radio 1 247m, 1214 KHz Med. wave. "POP" music, joins Radio 2 in evening.

BBC Radio 2 1500m, 200 KHz Long wave, 89.1 VHF. Popular music, sport and news

BBC Radio 3 464m, 647 KHz Med. wave, 91.3 VHF. Classical music and talks.

BBC Radio 4 330m, 908 KHz Med. wave, 93.5 VHF. News, plays and comment.

BBC Radio Birmingham 206m, 1457 KHz Med. wave, 95.6 MHz VHF. The local BBC radio station broadcasting information, traffic news, and music. Often joins BBC Radio 1, 2 or 4.

Fig. 26.2

For each survey random sampling methods are used and response rates are universally high. For areas outside London 70% or more of the selected sample complete a diary and in London a response rate of around 65% is achieved. The specification calls for a short interview at the placement stage including questions relating to radio listening. These questions, designed to provide crude listening levels for each individual interviewed, are included in the survey to establish whether there is any difference in listening behaviour between those individuals who complete a diary and those who do not.

The questions included take the following form:

SHOW CARD A

Q.1(a) Now some questions about your radio listening. Firstly, looking at this card, about how often these days do you listen to the radio?

ASK LISTENERS ONLY

Q.1(b) On a day when you listen to the radio, for about how many hours on average do you listen on the whole of that day?

SHOW CARD A

Q.2(a) Again, looking at this card, about how often these days do you listen to commercial radio—I mean stations like Radio Luxembourg, . . . (the Independent Local Radio), or any others that broadcast advertisements?

ASK LISTENERS ONLY

Q.2(b) On a day when you listen to commercial radio, for about how many hours on average do you listen on the whole of that day?

(Answers to parts (a) are recorded in days from the list given on Card A and answers to parts (b) are recorded in hours in the range 'less often than one' to 'more than seven'.)

The results confirm, as expected, that those individuals who do not listen to the radio at all or listen relatively infrequently are less likely to complete a diary than heavier listeners. To the extent that this is true it means that the levels of listening established by the diaries overstate the true level. However, the extent of this overstatement is slight and its effect on listening levels is negligible. These questions do, however, indicate that the diary method is likely to lead to overestimates of the radio audience but the nature of these overestimates can only be assessed by a more comprehensive investigation of non-respondents' listening behaviour.

The survey establishes broad listening data only for those individuals who are sampled and cooperate in the initial interview but who subsequently fail to fill in a diary. No information at all is available for those individuals who are sampled but not contacted at all or who refuse to give an interview. Clearly an investigation of the listening habits of this group is necessary before any definitive statement can be made about response bias.

Although more technical work is needed, the JICRAR surveys seem to produce results acceptable to the advertising industry. However, the specification set by JICRAR is an onerous one for the radio industry because the surveys are costly relative to the income of the stations. This burden is particularly heavy for the smaller stations and it is likely that the approach will have to be modified to cater for these smaller areas. More fundamentally, however, it is also questionable whether the advertising industry is prepared to handle and use the considerable quantity of data generated by surveys of this kind.

With expenditure on the radio medium at a relatively low level the amount of time and effort which can be devoted to media selection is also relatively small and detailed survey results can neither be absorbed nor used. On the other hand, the cost efficiency of ratio schedules can only be appraised through analyses of reach (cover) and frequency (repetition) based on data of the type produced by JICRAR surveys. So-called 'dipstick' surveys, which produce simple evidence of the weekly reach of a station, have little value in media research and in any event do not appear to conform to a common standard.

The system so far established by JICRAR could therefore be subject to modification in the future to take account of some of these problems but it seems likely that a diary approach will remain at the heart of UK radio audience research for some time to come.

Outdoor Advertising Research

The special feature of the poster which sets it apart from the other main advertising media is that its sole purpose in life is the transmission of an advertising message. While advertising may have an important economic role in the life of other media, their main role, so far as the public is concerned, is the dissemination of news or entertainment. The poster has no role other than advertising. An opportunity to see a poster advertisement cannot therefore be defined in terms of membership of the media audience, because the medium and the advertisement are one and the same.

Because the poster is purely an advertising medium, the public do not seek to become members of the poster audience. This again contrasts with the other main media, where it is necessary to get hold of a copy, turn on a set, or buy a ticket to become a member of the audience. The events which qualify an individual as a member of the cinema, TV, radio, newspaper or magazine audiences may be memorable to a greater or less degree but insofar as they are memorable they are measurable. With posters, the event which qualifies an individual for membership of the audience is incidental, and in view of the number and variety of posters seen in the course of one day by each of us, each of these events is scarcely memorable. Clearly it would be impossible to differentiate these countless events into individual exposures. The poster audience researcher has therefore approached the concept of 'opportunity to see' from the point of view of exposure to the environment of the advertisement.

A newspaper can be regarded as the environment of a press advertisement; exposure to the 'environment' through readership creates an opportunity to see. In the same way, the environment of a poster site is a locality within which that site can be seen. Exposure to this environment and, therefore, an opportunity to see, arises when an individual moves into or through this locality. An opportunity to see thus defined seems less closely related to advertisement exposure than an opportunity to see advertisements in other media, because the 'event' is less directly related to the advertisement. However, so far as posters are concerned, this seems to be the only feasible starting point for audience research. It has been used and accepted as a reasonable measurement although many would say it is only the starting point and we should go on to try to evaluate what percentage of opportunities to see are, in fact, converted into people who actually look at the poster site. This would produce a measure similar to noting scores for press media.

A member of the poster audience is therefore defined as a person who has an opportunity to see a poster, i.e. who 'passes by a place (on foot or in a vehicle) where a poster is or can be displayed'. It would clearly be an elaborate and expensive task to measure this in relation to all possible poster campaigns because the poster campaign is almost infinitely variable, consisting as it does of a selection of poster sites in a selection of towns. The researcher therefore has attempted to measure the audience to the medium by reference to the opportunities to see a campaign, consisting of a given number of average or representative sites distributed widely in a number of specific urban areas.

Audience measurement

The development of techniques for the measurement of poster audiences, and, in consequence, a poster audience model, was largely the responsibility of Brian Copland whose work must be standard reading for any student of outdoor research[10]. The poster audience consists of people moving about in their environment and, historically, the measurement of that audience has been made by determining the journey patterns of the population of specific towns. This produced estimates of the number of passages past each poster site (opportunities to see, or OTS) made by each member of the population.

The major UK study was carried out on behalf of Mills and Allen in 1955 in nine Midland towns ranging in size from Dunstable to Nottingham[11]. This survey was extended to the Birmingham conurbation in 1964 (using a modified technique). In each town a random sample of respondents was questioned about their journeys during the week prior to the interview. The journeys were recorded in detail and related to poster location, each location being a group of more or less adjacent sites. From these data we can deduce for each town:

(i) the total number of opportunities to see posters at each location;
(ii) the proportion of the population passing each location (i.e. coverage);
(iii) how many times on average each member of the audience passed each location in say a week (i.e. repetition).

Having established the audience for each poster site in a specific town, it is then possible to establish the audience for a campaign consisting of a number of sites in that town. This is done by selecting a sample of, say, 10 or 20 sites in the town and establishing by analysis the number of individuals who have passed at least one (cover) and the number of times each individual has passed any of the sites (repetition). By selecting a series of samples of this type from the poster locations in a specified town and averaging the results we can estimate the cover and repetition delivered by an 'average' campaign.

Copland carried out this procedure for each town and showed that certain patterns emerge:

(1) For each town the rate of increase in the percentage of population covered by campaigns of increasing size followed a simple exponential curve with a smaller rate of growth for larger towns (see Fig. 26.3).
(2) For each town the total OTS per head of population when plotted against the number of sites followed a straight line and the slope of this line increases as the size of the town falls (see Fig. 26.4). From this it can be seen that for any town the number of OTS per head of population was the product of the number of sites (S) and a constant (A) for that town.

Fig. 26.3 Cover provided by campaigns of varying size in towns W, X, Y and Z.

Fig. 26.4 (Source: The Size and Nature of the Poster Audience Study Two —
May 1955.)

(3) The repetition (or opportunities per head of audience–R) followed the same pattern as opportunities per head of population (A) but with the line shifted bodily upwards (see Fig. 26.5). (The extent of this displacement was almost identical in each town and subsequent work fixes this at a constant of 4.75.) Consequently, repetition can be written as $AS + 4.75$.

It has been noted that the value of A varies inversely with the size of town: the smaller the town the higher the value of A. This is, on reflection, not surprising as the smaller the town the greater the chance that an individual will pass any one site.

Figure 26.6 shows how that A value varied in practice between Dunstable, where it was estimated at 3.5 and Nottingham, where the observed A value was 0.5. It was found that the relationship could be described as log $A = 0.7250 \times \log$ population (000's) + 1.414. This formula therefore enables an A value and consequently OTS to be calculated for any town. The poster researcher has therefore a model from which he can calculate OTS, cover and repetition for any campaign in any town, cover being calculated from $(AS/AS + 4.75) \times 100$.

670

The measurements on which this model was based were obtained by reference to journeys in a seven-day time-period. Subsequent work has established that cover and repetition for periods which are multiples of one week can be predicted by a simple multiplication of the A value.

One feature of the model is that it has been found to apply generally with minor modifications in a wide variety of countries. The only major observed

Fig. 26.5

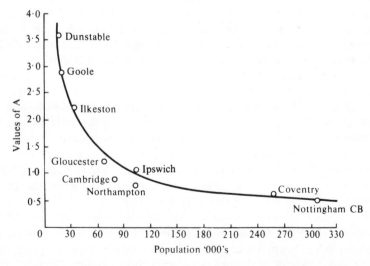

Fig. 26.6   (Source: The Size and Nature of the Poster Audience Study Two —
May 1955.)

671

difference is that the relationship between OTS per head of population and the OTS per head of audience can vary from country to country.

The model has been generalized as

$$\text{Cover} = \frac{tAS}{tkAS + b}$$

where t = time in weeks
A = a value for the urban area concerned
S = number of sites in the campaign
k = a constant for each country (GB = 1.0)
b = a constant for each country (GB = 4.75)

The majority of the work undertaken of course relates to posters on static sites but the model can be extended to advertising on mobile sites, e.g. advertising on the outside of public transport vehicles. The extension is complex and the work undertaken to date is limited. Again Copland is the main originator of this development and readers are referred to his work[12-15].

Data collection

The work to establish this model of the poster audience was undertaken in a number of countries and was spread over a long period of time. During the course of the work a number of modifications have been made to the data collection techniques.

The original approach was to collect by personal interview details of each individual's travel behaviour in the survey period. Details of each journey, including route and means of transport, had to be recorded and subsequently converted to passages past poster locations. There are two obvious disadvantages to this approach: it imposes a considerable strain on the memory of the respondent and the analysis of the data was very time consuming.

The difficulties have led to a change in approach, adopted in Britain and France, in which a random sample of sites are listed in the questionnaire and respondents are called upon to provide details of their journeys made past these 'key points' in a seven-day period. In Britain interview aids, known as location cards, were devised. These cards consist of a photograph and sketch map of each site location sampled, which serves to describe the precise location to the respondent and as a memory jogger.

Using a pack of such location cards, the interview proceeds on the following lines. 'Now, we just want to check the flow of traffic past various key points in the town. To make the inquiry easier we have prepared these pictures and diagrams of the places we want to ask about.'

NOW TAKE INFORMANT THROUGH THE LOCATION CARDS IN TURN ASKING ABOUT EACH ONE.

'Do you know where this is?'

IF 'NO' TRY TO EXPLAIN.

IF 'YES' ASK 'Have you ever been to this place?' (meaning the area marked by dotted lines on the location card map).

IF 'YES' ASK 'When were you last there, either *at* the exact spot or *passing through* it?' Probe: 'How long ago was that?', 'How were you travelling on that occasion?', 'How many times do you go there, or through there, in an average week these days?' IF LESS OFTEN THAN 'ONCE A WEEK' ASK 'How often do you go there?'

It was found when this technique was first applied that it produced slightly different results to the original approach. In particular, the levels of cover and repetition obtained using location cards was higher, either because memory is more effectively stimulated or as a result of overclaiming. (A more detailed discussion of this is to be found in the IPA Poster Audience Surveys 1964.) More recently, in 1974, the technique has been further modified to permit the collection of 'passage' data over a wide area in the larger conurbations. The earlier surveys had a limit of 60 poster locations: a limit imposed because of the burden which would have been placed on the interviewer in recording passages or in presenting location cards for a larger number of sites. Research Services Ltd. in surveys for Gallaher[16] and British Posters[17] developed a much simpler technique for recording locations passed which made it possible to log passages by a very large number of sites—1000 in the case of the London survey. The recording technique used relied on document reading facilities for registering the code number of each site in the area.

Demographic data

The poster audience model described gives basic data for the advertiser on the cover and repetition produced by campaigns of varying size and length but it does so only by reference to the adult population as a whole. It might be expected that cover and repetition would vary for different population sub-groups and the evidence available suggests that this is so.

In a section of the Newport survey it is shown that much higher exposure levels are achieved among men, young people and members of socio-economic group C, with 147%, 131%, and 121% of average exposure. House-wives, on the other hand, achieve only 59% of average exposure.

Results from the two 1974 surveys are less clear cut. Although the observed A values for men continue to be much higher than for women, the age and social class results seem to be inconsistent from area to area. However, the

1974 surveys do represent a considerable step forward in próviding coverage and repetition data for important population sub-groups.

The 1974 survey also represents a substantial step forward in terms of generally updating the data base for the poster audience model, thus rectifying a long-felt need. It is, however, somewhat surprising to note that the A values observed in these surveys are if anything lower than those estimated from the 1955 work. Because of an observed reduction in the value of b in these surveys there is little overall change in levels of cover and repetition. However, in view of the increase in traffic and mobility which has taken place in the last twenty years it would have been reasonable to expect a general increase in the value of A.

One might conclude that either the previous research tended to overstate the traffic parameter A or the 1974 surveys understate it. It is unfortunate that the latter surveys incorporated a change in technique with no attempt to calibrate the data to previous surveys. Certainly the nature of the task given to interviewers in the 1974 surveys may have led to fatigue and a consequential under-recording of journeys or passages.

The 1974 surveys also showed new values for b ranging from 4.52 in West Midlands to 3.43 in Crewe compared with the previously accepted figure of 4.75 based on the Newport work and 4 based on the original nine towns work. That there should be such variability in the value of b is perplexing. That its value in the recent surveys should be generally below previous levels may be due to the exclusion from the sample of those aged 65 and over. The reader will recall that b represents the extent to which the line representing OTS per head of population is shifted upwards when presented as OTS per head of audience. This value must therefore represent an 'immobility element' indicating that there are members of the population who never become part of the audience because they do not move around. As immobility is related to age and infirmity it seems likely that the absence of the oldest age groups from the sample could lead to a reduction in the value of b.

Other problems

The poster model relates to the levels of exposure generated by a random sample of sites. One question which needs to be answered is: how far do the sites selected for a typical campaign approximate to a random sample? To the extent that posters are bought on a package basis, i.e. where individual site selection is minimal, it might be expected that variations in the performance of individual sites would indeed cancel out and the package would approximate to a random sample of sites. However, this is not in fact the case because many sites are individually selected and many are virtually permanently allocated to a number of major advertisers. To the extent that these specially selected sites are the 'better' sites, it should be expected that the remainder are of lower quality and consequently the delivery of a package of the latter would be below average. It would be a relatively simple matter to

674

tabulate recent survey results by reference to available packages and report the cover and repetition levels delivered by these packages.

An elaborate system of site classification has been established by the poster industry which attempts to take into account traffic size and the aspect of sites. In the Newport study the A values for four different categories of sites were examined showing that the variation between 'best' and 'worst' was as much as 50%. If the variation is as great as this, then the pre-empting of better sites by special selection must have a considerable effect on the delivery of a package of sites. There seems to be little doubt that the advertiser would be better served if the A values basic to the model could be measured with reference to packages of sites available in practice for sale rather than a random sample of sites as a whole.

Opportunities and realities

The audience data for the outdoor medium depends, as we have said, on a concept of opportunity to see, which is substantially different to that for any other advertising audience. Its relevance to the advertiser depends on the relative value of different opportunities and the extent to which those opportunities are converted into 'sightings'.

In the poster model as presently constructed all opportunities to see are equal. Whether the member of the audience passes the site in a car, on a bus, or on foot, his opportunity is equal. For example, the opportunity to see a poster on the right hand side of a road from a seat on the left of a bus might be described as limited to say the least!

Clearly, the conversion of an opportunity into a sighting is likely to be dependent on the method of transport as well as speed of passage. While the audience can be differentiated in terms of method of transport, there are few data to assist in assigning a relative value to each. Furthermore, there are few general data to enable the conversion of opportunities into sightings. There is no poster equivalent of 'reading and noting' or 'presence and attention'. Given the difficulty of obtaining such measurements, the absence of data is perhaps not surprising. As an alternative, attempts have been made to relate opportunities to see to campaign recall and poster recognition. The number of published case histories is limited but sufficient to indicate that even a substantial number of opportunities to see produced relatively low levels of recall and recognition.

Undoubtedly the poster audience model is an easily used means of estimating the coverage and repetition provided by a specific advertising campaign. It is unfortunate that over the years the data input for this model has been collected by different methods, thus making comparisons across time very difficult. However, with minor modifications the data available are probably adequate for most users' needs given the relatively limited spend on each campaign.

Cinema Audience Research

On the face of it, the cinema should be the simplest of all media for the researcher. The cinema audience is easy to define because qualification for membership depends on the purchase of a ticket and the total 'opportunities to see' delivered by the medium must equal sales for tickets. Although this tells us nothing about the composition of the audience or the number of people represented by the total number of admissions, it is a reliable and accurate measure of 'opportunities' which can be used in conjunction with other research data. Admission figures are published monthly by the Department of Industry, but these figures in themselves are inadequate for campaign planning purposes because the only breakdowns published are by cinema size and the Registrar General's standard region. They do not tell us the total admission for a given period for a given selection of cinemas.

However, reasonable estimates of admissions can be made for individual cinemas because Department of Industry statistics show the percentage of capacity filled (for cinemas in each of four categories of seating capacity) and the average number of performances at these cinemas. Rank Advertising have been able to improve this further by taking into account the actual admissions to individual Rank and ABC cinemas. By deduction they can ascertain average admissions per seat per week to independent cinemas for each of 176 cells (seating capacity by region by quarter of year). By calculating a weekly admission factor for each cell and by applying this to the known seating capacity of an independent cinema, an admission figure can be calculated. Estimates of this kind for independent cinemas can be checked against actual admissions figures from certain independent cinemas who are prepared to supply them. Therefore, although admissions to individual cinemas are not available, reasonable estimates of admissions to cinemas selected for a campaign can be provided by the screen advertising industry through the co-operation of the major cinema chains and a number of independent cinemas.

However, admissions themselves are only part of the story. We need to know the nature of the audience in demographic terms and the number of people attending the cinema at least once in the campaign period, i.e. the cover of the campaign. The calculation of repetition would then be a simple matter of dividing admissions by the cover. Preferably, this information should be available for each demographic sub-group.

The major screen advertisers publish surveys concerning the cinema audience from time to time which have been useful in defining the audience in accurate terms, but the only continuous information available on the cinema audience is derived from the National Readership Survey (NRS). This survey contains three questions concerning cinema-going. These are:

1. *how often these days do you go to the cinema?*
   coded answers: twice a week or more; once a week; once a fortnight; once a month; three or four times a year; less often; never.

2. *how long ago was the last occasion you went to the cinema?*
   coded answers: within last seven days; over seven days to four weeks ago;
   over four weeks to three months ago; over three months to six months ago;
   over six months ago; can't remember.
If the answer to question two is 'within last four weeks':
3. *how many times have you been in the last four weeks?*
   coded answers: once; twice; three times; four times; five or six times; seven
   or eight times; over eight.

On the basis of these questions it is possible to classify individuals into seven
cinemagoing frequency categories based on their claimed frequency of
visiting the cinema (Q.1). This frequency distribution has been used to make
estimates of the coverage given by campaigns of varying lengths and
estimates can be made for any population sub-group classified in the NRS.
The obvious method of calculating coverage is to assign probabilities of
visiting the cinema in any given period based on an individual's claimed
frequency. Thus, those who visit the cinema once or twice a week or more
frequently have a probability of one of being covered by a one week
campaign. Those who claim to go once in two weeks have a probability of a
half, and so on. A probability estimate has to be made about the group who
visit the cinema less often than once per month.

   In a two-week campaign covering all cinemas, the following table
illustrates how cover would be calculated, assuming for the sake of simplicity
that all cinemagoers go at least once in every four weeks, and that data are
available for four groups of people. Having calculated the cover of a
campaign using all cinemas, the assumption then made is that a campaign
covering half of all admissions would have half the 'national' cover, i.e. for
the above example, 7%. Unfortunately, however, calculations of this kind are

Frequency category	Percentage of Population, say,	Probability of visit in two Weeks	Cover
1 per week	7	1	7%
1 every 2 weeks	4	1	4%
1 every 3 weeks	3	$\frac{2}{3}$	2%
1 every 4 weeks	2	$\frac{1}{2}$	1%
Total			14%

invalid because individuals tend to overestimate their cinemagoing
frequency. This can be evaluated by analysing their replies to the second
question on the survey. This shows, for example, that only 96% of the group
who claim to go twice a week or more often went to the cinema in the last four
weeks preceding the interview.

   Stephen Grey, of Computer Projects Ltd., has calculated[18] a cinemagoing
probability for each of the seven frequency claim groups and for each of a

number of demographic sub-groups. Through this work we can allocate to each individual in the survey a probability that he has visited the cinema in a four-week time-period. For those who claim to visit the cinema once a month, for example, the probability that they have been in the last four weeks is 0.617. The probabilities derived from this analysis can then be substituted for probabilities based on claimed frequency.

It can be demonstrated that the cinemagoing estimates obtained from this analysis are more accurate than estimates based on claimed frequencies. An analysis of question three produced an estimate of 15.4 million admissions in a four-week period compared with the Department of Industry estimate of 16.5 million for a similar period.

The technique developed by Grey can be used for much more sophisticated analysis. Cinema campaigns vary in length but are generally considerably longer than four weeks. It is, therefore, important to be able to estimate cover for various campaign periods. By a simulation process in which cinemagoing probabilities are derived for half-weekly periods it is possible to expand the survey information to give coverage estimates for campaigns of any length. For each individual in the survey the method adopted was to compute his probability of visiting the cinema in a half week and to allocate his visits in an 18-week period on a random basis. Thus, in the case of an individual who goes to the cinema weekly and has a probability of visiting of 0.5 in a half week, he should have made 18 visits in the chosen period. These visits would be randomly allocated to 18 half-weeks out of the total of 36. From a file of this kind it is possible to estimate the cover and repetition given by campaigns of any length up to 18 weeks for any sub-group of the population. A complete frequency distribution of opportunities to see the campaign can also be derived.

Estimates of this kind, of course, assume that the campaign is using all cinemas. The method used to relate cover to campaigns using only a proportion of cinemas is a crude one. The assumption made is that if a campaign is using, say, 50% of the total cinema potential (measured in terms of cost) it would achieve 50% of the coverage of a similar campaign using all cinemas. It would, of course, be preferable to use admissions data for the cinemas in question compared with total admissions, but this is not always readily available.

A further problem in making this type of calculation is that it assumes that everyone visits only one cinema. The assumption built into the model is that a person's frequency of visiting a particular cinema is the same as his frequency of visiting any cinema. However, about one-quarter of those who go to the cinema in a four-weekly period visit more than one and as we move from a consideration of national coverage estimates to the coverage given by a selection of cinemas we should take into account an individual's probability of visiting a particular cinema or selection of cinemas rather than any cinema. Coverage estimates made without taking this point into account are probably too low. The extent of that underestimate will depend on which cinemas are

678

actually chosen for the campaign. A cinema in the centre of a large city will attract an audience from a wide area and many of the people visiting it will do so only infrequently. On the other hand, a suburban cinema or a cinema in a small town will tend to attract the same people week after week. It follows, then, that a town centre cinema will give a wider coverage than other establishments. In order to establish the effect of this on coverage estimates, we need to know how many cinemas have been visited by each individual during the campaign period and we need more reliable admissions information.

Apart from coverage and admissions estimates, there are one or two aspects of cinema audience research which are worth a mention. First, the relationship between the total cinema audience and the advertisement audience has always been of interest to advertisers. In the cinema the two must be very close in absolute terms. As any cinemagoer knows, it is almost impossible to avoid seeing the advertisements. Anyone in the auditorium when the advertisements are being shown must be exposed to them. It is, therefore, not unreasonable to assume a one to one relation between the audience of the medium and the audience of the advertisement, though this relationship might be more reliably estimated by determining the proportion of the audience which arrives before and leaves the cinema after the advertisements are screened. The screen advertising industry has also carried out work which demonstrates the high re-call of cinema advertising which makes the medium such a potent one for its relatively small audience. Second, although we have information about the cinema audience in terms of its demographic characteristics, we do not know whether or how this varies according to the location and type of cinema or the type of film screened. Is it possible to grade films or cinemas in terms of the composition of the audience they attract? Perhaps if we knew a little more about why people go to the cinema we could move closer to answering this type of question. Third, what is the catchment area of a cinema? What determines its size and how do these areas overlap? These questions may be important for campaign planning, especially as the number of cinemas declines.

The advertisers' basic requirements are, therefore, reasonably well met so far as the cinema is concerned. The problem of the advertiser lies generally in terms of utilizing the information available. Because of the relatively low level of expenditure on cinema advertising, the amount of effort which goes into campaign planning for this medium is small compared with television and the press. However, the usefulness of analysis based on NRS data will, no doubt, encourage more advertisers to utilize the coverage estimation methods outlined in this chapter, and thus improve cinema campaign planning.

Bibliography

Chapter 1

1. PROUT, T. D. *Industrial Market Research Workbook*, Gower Press, 1973
2. ANDERSON, P. *A Monograph on Desk Research*, ISBA
3. HULL, C. *Principal Sources of Marketing Information*, Times Newspapers, 1971
4. TUPPER, E. and WILLS, G. *Sources of UK Marketing Information*, Ernest Benn, 1974
5. EDWARDS, B. *Source of Economic and Business Statistics*, Heinemann, 1972
6. DANIELS, L. M. *Business Information Sources*, University of California Press / Centre for Business Information, 1976

Chapter 2

1. GELLERMAN, S. W. *Motivation and Productivity*, American Management Association, 1963
2. LUNN, J. A. *Recent Developments in Market Segmentation*, ESOMAR Congress, 1969
3. SAMPSON, P. *An Examination of Exploratory Research Techniques*, ESOMAR Congress, 1969
4. SAMPSON, P. 'Research to Aid Personnel Selection for British Airways Cabin Staff: A Qualitative Research Approach', *Market Research Society Annual Conference, Proceedings*, March 1975
5. KING, R. H. 'A Study of the Problem of Building a Model to Simulate the Cognitive Processes of a Shopper in a Supermarket', in HAINES, G. H. *Consumer Behaviour, Learning Models of Purchasing*, The Free Press, New York, 1969
6. PALMER, J. and FAIVRE, J. P. 'The Information Processing Theory of Consumer Behaviour', *European Research*, **1**, No. 6, November 1973
7. SAMPSON, P. 'Commonsense in Qualitative Research', *Commentary*, **9**, 1, 1967
8. SHETH, J. 'The Role of Motivation Research in Consumer Psychology', *ESOMAR Seminar on Developments in Consumer Psychology*, Maidenhead, Berks, 1973
9. GOLDMAN, A. E. 'The Group Depth Interview', *Journal of Marketing*, **9**, 1, 1967
10. GORDON, W. J. J. *Synectics: the Development of Creative Capacity*, Harper and Row, New York, 1961
11. GETZELS, J. W. and JACKSON, P. W. *Creativity and Intelligence*, Wiley, New York, 1962
12. HUDSON, L. *Contrary Imaginations*, Methuen, London, 1966
13. DE BONO, E. *The Five-Day Course in Thinking*, Basic Books, New York, 1967
14. SAMPSON, P. 'Can Consumers Create New Products?', *Journal of the Market Research Society*, **12**, 1, 1970
15. COWLING, A. B. 'Use of Elicitation Technique for Producing Dimensions of Brand Choice', *Market Research Society Annual Conference, Proceedings*, March 1973
16. KELLY, G. A. *Psychology of Personal Constructs, Vols I and II*, Norton, New York, 1955
17. BANNISTER, D. 'Personal Construct Theory: a Summary and Experimental Paradigm', *Acta Psychologica*, **20**, 2, 1962

18. BANNISTER, D. 'A New Theory of Personality', in FOSS, B. M. (Ed.) *New Horizons in Psychology*, Penguin Books, London, 1966
19. FROST, W. A. K. and BRAINE, R. L. 'The Application of the Repertory Grid Technique to Problems in Market Research', *Commentary*, **9**, 3, 1967
20. BANNISTER, D. and MAIR, J. M. M. *The Evaluation of Personal Constructs*, Academic Press, London, 1968
21. RILEY, S. and PALMER, J. 'Of Attitudes and Latitudes: A Repertory Grid Study of Perceptions', *Journal of the Market Research Society*, **17**, 2, 1975
22. SAMPSON, P. 'Using the Repertory Grid Test', *Journal of Marketing Research*, **9**, 1972
23. FROST, W. A. K. 'The Development of a Technique for Television Programme Assessment', *Journal of the Market Research Society*, **11**, 1, 1969
24. CLEMENS, N. J. S. and THORTON, C. 'Evaluating Non-existing Products', *Admap*, **4**, 5, 1968
25. SAMPSON, P. 'Methods of Obtaining Salient Beliefs', Burke Marketing Research (Interscan) *Technical Note No. 4*, 1974
26. OPPENHEIM, A. M. *Questionnaire Design and Attitude Measurement*, Heinemann, London, 1966
27. CHAPLIN, J. P. *Dictionary of Psychology*, Dell, New York, 1968
28. MURSTEIN, B. I. (Ed.) *Handbook of Projective Techniques*, Basic Books, New York, 1965
29. ABELSON, H. I. 'A Role Rehearsal Technique for Exploratory Research', *Public Opinion Quarterly*, **30**, 1966
30. BERENT, P. H. 'The Depth Interview', *Journal of Advertising Research*, **6**, 2, 1962
31. WILSON, A. 'Industrial Marketing Research in Britain', *Journal of Marketing Research*, **6**, 1, 1969
32. SAMPSON, P. *A New Look at Qualitative Research*, Market Research Society Seminar on Psychological Methods in Market Research, 1967
33. BELSON, W., 'Tape Recording: Its Effect on Accuracy of Response in Survey Interviews', *Journal of Marketing Research*, **4**, 1967
34. BERELSON, B. 'Content Analysis', in Lindzey, G. (Ed.) *Handbook of Social Psychology*, Addison-Wesley, Cambridge, Mass., 1954
35. HOLSTI, O. R., LOOMBA, J. K. and NORTH, R. C. 'Content Analysis', in Lindzey, G. and Aronson, E. (Eds.) *The Handbook of Social Psychology*, Addison-Wesley, Cambridge, Mass., 1967
36. MCDONALD, C. D. P. and BLYTH, W. G. 'How to Handle Soft Data — a Linguistic Approach', *Thomson Medals and Awards for Advertising Research*, 1971
37. MCDONALD, C. D. P. 'Linguistic Coding — a New Solution to an Old Problem', *Journal of the Market Research Society*, **15**, 3, 1973
38. RING, E. 'Interpretation in Motivation Research', *ESOMAR Seminars on Developments in Consumer Psychology*, Maidenhead, Berks, 1973
39. DRAKEFORD, J. *Critical Appraisal of Pilot Techniques used Prior to Attitude Quantification*, ESOMAR seminar on attitude and motivation research, Elsinore, 1970
40. AAKER, D. A. *Multivariate Analysis in Marketing: Theory and Application*, Wadsworth Publishing Co., Belmont, Calif., 1971
41. GREEN, P. E. and CARMONE, F. J. *Multidimensional Scaling and Related Techniques in Marketing Analysis*, Marketing Science Institute / Allyn and Bacon, Cambridge, Mass., 1970
42. FROST, W. A. K. 'Cost-Effective Market Mapping Using the "Item-by-use" Concept', *ESOMAR Seminar on Diversification in the Pharmaceutical Industry*, Brussels, 1973
43. COLLINS, L. and MONTGOMERY, C. 'The Origins of Motivational Research', *British Journal of Marketing*, Summer 1969

Chapter 3

1. BELSON, W. A. *Studies in Readership*, published on behalf of the institute of Practitioners in Advertising by Business Publications Ltd., 1962
2. COX, D. R. *The Planning of Experiments*, Wiley, New York, 1958
3. HOOFNAGLE, W. S. 'Experimental Designs in Measuring the Effectiveness of Promotion', *Journal of Marketing Research*, May 1965
4. GREENHALGH, C. 'Some Techniques and Interesting Results in Discrimination Testing', *Journal of the Market Research Society*, January 1967

5. EHRENBERG, A. S. C. 'The Pattern of Consumer Purchases', *Applied Statistics*, 8, 26—41, 1959

6. COLLEY, R. H. *Defining Advertising Goals for Measured Advertising Results*, Association of National Advertisers Inc., New York, 1961

7. *Thomson Medals and Awards for Media Research*, Silver Medal papers, 1966

8. COOMBS, C. H. *A Theory of Data*, John Wiley and Sons, New York, 1964

9. ROSENBERG, M. J. and ABELSON, R. P. 'An Analysis of Cognitive Balancing' in HOVLAND, C. I. and ROSENBERG, M. J. (Eds.), *Attitude Organisation and Change*, Yale University Press, 1960

10. HENDRICKSON, A. E. *Choice Behaviour and Advertising*, ADMAP World Advertising Workshop, Southampton, October 1967

11. COWLING, A. B. and NELSON, E. H. *Predicting the Effects of Change*, Brighton Market Research Society Conference Paper, 1969

12. EHRENBERG, A. S. C. 'The Practical Meaning and Usefulness of the NBD / LSD Theory of Repeat Buying', *Applied Statistics*, 17, 17—32, 1968

13. EHRENBERG, A. S. C. and GOODHARDT, G. J. 'Practical Applications of the Duplication of Viewing Law', *Journal of the Market Research Society*, January 1969

14. ENIS, B. M. and COX, K. K. 'Ad Experiments for Management Decisions', *Journal of Advertising Research*, 15, 2, 1975

15. *The Effect of Alternative Wording on the Outcome of the EEC Referendum*, N.O.P. Market Research Ltd., February 1975

16. WOODSIDE, A. G. and WADDLE, G. C. 'Sales Effects of In-Store Advertising', *Journal of Advertising Research*, 15, 3, 1975

17. SHETH, J. A. and ROSCOE, A. M. 'Impact of Questionnaire Length, Follow-Up Methods and Geographical Location on Response Rate to a Mail Survey', *Journal of Applied Psychology*, 60, 2, 1975

18. BANKS, S. *Experimentation in Marketing*, McGraw-Hill 1965

19. CAMPBELL, D. T. and STANLEY, J. C. *Experimental and Quasi-Experimental Designs for Research*, Rand McNally and Co., 1963

Chapter 4

It has been possible here to give only a broad outline of a quite complex subject. Similarly basic treatments will be found in two complementary books on survey methods, by Moser and Katlon[2], and by Hoinville and Jowell[3].

The most comprehensive — if rather advanced — coverage is provided by Kish[4], and a less difficult treatment by Stuart[5]. A quite different, but equally valuable, treatment of sampling concepts will be found in Ehrenberg[6].

1. *National Readership Survey*, JICNARS and Research Services Ltd.

2. MOSER, C. A. and KALTON, G. G. W. *Survey Methods in Social Investigation*, Heinemann

3. HOINVILLE, G. W., JOWELL, R. M. *et al., Survey Research Practice*, Heinemann

4. KISH, L. *Survey Sampling*, John Wiley and Sons

5. STUART, A. *Basic Ideas in Scientific Sampling*, Charles Griffin and Co.

6. EHRENBERG, A. S. C. *Data Reduction*, John Wiley and Sons

Chapter 5

Further Reading

GLOCK, C. V. (Ed.) *Survey Research in the Social Sciences*, Russell Sage Foundation, New York, 1967

GARDEN, R. L. *Interviewing: Strategy, Techniques and Tactics*, Dorsey Press, Homewood, Illinois, 1975

HOINVILLE, G., JOWELL, R. M. *et al., Survey Research Practice*, Heinemann, 1978

LEMON, N. *Attitudes and their Measurement*, Batsford, 1973

LINDZEY, G. and ARONSON, E. *The Handbook of Social Psychology, Vol. 2: Research Methods,* Addison-Wesley, 1968
OPPENHEIM, A. N. *Questionnaire Design and Attitude Measurement,* Heinemann, 1966

References

1. PAYNE, S. L. *The Art of Asking Questions,* Princeton University Press, Princeton, New Jersey, 1951
2. BELSON, W. A. *Respondent Understanding of Survey Questions,* Polls, Survey Research Centre Reprint Series 40, **3,** No. 4, 1968
3. BELSON, W. A. *The Impact of Television,* London, Crosby Lockwood, 1967
4. BELSON, W. A. *Studies in Readership,* London, Business Publications, on the behalf of the IPA, 1962
5. FISHBEIN, M. (Ed.) *Readings in Attitude Theory and Measurement,* John Wiley and Sons, 1967
6. FISHBEIN, M. *Readings in Attitude Theory and Measurement, A Consideration of Beliefs and Their Role in Attitude Measurement,* John Wiley and Sons, 1967
7. McKENNELL, A. C. *Aircraft Noise Annoyance Around London (Heathrow) Airport,* Social Survey Report 337, Central Office of Information
8. BELSON, W. A. *A Study of the Effects of Reversing the Order of Presentation of Verbal Rating Scales,* Survey Research Centre Report, 1965
9. OSGOOD, C. E., SUCI, G. J. and TANNENBAUM, P. H. *The Measurement of Meaning,* Urbana, University of Illinois Press, 1957
10. JOYCE, T. *Techniques of Broad Image Measurement,* paper read at Market Research Society Annual Conference, 1963
11. THURSTONE, L. L. 'Attitudes can be measured', *American Journal of Sociology,* **33,** 529—554, 1928 (Reprinted in *Readings in Attitude Theory and Measurement,* FISHBEIN, M., (Ed.) John Wiley and Sons, 1967)
12. LIKERT, R. 'The Method of Constructing an Attitude Scale', *Readings in Attitude Theory and Measurement* FISHBEIN, M. (Ed.) John Wiley and Sons, 1967
13. STOUFFER, A. A., GUTTMANN, L., SUCHMAN, E. A., LAZARSFELD, P. F., STAR and CLAUSEN 'Studies in Social Psychology in World War II', *Measurement and Prediction* **4,** Princeton University Press, 1950
14. MORTON-WILLIAMS, J. 'Research on the Market for National Savings', Case Study No. 3 in ADLER, M. K. (Ed.) *Leading Case Histories in Market Research,* Business Books Ltd., 1971
15. McKENNELL, A. C. 'Surveying Attitude Structures: Discussion of Principles and Procedures', *Quality and Quantity,* **7,** 2, 1974
16. McKENNELL, A. C. 'Attitude Measurement: use of Coefficient Alpha with Cluster or Factor Analysis', *Sociology* **4,** 2, 1970
17. McQUITTY, L. L. 'Hierarchical Linkage Analysis for the Isolation of Types', *Educ. and Psychol. Measurement* **20,** 1960
18. HOINVILLE, G. 'Multidimensional Trade Offs: An Appraisal of the Priority Evaluator Approach' (1975 Paper awaiting publication, available from Social and Community Planning Research)
19. HOINVILLE, G. and JOWELL, R. *Classification Manual for Household Interview Surveys in Great Britain,* Social and Community Planning Research, 1969
20. *The Classification of Occupation,* HMSO, 1966
21. *National Readership Survey,* JICNAS
22. WOLFE, A. (Ed.) *Standardised Questions,* Market Research Society, 1974

Chapter 6

1. ATKINSON, J. A. *A Handbook For Interviewers,* The Government Social Survey, 1968
2. ATKINSON, P. L. and OGDEN, A. J. 'Sample Surveys at the Point-of-Sale: a Case History from the Petrol Market', *Journal of the Market Research Society,* **16,** 2
3. BELSON, W. A. *Studies in Readership,* Business Publications Ltd., 1962

4. BELSON, W. A. *Tape Recording: its Effect on Accuracy of Response in Survey Interviews*, The Survey Research Unit, the London School of Economics, 1963
5. BELSON, W. A. *Respondent Understanding of Questions in the Survey Interview*, The Survey Research Unit, The London School of Economics, 1968
6. BERENT, P. H. *Interview Recruitment and Training*, ESOMAR Congress, Evian, 1962
7. BRANDSMA, P. 'The Role and Influence of the Interviewer', *European Marketing Research Review*, **4**, 1, 1969
8. DRAKEFORD, J. F. *A Critical Appraisal of Pilot Techniques in Qualitative Research*, ESOMAR Seminar on Attitude and Motivation Research, 1970
9. FERBER, R. and WALES, H. G. 'Detection and Correction of Interviewer Bias', *Public Opinion Quarterly*, **XVI**, 1, 1952
10. HAUCK, M. and STEINKAMP, S. *Survey Reliability and Interviewer Competence*, Studies in Consumer Savings No. 4, Bureau of Economics and Business Research, University of Illinois, Urbana, 1964
11. HAUCK, M. 'Interviewer Compensation on Consumer Surveys', *Journal of the Market Research Society*, **14**, 1964
12. HORNE, A., MORGAN, J. and PAGE, J. 'Where Do We Go From Here' (Gold Medal Winning Paper), *Journal of the Market Research Society*, **16**, 3
13. HYMAN, H. *et al. Interviewing in Social Research*, Chicago, 1954
14. MCFARLANE-SMITH, J. 'Selection and Training of Interviewers', *Journal of the Market Research Society*, **12**, 2, April 1970
15. MCFARLANE-SMITH, J. *Interviewing in Market and Social Research*, Routledge and Keegan Paul, 1972
16. MARKET RESEARCH SOCIETY *First Report, Working Party on Interviewing Methods*
17. MAYER, C. S. 'Evaluating the Quality of Marketing Research Contractors', *Journal of the Market Research Society*, May 1967
18. STROTHMANN, K.-H. 'The Attitude to Interviews of Industrial Staff', *Journal of the Market Research Society (Commentary)* **VIII**, 1
19. TWIGG, J. *What is Interviewer Bias?* ESOMAR Congress, 1969

Chapter 7

1. MELHUISH, R. M. 'The use and operation of the Nielson Indices', *Journal of the European Society for Opinion and Market Research*, **1**, 64—71, 1954
2. NOWIK, H. *The use of Retailer Panel for Test Marketing*, ESOMAR Conference, 1963
3. YATES, W. A. *Shop Audits in Marketing Evaluation, Now and in the Future*, Market Research Society Conference, 1967

Chapter 8

1. PARFITT, J. H. *'Tailor-Made' Panels—Combining the Advantages of Ad Hoc Survey and Consumer Panel Methods*, ESOMAR, Montreux Conference, 1975
2. PARFITT, J. H. 'A Comparison of Purchase Recall with Diary Panel Records', *Journal of Advertising Research*, **7**, 3, September 1967
   Also *How Accurately can Product Purchasing Behaviour be Measured by Recall at a Single Interview?*, Paper 26, ESOMAR, Vienna Congress, August 1967
3. BROADBENT, S. and MOONEY, P. *Can Informant Claims on Product Purchase made at an Interview be used for Media Planning?*, Paper 14, ESOMAR, Opatija Congress, September 1968
4. COLLINS, B. J. K. and PARFITT, J. H. 'The use of Consumer Panels for Brand-share Prediction', *Journal of Marketing Research*, **V**, May 1968
   MCGLOUGHLIN, I. and PARFITT, J. H. *The use of Consumer Panels in the evaluation of promotional and advertising expenditure*, Paper 28 ESOMAR, Opatija Congress, September 1968
5. EHRENBERG, A. S. C. *Pack-Size Rates of Purchasing*, Paper 33, ESOMAR, Opatija Congress, September 1968
   EHRENBERG, A. S. C. 'The Practical Meaning and Usefulness of the NBD/LSD Theory of Repeat-Buying', *Applied Statistics*, **17**, 1968
   EHRENBERG, A. S. C. 'The Discovery and Use of Laws of Marketing', *Journal of Marketing*, **32**, 1968

Chapter 9

1. JENKINS, J. and KENDALL, J. *Formulating Quantified Objectives and Evaluating progress with Profit or Sales*, ESOMAR Conference, 1969
2. *Organisations Providing Market Research Services in Great Britain*, published annually by The Market Research Society

Chapter 10

1. MILN, D., STEWART HUNTER, D. and MARCHANT, L. *The Telephone on Consumer Research*, ESOMAR Conference Proceedings 1974, p. 229 (see also detailed Bibliography to this paper)
2. Plain Man's Guide to TGI, BMRB, 1977
3. ERDOS, P. L. *Professional Mail Survey*, McGraw-Hill, 1970
4. SCOTT, C. 'Research on Mail Surveys', *Royal Statistical Society Journal*, **124**, 2, 1961
5. ALLT, B. in Worcester, R. M. (Ed.) *Consumer Market Research Handbook, 1st edition*, McGraw-Hill, 1972
6. DAY, P. S. and DUNN, J. 'Estimating the Audience for Advertising on the Outside of Buses', *Applied Statistics*, **18**, 3, 1961
7. KONIG, G. and LOVELL, M. *The Measurement of Pupil Dilation as a Research Tool*, ESOMAR Conference Paper, 1965
8. CAFFYN, J. A. and BROWN, N. A. 'The Application of Psychological Ironmongery to Commercial Problems', *Commentary*, January 1965
9. FLETCHER, R. *Reading Behaviour Reconsidered*, ESOMAR Conference Paper, 1969
10. HOINVILLE, G. Paper given at Market Research Society Seminar Research for Social Policy, February 1970
11. MADGE, C. and HUXLEY, J. *Mass-Observation*, 1937 (see also HARRISON, T., *Pub and the People*, Gollancz, 1943; *War Begins at Home*, Chatto and Windus, 1940)
12. SELLTIZ, J. DEUTSCH and COOK *Research Methods in Social Relations*, Methuen, 1960
13. PATRICK, M. 'How to do the Washing Up in 41 Easy Stages', *Campaign* **20**, 4, 70
14. *Development of Method of Systemization of observation of Driver Behaviour*, Road Research Laboratory, LR213, 1968
15. MALINOWSKI, R. *A Nation-Wide Intelligence Service, First Year's Work*, Lindsay Drummond, 1938

Chapter 12

References

1. STUART, A. 'Standard Errors for Percentages', *Journal of the Royal Statistical Society*, Series C, Applied Statistics, **12**, No. 2, 87—101, 1963
2. COCHRAN, W. G. 'Some Methods for Strengthening the Common X^2 tests', *Biometrics*, **10**, 417—451, 1964
3. DAVID, H. A. *The Method of Paired Comparisons*, Charles Griffin
4. SCHEFFÉ, H. 'An Analysis of Variance for Paired Comparisons', *Journal of The American Statistical Association*, **47**, 381—400, 1952
5. SNEDECOR, G. W. and COCHRAN, W. G. *Statistical Methods (Sixth Edition)*, Iowa State University Press

Suggested Further Reading

FERBER, R. *Statistical Techniques in Market Research*, McGraw-Hill
QUENOUILLE, M. H. *Introductory Statistics*, Pergamon
MOOD, A. M. and GRAYBILL, F. A. *Introduction to the Theory of Statistics*, McGraw-Hill
MAXWELL, A. E. *Analysing Qualitative Data*, Methuen
SIEGEL, S. *Non-Parametric Statistics for the Behavioural Sciences*, McGraw-Hill
QUENOUILLE, M. H. *Rapid Statistical Calculations*, Charles Griffin
KENDALL, M. G. *Rank Correlation Methods*, Charles Griffin

Chapter 13

1. COLLINS, M. A. Three Approaches to a Multi-dimensional Problem, *Journal of the Market Research Society*, **11**, 3, 1969
2. KENDALL, M. G. *A Course in Multivariate Analysis, Introduction*, Chas. Griffin, 1965
3. EHRENBERG, A. S. C. 'Some Queries to Factor Analysts', *The Statistician*, **13**, 4, 1963
4. SIEGEL, S. 'Measures of Correlation and their Tests of Significance', *Non-parametric Statistics for the Behavioural Sciences*, McGraw-Hill, New York, 1956
5. HOPE, K. 'Principal Components', *Methods of Multivariate Analysis*, University of London Press, 1968
6. CHRISTOPHER, M. A. *A Cluster Analysis of Towns in England and Wales according to their Suitability for Test Market Locations*, University of Bradford Research Project Series in Marketing, 1969
7. HOLMES, C. 'Construction and Stratification of a Sampling Frame of Primary Sampling Units', *The Statistician*, **19**, 1, 1969
8. HARMAN, H. H. 'Foundation of Factor Analysis', *Modern Factor Analysis, 2nd edition*, University of Chicago Press, 1967
9. COOLEY, W. W. and LOHNES, P. R. 'Factor Analysis', *Multivariate Procedures for the Behavioural Sciences*, Wiley New York, 1962
10. LAWLEY, D. N. and MAXWELL, A. E. *Factor Analysis as a Statistical Method*, Butterworth, 1963
11. KAISER, H. F. *Comments in Communality and the Number of Factors*, Read at Conference, Washington University, St. Louis, 1960
12. THURSTONE, L. L. *Multiple Factor Analysis*, University of Chicago Press, 1947
13. HENDRICKSON, A. E. and WHITE, P. O. 'PROMAX—A Quick Method for Rotation to Simple Structure', *British Journal of Statistical Psychology*, **17**, Part 1, 1964
14. HILL, P. B. 'Multivariate Analysis—What Payoff for the Marketing Man?', *Journal of the Market Research Society*, **12**, 3, 1970
15. FROST, W. A. K. 'The Development of a Technique for TV Programme Assessment', *Journal of the Market Research Society*, **11**, 1, 1969
16. SOKAL, R. R. and SNEATH, P. H. A. *Principles of Numerical Taxonomy*, W. H. Freeman, 1963
17. JOYCE, T. and CHANNON, C. 'Classifying Market Survey Respondents', *Applied Statistics*, **XV**, 3, 1966
18. INGLIS, J. and JOHNSON, D. 'Some Observations on the Developments in the Analysis of Multivariate Survey Data', *Journal of the Market Research Society*, **12**, 2, 1970
19. EMMETT, B. P. 'The Exploration of Inter-relationships in Survey Data', *Journal of the Market Research Society*, **10**, 2, 1968
20. *Users Guide to Cluster Analysis Program*, Scientific Control Systems Ltd.
21. *CRC Cluster Analysis Program*, Cybernetics Research Consultants Ltd.
22. MORGAN, N. and PURNELL, J. M. 'Isolating Openings for New Products in a Multi-Dimensional Space', *Journal of the Market Research Society*, **11**, 3, 1969
23. *Journal of the Market Research Society*, **11**, 1, 1969
24. GREEN, P. E., CARMONE, F. J. and FOX, L. B. 'Television Programme Similarities: An Application of Subjective Clustering', *Journal of the Market Research Society*, **11**, 1, 1969
25. FERBER, R. 'Multiple Correlation Techniques', *Market Research*, McGraw-Hill, New York, 1949
26. GREEN, P. E. HALBERT, M. H. and ROBINSON, P. J. 'Canonical Analysis: An Exposition and Illustrative Application', *Journal of Marketing Research*, **3**, February, 1966
27. FRANK, R. E. and BOYD, H. W. 'Are private-brand-prone Grocery Customers Really Different?' *Journal of Advertising Research*, **5**, 4, 1965
28. BELSON, W. A. 'Principle of Biological Classification', *Applied Statistics*, **VIII**, 2, 1959
29. SONQUIST, J. A. and MORGAN, J. N. *The Detection of Interaction Effects*, Monograph 35, Survey Research Center, University of Michigan
30. NEIDELL, L. A. 'The Use of Non-metric Multi-dimensional Scaling in Marketing Analysis', *Journal of Marketing*, **33**, October 1969
31. GREEN, P. E. and FRANK, R. F. *A Manager's Guide to Marketing Research*, Wiley, New York, 1967
32. MOSER, C. A. and SCOTT, W. *British Towns — A Statistical Study of their Social and Economic Differences*, Oliver and Boyd, 1961

33. *Reader Categorisation Study: Indirect Measures of Exposure to Contents of Publications*, JICNARS, 1972
34. THOMPSON, V. R. 'Sequential Dichotomisation: Two Techniques', *The Statistician*, **XXI**, 3, 1972
35. WILLSON, E. J. 'Computational Segmentation in the Context of Multivariate Statistics and Survey Analysis', *Journal of the Market Research Society*, **16**, 2, 1974
36. SAMPSON, P. 'The Selection of Cluster Defining Variables', *Journal of the Market Research Society*, **16**, 4, 1974
37. ASSAEL, H. 'Segmenting Markets by Group Purchasing Behaviour: An Application of the A.I.D. Technique', *Journal of Marketing Research*, **VII**, May 1970
38. DOYLE, P. and MCGEE 'Perceptions of the Preferences for Alternative Convenience Foods', *Journal of Market Research Society*, **15**, 1, 1973
39. SHETH, J. N. 'The Multivariate Revolution in Marketing Research', *Journal of Marketing*, **35**, 1971

Chapter 14

1. HOLMES, C., Chapter 13 in WORCESTER, R. M. (Ed.) *Consumer Market Research Handbook*, 1st edition, McGraw-Hill, 1972
2. LUNN, J. A. 'Psychological Classification', *The Journal of the Market Research Society*, **8**, 3, 161—173, July 1966.
3. LUNN, J. A. 'Perspectives in Attitude Research', *Journal of the Market Research Society*, **11**, 3
4. STEFFLRE, V. 'Market Structure Studies: New Products for Old Markets', in FRANK BASS *et al. (Eds.) Applications of the Sciences in Marketing Management*, Wiley, New York, 1968
5. HILL, P. B. 'Multivariate Analysis—What Payoff for the Marketing Man?', *Journal of the Market Research Society*, **12**, 3, July 1970
6. SMITH, W. 'Product Differentiation and Market Segmentation as Alternative Marketing Strategies', *Journal of Marketing*, July 1956
7. LUNN, J. A. 'Market Segmentation—an Overview', in AUCAMP, J. (Ed.) *The Effective Use of Market Research Stapel Press, 1972*
8. FRANK, R., MASSY, W. and WIND, J. *Market Segmentations*, Prentice-Hall, 1972
9. BARNETT, N. L. 'Beyond Market Segmentation', *Harvard Business Review*, January–February 1969
10. HALEY, R. I. 'Benefit Segmentation: a Decision-Oriented Research Tool', *Journal of Marketing*, **32**, 30—35, July 1968
11. HANSEN, F. *Backward Segmentation using Hierarchical Clustering and Q-Factor Analysis, Proceedings of ESOMAR Seminar on Segmentation and Typology*, Brussels, 1972
12. LUNN, J. A. *Classifying Consumers in the 1970's, Proceedings of ESOMAR Seminar on Segmentation and Typology*, Brussels, 1972
13. BROADBENT, S. and MASSON, P. 'Informant Classification in Media and Product Surveys', *Admap*, January 1969
14. JAIN, S. C. *Life Cycle Revisited: Applications in Consumer Research, Proceedings of the 5th Annual Conference of the Association for Consumer Research*, 1975
15. AGOSTINI, J. M. 'New Criteria for Classifying Informants in Market Research and Media Strategy', *Admap.*, **3**, 9, 1967
16. BELK, R. W. 'Situational Variables and Consumer Behaviour', *Journal of Consumer Research*, **2**, 3, 1975
17. TWEDT, D. W. 'How Important to Marketing Strategy is the "Heavy Half" Theory?' *Journal of Marketing*, **28**, 1, 1964
18. FRANK, R. E. *But the Heavy Half is Already the Heavy Half*, Paper presented to the American Marketing Association's Conference in Philadelphia, June 17—19, 1968
19. MASSY, W. F., FRANK, R. J. and LOUDAHL, T. M. *Purchasing Behaviour and Personal Attributes*, University of Pennsylvania Press, Philadelphia, 1968
20. BASS, F. M., PESSEMEIR, E. A. and TIGART, D. J. 'Complementary and Substitute Patterns of Purchasing and Use', *Journal of Advertising Research*, **9**, 2, 1969
21. WELLS, W. D. (Ed.) *Life Style and Psychographics*, American Marketing Association, 1974
22. MONK, D. 'Burnett Life Style Research', *European Research*, **1**, 14—19, 1973

23. SEGNIT, S. *Practical Applications of Life Style Research*, paper given at the Seminar on 'The Life Style Concept in Marketing' organised by the Market Research Society and the College for the Distributive Trades, London1975
24. WELLS, W. D. 'Psychographics: A Critical Review', *Journal of Marketing Research*, **12**, 196—213, 1975
25. HOWARD, J. A. and SHETH, J. N. *The Theory of Buyer Behaviour*, Wiley, New York, 1969
26. BALDWIN, E. S. and LUNN, J. A. *Researching the Changing Consumer, Proceedings of the ESOMAR Annual Conference*, 1972
27. BEAZLEY, D. and LUNN, J. A. *Shopping Styles and Strategies and their Relationships to In-Store Factors, Proceedings of ESOMAR Seminar on Management Information for Retail Organisations*, Lucerne, 1974
28. WINKLER, A. 'Problems in Connection with the Use of Segmentation Methods with Examples from the Field of Consumer Goods', in DURAND, J. (Ed.) *Market Segmentation*, papers from the conference organized by ADETEM, Paris, March 1969
29. SONQUIST, J. A. and MORGAN, J. N. *The Detection of Interaction Effects*, Monograph No. 35, Survey Research Centre, University of Michigan, 1964
30. NUNNALY, J. *Psychometric Theory*, McGraw-Hill, 1967
31. KOGAN, M. and WALLACE, J. C. 'A New Coefficient for Cluster Discrimination', *Australian Journal of Psychology*, **6**, 1969
32. HELLER, H. E. 'Defining Target Markets by their Attitude Profiles', in ADLER, L. and CRESPI, I. (Eds.) *Attitude Research on the Rocks*, American Marketing Association, 1968
33. SHERAK, B. 'A Beer Segmentation and Brand Mapping Study', in DURAND, J. (Ed.) *Market Segmentation*, papers from the conference organized by ADETEM. Paris, March 1969
34. HENDRICKSON, A. E. *Choice Behaviour and Advertising: A Theory and Two Models*, paper read at the Admap World Advertising Workshop, Southampton, October 18—22, 1967
35. FRANK, R. E. 'Market Segmentation Research: Findings and Implications', in FRANK, BASS et al. (Eds.) *Applications of the Sciences in Marketing Management*, Wiley, New York, 1968
36. MOSS, M. *A Marketing Man's View of Research*, paper given at MRS Annual Conference, Brighton, 1967
37. BEAZLEY, D. 'Alternative Approaches to Brand Positioning Research: How Do We Choose?' in GREEN, P. E. and CHRISTOPHER, M. (Eds.) *Brand Positioning*, Cranfield Institute of Technology, UK, 1973
38. MORGAN, N. and PURNELL, J. M. 'Isolating Openings for New Products in a Multi-dimensionsl Space', *Journal of the Market Research Society*, **11**, 3, 245—266, 1969
39. BUCKLE, M. and HUGHES-HALLETT, A. *Getting the Best out of Brand Image Work, Proceedings of ESOMAR Annual Conference*, 1975
40. GREEN, P. E. and TULL, D. S. *Research for Marketing Decisions*, Prentice Hall, New Jersey, 1978
41. LUNN, J. A. *Attitudes and Behaviour in Consumer Research: a Re-appraisal, Proceedings of ESOMAR Seminar on Attitude and Motivation Research*, 1970
42. NICOSIA, F. M. *Consumer Decision Processes*, Prentice-Hall, New Jersey, 1968
43. SHETH, J. N. *Relevance of Segmentation for Market Planning, Proceedings of ESOMAR Seminar on Segmentation and Typology*, Brussels, 1972
44. TWIGG, J. and WOLFE, A. 'Problems of Communicating the Results of Market Segmentation Studies', *Journal of the Market Research Society*. **10**, 4, 264—278, October 1968

Chapter 15

Comprehensive Descriptions of New Product Development Procedures

1. BOYD, H. W. and WESTFALL, R. 'Product Research', in *Marketing Research: Text and Cases*, Richard D. Irwin, 1964
2. KING, S. J. *Developing New Brands*, Pitman 1973
3. KRAUSHAR, P. M. *New Products and Diversification*, Business Books Ltd., 1969
4. LUCK, D. J., WALES, H. G. and TAYLOR, D. A. 'New Product Research', in *Marketing Research*, Prentice-Hall, 1961
5. SMITH-WARDEN LTD. *Product Assessment Decision Series*, 1968
6. WOOD, J. F. New Product Development, *Admap*, 3, 1—10, 1967

Specific Techniques Referred to in this Chapter

7. GREENHALGH, C. *Generating New Product Ideas: a Review Paper*, ESOMAR, 1971
8. TAUBER, E. M. 'Heuristic Ideation Technique — A Systematic Procedure for New Product Search', *Journal of Marketing*, **36**, 1, 1972
9. LANITIS, T. 'How to Generate New Product Ideas', *Journal of Advertising Research*, **10**, 3, 1970
10. TAUBER, C. M. 'Discovering New Product Opportunities with Problem Inventory Analysis', *Journal of Marketing*, **39**, 1, 1975
11. GOODYEAR, J. R. 'Qualitative Research Studies', in AUCAMP, J. (Ed.) *The Effective Use of Market Research*, Staples Press, 1971
12. BROWN, L. O. 'Product Research', in *Marketing and Distribution Research*, Ronald Press 1955
13. KUEHN, A. and DAY, R. L. 'Strategy of Product Quality', *Harvard Business Review*, **40**, 6, 1962
14. BARNETT, N. L. 'Beyond Market Segmentation', *Harvard Business Review*, **47**, 1, 1969
15. CLEMENS, N. J. S. and THORNTON, C. 'Evaluating Non-Existent Products', *Admap*, **4**, 5, 1968
16. O'MULLOY, J. B. 'Research and the Development of New Products', *Admap*, **5**, 8, 1969
17. MORGAN, N. and PURNELL, J. M. 'Isolating Openings for New Products, *Journal of the Market Research Society*, **11**, 3, 1969
18. ROTHMAN, L. J. and TATE, B. Research Techniques for Minority or Maniple Marketing, in *Research in Marketing*, Market Research Society, 1964
19. STEFFLRE, V. 'Market Structure Studies: New Products for Old Markets', in BASS, F. *et al.* (Eds.) *Applications of the Sciences in Marketing Management*, Wiley, New York, 1968
20. THORNTON, C. *Ranking New Product Openings in Multi-Dimensional Space*, Market Research Society Conference, 1970
21. CLUNIES-ROSS, C. 'Different Uses of Market Segmentation', In AUCAMP, J. (Ed.) *The Effective Use of Market Research*, Staples Press, 1971
22. SKELLY, F. and NELSON, E. H. 'Market Segmentation and New Product Development', *Scientific Business*, **4**, 13, 1966
23. GORDON, W. J. J. *Synectics*, Harper and Row, 1961
24. HAEFELL, J. W. *Creativity and Invention*, Reinhold, 1962
25. SAMPSON, P. 'Can Consumers Create New Products?', *Journal of the Market Research Society*, **12**, 1, 1970
26. NATIONAL INDUSTRIAL CONFERENCE BOARD, *New Product Development* (Studies in Business Policy No. 69), NICB, 1954
27. WILSON, A. 'Selecting New Products for Development', *Scientific Business*, **1**, 3, 1963
28. SHERAK, B. *Testing New Product Ideas* 1966
29. KING, S. J. 'How Useful is Proposition Testing?' *Advertising Quarterly*, Winter 1965 / 66
30. LOVELL, M. R. C., JOHNS, S. and RAMPLEY, B. 'The Pre-Testing of Press Advertisements', *Admap*, **4**, 3, 1968
31. HENRY, H. *Motivation Research*, Crosby Lockwood, 1963
32. IUSO, W. 'Concept Testing: An Appropriate Approach', *Journal of Marketing Research*, **12**, 2, 1975
33. CAFFYN, J. M. and LOYD, A. *Predicting Effects of Brand Name and Consumer Proposition on Consumer Purchase Decisions: A Case History*, ESOMAR, 1968
34. JOHNSON, R. M. 'Trade-off Analysis of Consumer Values', *Journal of Marketing Research*, **11**, 2, 1974
35. WESTWOOD, R., LUNN, A. J. and BEAZLEY, D. 'The Trade-off Model and its Extensions', *Journal of the Market Research Society*, **16**, 3, 1974
36. TAUBER, E. M. 'Reduce New Product Failures: Measure Needs as well as Product Interest', *Journal of Marketing*, **37**, 3, 1973
37. TWEDT, D. W. 'How to Plan New Products, Improve Old Ones and Create Better Advertising', *Journal of Marketing*, **33**, 1, 1969
38. COLLINS, M. 'Product Testing', in AUCAMP, J. (Ed.) *The Effective Use of Market Research*, Staples Press, 1971
39. CLARKE, T. J. 'Product Testing in New Product Development', *Journal of the Market Research Society*, **9**, 3, 1967
40. PENNY, J. C., HUNT, I. M. and TWYMAN, W. A. 'Product Testing Methodology' in 'Relation to Marketing Problems: a Review', *Journal of the Market Research Society*, **14**, 1, 1972

41. BROWN, G., COPELAND, A. and MILLWARD, M. 'Monadic Testing of New Products — an Old Problem and some New Solutions', *Journal of the Market Research Society*, **15**, 2, 1973
42. KONDOS, A. and CLUNIES-ROSS, C. *Sources of Bias in Sensory Evaluations as Applied to Food and Beverages*, ESOMAR, 1966
43. DIETZ, L. 'Projective Techniques Applied', in *The Human Equation in Marketing Research*, American Management Association, 1967
44. DEAN, J. P. 'Pricing Policies for New Products', *Harvard Business Review*, **28**, 6, 1950
45. TAYLOR, B. and WILLS, G. *Pricing Strategy*, Staples Press, 1969
46. GABOR, A. and GRANGER, G. 'The Pricing of New Products', in TAYLOR, B. and WILLS, G. (Eds.) *Pricing Strategy*, Staples Press, 1969
47. KRAUSHAR, P. M. and SOWTER, A. P. *Pricing Research*, Market Research Society Conference, 1972
48. MILN, D. A. and TOPPING, N. *An Application of Market Research to Pricing and Price Elasticity*, Market Research Society Conference, 1971
49. GREENHALGH, C. 'Some Techniques and Interesting Results in Discrimination Testing', *Journal of the Market Research Society*, **8**, 4, 1966
50. GREENHALGH, C. *Discrimination Testing: Further Results and Developments*, ESOMAR, 1970

Chapter 16

References

1. LOVELL, M. R. C. and LANNON, J. M. *Difficulties with Recall*, ESOMAR, WAPOR Congress, August 1967
2. AXELROD, J. N. 'Attitude Measures that Predict Purchase', *Journal of Advertising Research*, March 1968

The divisions between 'Theoretical' and 'Practical' are arbitrary, and signify degree, rather than category.

Theoretical

APPEL, V. and BLUM, M. 'Ad Recognition and Respondent Set', *Journal of Advertising Research*, **1**, 4, June 1961
DEMBAR, W. N. *Psychology of Perception*, Holt, New York, 1965
HASKINS, J. B. 'Factual Recall as a Measure of Advertising Effectiveness', *Journal of Advertising Research*, **4**, 1, March 1964
HEDGES, A. *Testing to Destruction*, Institute of Practitioners in Advertising, London, 1974
JOYCE, T. *What do we Know about the Way Advertising Works?*, ESOMAR Seminar, 1967
KING, S. 'How Useful is Proposition Testing?' *Advertising Quarterly*, Winter 1965 / 6
KRUGMANN, H. E. 'The Measurement of Advertising Involvement', *Public Opinion Quarterly*, Winter 1966—67
LEAVITT, C. *Classic Models of Communication Effects and Innovations in These Models*, Annual Conference of American Association for Public Opinion Research, May 1970
LOVELL, M. R. C. and LANNON, J. M. *Difficulties with Recall*, ESOMAR WAPOR Congress, August 1967
LOVELL, M. R. C., JOHNS, S. and RAMPLEY, B. 'Pre-testing Press Advertisements', The Thomson awards for Advertising, *Research*, 1967
LUCAS, D. B. 'The ABC's of ARF's PARM', *Journal of Marketing*, July 1960
MORGENSZTERN, A. *How to Determine the Optimum Screening Frequency of a Movie Commercial*, ESOMAR, 1967
WELLS, W. D. 'How Chronic Overclaimers Distort Survey Findings', *Journal of Advertising Research*, **3**, 2, June 1963

Practical

AXELROD, J. N. 'Attitude Measures that Predict Purchase', *Journal of Advertising Research*, March 1968

BUCHANAN, D. I. 'How Interest in the Product Affects Recall: Print Ads. vs. Commercials', *Journal of Advertising Research*, March 1964

CAFFYN, J. M. and BROWN, N. A. *The Application of Psychological Ironmongery to Commercial Problems*, ESOMAR Congress, 1964

HESS, E. 'Attitudes and Pupil Size', *Scientific American*, April 1965

KING, S. 'Can Research Evaluate the Creative Content of Advertising?' *Admap*, June 1967

KONIG, G., LAKASCHUS, C. and LOVELL, M. R. C. *The Management of Pupil Dilation as a Market Research Tool*, ESOMAR-WAPOR Congress, September 1965

POTTER, J. 'Commercial Pre-testing', *Admap*, September 1971

SEGNIT, S. and BROADBENT, S. R. *Area Tests and Consumer Surveys to Measure Advertising Effectiveness*, ESOMAR Congress, 1970

STARCH, D. Measuring the Effect of Advertising on Sales (5 articles) *Printers Ink*, March—May 1964

WINICK, C. 'Three Measures of the Advertising Value of Media Context, *Journal of Advertising Research*, **2**, 2, June 1962

WOOD, J. F. 'Pre-testing the Advertising', *Admap*, Sepember 1967

See also

LOVELL, M. R. C. and POTTER, J. *Assessing the Effectiveness of Advertising*, Business Books, London, 1975

Chapter 17

Books

ADLER, M. K. *Marketing and Market Research*, 1967 (see section p. 277, 'Package Tests Are Fashionable': refers to visual instrumentation and other psychological and physiological tests)

AGNEW, H. E. and HOUGHTON, D. *Marketing Policies, 2nd edition*, 1951 (see p. 363, Chapter 'Package Sales Tests')

CORAM, T. (ed.) *Cases in Marketing and Marketing Research*, 1969 (see section 11, p. 92, David Greig Package Designs contributed by Gordon Wills article in *Packaging*, January 1967)

GILMER, VON HALLER, *Psychology*, 1970

HEPNER, H. W. *Advertising—Creative Communication with Consumers*, 1964 (see pp. 199—201, 205—206)

LEDUC, R. *How to Launch a New Product*, 1966 (see p. 61 for package-testing)

LE GRAND, Y. *Form and Space Vision*, 1967 (see chapter 10 pp. 158—177, 'Movements to the Eye' for discussion of different types of experimental method in this connection, including instruments and apparatus; also findings)

RODGER, L. W. *Marketing in a Competitive Economy*, 1965 (see p. 120, ratings chart, p. 124 section on 'Test Marketing'. Text and charts include package research under product research)

On Packaging

INSTITUTE OF PACKAGING, *Fundamentals of Packaging*, 1962

GRAY, M., *Package Design*, 1955 (chapter 2, 'The Science of Distribution')

GUSS, L. M. *Packaging Is Marketing*, AMA, 1967

JONES, H. *Planned Packaging*, 1950 (see chapter 17, p. 89, 'The Value of Research')

PILDITCH, J. *The Silent Salesman*, 1973 (see chapter 8, 'When to Use Research', pp. 85—97.)

On Motivational and Visual Research

BERLYNE, D. E. *Conflict Arousal and Curiosity*, 1960

CHESKIN, L. *Basis for marketing decision through controlled motivation research*, 1962; *Color for Profit*, 1951; *Colours and what they can do*, 1951; *Why People Buy*, 1960

CIRLOT, *A Dictionary of Symbols*, English translation, 1962

DICHTER, E. *The Strategy of Desire*, 1960; *Handbook of Consumer Motivations*, 1964

Articles and Papers

BERLYNE, D. E. 'Conflict and Information Theory Variables as Determinants of Human Perceptual Curiosity', *J. Exp. Psychol.*, **53**, 1957

BERLYNE, D. E. 'Influence of Complexity and Novelty in Visual Figures on Orienting Responses', *J. Exp. Psychol.*, **55**, 1958

BERLYNE, D. E. 'Complexity and Incongruity Variables as Determinants of Exploratory Choice and Evaluative Ratings', *Canad. J. Psychol.*, **17**, 1963

BERLYNE, D. E., CRAW, M. A., SALAPAIER, P. H. and LEWIS, J. L. 'Novelty, Complexity, Incongruity, Extrinsic Movitation and the GSR', *J. Exp. Psychol.*, **66**, 1963

BERLYNE, D. E. and PECKHAM, S. 'The Semantic Differential and Other Measures of Reaction to Visual Complexity', *Canad. J. Psychol.*, **20**, 1966

DILLON, P. J. *The Tachistoscopic Falacy: a Case of Invalid Research*, paper given to Market Research Society Annual Conference (UK), March 1969

ENOCH, J. M. 'Effect of the Size of a Complex Display upon Visual Search', *J. Opt. Soc. Amer.*, **49**, 1959 (Use of 'opthalmograph unit')

FORD, A., WHITE, C. J. and LICHTENSTEIN, M. 'Analysis of Eye-Movements during Free Search', *J. Opt. Soc. Amer.*, **49**, 1959 (use of electrodes, cathode ray oscilloscope and automatic camera to obtain electro-oculographic plots of eyeball movements)

FLETCHER, R. and MABEY, B. 'Effects of Set and Expectation in Tachistoscope Testing', *Admap*, January 1970

GOULD, J. D. and SCHAFFER, A. 'Eye-Movement Patterns in Scanning Numberic Displays', *Perceptual and Motor Skills*, **20**, 1965 (excerpt from this comprises reading twenty-four from M. D. Vernon *Experiments in Visual Perception*, q.v.)

JAHODA, G. 'Sex Differences in Preference for Shapes: a Cross-Cultural Replication', *Brit. J. Psychol.*, **47**, 1956

MACKWORTH, J. F. and MACKWORTH, N. H. 'Eye Fixations Recorded on Changing Visual Scenes by the Television Eye-marker', *J. Opt. Soc. Amer.*, **48**, 1958 (use of television camera to record the position of a man's gaze, use of second television camera to record scene he is looking at, and television monitor showing same scene: total composite eye-scene picture recorded with motion-picture camera: primarily intended for use with moving display)

MACKWORTH, N. H. and LLEWELLYN-THOMAS, E. 'Head-mounted Eye-market Camera', *J. Opt. Soc. Amer.*, **52**, 1962 (device consists of a small move camera and a periscope that transmits a spot of light reflected from the eye)

NEISSER, U. 'Decision without Reaction Time: Experiments in Visual Scanning', *Amer. J. Psychol.*, **76**, 1963

POTTER, J. 'Packaging Research: Is It Adequate?', *Advertisers Weekly*, 21 July 1967

ROCHE, M., LODGE, G. and YASIN, J. 'A Pre-test Market Programme', *Admap*, April 1970

SCHLACKMAN, W. 'Evaluating the Pack Design in Marketing', *Scientific Business*, 1963

TINKER, M. 'Recent Studies of Eye Movements in Reading', *Psychol. Bull.*, **55**, 1958

Pamphlets

(a) AMA Management Bulletins

Especially:

No. 53, 1964: *The Package: Key Components of Marketing Strategy*, Articles by Murphy and Gee

No. 96, 1967: *The Uses of Imagination in Packaging*, Articles by Siebel, Hoffman, and Solomon

No. 106, 1968: *Consumer Oriented Packaging*, Articles by Goldberg, Mahaney, Friedman, and Wuerther

No. 118, 1968: *Effective Beverage Marketing through Better Packaging*, Artilces by Glazier and Bergwall

(b) Other Publications

AMA Management Report No. 65, 1961: *The Power of Packaging*, See Part III, Consumer Packaging, articles by Barksdale and Thomas

AMA Packaging Series No. 53, 1957: *Marketing Research Reports on Packaging*, Articles by Nielsen and Trelogan

Institute of Packaging Advisory Service Report No. 350, 1960: *Fundamentals of Packaging*
'How Much Value can be Added by Packaging?' *Journal of Marketing*, January 1968
'The Coming Battle of the Packages', *Sales Management*, 4 May 1962

Chapter 18

References

1. SIMMONS, M. 'Evaluating Promotions: a New Syndicated Method', *Advertising Management*, February 1968
2. PARFITT, J. and McGLOUGHLIN, I. 'The Use of Consumer Panels in the Evaluation of Promotions', *Admap*, December 1968
3. EHRENBERG, A. S. C. and GOODHARDT, G. J. *Evaluating a Consumer Deal*, extracts from a case-study for the J. Walter Thompson Co.
4. BARNES, M. C. J., McDONALD, C. D. P. and TUCK, R. T. J. *Evaluating 'Below the Line' Expenditure*, The Thomson Medals and Awards for Advertising Research, 1969
5. SIMMONS, M. 'Point-of-Sale Advertising', *Journal of the Market Research Society*, **10**, 2, April 1968

Bibliography

SAMPSON, P. and HOOPER, B. *Evaluating 'Below the Line' Expenditure*, The Thomson Medals and Awards for Advertising Research, 1969
KENNEDY, R. W. 'Merchandising and Point-of-Sale Evaluation', *Advertising Management*, April 1968
WEBER, J. H. 'Can the Results of Sales Promotion be Predicted?,' *Journal of Marketing*, January 1963
'Retailer Attitudes to Promotions', *The Grocer*, 6 July 1968
HEARNE, J. J. 'Does 'Below the Line' Promotion Pay?' *The Financial Times*, 4 July 1968
ALTMAN, W. 'The Point of Point-of-Sale', *Marketing*, March 1969
CHRISTOPHER, M. 'The Whys and Wherefores of Below the Line', *The Financial Times*, 3 July 1969
'Buyers Attitudes to Below-the-Line', *The Grocer*, 1 June 1968
WILLETT, R. P. and KOLLAT, D. T. 'Customer Impulse Purchasing Behaviour: Some Research Notes and a Reply', *Journal of Marketing Research*, **V**, February 1967
HOOFNAGLE, W. S. 'Experimental Designs in Measuring the Effectiveness of Promotion', *Journal of Marketing Research*, **11**, May 1965
ADLER, E. *The neglect of Promotions Research During Economic Recession and Expansion*, Market Research Society Conference, April 1978

Chapter 19

References

1. CHRISTOPHER, M. *A Cluster Analysis of Towns in England and Wales According to their Suitability for Test Market Locations*, University of Bradford Management Centre, 1969
2. SCHLAIFER, R. *Probability and Statistics for Business Decisions*, McGraw-Hill, New York, 1959
3. DAVIS, E. J. *Experimental Marketing*, Nelson, 1970

Further Reading

GOLD, J. A. 'Testing Test Market Predictions', *Journal of Marketing Research*, August 1964
GREEN, P. E. and FRANK, R. E. 'Bayesian Statistics and Marketing Research', *Journal of the Royal Statistical Society*, Series C, **XV3**, November 1966

PARFITT, J. H. and COLLINS, B. J. K. 'The Use of Consumer Panels for Brand-Share Prediction', *Journal of Marketing Research*, May 1968

PYMONT, B. C. *The Development and Application of a New Micro Market Testing Technique*, ESOMAR Congress Papers, 1970

WILLS, G. 'Cost Benefit of a Test Market', *Management Decision*, Winter 1967

'Test Marketing Reduces Risks', *The Nielsen Researcher* (Oxford edition), January—February 1973

Chapter 20

1. PALMER, J. *A Survey of Market Modelling Practice*, Proceedings of ESOMAR Seminar on Market Modelling (Part 1), 1975
2. LUNN, J. A. *A Review of Consumer Decision Process Models*, Proceedings of ESOMAR Annual Conference, 1971, reprinted in SHETH, J. N. (Ed.) 1974 (reference 6)
3. LUNN, J. A. 'Applications of Behavioural Models to the Study of Individual Consumers', in NICOSIA, F. M. and WIND, Y. (Eds.) *The Uses of Theories and Models in Marketing. An Introduction*, Dryden Press, Illinois, 1977
4. KOTLER, J. A. *Marketing Decision-Making: A Model Building Approach*, Holt Rinehart and Winston, New York, 1971
5. MASSY, W. F., MONTGOMERY, D. B. and MORRISON, D. G. *Stochastic Models of Buying Behaviour*, MIT Press, Cambridge, Mass., 1970
6. SHETH, J. N. *Models of Buyer Behaviour: Conceptual, Quantitative and Empirical*, Harper and Row, New York, 1974
7. NICOSIA, F. M. and WIND, Y. (Eds.) *The Uses of Theories and Models in Marketing: An Introduction*, Dryden Press, Illinois, 1977
8. ROTHMAN, J. 'Experimental Designs and Models', chapter 3, in WORECESTER, R. M. (Ed.) *Consumer Market Research Handbook*, McGraw-Hill, 1972
9. FAIVRE, J. P. *Consumer Models as a Way to Improve Management Decision Making*, Proceedings of ESOMAR Seminar on Development in Consumer Psychology, 1973
10. ZALTMAN, G. 'The Structure and Purpose of Marketing Models', in NICOSIA, F. M. and WIND, Y. (Eds.) *The Uses of Theories and Models in Marketing: An Introduction*, Dryden Press, Illinois, 1977
11. WESTWOOD, R. A., LUNN, J. A. and BEAZLEY, D. 'The Trade-off Model and its Extensions', *Journal of the Market Research Society*, **16**, 3, 227—241, 1974
12. HOWARD, J. A. and SHETH, J. N. *The Theory of Buyer Behaviour*, John Wiley, New York, 1969
13. ZALTMAN, G., PINSON, C. R. A. and ANGELMAN, R. *Metatheory and Consumer Research*, Holt, Rinehart and Winston, New York, 1973
14. SAMPSON, P. *Consumer Behaviour Prediction and the Modelling Approach*, Proceedings of the ESOMAR Annual Conference, 1974
15. BETTMAN, J. R. and JONES, J. M. 'Formal Models of Consumer Behaviour: A Conceptual Overview', *Journal of Business*, **45**, 4
16. NICOSIA, F. M. 'Brand Choice: Toward Behaviour — Behaviouristic Models' in DAVIS, H. L. (Ed.) *Behavioural and Management Science in Marketing*, Ronald Press, New York, 1976
17. EHRENBERG, A. S. C. 'Towards an integrated Theory of Consumer Behaviour', *Journal of the Market Research Society*, **11**, 4, 305—337, 1969
18. WILKIE, W. L. and PESSEMIER, G. A. 'Issues in Marketing's Use of Multi-Attribute Attitude Models', *Journal of Marketing Research*, **10**, 4, 428—491, 1973
19. FISHBEIN, M. *Belief, Attitude, Intention and Behaviour: An Introduction to Theory and Research Reading*, Addison-Wesley, New York, 1975
20. ENGEL, J. F., KOLLAT, D. T. and BLACKWELL, R. D. *Consumer Behaviour*, Holt, Rinehart and Winston, New York, 1972
21. NICOSIA, F. M. *Consumer Decision Processes*, Prentice Hall, New Jersey, 1966
22. JACOBY, J. 'Consumer Psychology as a Social Psychological Sphere of Action', *American Psychologist*, October 1975
23. SHETH, J. N. 'The Next Decade of Buyer Behaviour Theory and Research', in SHETH, J. N. (Ed.) *'Models of Buyer Behaviour*, Harper and Row, New York, 1974

24. McGuire, W. J. *The Guiding Theories Behind Attitude Change Research*, Proceedings of the Third Annual Attitude Research Conference, American Marketing Association, 1970
25. Palmer, J. and Faivre, J. P. 'The Information Processing Theory of Consumer Behaviour', *European Research*, **1**, 6, 1973
26. Hughes, G. D. and Ray, M. (Eds.) *Buyer/Consumer Information Processing*, University of North Carolina Press, Chapel Hill, 1974
27. Lunn, J. A. and Beazley, D. *The Role of the Threshold Model in the Assessment of Belief Importance and in Conumer Information Processing*, Proceedings of the ESOMAR Seminar on Market Modelling (Part 1), 1975
28. Beazley, D. and Westwood, R. A. *Modelling Choice Behaviour*, Proceedings of the Market Research Society Annual Conference, 1976
29. Van Raaij, W. F. *Evaluation Process Models: An Overview*, Proceedings of the ESOMAR Seminar on Market Modelling (Part 1), 1975)
30. Westwood, P. A., Lunn, J. A. and Beazley, D. 'Models and Modelling: Part 1, New Approaches to Measuring Belief Importance', *European Research*, **2**, 3, 1974
31. Little, J. D. C. 'Models and Managers: The Concept of a Decision Calculus', *Management Science*, **16**, 8, 1970
32. Gunter, P. and Beazley, D. *An Application of Micro-Simulation Modelling to the Marketing of a Consumer Durable*, Proceedings of the ESOMAR Annual Conference, 1976
33. Palmer, J. B. *Structures of Buyer Behaviour*, Proceedings of ESOMAR Seminar on Developments in Consumer Behaviour, 1973
34. Faivre, J. P. and Sanchez, C. *The Validation of Marketing Models*, Proceedings of the ESOMAR Conference on Market Modelling (Part 1), 1975
35. Westwood, R. A., Lunn, J. A. and Beazley, D. 'Models and Modelling: Part II, Modelling Markets for Management Decision', *European Research*, **2**, 4, 186—189, 1974
36. Lunn, J. A. and Blackston, M. *Micro Behavioural Modelling as a Cost Effective Tool*, Paper to be given at the 1978 ESOMAR Annual Congress
37. Oppedijk van Veen, W. M. and Beazley, D. 'An Investigation of Alternative Methods of Applying the Trade-Off Model', *Journal of the Market Research Society*, **19**, 1, 1977

Chapter 21

1. Macleod, J. S. *The Marketing Power of Brand and Corporate Images*, Opinion Research Corporation, December 1961
2. Brien, A. 'Pleasure', *Punch*, 648, 22 October 1969
3. Lowe Watson, D. *Advertising and the Buyer / Seller Relationship*, IPA Thesis Competition, 1967
4. Burnett, L. 'Advertising', *The New York Times*, 14 December 1969
5. Paterson, W. 'Try to Use the Same Language', *IAM* 12—14 June 1970
6. Shaw, J. F. *Trust Houses Forte: A Case Study in Corporate Advertising*, Thames Television Limited, 1974
7. Pilditch, J. *Communication by Design*, McGraw-Hill, 1970
8. Roberts, L. D. Letter to the Editor, *The Financial Times*, 19 March 1970
9. Worcester, R. M. and Cook, L. 'Do you know what your employees think?' *Delta Review*, 21—23, Summer 1975

Chapter 22

1. *How does Britain save?* The Stock Exchange Council, 1966
2. *Savings and Investments*, The Building Societies Association, 1969
3. *The GEC bid for AEI*, J. Walter Thompson's, 1969
4. 'Business Opinions' Taylor Nelson Group; and printed monthly in the *Financial Times*
5. *The Target Group Index*, British Market Research Bureau, annually
6. *Applied Economics*, Glynn, August 1969
7. *CBI Review*, Price, 1974
8. *NIES Review*, August 1975

9. Proceeding of the CIRET Conferences in 1970 and 1974
10. 'Financial Expectations', British Market Research Bureau, and printed monthly in the *Financial Times*
11. Proceedings of the ESOMAR Annual Congress, 1975
12. Proceedings of the ESOMAR 'Financial and Banking' seminar, January 1975
13. Savings, Investment and Insurance Market Surveys, NOP, 1969—71
14. WORCESTER, R. M. 'Marketing Research for Financial Services', chapter 20 in HANDSCOMBE, R. (Ed.) *Bankers' Management Handbook*

Chapter 23

1. ALLEN, D. E. *British Tastes*, Hutchinson, London, 1968
2. BERENT, P. H. 'International Research is Different', *A.M.A. Conference*, USA, April 1975
3. COLEMAN, K. M. H. 'The Problem of International Pharmaceutical Marketing Research', *ESOMAR Seminar on Practice and Problems of International Pharmaceutical Research*, 1971
4. CZARTORYSKI, R. 'Research Before You Leap', *Trade and Industry*, 28 February 1975
5. DAY, R. 'The Meaning of "Comparability" in Multi-Country Research and How to Achieve It', *ESOMAR Congress paper*, 1966
6. DE JONG, P. and MEYERS, F. 'Some Reflections on the Measurement of Basic Attitudes in a Multi-Country Context', *ESOMAR Seminar on Multi-Country Research*, 1971
7. DOUGLAS, S. and WIND, Y. 'Environmental Factors and Marketing Practices', *European Journal of Marketing*, 7, 3, 1973 / 4
8. DOWNHAM, J. S. 'Marketing Research in the Multi-National Corporations', *A.M.A. Conference*, USA, April 1972
9. *Europe Today*, The Reader's Digest, London, 1970
10. *European Guide to Industrial Marketing Consultancy* (contains a section on the use and selection of consultants and a list of firms), Industrial Marketing Research Association, Lichfield, UK, 1975
11. *Export Marketing Research Scheme* (leaflet), British Overseas Trade Board, London, 1976
12. HANSZ, J. E. and GOODNOW, J. D. 'A Multivariate Classification of Overseas Country Market Environments', *A.M.A. Conference*, USA, April 1972
13. *International Directory of Market Research Organisations*, Market Research Society, London, 1973
14. *International Directory of Published Market Research*, British Overseas Trade Board, in association with Research and Finance Management (International) Limited, BOTB, London, 1976
15. *International Marketing Research*, Supplement to the Market Research Society Newsletter, London, March 1976
16. *International Marketing Research*, Report of ESOMAR Seminar, 1976
17. KEEGAN, W. J. 'Five Strategies for Multi-National Marketing', *European Business*, January 1970
18. LIANDER, B. (Ed.) *Comparative Analysis for International Marketing*, Marketing Science Institute, Boston, Allyn and Bacon, 1967
19. LINTON, A. and BROADBENT, S. 'International Life-Style Comparisons', *European Research*, March 1975
20. LOUDON, D. L. 'The Influence of Environmental Variables on the Use of Marketing Research', *Management International Review* (Germany), 2 / 3, 1975
21. LOVELL, M. R. C. 'Examining the Multi-National Consumer', *ESOMAR Seminar on Developments in Consumer Psychology*, 1973
22. *Marketing Research in Europe* (ESOMAR Yearbook), ESOMAR, Amsterdam
23. *The Market Research Society Yearbook* (contains a list of market research organizations — i.e. professional associations — overseas, and also a guide to the commissioning of survey research), Market Research Society, London
24. MARSH, C. *Guidelines for Commissioning an Interview Survey from a Research Company*, Survey Unit, Social Science Research Council, London, 1976
25. MAYER, C. S. 'Evaluating the Quality of Marketing Research Contractors', *Journal of Marketing Research*, May 1967

26. *Multi-Country Research*, Report of ESOMAR Seminar, 1971
27. *Organisations providing Market Research Services in Great Britain* (notes overseas affiliations of UK agencies), Market Research Society, London, 1976
28. RUSBY, P. 'Some Problems in Multi-Country Advertising Research', *ESOMAR Seminar on Multi-Country Research*, 1971
29. SORENSEN, R. Z. and WIECHMANN, U. E. 'How Multinationals View Marketing Standardisation', *Harvard Business Review*, May—June 1975
30. SQUIRES, C. K. 'International Industrial Market Research — Some Aspects', *ESOMAR Congress*, 1965
31. *Standards in Appraising Market Research Agencies and the Services They Provide*, Incorporated Society of British Advertisers Limited, London, 1968
32. WEBSTER, L. 'Comparability in Multi-Country Surveys', *Esomar Congress*, 1965
33. WHITLEY, E. W. 'Case History of a 16-Country Survey', *ESOMAR Seminar on Multi-Country Research*, 1971

Chapter 24

1. EPHRON, E. H. 'Some Observations on Media Planning in the United States', *Admap*, 6, 1, 1970
2. *Development Research for the 1968 National Readership Survey*, Joint Industry Committee for National Readership Surveys, 1968
3. BELSON, W. A. *Studies in Readership*, Business Publications, 1962
4. 'Introduction, Comparisons with Other Data', *Target Group Index*, British Market Research Bureau Ltd., 1969
5. SMITH, H. A. 'The Use of Panels for the Collection of Readership Data', *The Thomson Medals and Awards for Media Research 1966*, Thomson Organization, 1967
   AGOSTINI, J. M., *ibid.* 'The Possible Role of Readership Panels in Media Research and Media Planning'
   JOYCE, T. and BIRD, M., *ibid.* 'The Use of Panels for the Collection of Readership Data'
   PARFITT, J. H., *ibid.* 'The Use of Panels for the Collection of Readership and Other Data'
6. 'A New Measurement Study of Women's Magazines', *Woman*, 1963
7. NOELLE-NEUMANN, E. Winning Paper, *The Roy Thomson Medals and Awards for Media Research 1962*, Thomson Organization, 1962
   JONES, H. J. M., SCHLAEPPI, A. C., NUTTALL, C. G. F. and AGOSTINI, J. M., *ibid.* other published papers, untitled
8. SMITH, H. A. and others, *op. cit.*
9. CORLETT, T. *An Introduction to the Use and Interpretation of Reading Frequency Data*, Institute of Practitioners in Advertising, 1967
10. METHERINGHAM, R. A. 'Measuring the Net Cumulative Coverage of a Print Campaign', *Journal of Advertising Research*, 4, 4, 1964
11. SHEPHERD-SMITH, N. H. 'Computers and the Advertising Agency: A Practical Approach', *Admap*, 5, 9, 1969
12. LUCAS, D. B. and BRITT, S. H. 'Exposure of Advertisements', *Measuring Advertising Effectiveness*, McGraw-Hill, New York, 1963
13. *Development Research for the 1968 National Readership Survey, op. cit.*
14. *Reader Categorisation Study: Indirect Measures of Exposure to Contents of Publications*, Joint Industry Committee for National Readership Surveys, 1972
15. *Reading Intensity Scale: Interim Report on Calibration*, Joint Industry Committee for National Readership Surveys, 1970
16. *A Study of Printed Advertisement Rating Methods*, Advertising Research Foundation, 1956
17. FLETCHER, R. *Reading Behaviour Reconsidered*, ESOMAR-WAPOR Congress, 1969
18. TWYMAN, W. A. *The Measurement of Page Advertisement Exposure*, Agencies Research Consortium, 1972
19. *The Target Group Index*, British Market Research Bureau Ltd., 1969
20. *Markets and Media*, National Magazine Co. Ltd., 1969
21. *A Qualitative Study of Regional Evening Newspapers*, Evening Newspaper Advertising Bureau, 1963

22. Qualitative Media Assessments, *TV Times*, 1967
23. Publication Q, *Reader's Digest*, 1972
24. WINICK, C. 'Three Measures of the Advertising Value of Media Context', *Journal of Advertising Research*, **2**, 2, 1962
25. BROADBENT, S. R. and SEGNIT, S. 'Beyond Cost per Thousand—an Examination of Media Weights', *The Thomson Medals and Awards for Advertising Research 1968*, Thomson Organization, 1968
26. 'Page Traffic and Page Frequency of Three Leading Publications', *Radio Times*, 1965
27. Usage of Weekly Magazines, *TV Times*, 1974
28. AGOSTINI, J. M. 'The Marriage of Data from Various Surveys: an Expedient or a Unique Way to Make Progress', *Admap*, **3**, 9, 1967
29. JOYCE, T. 'YES—or How the TGI can Help You', *Admap*, **6**, 1, 1970
30. BROADBENT, S. R. 'Media Planning and Computers by 1970', *The Thomson Medals and Awards for Media Research 1965*, Thomson Organization, 1966
31. GENSCH, D. H. 'Computer Models in Advertising Media Selection', *Journal of Marketing Research*, **5**, 1968
32. BROWN, M. M. 'Media Selection Models Compared and Contrasted', *Admap*, **4**, 10, 1968
33. Media Research Group, 'Media Model Comparison', *Admap*, **5**, 3, 1969
34. BROADBENT, S. 'How to Approach the Computer', *Spending Advertising Money*, Business Books, 1970
35. CAFFYN, J. *Experimental Intermedia Studies*, Twelfth Annual Conference, Market Research Society, 1969
36. McDONALD, C. D. P. *ibid. Relationships between Advertising Exposure and Purchasing Behaviour*
37. 'A Major Advertiser Tests the Effectiveness of General Magazines and Television', *Admap*, **6**, 4, 1970
38. WOLFE, H. D., BROWN, J. K., CLARK THOMPSON, G. and GREENBERG, H. *Evaluating Media* (Business Policy Study, No. 121), National Industrial Conference Board, 1966
39. MOONEY, P. B. and WICKS, A. *The Use of Market Research in the Launching of a New Evening Newspaper—a Case History*, Market Research Society Annual Conference, 1967
40. BUSH, C. F. (Ed.) *News Research for Better Newspapers*, American Newspaper Publishers Association Foundation, Vol. 1, 1966; Vol. 2, 1967; Vol. 3, 1968; Vol. 4, 1969

Chapter 25

1. *Report of the Committee on the Future of Broadcasting*, Chairman Lord Annan, HMSO, London, March 1977
2. HULKS, B. *Landmarks in Televesion Research*, Admap Publications Ltd., London, March 1974
3. EHRENBERG, A. S. C. and TWYMAN, W. A. 'On Measuring Television Audiences', *Journal of the Royal Statistical Society*, Series A (General), 130, 1967
4. TWYMAN, W. A. *Research into Methods of Measuring Television Audiences and Data Requirements for the British Television Advertising Industry*, ESOMAR, 1969
5. TWYMAN, W. A. *Review of Media and Product Consumer Research Sources*, Institute of Practitioners in Advertising, London, April 1976
6. BUCK, S. F. and WEST, M. J. 'Consistency of Purchasing and Viewing Behaviour; Optimum period for study', *Journal of the Market Research Society*, **10**, 4, 1968
7. *JICTAR, Reference Manual*, AGB Ltd., 1970 and revisions thereafter
8. BALLINGTON, G. (Ed.), *The Computer Comes to Media Buying*, Admap, February 1975
9. IPA, *The Case for Integrating Media & Product Research*, Occasional Paper No. 19, 1967 and revision 1975
10. AGOSTINI, J. M. *The Marriage of Data from Various Surveys: An Expedient or a Unique Way to Make Progress?* Admap, October 1967
12. BUCK, S. F. and TAYLOR, L. *Consistency of Housewives ITV Viewing Intensity over Time*, Admap, July / August 1970
13. BUCK, S. F., SHERWOOD, R. and TWYMAN, W. A. *Panels and the Measurement of Change*, ESOMAR / WAPOR Congress, Montreux, 1975
14. TWYMAN, W. A. *Attention and the Measurement of Media Exposure for Press and Television*, ESOMAR Congress Proceedings, 1973

15. TWYMAN, W. A. *A Review of Research into Viewership of Television Advertising Breaks*, Institute of Practitioners in Advertising, London, 1971
16. ARF, *Electronic Test of In Home TV Viewing among those Families who Fail to Respond to the Doorbell*, Arrowhead Study No. 8, ARF 1968
17. TAM *Comparison Survey of Audience Composition Techniques*, Television Audience Measurement 1961
18. BMRB, *Television Presence Research, Report to IPA/ISBA Presence Working Party*, British Market Research Bureau, 1968 (see also earlier reports on Pilot Work)
19. JICTAR/BMRB, *Television Audience Presence and Comparison with JICTAR Data*, JICTAR, London, March 1976
20. CONTAM, *How Good are Television Ratings?* (continued) CONTAM, 1969 (and ARF Conference, 1969)
21. LONDON PRESS EXCHANGE, *The Audience to Television Advertisements*, Research Services, 1961
22. TAM, *Two Studies in Housewife Attention During Commercial Breaks*, Television Audience Measurement, 1965
23. TWYMAN, W. A. *Techniques for Measuring Program vs. Commercial Audiences*, ARF 15th Annual Conference, 1969 (see also IPA Forum No. 25, January 1969)
24. McCANN-ERICKSON LTD., *Television Audience Research: Presence and Attention Check*, London, September 1972
25. *Audience Research in the United Kingdom: Methods & Services*, British Broadcasting Corporation, 1970
26. EHRENBERG, A. S. C. 'A Comparison of TV Audience Measures', *Journal of Advertising Research*, **4**, 4, 1964
27. SIMMONS, W. R. *Evaluating Television Measurement Systems*, ARF 14th Annual Conference, 1968
28. LYONS, J. D. *The Storage Instantaneous Audimeter System*, Proceedings of the ARF Conference, pp. 43—44, New York, 1974
29. CONSTERDINE, G. *AMPS TV Diaries*, Admap, February 1968
30. LONDON WEEKEND TELEVISION, *Viewing and Reading; Multi Media Audience Measurement Study*, London, March/November 1973
31. RKO General Broadcasting, *1967—8 Television Research Manual*, RKO, 1967
32. MAYER, M. *How Good are Television Ratings?* CONTAM, 1966
33. EHRENBERG, A. S. C. *Surprise at Poly Channel*, ADMAP, December 1966
34. JWT, *Television Viewing Diaries*, British Market Research Bureau, 1967 (see also *Television Attention Research Reports*, 1961—66)
35. LINTAS, *Television in the Family Setting*, Research Bureau, 1962
36. STEINER, G. A. 'The People Look at Commercials', *Journal of Business*, **39**, 2, 1963 (and also *The People Look at Television*, Knopf, 1963)
37. TELEVISION ADVERTISING REPRESENTATIVES, *Observiewing*, 1965
38. CBS, *Taking the Measure of Two Media*, CBS Television Network, 1962
39. ALLEN, C. L. 'Photographing the TV Audience', *Journal of Advertising Research*, **5**, 1, 1965
40. STUART, A. *Reports to JICTAR* (unpublished) 1964
41. BBM BUREAU OF MEASUREMENT, *Quality Control Test*, BBM Toronto, April 1973
42. BBM BUREAU OF MEASUREMENT, *A Review of the 1974—5 Research Programme*, BBM Toronto, June 1975
43. CORDELL, W. N. and RAHMEL, H. A. 'Are Nielsen Ratings Affected by Non-Co-operation, Conditioning or Response Error?', *Journal of Advertising Research*, **2**, 3, 1962
44. JOYCE, T. *Examples of Experimental Work with Media Panels*, Admap, September 1967
45. HARVEY, B. 'Non-Response in TV Meter Panels', *Journal of Advertising Research*, **8**, 1968
46. STUART, A. *Sampling in Television Research, ATV Technical Research Study*, Associated Television, 1960
47. SILVEY, R. and EMMETT, B. 'What Makes Television Viewers Choose?', *New Society*, **24**, 14th March 1963
48. AMERICAN RESEARCH BUREAU, *Arbitron Replication: A Study of the Reliability of Broadcast Ratings*, ARB New York, 1974
49. SHERWOOD, R. *Basics of TV Research: Organisation, Methods, Use*, Admap, March 1976
50. GREEN, P. E., CARMONE, F. J. and FOX, L. B. 'Television Programme Similarities; an Application of Subjective Clustering', *Journal of Market Research Society*, **11**, 1, 1969
51. ROTHMAN, J. and RAUTA, I. 'Towards a Typology of the Television Audience', *Journal of the Market Research Society*, **11**, 1, 1969

52. BROADBENT, S. *Spending Advertising Money, 2nd edition*, Business Books, 1975
53. BROADBENT, S. and SEGNIT, S. *Response Functions in Media Planning*, Thompson Silver Medal Paper, 1967
54. HASKINS, J. *How to Evaluate Mass Communications*, ARF Monograph, 1968
55. LAWRENCE, R. J. 'Report on a Research Programme', *BBTA Bulletin*, **2**, March 1968
56. SEGNIT, S. and BROADBENT, S. *Area Tests and Consumer Surveys to Measure Advertising Effectiveness*, ESOMAR, 1970
57. BLOOM, D., JAY, A. and TWYMAN, T. *The Validity of Advertising Pretesting*, Market Research Society Conference, Brighton, 1976
58. ADLER, J. and KUEHN, A. A. *How Advertising Works in Market Experiments*, ARF 15th Annual Conference, 1969
59. INSTITUTE OF PRACTITIONERS IN ADVERTISING, *Attitudes Towards Advertising*, IPA, London, May 1975
60. GOODHARDT, G. J., EHRENBERG, A. S. C. and COLLINS, M. A. *The Television Audience: Patterns of Viewing*, Saxon House, Lexington Books, Farnborough, Hants. England, 1975
61. FROST, W. A. K. 'The Development of a Technique for the Programme Assessment', *The Journal of the Market Research Society*, **11**, 1, 1969
62. HALDANE, I. R. *Measuring Television Audience Reactions*, MRS Conference, 1970
63. KIRSCH, A. D. and BANKS, S. 'Program Types Defined by Factor Analysis', *Journal of Advertising Research*, **2**, 3, 1962
64. BELSON, W. A. *The Impact of Television*, Crosby Lockwood, 1967
65. BBC, *The Peoples Activities*, BBC Audiences Research Department, 1966
66. EMMETT, B. P. *A New Role for Broadcasting Research?* WAPOR Conference, 1967
67. HTI, *Programme Idea Q*, Home Testing Institute, 1966
68. BROWN, M. M. *Attitudes to Programmes and the Effect of Commercials*, ADMAP, January 1967
69. BOGART, L. *Strategy in Advertising*, Harcourt Brace and World, 1967
70. CORLETT, T. and RICHARDSON, D. *TV Attention — A Further Step*, Admap, September 1970
71. TWYMAN, W. A. *Setting Television Advertising in Context*, in *ESOMAR Seminar, Beyond Vehicle Audiences*, Budapest, March 1976
72. DE SOLA POOL, I. and SCHRAMM, W. (Eds.) *Handbook of Communication*, Chicago, 1973
73. TWYMAN, W. A. *JICTAR Investigations of the Factor Approach*, IPA Forum No. 34, Institute of Practitioners in Advertising, London, April 1971
74. FIVE-AGENCIES STUDY GROUP, *The Importance of Product Purchase in Relation to ITV Viewing Patterns*, FASG, London 1967
75. TWYMAN, W. A. *Do Housewife Product Purchasing Groups View Differently from All Housewives?* AMPSAC, 1968
76. TWYMAN, W. A. *How the AMPS Survey was used by its Subscribers*, AMPSAC, 1969
77. TAM, *Studies of Housewives who are Light ITV Viewers*, Television Audience Measurement, 1963 and 1966
78. EHRENBERG, A. S. C. and GOODHARDT, G. T. 'Practical Applications of the Duplication of Viewing Law', *Journal of the Market Research Society*, **11**, 1, 1969
79. GOODHARDT, G. T. 'Constant in Duplicated Television Viewing', *Nature*, **212**, p. 1616, 1966
80. PIEPE, A., EMERSON, M. and CANNON, J. *Television and the Working Class*, Saxon House, Lexington Books, Farnborough, Hants, England, 1975
81. JOHNSON, D. S. and PEATE, J. L. *The Estimation of Television Viewing Frequency*, Admap, July / August 1966
82. AUDITS OF GREAT BRITAIN *AGB Coverage and Frequency Guide*, London, 1972
83. TWYMAN, W. A. *The Prediction of Frequency Patterns*, An Experiment for JICTAR carried out by the Media Circle, 1967
84. HULKS, R. and THOMAS, S. *An International Model for the Prediction of Television Coverage and Frequency Distribution — The Key to the Medium?* ESOMAR / WAPOR Congress, Budapest, 1973
85. BBDO, *The Repetition of Advertising, 3rd edition*, Batten, Barton, Durstine and Osborn, New York, January 1970
86. GRASS, R. C. *Satiation Effects of Advertising*, ARF 14th Annual Conference, 1968
87. KRUGMAN, H. E. and HARTLEY, E. *Passive Learning from Television*, ESOMAR / WAPOR, 1969

700

88. KRUGMAN, H. E. *Processes Underlying Exposure to Advertising*, ARF 14th Annual Conference, 1968
89. BROADBENT, S. R. *Media Planning and Computers by 1970*, Thomson Award Papers, 1965

Chapter 26

Radio

1. Radio Luxembourg Audience Surveys
2. Westinghouse Broadcasting Corporation, *Radio's New Math*
3. Radio Luxembourg Audience Panel, November 1968
4. Television Audience Measurement Limited, *Comparison Surveys*, 1963
5. American Research Bureau / RKO General Broadcasting, *The Individual Diary Method of Radio Audience Measurement*, February 1965
6. ARMS, *All Radio Methodology Study*, 1967
7. BBM, *Tests of Revised and Single Media Diaries*, February 1974
8. Radio Advertising Representatives, *Polyphase: Radio Listening and the problems of its measurement*
9. *JICRAR, Radio Audience Surveys*, AIRC

Posters

10. Copland, B. D. *A review of Poster Research*, Business Publications Ltd., 1963
11. Copland, B. D. *The Size and Nature of the Poster Audience Study II*, Mills and Rockley, 1955
12. Copland, B. D. *Transport Advertising Research*, Institute of Practitioners in Advertising, 1964
13. Copland, B. D. *The Audience for Advertising on the Outside of the Red London Bus*, London Transport Advertising, 1967
14. Copland, B. D. *London Travel Survey 1949*, London Transport Executive, 1950
15. COPLAND, B. D. *La Audience Della Publicita Esterna Sui Meggi di Transporto Pubblici*, Impresa Generale Pubblicita, 1968
16. RESEARCH SERVICES LIMITED, *London and Leeds Poster Study for Gallaher Ltd. and Advertising Agency Poster Bureau*, 1974
17. Research Services Limited, *British Posters Traffic Study*, 1974

Cinema

18. GRAY, S. *Simulation of Cinema Going Habits*, Computer Projects Limited, 1969 (unpublished)

See also:
The Cinema Audience: Duplication of Media Survey, Screen Advertising Association, 1964
The Cinema Audience: A National Survey, Screen Advertising Association, 1961

Biographies of the contributors

MICHAEL BROWN is an independent marketing and research consultant. He obtained a BA degree from the University of Cambridge in natural sciences and economics. In 1954 he entered advertising, initially as an account executive, and then moved to the marketing and research side. Mr. Brown joined Lintas Ltd. in 1959 as Head of Media Research. In 1962 he moved to Research Bureau Ltd. (the Unilever market research company). In 1963/4 he was attached to the Research Department of Sullivan, Stauffer, Colwell and Bayles, New York. He then returned to RBL as Technical Manager, with responsibility for basic research in the advertising and product areas within an international program. In 1968 he joined the Newspaper Publishers Association and was later appointed their Head of Marketing, before leaving to start his own business in 1971. He is Technical Consultant to the Joint Industry Committee for National Readership Surveys and to the South African Advertising Research Foundation.

MICHAEL BURROWS was until his death Director, British Market Research Bureau Ltd., and Head of Industrial and Financial Research. Mr. Burrows joined the British Market Research Bureau as a research executive in 1958 and was primarily concerned with continuing studies of the markets for consumer durables and the motor industry. Between 1962 and 1967 he was a director of 'Windett, Burrows and Bonar Law Ltd.', a specialist research company in which a merchant bank had an equity interest: as a result, he became particularly involved in portfolio investment research and specialized surveys for City clients. In 1967, Mr Burrows returned to BMRB to develop new business in the industrial and financial field: he was appointed an associate director in 1968 and a director in 1970.

DAVID CHITTENDEN took an honours degree in Social Anthropology at Cambridge, and began his research career with Ogilvy Benson and Mather, subsequently moving to management positions with Ford Motor Company (Research Coordinator), Attwood Statistics (Director, Surveys Division),

Marplan, London (Director) and Packaging and Perceptual Research Ltd. (Managing Director), where he was heavily involved in the control of projects using the specialist techniques outlined in this article. In 1976 he became Research Director at Business Decisions Ltd., a Business and Market Research Consultancy, where he controls the projects conducted for a number of clients, as well as the development of new techniques and services marketed by the company.

MARTIN COLLINS is a Research Director of Social & Community Planning Research and a consultant with Aske Research Ltd. He is a former Director of that company and of Research Services Ltd., and a graduate in economics of University College, London.

JOHN DAVIS is a member of the Senior Faculty at Henley — the Administrative Staff College. After graduating in 1948 he worked in statistics and operational research with Gillette, BOAC and the Attwood/TAM group of companies, before going to the British Market Research Bureau Ltd. in 1956. After three years as a Group Head in the General Research Division he was appointed Head of the Retail Audit Division, and was responsible for setting up the first permanent store audit test panels based on television areas. In 1966 he moved from BMRB to J. Walter Thompson to set up the Operational Research Unit, carrying out basic research into problems of advertising and marketing. He left JWT in 1974 to devote more time to academic work. He is the author of *Experimental Marketing* and numerous papers, and was awarded the Gold Medal of the Market Research Society for his work on test marketing.

JOHN DOWNHAM is Head of Market Research, Marketing Division, in Unilever Ltd., where he is concerned with Unilever's development and application of market research facilities and methods internationally. After taking a degree in philosophy, politics and economics at Oxford, Mr Downham joined the British Market Research Bureau in 1948 as a research officer. Subsequently, he reconstructed and developed the BMRB Retail Audit (now a part of Retail Audits Ltd.), before assuming responsibility for all consumer research. He became the Managing Director of BMRB in 1960 and towards the end of 1963 joined Unilever. Mr Dowham was a Council member of the Market Research Society from 1956 to 1962, becoming Chairman in 1959 to 1960. Both then and later he was contributor to Market Research Society courses and to various Committee activities. He is a Council member of ESOMAR and has given papers at three of its conferences. During 1976 he was the member of a joint ESOMAR/ICC Working Party responsible for preparing a revised International Code of Marketing Research Practice. He is co-author of *The Communication of Ideas*, and author of a number of papers and articles on market research.

JOHN DRAKEFORD, after graduating in classics at Cambridge University, spent two years in local government accountancy, before joining the Research Department of the leading advertising agency, Mather and Crowther Ltd. in 1957. He was Research Manager there from 1960–1963, heading a department which serviced the continuous and *ad hoc* research requirements of agency clients. He then joined AGB Research, specializing in *ad hoc* surveys. He was a Director of Audits of Great Britain Ltd. and then of RSGB Ltd., responsible for a wide variety of *ad hoc* research projects, conducted on behalf of manufacturers, retailers, advertising agencies, media owners, central and local government and nationalized industries. He left the AGB group in 1974 to set up on his own research and consultancy company, Drakeford Survey Research Ltd. John Drakeford is a full member of the Market Research Society and has a particular interest in training courses for research. He has lectured on research topics both in the UK and in Europe, and also holds the Diploma of the Institute of Practitioners in Advertising.

LEONARD ENGLAND formed England, Grosse and Associates Ltd. with Wendy Grosse in 1969. Mr England began his market research career as an interviewer with Mass-Observation Ltd. and was trained in many of the techniques described in his chapter; subsequently, he became Managing Director of the Company, a post which he held for over twenty years. He has been Chairman of both the Market Research Society and of the Association of Market Survey Organizations. Among his main research interests are the need to maximize the use of market research techniques in fields such as social welfare, and to improve effective communication of results to management.

COLIN GREENHALGH took a BA with honours in mathematics at Jesus College, Oxford, and started his market research career in 1955 with the British Market Research Bureau. He then moved to Tyne Tees Television, where he was responsible for introducing the market research services supplied to advertisers who were test marketing in that region and, subsequently, to the Research Bureau (Unilever). In 1963 he joined the Phillips Scott & Turner Company (now Sterling Health Products) where he was largely responsible for setting up and managing a substantial market research department. Later he became Management Services Controller of that company and had new product development responsibilities in Phillips Laboratories, its proprietary medicines division. He joined Taylor, Nelson & Associates as a Director in 1969, but in 1974 established his own company, Product Testing Research, to specialize in research of that type. He has frequently presented papers on product testing and new product development to market research courses and conferences in the UK and Europe. He is a former Council Member of the Market Research Society, and winner of the Society's Gold Medal both in 1968 and in 1973.

PAUL HARRIS is the Chief Statistician of NOP Market Research Ltd. He was formerly with the market research department of the Electricity Council and before that with the planning department of the Central Electricity Generating Board. He studied statistics at the Regent Street Polytechnic (now the Polytechnic of Central London) and is a fellow of the Institute of Statisticians. His interests include the application of multi-variate statistical methods to market research data, and the use of computers in statistical analysis, subjects on which he has given lectures for The Market Research Society.

CLIFF HOLMES is Technical Director of Marplan Limited. After a period of five years in industry, he began his market research career with Marplan as a statistican. In 1967 he joined Research Services Ltd. as Head of Sampling and Statistics. He returned to Marplan in 1972 and became a Board Director in 1975. Mr. Holmes qualified with honours as a Member of the Institute of Statisticians and he is, at present, on the Examining Board of the Institute. He is a frequent lecturer for the Market Research Society where he is Member of Council and is convenor of the residential course on Sampling and Statistics.

BRIAN HUGHES joined the Operational Research Division of Shell-Mex and BP Limited in 1966 after graduating with a first class honours degree in mathematics. In 1968 he was sponsored by the Company at business school were he gained a MA (with distinction) in marketing. He returned to take up an appointment in the Market Research Department where he was made Market Research Manager in 1970. With the separation in 1975 of the joint Shell and BP operation in the UK, he took up the appointment of Manager of Marketing Research and Management Sciences in BP Oil Limited. In 1977 he became the Retail Manager in the Company's Northern Region. He has convened a number of courses and seminars and delivered papers on various aspects of marketing and research practice. He has been Chairman of the Association of Users of Research Agencies, a member of the Market Research Society Education and Meetings Committees, Chairman of the Research Committee and member of the Executive Committee of the Incorporated Society of British Advertisers and a member of the Research Committee of the Advertising Association.

JOHN KENDALL is the Director of Economics and Market Research in the International Wool Secretariat, responsible for the control and coordination of economic and market research in the 25 or so countries where the IWS operates. He read mathematics and economics at St. John's College, Cambridge and joined the British Market Research Bureau in 1959 as a research executive. In 1962 he moved to Masius Wynne-Williams, the leading London advertising agency, where he supervised a wide range of accounts as a research group head. In 1966 he joined the Wool Secretariat to build up and coordinate economic and market research activity throughout Europe. In this position he was involved in great depth in the use of the type of omnibus surveys mentioned in his chapter and was concerned with a number of studies to improve the accuracy and use of this type of research. Finally, in 1974, he took over global responsibility for market research and economics for the Wool Secretariat where he has been responsible for a number of international comparative research programs, often using omnibus surveys.

MARK LOVELL is Vice-President of the Creative Research Group Ltd., the Toronto-based consumer research company. He is also Vice-President of the Professional Marketing Research Society of Canada. From 1970 to 1975, he was Research Director at Leo Burnett Ltd., joining their main board in 1972. He took a double first in classics and psychology at Cambridge. In 1959, he joined the British Market Research Bureau, where he was made a group head with responsibility for research on a range of consumer accounts. In 1963, he joined Marplan, where he was appointed to the board. Here he had responsibility for the Communication Research Unit. Communication Research Ltd., then a subsidiary of the London Press Exchange, invited him to join their board in 1965. He transferred shortly to the LPE Ltd. (later merged with Leo Burnett), where he was in charge of the Research Department from that year onwards. He has delivered many papers at ESOMAR, for the A.M.A., and at other international conferences. He has won several Thomson Awards for Advertising and Media Research: the Silver Medal 1966, and Gold Medals 1967 and 1968. He has published several books on child psychology, including *Gifted Children* and *How Children Grow*. He is the joint author (with Jack Potter) of *Assessing the Effectiveness of Advertising*, published by Business Books in 1976.

TONY LUNN is an Executive Director of Research Bureau Ltd., the wholly-owned Unilever subsidiary, and a member of the Research International Group of Companies. He joined RBL in 1964 after four years with Attwood Statistics Ltd. His particular interests include market segmentation, attitude research and consumer modelling, and he has published extensively on these and other topics concerning the application of the behavioural sciences to management problems. He has lectured widely in the UK, Europe and the USA, in both business and academic circles, and has convened and chaired a number of seminars. He has been a Council member of the Market Research Society since 1974, and has chaired the Society's Education and Academic Standards Committee. He won the Coglan Award in 1969 and the Society's Gold Medal in 1974. He took a BA in psychology and philosophy at St. John's College, Oxford and an MA in occupation psychology at Birkbeck College, London.

JEAN MORTON-WILLIAMS joined Social and Community Planning Research in 1970, an institute specializing in surveys for government

706

departments, local government and universities, where she is a research director running a group mainly concerned with attitude research and surveys in the area of health. She is a psychologist with a BA (Hons) from London University and a postgraduate diploma in occupational psychology. She came into survey research via the BBC Audience Research Department where she worked with Dr. W. A. Belson on studies of the comprehensibility of programs and of the effects of programs on attitudes and knowledge. She joined McCann-Erickson Research Department under Harry Henry in 1957, became a Director of Marplan on its foundation in 1959, and, later, Assistant Managing Director. She moved to Market Investigations Ltd. in 1966 as Director in charge of psychological research where she was involved in several large-scale government attitude studies as well as commercial surveys. She has been a frequent speaker at Market Research Society weekend courses and winter and summer schools on motivation research and attitude measurement and has organized weekend courses on psychological methods, questionnaire design and qualitative research. She has also lectured on various aspects of survey research at the Institute of Marketing and at Birmingham University courses for social services research officers. Her main interests are in the development of attitude research techniques for use in large scale surveys and in research on health topics.

NIGEL NEWSON-SMITH is Commercial Research Manager at Imperial Group Ltd. After taking a degree in theology and a post-graduate diploma in social science at Oxford, he began his research career with a spell as an interviewer with the Gallup Poll in 1958. He joined Nestle in 1959 as a research assistant, later moving to Mather & Crowther (now OBM) as a research and marketing executive. His next job was as Market Research Manager at J. Lyons from where he moved to Imperial, first as Market Research Coordinator of Imperial Foods and then as Planning Coordinator at the Group HQ. He is Past Chairman of AURA and of the ISBA Research Committee, and Chairman of the Advertising Association's Research Committee, and has convened and lectured at MRS and IMRA courses. He is the author of several articles on market research and a member of the MRS and IMRA.

JOHN PARFITT graduated at LSE with a BSc (Econ.) first class and entered Unilever as a Management Trainee in 1952, and joined Market Research Division, as Manager of the TV Research department. Later Managing Director of Attwood Statistics in charge of the British and European Panel operations, he is currently Chairman / Managing Director of Mass Observation. He was Chairman Market Research Society in 1970.

JAMES ROTHMAN is an independent marketing and research consultant and holds a Cambridge MA degree in natural sciences (Part I) and economics (Part II). After starting his career in the electronics industry he entered market research as an executive with BMRB, where he was subsequently appointed a Group Head. He next became Chairman of Sales Research Services and following the sale of that company to the Taylor Nelson Group he combined the functions of Joint Managing Director of Taylor Nelson Investment Services and Technical Director of Taylor Nelson & Associates. His main work interests now are social, economic and financial research and European comparative studies. He also acts as a consultant on survey re-analysis and the efficient design of complex research projects and provides a second opinion on research studies. James Rothman is a Visiting Research Fellow at Lancaster University and has received the Coglan Award, the Thomson Gold Medal and Award for Media Research and the Market Research Society Gold Medal. He is an external examiner at Surrey University and Joint Editor of the Journal of the Market Research Society.

GEOFFREY ROUGHTON is Chairman of MAS Survey Research Ltd. He is a graduate of Trinity College Cambridge, where he studied the unusual combination of English literature and engineering. His first job was with George Newns Ltd. in a trainee position. In 1956 he joined the Attwood group of companies as a Client Service Executive with TAM. He then became a marketing consultant for a short time early in 1958 before founding MAS with John Robertson. Mr Roughton is a member of the Market Research Society and the Royal Statistical Society. He has been a council member of the Association of Market Survey Organisations since 1965. He has contributed a number of articles on data processing in market research, and has been a regular speaker and participant in seminars on data processing and related subjects.

PETER SAMPSON is joint UK Manager of Burke Marketing Research, London and Technical Director for Burke, Europe. A full member of the Market Research Society, Mr. Sampson graduated from the University of Exeter in 1959 with a degree in social science. He entered market research straight away and worked in the research departments of a number of leading advertising agencies. He has lectured on market research and psychology for the Market Research Society and was a part-time tutor in psychology for the University of London Extra-Mural Department. He has published a number of articles on market research topics, covering consumer psychology from both qualitative and quantitative standpoints, and given papers at conferences in Europe, Mexico City and New Zealand.

WILLIAM SCHLACKMAN received his education in psychology at Brooklyn College, the City College and New York University. Prior to his work in market research he was a clinical psychologist working in the area of personnel selection. This was followed by a period of freelance psychology in the area of motivational research. In 1956 he joined the Dichter organization.

708

Between 1960 and 1962 he was Managing Director of Ernest Dichter Associates in London. He founded William Schlackman Ltd. in 1963.

MARTIN SIMMONS is Joint Managing Director of Gordon Simmons Research Ltd., responsible for its consumer research activities including 'below the line' research. He was previously a Director of the Gallup Poll and before that a Director of Sales Research Services Ltd. He has extensive experience in all forms of consumer and trade research. He has frequently presented papers on Market Research Society and ESOMAR meetings. He has served on the Market Research Society's Governing Council and is a Fellow of the Royal Statistical Society. Mr Simmons graduated from the London School of Economics with an honours degree in statistics.

FRANK TEER is the Joint Managing Director of The Dangar Research Group, Sydney, Australia. Until 1977 he was Managing Director of Research Surveys of Great Britain Limited, a post which he held from 1972. Previously he was for 6 years Joint Managing Director of NOP Market Research Limited. A graduate of the London School of Economics, Mr. Teer has lectured and broadcast on market research and opinion polling and is joint author with J. D. Spence of *Political Opinion Polls*. He is a Vice President and former Chairman of the Market Research Society, a fellow of the Royal Statistical Society and a member of the European Society for Opinion and Marketing Research and the World Association for Public Opinion Research.

ANTHONY TWYMAN is an Executive Director of Research Bureau Ltd. — Research International, where he is responsible for a wide range of *ad hoc* marketing and social research surveys. He has also been responsible for some years for a program of basic methodological research. As an independent media research consultant, he is Technical Associate of JICTAR and is technical consultant to the Association of Independent Radio Companies and to the Joint Industry Committee of Medical Advertisers for Readership Surveys. He was formerly a director of TAM and taught experimental psychology at Birkbeck College, London.

ROBERT M. WORCESTER is Chairman and Managing Director of Market & Opinion Research International (MORI). Prior to his London appointment nearly a decade ago, Mr. Worcester served in client liaison and research direction posts and as Controller and Assistant to the Chairman of the Board of Opinion Research Corporation Princeton, New Jersey, USA. He was also Chairman of the Board of Market Insights, a Vice President and Director of E. L. Reilly Co. Inc. and Director of Market Dynamics Inc., ORC subsidiaries. Prior to that he was a consultant with McKinsey & Company. Mr. Worcester is a Fellow of the Institute of Directors and is a member of the American Marketing Association, the World Association for Public Opinion Research (WAPOR), the European Society for Opinion and Marketing Research (ESOMAR), the Market Research Society of Great Britain and the British Institute of Management. A graduate of the University of Kansas, Mr. Worcester has contributed papers to ESOMAR, WAPOR, and the Market Research Society Conferences, and articles to a number of journals. He is Editor-in-Chief of *Consumer Market Research Handbook* and has lectured both in this country and abroad on topics relating to opinion and attitude research.

ICC/ESOMAR International Code of Marketing and Social Research Practice

International Chamber of Commerce and European Society for Opinion and Marketing Research

Market (and social) research has for more than 25 years been regulated by various voluntary Codes of Practice. These have been extended and elaborated over time as the techniques and practices of research have become more complex. Their primary objective is to help ensure that the rights of the public, particularly as respondents, are adequately protected, and also that the interests of both research agencies and their clients are mutually respected.

International Codes have existed since 1948, that prepared by the European Society for Opinion and Marketing Research being the first of its kind. In 1977 this and the Code of the International Chamber of Commerce were combined into a new joint International Code. This is reprinted here by permission of the two bodies involved. It is now the sole Code regulating research *internationally*, and has in addition been adopted by an increasing number of countries as their local national Code of Practice.

There are also certain Codes drawn up by national bodies, of which that prepared by the UK Market Research Society is the most extensive. The latter is in fact fully compatible with the International Code, although it covers a few additional aspects of research activities.

In carrying out research studies researchers must conform to the International Code, as well as (where relevant) any extra provisions of local Codes or national legislation. Good research is therefore not just a question of an intelligent approach to problem solving, and the creative application of sound techniques: it must also follow the high standards of professional and ethical practice exemplified by this Code.

Foreword

For many years the ICC and ESOMAR have promoted the application by all sectors concerned of rules reflecting a high level of ethics in marketing and opinion research.

The new code of ethics set out in this publication drawn up jointly by the ICC and ESOMAR reflects the conviction common to both organizations that professional self-regulation can safeguard the legitimate interests of the community, while at the same time assuring the harmonious development of relations among the sectors directly involved.

The ESOMAR constitution requires the members of that organization to abide by this Code.

The ICC for its part recommends that all national and international professional associations representing the users and practitioners of market research adopt these rules as rapidly as possible.

Both organizations wish to emphasize that the Code includes provisions for examining any alleged failure to observe its rules of conduct.

In the near future, the ICC and ESOMAR plan to pursue their reciprocal efforts to foster the unification of commercial practice by issuing recommendations intended to facilitate the establishment of contracts between users and practitioners of marketing research.

Carl-Henrik Winqwist
Secretary General of the ICC

C.C.J. de Koning
President, ESOMAR

Introduction

Effective two-way communication between the suppliers and the consumers of goods and services of all kinds is vital to any modern society. Growing international links and interdependence reinforce this need. The supplier seeks to inform the consumer of what is available and where, using advertising and other forms of publicity to do so. In the other direction, the varied requirements of consumers must be made known to those who cater for their needs in both the private and public sectors of the economy, and this increasingly calls for the use of research.

Marketing research is concerned with analysing the markets for products and services of all kinds. In particular it involves the systematic study of behaviour, beliefs and opinions of both individuals and organizations. The measurement of public opinion on social, political and other issues has also long been linked with the field of marketing research; and in recent years similar approaches have been applied throughout very much wider fields of social research.

712

Although the subjects of study tend to differ, marketing research and social research have many interests, methods and problems in common. Both are involved with the analysis of available data, or the collection and analysis of new information, using sampling, questionnaire and other appropriate techniques. The issues dealt with in this Code therefore apply equally to both fields of research where they use similar methods of study.

It is against this background that Codes of Marketing Research Practice have been developed. The first, published in 1948 and last revised in 1972, was that of the European Society for Opinion and Marketing Research (ESOMAR). This was followed by a number of Codes prepared by national marketing research organizations. In 1971 the International Chamber of Commerce (ICC), representing the international marketing community, set out to bring together and rationalize the major points contained in the existing Codes, publishing its own International Code after consultation with the marketing research and marketing bodies concerned.

Since 1971 the practice of marketing research has continued to evolve. New issues have arisen and additional safeguards have been incorporated into certain national Codes. In 1976 ESOMAR and the ICC both decided that it was necessary to revise their existing Codes to take account of these changes, and that it was at the same time highly desirable that there should be one international Code rather than two differing ones. A Joint Working Party representing both bodies was therefore set up to prepare a single revised Code, and this has now been adopted by the two organizations.

This international Code is designed to provide individuals and organizations concerned with a basic set of rules which are generally acceptable internationally. It applies to all international and national projects. Where in a given country there is already a national Code, the latter may on occasion go further than this international Code in dealing with certain detailed points of practice: in such cases the national Code will be followed. National and international practice must of course in all cases conform to the legislation and legal practice of the countries concerned.

Basic Principles

Marketing and social research depend upon public confidence: confidence that the research is conducted honestly, objectively, without unwelcome intrusion and without disadvantage to informants, and that it is based upon the willing cooperation of the public.

The general public and anyone else interested shall be entitled to complete assurance that every marketing research project is carried out strictly in accordance with this Code, and that their rights of privacy are respected. In particular, members of the general public must be assured absolutely that personal and/or confidential information supplied during the course of a marketing research study will not be made available without their agreement to any individual or organization, whether private or official, outside the researcher's own organization (as laid down in Section C), and that such information will not be used for any purposes other than marketing research.

Research should also be conducted according to accepted principles of fair competition, as generally understood and accepted, and to high technical standards. Marketing and social researchers should always be prepared to make available the necessary information whereby the quality of their work and the validity of their findings can be adequately assessed.

Definitions

In this Code:

(a) The term **marketing research** is defined as the systematic collection and objective recording, classification, analysis and presentation of data concerning the behaviour, needs, attitudes, opinions, motivations, etc. of individuals and organizations (commercial enterprises, public bodies, etc.) within the context of their economic, social, political and everyday activities. For the purposes of this Code, the term marketing research is taken to cover also social research, insofar as the latter uses similar approaches and techniques in its study of issues and problems not directly connected with the marketing of goods and services. Reference to the term marketing research shall throughout this Code therefore be held to include **social research** equally. The term also includes those forms of research commonly referred to as **industrial marketing research** and as **desk research,** especially where these are concerned with the acquistion of original data from the field and not simply the secondary analysis of already available data.

(b) The term **researcher** is defined as any individual, company, group, public or private institution, department, division, etc. which directly or indirectly conducts, or acts as a consultant in respect of, a **marketing research** project, survey, etc. or offers its services so to do. The term researcher also includes any department or division, etc. which may belong to or form part of the same organization as that of the **client.** The term researcher is further extended to cover responsibility for the procedures followed by any subcontractor from whom the researcher commissions any work (data collection or analysis, printing, professional consultancy, etc.) forming only part of the research project; in such cases the researcher is held responsible for ensuring that any such subcontractor fully conforms to the provisions of this Code.

(c) The term **client** is defined as any individual, company, group, public or private institution, department, division, etc. (including any such department or division, etc. which may belong to, or form part of, the same organization as the **researcher)** which wholly or partly commissions, requests, authorises, or agrees to subscribe to a **marketing research** project or proposes so to do.

(d) The term **informant** is defined as any individual, group or organization from whom any information is sought by the **researcher** for the purposes of a **marketing research** project, survey, etc., regardless of the type of information sought or the method or technique used to obtain it. The term informant therefore covers not only cases where information is obtained by verbal techniques but also cases where non-verbal methods such as observation, postal surveys, mechanical, electrical or other recording equipment are used.

(e) The term **interview** is defined as any form of direct or indirect contact (including observation, electro-mechanical techniques, etc.) with **informants** the result of which is the acquisition of data or information which could be used in whole or in part for the purposes of a given **marketing research** project, survey, etc.

(f) The term **record(s)** is defined as any brief, proposal, questionnaire, check list, record sheet, audio or audio-visual recording or film, tabulation or computer print-out, EDP tape or other storage medium, formula, diagram, report, etc., in whatsoever form, in respect of any given **marketing research** project, survey, etc., whether in whole or in part. It includes records prepared by the **client** as well as by the **researcher.**

Rules

A. Responsibilities towards informants

Article 1

Any statement made to secure cooperation and all assurances given to an informant, whether oral or written, shall be factually correct and honoured.

Anonymity of Informants

Article 2

Subject only to the provisions of article 3, the informant shall remain entirely anonymous. No information which could be used to identify informants, either directly or indirectly, shall be revealed other than to research personnel within the researcher's own organization who require this knowledge for the administration and checking of interviews, data processing, etc. Such persons must explicitly agree to make no other use of such knowledge. All informants are entitled to be given full assurance on this point.

Article 3

The only exceptions to the above article 2 are as follows:

(a) If informants have been told of the identity of the client and the general purposes for which their names would be disclosed and have then consented in writing to this disclosure.
(b) Where disclosure of these names to a third party (e.g. a subcontractor) is essential for data processing or in order to conduct further interviews with the same informants, provided that the provisions of article 4 are followed. In all such cases the researcher responsible for the original survey must ensure that any third parties so involved will themselves observe the provisions laid down in this Code.
(c) Where the informant is supplying information not in his private capacity but as an officer of an organization or firm, provided that the provisions of article 5 are followed.

Article 4

With the exception noted below, further interviews with the same informants shall be carried out only if:

(a) Informants' permission has already been obtained at a previous interview; *or*
(b) It is pointed out to informants at the time they are recontacted that this interview is consequent upon one they have previously given and they then give their permission before the collection of further data.

The only exception to this procedure is in the case where it is an essential feature of the research technique involved that informants do not realize that this further interview is consequent upon one they have previously given.

Article 5

If the informant is supplying information not in his private capacity but as an officer of an organization or firm, then it may be desirable to list his organization in the report. The report shall not however enable any particular piece of information to be related to any particular organization or person except with prior permission from the relevant informant, who shall be told of the extent to which it will be communicated. This requirement does not apply in the case of secondary analysis of published data.

Rights of the Informant

Article 6

All reasonable precautions shall be taken to ensure that the informant, and others closely associated with him, are in no way adversely affected or embarrassed as a result of any interview. This requirement covers the

716

information to be obtained, the interviewing process itself, and the handling and testing of any products involved in the research. The purpose of the enquiry shall be revealed in cases where information given in ignorance of this knowledge could adversely affect the informant.

Article 7

The informant's right to withdraw, or to refuse to cooperate at any stage of the interview, shall be respected. Whatever the form of the interview, any or all of the information given by the informant must be destroyed without delay if the informant so requests. No procedure or technique which infringes this right shall be used. Informants shall be told in advance where observation or recording techniques are to be used. This requirement does not apply where the actions or statements of individuals are observed or recorded in public places and are normally liable to be observed and / or overheard by other people present. In the latter case at least one of the following conditions shall be observed:

(a) all reasonable precautions are taken to ensure that the individual's anonymity is preserved; *and/or*
(b) the individual is told immediately after the event that his actions and / or statements have been observed or recorded or filmed, is given the opportunity to see or hear the relevant section of the record, and, if he wishes, to have it destroyed or deleted.

Wherever questions are subsequently asked to the person observed, condition (b) above shall apply.

Article 8

The name and address of the researcher shall normally be made available to informants at the time of interview. Where an accommodation address is necessary for postal surveys, or where a 'cover name' is used for interviews, arrangements shall be made so that it is possible for informants subsequently to find without difficulty the name and address of the researcher.

Interviewing Children

Article 9

Special care shall be taken in interviewing children. Before they are interviewed, or asked to complete a questionnaire, the permission of a parent, guardian, or other person currently responsible for them (such as the responsible teacher) shall be obtained. In obtaining this permission, the interviewer shall describe the nature of the interview in sufficient detail to enable the responsible person to reach an informed decision. The responsible person shall also be specifically informed if it is intended to ask the children to test any products or samples.

B. Relations with the general public and the business community

Article 10

No activity shall be deliberately or inadvertently misrepresented as marketing research. Specifically, the following activities shall in no way be associated, directly or by implication, with marketing research interviewing or activities:

(a) enquiries whose objectives are to obtain personal information about private individuals *per se*, whether for legal, political, private or other purposes;
(b) the compilation of lists, registers or data banks for any purposes which are not marketing research;
(c) industrial, commercial or any other form of espionage;
(d) the acquisition of information for use by credit-rating or similar services;
(e) sales or promotional approaches to the informant;
(f) the collection of debts;
(g) direct or indirect attempts, including the framing of questions, to influence an informant's opinions or attitudes on any issue.

Article 11

Researchers shall not misrepresent themselves as having any qualifications, experience, skills or access to facilities which they do not in fact possess.

Article 12

Unjustified criticism and disparagement of competitiors shall not be permitted.

Article 13

No one shall knowingly disseminate conclusions from a given research project or service that are inconsistent with or not warranted by the data.

C. The mutual responsibilities of clients and researchers

Article 14

The relationship between a client and a researcher will generally be subject to a form of contract between them. This Code does not aim to limit the freedom of the parties to make whatever agreement they wish between themselves. However, any such agreement shall not depart from the requirements of this Code except in the cases of certain specific articles, namely articles 15–21 inclusive, 28 and 30. These are the only articles which may be modified in this way by agreement between client and researcher.

Property of Marketing Research Records

Article 15

Marketing research proposals and quotations provided by a researcher at the request of a client and without an agreed payment remain the property of the researcher submitting them. In particular, prospective clients shall not communicate the proposals of one researcher to another researcher *except* where the latter is acting directly as a consultant to the client on the project concerned; nor shall the client use the proposals or quotations of one researcher to influence the proposals of another researcher. Similarly, the marketing research brief and specifications provided by a client remain the property of the client.

Article 16

The research findings and data from a marketing research project are the property of the client. Unless the prior written consent of the client has been obtained, no such findings or data shall be disclosed by the researcher to any third party.

Article 17

The research techniques and methods used in a marketing research project do not become the property of the client, who has no exclusive right to their use.

Article 18

All records prepared by the researcher other than the report shall be the property of the researcher, who shall be entitled to destroy this material two years after completion of the study without reference to the client.

Article 19

After the researcher has submitted his report upon the study to the agreed specification, the client shall be entitled to obtain from the researcher duplicate copies of completed questionnaires or other records, provided that the client shall bear the reasonable cost of preparing such duplicates, and that the request is made within the time limit set by article 18. Article 19 shall not apply in the case of a project or service which is developed by a researcher and where it is clearly understood that the resulting reports are to be available for general purchase on a syndicated or subscription basis. Any duplicates provided shall not reveal the identity of informants.

Confidentiality

Article 20

Unless authorized to do so by the client, the researcher shall not reveal to informants, nor to any other person not directly concerned with the work of the study, the name of the client commissioning the study.

Article 21

All confidential information and material relating to the client shall not be divulged except to persons wholly or substantially engaged in the service of the researcher, including subcontractors, who need such information or material in order effectively to carry out the research work.

Client's Rights to Information about a Project

Article 22

The researcher shall clearly indicate to the client what parts of a project will be handled by subcontractors.

Article 23

On request the client, or his mutually acceptable representative, may attend a limited number of interviews to observe the standards of the fieldwork (he then becomes subject to Section A of this Code). The researcher is entitled to be recompensed if the client's desire to attend an interview interferes with, delays or increases the cost of the fieldwork. In the case of a multiclient study, the researcher may require that the observer in charge of checking the quality of the fieldwork is independent of any of the clients.

Article 24

When two or more projects are combined in one interview, or one project is carried out on behalf of more than one client, or a service is offered on the basis that it is also available on subscription to other potential clients, each client concerned shall be informed of this fact in advance.

Multiclient Studies

Article 25

The client shall not give any of the results of a multiclient study to other potential purchasers of the study unless he has first obtained the researcher's permission to do this.

Publishing of Results

Article 26

Reports and other records relevant to a marketing research project and provided by the researcher shall normally be for use solely by the client and his consultants or advisers. Whether or not the copyright of the research findings is reserved to the researcher in the form of contract for the project, if the client intends any wider circulation of the results of a study either in whole or in part:

(a) the client shall agree in advance with the researcher the exact form and contents of publication or circulation: if agreement on this cannot be reached between client and researcher, the latter is entitled to refuse permission for his name to be quoted in connection with the study;

(b) where the results of a marketing research project are given any such wider circulation the client must at the same time make available the information listed under article 31 about the published parts of the study. In default of this, the researcher himself is entitled to supply this information to anyone receiving the above-mentioned results.

(c) the client shall do his utmost to avoid the possibility of misinterpretation or the quotation of the results out of their proper context.

Article 27

Researchers shall not allow their names to be used as an assurance that a particular marketing research project has been carried out in conformity with this Code unless they are fully satisfied that the project has in every respect been controlled according to the Code's requirements.

Exclusivity

Article 28

In the absence of any contractual agreement to the contrary the client does not have the right to exclusive use of the researcher's services, whether in whole or in part.

D. Reporting standards

Article 29

The researcher shall, when presenting the results of a marketing research project (whether such presentation is oral, in writing or in any other form), make a clear distinction between the results themselves and the researcher's interpretation of the data and his recommendations.

Article 30

Normally every report of a marketing research project shall contain an explanation of the points listed under article 31, or a reference to a readily available separate document containing this explanation. The only exception to this article is in the case where it is agreed in advance between the client and the researcher that it is unnecessary to include all the listed information in the formal report or other document. Any such agreement shall in no way remove the entitlement of the client to receive any and all of the information freely upon request. Also this exception shall not apply in the case where any or all of the research report or findings are to be published or made available to recipients in addition to the original client.

Article 31

The following information shall be included in the report on a research project:

Background
(a) for whom and by whom the study was conducted;
(b) the purpose of the study;
(c) names of subcontractors and consultants performing any substantial part of the work.

Sample
(d) a description of the intended and actual universe covered;
(e) the size, nature and geographical distribution of the sample, both planned and achieved;
(f) details of the sampling method and of any weighting methods used;
(g) where technically relevant, a statement of response rate and a discussion of possible bias due to non-response.

Data collection
(h) a description of the method by which the information was collected (that is, whether by personal interview, postal or telephone interview, group discussion, mechanical recording device, observation or some other method);
(i) adequate description of field staff, briefing and field quality control methods used;
(j) the method of recruitment used for informants and the general nature of any incentives offered to them to secure their cooperation;
(k) the time at which the field work was done;
(l) in the case of 'desk research', a clear statement of the sources and their reliability.

Presentation of results
(m) the relevant factual findings obtained;
(n) bases of percentages, clearly indicating both weighted and unweighted bases;
(o) general indications of the probable statistical margins of error to be attached to the main findings, and of the levels of statistical significance of differences between key figures;
(p) questionnaires and other relevant documents used (or, in the case of a shared project that portion relating to the matter reported upon).

722

E. Implementation of the Code

Article 32

Any person or organization involved in, or associated with, a marketing research project and/or proposal is responsible for actively applying the rules of this Code in the spirit as well as the letter.

Article 33

Any alleged infringements of the Code relating to a single country shall be reported without delay to the appropriate national body which has adopted this Code. Problems of interpretation and enforcement in such cases shall in the first place be the responsibility of the said national bodies which have adopted this Code and which are representative of all the interests directly concerned. Where such a suitable national body does not already exist it is urged that one be established speedily. The national body shall take such actions as it deems appropriate in relation to implementation of the Code, taking due account of any relevant national marketing research Codes and the laws of the country concerned. It is important that any decision taken under this Article should be notified to the secretariats of the ICC and ESOMAR, without revealing the names of the parties concerned.

Article 34

In cases where:

(a) an appropriate national body *does not exist;* or
(b) the national body concerned is for any reason *unable* to provide an interpretation of, or take action to enforce, the Code; or
(c) any of the parties involved *wishes to refer the problem to an international body* (either immediately or for a subsequent second opinion); or
(d) the problem involved *parties from different countries* (for example with an international marketing research project), the problem shall be referred to the secretariats of the ICC or of ESOMAR. The secretariats will then convene the special body set up jointly by ESOMAR and by the ICC for the purpose of dealing with problems of these kinds.

Index

726

BRMB, 665
Broad spectrum, 568
Broadbent, S., 185, 592, 598, 643, 644, 651, 653, 684, 687, 691, 696, 698, 700, 701
Brown, 403
Brown, G., 690
Brown, J. K., 698
Brown, L. O., 689
Brown, M., 578–603, 700
Brown, N. A., 685, 691
Buchanan, D. I., 691
Buck, S. F., 610, 614, 635, 639, 698
Buckel, 369, 688
Building Societies Association, 695
Bureau of Broadcast Measurement, 634, 637
Burnett, L., 695
Burrows, M., viii, 537–550
Burt, 317
Bus advertising, see Public transport advertising
Bush, C. R., 698
Business analysis, 395
Business International, 22
Business Monitor, 18
Business opinions survey, 544
Business Statistics Office, 16
Business Surveys Ltd., 20

Caffyn, J., 685, 689, 691, 698
Camera, use of in research, 229, 629, see also Eye camera
Campbell, D. T., 682
Canadian Facts Co. Ltd., 216
Cannon, J., 700
Canonical analysis, 311
Canonical correlation, 327–328
Car cards, see Public transportation advertising
Cards, punch, see Punch cards
Cards, show and prompt, 98, 100
Carmone, F. J., 325, 681, 686, 699
Carroll, 46
Carry-over effects, 57
Cars, 362
Cartoon completion, 36
Catering, 10
CBD Research, 19, 23, 24, 164
CBI, 19, 539, 545, 695
CBS, 699
CEIR, see Scientific Control Systems Ltd.
Central Statistical Office, 14, 16
CEST, 614
Census, 18, 87
Chang, 46
Channon, C., 322, 686
Chaplin, J. P., 36, 681
Chemists Register, 164
Cheskin, L., 691
Children, television viewing by, 633
Chi square table, 282, 284, 329

Chittenden, D., 450–469
Christopher, M. A., 316, 686, 688
Christopher, M. D., 492, 693
Cinema research, 676, 679
Circulation research, 603–604
CIRET, 696
Cirlot, 691
'City block' measure, 67, 71
Clarke, T. J., 689
Clark Thompson, G., 698
Classification data, 118–122
Classification of respondents, 118–122, 251, 264–265, 590, see also Demographic classification, Television viewing
Classification page 121–125
Clausen, 683
Clemens, N. J. S., 34, 681, 689
Clumping, 324
Clunies-Ross, C., 689, 690
Cluster analysis 311, 321, 324, 356, 360, 361, 370, 492, 566
'Clustering', analysis, 324, 566
'Clustering', sampling, 79
Cochran, W. G., 685
Coding, 238–263
Coding frame, 246–248
Coding instructions, 246
Coefficient of responsibility, 113
Coincidental technique, 619
Colley, R. H., 682
Collins, B. J. K., 684, 694
Collins, L., 681
Collins, M. A., 74–90, 311, 650, 686, 689
Colour television, in advertising testing, 433
Commercial break, behaviour during, 520–521
Commercials, see Television commercials
Commercials, radio, see Radio commercial
Communality, 318
Communication with respondents, 92–101, 553
Community Antenna Television, 488
Community leaders, 532
Companies House, 21, 539, 542
Companion brands, 410
Company image, see also Corporate image, 538
Competitions, see 'Below the line' expenditure
Computer input requirements, 261–262
Computer media programs, 586
Computer output, checking, 262–263
Computer projects, 260–261
Computers, 257–263
in editing, 245–246
in media research, 595–599, 613, 614
Concept association test, 455–457
Concept development, 27, 345, see also New product development
Concept evaluation, 387

730

731

Product compatibility research, 531
Product concept, 366–370, 379
Product development, 9, 10, 345, 365,
    377–411
Product segmentation, 366–370
Product testing, 50, 54, 55–56, 65
    panels, 178, 390
    product development, 394–404
    qualitative, 404
    see also Market testing
'Profile chart', 320
Projections, 493–495
Projective techniques, 28–35, 111
Promax, 319
Promotions, 174–175, 199–200, 470–482, 487
Pronunciation, in name testing, 467
Propensity to purchase, 407–408
Prout, T. P., 17, 680
Pseudo-product test, 457
Psychogalvanometer, 219, 230, 433
Psychological classification, 186, 350
Psychologist, 42, 130, 317, 421, 434
Psychometrics, 350
Public attitude services, 216
Pull-out costs, 490
Punch cards, 245, 252–255
Pupil dilation, 229, 433
Purnell, J. M., 324, 394, 396, 686, 688, 689
Pymont, B. C., 694

Quadratic function, 66
Qualitative research, 4, 5, 25–48
    advertising research, 421
    costs, 44
    financial research, 541
    interpretation, 41, 42
    new product development, 382–383, 402
    segmentation research, 354
    techniques, 28–37
    uses, 27
Quality control of interviewing, 139–142
Quantitative Media Assessments, 698
Quantity control test, 634
'Quasi-random sampling', 84, 559
Quenouille, M. H., 685
Questionnaire design, 91–125, 312
    advertising post-testing for, 441–442
    mail surveys for, 223, 224, 225–226
    omnibus surveys for, 204–205, 211, 212
    product development surveys, 393, 402–404
    self-completion, 227–228
    see also piloting
Questioning techniques, 10, 107–111
Questions, types of, 102–118
Quota controls, 82–84, 84–87, 118
Quota sampling, 82–84, 118, 559
'Q-technique', 322

Radio, 634, 635, 657–679
Radio, commercial, 657, 658, see also Radio
    research

Radio Luxembourg, 658, 659, 665, 666, 701
Radio, pirate, see Pirate radio
Radio Times, 593
Radio, UHF, see UHF radio
Rampley, B., 689, 690
Random numbers, 89
Random-route, sampling of, 84, 224
Random sampling, 74–81, 87–90, 559
    for omnibus surveys, 206
    see also Quasi-random sampling
Rank Advertising, 676
Ranked data, 265–266
'Rapport' with respondent, 94
    on telephone, 221–222
Rating scales, 107–110, 287–291, 296, 320,
    328, 431
Ratings services, 613
Rauta, I., 647, 699
Ray, M., 695
RBL, see Research Bureau Ltd.
'Reader', definition of, 580–581
Reader's Digest, 592, 696
Readership parallel, 583
Readership replicated, 583
Readership research, 548–550, 578–605
Readership scales, 58
'Reading days', 593
Reading frequency, 583–586
Reading scale, 593
Recall questions, 432, 437, 581, 582
    re TV viewing, 621–624, 632
Recognition methods, 582
Recordimeter, 627, 632, 636
Recruitment, personnel, 532
Re-cycling, of products, 338, 378, 408
Refusals, 620
Register, electoral, see Electoral register
Regression analysis, 311, 325–327, 356, 566,
    see also Multiple regression analysis
'Regret at loss' question, 592
Reminders, for mail surveys, 224
Repeat purchase analysis, 198
Repertory grid, 28, 32–35, 109
    analysis, 311
    cost, 45
    example, 34–35
    TV research, use in, 646
Reputation, company's see Corporate image
    research
Research Bureau Ltd., 171, 174, 476, 629
Research Marketing Services Ltd., 216
Research Services Ltd., 512, 637, 673, 701
Research Surveys of G.B., 216, 661, 664
Response function, 597
Response rate, 82, 83, 223, 224, 535
Retail audits, see Audits
Retail Audits Ltd., 151
Retailer research, 163
    packaging, 450–451
    see also 'Below the line' expenditure

Richardson, D., 649, 700
Riley, 32, 681
Ring, E., 681
Roberts, L. D., 695
Robinson, P. J., 686
Roche, M., 692
Rodger, L. W., 691
Role research, 37–38
Rorschach Ink Blot test, 36
Roscoe, 62, 682
Roskill, O. W., 19
Roughton, G. R., 238–263
Rosenberg, M. J., 71, 508, 682
Rotation, of factors, 319
Rothman, J., 47–73, 503, 647, 694, 699
Rothman, L. J., 689
Round robin, 57
Roy Morgan Research Centre, 216
'R' technique, 322
Rusby, 558, 697

'SABLE', 260–261
Salapaier, P. H., 692
Sales Research Services Ltd., 59
Saliency, 105–106
  brand, 441, 442
'SAMPLE', 261
Sample size
  calculation of, 84–87
  experimental design in, 51
Sampling, 74–90
  costs, 81
  cumulative, 209–210
  disproportionate, 86, 151
  equal cell, 161
  financial research for, 539–540
  mail surveys for, 222, 223, 224–225
  methods, examples of, 87–90
  multi-phase, 86–87
  omnibus survey, for, 206, 209–210, 214
  panels, for, 178–179
  quota, 82–84, 118–120
  random, 74–79, 87–90
  random route, 84
  retail audits, for, 151–153
  sequential, 85–86, 209–210
  serial, 88–89
Sampling, distribution of the test statistic, 273
Sampling error, 10, 50, 74–77
  table, 307–309
Sampling frame, 82, 87, 89
Sampling interval, 88
Sampson, P. M. J., 25–48, 34, 109, 331, 354, 680, 681, 687, 689, 693, 694
Sanchez, 515, 695
Saving, 538
  examples of research on, 115–116, 549
  see also Financial research
Scales, 33, 35, 367, 368 see also
  Diagrammatic, Numerical, Nominal,

Oblique, Rating, Ratio, Readership, Semantic differential, Verbal
Scalogram, 113
Scatter diagram, 326
Schaffer, A., 692
Scheffe, H., 685
Schewerin, H., 435
Schlackman, W., 450–469, 692
Schlaeppi, A. C., 697
Schlaiffer, R., 693
Schramm, 649, 700
Scicon, 260, 261
Scientific Control Systems Ltd., 324, 327, 686
Scott, C., 317, 685
Scott, W., 686
Screening, new product ideas, 387
Secondary data, 7, 14
Segment exposure research, 618
Segmentation criteria, 348–352
Segmentation, market, see Market segmentation
Segmentation models, 65
Segnit, S., 351, 644, 688, 691, 698, 700
Self-completion questionnaires, 227–228
Self Service and Supermarkets Directory, 164
Self-service shops, 470
Sellitz, J., 685
Semantic differential, 71
  scales, 109–110, 111, 266
Semi-structured interview, 28
Sentence completion tests, 36
Sequential dichotomization techniques, 329–331, 356
Sequential sampling, 85–86, 209–210, 567, 611
SETMETER, 624
Set switching data, 624–626
'Seven day aided recall', 623–624
Shaving, 516–519
Shaw, J. F., 695
Shelf space allocation, 481–482
Shepherd Smith, N. H., 697
Sherak, B., 362, 371, 688, 689
Sherwood, 635, 639, 698, 699
Sheth, J. N., 62, 333, 373, 680, 682, 687, 688, 694
Shop fronts, research on, 60–61
Shopping list, 454, 473–474
Shopping panels, 177–178
Seigel, S., 315, 685, 686
Significance level, 276
Significance testing, 264–309
'Significant', 276
Significant differences table, 306–309
Significant results, 304–305
  interpretation of, 304–305
Sign test, 290–291
Silvey, R., 699
Similarity coefficient, 322
Simmons Research Ltd., Gordon, 216

Simmons, 594, 634
Simmons, M., 470–482, 623, 693
Simulation approach, 597
Skelly, F., 689
Skip instructions, on questionnaires, 100
Smith, H. A., 697
Smith, W., 687
Smith-Warden Ltd., 688
Sneath, P. H. A., 321, 686
Snedecor, G. W., 685
Social and Community Planning Research, 119
Social class in group discussions, 44, *see also* Classification, Demographic classification
Socio-economic classification, 122, 590
SOFRES, 216
Software package, 257–261
Sobal, R. R., 321, 686
Sonquist, J. A., 331, 358, 686, 688
Sorenson, R. Z., 697
Sowter, A. P., 690
Spearman, 317
Spearman's rank correlation coefficient, 315
'Spherical' map, 320
Split run, 50, 52, 59, 210, 488, 496
Split sample, *see* Split run
SPS, 261
Squires, 697
SRI, 22
SRS, *see* Sales Research Services
STAFCO consumer panel, 181
Standard deviation, 269, 270, 271
Standard error, 76–77, 84, 272
'Stand-out' problem, packaging, 460, 463–464
Stanley, J. C., 682
Star, 683
Starch, D., 691
Starch tests, 434
Statistical analysis machines, 255–257
Statisticians, Institute of, *see* Institute of Statisticians
Statistical Model, 506
'Statistical News', 14
Statistical significance, 25, 264–309
Statistics, 264–309
Stats, M. R., 151
Stefflre, V., 354, 687, 689
Steiner, 629, 648, 651, 699
Steinkamp, S., 684
'Stepwise' program, 597
Stewart Hunter, D., 685
St. James Model, 71, 364, 403
Stockbrokers, 539
    reports, 21
Stock Exchange Council, 695
Stock Exchange Yearbook, 539
STONEWALL, 261
Store checks, 478
Store tests, 61

Stouffers, A. A., 683
Stratification, in sample design, 80, 317
Strothman, K. H., 684
Stuart, A., 682, 685, 699
Sub-groups, *see* Minority groups
Suchman, E. A., 683
Suci, G. J., 683
Suemen Gallup, 216
Supervisor, of interviewers, 132–133, 135–136, 138
Switzerland, 554
Symbol research, 450–469
Syndicated research, 154, 162, 215, 547, 569, 570, *see also* Omnibus surveys, Panels, Audits
Synectics, 30, 386
Systematic cross-border analysis, 563

TABLEAU, 261
Tabulations, interpretation of, 70
Tabulator, 255–256
Tachistoscope, 219, 230, 438, 461, 464, 465
TAM, 175, 620, 623, 625, 626, 627, 628, 629, 632, 633, 637, 646, 649, 652, 655, 662, 699, 700, 701
TAM meters, 632, 637
Tannenbaum, P. H., 683
Tape,
    paper, 253–256
    magnetic, 256
Tape recorder, 7, 39–41, 135
Target group definition, 356–365
Target Group Index, 222, 223, 545, 547, 552, 582, 591
TAT, *see* Thematic apperception test
Tate, B., 689
Tauber, 382, 394, 689
Taxonomic models, 65
Taxonomy, 311, 321, 324–325
Taylor, 614
Taylor, B., 690
Taylor, D. A., 688
Taylor, L., 698
Taylor Nelson & Associates, 544
Teer, F., 657–679
TCA, 172, 173, 614
t distribution, 304
Telephone interviewing, 7, 99, 130, 164, 165, 218–222, 541, 560, 582
    radio research in, 659
    TV viewing research in, 620, 655
Television areas, 491, 607–608
    definition of, 611
Television Audience Measurement, *see* TAM
Television audience measurement, 613–631
Television, colour, *see* Colour television
Television commercials, 607–608, 651–652
Television commercial testing, 430–435, 642–646
Television Consumer Audit, 439